THE CHURCH IN
ANGLO-SAXON SOCIETY

The Church in
Anglo-Saxon
Society

JOHN BLAIR

OXFORD
UNIVERSITY PRESS

OXFORD

UNIVERSITY PRESS

Great Clarendon Street, Oxford OX2 6DP

Oxford University Press is a department of the University of Oxford.
It furthers the University's objective of excellence in research, scholarship,
and education by publishing worldwide in

Oxford New York

Auckland Bangkok Buenos Aires Cape Town Chennai
Dar es Salaam Delhi Hong Kong Istanbul Karachi Kolkata
Kuala Lumpur Madrid Melbourne Mexico City Mumbai Nairobi
São Paulo Shanghai Taipei Tokyo Toronto

Oxford is a registered trade mark of Oxford University Press
in the UK and in certain other countries

Published in the United States
by Oxford University Press Inc., New York

© John Blair 2005

British Library Cataloguing in Publication Data
Data available

Library of Congress Cataloging in Publication Data
Data available

ISBN 0-19-822695-0

1 3 5 7 9 10 8 6 4 2

Typeset by SNP Best-set Typesetter Ltd., Hong Kong
Printed in Great Britain
on acid-free paper by
Biddles Ltd, King's Lynn,
Norfolk

FOR MY FATHER

who first inspired my interest in churches

AND IN MEMORY OF MY MOTHER

Acknowledgements

This book brings to fruition a seed sown when, as a small child, I used to play in a ditch near my parents' home, in fact the boundary between the residual Anglo-Saxon parish of Leatherhead and its Norman chapelry of Ashtead (see below, p. 488 n). Most of the research and all the writing, however, have taken place during my tenure of a fellowship at The Queen's College, Oxford. To Queen's, and to my successive colleagues in History there—the late Alastair Parker, Kenneth Morgan, John Davis, and Christine Peters—I owe a big debt for support, encouragement, and tolerance. As a graduate student supervised by Barbara Harvey, I was on of the many who 'in necessitatibus suis . . . ab ea consilium quaererent et invenirent', as Bede said of another great teacher.

The text has passed through many drafts, and has been much improved by those who took the trouble to read and comment on it, notably Mick Aston, Thomas Charles-Edwards, Rosamond Faith, Helen Gittos, Henry Mayr-Harting, Christopher Whittick, and Barbara Yorke. Especially warm thanks are due to three readers—Felicity Clark, Christine Peters, and Patrick Wormald—for their searching and constructive criticisms (made unselfishly when all of them were under special pressures, both academic and personal), and for re-thinking so many of my thoughts more clearly than I could have done myself. Sarah Blair lived with the writing of this book, and visited many Anglo-Saxon church sites with me.

Among those who showed me their work in advance of publication, I owe particular thanks to Susan Wood, Patrick Wormald, and Barbara Yorke for access to fundamentally important books at draft stage. Martin Biddle and Birthe Kjølbye-Biddle provided information on Winchester, and good-humouredly debated hypotheses contrary to their own. More others than I can remember have helped by commenting on individual chapters, answering questions, providing information, or just giving moral support: I am profoundly grateful to them all, especially Julia Barrow, Stephen Baxter, Brad Bedingfield, Tyler Bell, Claude Blair, Nicholas Brooks, Martin Carver, Katy Cubitt, Scott DeGregorio, Fiona Edmonds, Sarah Foot, Richard Gem, Dawn Hadley, Alaric Hall, Barbara Harvey, Jane Hawkes, Joy Jenkyns, Drew Jones, Elisabeth Lorans, Simon Loseby, Ben Palmer, Aliki Pantos, Jonathan Pitt, Philip Rahtz, Andrew Reynolds, Christopher Scull, Sarah Semple, Richard Sharpe, John Steane, David Stocker, Victoria Thompson, Francesca Tinti,

Sam Turner, Ann Williams, Susan Wood, and Susan Youngs. Finally, thanks to Kanerva Heikkinen for being there at the end.

For permission to reproduce illustrations, and for providing copy for them, thanks are due to: Keith Baker, Fig. 47; Steven Bassett, Fig. 34; British Museum, Figs. 5, 15; Robert Carr, Fig. 25; Durham Cathedral Chapter, Fig. 54; Richard Gem, Fig. 15; Hartlepool Museum Service, Fig. 32; Jane Hawkes, Fig. 20; Carolyn Heighway and Richard Bryant, Fig. 40; English Heritage, Fig. 20; Simon Hill, Figs. 12, 13; Humberside Archaeological Unit, Fig. 16; Terrence James, Fig. 4; Christopher Loveluck, Figs. 16, 25; Ian Meadows, Fig. 44; Audrey L. Meaney, Fig. 21; Philip Rahtz and Lorna Watts, Fig. 16; Dommuseum zu Salzburg, Fig. 17; Suffolk County Council Archaeological Service, Fig. 26; Tim Tatton-Brown, Fig. 10; Andrew Tester, Fig. 26; Leslie Webster, Figs. 17, 32; York Archaeological Trust, Figs. 12, 13; and Susan Youngs, Fig. 5.

The staff of Oxford University Press, especially Ruth Parr, Anne Gelling, and Kay Rogers, have shown extraordinary enthusiasm and tolerance for a book which has reached them several years late and at several times the projected length.

J.B.

Contents

List of Illustrations

Abbreviations and Primary Sources

Abingdon	S. E. Kelly (ed.), *Charters of Abingdon Abbey* (2 vols., *Anglo-Saxon Charters* vii–viii, Oxford, 2000–1)
Actes Norm.	M. Fauroux (ed.), *Recueil des actes des ducs de Normandie de 911 à 1066* (Caen, 1961)
Ælfric Supp.	*Homilies of Ælfric: A Supplementary Collection*, ed. J. Pope (EETS 259–60, 1967–8)
Æthelweard	*The Chronicle of Æthelweard*, ed. A. Campbell (Oxford, 1962)
Alc. Ep.	*Alcuini sive Albini Epistolae*, ed. E. Dümmler (*MGH, Epistolarum*, 4 (Berlin, 1895), 1–493)
AntJ	*Antiquaries Journal*
AO	*Aldhelmi Opera*, ed. R. Ehwald (*MGH, Auct. Ant.* 15, 1919)
ArchJ	*Archaeological Journal*
ASC	'Anglo-Saxon Chronicle' (cited with letter-symbol indicating version, except where the entry is from the common stock, and with corrected AD date), ed. C. Plummer, *Two of the Saxon Chronicles Parallel* (2 vols., Oxford, 1892–9)
ASE	*Anglo-Saxon England*
ASSAH	*Anglo-Saxon Studies in Archaeology and History*
Asser	Asser, 'De Rebus Gestis Ælfredi', ed. W. H. Stevenson, *Asser's Life of King Alfred* (Oxford, 1904); trans. Keynes and Lapidge 1983: 67–110
BAR	British Archaeological Reports
BOE	*Baedae Venerabilis Opera*, ii: *Opera Exegetica*, ii–iia, ed. D. Hurst (*CCSL* 119–119a, Turnhout, 1962, 1969)
Bon. Ep.	*S. Bonifatii et Lullii Epistolae*, ed. M. Tangl (*MGH Epistolae Selectae*, I, Berlin, 1916)
C&S	D. Whitelock, M. Brett, and C. N. L. Brooke (eds.), *Councils and Synods, with Other Documents Relating to the English Church*, i: *AD 871–1204* (2 vols., Oxford, 1981)
Capitularia	A. Boretius and V. Krause (eds.), *Capitularia Regum Francorum* (2 vols., *MGH Legum, sec. II, Capitularia*. Hannover, 1881, 1897)
CBA	Council for British Archaeology
CCSL	*Corpus Christianorum, Series Latina*

CED	A. W. Haddan and W. Stubbs (eds.), *Councils and Ecclesiastical Documents Relating to Great Britain and Ireland* (3 vols., Oxford, 1869–71)
CG1	C. Munier (ed.), *Concilia Galliae a. 314–a. 506* (*CCSL* 148, Turnhout, 1963)
CG2	C. de Clercq (ed.), *Concilia Galliae a. 511–a. 695* (*CCSL* 148a, Turnhout, 1963)
Chron. Battle	E. Searle (ed.), *The Chronicle of Battle Abbey* (Oxford, 1980)
Chron. Ram.	W. D. Macray (ed.), *Chronicon Abbatiae Rameseiensis* (Rolls Ser. 83, 1886)
Clof.747	Acts of the Council of *Clofesho*, 747 (ed. *CED* iii. 362–76)
DA	Æthelwulf, 'De Abbatibus', ed. A. Campbell (Oxford, 1967)
DB	Domesday Book. Citations are by folio in Great Domesday (DB i), Little Domesday (DB ii), and Exeter Domesday (DB Exon.). They are cited from: *Great Domesday: Facsimile* (Alecto Historical Editions, London, 1986); *Little Domesday: Facsimile* (Alecto Historical Editions, London, 2000); and (for Exon.) *Domesday Book: Additamenta* (London, 1816)
DEB	Gildas, 'De Excidio Britonum', ed. M. Winterbottom, *Gildas: The Ruin of Britain and Other Works* (Chichester, 1978), 87–142
Dialogue	Ecgberht, 'Succinctus Dialogus Ecclesiasticae Institutionis' (ed. *CED* iii. 403–13)
EAA	*East Anglian Archaeology*
ECEE	C. R. Hart, *The Early Charters of Eastern England* (Leicester, 1966)
ECWM	H. P. R. Finberg, *The Early Charters of the West Midlands* (Leicester, 1972)
EEA	*English Episcopal Acta*
EETS	Early English Text Society
EHR	*English Historical Review*
EME	*Early Medieval Europe*
Encyc.	M. Lapidge and others (eds.), *The Blackwell Encyclopaedia of Anglo-Saxon England* (Oxford, 1999)
Ep. E.	Bede, 'Epistola ad Ecgbertum Episcopum', ed. C. Plummer, *Venerabilis Baedae Opera Historica* (i–ii, Oxford, 1896), i. 405–23
EPNS	English Place-Name Society
Feodarium	W. Greenwell (ed.), *Feodarium Prioratus Dunelmensis* (Surtees Soc. 58, 1872)
Gesetze	F. Liebermann (ed.), *Die Gesetze der Angelsachsen*, i (Halle, 1903)

GP	William of Malmesbury, *De Gestis Pontificum Anglorum*, ed. N. E. S. A. Hamilton (Rolls Ser. 52, 1870)
GR	William of Malmesbury, *Gesta Regum Anglorum*, ed. R. A. B. Mynors, R. M. Thomson, and M. Winterbottom (2 vols., Oxford, 1998–9)
HA	Bede, 'Historia Abbatum', ed. C. Plummer, *Venerabilis Baedae Opera Historica* (i–ii, Oxford, 1896), i. 364–87
HE	Bede, 'Historia Ecclesiastica Gentis Anglorum', ed. B. Colgrave and R. A. B. Mynors (Oxford, 1969)
Hib.	H. Wasserschleben (ed.), 'Collectio Canonum Hibernensis', *Die Irische Kanonensammlung* (2nd edn., Leipzig, 1885)
Hist. Abb. ii	J. Hudson (ed.), *Historia Ecclesie Abbendonensis*, ii (Oxford, 2002)
Hom. Wulf.	*The Homilies of Wulfstan*, ed. D. Bethurum (Oxford, 1957)
JBAA	*Journal of the British Archaeological Association*
JEH	*Journal of Ecclesiastical History*
JW	*The Chronicle of John of Worcester*, ed. P. McGurk and others (ii–iii, Oxford, 1995, 1998)
Lawsuits	R. C. Van Caenegem (ed.), *English Lawsuits from William I to Richard I* (2 vols., Selden Soc. 106–7, 1990–1)
Leechdoms	O. Cockayne (ed.), *Leechdoms, Wortcunning and Starcraft* (3 vols., Rolls Ser. 35a–c, 1864–6)
Lib. El.	E. O. Blake (ed.), *Liber Eliensis* (Camden 3rd ser. 92, 1962)
LS	*Ælfric's Lives of the Saints, 1*, ed. W. W. Skeat (EETS, 76, 82, 1881, 1885)
MA	*Medieval Archaeology*
MGH	*Monumenta Germaniae Historica*
Nectan	P. Grosjean (ed.), 'Vita', 'Inventio', 'Miracula S. Nectani Martyris', *Analecta Bollandiana*, 71 (1953), 397–414
NMW	S. Miller (ed.), *Charters of the New Minster, Winchester* (*Anglo-Saxon Charters* ix, Oxford, 2001)
NPL	'The Northumbrian Priests' Law', ed. *Gesetze*, 380–5, ed. and trans. *C&S*, 449–68
OEB	*The Old English Version of Bede's Ecclesiastical History*, ed. T. Miller, 1. i (EETS 95, 1890)
OS	Ordnance Survey maps
P&P	*Past and Present*
PL	*Patrologia Latina*

P-N	Volumes in the English Place-Name Society series are cited by this abbreviation, followed by the county name
PT	'Poenitentiale Theodori', ed. P. W. Finsterwalder, *Die Canones Theodori Cantuariensis und ihre überlieferungsformen* (Weimar, 1929)
RASC	A. J. Robertson (ed. and trans.), *Anglo-Saxon Charters* (Cambridge, 1956)
Regesta W. I	*Regesta Regum Anglo-Normannorum: The Acta of William I (1066–1087)*, ed. D. Bates (Oxford, 1998)
RHEF	*Revue d'histoire de l'église de France*
Rituale	U. L. Lindelöf (ed.), *Rituale Ecclesiae Dunelmensis* (Surtees Soc. 140, 1927)
S	Anglo-Saxon charters are cited by their 'S' number in P. H. Sawyer, *Anglo-Saxon Charters: An Annotated List and Bibliography* (London, 1968); the revised version edited by S. E. Kelly, currently available in typescript or on-line at www.trin.cam.ac.uk/sdk13/chartwww/chartholme.html, has been used
SCH	*Studies in Church History*
Selsey	S. E. Kelly (ed.), *Charters of Selsey* (Anglo-Saxon Charters vi, Oxford, 1998)
Sherborne	M. A. O'Donovan (ed.), *Charters of Sherborne* (Anglo-Saxon Charters iii, Oxford, 1988)
Southwell	A. F. Leach (ed.), *Visitations and Memorials of Southwell Minster* (Camden Soc. cliv, 1891)
SSCI	*Settimane di Studio del Centro Italiano di Studi sull'Alto Medioevo*
St. Aug.	S. E. Kelly (ed.), *Charters of St. Augustine's Abbey, Canterbury, and Minster-in-Thanet* (Anglo-Saxon Charters iv, Oxford, 1995)
Stoke Cart. i, iii	*Stoke-by-Clare Cartulary*, ed. C. Harper-Bill and R. Mortimer, i, iii (Suffolk Records Soc. 1982, 1984)
Symeon Lib.	Symeon of Durham, 'Libellus de Exordio atque Procursu istius, hoc est Dunhelmensis Ecclesie', ed. D. Rollason (Oxford, 2000)
Symeon Op.	*Symeonis Monachi Opera Omnia*, ed. T. Arnold (Rolls Ser. 75a–b, 1882, 1885)
TBGAS	*Transactions of the Bristol and Gloucester Archaeological Society*
Theodulf	*Theodulfi Capitula in England*, ed. H. Sauer (Munich, 1978)
TRHS	*Transactions of the Royal Historical Society*
VCA	'Vita Sancti Cuthberti Auctore Anonymo', ed. B. Colgrave, *Two Lives of St. Cuthbert* (Cambridge, 1940), 60–138

VCB	Bede, 'Vita Sancti Cuthberti', ed. B. Colgrave, *Two Lives of St. Cuthbert* (Cambridge, 1940), 142–306
VCH	*Victoria Histories of the Counties of England* (cited by county and volume)
Vercelli	D. G. Scragg (ed.), *The Vercelli Homilies and Related Texts* (EETS 300, 1992)
VG	Felix, 'Vita Sancti Guthlaci', ed. B. Colgrave, *Felix's Life of Saint Guthlac* (Cambridge, 1956)
Vita Wulf.	William of Malmesbury, 'Vita Wulfstani', ed. M. Winterbotton and R. M. Thomson, *William of Malmesbury, Saints' Lives* (Oxford, 2002), 8–154
VS	'Vita Prima S. Samsonis', ed. R. Fawtier, *La Vie de Saint Samson* (Bibl. de l'école des Hautes études 197, 1912)
VW	Stephen of Ripon ['Eddius Stephanus'], 'Vita Wilfridi', ed. B. Colgrave, *The Life of Bishop Wilfrid by Eddius Stephanus* (Cambridge, 1927)
W. Æth.	*The Will of Æthelgifu* [= S 1497], ed. D. Whitelock, N. Ker, and Lord Rennell (Roxburghe Club, Oxford, 1968)
Walt. Chron.	L. Watkiss and M. Chibnall (eds. and trans.), *The Waltham Chronicle* (Oxford, 1994)
Wills	D. Whitelock (ed.), *Anglo-Saxon Wills* (Cambridge, 1930)
Winch. Acta	M. J. Franklin (ed.), *EEA* viii: *Winchester 1070–1204* (Oxford, 1993)
Writs	F. E. Harmer (ed.), *Anglo-Saxon Writs* (Manchester, 1952)
WVG	'Liber Beati et Laudabilis Viri Gregorii Pape', ed. B. Colgrave, *The Earliest Life of Gregory the Great* (Lawrence, Kan., 1968)

Introduction

This is a study of the Church, and of churches, as forces for change: in ritual and social behaviour, in economic life, and in the organization of landscape and settlement. It is not a book about theology and learning, nor even primarily about conversion. Its concerns are with the externals of Christian culture rather than its spirituality; with churches as social and economic centres rather than as sites of scholarship or the religious life; with the topographical and tangible rather than the intellectual and conceptual. At the same time, it explores the central importance of ritual activity and organized devotion in the Anglo-Saxons' perceptions of themselves and the world around them, in their senses of identity, and in their ways of articulating the communities in which they lived. Above all it is a book about *places*, and the various functions in a wider world which stemmed from their religious character.

Inevitably it is institutions which often dominate the narrative, both because they provide most of the evidence and because the central debates focus on them. At every stage, however, I have tried to ask questions which explore the institutions' wider social impact. Why did a para-monastic system based on complex religious sites prevail in England, as in other parts of northwestern Europe, over more orthodox modes of Church organization? Why did its high culture enjoy such a spectacular but short-lived boom between 670 and 740? How important was episcopal as against monastic power in the governance of the pre-Viking local Church? What was the physical impact of monastic centres on the seventh- to ninth-century landscape? How far did religious culture and pastoral care percolate from these centres to the ordinary laity, and were there alternative sites of cult and devotion? How much did monastic settlements contribute to economic growth, and why did so many of them eventually become towns? How much continuity was there in local ecclesiastical organization through the first Viking age and after, and what were the experiences of religious communities in this fast-changing world? Why, when, and how did a tier of local churches—the eventual 'parish churches'—come into existence, and how did this process relate to others which transformed the social, economic, and topographical face of England during the tenth and eleventh centuries? How did the growing coherence of

parishes, and the crystallizing obligations of parishioners, affect more traditional and autonomous modes of lay ritual and devotion? Such issues are
more than simply strands in ecclesiastical history: they are fundamental for
understanding the formation of English society at large.

My themes are the local and the ordinary, and my main approach is topographical. I have tried, even if I have not always succeeded, to frame my
account around the generality of places which were typical rather than the
few which are constantly discussed. To attempt this is to confront the inad-
equacy of written sources which, in James Campbell's phrase, 'give a certain
amount of light, sometimes a bright flash, more frequently a dim flicker, in
a darkness which for long periods and large areas is all but complete'.[1] The
only comprehensive document, though written on many times over, is the
landscape itself. My starting-point is a lifelong fascination with English parish
churches and the English landscape, and it is through the spatial and local
context that I have tried to explore the wider role of Christian culture. Early
medievalists can too easily retreat into the comforting assumption that issues
known to us from written sources are the only issues that mattered, and that
a small number of well-documented places can be taken as typical. A topographically based study has to ask 'What was going on *here*?', and to recognize that *something* must have been going on there, even if no documents
survive to tell us what it was.

In recent years, the evidence and the possibilities have been transformed
by the growth of landscape archaeology in general and church archaeology
in particular.[2] England was spared the bombing, and subsequent reconstruction, which gave rise to large-scale church excavations in Germany, and
until the 1970s progress was retarded by legal and ethical obstacles, and by
perceptions that the archaeology of church sites held few surprises. Advances
have come partly through academic stimuli and a series of major excavations,
partly through a gradual tightening of the Church of England's planning
process. The fashion for whole-landscape studies has meant that churches are
often now discussed in their local contexts rather than as entities in isolation.[3] The archaeological data are of paramount rather than (as historians
can still sometimes assume) secondary importance in understanding how the
early Church functioned, and at every stage I have drawn freely on physical
as well as documentary evidence.

It is not only these technical advances which invite reappraisal of the whole
subject, but also some shifts of perception and emphasis. Central among

[1] Campbell 1986: 138.   [2] See Blair and Pyrah 1996.
[3] As, most substantially and successfully, by R. Morris 1989, an excellent book to which I owe
a great deal.

them are the dawning realization that a simple classification of ecclesiastical sites as 'monasteries' or 'parish churches' is anachronistic for Anglo-Saxon England, and the recognition of a broad, pre-eminently important category which can be described generically as 'minsters'. Since these places are the main theme of this book, the term needs to be explained at the outset. It is now generally accepted that Latin *monasterium*, and its Old English derivative *mynster*, were used extremely broadly, to denote any kind of religious establishment with a church.[4] They thus differed substantially from 'monastery', the modern English loan-word from *monasterium*, which in normal usage means an enclosed and primarily contemplative community living by a clear-cut normative rule. Certain Anglo-Saxon establishments, such as Wearmouth-Jarrow in the eighth century or Abingdon in the late tenth, are commonly and correctly called 'monasteries' in that sense. The problem is that we simply do not know what went on in the great majority of Anglo-Saxon religious communities, though it is likely that a high proportion of them were neither very regulated nor very enclosed. If we call Wearmouth-Jarrow a 'monastery' and a community of unknown character a 'minster'—by implication something different—we are making an unwarranted judgement on the latter, and are also implying a simple, binary contrast which would have puzzled contemporaries before the tenth century.

The great attraction of *mynster*, modernized as 'minster', is that we can use it, as contemporaries did, to mean *any* kind of community, strict or lax, well documented or obscure. If it sounds odd to speak of Augustine, Aidan, or Bede inhabiting 'minsters', the oddness simply exposes the anachronistic assumptions which selective translation has imposed on the sources. I shall work with the following inclusive definition of the kind of place which, in the Anglo-Saxon context, I shall call a 'minster', but which existed under other names throughout north-western Europe:[5]

A complex ecclesiastical settlement which is headed by an abbess, abbot, or man in priest's orders; which contains nuns, monks, priests, or laity in a variety of possible combinations, and is united to a greater or lesser extent by their liturgy and devotions; which may perform or supervise pastoral care to the laity, perhaps receiving dues and exerting parochial authority; and which may sometimes act as a bishop's seat, while not depending for its existence or importance on that function.

I have, however, baulked at inventing an abstract noun 'minsterism' or an adjective 'minsterish': 'monasticism' and 'monastic' will have to do, though in senses much wider than their modern ones.

A further problem arises from some historians' practice of using 'minster'

---

[4] Foot 1992*b*; Blair 1995*a*: 194–6.   [5] See further below, pp. 73–4.

to mean a parochial mother-church identified from post-Conquest sources, even when there is no direct evidence that it had housed a religious community. Given that so many early minsters did in fact survive as late mother-churches, this usage must often be correct, but in individual cases it can certainly be criticized for turning hypothesis into assumption. Experience of the fragmentary and uneven sources shows that minsters can often be identified by matching them against a recurrent set of criteria, of which late-recorded status as a parochial mother-church is one.[6] Places for which this is the *only* known criterion generally appear in this book as 'mother-churches' rather than 'minsters', though in generalized accounts of regional patterns I have not signalled every such case. Since the parochial evidence is mostly late, and distinct from sources for the age or character of the churches themselves, I generally refer to the dependent districts as 'mother-parishes' rather than 'minster-parishes'.

As this last usage of 'minster' illustrates, recent decades have also seen the emergence of what has been called (not altogether helpfully) the 'minster model' of parochial organization: the view that minsters were the centres of proto-parishes through most of the Christian Anglo-Saxon period. Initially suggested by Bede's emphasis on the pastoral role of monks, and by hints that some early monasteries interacted in various ways with the secular land-units in which they stood, this line of argument gathered momentum from the 1950s.[7] At that stage, the usual approach was to look backwards from late evidence.[8] The pattern of old-established churches at the centres of large, fragmenting 'mother-parishes' in the eleventh and twelfth centuries, which a series of local studies showed to be near-ubiquitous, was seen as the last pale reflection of much older arrangements; a law of the 960s, protecting the tithe-rights of 'the old minster to which obedience pertains', encouraged this view.

From the late 1980s, notably in an essay by Sarah Foot (1989) and a collection of conference proceedings (1992),[9] the pre-Viking written sources were scrutinized more closely. The emphasis in eighth-century texts on the controlling hand of bishops, and the lack of clear statements that monasteries were centres of pastoral care, began to raise doubts: as Catherine Cubitt put it, 'the discrepancy between the [episcopal] office-centred view of the canons and the institution-based theory of the topographers is not a trivial one, and should alert us to some of the problems of the topographical model'.[10] A sustained critique in 1995, and the challenge of responding to it,[11] forced me to confront some weaknesses of the topographical approach,

[6] Cf. Blair 1995*a*: 199–203.
[7] For instance: Addleshaw 1953; Deanesly 1961: 191–210; Hill 1966.
[8] Below, p. 153. This phase in the development of the model culminated with the essays in Blair 1988*a*.
[9] Foot 1989*b*; Blair and Sharpe 1992.   [10] Cubitt 1992: 207.   [11] Below, p. 153.

and (I hope) to treat the early evidence more cautiously.[12] As will be clear from this book, my belief in the central and enduring importance of minsters in local religious life, and as the basis of the first English parochial system, still stands. But for my own part I never meant to create an inflexible model, destined to stand or fall in its entirety, but rather to suggest an explanatory framework which could develop, and if necessary change, with the growth of knowledge. For that reason, I hope that the phrase 'minster model' can now be abandoned.

A new account of local religious organization can now, happily, be emancipated from those imaginary constructs, the 'Celtic Church' and the 'Roman Church'.[13] England in the seventh and eighth centuries was influenced by Ireland on the one hand, Italy and Gaul on the other, but to think of these as two self-contained and contrasting 'packages' is unrealistic and unhelpful. In the melting-pot of early insular culture, influences from many sources re-combined and a wide range of alternatives was on offer. The ecclesiastical textures of the various regions of the British Isles were not imposed, but evolved: basic political, social, and chronological conditions—the state of development at the point of conversion, the size of kingdoms, the relationship between land and kindred, the presence or absence of towns, the memory or otherwise of a Romano-British past—were variables around which heterogeneous traditions grouped themselves in new combinations, and flourished if the contexts suited them. For instance, the English monastic culture was moulded both by Irish and by Gallic traditions, but in my view its extraordinary growth after *c.*670 owes far more to its success in bonding with native kindred structures, to the cultural and economic possibilities which it could offer, and to the absence of Roman-style *civitates* and bishoprics, than to any one channel of religious influence. Ecclesiastical similarities or differences between the English and their neighbours can be highly illuminating, and are explored several times in this book, but in the end they may often amount to little more than similarities or differences between the societies in general.

Parallels between different parts of the British Isles can reflect direct influences, but beyond a certain point they become comparative anthropology. In trying to broaden the scope of plausible interpretation I have ranged more widely, both to better-documented Christian societies (notably the colonial New World and rural Spain) and to non-Christian ones. Some readers may be disconcerted by comparisons between the impact of monasticism in England and in Tibet, between the economic roles of eighth-century minsters and of early Chinese cities, or between Alcuin's view of lay Christianity and those of Spanish priests in Mexico. I have chosen such analogies to

[12] Below, pp. 155–8.   [13] Cf. Davies 1992; Charles-Edwards 2000: 241.

illustrate what can happen when an alien and highly organized socio-religious culture, based upon elite ceremonial centres, implants itself into a relatively primitive society with fluid economic and settlement structures. Such perspectives offer antidotes to the insidious assumption that the role of the Church in the seventh and eighth centuries resembled what it would be in the better-documented high middle ages, when non-ecclesiastical forms of organization were in reality utterly different and far more developed. Even the best-chosen anthropological parallels can never tell us what *did* happen, but they are a better guide to what *might* have happened than an unthinking extrapolation of England in 1200 to England in 700.

It is in fact an odd feature of the English historiography that, while the importance of the early medieval Church is in a general sense taken for granted, churches are accorded a less dynamic role in social and economic formation than in other parts of Europe.[14] To redress this imbalance, I have made a point of presenting minsters as initiators and leaders of new practice, rather than merely as beneficiaries of secular enterprise. Have I gone too far? It may be useful to say at the outset that my argument for the Church's distinctive economic role is qualitative rather than quantitative. I do not know what proportion of English wealth was in ecclesiastical hands in, say, 750, and readily acknowledge that the proportion in royal and noble hands may have been much greater. What I do argue, though, is that religious communities had ways of gathering, increasing, and using wealth which were new and very important, and which generated more complex, structured, and permanent sorts of place than the English could have created if they had not been exposed to this external cultural stimulus.

As in any book which tries to be a general study of local developments, almost every argument is to some degree qualified and compromised by regional variation. This is true in some major and obvious ways—the Britishness of the seventh-century west, the brilliance of eighth-century Northumbria, the distinctiveness of the tenth-century Danelaw, the wealth of eleventh-century East Anglia—to which I have tried to give due weight, but also in a host of small ones which are inevitably skated over. To extrapolate, as I must, from scattered fragments of evidence and from localized clusters of sources (Northumbrian narratives, Worcestershire charters, East Anglian Domesday entries) runs the risk of building up a composite picture which does not perfectly fit any one region. For the sake of understanding the main lines of what was fundamentally an interconnected and relatively homogeneous religious culture, I believe that this is a tolerable price to pay.

[14] Below, pp. 265–6. Even now, few English studies of urbanization would give monasteries so central a role as does, for instance, Verhulst 2000.

After surveying background processes and influences before the mid seventh century (Chapter 1), I proceed through a series of themes and problems spanning the period 650–850: the political and tenurial context of minsters (Chapter 2); their role in social, devotional, and parochial organization (Chapter 3); and their impact on the ritual landscape, settlement growth, and urbanization (Chapters 4 and 5). These themes are then taken up for the period between the first Viking invasions and Domesday Book: the fortunes of minsters as religious and economic centres (Chapter 6); the foundation of new churches (Chapter 7); and the crystallization of parochial authority over the ritual lives of the laity (Chapter 8). This division of the book into 'pre-Viking' and 'post-Viking' halves is conditioned by the sources, and to some extent by a genuine though gradual shift from a world in which minsters were wealthy by aristocratic standards and pre-eminent in the ecclesiastical sphere, to one where they succumbed progressively to asset-stripping, the encroachment of secular activities, and the rival claims of newer and more local churches. But it is emphatically not meant to imply that the Viking invasions wiped the slate clean, or constituted a hiatus between an earlier 'monastic' Church and a later 'parochial' one. The evolution of institutions through the whole period is a central argument of the book, and its two halves tell one continuous story.

This is, to repeat, a book about local phenomena. Other aspects of the Anglo-Saxon Church have been extremely well discussed in recent years (three obvious examples are the origins and character of royal nunneries, the role of church councils, and the relationship between reformed monasticism and tenth-century kingship[15]), and to try to do them justice would have made an already large book enormous. Some readers will be more surprised to find that the problems which were so much discussed in the 1980s and 1990s—the reconstruction of mother-parishes and the analysis of parish boundaries—are given relatively little space. This is simply because the debate has, in my view, reached a point beyond which it cannot progress significantly without another generation of local studies, and ultimately a complete catalogue of Anglo-Saxon religious sites supported by a cartographic database. For now, reassessing the processes which influenced, and resulted from, the foundation and evolution of churches and parishes seemed a more useful and creative exercise. This book will have fulfilled its central aim if it helps to form a clearer view of what local churches and local communities meant to each other.

[15] Yorke 2003*b*; Cubitt 1995; below, p. 350 n.

I

The English and their Christian Neighbours
c.550–650

Perched on the edge of the Roman world, the sixth-century English occupied an ambiguous position between 'civilized' Europe and the 'barbarian' north. Christianity was remote, yet accessible; alien, yet the religion of the sub-Roman British culture which the Anglo-Saxon migrations had overlain. A pagan warrior people knowing little of Rome, they had infiltrated a former province in which the ruins of towns, forts, and villas remained widely visible. Although those monuments were massive and relatively recent, their social and economic functions were remote from the experience and comprehensions of the settlers, and even of the remaining British. But not so far away, another 'barbarian' people, the Franks, had assumed in a more purposeful fashion the authority, religion, and urban culture of what had been Roman Gaul. To the west, in some of the least Romanized parts of former Britannia, autonomous British aristocracies had preserved and transformed the religion of the late Empire within a non-urban, kin-based culture like that of their Germanic rivals. Further west still, beyond the Irish Sea, a continuing Iron Age society, without any direct experience of Roman rule, was developing a powerful Christian civilization.

Occupants of former Roman territory though they were, the Anglo-Saxons resembled their pagan Scandinavian relatives more than their Christian Frankish neighbours. Even if—as seems likely—they had absorbed large numbers of British-descended people, the imported material culture prevailed. If Christian doctrines, institutions, and practices were to reach the English it had to be mainly from outside, as they would later reach the peoples of Scandinavia and of central and eastern Europe. But there was a difference. Latin Christendom, and the English themselves, knew that Britain had once been a Roman province; the ruins of its important places were obvious, and the names of many of them were known. From as early as c.600, when Pope Gregory directed (unrealistically as it turned out) that London and York were to have metropolitan bishops controlling twenty-four episcopal sees at what were probably thought of as the old *civitas* capitals, the memory and the physical remains of Britannia were pressed into the service of its re-connection with a transformed Christendom.

The course of this re-connection, visible to us in the formal conversions of the Anglo-Saxon royal dynasties, can be understood in five phases.[1] The first opened in 597 with the mission to the tiny but powerful kingdom of Kent, launched by Pope Gregory and led by the monk-bishop Augustine, and ended in 616 with the death of the convert King Æthelberht. At this point Christian allegiance was still extremely limited, being confined to Kent and—rather shakily—the Kentish-influenced East Saxon and East Anglian courts; during the second phase (*c.*616–25) it contracted even there with the accession of an unbaptized or apostate king in Kent. The third phase (*c.*625–42) saw major and sustained expansion: the resumption of Christianity by King Eadbald of Kent, perhaps in the context of his daughter's marriage to King Eadwine of Northumbria, leading in turn to a Canterbury-sponsored mission to the Northumbrians under the Italian Paulinus; the replacement of Eadwine by Oswald, head of a rival dynasty, who initiated in Northumbria a completely different mission of Irish monks from Iona; and the conversion of the courts of the East Anglians and Gewisse (the people of the upper Thames region) under the tutelage of Continental missionaries, Felix the Burgundian and Birinus the Italian. Another formative decade (phase four) during *c.*653–64 opened with the Northumbrian-sponsored conversion of the East Saxon, Middle Anglian, and Mercian rulers, and culminated with the Synod of Whitby and Northumbria's acceptance of a Roman rather than Ionan liturgical tradition. With the fifth phase, the conversion of Sussex and finally the Isle of Wight during the 670s and 680s, all English kings were baptized and all English peoples were nominally Christian.

In the course of these conversions, the ecclesiastical structures and systems analysed in this book first took root. Why did they come when they did, and what determined their character? The usual answer appeals to the timing of the missions, and to the spiritual traditions and modes of organization and authority in the Churches which launched them. There is of course truth in this, but it is an inadequate explanation on its own: if the seeds were sown from outside, their germination depended on a series of changes in English society which came to a head around 600. The formation of Church

---

[1] Among the huge literature, see especially: Mayr-Harting 1991, the classic account; P. Brown 1996; Fletcher 1997 for the conversion of the English in the context of the conversion of Europe; the many essays in Carver 2003; and Mayr-Harting 1994 for an enlightening comparison. Higham 1997 is an uncompromisingly political account, which largely ignores both spiritual and cultural factors, but contains much of interest. Carver 1998 gives a stimulating archaeological view.

organization may be envisaged in terms of ingredients—the various influences and traditions—combined in accordance with a recipe—the political, social, and cultural complexions of the seventh-century kingdoms. Among the ingredients, the Christianity already long established in Britain was the least important but the most immediate.

Influences (i): the Roman inheritance in Britain

For most of the fourth century, Britain was part of an officially Christian empire. In practice Christianity was probably still a minority religion, overlaid on the Celtic polytheism of the late Iron Age British and varying both regionally and by social class. Most obviously, it was one aspect of a colonial civilization which was bound to be most successful in towns and their relatively Romanized hinterlands. Recent work has tended to raise estimates of rural and middle-class Romano-British Christianity, but it remains clear that in the countryside it was both more diluted and more permeated with indigenous pagan practice.[2] Geographically, then, it tended to reflect the distribution of towns, villas, and forts. The latest review of the evidence of inscriptions, artefacts, and burials suggests that it was most prominent around the Thames estuary and in the east midlands, followed by the Severn estuary, the Cotswolds, Somerset and Dorset, and parts of the militarized north. By contrast, Lancashire, Wales (apart from Gwent), the marches, and the whole south-western peninsula essentially lack evidence for Christianity under Roman rule (Fig. 2, inset).[3]

The Christian communities of Britain after 400 grew directly out of this official late Romano-British Church, but two mutually reinforcing processes transformed it. One was the collapse and abandonment of towns and villas, with the social and economic systems which supported them.[4] The second was the drastic reorientation from eastern to western Britain, prompted by the Anglo-Saxon raids and settlements which brought the main Romanized and Christianized zones under hostile pagan control. Britain would thus be fundamentally different from Gaul, where cities survived as seats of bishops and nuclei for expanding evangelization in the countryside.[5] Its ecclesiastical structures would inevitably be decentralized and rural, perhaps drawing more on organic grass-roots support than in those European regions which maintained a contrast between town and country, but also perhaps more permeated by an older layer of syncretic polytheism.

[2] Thomas 1981: 136–41; Watts 1991: 215–16, 224; Dark 1994*b*: 32–9.
[3] Watts 1991: 216–21.
[4] Loseby 2000: 331–5, for the latest survey; cf. below, pp. 271–4.
[5] Ibid. 335–8.

But the familiar image of the British Church as eccentric, introverted, and feeble should be rejected.[6] It kept an episcopal hierarchy, with which Germanus and Patrick dealt in the early fifth century, and which survived to be denounced in Gildas's polemical treatise of the early sixth. There is strong evidence that Gildas himself was trained in the late Roman rhetorical tradition, and hints that his sixth-century British world was one in which complex Latinity was appreciated in the same circles as vernacular praise-poetry.[7] If this survival of classical learning and literacy without their normal economic support-systems is remarkable, so is the growth of a minority religion in 400 into an officially universal one by 550, in some regions much sooner. Gildas castigated his 'tyrants' as bad Christians, not as pagans, and even Bede, who had few good words for the British, blamed them for lack of charity and pastoral zeal rather than lack of Christian learning.[8]

Rather than an idiosyncratically 'Celtic' Church, we should envisage a continuing Roman one limited by the peculiarly severe collapse of material civilization around it. The physical sites of Christian ritual and governance belonged to this doomed civic world, and generally had no future. Villas of fourth-century Christian proprietors may occasionally, on a pattern well known in Gaul, have evolved into early medieval churches (Fig. 1),[9] though the siting of churches over Roman remains more usually reflects early medieval re-use after a substantial break.[10] Potentially more important were the tombs of martyrs in certain late Roman cemeteries: cult sites which were free-standing from the towns which generated them and could prosper in the new environment, even to the point of being adopted or imitated by the first Christian English.

The origin of extramural martyr cults lay in the Roman ban on burying within city walls, which meant that approach-roads to towns and cities throughout the Empire were lined with cemeteries. Here Christian martyrs and saints were buried, and here in turn the graves of the faithful clustered around their tombs (*martyria*). From the mid fourth century great churches were built over these tombs, magnets for devotional and then for social communities. Thus, as St Jerome wrote of Rome, 'the city moved house': the old public and ritual spaces within the walls were rivalled by new ones outside

---

[6] Sharpe 2002*a*: 75–112, for a recent powerful argument on which I have drawn heavily here.

[7] *DEB*; Lapidge 1984; Sims-Williams 1984. David Howlett's arguments for a complex numerical structure in British Latin prose (e.g. Howlett 1995) have not been universally accepted, but for a balanced critique see Hood 1999.

[8] Below, pp. 15, 19, 28–9.

[9] Robinson 1988; Selkirk 1996; Bell 1998*b*: 8–10; Bell 2001: 37–45, 198–9, 303–4; Petts 2002: 30–1. The forthcoming Llandough report (N. Holbrook and A. Thomas, *An Early Medieval Monastic Cemetery at Llandough*) is more cautious about the early origins of the cemetery. Below, pp. 38–9, for the Gallic model.

[10] Below, pp. 188–90.

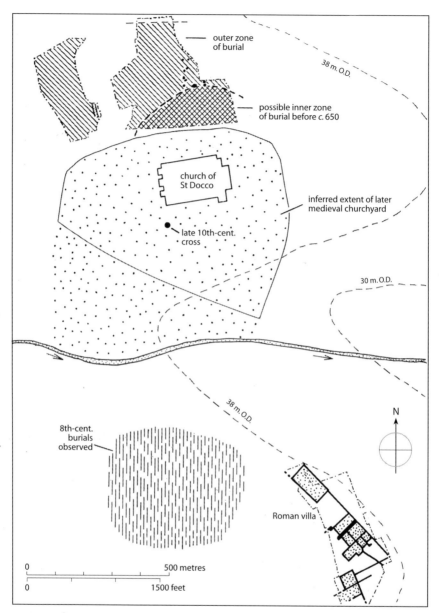

outer zone
of burial

38 m. O.D.

possible inner zone
of burial before c. 650

church of
St Docco

inferred extent of later
medieval churchyard

late 10th-cent.
cross

30 m. O.D.

8th-cent.
burials
observed

38 m. O.D.

N

Roman villa

| 0 | | | | 500 metres |
| 0 | | | | 1500 feet |

1. *Llandough* (Glamorgan): from Roman villa to cemetery and minster. The villa, abandoned in the fourth century, remained visible through the early middle ages. The graveyard zone immediately north of the churchyard contained graves of the seventh to tenth centuries, probably with a curvilinear inner zone established by *c.*650. A cemetery between the villa and the churchyard included eighth- to ninth-century graves. A monastery at Llandough ('St Docco's *llan*') is recorded between *c.*650 and *c.*1075. This is a potential—if still inconclusive—instance of the 'villa-to-monastery' sequence. Contours are at eight-metre intervals. (After Robinson 1988: figs. 59 and 64, and Selkirk 1996, with revisions supplied by Neil Holbrook.)

them, focused on the increasingly complex ecclesiastical buildings above the holy dead. In Italy, Gaul, and the Rhineland the extramural martyrial and cemetery site, often the counterpart of a cathedral inside the city, was one of the main links between classical and medieval urbanism: the very name of the Rhenish town of Xanten means 'at the saints' (*ad sanctos*).[11]

In Britain the cult of Albanus, martyred outside the walls of *Verulamium* and buried there in a cemetery where the abbey and town of St Albans now stand, is unique and extraordinary. Visited by St Germanus of Auxerre in 429, and described in a *passio* known to Gildas and Bede, it shows that a Christian shrine could survive through the fifth and sixth centuries in an enclave within the Anglicized south-east, to be embraced by the English themselves by the early eighth.[12] And there are other glimpses: of a St Sixtus who received popular veneration somewhere in the south-east around 600; of 'Augulius', possible martyr of London; and of Aaron and Julius at Caerleon, deep in British territory and also known to Gildas.[13] Others have been conjectured on archaeological or topographical evidence.[14] But the essential point is that this kind of cult practice—of which perhaps only a small minority of the sites are recorded—provides a thread of influence from mainstream late Roman Christianity to the localized religious landscapes of early medieval west Britain, with their innumerable *llans* of holy men and women.

With the post-Roman fragmentation of Britain, it becomes impracticable to discuss its Christian culture as one entity (Fig. 2). The subjection of part but not all of the former province to pagan Anglo-Saxons meant that its religious development would follow divergent paths. Even in the non-English zone, some areas must have been more Christian than others: the Severn estuary, for instance, had an established late Roman tradition, whereas the lands north of Hadrian's Wall are unlikely to have been significantly influenced until after 400, or Cornwall until after 500.[15] The rituals of Romano-Celtic polytheistic cults can hardly have been eradicated totally, and syncretic fusions with Germanic paganism are not impossible.[16] No scheme of

[11] For continental Europe see principally: Brown 1981; Thomas 1981: 159–63; Markus 1990: 142–55; Pearce 2003: 68–74; Keller 2003. Biddle 1986: 1–5 considers some of the Rhineland sites as a context for St Albans.

[12] *DEB* cc. 10–11 (p. 92); for a recent full account see Sharpe 2002*a*: 112–18. Bede says that 'when the calm of Christian times returned, a church of wonderful workmanship and worthy of his martyrdom' was built on the site, where a cult and miracles continued until his own day (*HE* i. 7, p. 34). See Biddle and Kjølbye-Biddle 2001*a*: 46–66, for archaeological evidence for the Roman cemetery and post-Roman activity on its site.

[13] Below, p. 24; *DEB* c. 10 (p. 92); Sharpe 2002*a*: 112, 118–23.

[14] R. Morris 1989: 30–4; Sharpe 2002*a*: 125–30. Cf. Edwards and Lane 1992*b*: 8, for Caerwent.

[15] Thomas 1981: 266–94 was the first serious attempt to plot the incidence of fifth-century Christianity, and remains the fullest; cf. Thomas 1994*b*: 270–1.

[16] St Samson found renegade Christians venerating an 'abominable image' on a hilltop in north-east Cornwall (*VS* I. 48–9, pp. 143–5); below, p. 52, for shrine structures.

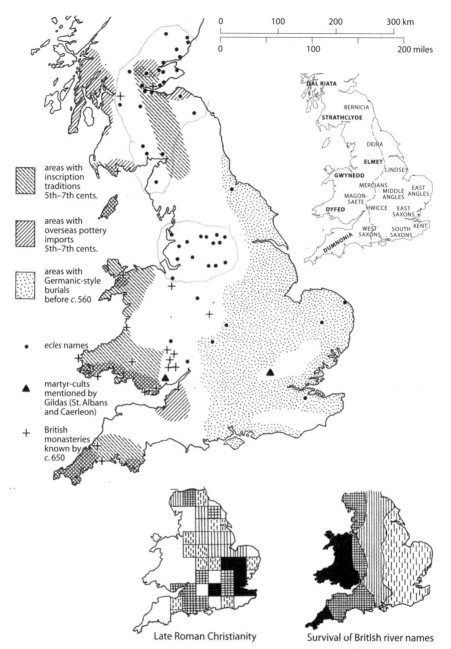

areas with
inscription
traditions
5th–7th cents.

areas with
overseas pottery
imports
5th–7th cents.

areas with
Germanic-style
burials
before c.560

• *ecles* names

▲ martyr-cults
mentioned by
Gildas (St. Albans
and Caerleon)

+ British
monasteries
known by
c.650

DÁL RIATA
BERNICIA
STRATHCLYDE
DEIRA
ELMET
GWYNEDD   LINDSEY
MERCIANS   EAST
MAGON-   MIDDLE   ANGLES
SAETE   ANGLES
DYFED   HWICCE   EAST
SAXONS
KENT
WEST   SOUTH
DUMNONIA   SAXONS SAXONS

Late Roman Christianity   Survival of British river names

2. British Christianity and the English: the relationship between the zone of Anglo-Saxon
cultural dominance up to *c.*560 and selected evidence for fifth- to seventh-century British
Christianity. The maps below, with weight of shading representing strength of evidence,
show: the known incidence of late Romano-British Christianity (after Watts 1991: fig.
28); and the post-Roman survival of British river-names (K. Jackson, after Gelling 1978:
fig. 3). The map of polities (top-right) marks non-English states in bold.

division into zones—and certainly not the traditional bipartite one between British and English—can do full justice to what must be envisaged as a multiplicity of local experiences rather than a westwards-rolling frontier.

Some kind of framework is, however, necessary, so I shall use a tripartite one, which sustains not just the contrasts between British and English, but also the potential for the Christianity of the one to influence the other. It proposes two cultural frontiers: the more westerly running from Midlothian and Peebles through the Lake District to the heads of the Ribble and Mersey estuaries, through the Welsh marches to the Wye, and across the Severn sea to the south coast near Exeter; the other from Tyneside to the vale of York, south-westwards across the midlands from the Trent to the Severn–Avon confluence, and southwards again through the western Cotswolds and Salisbury Plain to Poole harbour.[17] The zone between these frontiers, the only likely arena of British religious influence carrying through into the age of mature English Christianity after the 650s, will need special attention.

The natural starting-point is, however, the westernmost zone, never subjected to English rule until after—sometimes centuries after—the English were Christian themselves. It mainly comprises upland territory facing the Irish Sea, from Dumbarton through Cumbria to Wales, western Devon, and Cornwall. Its political and cultural identity, and its social organization, were in some respects a reversion to the tribal warrior society of the pre-Roman Iron Age.[18] This culture supported an intellectual tradition which perpetuated the late classical milieu of Gildas to produce scholars whom even the prejudiced Bede could call 'most learned men', and which may become visible again in ninth- and tenth-century texts from Wales.[19]

The nuclei of rural Christianization after 400 are likely to have been the hinterlands of the former Roman towns, notably the Severn estuary with its *civitas* capital of *Venta Silurum* (Caerwent) and its many villas in the vale of Glamorgan.[20] As the religion spread, it did so in a world of wider contacts: between Wales and Brittany via Cornwall; with Irish settlers up the west coast; with merchants from Gaul and the eastern Mediterranean. From the evidence of inscribed stones and later traditions, Charles Thomas has constructed a model of a Christian culture which expanded in western Wales in an Irish-influenced milieu during the fifth century and was exported around

---

[17] This scheme bears a close though not exact resemblance to Jackson's division of Britain into zones according to the survival or otherwise of British river-names (Fig. 2, inset): Gelling 1978: 88–90.

[18] Ward-Perkins 2000: 527–30; cf. Dark 1994*b*: 246–9, 255–7, for a rather different emphasis.

[19] *HE* ii. 2 (p. 136); Lapidge 1986: 102; Stancliffe 1999: 116; Charles-Edwards 2000: 176–81. Cf. above, p. 11.

[20] Pryce 1992*a*: 47–8; Thomas 1994*a*: 41–64; Edwards 1996: 49–50.

500 to eastern Cornwall, where St Samson encountered it shortly afterwards on his travels between Breton and Welsh monasteries.[21] North of Hadrian's Wall, the collapse of the frontier and increasing exchange across the Irish Sea may have facilitated Christian contacts. It seems likely (to cut a long and contentious story short) that the British and Pictish groups in what is now southern and central Scotland converted during the fifth and sixth centuries through a combination of British and Irish influences.[22] Cumbria and north Lancashire—probably very lightly populated—are by contrast thin in Christian evidence, and remind us that there may have been great regional contrasts.

The expansion of the western British churches must still, despite reservations introduced by recent work, be seen against the background of two related stimuli: Gallic influence, and the rising popularity of monasticism. In the context of this book these trends are important, for they suggest ways in which western Britain during *c.*550–650 may have been moving, in some respects though not in others, towards modes of organization which the English Church would display by *c.*700.

The Atlantic zone of Britain is rich in two kinds of physical evidence which, for their eloquence amidst an otherwise deep silence, have attracted strong interest: inscribed stones, and pottery imports from the Mediterranean and western Gaul. The pottery shows that people in west Cornwall, south Wales, Galloway, and Argyll were in contact, at least intermittently, with sailors from Christian Europe. The inscriptions show that some inhabitants of Wales, Cornwall, and north Britain were commemorated by epitaphs, often of an explicitly Christian nature, drawing on earlier epigraphic traditions (Fig. 3). This is extremely important evidence, but scholars have gone too far in using it—precisely because they have so little else—to define the whole essence of post-Roman Christianity in terms of Continental and Irish influence rather than indigenous survival.[23] The visible material culture of the Atlantic and Irish Sea provinces need have had little impact on Christianity further inland, and even in its own area may have been merely the exotic icing on a British cake.

As an index of contacts with more developed economies abroad, the imported pottery[24] shows an early phase (*c.*475–550) of carefully targeted voyages from the Mediterranean to the tin-producing zones of Cornwall,

---

[21] Thomas 1994*a*: 67–108, 218–300; note, however, the much more cautious conclusions on dating reached by Okasha 1993: 50–7. Cf. Campbell 1987: 333–5, and Charles-Edwards 2000: 158–76.

[22] Thomas 1981: 291–4; Bullough 1982: 82–5; Smith 1996: 20–8; Carver 1998: 26–37; Charles-Edwards 2000: 227–30, 299–308; Carver 2001: 10–12.

[23] Here I follow the argument of Sharpe 2002*a*: 93, 96–8.

[24] Campbell 1996 for the following.

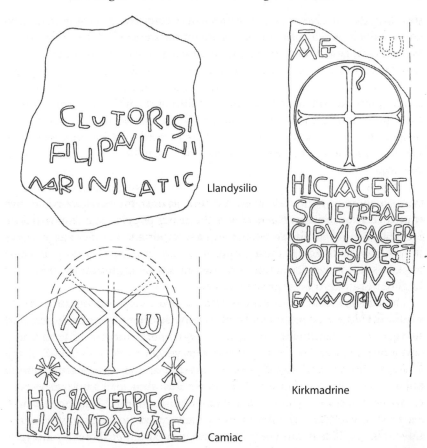

Llandysilio

Kirkmadrine

Camiac

3. Latin culture and commemoration in fifth- and sixth-century western Britain. The inscription at *Llandysilio* (Pemb.), '(Of) Clutorix son of Paulinus Marinus from Latium', illustrates the presence in post-Roman Wales of people who were—or claimed to be— genuine Romans. Ecclesiastical organization becomes overt in the more ambitious monument at *Kirkmadrine* (Galloway), with its Christian iconography and legend 'Here lie the holy and outstanding priests [*or* bishops], that is Viventius and Mavorius'. Its resemblance to the slab at *Camiac*, near Bordeaux, illustrates the coherence of north-west European Christian culture, including Britain. (After Thomas 1994*a*: figs. 5.6 and 12.3, and Knight 1992: fig. 6.3.)

Somerset, and south Wales, suggesting a world in which British potentates at sites such as Tintagel lived well on foreign luxuries in exchange for tin. A later and distinct trade from south-western Gaul, spanning the period *c.*580–680 and at its height in the early seventh century, brought pottery, glass, and presumably wine to a more diffused range of sites, in the same areas but also in Galloway, the western isles, and Ireland. These trade patterns finally broke down after *c.*680 at about the time of the rise of the North Sea emporia, facing the English kingdoms in the east rather than the British ones in the west.[25] While they lasted, they could clearly have brought intellectual as well as purely material imports, which could have included elements from the expanding Continental ascetic and monastic movements.

By the sixth century there was thus a Christian social nexus operating against the background of contacts with the eastern Mediterranean, Gaul, and the developing churches in Ireland. In this nexus monasticism, which had arisen in the eastern Mediterranean in the years around 300 and was practised in Gaul by the late fourth century, was known and becoming increasingly important. Where pottery and wine could travel, so could religious aspirations and monastic ideals. To identify specific routes, however, is probably unrealistic, and to picture a new and self-contained religious world cut off from its British roots goes much too far. Crucially, it now seems that the Christian memorial inscriptions, which appeared during the fifth and sixth centuries up the west coast of Britain, stemmed not, as has often been thought, from Gallic influence but directly from the fourth-century British tradition.[26] Monasticism was all-pervasive in the sixth-century Church, and coexisted with continuing episcopal power—most conspicuously in Gaul, where bishops were the main agents for spreading it.[27] The aspect of the 'Celtic Church' myth which pictures an idiosyncratic all-monastic culture, isolated both from its Roman background and from mainstream aspects of Church governance, is thus fundamentally misleading. This is in no way to deny the importance of monasticism: its advent was indeed transformative, and set insular Christianity on a course which would enable it to integrate in entirely new ways with the various lay societies which it encountered.

For Gildas, writing his 'De Excidio Britonum' in the early to mid sixth century, the monasticism which he contrasted with the worldliness of the British clergy was still a relatively youthful reform movement.[28] His 'fragments' suggest an expanding monastic society embodying a range of lifestyles, including an extreme ascetic element which he rebuked for pride and cold-heartedness.[29] An eremitic tradition is implied by the reference in 'De

---

[25] Below, pp. 256–7.

[26] For the Gallic argument see Knight 1992; Thomas 1994*a*: 197–207; Thomas 1994*b*: 271–5; Knight 1996; Knight 1999: 85–111, 135–8. It is now called into serious question by Handley 2001.

[27] Sharpe 2002*a*: 96–102. As Sharpe observes (pp. 99–100), the great Gallic monastery of Lérins was a nursery of bishops, and it is implausible to see monastic influence as something remote from Augustine who travelled to England through the same sites.

[28] Herren 1990; Stancliffe 1999: 116–17.

[29] Sharpe 1984*b*: 197, 199–200; Stancliffe 1999: 110.

Excidio' to the 'caves and consolations of holy men', and by St Samson's residence in a cave on the Cornish coast.[30] If these people were proud of their learning, the few surviving texts suggest that their pride was justified. So Bede's account (probably from a British source) of the debate between Augustine and the western British bishops rings true in the prominence which it gives to a 'holy and wise' hermit, in its reference to monastic austerity, and in noting the involvement both of bishops and of 'many most learned men (*viri doctissimi*)'.[31]

Gildas, saints' Lives, inscribed stones, and charters are all consistent with this image of a complex ecclesiastical milieu, in which a strong monastic element coexisted with bishops and priests—the *sacerdotes* and *presbyteri* of inscriptions in north-west Wales and Galloway. Modes of life are rarely described in detail, but if we concentrate on structures and functions rather than striving to recognize invisible boundaries between clerical and monastic, we can observe an important development: the emergence of big ecclesiastical settlements which might house bishops, abbots, priests, deacons, and monks in a variety of combinations.[32]

These settlements have proved rather elusive in the written and even the archaeological record. Bede's account of Bangor-is-Coed, near Wrexham, implies an extremely large, structured, and populous settlement in the 610s; St Kew (*Landochou*) in Cornwall features in the seventh-century Life of St Samson as a (rather easy-going) cenobitic community; the same text, and the Life of St Paul Aurelian, mention other early *monasteria* at Golant (or Fowey) and Paul.[33] Other Cornish monastic sites have produced fragmentary physical remains (though rarely as early as the sixth or seventh centuries), and hints of large sub-circular enclosures around them.[34] The most solid evidence comes from south Wales, thanks to Terrence James's aerial reconnaissance which has revealed cropmarks of large, complex, and sometimes concentric enclosures around early churches (Fig. 4).[35] As well as corroborating theories that the road-patterns of some Welsh towns may fossilize monastic enclosures,[36] these discoveries suggest that the lack of known major sites on the Irish pattern may be less because they never existed in Britain than because

---

[30] *DEB* c. 34 (p. 102); *VS* I. 50 (p. 146), and Olson 1989: 10–14.

[31] *HE* ii. 2 (p. 136); Stancliffe 1999: 130–2.

[32] Davies 1978: 124–8; Davies 1982: 146–57; Pryce 1992a: 47–55; Knight 1999: 138–40, 143–6.

[33] Below, p. 34; *VS* I. 45–6 (pp. 141–3); Olson 1989: 10–16, 20–5, 81–4; Thomas 1994a: 231–3. Cf. Turner 2003: 178.

[34] Preston-Jones 1992: 120–1; Olson 1982 (Crantock); Olson 1989: 106–7 (Padstow).

[35] T. James 1992; cf. Edwards and Lane 1992b: 8–10.

[36] For instance Bangor (Caerns.) or Llandeilo Fawr (H. James 1992: 100–1; T. James 1992: 74–5), or the sites discussed by Butler 1979. But cf. Petts 2002: 30–2, who observes that internal subdivision of Welsh (in contrast to Irish) monastic sites is still not clearly attested.

4. *Llangan* (Carms.): cropmarks of concentric ditched enclosures, showing that the present small church perpetuates a larger and more complex ecclesiastical site. (Terrence James, © Cambria Archaeology.)

later development has effaced them. Here is one of the several potential sources for the complex morphology of later English minsters.[37]

By the tenth century, and probably a good deal earlier, a much larger and more visible category of ecclesiastical settlement had become widespread in Wales, Cornwall, and possibly to some extent the north-west.[38] It comprises the small religious sites, often associated with early inscribed memorial stones or curvilinear churchyards, which are characteristically identified by place-names in *llan/*lann* compounded with the names of saints or founders.[39] The traditional view that these sites were the churches, hermitages, and cemeteries of a pioneer generation of sixth-century holy men, the bedrock of an intensely localized Christian culture, has now been heavily criticized: scholars have pointed out that neither *llan* names nor enclosed cemeteries are attested until well after the sixth century, and have even argued that the proliferation of western church sites occurred mainly after 900.[40] These are important correctives, but they may have gone too far. There is explicit evidence for *llan*-type sites associated with saints' names by the late ninth century, and some persuasive indirect pointers to them in the seventh.[41] And while some inscribed stones may have been brought to church sites in recent times,[42] others have not: it is hard to discount a case like Llansadwrn (Anglesey), where an inscription to *beatus . . . Saturninus,* presumably the eponymous Sadwrn, was dug up in the churchyard before 1742.[43] The natural interpretation remains that sixth- to eighth-century west Britain, like contemporary Ireland, contained relatively large numbers of small monastic or clerical settlements whose rulers and patrons tended to be venerated in them as saints, even if they are harder to date and quantify than has been assumed. The spiritual milieu of Gildas had a broad topographical base, and in its strong identification with local holy figures it recalled the Roman martyr-cults.

[37] Below, pp. 196–8.

[38] O'Sullivan 1985: 31–2, treats with due scepticism the idea that Cumbrian curvilinear churchyards are necessarily British. It is, however, fair to say that the curvilinear form concentrates overwhelmingly in western Britain; whatever the origins of the specific Cumbrian cases, they must surely in general terms reflect British influence. Cf. Brook 1992.

[39] For Wales: Davies 1978: 37–8, 121–4; Pryce 1992a: 57–60; Edwards 1996: 50–1. For Cornwall: Padel 1976–7; Preston-Jones and Rose 1986: 154–7; Preston-Jones 1992; Thomas 1994a: 310–21; Padel 2002.

[40] Davies 2002 (south Wales) and Padel 2002: 310–26 (Cornwall) for measured critiques; Petts 2002 (Wales) and Turner 2003 (Cornwall) for rather more extreme ones. The convincing case that enclosed cemeteries are a late phenomenon (cf. below, pp. 374–5) seems to have become extended into a less convincing one that small ecclesiastical sites *of all kinds* are generally late.

[41] Olson and Padel 1986; Padel 2002: 313–26; Davies 2002: 391–4; Petts 2002: 40–2. In addition, the British name for the minster at Sherborne (Dorset), 'Lanprobus', is surely likely to pre-date the English annexation of the site in the late seventh century: Edwards 1988: 245, 251.

[42] Petts 2002: 27–8; Edwards 2001.

[43] Nash-Williams 1950: 61–3.

It is even harder to know how far this seemingly decentralized ecclesiastical world, probably based to an important extent on patterns of local aristocratic landholding,[44] embodied order and hierarchy. From the fragmentary material preserved in the much later 'Book of Llandaf', Wendy Davies argued that by the seventh century the property accumulated by some major monastic houses in south-east Wales included older churches, creating constellations of dependencies identified with the saint of the central site ('the Teilo connection', 'the Cadog connection', and so forth).[45] Her chronological scheme has been disputed,[46] and it does not really seem possible with much conviction to recognize this consolidation of monastic power before the ninth to tenth centuries. This is not to say that all ecclesiastical sites were equal— Bede's Bangor-is-Coed must have been hugely bigger than the average—and a contrast between large, complex monasteries and church sites housing three or four monks or priests could well have been obvious in Wales and Cornwall by the mid seventh century. The small sites, the eventual *llans*, represent a bottom layer of Christian topography that was common to Atlantic Britain, Brittany, and Ireland, even though decisively different from what would emerge in early Christian England.

It is evident that the major sites were in some sense monastic, and their abbots or other rulers must have built up wide territorial powers. For the institutional context of these powers, we are largely dependent on saints' Lives and on the controversial, heavily re-worked core of the Llandaf texts. While the theoretical subjection of abbots to bishops is not in doubt, and while bishops are depicted supervising the religious lives of their dioceses, it is hard to gauge the precise relationship between monastic and episcopal power in a Church so dominated by wealthy monasteries. Bishops were themselves based in religious communities which were not, so far as the sources show, significantly different from others in any respect but this.[47] The growth of complex monasteries, the consolidation of territorial power, and the difficulty of defining the interface between episcopal and monastic jurisdiction, are central themes in the formation of the English Church, and will become familiar through this chapter and the next.

To move from the western to the eastern side of Britain is to enter a different world. By the seventh century this formerly most Romanized sector, containing the most low-lying and fertile soils, had been carved up into English kingdoms whose kings identified with Scandinavian and Germanic pasts, and looked overseas for their political and cultural inspiration. The

---

[44] Faith 1997: 4–28, for an attempt to reconstruct the territorial and seigneurial context.

[45] Davies 1978: 124, 130–1, 139–46.

[46] Sims-Williams 1982; Dumville 1984: 23; Dark 1994*b*: 140–8; Davies 2002.

[47] Davies 1978: 146–52, 158–9; Davies 1982: 157–64; Davies 1992: 15.

most striking feature of its early medieval archaeology is the plethora of fifth- and sixth-century burials and cremations, furnished with objects of a southern Scandinavian and north Germanic character. The simple and seemingly obvious explanation, that these people were the invaders described by Gildas as a scourge of God and by Bede as the ancestors of the English, has been intensively scrutinized during the last decade. Various positions are now taken, between the traditional model of a mass-migration displacing the native British, and the view that a British majority adopted the language and cultural markers of an invading warrior elite.[48]

This debate has often lost sight of the contrasts between micro-communities within the region. In parts of East Anglia, for instance, it is surely perverse to ascribe the vast and purely Scandinavian cremation cemeteries to anything other than migration.[49] On the other hand, the zone contains pockets with few or no Germanic burials—notably the region extending eastwards from the upper Thames along the Chilterns and Icknield Way, and significantly including the St Albans martyr site. Between these two extremes, it may be right to envisage a very widespread process of assimilation, in which large numbers of Britons 'became English' of their own free will because they could see that it was in their best interests to do so.[50]

It seems likely that this process gathered its own momentum, as pressure to acculturate intensified on Britons living in what was increasingly perceived as English territory. Distribution-maps of furnished burials show that whereas expansion up to a western boundary visible by *c.*500 looks (apart from the Chiltern enclave) essentially unrestrained, the next sixty or seventy years show considerable consolidation inside this frontier but little advance beyond it.[51] Also during the sixth century, the emergence of stronger regional styles in dress accessories suggests the construction of 'Anglian' and 'Saxon' culture-groups out of the ethnic (and presumed linguistic) melting-pot of the migration period, culminating in 'a common "Anglo-Saxondom" of material and social culture' by the late sixth century, and a linguistically distinct *gens Anglorum* by the time of Bede.[52]

In striking contrast to the Franks, who in re-inventing themselves embraced Gallo-Roman Christianity with enthusiastic native support, the

[48] Currently the best guides to this debate are Hamerow 1997 and Ward-Perkins 2000.
[49] Hamerow 1997: 40. As she shows, the range and depth of cultural attributes over a much wider area goes well beyond what can plausibly be attributed to a tiny warrior elite.
[50] Ward-Perkins 2000: 523–7.
[51] Hines 1990: 26–8 and figs. 1–3. The only significant exceptions are zones of limited expansion in the Gloucestershire/Warwickshire area, towards the Peak District, and in northern Deira.
[52] Hines 1990: 30–3: despite the diverse origins of the migrants, English dialects as first recorded seem not to descend from dialects in the earlier Germanic world. Cf. Dark 1994*b*: 246–51, for a scheme dividing the eastern zone into Anglian and Saxon areas plus a British enclave.

English made polytheistic paganism an integral part of their self-created identity. It seems possible that Anglo-Saxon elites were keen to distance themselves from the Christian rulers of independent British states, or at least had no use (in the absence of a continuing material culture such as survived in Gaul) for the intellectual culture which their Christianity preserved.[53] Britons who became English for reasons of self-advancement may thus in the process have become pagan, like those post-Roman Greek- and Latin-speaking Christians in the eastern Mediterranean and north Africa who learnt Arabic, became Arabs, and converted to Islam.[54] This would have been all the easier if grass-roots Christianity still embodied traits from Romano-Celtic polytheism, as it had in the fourth century. Conversely, British communities which chose to keep their own identity, with all its social disadvantages, were thereby all the more likely to remain Christian.

The tenuous scraps of evidence seem consistent, so far as they go, with this level of survival and contact. Hanging-bowls with cruciform mounts (Fig. 5), known from Anglo-Saxon graves, are of British manufacture and show that products of the Christian culture of northern and western Britain were available to high-status Angles after 600, though their symbolism need not necessarily have been understood.[55] Two Norfolk place-names in *eclēs*, '(British?) church',[56] and one in Kent, are isolated but persuasive indications of surviving cult sites. And somewhere in or near Kent, Augustine found the shrine of a St Sixtus being venerated by local people who were, however, ignorant of their martyr's life and death.[57] Pope Gregory's negative response—to suppress the cult and substitute relics of the Roman martyr Sixtus—may help to explain why no other evidence has survived for indigenous Christianity in the Kentish ambit.[58] The story is also interesting for the rustic ignorance of the saint's devotees (assuming that the problem lay in their inability to explain rather than in their questioners' unwillingness to understand): it is not even clear that they had any clergy, and they look far removed from the learned and fastidious *doctores* of contemporary Wales.

If Roman Christianity flourished in the west by transforming itself, it is unlikely in the east to have enjoyed more than a ghost-life. And it is hard to see how the religion of groups who were enemies outside the Anglo-Saxon frontier, and second-class citizens within it, could have had much impact on

---

[53] Stancliffe 1999: 135–7; Ward Perkins 2000: 528–30; Sharpe 2002a: 88.

[54] Ward-Perkins 2000: 525.

[55] Work in progress by Susan Youngs (pers. comm.); Geake 1999 for the context of deposition.

[56] Below, p. 27, for these names, and p. 236 n. for the special case of Eccles on the Medway.

[57] Brooks 1984: 20; Stancliffe 1999: 121–3; Brooks 2000: 237–9; Sharpe 2002a: 123–5.

[58] Below, n. 238, for arguments against the view that people in Kent around 600 had learnt ideas of ritual purity from British bishops.

5. Escutcheon-plate with Christian imagery from a British-made hanging-bowl, found in an early seventh-century English grave at *Faversham* (Kent). Actual size. (British Museum.)

kings and nobles who had defined themselves, perhaps self-consciously, in contradistinction to the British and their culture. Augustine of Canterbury began his mission with an almost clean slate.

If there is was any territory where these two seemingly antagonistic cultures could have met on more equal terms, and influenced each other, it must have been in the intervening central zone of Britain. Its northern expanse was essentially, as viewed from the east coast, a hilly hinterland to Northumbria: the Scottish southern uplands, the Cheviots and Pennines. Further south, it was split between the two great English kingdoms of the future: the Mercians (*Mierce*, 'border people'), expanding from the Trent valley, through the central and west midlands to the Cotswolds and Severn; and the Saxons of Hampshire and Wiltshire, the future West Saxons, pushing steadily westwards into Dorset, Somerset, and east Devon. This is a diverse swathe of territory, but its regions did have in common that although by *c.*680 they were formally 'English' in a variety of political configurations, they were much less thoroughly acculturated than the lands to their east.

A tangible mark of cultural difference is that whereas in the eastern zone furnished burial and cremation were overwhelmingly the dominant rites throughout the pagan Anglo-Saxon period, in much of the central zone they occur more sparsely, and sometimes as a minority element among native or mixed practices. It has been tempting to conclude, especially for the west midlands, that incoming Anglo-Saxons were converted by the native British to Christianity and thus to unfurnished burial.[59] Such arguments need, though, to be seen against a background of long-term regional diversity. The west midlands, the Welsh marches, and large areas of north Britain had practised archaeologically invisible burial rites since before the Roman conquest:[60] the scarcity of diagnostic grave-deposits from *c.*400–700 implies the persistence of indigenous but not necessarily Christian practice.

It remains significant that such a high proportion of the few burials from this intermediate zone which do have Germanic-style metalwork also show indigenous traits, for instance stone grave-linings, or single rather than paired brooches.[61] This is clearest in two regions where distinctive rites can in fact be identified in the Romano-British period. One is the Peak District, where a prehistoric and Roman tradition of barrow-burial re-emerged in the later seventh century, combining local traits—rock-cut graves, quartz pebbles, antler tines—with prestige Anglo-Saxon grave-goods.[62] The other is the formerly quite Romanized zone of Dorset and Somerset, where several excavated cemeteries (in common with those of Gwent across the Severn) show a striking continuity of both site and practice during *c.*300–700, and incorporate occasional Anglo-Saxon traits into a dominant native culture.[63] At Cannington (Somerset), for instance, knife-furnished graves show one group among the various users of the cemetery practising a seventh- to eighth-century English rite: as the excavators put it, 'Cannington was a burial place for people who lived in the area, whoever they might have been'.[64] These patterns suggest incomplete acculturation of the Britons, or even some acculturation of the Angles to British practices. By 700 the inhabitants of the Pennines, the midlands, and the south-west had accepted (from what must surely have been an ethnic minority) an English political and linguistic identity, but they did so without having constructed the homogeneous cultural identity, reinforced by a rejection of all things British, of their eastern neighbours.

Without even the few sources available further west, it is hard to see when, and how fully, the British of these regions were Christianized. The Roman heritage is likely to have been strongest in Somerset and Dorset, weakest in

---

[59] Sims-Williams 1990: 64–71, 83, and Bassett 1992: 15–17, for this argument. Bassett 2000: 113–16 shifts to the model of a British Christian majority resisting acculturation of its burial rites, even though eventually accepting an English identity.

[60] O'Brien 1999: 38, 62–70, 78, 185.

[61] Geake 1997: 17 and e.g. 172–3 (Northumbria), 176 (Bromfield: see also Hadley 1995), 186–8 (Monkton Deverill and West Knoyle), 190 (Occaney Beck); O'Brien 1999 for these and others; Hope-Taylor 1977: 246–7, and Lucy 1999 (sceptical), for the north-east.

[62] Loveluck 1995; Geake 1997: 148–50; O'Brien 1999: 86–94. Loveluck argues that these rich burials represent mutual emulation by native and immigrant elites, financed by sales of lead to the new minsters of Northumbria and Mercia.

[63] Rahtz 1991: 13–18; Geake 1997: 150, 176; O'Brien 1999: 32–4; Rahtz and others 2000: 418.

[64] Rahtz and others 2000: 92–3, 96–7, 423–5. See below, p. 240, for the knife-burial rite.

the north midlands and south-eastern Scotland. There seems no reason why the developing Christianity of the west-coast regions should not have extended as far east as did the autonomous British states which supported it. Sub-Roman Christian sites are, however, archaeologically visible only on the western fringe, mainly in the Severn estuary zone where a series of pagan temples have been interpreted (with varying degrees of plausibility) as con-verted to Christian cult-use in the fifth century.[65] Further north, the char-acteristic sub-circular churchyards and church enclosures of Wales extend into the west midlands, especially parts of Herefordshire and Shropshire, and include some large examples such as the parochial mother-church of Eccle-ston (Cheshire).[66] These sites show the material culture of the British Church penetrating at least a zone of interface between British and English.

Eccleston also illustrates a different category of evidence, suggestive of British Christians not just on the edges of the central zone but in its heart. Place-names in 'Eccles-' are generally agreed to embody Brittonic *eclēs* 'a church', a loan-word from Latin *ecclesia* which developed into modern Welsh *eglwys*.[67] The distribution of this element is unexpected and intriguing (Fig. 2). Unknown in the western heartland of British Christianity, *eclēs* names cluster instead in two groups: one around the Forth estuary, the other in Lancashire, Cheshire, and western Yorkshire. There are light scatters around the Solway and in the south midlands, two instances in Norfolk, and one in Kent.

What the main concentrations have in common is that they lie in terri-tories colonized during the seventh century by the expanding kingdoms of Northumbria and Mercia. Although it is uncertain if *eclēs* ever entered the English language as a generic noun, it does seem likely that these place-names became established through English practice.[68] In other words, it was the British who used a Latin loan-word for their 'churches' (whatever exactly those were), but the English who picked it up as descriptive of specific places.

[65] Rahtz 1991; Dark 1994*b*: 60–3; Woodward and Leach 1993: 66–79, for Uley (a temple of Mercury replaced in the fifth century by a series of structures including a possible baptistery).

[66] Brook 1992; Gelling 1992: 86–92; Hadley 1995: 150; *VCH Cheshire*, i. 240–1 and pl. 19; Ray 2001: 109–23; Blair 2001*a*: 3–6. Above, n. 38, for Cumbria. See Petts 2002 for some chronological doubts.

[67] For the debate on the origin and distribution of this element: Cameron 1968; Cameron 1975; Gelling 1978: 82–3 (suggesting that the south-eastern outliers may be direct borrowings from Latin to English); Fellows-Jensen 1987: 295; Gelling 1992: 87; Sharpe 2002*a*: 121, 146–7; Petts 2002: 42–3. For the northern group: Barrow 1983; Thomas 1981: 262–5; Smith 1996: 27.

[68] The contrast between the diverse vocabulary for church sites in Ireland and the ubiquity of *llan* names in Wales may suggest that the latter were overlaid on earlier and more varied terms which could have included *eclēs* (cf. Petts 2002: 41–2 and Davies 2002: 392–4). On the southern and western Gallic pattern, it may be that *ecclesia* originally meant specifically an episcopal church, though it is hardly likely that this distinction was carried over into English perceptions (cf. below, p. 74 n.). I am grateful to Thomas Charles-Edwards for his advice on this problem.

The implication seems to be that when Anglo-Saxon rulers established political hegemony in the Scottish lowlands and the north midlands they found the landscape dotted with places of Christian cult, and grasped something of their special character by talking to the locals. Since several emerge later as parochial mother-churches, it even looks as though they maintained some status as ecclesiastical centres. The smaller group in the south-west midlands[69] would then suggest more limited continuity, while the three cases in eastern England are consistent with an exiguous survival of Christian enclaves. The tendency for toponymy to vary regionally—especially in a multi-lingual culture—means that this line of reasoning cannot be pushed too far, but it does at least suggest a more widespread survival of localized Christian sites than the texts or the archaeology would imply.

In the north there are signs of the process—already dimly perceived in Wales—whereby larger and more complex sites of a broadly monastic character arose among the small ones. To monasteries mentioned in the rather less unreliable hagiographies of British and Pictish founder-saints—Culross, Glasgow, Hoddom—can perhaps be added others which emerge by the later seventh century in English hands—Melrose, Abercorn, Carlisle.[70] Especially interesting, thanks to recent excavations, is Whithorn on the Solway Firth, which by the mid sixth century had apparently been organized as an inner precinct containing graves and shrines (and presumably the main church), surrounded by an outer residential area:[71] a glimpse, like the Welsh crop-mark sites, of the sort of concentric monastic site known mainly from Ireland. Further south there are no clear cases east of Bangor-is-Coed (unless we take seriously a later reference to a bishop and monks at *Letocetum*, the predecessor of Lichfield, Staffs., around the early seventh century), but a British background to some of the great west midland minsters is no less plausible for being impossible to verify.[72]

So some British infrastructure remained: could it contribute anything to the English ecclesiastical infrastructure being established by the 680s? For Bede, the manifold crimes of the Christian British included 'this one, that they never preached the faith to the Saxons or Angles who inhabited Britain with them'.[73] It is possible that this famous comment arose from a simple misunderstanding,[74] and it fits the ideological framework of Bede's 'History'

---

[69] Sims-Williams 1990: 79–80.

[70] Smith 1996: 22–4, 26–7; below, p. 152.

[71] Hill 1997. Note, though, that only a small proportion of the total area was excavated.

[72] Below, pp. 30, 151–2.

[73] *HE* i. 22 (p. 68).

[74] For the argument that the neglectful 'priests of the neighbourhood' *(sacerdotes e vicino)*—blamed by Gregory for not converting the English—were Frankish not British, but that Bede

too conveniently to be accepted without question. This is not to say that his strictures were completely baseless: it is easy to picture embattled and rather purist British ecclesiastics who had inherited the late Roman Church's distaste for evangelizing 'barbarians'. On the other hand the eastern English can hardly have been receptive to British missionaries, however diligent, and it is arguable that when, around 602–4, Augustine met a contingent of British bishops and *doctores* near the Somerset/Gloucestershire border, intransigence was not all on their side.[75] If local contacts had fostered any goodwill, Augustine's mandate from the pope to subject British bishops to the 'new Church of the English', his insistence on his own supremacy, and maybe his low opinion of native ecclesiastics formed from circumstances and attitudes in Kent, are together likely to have stifled it. As the suppression of the cult of 'St Sixtus' illustrates, the Gregorian agenda offered no encouragement or protection to native Christian culture.

Outside Augustine's sphere, and in a more secular context, things look rather different. Vernacular sources such as the 'Gododdin' suggest a web of local feuds and alliances between British, Pictish, Irish, and Anglian groups which, while involving fierce antipathies, also left scope for Anglo-British co-operation (most famously the alliance between Penda of Mercia and Cadwallon of Gwynedd around 630[76]). As English dynasties emerged and consolidated their power in the decades around 600, it is possible that they became more rather than less open to influence from the aristocratic culture of Celtic Britain.[77] There is nothing to suggest that ecclesiastical politics were any different. In the 630s King Oswald of Northumbria looked to Iona rather than Canterbury for his missionaries, and there was no evident barrier between British and Irish Christians, or the English converts of either, until the Easter controversy drove a wedge between them in the 660s, and marginalized both the British and the Irish non-conformists.[78]

Religious communities could suffer in warfare, most spectacularly in *c.*615 when the pagan King Æthelfrith of Northumbria slaughtered some 1,200 priests from the monastery of Bangor-is-Coed near Wrexham.[79] But

---

understood the phrase in the latter sense and built his picture accordingly, see for instance Stancliffe 1999: 109. It is, however, rejected by Brooks 2000: 243–4 n. 57, and Patrick Wormald observes to me that the Stancliffe interpretation entails a circumlocution which would fit badly with Gregory's normal forthright style. In the last analysis the phrase is ambiguous.

[75] *HE* ii. 2 (pp. 134–40); Stancliffe 1999: 114–15, 122–34.

[76] *HE* ii. 20 (p. 202): for Bede an especially unholy alliance between a pagan Angle and a Briton with 'the name and profession of a Christian but a barbarian in heart and habits'.

[77] Blair 1995*b*: 21–2 interprets the possible influence of Romano-Celtic square shrines (below, p. 52) in this context.

[78] Stancliffe 1995*a*: 37–46. Sharpe 2002*b* proposes British influence on new names taken in the 650s by the first native English bishops.

[79] *HE* ii. 2 (pp. 140–2).

Æthelfrith's motivation was seemingly neither racial nor anti-Christian, but simply that he considered the clergy to be part of the opposing army. If we are to trust the later 'Lament for Cynddylan', it was a Welsh rather than an English raid in around the 630s which gave no quarter to the (presumably British) bishop and 'book-holding monks' in the former Roman town of *Letocetum* (Staffs.).[80] On the other side, the resolutely pagan King Penda of Mercia (*c.*630–655) was happy for his subjects—presumably either Anglian or British—to practise Christianity provided they did so properly.[81]

In the north and midlands, some assimilation of British ecclesiastical sites by the English clearly did occur during the seventh century. The fact that Carlisle, Abercorn, and Melrose all kept their British names (*Luel, Aebbercurning, Mailros*) suggests some element of continuity in the process of transfer,[82] but the form that this took, on the spectrum between gentle acculturation and violent displacement, is unknown. The early eighth-century Northumbrian takeover of Whithorn maintained its site and pre-served some of its traditions, but overbuilt at least part of the British monastic complex with a layout and buildings of a purely English kind.[83] Most explic-itly and starkly, St Wilfrid's biographer describes how, at the dedication of the great Yorkshire minster of Ripon in the mid 670s, he announced his acquisition of 'holy places (*loca sancta*) in several regions which the British clergy had abandoned as they fled the sharpness of the hostile sword in our people's hand'.[84] If—as seems likely—these lay in recently annexed British territory southwards and westwards, in Elmet and the valleys of the Ribble, Mersey, and Lune,[85] they could have included some of the **eclēs* sites there.

While the message of this case is bleak, its context was the more central-ized and perhaps less tolerant religious-political world developing after the 660s. There is, as Clare Stancliffe observes, a contrast between the **eclēs* sites between Tweed and Forth, which mostly emerge as the mother-churches of big parishes with dependent chapels, and those near Ripon, which tend to be humble churches later: is this because King Oswald and St Aidan had allowed more continuity of religious personnel and structures, when absorb-ing British territory in the 630s, than King Ecgfrith and St Wilfrid would do

---

[80] Kirby 1977: 37; Bassett 1992: 34 (as against Brooks 1989: 169).

[81] *HE* iii. 21 (p. 280). Could Penda's insistence on strict standards reflect the purist attitudes of *British* bishops advising him or his allies?

[82] Thomas 1981: 291–4; Stancliffe 1995*a*: 78–9.

[83] Hill 1997: 16–18; below, p. 187.

[84] *VW* c. 17 (p. 36).

[85] This remains the common-sense interpretation, and is supported by current work by Felicity Clark, but it has been contested: see Sims-Williams 1988: 180–3, as against Potts 1994. This passage, and King Ecgfrith's reputed gifts to Cuthbert of land at Carlisle and Cartmel, are the first evidence for English administration west of the Pennines: Potts 1994: 63–4; Stancliffe 1995*a*: 56–7.

in the 670s?[86] In any case, it would not be surprising if Wilfrid's behaviour towards British clergy within his power was harsher than that of many of his contemporaries.

Further south, in the west midlands, the search for the British roots of English Christianity has been intense. In 1990 Patrick Sims-Williams observed that the Hwicce and Magonsæte (the people of Gloucestershire, Worcestershire, Warwickshire, Herefordshire, and Shropshire) were evidently Christian by *c.*660—a conversion of which Bede evidently knew nothing— and suggested that they 'were converted in an unobtrusive and ultimately unmemorable way by the Britons among them'.[87] Coming to the same point from a different direction, Steven Bassett was meanwhile developing the hypothesis that the huge and topographically coherent mother-parishes which can be recognized later around important ex-Roman places— Worcester, Gloucester, *Letocetum*, Wroxeter—began as territories of British churches of a status likely to have housed bishops.[88] This must be accepted as a serious possibility, and it does seem suggestive that only some thirty years after the supposed raid on the bishop and monks at *Letocetum*, its successor site at Lichfield was considered 'well prepared' to be an episcopal seat.[89] It is, however, inherently difficult for this kind of topographical argument to move from hypothesis to proof, and archaeological support remains elusive.[90]

Southwards into Wessex, we again find intriguing pointers but few hard

---

[86] Stancliffe 1995*a*: 78; cf. Barrow 1973: 28–30, 36–9, for the later high status of the more northerly **eclēs* sites, and Smith 1996: 27–31, for an evolutionary view of Anglian dominance in southern Scotland. Stancliffe's idea would, by extension, imply a high degree of continuity in cases like Eccleshall (Staffs.) with its huge mother-parish (Spufford and Spufford 1964: 5–10). It looks more than coincidence that the Lancashire hundreds of Salford, Blackburn, Amounderness, Leyland, and West Derby each contains one 'Eccles-' site (*VCH Lancs. passim*).

[87] Sims-Williams 1990: 55–9, 75–9, 84; cf. Bassett 2000 for the plausible argument that the region was largely populated by acculturated Britons.

[88] Bassett 1989*a*; Bassett 1992. Another possible candidate for this list (though not ex-Roman) is Leominster: Hillaby 1987; Blair 2001*a*: 3–5, 10–11.

[89] Below, p. 99.

[90] Discoveries which at one stage looked encouraging, in the form of post-Roman but pre-English burials under the church of St Mary-de-Lode, Gloucester, and beside Worcester cathedral, turn out to be inconclusive in the first case and mistaken in the second: Bryant and Heighway 2003: 112–17; Bassett 1989*a*: 254 n. 107. At St Mary-de-Lode the burials were in a timber building on padstones (Period 3), overlying and exactly aligned on a Roman building with a mosaic floor. Undoubtedly this was the first phase of the church, which had a continuous existence thereafter, but there is no even vaguely reliable date until the next phase but one (Period 5), which has a radio-carbon determination centred on the tenth century. The one pointer to a pre-English date is that the post-pad technique is closer to late or sub-Roman than to Anglo-Saxon building technology; but this is hardly conclusive, and it remains possible that St Mary's was first built, within a visible Roman ruin, as an adjunct to the late seventh-century minster. Dating of the Worcester burials depends on two radiocarbon determinations, the earlier of which has a calibrated range extending up to 680 at 68% confidence and 852 at 95% confidence.

facts.[91] Susan Pearce's argument that villa estates and sub-Roman lordships may be perpetuated as Anglo-Saxon mother-parishes shares both the possibilities and the problems of Bassett's west midland hypothesis.[92] Some of the more westerly minsters, such as Wareham, Sherborne, and Exeter, have evidence for some kind of British background,[93] and the scatter of continuing British saints' cults in western Wessex carries its own message.[94] In about 664 an episcopal consecration, apparently at Winchester, involved two British bishops who had presumably come there from the south-west.[95] This impression of ecclesiastical interchange between Wessex and the British lands to its west is strengthened by a poem of the West Saxon scholar-abbot Aldhelm, describing a journey from Cornwall into Devon where he celebrates mass in a timber church in the company of its religious community.[96] In a further crucial text, a letter of (probably) the 690s, Aldhelm could address Gerent, king of free British Devon and Cornwall, in respectful tones, urging him to bring his bishops into conformity with the Roman Easter and tonsure; Bede adds the interesting information that this letter convinced 'many of the Britons who were subject to the West Saxons'.[97]

In warning Gerent against the Welsh bishops across the Severn who, 'glorying in the private purity of their own way of life, detest our communion to such a great extent that they disdain equally to celebrate the divine offices in church with us and to take courses of food at table for the sake of charity', Aldhelm proposes a union of West Saxons and Dumnonians in the catholic faith which will distance them from their schismatic and hypocritical British neighbours. If this sounds benign, it also reflects a sense of English superiority—not necessarily as harsh or as ideologically motivated as Bede's—which may nonetheless have suppressed native culture on the annexed sites. To quote Barbara Yorke, 'it can only be an assumption that there was a place for British priests and monks who were prepared to adapt in the Anglo-Saxon church structure because no firm indicators of their presence exist. If they

---

[91] Hase 1994: 50–2, for a maximalist view, and Hall 2000: 29, for a minimalist; Yorke 1995: 177–81 is judiciously in the middle.

[92] Pearce 1982*b*; Pearce 1985. See Dark 1994*b*: 160–2, for a supportive reaction, and Hall 2000: 21–4, for a sceptical one. Bell 2001 discusses the individual villa sites.

[93] Yorke 1995: 69–72, 177–81; Henderson and Bidwell 1982; Edwards 1988: 243–53; Probert 2002: 279–81; and note the Anglo-Saxon window-glass on the Roman temple site at Uley (Woodward and Leach 1993: 189–92). However, I reject the claim of Rodwell 2001: 40–54, that the Wells complex developed from a late Roman mausoleum: see Blair 2004.

[94] Blair 2002*a*: map p. 458: Nectan (Hartland), Urith (Chittlehampton), Sativola (Exeter), and Juthwara (Halstock), to whom Decuman (Watchet) should perhaps be added. I owe this point to Barbara Yorke.

[95] *HE* iii. 28 (p. 316); cf. Stancliffe 1999: 109–10, and Probert 2002: 278–9.

[96] *AO* 524–8 (Lapidge and Rosier 1985: 177–9); cf. Probert 2002: 265–7.

[97] *AO* 480–6 (Lapidge and Herren 1979: 140–3, 155–60); *HE* v. 18 (p. 514); cf. Probert 2002: 267–78.

did, they must soon have abandoned British names as these do not appear
in witness-lists.'[98]

In the end, the debt of the institutionalized English Church to the British
still seems limited. If British Christians did convert any of their conquerors,
it was at the level of micro-communities. Coexistence of British, English, and
Irish groups—and therefore of Christians if that was what they were—may
have been widespread at a local level in the late sixth and seventh centuries,
a possible but unverifiable undercurrent in the 'official' conversion of the
Anglo-Saxon laity. Adoption of church sites may have been common, though
if the Ripon episode was at all typical they may often have been abandoned
by their British clergy, and reduced to the status of satellites of English minsters. In British border zones (Ergyng in south-western Herefordshire is a particularly striking case), groups of these small establishments could have given
the mature Anglo-Saxon Church a more localized character than it would
have elsewhere.[99] But there are few signs that either personnel or structures
were assimilated, or that there were contacts at the level of scholarship and
literate devotion.[100] As population groups gradually saw political and social
advantage in 'opting for a future labelled Anglo-Saxon',[101] they turned their
eyes away from Welsh bishops and monasteries and towards the Gregorian
east. Thus the probably extensive grass-roots influence was neutralized and
silenced by the larger-scale political and cultural structures, which aligned
Christianity inexorably to Lindisfarne, Whitby, or Ripon on the one hand,
to Canterbury or its daughter sees on the other. Bede is merely the culmination of a project to construct a new English Christian identity, founded
on Gregorian Rome, which encouraged a British cultural amnesia and cold-
shouldered any help—if in fact there was any—on offer from the learned
and well-organized Churches of western Britain.[102]

Yet the organizational modes developed in British Christian settlements
may have something to contribute to the themes of this book. Among the

---

[98] Yorke 1995: 179–81.   [99] Below, pp. 151–2; Ray 2001: 109–33.

[100] Cf., for the west midlands, Charles-Edwards 1991: 'If the Christianity of the area had begun
by being native and British, it ended by being emphatically non-British. Evidence from several
genres—biblical exegesis, letter-writing, visions, collections of prayer and poetry—shows a remarkably full participation in Christian Latin culture, but, with hardly any exception, it is a culture
whose ties run in all directions except west to Wales.'

[101] Bassett 2000: 115–17, on the re-alignment of the west midlands, with the striking suggestion
that 'there were far more British christians in the region who became English than there were
Germanic immigrants who became christian'. Cf. Charles-Edwards 2001 for the intermixture of
British and English communities around the Welsh border, and the hardening of the confessional
frontier.

[102] For recent thoughts along these lines: Stancliffe 1999: 138–40; Brooks 2000: 244–6;
Bassett 2000: 116. Thomas Charles-Edwards observes (pers. comm.): 'I suspect that attitudes were
formed as much by what the Franks thought of the Bretons (not distinguished from Britons) as
by any ideas of Gregory the Great.'

large monastic sites which the British Church generated during the sixth century, at least a few were perpetuated as such English minsters as Whithorn, Melrose, Leominster, Lichfield, or Sherborne. Even the pagan Northumbrians who slaughtered its priests must have been impressed by the 'most noble minster' of Bangor-is-Coed, 'where there was said to be so great a number of monks that, when it was divided into seven parts with superiors (*praepositi*) over each, no division had fewer than 300 men, all of whom were accustomed to live by the labour of their hands'.[103] Exaggeration notwithstanding, Bangor surely exemplified the most complex and structured kind of place which they could have known at first hand. Fusing with similar influences from other directions, the British monastery could have had some impact as a settlement-form.

Influences (ii): the Roman inheritance in Italy and Gaul

When Pope Gregory launched his mission to the English, he probably did so mainly because leaders of Kentish society were coming to see Rome as a fountainhead of spiritual and temporal authority and of fashionable taste, and wanted to draw their Christianity from it.[104] If Augustine thought the British Church contemptible beside the Roman, his Kentish converts are likely to have shared this prejudice. Conversely, any Roman model for local ecclesiastical organization had a good chance of being received enthusiastically in the first instance. All the major mission leaders up to the 630s— Augustine and Mellitus in Kent and Essex, Paulinus in Northumbria, Felix in East Anglia, Birinus in the upper Thames valley—came direct from Italy or Gaul, and there must be a strong presumption that they tried to reproduce forms of Church organization which they knew. What are those likely to have been?

Northern and central Italy, and central and southern Gaul, had been more thoroughly Romanized than the regions to their north (Fig. 6). They also still remained city-based societies, in which the *civitates* (city-territories) retained much of their old identity as the social and economic hinterlands of urban centres. Under Lombard and Frankish rule, political power, administration, taxation, and justice continued, if often in a fragmented and attenuated form, to be exercised from the cities.[105] In sharp contrast to

[103] *HE* ii. 2 (pp. 136–7, 140).
[104] Cf. Stancliffe 1999: 137–8. Bassett 1989*a*: 226–9 is more inclined to envisage an aim of re-creating the lost province. For Gregory's attitudes to the English see also Markus 1970; P. Brown 1996: 134–47. Below, pp. 39–40, for Roman taste in English early seventh-century grave-goods.
[105] Wickham 1981: 80–92, for Italy; Loseby 1998: 239–52, for Gaul.

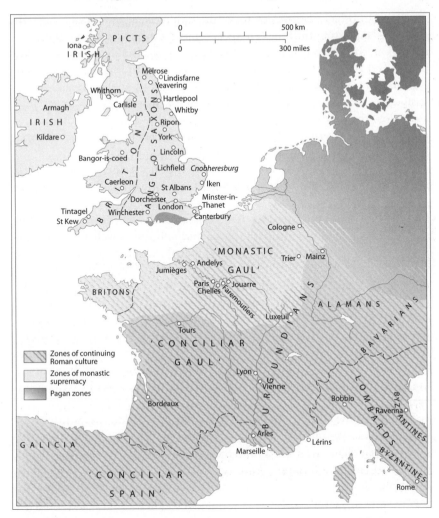

6. Christian north-west Europe in the 660s: a schematic illustration of the contrast between zones of continuing Roman culture and urban life (diminishing in intensity from south to north), and those of predominantly monastic ecclesiastical organization.

post-Roman Britain, large elements of the architectural and social civic fabric survived. But during the fourth to sixth centuries there was a profound transformation, from a secular urban landscape of public buildings and amenities to a sacred one of churches. Fora, baths, theatres, and aqueducts decayed; cathedrals rose inside city walls, ringed by groups of satellite churches, and basilicas marked graves of the holy dead in extramural cemeteries.[106] Initiated when the Empire and its economy remained intact, this Christian component grew in relative importance under barbarian rule as other urban functions declined.

As cathedrals came to dominate cities, their bishops emerged as one of the main institutional links from imperial past to Lombard or Frankish present. In some regions, notably the sixth-century central Gaul pictured for us by Gregory of Tours, bishops exercised functions of government and public administration, and were truly the social and political as well as the spiritual leaders of their city-territories.[107] So the gradual extension of Christian belief from civilized citizens to the *pagani* of the countryside, as it proceeded through the late fourth to seventh centuries, was a centre-outwards movement: controlled by bishops, based on the inherited fabric of territorial division and settlement hierarchy, and administered in Roman fashion by bureaucratic means. Just as minor urban churches were conceived as diocesan property, so the initial assumption was that new rural churches and their clergy were the bishop's; just as the cathedral of a *civitas* stood in its city, so the focal settlements of the main provincial districts (*plebes* in Italy, *vici* in France) became the next tier of pastoral centres.

Despite all the complexities and limitations in practice, it is thus possible to adduce a clear-cut ideal model of how the ministry to the laity was supposed to be organized.[108] Pastoral care, and above all the initiatory sacrament of baptism, were the responsibility of the bishop and of clergy under his direction. In his city the bishop therefore had a group of buildings, including his cathedral church (*ecclesia*, a word often apparently denoting the whole

---

[106] North and central Italy: Ward-Perkins 1984: 51–84. Gaul: Février and others 1980; Knight 1999: 63–84; Pearce 2003; and further references in Blair 1992: 235–46.

[107] P. Brown 1996: 61, 104, 112–17; Wickham 1981: 87 for Italy; Loseby 1998: 252–6 for Gaul.

[108] For Italy: Boyd 1952: 49–57. For Gaul: Imbart de la Tour 1900: 3–105; Griffe 1949; Aubrun 1986: 12–131; Treffort 1996a: 35–7; Knight 1996: 113; Charles-Edwards 2000: 244, 249; Delaplace 2002. Wood forthcoming will provide much new material. Some conciliar statements of the relationship between cathedrals and *parochiae* are: Vaison 529, c. 2 (*CG2* 78–9): priests can preach 'non solum in civitatibus sed etiam in omnibus parrociis'. Orleans 538 c. 5 (*CG2* 116): *basilicae* in *civitates* distinguished from *parrociae* or *basilicae* in *pagis civitatum*. Orleans 541, cc. 26, 33 (*CG2* 139–40): clergy serving *parrociae* in the houses of great men are subject to the archdeacon of the *civitas*; anyone who has, or asks to have, a *diocessis* on his estate must provide adequate land and clergy. These and other passages in the councils and Gregory of Tours are collected by Delaplace 2002: an important new analysis of the terminology. See also below, p. 38 n.

complex) and a baptistery.[109] Public churches were built at the largest and most accessible centres of rural population, were staffed by contingents of the bishop's clergy under archpriests, and were provided with the baptismal rights and facilities which give them their distinctive status as baptismal or 'parish' churches (*ecclesiae baptismales, baptisteria, parochiae*);[110] the property, personnel, and activities of these churches remained, however, under the bishop's oversight. It was permissible for private individuals, such as substantial landowners, to build churches (*oratoria, basilicae, dioceses*) on their own property, but these were to be properly consecrated and supervised, and were not to accroach the functions—above all baptism—of public churches.

Naturally this model can rarely have worked in a completely pure form. There were regional and chronological contrasts both in the impact of barbarian invasion and administrative collapse, and in the enthusiasm of bishops for extending pastoral networks around their cities. Central Gaul, with its strong bishops and its assimilation to Frankish rule, may have been especially coherent. Thus the well-documented Touraine shows the progressive foundation during *c.*370–591 of *vicus* churches staffed by groups of clergy under archpriests, spinning a web which left few people living more than seven miles from a centre of pastoral care, but whose main filaments ran straight back to the bishop in Tours.[111] In Italy on the other hand, where letters of Pope Gelasius I (492–6) show the controlled foundation of baptismal churches, the Lombard and other wars left a disrupted fabric which Gregory the Great (590–604) embarked energetically on rebuilding and extending.[112] It was also only slowly that the baptismal churches—initially viewed as extensions of their parent cathedrals, even if serving territories which were well defined in social or administrative terms—acquired the kind of autonomy over stable ecclesiastical districts which makes it possible to call them 'parish churches' in something like the later sense. In Italy, where this problem has been most closely examined, the *sistema pievano* of mother-parishes centred

---

[109] Carrié 1996: *passim,* and the works cited in n. 106 above, for baptisteries as elements in church groups.

[110] For Gaul, Delaplace 1999: 167–70 proposes an evolutionary development: initially mere oratories in the *vici,* which only during the sixth century acquired archpriests, fixed clergy, and baptismal rights; cf. Delaplace 2002. A remarkable allegory of the Italian mother-church is the model at Monza of a hen and seven chicks, supposedly given by Gregory the Great to Queen Theodolind of the Lombards and representing the church which she founded with its seven parishes: Gannon 2003: 124.

[111] Stancliffe 1979; Fletcher 1997: 40–8; Delaplace 2002. For other regions see Griffe 1975: 3–7, and Delaplace 1999: 156–66. Ibid. 166–7 notes that the earliest rural churches were sometimes on the peripheries rather than in the core areas of dioceses, perhaps a reflection either of missionary concerns or of a need to define frontiers.

[112] Violante 1986: 113–44.

on the baptismal churches of *plebes* (*pievi*) took shape very gradually during the seventh to ninth centuries.[113]

This definition of baptismal parishes was part of a larger process which ultimately tended towards parochial fission: the pressure for churches at any level to gain sacramental, financial, and territorial independence from the level above. In particular, private *oratoria* on estates of both Roman and barbarian landlords (the churches of mere *villae* rather than *vici*) multiplied hugely during the fourth to seventh centuries.[114] Papal correspondence and Gallic church councils show a determination to keep them under control, but also by implication a persistent fear that they might break free. By the start of the Carolingian period, generations of encroachments and pragmatic compromises had produced a continuum in which the boundary between public and private was becoming blurred, for instance by secular lords acquiring baptismal churches or establishing baptisteries at their oratories. But when Carolingian legislators sought to re-impose order,[115] they could at least recognize in some parts of their Empire a coherent underlying framework which might be appealed to, and if possible restored. As we will see, that was not true of all parts.

During the fourth century a radically new mode of Christian life spread into western Europe which, though in theory antithetical to lay settlement, parochial organization, and pastoral care, would in practice intermesh with them in multifarious ways: monasticism. An ideal which had begun with solitary flight into the Egyptian desert, and had flourished in communities of ascetics living apart from the world, became, paradoxically, an inspiration for evangelistic zeal and a model for complex settlement forms. It illustrates the ambiguities that Martin (d. 397), the bishop of Tours who initiated the conversion of the countryside around his city, was the monastic pioneer of Gaul, and that Augustine, bishop of Hippo (d. 430), had a household monastery of clergy (*monasterium clericorum*) as a base for his administrative and pastoral duties.[116] The earliest monasteries were often attached to cathedrals or sited in aristocrats' town houses, though many in fourth- to sixth-century

---

[113] Violante 1986: 139, 145–82; Castagnetti 1979: 7–21; Boyd 1952: 58–60.

[114] Wood forthcoming will be fundamental. For Italy: Boyd 1952: 55–7; Violante 1986: 133–9. For Gaul: Knight 1999: 126–7; Griffe 1975: 8–26; Stancliffe 1979: 51; Chaume 1937 (controlled episcopal devolution of parochial functions in the Mâconnais). Some conciliar restraints on encroachment by oratories are: Agde 506, c. 21 (*CG1* 202): anyone *extra parrocias* who wants to have an *oratorium in agro* cannot hold masses there on major feasts, which must must be celebrated 'nonnisi in civitatibus aut in parrociis'. Orleans 511, c. 17 (*CG2* 9): all the *baselice* which have been built in many places or are daily being built to be in the power of the bishop in whose *territurium* they are. Epaon 517, c. 25 (*CG2* 30): relics not to be placed *in oratoriis villarebus* unless 'clericus cuiuscumque parrochiae vicinus esse contingat'. Clermont 535, c. 15 (*CG2* 109): control over priest or deacon 'qui neque in civitate neque in parrochiis canonecus esse dinuscitur, sed in villolis habitans'.

[115] Below, p. 118.

[116] For some recent accounts: P. Brown 1996: 41–4; Fletcher 1997: 40–3; Langefeld 1996: 23–4.

Gaul developed from the country villas of devotees.[117] This was the monasticism familiar to the first monk-pope, proprietor of his own house-monastery in Rome, who in 596 sent a monk as first bishop of the English: an action contradicting his own view, firmly stated only the previous year, that the administrative and pastoral duties of priests could not properly be combined with the monastic discipline. Pope Gregory's complex attitudes to the relationship between monks, bishops, and pastoral care would resonate in the behaviour of his disciples at Canterbury.[118]

The modes of organization which those disciples are likely to have tried to replicate in England are thus fairly clear. In the first instance they would have founded cathedrals in such places as they could recognize as *civitates*, and as the mission expanded they would have proceeded to build neighbourhood baptismal churches. They would probably have sited them at the centres of whatever territories or folk-groupings they perceived as analogous to *vici* or *plebes*. They would have envisaged a major role for monasticism, but would have been alive to the dangers of its undermining the episcopally directed structures of parochial governance. They would not have viewed the building of oratories on aristocrats' estates as anomalous or necessarily undesirable, but would have insisted on their subordinate status and limited functions.

But how adequate to fulfil such aims were the economic and territorial realities of the English kingdoms? Before trying to answer this question directly, it may be useful to look at those more northerly parts of the Continent where Christianity was also expanding, but which preserved less classical urban culture than northern Italy or southern Gaul.

Influences (iii): the Frankish world

Grave-goods, which tell us less about conversion itself than was once thought, do say a good deal about its context. From the end of the sixth century there was a dramatic change in the nature of the objects deposited. Many familiar items disappear, notably jewellery of a conspicuously Germanic character, and regional dress-fashions are replaced by a simpler, homogeneous style. New jewellery types reflect Frankish fashions (especially in Kent), but also, and increasingly, the luxury goods of the Roman and Byzantine worlds, whether as imported originals or as copies. Suddenly, the English turned their backs on a range of cultural markers from their Germanic inheritance, and

[117] Percival 1997, and Bell 2001: 37–47, for monasteries overlying villas. Charles-Edwards 2000: 378–80 emphasizes the attachment of monasteries to cities; cf. Atsma 1976.

[118] The very same year, Gregory agreed that urgent pastoral necessity justified the removal of monks from monasteries in Orvieto diocese to make way for priests: Violante 1986: 143–4.

replaced them with new ones redolent of Frankish and eventually of Mediterranean culture.[119] In Kent, the critical changes were happening from *c*.580: St Augustine arrived in a kingdom whose richer inhabitants were already adopting the fashions of their northern Frankish neighbours across the Channel. If this Christian milieu was ultimately less glamorous than that of Rome, it was also—both physically and culturally—less remote.

The heartlands of continuing Roman civilization and city-based life were bordered by the Alps, the Saône, and the lower Loire. As we move further north[120]—into areas less Romanized in the first place and more heavily overlain by barbarian immigration; from Romance to Germanic speech; and eventually across the imperial frontier—the Roman substrate becomes thinner and more disrupted, and urban survival more tenuous. The map should, however, be visualized as a patchwork rather than a spectrum, with diverse zones in which Roman organization had existed, had survived or was revived to greater or lesser degrees. On the Moselle and middle Rhine frontier, as also in the Paris basin and Normandy, they were battered but not broken. In the Low Countries to the north, and in the emergent Alamannic and Bavarian territories to the south-east, disruption was significantly more severe. Across the Rhine into south-west Germany, where Frankish kings expanded their power and where Irish- and English-led missions dominate the narrative of conversion, any re-creation of Roman modes had to be done from scratch.

It is therefore unsurprising that during the fifth to eighth centuries the Rhineland and north-central France displayed—partly surviving, partly reconstructed—the late Roman organizational forms: cathedrals in major centres, suburban churches near their walls, baptismal churches built by bishops in the territories around.[121] Christian Frankish rulers drew heavily on expertise from the south, which must have helped to give mangled but recognizible structures a new lease of life. But if the ideal was a restored and homogeneous Gallic Church, it was in practice patchy and threadbare in the northern territories. Bishops had only limited resources to establish an effective pastoral network, and only limited authority to control the public and sacramental functions of such churches as did exist; they responded with a mixture of suspicion and support to the growing alternative power-structures of the monastic networks.[122] The further from the pockets where some

---

[119] Geake 1997: 107–39; Hawkes 1981 for Frankish buckles in Kent.

[120] For definitions of the frontier: Lemarignier 1966: 452–5; Fouracre 1979: 80; Loseby 1998: 248–9, 273–4.

[121] The Rhineland: Ewig 1976: 41–2; Semmler 1982: 836–44; Damminger 1998: 73–4; Green 1998: 343; Keller 2003. Normandy: Musset 1948. Alamannia and Bavaria: Burnell 1988: 494–530.

[122] Stancliffe 1999: 135–6, and Verhulst 2000: 104–6, for the disrupted state of northernmost France and the Low Countries; Semmler 1982: 844–50, for private initiatives in the Rhineland,

Roman infrastructure survived, the less the theory of a hierarchy of public churches under episcopal governance had real substance.

The traditional view is that new and vigorous brands of northern monasticism filled the gap: Columbanus and his Irish followers re-vitalized the northern Frankish Church early in the seventh century, and Anglo-Saxon monastic missions under Wilfrid, Willibrord, and Boniface converted Frisia and west Germany in the late seventh and eighth.[123] To an extent this stands: it is precisely my argument here that monastic organization was destined to prevail in northern Christendom, and took over where episcopal cities left off. But there are two qualifications, the effect of which is to root changes less in any distinctive 'national' character of ecclesiastical traditions, and more in the varied fabric of the societies upon which Christianity operated.

First, recent work stresses the importance of small to middle-range churches at grass-roots level, founded in great numbers by nobles on their own estates throughout the sixth- to eighth-century Frankish world. Archaeology has shown how churches built over ancestral burial-grounds, or as aristocratic mausolea, sometimes acquired public community functions and eventually emerged as parish centres.[124] These 'private' churches proliferated not only in regions where cathedral-centred structures of authority remained important, but also in those such as northernmost Gaul, the Low Countries, south-west Germany, and Bavaria where they were tenuous or absent. The monastic missions were thus not launched into a vacuum: as Simon Burnell observes of the Alamannic regions, 'the existence of a Christian aristocracy was the prerequisite for monastic foundations and not their first-fruits'.[125] The fact that when structures did develop they tended to assume a monastic character may have less to do with contrasting missionary cultures than with needs and expectations on the ground.

---

including the revealing case of the baptismal church at Tholey in 634; Fouracre 1979: 77–90, for bishops and monasteries in Rouen and Noyon dioceses. These issues are reviewed by Wood forthcoming. Defensive statements from councils held in the 'conciliar/monastic' border region are: Chalons-sur-Saône 647 × 53, c. 14 (*CG2* 306): magnates with *oraturia* at their *villae* not to exclude archdeacons; Clichy 626, c. 21 and Saint-Jean-de-Losne 673–5, c. 9 (*CG2* 295, 316): laymen not to become archpriests of *parrochiae*.

[123] Fletcher 1997: 136–59, 193–227, for an excellent recent account; see also Green 1998: 344, and Bierbrauer 2003: 436–41.

[124] Lemarignier 1966: 452–60; Fournier 1982: 502–25; Burnell 1988, esp. 64–70, 534–45; Halsall 1995*a*: 272; Damminger 1998: 58, 70–1, 92, 94–5; see also below, p. 235. Schulze 1967: 44–52, shows how in Thuringia, on the furthest eastern periphery, the eighth-century monastic expansion coexisted with important and sometimes baptismal churches founded by lay lords at their strongholds. Again, Wood forthcoming will provide a new and comprehensive survey of the written evidence.

[125] Burnell 1988: 583; cf. Werner 1976 for aristocratic interest in church-building as a context for monastic expansion.

Secondly, it is untenable to conceive 'Columbanian monasticism' as a distinct and coherent entity to be contrasted with old-fashioned Gallo-Roman monasticism.[126] Frankish rulers drew on monastic traditions from the south as well as from Ireland, and there was considerable interpenetration of the two in Burgundy and the Seine valley. The Irish character of Columbanus's own foundations also seems to have been quickly diluted and overlain by an influx of Frankish personnel, and by re-alignments determined by the political and familial links of royal and aristocratic patrons. The point is not that the Franks embraced monasticism because they were exposed to Columbanus, but rather that he and his colleagues offered versions of something that the northern Frankish royalty and aristocracy found highly appealing: monastery and estate church in one.

The proof of this is the extraordinary proliferation of rich monasteries in the zone between the Loire, the Saône, the Rhine, and the English Channel during the seventh century.[127] The founders and prime movers were usually monks, bishops, or monk-bishops; Columbanus' monastery of Luxeuil in Burgundy became a training-school for bishops. These monasteries tended, however, to be less closely associated with sites from the Roman past than in the south,[128] and the major communities were endowed and supported by competing branches of the Neustrian royal dynasty and by upwardly mobile kindreds. Important here is the early to mid seventh-century fashion for double houses containing aristocratic female communities under princess-abbesses, exemplified by a group in the Seine valley which were closely associated with the court: Chelles, Jouarre, Faremoutiers. Ruled by women whose families intermarried with the dynasties of Kent and East Anglia, they would be a prime source for the monastic civilization adopted by eastern English courts.[129]

The impression that the slighter the Roman inheritance, the more central the importance of free-standing religious communities, is reinforced if we consider Brittany, an anomalous corner of the Frankish land-mass. Marginal

---

[126] For recent perspectives on Columbanus, and on the appropriateness of the term 'Hiberno-Frankish', see Dierkens 1989: 372–88; Green 1998: 344–5; Charles-Edwards 2000: 364–90; Lebecq 2000: 123–4.

[127] Prinz 1965 is an encyclopaedic survey. For other accounts: Campbell 1986: 60–4; Lemarignier 1966; Wood 1994; Atsma 1976.

[128] Thus there is little evidence in the Frankish north for monasteries developing out of Roman villas: Percival 1997: 16–17.

[129] Campbell 1986: 53–9, 65–6; Thacker 2002: 58–61; Yorke 2003*b*: 17–46; Story 2003: 37–41; Sims-Williams 1975. See also Lebecq 1989: 409–11, for geographical links between other northern Frankish monasteries and England; Le Jan 2001 for the role of these female-ruled houses in inter-family competition, and in kindreds' attempts to 'capture the sacred forces of rural areas in the process of christianisation' (p. 262); and Cramp 1993: 68–70, for sculptural parallels between the Chelles area and minsters of the Northumbrian coast.

to Roman Gaul, the Armorican peninsula became 'little Britain' as a result of cross-channel migration during the fifth and sixth centuries; it shared a language with Cornwall, and like western Britain it withstood 'barbarian' takeover through the sixth and seventh centuries. Also like western Britain, it acquired a plethora of localized Christian sites identified by place-names in 'Lan-', and a category of more important ones housing religious communities. An exceptional ninth-century source, the Redon group of charters, shows that these larger sites housed groups of priests and served as the social and proto-parochial centres of administrative territories known as *plebes*.[130] While these establishments might be compared with the baptismal churches of southern *plebes* or *vici*[131] they seem essentially rural and non-Roman, and it is unclear how far, if at all, they operated under episcopal direction. Here is clear evidence that the post-Roman and pre-Carolingian fringe could generate sites which were at once religious communities, centres of organized pastoral care, and foci for lay society and settlement growth.

The Breton *plebs* churches were of course very different from the royal monasteries of north Francia. But they fall on the same side of a broader divide which follows the grain of economic and cultural variables: on the one hand, regions still dominated by cities, with their episcopal and centripetal systems of church organization; on the other, rural regions with fluid settlement patterns, where free-standing monastic communities (using the term in the broadest sense, and irrespective of the kinds of spiritual discipline practised in them) could stimulate new modes of political, administrative, economic, and topographical organization. It was essentially this distinction that J.-F. Lemarignier made—if rather too rigidly—between two juxtaposed but different Gauls: 'conciliar Gaul' of the bishops and their legislation, and 'monastic Gaul' of the Frankish north.[132] These Gauls overlapped—the monasticism of the north owed much to the south, and northern Burgundy and the Paris basin were both conciliar and monastic—but what matters here is the recognition of a cultural frontier, on the northern side of which lay the Frankish heartland, Brittany, Britain, and Ireland.

Influences (iv): the Irish

Even with this wider perspective, the contribution of the Irish still looks remarkable. Converted after 400 by missionaries from Britain, they were

---

[130] Davies 1983; Tanguy 1988. Cf. Dumville 1984: 20–2, for ecclesiastical connections between Ireland, western Britain, and Brittany during the sixth to tenth centuries.

[131] Davies 1983: 191–3 makes this comparison.

[132] Lemarignier 1966: 458–62.

among the first people outside the former Empire to accept Christianity. At the point of conversion they were politically fragmented but socially homogeneous; a kin-based, non-urban society aware of the Roman world but not dominated by it; marked by rich indigenous traditions of art and oral composition; and enjoying an economic boom.[133] All these things—with one or two important variants—could be said of the English two centuries later. Despite a rhetoric of conflict (St Patrick versus druids), the Irish showed what other northern peoples would show in their turn: the capacity of tribal, warlike, and non-urban societies to develop a well-integrated and expansionist Christianity. It is a truism, but nonetheless true, that modes of organization and mission grounded in vernacular cultures were more successful among northern 'barbarians' than urban and Latinate ones; it is another that they tended to take monastic forms.[134] Before we examine recent debates on Irish Church organization, it is worth recalling Bede's unambiguous comment on the Ionan mission to Northumbria: 'they were mainly monks who had come to preach.'[135] But then, what was a monk?

Irish missionaries in England were the culmination of a larger monastic diaspora: Columba in Irish western Scotland (Dál Riata) at Iona in 563, Columbanus among the Franks at Luxeuil in the 590s, Aidan among the Northumbrians at Lindisfarne in the 630s.[136] Bede's highly controlled narrative emphasizes Lindisfarne at the expense of the broader background, both cultural and political. Irish ecclesiastics were important among the western British, their own former teachers, as also in at least some pockets of midland and southern England.[137] Iona was itself the product of Irish expansion in Scotland, and connections between Anglian, Pictish, and Dál Riatic nobles (including perhaps a Northumbrian claim to hegemony in the western isles) facilitated the Ionan mission to Northumbria; metalworking debris from the princely site of Dunadd, in western Scotland, shows motifs from early seventh-century English art alongside others from Ireland.[138] In the south, Frankish ecclesiastical contacts with the courts of Kent, East Anglia, and the Gewisse had a major Irish component.[139] It is best to envisage a web of influences between the insular peoples and their neighbours: factors such as the relative proximity of different parts of the Continent, the cultural vitality and

---

[133] The outstanding account of all this is now Charles-Edwards 2000: 145–240. See also Dumville 1984.

[134] e.g. Fletcher 1997: 136–8, 232–4.

[135] *HE* iii. 3 (p. 220).

[136] Charles-Edwards 2000: 293–308 (Iona), 344–90 (Columbanus), 308–26 (Lindisfarne). For Lindisfarne see also Bullough 1982: 85–8.

[137] Bullough 1982: 81–9; Campbell 1987: 337–43.

[138] Campbell 1987: 335–7; Campbell and Lane 1993.

[139] Campbell 1986: 56–9.

missionary ethic of the Irish, the fastidious reserve of the British clergy combined with the English hierarchy's contempt of them, meant that the Irish had much the strongest impact on some parts of England, and some impact on all.

The outstanding influence remains that of Dál Riata upon the northern Angles. The expansion of Irish monastic federations into Pictish territory during the sixth and seventh centuries produced a group of major communities and their satellites—Iona, Lismore, Eigg, Applecross, Kingarth—which may have had much in common, at least physically, with the British monasteries developing in northern Britain at the same time.[140] When Oswald gave Lindisfarne to Iona, a great English king for the first time sponsored an insular monastic culture, giving it influence in a huge tract of territory that had accepted an Anglian ethnic identity while rejecting, at least in any overt and organized form, the British Christian option. It was in this context that Bede wrote his famous comment on Iona which—though it describes the customs of merely one monastic federation—has been considered a defining account of the 'Irish Church':

This island is accustomed always to have as its ruler an abbot [who is also a] priest, to whose authority both the whole province and the very bishops themselves are required, by an abnormal mode of organization (*ordine inusitato*), to be subject. This is in accordance with the example of its [Iona's] first teacher [Columba], who was not a bishop but a priest and a monk.[141]

Of the various traditions that went into the making of the English Church, that of the Irish is the most complex, perplexing, and contentious.[142] Seventh- and eighth-century texts in both Latin and the vernacular survive in abundance, but use of them is complicated by their often formalized and allusive style, and by an idiosyncratic vocabulary which (it now emerges) was used in different registers. The model which long enjoyed a consensus, and which was expounded by Kathleen Hughes in 1966, ran as follows: St Patrick and his followers initially set up a conventional structure of territorial dioceses ruled by bishops. During the sixth century, however, this was subverted by the rise of great monasteries and their dependencies, creating dispersed federations (*paruchiae*) which cut across diocesan boundaries. Administrative and coercive power was concentrated into the hands of the abbots, heirs of the monastic saint-founders, to the point of negating episcopal authority. Bishops, exceptionally numerous though they were, thus became simple

---

[140] Bullough 1982: 89–91; Fisher 1996: 38–40; cf. above, p. 28.　　[141] *HE* iii. 4 (pp. 222–4).
[142] The development of the debate, summarized here in merest outline, can be followed through: Hughes 1966; Sharpe 1984*a*; Charles-Edwards 1992; Sharpe 1992; Etchingham 1999; Charles-Edwards 2000.

preachers and purveyors of the sacraments, subject in all other respects—
Bede's 'abnormal mode'—to the abbots in whose communities they resided.
In 1984 and 1992, two articles by Richard Sharpe largely demolished
and partly rebuilt this edifice; Colmàn Etchingham and Thomas Charles-
Edwards have now picked up more of the pieces. This recent work, despite
some slightly different emphases, shows a broad consensus: it makes it possible to gain a clearer view of aspects of Irish organization which may have
influenced the English, and to suggest that they did so in a more inclusive
and flexible context than the traditional interpretative straitjacket of 'Celtic
versus Roman'.

Rather than an imposed diocesan framework being replaced by a monastic one, ecclesiastical structures apparently developed from the grass roots to
suit the needs of local communities.[143] Early Ireland contained very large
numbers of small church sites, which are listed for a few districts in sources
as early as the seventh century and can be identified elsewhere from field evidence.[144] In scale and density these look comparable to the *llans/*lanns* of
western Britain, though their nomenclature is more varied. For Sharpe they
'bear witness to what in its time was one of the most comprehensive pastoral
organizations in northern Europe',[145] but it is not clear that they were initially regulated in any systematic way. Ascetic monasticism may likewise have
developed from St Patrick's time onwards in an organic and unstructured
fashion:[146] a growing inspiration which ultimately caused a much wider circle
of right-living Christians to be known generically as 'monks', but never made
this the only or even most common form of the religious life.

Yet by the seventh century, hierarchies and structures had emerged. A
range of sources mention religious sites perceived to be locally superior: the
'primary churches of Ireland'; the 'old (*andóit*, from *antiquitatem*) churches';
the '*domnach* (from *dominicum*) churches'; even, in the case of the largest
and most important, the *civitates*. Characteristically they are linked to peoples
inhabiting defined territories, in formulations such as 'the great *domnach* of
the plain of *X*'.[147] The lay community and its principal church are assumed
to enjoy a close personal bond and reciprocal obligations, and lesser churches
often or usually look to the head church for their ecclesiastical personnel and
resources. The heads of the great churches are described sometimes in the
language of secular lordship (*princeps/airchinnech*), sometimes of monasticism
(*abbas/ap*), and careful analysis shows that these are often the same people

---

[143] Sharpe 1984*a*: 239–42.   [144] Sharpe 1992: 84–91.
[145] Ibid. 109.
[146] Sharpe 1984*a*: 265–6; Charles-Edwards 2000: 223–6.
[147] Charles-Edwards 1992: 64–71; Sharpe 1992: 93–7; Charles-Edwards 2000: 119, 239–40.

wearing different hats: the 'prince' of 'subjects' (*subiecti/subditi*), who governs his *civitas*, administers its property, and regulates its activities, can appear as an 'abbot' of 'brethren/monks' (*fratres/monachi*) when his role as spiritual father is at issue.[148] He can alternatively be a layman, though his legitimacy depends on good conduct and acceptance of due spiritual discipline.

At the same time, there were bishops in abundance. The sources envisage that a *túath* (local kingdom or folk-district) will typically have its head-bishop, in a hierarchy with other bishops above and below him. His diocese (*paruchia*) is in its basic form territorial and compact, and characteristically equivalent to the *túath*.[149] It should follow from this that the sphere of such a bishop's authority will often have been identical with a district or people centred on a *domnach*-type establishment, and indeed it is envisaged that a church of that status will normally house a bishop. A good *airchinnech* or secular lord submits himself to a bishop's correction, or can sometimes even be a bishop himself. There is no evidence that bishops' spiritual authority within their *paruchiae* declined during the sixth to eighth centuries, and some signs that it may actually have increased.

One level of confusion can be avoided by grasping the distinction between spiritual authority on the one hand, and rulership over people, places, and territories on the other.[150] In Ireland as everywhere else, the former flowed from bishops, whose presence in such numbers and at such a local level made them an all-pervasive force. But the emergence and growth during the sixth to seventh centuries of complex para-monastic sites, bound up with the iden-tities and aspirations of lay kindreds and ruled by their members, is certainly no fiction. If we can accept an inclusive model, which allows room for the authority of bishop, abbot, and lord to be combined in various permutations, the worst perplexities disappear. As Charles-Edwards puts it, 'it would be unsurprising to find the chief church of a *túath* to be both episcopal and monastic, and for the bishop to be head of the church, *princeps*, and also, in relation to the monks, *abbas*'.[151] In society at large the great churches—what-ever their composition—were becoming increasingly powerful, and it was their 'rulers'—of whatever spiritual grade or none—who wielded that power.

Affiliations and rivalries at a higher level of ecclesiastical politics, and the failure of many kindreds and polities to conform to the tidy compact model just outlined, introduce further complexities. Just as familial associations in the secular world could be far-flung and disparate, so could ecclesiastical

---

[148] Sharpe 1984*a*: 260–5; Etchingham 1999: 47–99.
[149] Sharpe 1984*a*: 235–6, 251, 258–9; Etchingham 1999: 148–68; Charles-Edwards 2000: 258–60.
[150] Sharpe 1984*a*: 263–6.
[151] Charles-Edwards 1992: 67.

ones.[152] The *familia* equivalent to the kin of a dominant saint could embrace a mother-house and many scattered daughters; ordinary 'head' (*domnach*) churches could subject themselves to major monastic federations to avoid worse forms of domination; the greatest churches, Armagh and Kildare, aspired to overriding jurisdiction. Already by the seventh century the hierarchies of churches could be multi-layered and extremely complex, an elaborate and unstable jigsaw of alliances.[153] This is the context of the traditional model's 'dispersed monastic *paruchia*', exemplified most strikingly (though perhaps not very typically) by Iona as described by Bede.

That model was deficient in two fundamental ways. First, it failed to make a clear distinction between bishops' spiritual rulership over Christians and monastic heads' territorial rulership over lands and people: conflicts arose from the competing claims of individual churches, not from a basic tension between episcopal and monastic forms of governance. Secondly, it put such an emphasis on forms of authority at the top level that it neglected the realities of local arrangements. The latter invite comparison with structures encountered elsewhere on our tour: the *domnach* churches of *túatha* with the head-churches of Breton *plebes*; the saints' dispersed *familiae* with the dominant monastic communities of Wales; the secular rulers of ecclesiastical *civitates* with the northern Frankish nobility and their family monasteries. The Irish sources are unusual in being so explicit about lay rulership,[154] and anomalous in their use of monastic terminology for such a wide range of people.[155] Yet the Irish integration of ecclesiastical structures into territorial and familial ones, balancing 'the demands of family, dynasty, property interests and so on, with the duties of maintaining the services of religion',[156] seems essentially characteristic of northern Europe.

At this point some statements can be made about the ecclesiastical cultures which influenced the seventh-century English. In all of them bishops were important pastorally, and to varying degrees administratively. However, bishops' top-downwards control over hierarchies of churches was only clear-cut south of the Alps and the Loire, and increasingly equivocal and compromised further north. All the systems had an infrastructure of local churches: oratories of *villae* in the south; family burial churches in northern

---

[152] Sharpe 1984a: 243–7, 262–3, 270; Etchingham 1999: 106–48, 168–71, 223–38, 458; Charles-Edwards 2000: 121–3, 241–64.

[153] Sharpe 1992: 96–8; below, p. 97, for the most striking English analogue, Wilfrid's 'realm of churches'.

[154] Presumably because their terminology was established before Bede, Boniface, and the Carolingians started the tradition of hostility to lay-abbacy: below, p. 107 n.

[155] Sharpe 1992: 102; Etchingham 1999: 456–8, 465.

[156] Sharpe 1984a: 269.

Francia; *llans* in Wales, Cornwall, and Brittany; the countless, now abandoned church sites of Ireland. In all of them complex religious sites, housing
communities of a broadly monastic character, became progressively more
important.

The Anglo-Saxon kingdoms: political and social contexts

We have seen that this para-monastic form, capable of being endowed,
adopted, or controlled by individuals or dynasties, was attractive to the kings
and nobles of northern Europe, where the monastic sites tended to become
nodes of interconnections based on familial and territorial structures. Eventually it proved enormously attractive to English kings too, though this only
becomes apparent some time after the initial conversions. As elsewhere, the
chronology of its development and the form that it took were profoundly
influenced by the local political structures.

In the absence of contemporary written sources, the recently fashionable
argument that the seventh-century English kingdoms emerged from a
plethora of tiny folk-groups is vulnerable to the charge that it takes no evidence as negative evidence.[157] On the other hand, our archaeological data are
consistent, to put it no more strongly, with the proposition that some radical
changes occurred in social hierarchies, and in means of controlling resources,
at the end of the sixth century. A recent judicious approach from the perspective of theoretical archaeology concludes that

[t]he ranked societies of the fifth and sixth centuries were capable of political integration to the extent that would support local chieftains and an impermanent or
cyclical regional hegemony, but the establishment and maintenance of any permanent regional overlordship required, and precipitated or accelerated, permanent
social and political change. . . . Some local chieftains of the fifth and sixth centuries
may have considered themselves kings, but we may doubt whether they would have
been recognized as such by the major rulers of the seventh century, or by contemporary Frankish monarchs.[158]

While our written sources (notably Bede) may over-stress the reception of
specific missionaries by specific great kings, it remains essentially true that
organized Christianization proceeded from the top downwards, via courts to
wider kindreds and dependants. One reason for the late conversion of the
English may therefore lie in the relatively slow emergence of coherent polities. This cannot be a complete explanation—tiny Irish kingdoms had converted in the fifth and sixth centuries—and we should probably also contrast

---

[157] Bassett 1989*b*, and the caveats of Yorke 1999*b*.   [158] Scull 1999: 23.

the long-term stability of Irish society with the urge for emergent Anglo-Saxon communities to forge a new, Germanic, and therefore pagan identity: it was only as they moved towards a more 'political', less 'tribal' organization that they reorientated themselves towards the Christian world.

At all events, it was the major English rulers of the years around 600 who first showed a need for Europe, Rome, and the Church, and whom Italian and Frankish ecclesiastics were first concerned to target. Thus Christianity made its fastest progress, in the early to mid seventh century, at a time when the territory under English control had mostly coalesced into half a dozen substantial kingdoms. In marked contrast to Ireland and (probably) the British west, it was *great* kings who took the lead in converting, appointing bishops, and in due course endowing Christian sites. Thus a huge tract of land, which in Ireland would have had many kings and bishops, would in England have had only one of each. This was to have profound implications, when the mature monastic Church developed after 660, for the nature of minsters' relations with their lay patrons and with bishops.

Integral to the changing quality of English society and kingship around 600 was a larger process of cultural assimilation. The new dynasties were in growing contact with a wider world around them, insular as well as Mediterranean, which despite its diversity was unified by one religion. The more that the English came to know their Christian neighbours, the more they may have felt themselves a pagan backwater. English Christianity was preceded by a package of cultural imports from a variety of sources, the sudden and enthusiastic acceptance of which shows a people with a new openness to different cultures. Whether this widening of horizons stemmed directly from the English rulers' enhanced control over land, people, and resources, or was simply a facet of the accelerating interchanges between the peoples of northwestern Europe, it is the key to understanding why, when the time was ripe, the same rulers converted so readily.

This Christian European culture also had a capacity to equip 'barbarian' kings with new ideals of royal power expressed in new kinds of places. It has often been observed that Christianity, as an exclusive and hierarchical religion offering normative regulation and written record, had particular attractions for emergent rulers deploying wider and more systematic power.[159] It is notable that in some societies approaching both conversion and state-formation, the English probably included, paganism (which is likely to have shared the organic, decentralized character of other polytheisms) began to assume features of the religion around the corner, notably the emergence of

[159] Urbańczyk 2003; P. Brown 1996: 27, 32; Higham 1997: 25–34.

one dominant deity in the pantheon and the building of imposing ceremonial centres.[160] On conversion, kings who spent their itinerant lives in tents and timber halls might hope to learn about, and imitate, imperial palaces; more realistically, institutionalized Christianity brought grand ceremonial architecture in the form of cathedrals, church groups, and monastic sites. Political, spiritual, material, and aesthetic aspirations all had something to gain from these new modes, which also offered ways of breathing new life into massive but largely meaningless Romano-British ruins.

Yet there were strict limits on the exportability of Mediterranean culture. The gulf between the reality of a decentralized tribal society and the ideal of a lost province reclaimed for Rome has complicated perceptions of seventh-century England. Historians—and scholars of Old English literature—have tended to emphasize the former, whereas archaeologists have sought political, organizational, and religious continuities to explain the use of Roman places by Anglo-Saxon rulers. It deserves stressing how far the Latin vocabulary of our sources, projected from a different world onto Anglo-Saxon England, is an expression of the ideal rather than a description of the reality. From the urbanized and literate Mediterranean, Christianity brought with it a baggage of terminology: *civitas* (city-territory), *metropolis* (capital), *imperium* (empire), *episcopus* (bishop), *dioecesis* (diocese). But centralized power and developed economies could not be imported along with the words describing them. Without urban life, a *civitas* centre was a city only in name, even if it occupied a Roman ruin; an English bishop's *dioecesis* could be like a Gallic bishop's only if it had access to comparable means of administration.

The monumentalization of cult[161]

Turning now to how the recipe assimilated the ingredients, the emergent dynasties' needs to define, project, and commemorate themselves in tangible forms make a good starting-point. In some other developing societies the advent of more coherent belief-systems and rituals, sanctioning new endeavours and underpinning the legitimacy of new status-groups, has had a physical dimension: the building of monuments and ceremonial sites, testifying to the centrality of the new values and vindicating the deployment of

---

[160] Urbańczyk 2003: 18–19; Murray 1992: 199–200. For Anglo-Saxon paganism: Meaney 1985; Hines 1997*b*; other works listed by Higham 1997: 44 nn. 3–7.

[161] Readers may find it interesting to compare this section with various papers by Martin Carver, synthesized in Carver 2001, which interpret the same phenomena in a different light: as political, ideological, and antagonistic, whereas I tend to see them as cultural, assimilatory, and consensual. There is scope here for further debate.

resources, manpower, and technology in their service.[162] Among the English around 600, a new interest in the formal articulation of the landscape can be recognized in such apparently diverse phenomena as the planning of cemeteries in orderly rows and the alignment of buildings and ritual foci on strict axes. The relatively rapid appearance of monuments—princely barrows and halls, churches and monastic sites—is better understood by reference to this broad developmental model than by dividing them into 'pagan' or 'Christian' categories. Monument-building defined the Christian religious landscape, but its foundations were laid by the last pagan generations.

A small group of square fenced or ditched enclosures, usually built over prehistoric mounds, can be interpreted as the first (and almost the only) structural 'shrines' or 'temples' of the pagan Anglo-Saxons.[163] The type seems to derive from a Romano-Celtic tradition perpetuated in a British context since the fourth century, but the English can be perceived to have adopted it only from the late sixth. At the Northumbrian royal site of Yeavering, an enclosure of this type was replaced by a roofed ritual building—perhaps one of those 'well-built' pagan shrines which missionaries seem to have encountered in Kent—at a date only shortly before King Eadwine's baptism in the 620s.[164] Here is one hint that this pagan culture, like others confronted by the Church, began to assimilate outward and visible forms of the rival religion a generation or so before formally adopting it.

This may have been more a cultural than a strategic response: not an attempt to fight Christianity with its own weapons, but rather an acknowledgement that a religion equipped with buildings and rich accoutrements could have had more impact than a religion located merely in the natural landscape. Lay responses to Christianity cannot be straitjacketed into opposed categories of 'conversion' and 'pagan reaction', especially among a laity who did not share the Christians' own exclusive attitudes to religious orientation. Missionaries, and the writers through whom we know them, assumed clear boundaries between true and false faith: they classified the laity with whom they came into contact as either accepting or rejecting Christ, and many of their traditional social customs as pagan rites. It is unlikely that their converts recognized these boundaries:[165] King Raedwald of East Anglia, who to Bede's disgust 'had in the same temple both an altar for the Christian sacrifice and a little altar for [offering sacrificial] victims to demons',[166] was behaving less oddly than the uniqueness of this reference might suggest.

---

[162] For monument building and re-use see: Bradley 1987; Bradley 1993: 113–29; Blair 1994: 32–4; Blair 1995*b*: 21–2; and (for sociological approaches) Adams 1966: 121–2 and Wheatley 1971: 305, 321. Helms 1993, esp. 77–87, offers an ethnographic perspective on the prestige gained by kings as builders and acquirers of exotic monuments and artefacts.

[163] Blair 1995*b*.   [164] Hope-Taylor 1977: 95–118; Blair 1995*b*: 2, 16–17; cf. *HE* i. 30 (p. 106).

[165] Markus 1990: 1–17; Yorke 2003*a*: 243–5.   [166] *HE* ii. 15 (p. 190).

One important development of around 600, the rise of richly furnished barrow-burials, needs to be seen in this context.[167] Between the late fifth and early eighth centuries, barrows were built in England, southern Scandinavia, the Rhineland, and northern Switzerland. A small minority, exemplified in England by the mounds at Sutton Hoo (Suffolk) and Taplow (Bucks.), are remarkable for the extraordinary range and richness of their grave-goods, and must commemorate people of more than simply local status. Both the date and the distribution of these barrows are important: they appeared around the fringes of Christian Francia, and they did so well after the adoption of church burial by royal and some noble Franks. So they are not relics of entrenched pagan practice, even if one purpose of them was to manufacture links with an imagined past suggested by prehistoric barrows. Rather, they share with other signs of the times a striving for a monumental expression of status, achieved in more developed cultures by means of funerary churches, above-ground sarcophagi, and tomb-sculpture.[168] When, more than a century after Sutton Hoo, a Mercian king or prince was buried beside the minster of Repton (Derbs.), his free-standing mausoleum on a bluff above the Trent could have been perceived as a barrow executed in stone rather than earth.[169] The occupants and builders of the rich barrows were competitive, insecure potentates, concerned to show themselves as good as their Frankish contemporaries and better than their English rivals. We cannot know how often they were already Christian; what is clearer, and may be more important, is that they valued permanent and conspicuous commemoration, for that is something that the Church was supremely well placed to provide.

Analogous to barrow-building, and widespread in the same regions during the same period, was the insertion of burials into mounds, earthworks, and buildings inherited from the prehistoric and Roman past.[170] Prehistoric

---

[167] For the plethora of views see especially: Shephard 1979; Bullough 1983: 194; Webster 1992; Carver 1992*b*; Campbell 2000: 55–83; Van de Noort 1992; Van de Noort 1993; Carver 2001: 5–9. Contrary to Carver, I am not persuaded that barrow-burial was an ostentatiously anti-Christian demonstration of paganism, nor indeed specifically pagan at all. (The 'princely' burial at Prittlewell (Essex), which became public as this book was in press, had gold-foil crosses—a Lombard fashion— laid on the face: surely a clear statement of Christian affiliation?) I am unconvinced by the argu- ment that the early seventh-century 'princely' burials are merely lucky survivals rather than examples of a new type. I accept that the richness of the 'princely' burials was stimulated by competition and insecurity, so that they may show greater investment in funerary pomp rather than necessarily an absolute increase in assets; but I think nonetheless that they are the tombs of a decisively new kind of elite with decisively new attitudes.

[168] Halsall 1992: 269, 278; see Carver 1986 for a stimulating but rather different approach. Cf. Van de Noort 1992: 32: 'churches themselves were, to Germanic eyes, a grandiose innovation of the funerary rite. Moreover, such graves were monuments, to be admired by the generations that followed.' This is a good example of 'stimulus diffusion': Knight 1992: 49.

[169] Biddle 1986: 22.

[170] Bell 2001 and Semple 2002 are now fundamental. See also e.g. Van de Noort 1993: 66–9; Le Maho 1994.

barrows had been used in this way in northern Gaul, Wales, and Ireland through the Iron Age and Roman periods,[171] but among the English the practice of burying in them, and in Roman ruins, was widely adopted only from the later sixth century. While it is possible that they first learnt it from their insular neighbours, it is part of a wider phenomenon, again found around the fringes of Merovingian culture.[172]

Like other state-forming societies, the late sixth-century English apparently became concerned to *create* continuity: to forge links with perceived heroes, ancestors, or gods through ritual appropriation of their monuments.[173] These patterns of behaviour, which again hovered on the fringes of Christianity without being specifically Christian, merged easily (and for us invisibly) into that recycling of Roman villas, baths, and forts which was commonplace in the homelands of Italian and Frankish missionaries, and was to guide the establishment of English ecclesiastical sites.[174] Idioms for Christianizing the classical landscapes of fourth- and fifth-century Europe were exported, with Christianity, to the edges of the former Empire; there they reinforced practices which emerging aristocracies, newly conscious of the wider (and Roman) world, had themselves recently evolved.[175]

Here Yeavering is uniquely informative. Bede tells how St Paulinus, after King Eadwine's baptism in the late 620s, taught 'the people who flocked to him from all the hamlets and places' at this Bernician royal vill, and baptized them in the nearby river.[176] Excavation has revealed a remarkable complex, undoubtedly to be identified as Eadwine's vill and Paulinus's preaching-point (Fig. 7).[177] At either end of a ridge, the first Anglian settlers had found a

---

[171] H. James 1992: 90–4, 98; O'Brien 1992; Blair 1995*b*: 3–5; Petts 2002: 35–9; Zadora-Rio 2003: 4, 7–9.

[172] H. Williams (1997, 1998) denies the novelty of barrow re-use (contrast Blair 1994: 32–4), and his sample certainly includes more fifth- and sixth-century cases than I had realized. I still think, though, that he understates a sharp rise in purposeful re-adoption around 600. For burials on Roman villas see Bell 2001: 52–95: he concludes (p. 64 and table 6) that datable cases have an extreme range between the fifth and eighth centuries, but most are of *c*.550–700, and 'on the whole, they appear to hinge upon the middle of the seventh century'. See Knight 1999: 140–1, and Edwards 2001: 18–28, for the idea that Welsh inscribed stones on prehistoric and Roman monuments indicate a deliberate identification with the past. Freke and others 1987 describe a cemetery over a large barrow in Cheshire which could reflect Welsh practice. Martin Carver (pers. comm.) regards monumental barrows and re-used Roman structures as contrasting rather than analogous forms, and certainly there must have been some rather different resonances. I think nonetheless that the growth of both practices at much the same time suggests a continuum rather than a contrast.

[173] Bradley 1987; Blair 1995*b*: 20–2; Blair 1996*c*: 6–9; Williams 1998: 102–4.

[174] Below, pp. 188–90.

[175] Below, p. 183.

[176] *HE* ii. 14 (p. 188).

[177] Hope-Taylor 1977; Meaney 1985: 9–14; Scull 1991; Bradley 1987: 5–10; Blair 1995*b*: 16–19. The phasing and interpretation proposed here are slightly different from those hitherto accepted.

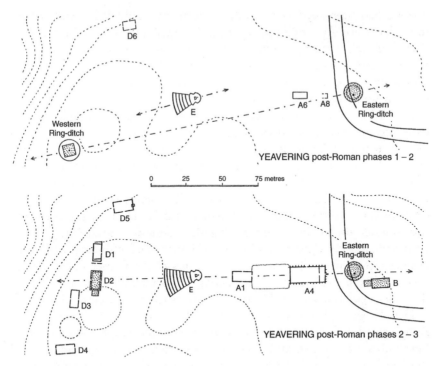

7. *Yeavering*: a ritual and royal site in seventh-century Northumbria. The phases of development are re-drawn here to illustrate how the dual ritual foci of the site pre-dated the royal halls. (After data in Hope-Taylor 1977.)

small stone circle (the 'western ring-ditch') and a Bronze Age barrow (the 'eastern ring-ditch'). Some time before *c.*600 these were refashioned into new forms: the circle by the substitution of a cob-walled square shrine, the barrow by the insertion of a large standing post. The two monuments now formed the poles of a ritual axis, on which the square shrine, and an extraordinary structure like a theatre segment (E) set a little way to the north, were aligned; they also became foci for small cemeteries. During the early years of the seventh century more buildings were added, notably a central complex with monumental timber halls (A1, A4, etc.). These were aligned on a new axis, which passed through the post in the eastern barrow, the focal point of the theatre segment, and a roofed 'temple' (D2) which had been built to the north of the 'western ring-ditch'. After a fire, probably in the 620s, the 'eastern ring-ditch' was replaced by a new ritual structure (B): a timber building, set directly over one of the earlier 'strings' of graves, around and

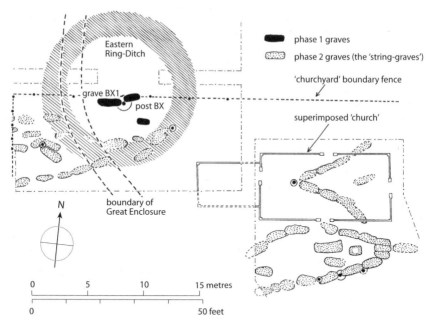

8. *Yeavering:* the 'eastern ring-ditch', one pole of the early axis, centred on a post stand-ing within a Bronze Age barrow-ditch. Anglian burials comprised 'string-graves' aligned on posts (phases 1 and 2), then haphazard graves (phase 3, not shown). The early seventh-century timber building was placed directly over one of the groups of 'string-graves'. (After Hope-Taylor 1977: figs. 31 and 33.)

within which a dense-packed cemetery of orientated graves developed (Fig. 8).

Yeavering offers perspectives on the interaction between ritual activity and high-status secular residence at the point of conversion. It looks as though the initial Anglian structures were an arena for religious cult and meetings, but not necessarily for the kind of hall-centred royal life that we know from 'Beowulf'. The site was formed around appropriated ancient monuments; its biggest structure was designed to house assemblies; and its name (*ad-gefrin*, probably from Brittonic 'the hill of the goats') suggests—in the light of the goat-head found with one Anglian burial—pagan cult by both British and English Bernicians.[178] It may have been only with the re-planning and the building of the major halls, perhaps by Eadwine's immediate predecessors, that it became the *regia villa* of Bede's account. It seems possible that an emergent kingship, anxious to establish formal centres, commandeered a

[178] Hope-Taylor 1977: 15, 67–9. It is conjectured that the name originally referred to Yeavering Bell and was transferred to the palace site.

place of long-standing popular assembly, and that Paulinus carried out his mass-baptisms at Yeavering less because it was a royal residence than because the inhabitants of a wide region met there.[179]

There is a parallel here with Scandinavian *things* of a few centuries later: public meetings which were sometimes held at pagan cult centres, and which were gradually assimilated into the processes of royal government.[180] It suggests a context for other sites of royal assembly which had names denoting pagan worship: the lost *Besingahearh* ('temple of the Besingas') in Wessex (688), Wye (*weoh*, 'shrine') in Kent (762), and Thunderfield ('Thunor's open ground') in Surrey (*c.*880 × 8).[181] The dynastic myth located in the 660s, in which a royal thegn called Thunor murders two princes and buries them under the high seat of the king's hall at Eastry (Kent), could recall another case.[182] At such places, royal status was built up on foundations of pagan cult.

Christianity built in turn on the same foundations. Although the orientated building and cemetery which supplanted the 'eastern ring-ditch' at Yeavering are not self-evidently Christian, the known history of the site encourages such an interpretation. At all events, Paulinus's preaching there put into practice Pope Gregory's advice, given to the Augustinian mission in 601, to Christianize established cult sites rather than destroy them.[183] The pagan past, focused on adopted prehistoric monuments, was being recycled—under the auspices of kings who had only recently bent it to their own political and dynastic ends—for the Christian future.

Told by their new mentors that Christian kings were expected to found churches, such rulers would have warmed to the idea of exotic buildings and grand complexes which could become identified with their own dynasties. One notable success of these novel cult monuments would be their ability to supplant the old cemeteries, and the more recent barrows, as dynastic mausolea.

[179] Cf. Morris 1991: 21–2.

[180] Sawyer and Sawyer 1993: 80–1; cf. Hedeager 2001: 478–81, for Scandinavian 'central complexes' of the third to sixth centuries combining ritual and residential functions. There are also analogies with the 'royal centres' of early Ireland: Aitchison 1994: 7–197; Charles-Edwards 2000: 469–74.

[181] S 235, S 25, S 1507; cf. Gelling 1978: 159, and Higham 1997: 25–6 and 49 n. 61. The witness-list of S 235 evokes the remarkable image of Wilfrid, Eorcenwald, Hædde, and Aldhelm gathered on a site of pagan cult. Thunderfield lay deep in the Wealden pastures, and was presumably a place of assembly and cult rather than a 'central place' in any developed sense: see Turner 1997, which rightly corrects Blair 1991*a*: 19.

[182] Below, p. 144; Hawkes 1979 for Eastry. Behr 2000: 39–45 argues that Eastry, Finglesham, and Woodnesborough ('Woden's *beorg*') constituted a major sixth-century royal centre associated with the cult of Woden. The reference to the high seat echoes the early Germanic belief (e.g. 'Beowulf' lines 168–9, and cf. Hedeager 2001: 479) in the sacred character of this feature.

[183] Below, p. 185.

Lay burial: church versus ancestors?

More than a century after the conversion of Kent, when the English were taking Christianity to their former homelands, King Radbod of the Frisians agreed to be baptized. He had put one foot into the font when a worrying thought struck him: would he meet more kings and nobles of his people in heaven or in hell? On being assured that all his pagan ancestors were damned, he walked away: he could never, he said, turn his back on his forebears and sit with a few people in heaven.[184] We have no such colourful story from the English conversions, but an aristocracy as committed as Radbod to their own heroic ancestors would have seen his point. Missionaries, however eager to smooth their converts' path, had to be pessimistic about the chances of former pagan heroes in the next world, and discourage their celebration in this one.[185]

The kings and nobles who did convert must somehow have resolved this dilemma in their own minds, but it was not by jettisoning their ancestors or even (in the guise of folk-heroes) their gods, as the appearance of both in later royal genealogies illustrates. They were far too central to their own identities, culture, status, and—probably at least by *c.*600—their territorial rights. And if re-negotiating relationships with ancestors was problematic, reconciling an extended and strongly self-conscious living kindred with the claims of an imported and centrally organized religion is likely to have been harder still. Such considerations may have encouraged English aristocracies, like Irish and Frankish ones before them, to embrace a form of religious life—the monastic—which could grow out of their own households, and enable ecclesiastical structures to intermesh with family ones.

The first Christian rite of passage was of paramount importance to the converters, but may have had only limited resonances for the converted; the reverse can probably be said of the last rite of passage. Baptism was required of all believers, but 'Christian burial' had not yet become clear-cut and prescriptive: it was a privilege rather than an obligation, and even the baptized did not necessarily have universal access to it. This had its advantages: the form and location of burial are likely to have carried ancestral and hierarchical associations which converts would have found hard to relinquish, and in practice did so only slowly. It follows that the value of funerary practice as direct evidence for conversion is strictly limited. The seventh century did nonetheless see fundamental changes, and the archaeology of cemeteries provides our only window—a small and murky one—on the responses of the laity at large.

---

[184] 'Annales Xantenses' s.a. 718: G. H. Pertz (ed.), *MGH Scriptores*, ii (Hannover, 1829), 221.
[185] For the 'damned ancestor' in Christian aristocratic culture see Wormald 1978: esp. 45–6, 49–50, 56–7, 66–7. Cf. P. Brown 1996: 305–15; Blair 1995*b*: 21; and (for the contrasting situation in Ireland) Charles-Edwards 2000: 199–202.

The assumptions that the Church forbade converts to be buried among their pagan ancestors, or to deposit objects in graves, are widespread but unsupported. Although Christian groups may sometimes have used distinct zones within cemeteries,[186] there is no real evidence that they ostentatiously distanced themselves: cemeteries had always gone in and out of use. As knowledge of settlement patterns and dynamics has grown, doubt has also been cast on the supposed shift of burial from the peripheries to the centres of settlements.[187] No known pronouncement of the western Church prohibits grave-goods, and furnished burial in churches and churchyards was established practice in the Frankish world. Recent studies have emphasized that the accelerating decline in grave-goods and the adoption of orientated burial may have economic and cultural, rather than primarily religious, causes (even though one of these might be contact with already Christian populations such as the British).[188] If furnished burial in this period rarely tells us that people were Christian, it certainly does not tell us that they were pagan.

Nor does a predilection for burial on traditional sites. The supposed dichotomy between 'pagan' burial determined within communities, and 'Christian' burial determined by the centralizing authority of a Church intent on reforming existing practice, was probably non-existent. There is no English evidence, outside the Kentish royal family, that Christian laity before at earliest the 670s expected to lie in holy ground near churches, nor that they allowed their new faith to undermine traditional funerary expressions of kinship, community, and status.[189] Religious affiliation could have been declared in unrecorded ways, most obviously in the liturgy: it did not need changes in the site or even accoutrements of the grave.[190]

Changes in ritual practice were normally led by kings and nobles, precisely the groups who had the strongest reasons, even after baptism, to retain traditional modes of burial. There is evidence from Ireland and (less clearly) Wales that ancestral graves were thought not merely to mark the boundaries of family lands, but to defend them against encroachers.[191] From seventh-century England a group of rich barrow-burials, set high on frontier

---

[186] Below, pp. 235–7.

[187] Reynolds 2002: 186–7.

[188] For recent models, and the development of the debate, see: Bullough 1983; Morris 1983: 49–62; Boddington 1990; Halsall 1992; Hadley 1995: 145–7 (with useful additional bibliography); Halsall 1995*b*; Geake 1997; Burnell and James 1999.

[189] See especially Bullough 1983; the next stages of the process are discussed below, pp. 228–45.

[190] The Lives of St Patrick by Muirchú and Tírechán mention cemeteries in which Christians were buried amongst pagans, their graves marked by wooden crosses: Sharpe 1992: 82; O'Brien 1999: 54.

[191] Charles-Edwards 1976; Fry 1999: 104–5. Handley 1998 makes a strong case that western inscribed stones with formulae in the genitive ('Cumregni fili Mauci' etc.) were Irish-influenced and could be both memorials and boundary-stones, marking burials on the estate boundaries; cf. Edwards 2001: 23.

zones and sometimes with their feet pointing towards open country, so strongly recall Irish and British descriptions of 'sentinel' burials that it seems reasonable to interpret them in the same light.[192] If so, the English kings and aristocrats who (at a crucial stage in the process of territorial formation) accepted Christianity would have faced the problem defined, in an Irish context, by Thomas Charles-Edwards: 'relegated to the graveyards of churches the dead lost their power to defend the land which they left to their heirs.'[193] Given also the plutocratic displays of status which had only recently been evolved, both in the monumental scale of barrows and in the wealth paraded at funerals, the great would have demanded that any alternative mode of burial not only avoided disempowerment of their heirs, but also made their rank known to the world in an equally emphatic (and if possible more permanent) way.

The Church did nonetheless offer believers an appealing alternative: to await the resurrection in ground sanctified by the proximity of holy relics (*ad sanctos*) or of an altar used for the mass, where a stream of prayer and liturgy could pour out forever for their souls. Because the saints' bodily relics still mostly lay under their basilicas outside the walls of towns, the major cemeteries of post-Roman Europe tended to form on the suburban sites where Roman cemeteries had been before them. Burial *ad sanctos* was not quite the same thing as later 'Christian burial': its essence was proximity to a sacred focus rather than inclusion within boundaries defined by consecration, and although it could be withdrawn from the unworthy it did not brand all other kinds of burial as shameful or un-Christian.[194] This tradition was the common inheritance of the immigrant clerics and monks who staffed the first English cathedrals and minsters; it is not, however, clear how quickly, during the slow interpenetration of ecclesiastical and secular cultures, the English laity aspired to a form of burial which their Continental peers had gradually adopted since the third century.

In Europe the incidence of the practice had varied greatly, both with proximity to towns and with the degree to which, as the fifth and sixth centuries advanced, existing or immigrant populations had preserved or assimilated Roman ways. Basilicas in Provence and western Gaul could attract many

---

[192] O'Brien 1999: 55–6, 91, 122, 163.

[193] Charles-Edwards 1976: 86. Cf. Williams 1998: 102–4, on the social context of the re-use of ancient barrows.

[194] Below, p. 464. Costambeys 2001 traces the growth of ecclesiastical control over burial arrangements in Rome during *c*.400–600, and questions the pre-eminent pulling-power of saints' relics in the origins of 'Christian burial'. Effros 1997, while emphasizing hierarchy, regulation, and exclusion in Merovingian *ad sanctos* burial, actually highlights its limitations compared with later medieval practice (and see the criticisms by Zadora-Rio 2003: 10–11).

thousands of burials, and must have served large rural areas as well as the towns: these were societies which the culture of church-focused burial had penetrated deeply.[195] Very different were the Frankish areas of northern Gaul, where 'row-grave' cemeteries remained the norm into the seventh century.[196] Here kings had to set an example which others slowly and hesitantly followed, and the links between cultural and religious affiliation were not straightforward. The pagan King Childeric (d. 481) was buried (with quasi-Roman insignia) in a traditional surburban cemetery outside Tournai. His Christian son Clovis (d. 511) was likewise buried in a civil cemetery outside the walls of his capital, Paris, but now in a funerary basilica over the grave of St Geneviève which set the pattern of burial *ad sanctos* for Frankish kings.[197] At the same time, the ban on intramural burial started to break down, occasionally even as early as the fourth century but much more widely from the sixth.[198] Two richly furnished sixth-century tombs under Cologne cathedral illustrate both the advent of intramural burial for the highest ranks, and the compatibility of grave-goods (including vessels and food) with a Christian funeral.[199]

Although the English could have known about *ad sanctos* burial among British Christians (for instance at St Albans), the chronology and the main cultural connections suggest that they would have absorbed the idea, in so far as they absorbed it at all, from Gallic or Italian sources. These influences, which could have included direct emulation of Frankish kings by English ones, probably explain its most striking manifestation, at Canterbury. Between the city and Queen Bertha's church of St Martin, on a road once flanked by Roman cemeteries, King Æthelberht built for Augustine the monastery of SS Peter and Paul. This zone developed (it is unclear precisely when) into Canterbury's main cemetery, and has produced the only persuasive late sixth- or early seventh-century burial with gold jewellery from an English churchyard.[200] The pseudo-basilican setting is almost certainly a case

---

[195] Young 1977: 11–12; Bullough 1983: 182; Burnell 1988: 211–33.

[196] Young 1977: 11–12: 'Dans le Nord, où l'Église était peu implantée dans les campagnes, elle n'eut pendant longtemps ni le goût ni les moyens d'organiser le domaine funéraire.' Cf. James 1979, and Knight 1999: 128–34.

[197] Young 1986: 383–90; E. James 1992; Périn 1992: 256; Ward-Perkins 2000: 529–30.

[198] The erosion of the old embargo, and the consequent *rapprochement* between living and dead, has been of central interest to recent French historians: see for instance Reynaud 1996; Treffort 1996*a*: 133–7; Treffort 1996*b*: 57. Burnell 1988: 233–46 stresses Byzantine imperial practice, and the bringing of martyrs' relics into cities, as the main factors behind the growth of lay intramural burial.

[199] E. James 1992: 247–8, 253.

[200] This statement is based on the inference that the four coin pendants and the Liudhard medalet from the so-called 'St Martin's hoard' are distinct from the other items, and derive from a single female grave: Webster and Backhouse 1991: 23–4. It should be noted that the attribution of the find to St Martin's is not wholly secure: the first published reference ascribes it to 'the grounds of the monastery of St Augustine'.

of created rather than genuine 'continuity': probably inspired by Augustine's desire to found a 'new Rome', it also recalls imitative extramural churches in Merovingian central Gaul such as those at Angers and Chartres.[201] It could have appealed to Æthelberht as well as to Augustine that the arrangement simulated an antique, classical setting for what was to be both a monastic and a mortuary church, 'in which', as Bede says, 'the bodies of Augustine himself and all the bishops of Canterbury and the kings of Kent might be placed'; Augustine was duly buried in the north *porticus* of SS Peter and Paul, and Æthelberht and his queen in the south.[202] Canterbury is also the only Anglo-Saxon town which paid at least lip-service to the Roman ban on intramural burial—a taboo decisively broken in 760 when the location for archiepiscopal tombs was transferred from St Augustine's to the cathedral.[203] This is one of those respects in which Canterbury was more like a Gallic than an Anglo-Saxon 'city'.

Outside Kent, there is no evidence that English Christian kings were buried in churches until the 650s, when Œthelwald of Deira envisaged being buried in Lastingham minster, and then 671, when Osuiu of Northumbria was buried at Whitby.[204] In fact earlier royal graves are totally unrecorded, beyond the confusing but suggestive cases of the Northumbrian kings Eadwine (d. 633/4) and Oswald (d. 642/3). Both were buried near the battle-fields where they fell, except that Eadwine's head was taken to his church in York, and Oswald's head and arms (fixed to a post by his slayer) were retrieved the following year and taken to Bernicia, where the head was buried in the monastic cemetery at Lindisfarne and the arms kept in the royal citadel of Bamburgh.[205] In the 680s or 690s the remaining bones were finally given monastic burial, Eadwine's at Whitby and Oswald's at Bardney.[206] It com-

---

[201] Below, pp. 66–8; Burnell 1988: 225–7, for the view that some suburban martyrial sites of central Gaul are imitative, rather than products of genuine continuity; and now see Wood 2002 and Pearce 2003 for the construction of Gallic cults.

[202] *HE* i. 33, ii. 3, ii. 5 (pp. 114, 142–4, 150).

[203] Brooks 1984: 35–6, 81–3; Sims-Williams 1990: 61–2, 344. The late story that Archbishop Cuthbert (d. 760) obtained papal permission for burials to take place inside the walls of English towns is clearly, as transmitted, nonsense; but given that he was himself the first archbishop to be buried inside the city, a garbled memory of a local change of practice seems likely.

[204] *HE* iii. 23, 24 (pp. 286, 292). Infant children of Eadwine were buried in the church at York *c.*630 (*HE* ii. 14, pp. 186–8), but they died as neophytes wearing the baptismal robe. The parallel description of the burial of their siblings in Francia (*HE* ii. 20, p. 204) suggests that this information reached Bede via his Kentish sources for Paulinus (cf. below, n. 237). York was a place of royal burial in 679 (*VW* c. 24, p. 50).

[205] *HE* ii. 20, iii. 12 (pp. 202–4, 250–2). The episodes are discussed by Thacker 1995, who notes the possible resonances of the head-relics with the ancient Celtic cult of the severed head, and stresses that at this date the enshrinement of Oswald's arms was highly abnormal. My own interpretation is compatible with Thacker's, but has a rather different emphasis. For Christian after-echoes of head-cults see also Merdrignac 1993: 60–1, and O'Brien 1999: 55.

[206] *WVG* cc. 18–19 (pp. 100–4); *HE* iii. 11 (p. 246).

plicates matters that both kings died in battle and came to be venerated as saints, but if their graves were thought dishonourable it is extraordinary that their kin did not trouble to retrieve the corpses, which they had opportunities to do, during the intervening half-century. The explanation may be that they lay, as kings of their generation normally did, in barrows, and were therefore thought to have received appropriate burial (the removal of their heads to church burial conceivably marking a transitional compromise between new and old rites).[207] Only towards the end of the century, when the great were starting to be buried in their new dynastic minsters, were the two kings thought to require graves matching their saintly rather than their heroic status. These stories serve only to highlight the singularity of Kent.

A rural form of the martyr-cult tradition probably survived among the western British,[208] and could have been reinforced by the same commercial and ecclesiastical contacts that brought pottery from western and southern Gaul, regions with a strong tradition of *ad sanctos* burial. Either or both explanations may be invoked for such archaeological phenomena as Whithorn, where graves focused on what seem to have been small outdoor shrines, or Cannington, where the large fourth- to eighth-century cemetery contained two shrine-like foci including a 'special' grave.[209] If English groups in Bernicia and the west midlands abandoned furnished burial under British influence,[210] they could also have absorbed the idea of burial near Christian relics from a similar source. But the extent to which the British, let alone the English, laity had adopted *ad sanctos* burial by the eighth century should not be exaggerated. Certainly in Wales, the late prehistoric tradition of burial in lay cemeteries and isolated spots continued well into the early middle ages, and it may not have been until the ninth or tenth century that the laity were automatically buried on church sites.[211]

Yet a trend towards church-associated burial was moving slowly across northern Europe during *c.*600–50. While the example of Clovis was followed by the highest Frankish aristocracy during the sixth century, it is unclear (and controversial) how widely it was adopted among lesser groups before the seventh.[212] At the suburban funerary churches of northern Gaul, such

[207] Halsall 1995*a*: 272 suggests this explanation for a seventh-century grave at Audun-le-Tiche containing the furnished but decapitated bodies of two young men. Cf. Fry 1999: 96–102, for separate head-burial in Ireland.

[208] Sharpe 2002*a*: 126–54; cf. Thomas 1971: 48–58, 132–66.

[209] Hill 1997: 67–133; Rahtz and others 2000: 45–57, 413–14. Cf. Bullough 1983: 182–3, suggesting that cemeteries like Cannington are the closest insular equivalent to the *ad sanctos* cemeteries of southern Gaul.

[210] Above, pp. 25–6.

[211] Davies 1982: 185–7 (perhaps not until the eleventh century); H. James 1992; Edwards and Lane 1992*b*: 6–7; Petts 2002: 43–4 (after the eighth century).

[212] Contrast Young 1986: 386–96 with the argument of Halsall 1995*a*: 272 that the decisive shift came only in the later seventh century.

as Saint-Denis and Sainte-Geneviève outside Paris, the accumulation of Merovingian graves of less than the highest status may be principally a seventh-century phenomenon.[213] In the countryside, two different initiatives by the Frankish upper classes extended the range of church burial: some favoured burial in family monasteries,[214] while others built small churches within long-standing community cemeteries to house their family graves.[215] These two strategies, of which the first was to influence the English profoundly and the second hardly at all, shared a concern to integrate Christian burial into traditional expressions of family and group identity. The effect was a steady percolation down through the Frankish laity, as the seventh century progressed, of the idea of burial in association with a church.[216]

There are signs that the non-English insular peoples experienced similar trends over a similar time-scale. Seventh-century Irish laws show the tension of loyalties divided between ancestral cemeteries and churches. Burial with ancestors or spouse is condoned; it is acknowledged but regretted that some Christians will be buried among pagans; a man who divides his gifts between his ancestral cemetery and his church must give more to the latter; and anyone who is 'joined to a church' (as a monk or monastic tenant) is to be buried there. Evidently the Church was trying to pull both the corpses and the allegiances of the laity into an ecclesiastical ambit, re-focusing family loyalties on the central churches of the folk-districts.[217]

In northern and western Britain, a 'point at which the importance of the Church is outstripping that of the ancestors', in Stephen Driscoll's useful phrase, may be signalled in the later seventh century by the ending of monumental traditions which had affirmed kindred and secular status: the Pictish 'Class I' symbol-stones, and Latin inscription traditions in Wales and Dumnonia. As Driscoll observes, the stately crosses on the new, 'Class II', Pictish slabs emphasize 'the adoption of a more powerful discourse, one capable of banishing the animal symbols and their possible regional or tribal associations, one which was supported by a highly centralised, hierarchical,

---

[213] At Saint-Denis the elite coffined burials inside the basilica certainly spanned the sixth and seventh centuries (Fleury and France-Lanord 1998), but the surrounding cemetery may not have developed much if at all before *c.*600 (Wyss 1996: 112–14). Cf. Périn 1992: 260–1, for Sainte-Geneviève, and Young 1977: 57, for Saint-Germain-des-Prés.

[214] Young 1986: 390–4; Burnell 1988: 204–7, 252–6, 264.

[215] Dierkens 1981: 67–9; Young 1986: 394–6; Demolon 1990; Burnell 1988: esp. 62–7, 162–77, 184–204, 247–52, 519–30, 584–5; Halsall 1995*a*: 272; Burnell and James 1999: 96–103.

[216] Cf. Young 1977: 66, on the fading-out of row-grave cemeteries around 700: 'Elle signifie que la longue évolution de l'inhumation *ad sanctos* avait porté ses fruits et que l'église était prête à assumer la pleine responsabilité qui incombait jadis à la famille.'

[217] Charles-Edwards 1992: 76; Sharpe 1992: 82–3; O'Brien 1992: 134–6; O'Brien 1999: 53–4; Treffort 1996*a*: 170–2.

transcendent institution'.[218] In Cornwall, the proportion of inscribed stones sited (at least eventually) at churches rather than in the open landscape may rise during the period *c*.500–700; after that they become less common, perhaps because commemoration was achieved, and status marked, in different ways and within a Christian framework.[219] A shift in both the form and the siting of stone monuments—towards Christian symbolism and association with churches—can also be recognized in seventh- to ninth-century Wales.[220] The new tone of this more clerical funerary milieu is evoked by one of the later British inscriptions, a metrical epitaph at Llanlleonfel (Brecon):

> *In sindone muti Ioruert Ruallaunque sepulchris +*
> *Iudicii adventum spectant in pace tremendum*

Silent in the shroud, Iorweth and Ruallaun in their tombs await in peace the dreadful coming of the Judgement.

This dignified, obviously clerical text, 'a fragment of contemporary manuscript cut into rock', does not even mention—as one of the earlier, tersely genealogical, inscriptions would have done—their parentage or titles.[221] The memory of these two noblemen was entrusted to forms of record and commemoration which were the preserves of an institutionalized Christian culture.

These trends, which had barely penetrated the Christian English by *c*.650, would affect them deeply over the next century. Like their neighbours, the English needed churches around which they could reorientate family identities, shielding them from King Radbod's worrying sense of faithlessness to a larger kindred. As English kings and nobles began their great phase of monastic endowment they created family shrines of a new kind, as expressive of worldly status as their parents' barrows and and much more able to preserve it in permanent, coherent memory. In such contexts, the new ways of burial would run no risk of disempowerment.

The first Christian sites and systems

English ecclesiastical sites founded before 650 need to be considered as a group, and free from hindsight. It is well known that the early bishops' seats

---

[218] Driscoll 1988: 184 (referring to the 'banishment' of Pictish symbols from the faces of 'Class II' stones which display crosses, not to their total disappearance). Cf. Carver 1998: 26–37.

[219] Thomas 1994*a*: 305–10; but again contrast Okasha 1993 for dating, and the rather later chronology of Petts 2002: 27–8, 43–4.

[220] Edwards 2001: 28–34, 38–9.

[221] Nash-Williams 1950: 77–8; Thomas 1994*a*: 322–3.

set a topographical pattern—association with Roman walled sites—which many minsters would adopt during the next century. It is less frequently noticed that the few identifiable smaller sites look really rather different in kind from later ones, and closer to potential Italian and Gallic prototypes. It seems possible that they represent a false start, before the later seventh-century Church sailed off on its monastic course: the doomed attempt of a narrow missionary group to reproduce local ecclesiastical organization as they had known it in their homelands.

To begin with the cathedrals, Canterbury was once again in a class of its own, both from its symbolic importance and from its purposeful topographical coherence (Fig. 9). In the years immediately after 597, Augustine and his colleagues set about transforming ruined *Durovernum* into a 'new Rome', evocative both of the authority behind his mission and of its supremacy, backed by the Kentish people and their king, over the surviving British hierarchy. Canterbury's Christian topography, the locations and dedications of its churches, and the liturgy observed in them, were all designed to mirror those of Continental cities in general and Rome in particular.[222] Most remarkable is the creation of a classic bi-polar 'holy city', framed around the cathedral of the Holy Saviour within the Roman walls and the extramural, pseudo-martyrial monastery of SS Peter and Paul. Despite later traditions which credited Augustine with re-using a Romano-British church as his cathedral, this scheme probably owed nothing to Canterbury's Christian past:[223] it was a statement that the Church in Britain was making a new start.

Yet nothing quite like it would happen in England again. Setting a pattern that many minsters followed after 650, the other leaders of the Gregorian mission—Mellitus at London, Justus at Rochester, Paulinus at both York and probably Lincoln—built their churches in the principal Roman walled places of their dioceses, as did the independent missionaries Felix at *Dommoc* and Birinus at Dorchester-on-Thames.[224] Although some or all of these founders

---

[222] Brooks 2000, arguing that 'Canterbury's prolonged campaign of *imitatio Romae* was an essential element in the process of English ethnogenesis'; Thacker 2002: 52–4.

[223] Here I differ somewhat from Brooks 2000. See Brooks 1988 and Loseby 2000: 340 for the likelihood of discontinuity, even at Canterbury (though the gap may be as little as twenty years), between sub-Roman and Anglo-Saxon occupation. Bede (*HE* i. 33, p. 114) repeats a Canterbury story that Augustine restored (*recuperavit*) a Roman church, but the recent excavation makes it seem almost impossible that the first cathedral was an *in situ* Roman building: Blockley and others 1997: 99–100. Cf. below, pp. 189–91.

[224] *HE* ii. 3, ii. 14, ii. 16, ii. 15, iii. 7 (pp. 142, 186, 192, 190, 232). See Tatton-Brown 1986 and Rodwell 1993*a* for London. Paulinus's church at York was probably built in the ruins of the Roman *principia*, where part of what may have been its cemetery has been excavated (Phillips, Heywood, and Carver 1995; cf. Rollason and others 1998: 125–38); I am unpersuaded by the alternative hypothesis of Norton 1998: 11–13. At Lincoln, the church (St Paul) found in the middle of the Roman forum resembles the early seventh-century Kentish group, which points to Paulinus, but there are

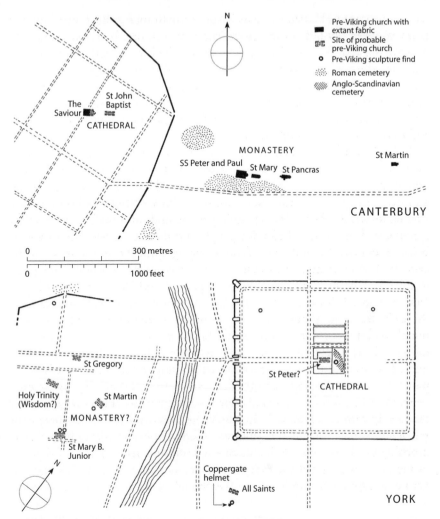

9. Above: *Canterbury* in the time of Æthelberht and Augustine, illustrating the probably deliberate modelling of the Christian topography on that of Rome and other Continental cities. Below: *York* by the late eighth century, showing the inferred sites of the seventh-century cathedral in the headquarters building of the Roman fort, and of the later complex beyond the Ouse which may have been founded in imitation of Canterbury's bi-polar arrangement. (After Brooks 1984: fig. 1, R. Morris 1986: figs. 59–60, and Phillips and others 1995: fig. 83, with additions.)

took advantage of Roman ruins to create formal settings for their churches, there is never any hint of the careful parallelism of dedications, nor of the bi-polar format.[225] Like Canterbury these are evocations of Christian civic topography, but in a more attenuated and less literal mode, without its reference to the dichotomy of *urbs* and *suburbium*.

Augustine's Canterbury also delineated—more clearly than any other English religious site before the tenth century—the dichotomy between pastoral and contemplative, though even there it had ambiguities. 'You, brother, have been trained in the monastic rules and should not be separated from your clergy (*clerici*) in the Church of the English,' Pope Gregory reminded Augustine. 'You must establish the way of life which was our fathers' in the early days of the Church, none of whom claimed anything as his own from among their possessions, for everything was held in common.'[226] This advice conspicuously fails to make a clear distinction between the lifestyles of monks and clerics, implying rather that all Augustine's religious personnel were to live 'the way of life which was our fathers''. Nonetheless, the division of his following between the intramural cathedral and the extramural monastery does look like an attempt to separate the archbishop's ordained staff, involved in administration and pastoral care, from those who were monks pure and simple and were cut off from the world to concentrate on spiritual labours.[227]

Yet outside Canterbury, there is no evidence that any English minster for centuries after would make this distinction, nor that bishops or their staffs were kept physically separate from contemplative monks.[228] Two Essex minsters of the 650s do sound like joint communities of episcopal clergy and monks: Bishop Cedd, says Bede, 'made churches through the districts (*fecit per loca ecclesias*) and ordained priests and deacons who would help him in teaching the Faith and baptizing, especially in the *civitas* called *Ythancaestir* [Bradwell-on-Sea] in the Saxon tongue and in that known as Tilbury . . . , in which, gathering a multitude of servants of Christ [i.e. monks], he taught them . . . to keep the discipline of regular life'.[229] Even so, it is unknown whether the monks and priests lived apart, and the relatively early date of

difficulties in reconciling this with the radiocarbon evidence (Jones 1994, tending towards a late Roman date; Sawyer 1998: 58–62, 226–30, arguing strongly for a seventh-century one). See Blair 1994: 1–6, 39–41, for Dorchester; Campbell 2000: 108–10, for *Dommoc*; below, pp. 188–9, for later minsters in Roman walled places.

[225] York looks deliberately bi-polar, but the monastic complex on the west bank of the Ouse may not have been established until the eighth century: Fig. 9 and below, p. 126 n.

[226] *HE* i. 27 (p. 80). Cf. Bede's (slightly disingenuous) use of this passage to justify the different arrangements at Lindisfarne: *VCB* c. 16 (pp. 206–8).

[227] Cf. Brooks 1984: 87–91.

[228] Below, pp. 98–9.

[229] *HE* iii. 22 (pp. 282–4).

Cedd's minsters prevents them from being indicative of what would happen after the 660s. Augustine's scheme—which historians as well as early medieval polemicists have tended to take as a norm—looks barely more than an aspiration, soon to melt away before the realities of insular culture.

The next tier down, the hypothetical equivalents of the baptismal churches built by bishops at Italian *plebes* and Gallic *vici*, are elusive. If we could find them anywhere it should be in east Kent, and that area does have its peculiarities. The addition to Canterbury cathedral around 750 of a free-standing baptismal church, unique in England and by then obsolete in Gaul, was a (deliberately archaizing?) symbol of its Roman dignity and maternal status.[230] Also uniquely, as a coherent system, the minsters of Canterbury diocese enjoyed in the eleventh century a virtual monopoly of the right to collect and distribute the archbishop's chrism, which in Nicholas Brooks's view 'is best understood as a jealously maintained relic of an age when the Kentish "monasteries" were true baptismal churches, taking a dominant role in the pastoral work of the diocese'.[231] If some of the east Kent minsters did indeed begin as would-be *pievi* they changed their character quickly, and given the very small size of the diocese it is hard to think that many of them were needed. But it is indeed possible that the late chrism-dues are a faint aftertaste of the distinctively Italian flavour of Canterbury under Augustine.[232]

When Paulinus moved from Kent to Northumbria in the mid 620s, he confronted a still-pagan territory far larger than his colleagues' dioceses in the south-east. It seems possible that here too he planned a network of *vicus*-type churches, elements of which lasted into the era of the Lindisfarne mission. In the years around 630, according to Bede, Paulinus preached from a series of what were probably ex-Roman sites in Deira, Lindsey, and Elmet, at one of which, the royal vill of *Campodunum,* he built a church (*basilica*).[233] Bede may have been thinking of such places when he wrote that Cedd (the Northumbrian missionary to Essex) 'made churches through the districts', a phrase which he also uses of Northumbria after the foundation of

---

[230] Below, pp. 101–2.
[231] Brooks 1984: 188–9, 202; cf. Foot 1992a: 181; Tatton-Brown 1988: 114–17; Barlow 1979: 182 n.
[232] This Italian aspect is emphasized by several contributors to Gameson 1999, notably Scharer, Cambridge, and R. Gameson. References (all post-1100) to the organized distribution of chrism through minsters in other regions are rare, but they do occur: at Southwell for the archbishop of York (Dixon and Stocker 2001: 262, 265), and at Leominster and Bishops Waltham (below, p. 442 n.).
[233] *HE* ii. 14 (p. 188); cf, below, pp. 271–2, Higham 1997: 172–5, and Charles-Edwards 2000: 314–15. The Whitby Life of St Gregory describes, in an episode involving Eadwine and Paulinus on an unknown site, a royal church near a hall and a *platea populi* (*WVG* c. 15, pp. 96–8; Rollason and others 1998: 127–9); there is nothing to identify this with York, as has sometimes been supposed.

Lindisfarne.[234] Aidan died in 651 at a royal vill near Bamburgh, in which he had 'a church and resting-place (*ecclesiam et cubiculum*) where he was used to turn aside and stay and go out thence to preach round about; he was also accustomed to do this in other royal vills, inasmuch as he had no private property except his church and the small landholdings attached to it (*ecclesia sua et adiacentibus agellis*)'.[235] The complex which replaced the 'eastern ring-ditch' at Yeavering (Fig. 8) possibly gives some impression of what a Christian adjunct to an early royal vill might have looked like.

It is intriguing that in one of this series of comments, Bede uses the language of Continental parochial hierarchy: Paulinus baptized his converts in the River Swale 'because oratories or baptisteries (*oratoria vel baptisteria*) could not be built in that first stage of the nascent Church there'.[236] 'Baptisteries' suggests episcopal baptismal churches, such as an Italian-trained bishop like Paulinus would have planned within his diocese. But seemingly they were hard to build not only 'in that first stage of the nascent Church' but in any later stage: this is the last as well as the first reference to *baptisteria* as a generic category in Anglo-Saxon England. It is almost as though Bede's phrase reflects assumptions current in the 620s, quite different from those of his own monastically dominated generation.[237]

Finally, the private oratories ubiquitous on the Continent are virtually invisible in England. The one context in which they can perhaps be inferred is, not surprisingly, the Frankish-influenced aristocratic milieu of east Kent.[238] When, some time before 597, King Æthelberht's Frankish queen had a Roman building outside Canterbury fitted up as a church dedicated to St Martin of Tours (Fig. 10), she was following practices familiar in her home circle.[239] It is conceivable that other Franks, or Frankish-influenced Kentish

---

[234] Above, p. 68; *HE* iii. 3 (p. 220): 'construebantur ergo ecclesiae per loca.' Note the resemblance of this to Gregory of Tours's phrase 'instituisse ecclesias per vicos', describing the episcopally directed foundation of subordinate churches with which he was familiar: Delaplace 2002: 20.

[235] *HE* iii. 17 (p. 262).

[236] *HE* ii. 14 (p. 188).

[237] Could these uses of *basilica* and *baptisterium* derive from a mid seventh-century Canterbury text which used Italian terminology? Bede obtained some and perhaps much of his information about Paulinus from Kent, for instance the reference to his cross and chalice (*HE* ii. 20, p. 204; and cf. above, n. 204). Cf. Cubitt 1992: 209–10. See below, pp. 201–2, for the lack of separate baptismal churches in England.

[238] There may have been a good deal more Frankish ecclesiastial influence here than Bede's Gregorian-centred narrative allows. Cf. Wood 1994; Higham 1997: 82–90; Stancliffe 1999: 120–1, for the view that concerns about purity among the Kentish laity, which Meens 1994 ascribes to British ecclesiastics, probably came from Frankish ones; and Cambridge 1999 for the Frankish character of the early Kentish churches.

[239] *HE* i. 26 (p. 76). For the building see Tatton-Brown 1980; R. Morris 1989: 20–5; Bell 2001: 184–5. The first phase is probably not, as Bede implies, an actual Roman church, and the dedication is best ascribed to Bertha and her bishop. There remains a doubt whether it is a Roman structure at all, or a church built in a Roman style at the end of the sixth century: the former seems more likely, but either would be consistent with contemporary Merovingian practice.

10. *St Martin's, Canterbury*: the first 'English' church, created in the 590s by remodelling a Romano-British structure. It illustrates a contemporary fashion in Queen Bertha's northern Frankish homeland. (Tim Tatton-Brown; model by J. Atherton Bowen in the Royal Museum, Canterbury.)

people, were doing the same. Kent has two further cases (Stone-by-Faversham and Lullingstone) of this kind of re-adoption, involving the construction of a church in or over a late Roman mausoleum: the idiom, always rare in England, was widespread around 600 in north-western France.[240] East Kent also gives us the only plausible English analogues for 'founder-grave' churches, as well as a stray reference (in 741) to an 'oratory of St Martin'.[241] But again these cases illustrate differences between Kent and the rest of England rather than similarities between England and the Continent.

The early Anglo-Saxon Church tends to be pictured in terms of modest episcopal preaching-churches attached to royal vills or scattered through the countryside, and of clergy trained by the bishop and working under his direction. But this picture rests purely on the short passages in Bede's 'History' cited above, all describing events between the late 620s and the late 650s. It looks very unlike the ecclesiastical world of *c*.700, and very small-scale by comparison. For Bede, with the hindsight of three generations, smaller was better: this had been an austere and zealous Church, which had enjoyed the firm rule of upright bishops and had despised riches that came from the laity with strings attached. As he wrote wistfully of the pre-664 community at

[240] Fletcher and Meates 1977; Bell 1998*b*: 11–14; Bell 2001: 187–9; Le Maho 1994: 14–16.
[241] S 24; below, pp. 236–7, 220.

Lindisfarne, 'they were so purified from all infection of greed that they did not accept any lands or possessions to build minsters (*monasteria*) unless coerced by secular powers, and this custom was universally observed in the Northumbrian churches for a little time afterwards'.[242]

Writing of the 640s, Bede also observes that 'because at that time not many minsters had yet been built in English regions, many people from Britain used to enter the minsters of the Franks or Gauls for the sake of the monastic life; they also sent their daughters to be taught in them and to be united with the heavenly bridegroom, especially at [Faremoutiers–en–]Brie, Chelles, and the minster of Andelys[-sur-Seine]'.[243] Such minsters as are recorded in the middle third of the century were mostly in the Hiberno-Northumbrian milieu (Lindisfarne, Hartlepool, probably Melrose), or products of other Irish missions (*Cnobheresburg,* possibly Malmesbury and Bosham).[244] In general, monastic settlements were still something that the English knew more through contacts with their Frankish, Irish, and British neighbours than at first hand. But life was changing: in another narrative, of the decisive battle between the Northumbrians and Mercians in 654/5, Bede himself sketches the shape of things to come. King Osuiu of Northumbria, he says,

vowed that if he gained the victory he would dedicate his daughter to the Lord as a holy virgin and give twelve estates to build minsters (*XII possessiones praediorum ad construenda monasteria*). . . . [After winning the battle he] gave his daughter Ælfflaed, who was scarcely a year old, to be consecrated to God in perpetual virginity. He also gave twelve small estates (*possessiunculis terrarum*) on which, as they were freed from concern with earthly warfare [i.e. from military service], a site and means might be provided for monks to wage heavenly warfare and to pray with unceasing devotion for the eternal peace of his race. Six of the estates which he gave were in the province of the Deirans and six in that of the Bernicians. Each estate consisted of ten hides, so that there were 120 hides altogether. King Osuiu's daughter who had been dedicated to God entered the minster named *Heruteu* [Hartlepool] . . . , then ruled by Abbess Hild, who two years later gained possession of ten hides in the place known as *Streanæshalch* [Whitby][245] and there built a minster. In it the aforesaid king's

---

[242] *HE* iii. 26 (p. 310)—though he also says of Aidan's Lindisfarne that 'donabantur munere regio possessiones et territoria ad instituenda monasteria' (iii. 3, p. 220).

[243] *HE* iii. 8 (pp. 236–8); cf. Le Jan 2001: 254–5.

[244] C. Plummer, *Venerabilis Baedae Opera Historica* (2 vols., Oxford, 1896), ii. 148–9, for most of these. Others are Bradwell-on-Sea and Tilbury (above, p. 68), Gateshead, and possibly Bury St Edmunds.

[245] Notwithstanding recent arguments (Barnwell and others 2003), I continue to believe that the place which Bede knew as *Streanæshalch* is Whitby, not Strensall near York. Bede's statement that it lay about thirteen miles from Hackness (*HE* iv. 23, pp. 412–14) is surely conclusive: Hackness is fourteen miles from Whitby, thirty-five from Strensall. Bede's Latin expression *sinus fari* (*HE* iii. 25, p. 298) clearly does not, as he implies, translate the English term, but in itself it is adequately explained by Bell 1998a. The compound *Streoneshalch* occurs twice in Worcestershire (Gelling 1978: 189); could it not have occurred twice in Yorkshire?

daughter was first a pupil in the regular life and then a teacher (*magistra*); then, about the age of sixty, the blessed virgin departed to the embrace and nuptials of her heavenly bridegroom. She is buried in that minster together with her father Osuiu, her mother Eanflaed, her mother's father Eadwine, and many other nobles, all in the church of the holy apostle Peter.[246]

Princess-abbesses; monastic endowments in round numbers of hides; networks of minsters created by rulers in co-operation with monastic experts; a family's minster as its burial-place and the repository of its history: all these things would be central to the expansion of the English Church over the next century.

The triumph of the monastic model

Monastic settlements, and relationships of proprietorship and allegiance centred on them, became after 650 the framework around which English ecclesiastical organization was built. To anticipate the next chapter, late seventh- and eighth-century England shows extremely little evidence for structures of authority that were episcopal in the strict sense, as distinct from the monastic networks over which bishops—among others—exercised lordship.[247] This was radically different from anything that could have been planned by Augustine and his colleagues, and leads us to something not unlike the unmodified Irish model of a monastic Church supplanting an episcopal one. The solution offered here is that the Irish and English Churches were both indeed 'monastic', but in a very broad sense of the word; and that English bishops lacked both the wealth, status, and authority of their Continental colleagues and the weight in numbers of their Irish ones.

   To understand the forces which shaped a distinctively monastic Church in England after 650, we must try to grasp the differences between the various possible modes of exercising authority and of controlling places. These are illustrated by the contrasting European systems of terminology for Church organization. The Latin usage of Gaul recognized a three-tier hierarchy of churches plus two categories apart: on the one hand, cities with their cathedral churches (*ecclesiae*), sites of pastoral care delegated from the bishop (*baptisterial/parochiae*), and mere oratories; on the other, extramural basilicas, and monasteries (*monasteria*) of enclosed monks. In the kaleidoscopic terminology of Ireland, a regionally important church (*civitas, ecclesia, domnach, domus*) would probably have a bishop, might or might not house an abbot and strict monks, but would certainly contain a religious community of some

[246] *HE* iii. 24 (pp. 290–2).   [247] Below, pp. 97–9.

kind and would probably oversee lesser churches (*ecclesiae, cellae*). The Latin and vernacular vocabulary developed in Germany from northern Francia drew the lines between bishops' cathedrals (*domus*), mere churches (*ecclesiae*), and monasteries (*monasteria*). That of England put the emphasis on minsters (*monasteria, coenobia*), while recognizing episcopal *sedes* (though these could be contained within minsters) and an unspecific category of *ecclesiae* (which were usually also minsters or their adjuncts).[248]

The vocabulary used to describe the English Church, like that used for its Irish and Franco-German counterparts, therefore differed from that of more southerly parts of Europe in having no word denoting a distinct tier of churches, immediately below the cathedral, which drew their authority from the bishop.[249] All of them also recognized—but in different terms—the existence of the kind of complex, multi-functional ecclesiastical settlement for which an inclusive definition is proposed on p. 3 above. The Irish did not usually apply *monasterium/mainister* to such a place. The English—probably influenced by the aristocratic monastic culture of northern Francia[250]—did, in the forms *monasterium* (Latin) and *mynster* (Old English).

If—as a wide range of other evidence suggests—the terminology points to a north-west European Church dominated by 'monastic' centres, we must try to understand why. Minsters were evidently a great success with kings and nobles, but if their flexibility and inclusiveness help to explain this appeal to the laity, it would also be quite wrong to minimize the role of strict living and arcane learning. All these monastic cultures supported scholars, ascetics, and hermits: if they monopolize the narrative sources unduly, and if we now realize that Columba, Columbanus, Fursey, and Cuthbert are not the whole story, they remain an essential part of it. Their example was the moral face and the conscience of the para-monastic boom, enabling patrons to feel that their wealth was financing both the learning of the Christian world and the exertions of the genuinely holy. Where traditional models fail is in perceiving rarefied lifestyles as the whole essence of early monasticism, before various kinds of corruption set in: in reality they were always one end of a broad spectrum. In northern Europe, the age of unalloyed monastic purity existed only in the minds of reformers.

If the monastic mode was generally attractive both to kings and to idealists, its success specifically among the English was enhanced by the minsters' capacity to fill a gap left by a notable weakness in episcopal governance: a

---

[248] Green 1998: 355–7, 366, for an interesting dialogue on the German vocabulary; Foot 1992*b* for English terminology, and above, p. 70, for the sole Anglo-Latin use of *baptisterium*.

[249] Cf. Charles-Edwards 2000: 249, for the insular uncoupling of the word *ecclesia* from the idea of episcopal oversight.

[250] Green 1998: 357–9.

peculiarity best explained by comparison with the two available models. Bishops in England would never be able to establish the centralized, city-based rule of Gallic ones, because the capacity for reconstructing that kind of cultural and economic milieu in former Britannia simply did not exist.[251] Of the civic geography which proclaimed the bishop's supremacy, and derived its meaning from him, the English occasionally replicated the show but virtually never the substance; a minster might house a bishop, but could get on very happily without him. On the other hand, the numerous bishops of Ireland (and probably western Britain), with their multiple grades and their direct involvement in Church life at all levels, belonged to a fragmented social and political structure very different from seventh-century England. Outside Kent, the convert English kings ruled huge tracts of territory, and tended to appoint single bishops over their realms. As the monastic tide started to rise in the late 660s, England had three bishops; Ireland at the same date must have had a hundred or more. Housing a bishop was standard for Irish *domnach* churches, exceptional for English minsters.

So a monastic Church was conspicuously well suited to the mid seventh-century English. But another English idiosyncrasy, the lack of purely local churches serving villages and homesteads, remains more puzzling.[252] There is the obvious chronological point that these proliferated in Francia, Ireland, and (probably) western Britain during the fifth and sixth centuries, whereas English thegns and husbandmen had no chance to build them before the seventh. Yet from the 650s, as royal patronage fuelled a monastic boom, one might have expected a parallel boom in the estate oratories ubiquitous elsewhere. The most promising explanations concern the extent to which ecclesiastical structures were established from above downwards, combined with the strength of kings' control over provincial districts and (compared with Francia) lesser proprietors' correspondingly looser control over land. Again we may contrast the governmental and exploitative capacities of great English kingdoms with the decentralized rulership and highly segmented dynasties of Ireland:[253] perhaps in most parts of England the model of a regional minster with its peripheral sites was the only one on offer. This is speculation: we know so little about English landholding before 700 that the lack of small churches is more readily adduced as evidence for background conditions than set in the context of them.

In the last analysis, the location, economy, and cultural orientation of the

---

[251] As is now very effectively brought out by Loseby 2000: 344–9.

[252] Below, pp. 118–21, for the argument that such churches remained uncommon in England before the tenth century. Martin Carver (pers. comm.) believes that the Picts, like the English, had crosses but not local churches.

[253] Cf. Charles-Edwards 1989: 39; Campbell 1986: 95–7, 108–16.

English kingdoms were the main determinants of their ecclesiastical structures (Fig. 6). Viewed from the south, they lay on the Roman fringe. As Patrick Wormald has observed of written law in post-Roman Europe, one can envisage a deeply hatched zone in Italy and Spain, 'shading off as the eye moves up [the map], though not sharply till one gets north of the Danube and the Loire–Saône watershed, and less sharply beyond the latter than the former. In such terms, southern England is merely stippled, the North effectively "blank".' These gradations trace 'the varying depth of Rome's imprint: not upon ideals, for the *élites* of sub-Roman Europe shared a hankering after its *exempla*, but upon the common practice of society'.[254] Extending this to Church organization, we might say that the outer margins of city-based episcopal governance stretched just across the Channel, to Canterbury but no further. The same dynamic operated in Galicia, another 'peripheral' part of the Empire, where a seventh-century boom in monastic foundations filled an episcopal vacuum and initiated processes which we will shortly meet in England: power-struggles between bishops and monasteries, a monastic lifestyle both sustained and compromised by secular culture, and family and community structures re-fashioned in a monastic guise.[255] Viewed from closer range, Ireland and parts of northern Francia had enough social and economic common ground with the English for their para-monastic institutions, rapidly developing around 600, to be powerful and mutually reinforcing influences. It would have been extraordinary if the English royal and noble dynasties had not favoured this form.

While the English were still largely pagan, Columbanus wrote of 'all the Churches of the whole West', a conception probably embracing Ireland, western Britain, Brittany, and the Loire valley.[256] During the next century this distinctive Christian zone would expand northwards and eastwards to become what Denis Bethell called a 'Northern Church':[257] not indeed with the coherence implied by the capital initials, but in the sense of a broad religious culture articulated around the societies of northern Europe and to be contrasted with that of the south. Bethell also recognized its central feature, the religious community as a social and topographical mode:

Kings in fact soon found that there was much to be said for having a monastery. It was sacred, its possessions were safe in war; it was a place of refuge. It was a craft centre where metal-workers, painters, musicians were trained. In that world without electricity it provided the great feasts of lighting, that aristocratic world which loved

---

[254] Wormald 1999*a*: 480 (developing Marc Bloch's image); Loseby 1998 makes a similar point about city life in Gaul.

[255] Díaz 2001.   [256] Dumville 1984: 20–1; Sharpe 1984*b*: 201–2.

[257] Bethell 1981: 45–8.

ceremony, rich ceremony . . . These were educational centres where there were learned men who could explain the movements of the stars, the workings of the universe, the course, reason and nature of human history, the purpose and ends of men. They were places of political use . . . [T]hey could be neutral meeting grounds; their large buildings allowed of large assemblies. They were homes of refuge for the aged . . . Many ordinary men and women joined or became attached to the monasteries as labourers and shared the name of 'monks' . . . Our nearest modern parallels to it [early Christian Ireland] are early twentieth century Tibet, and the still existing monastic/aristocratic societies of the Himalayas. In modern Bhutan we have an entire society living in such monasteries.[258]

For 'tribal' societies becoming more complex, the monastic form had the potential to be at once familiar and exotic, reassuring and dynamic. The sponsors of imported and more advanced religious cultures could create sites which flattered their vanities and accommodated their daily routines, but which at the same time claimed intellectual supremacy and purveyed a new kind of arcane wisdom supplanting that of older priesthoods.[259] In a kin-based culture the monastic community could itself be a family ('collegiate, or redolent of quasi-kinship, rather than essentially monastic'[260]), capable of developing in parallel with the secular families that supported it. But precisely because its other-worldly functions were universally accepted, and required the commitment of resources to supporting large concentrations of often aristocratic people, it could sometimes realize more advanced and complex organizational and economic forms than could the host societies themselves.

Here Buddhist cultures—as Bethell recognized—offer some striking analogies. In eighth- and ninth-century Tibet,[261] the official acceptance of Buddhism was followed immediately by the heaping of gifts and privileges on religious orders and the founding of huge numbers of monasteries. Exempt from tax and services, the monasteries owned lands and serfs, exercised jurisdiction over them, and increased their revenues by trade. Social hierarchies were observed, the rich monks owning extensive property and having poor monks as servants. Complex settlements resembling towns or

---

[258] Ibid. 44.

[259] Wheatley 1971: 302–5; Adams 1966: 121–2; Jigmei and others 1981: 160, on the reception of Buddhism in seventh-century Tibet, where it must 'have immensely impressed the comparatively barbaric Tibetans for the marvellously rich and refined civilization accompanying the religious message'. For a revealing ethnographical perspective on the prestige invested in far-away cultural worlds, and exotic artefacts acquired from them, see Helms 1993.

[260] Etchingham 1999: 223. Cf. Díaz 2001: 342–52, for the re-branding of Galician families and peasant communities as monasteries.

[261] The following sketch is based on Stein 1972: 140; Tucci 1980: 8–10, 158–60; Jigmei and others 1981: 163–71.

fortresses, the monasteries housed large, multi-functional communities and were divided into sections attached to specific families or villages.

This description could be applied, almost unaltered, to the English minsters discussed below. In both cultures the spectacular monastic supremacy proved in due course unstable, as wealth bred a dilution of internal standards and envy among the descendants of the first enthusiasts.[262] But the impact of the English minsters, both as settlement forms and as foci for the religious and social life of their regions, was transformative and permanent. It will be the theme of the next four chapters.

[262] Below, pp. 132–4, 290 (though in Tibet, unlike England, the monastic supremacy later reasserted itself).

2

Minsters in Church and State
c.650–850

The monastic boom started, in the years around 670, at a critical point in
the development of the English Church and its culture. If the Synod of
Whitby (664) was largely of symbolic importance, few areas of religious life
can have been left untouched by the plague which struck England in the
same year, and remained a feature of life for some decades.[1] Yet that disaster
(which could, like the fourteenth-century plague, have given survivors access
to higher material standards[2]) accompanied an extraordinary economic and
cultural expansion. As the first, essentially foreign, generations of religious
mentors passed from the scene, their place was taken by English-born men
and women trained from youth in Christian doctrine and scholarship.[3] The
really momentous change was not the triumph of 'Roman' over 'Irish', but
the formation of an indigenous ecclesiastical establishment which could stand
on its own feet.

The leaders of this establishment were bishops, but at this most formative
of junctures there were remarkably few of them. When the reforming Syrian
archbishop Theodore of Tarsus (669–90) arrived at Canterbury the English
episcopate was reduced to three: Wine, bishop of London by simony; Chad,
holding the Northumbrian see uncanonically; and Wilfrid, uncontrollable
and currently without a see. Theodore worked hard to consolidate the
English diocesan structure, which by his death comprised sees for Kent
(Canterbury and Rochester), the East Saxons (London), the West Saxons
(Winchester), the East Angles (Elmham and *Dommoc*), the Mercians (Lichfield), the Hwicce (Worcester), Bernicia (Lindisfarne and Hexham), Deira
(York), Lindsey (*Syddensis civitas*), and possibly the Magonsæte (Hereford?)

---

[1] Maddicott 1997, seeing these plagues as 'a brief and temporary intermission in an upward
trend', and suggesting (pp. 47–9) that the larger and more important minsters may have received
an influx of experienced monastic personnel from small communities struck down by plague.

[2] Campbell 2003: 12 n.

[3] Sharpe 2000*b* for the first generation, in the 650s, of English-born bishops.

and the Middle Angles (Leicester). In the process he trod heavily on some episcopal toes, most notoriously Wilfrid's but also those of at least one other bishop who, though appointed under Theodore's own aegis, resented the dismemberment of his see.[4] If Theodore achieved much, it was still a good deal less than had once been envisaged. Gregory the Great, perhaps with Roman Britain in mind, had proposed twenty-four diocesan and two metropolitan sees;[5] Theodore, nearly a century later and after great effort, achieved little more than half that number.

Theodore's pontificate in fact began just when it was becoming clear that ecclesiastical growth would be much more monastic than diocesan. New sees would continue to be founded, but slowly and painfully; increasingly it would be by means of monastic networks, cutting across diocesan boundaries, that bishops would build their power-structures. English bishops never ceased to claim the authority which the councils of the Church gave them, but as monastic endowments multiplied after 670 it was in the independence, lands, and rights of minsters that ecclesiastical power resided. How much the organizational framework of dioceses impinged on religious establishments within them is central to this chapter, where it will often be necessary to try to distinguish ideal from reality, especially when using prescriptive texts in which bishops asserted the scope of their own office.

Minsters and monasticism

Pre-Viking England lacked any normative monastic rule. Forms of the religious life are not in themselves a central concern of this book, but it is important here to reiterate their essentially eclectic and inclusive character, in England as in the cultures which influenced it.[6] *Monasterium/mynster* is a non-specific term, and the rules and lifestyles followed in most early English minsters are irrecoverable. Some founders, most famously the great Northumbrian nobleman-abbots Wilfrid and Benedict Biscop, constructed rules based heavily on St Benedict's, but they did so by choice rather than obligation, and in an eclectic spirit.[7] There was a deep-rooted perception— occasionally apparent even in place-names—that monastic founders and pro-

---

[4] *HE* iv. 2, 6 (pp. 334–6, 354); *VW* c. 25 (p. 50); Brooks 1984: 71–6; Bischoff and Lapidge 1994: 133–9; Cubitt 1995: 113–15; Cubitt 1999: 1220–1. The list of sees depends on interpretation: see Bassett 1989*a*: 229, for a slightly more inclusive one.

[5] *HE* i. 29 (p. 104).

[6] For monastic rules and the internal life of minsters, see especially: Mayr-Harting 1991: 148–219; Wormald 1976; Schneider 1985; Foot 1989*a*; Sims-Williams 1990: 87–143; Foot 2000; Yorke 2003*b*.

[7] *HA* c. 11 (pp. 374–5); Wormald 1976: 141–6.

prietors were autonomous rulers of households;[8] as we will see, the monastic ethic of obedience to abbot or abbess resonated strongly with the indigenous ethic of loyalty to lord or kin.

The temptation to pigeonhole a particular minster as following a 'Roman', 'Frankish', or 'Irish' observance should therefore be resisted: life was more complicated than that. Naturally a minster's character will have reflected the influences bearing on its founder and rulers, but the fragments of evidence that we do have show a weave of strands drawn from several sources.[9] If these influences were channels for high standards and sophisticated learning, it also follows that an eccentric, maverick, or ignorant founder is likely to have created a community in his or her own image. Because our sources mention such establishments only to attack them,[10] they construct a polarization of 'good' and 'bad' minsters which historians, influenced by later definitions of 'reformed' as against 'unreformed' or 'regular' as against 'secular', have taken too much at face value. The reality is likely to have been a spectrum containing a rich and varied mixture of forms, and if some were spiritually unappealing and pastorally supine when viewed from the moral heights of Jarrow, it need not follow that they were socially or culturally useless to the laity around them.

Something can be learnt about many of the early minsters from references to their heads. The Frankish model of a mixed-sex community with a nucleus of nuns under a noble or royal abbess, known since the 640s through contacts of Kentish, Northumbrian, and East Anglian princesses with the communities near Paris, is well attested in England after 670.[11] Given the lack of any explicit references to all-female communities, it seems probable that most or all princess-abbesses ruled double houses. Conversely, references to abbots or other kinds of male head are probably suggestive of all-male personnel.[12] But these were not inflexible categories: monastic sites could be transferred from monks to nuns, and either a male or female member of a

---

[8] Cf. Wormald 1976: 141–4; Campbell 2000: 98; Wood forthcoming: ch. 5. Bede sometimes uses phrases indicating the identification of a minster with its head, e.g. 'servatur adhuc in monasterio reverentissimi abbatis et presbyteri Thrythuulfi', or 'Tunna presbyterum et abbatem monasterii in civitate quae hactenus ab eius nomine Tunnacaestir cognominatur' (*HE* ii. 14, iv. 22, pp. 188, 402). Place-names comprising a personal name compounded with -*mynster* or -*burh* similarly suggest proprietorship: thus Bibury (Glos.), 'Beage's *burh*', was leased to the lady Beage in 718 × 45 (S 1254). See Sims-Williams 1990: 92–3; Blair 1992: 234; Smith 1956: 61–2. These cases should perhaps be distinguished from the British practice of naming holy sites after founder-saints, which the English hardly ever followed (below, p. 195).

[9] The best picture of this amalgam of monastic influences, within a particularly well-documented region, is provided by Sims-Williams 1990: 87–143.

[10] Below, pp. 100–15.   [11] Above, p. 42; below, p. 85.

[12] Sims-Williams 1990: 118–19. *Mynstres aldor* ('elder'), the generic vernacular term for the head of a minster in the later Anglo-Saxon period (below, p. 343), occurs in a Kentish law of 695 (Wihtred, c. 17, *Gesetze*, 13).

minster's ruling kin might potentially succeed to its headship.[13] Fundamentally, monastic property was conceived as a special kind of family property: it had a religious status, but one that was interpreted in traditional terms. This had consequences which by the mid eighth century were being identified as scandalous perversions, but the evidence suggests that in England, as in Ireland, it was fundamental to the forming and endowing of religious communities from the very start.[14]

Any minster with genuine religious functions would presumably have housed enough priests to meet at least the community's own sacramental needs, if not those of a wider lay group. A slightly more difficult question is whether there were minsters of priests only, containing neither monks nor nuns. We have seen that some of the few English minsters recorded before 660 seem to have been episcopal *monasteria clericorum*, housing and training the bishop's clergy on an ancient pattern that would be re-defined in the Frankish reforms under the Carolingians.[15] But finding such establishments in late seventh- and eighth-century England is remarkably difficult, as is finding any clear influence of the Carolingian divide between houses of monks and houses of clergy.[16] It may in fact be inappropriate to envisage English founders and rulers viewing their communities in this way at all: a minster was inherently a complex settlement form, which could include categories of ecclesiastical (and secular) personnel in addition to the one for which it was principally founded.

At this date *no* rule is likely to have excluded the presence of diverse groups of people within and around the minster enclosure, nor to have prevented social, economic, or pastoral contacts between the monastic personnel and a wider lay community. Sources for the leading double houses mention groups of subordinate and sometimes menial males, but also monks, priests, ascetics, and occasionally bishops.[17] The hierarchies of the secular world were replicated in these places.[18] They were less like homogeneous religious brotherhoods or sisterhoods than microcosms of lay communities, with the associated loyalties, rivalries, and tensions; a Kentish abbess who wrote to Boniface blames specifically the male monastics for the quarrels which were disrupting her community.[19] On the outer fringes were a category, only occasionally and indirectly visible, to whom we will return: low-status semi-monks, operating in an ambiguous zone between the manual work enjoined on true monks and the labour-services of tenants, reminiscent of the *manaig* or 'lawful laymen' in Irish sources.[20]

---

[13] Schneider 1985: 24–6. For cases see *VCB* c. 3 (pp. 160–2); *Dialogue*, XI (p. 408).
[14] Above, pp. 47–8; below, pp. 105, 107.   [15] Above, pp. 68–70.
[16] Below, p. 25; Langefeld 1996.   [17] Schneider 1985: 26–31.
[18] Cf. Yorke 2003*b*: 145–50.   [19] *Bon. Ep.* No. 14 (p. 23).
[20] Above, p. 77; below, p. 255.

Many minsters must have been smaller and simpler than the examples considered above. The written sources tend to emphasize the great communities, but archaeology has revealed a number of sites which can plausibly be considered monastic, but which were only a fraction of the size of, say, Whitby.[21] In an extreme case, the nunnery of Nazeing (Essex), apparently the recipient around 700 of grants totalling forty hides, has been identified as two (successive) tiny timber churches and a cemetery, fitted into the earthworks of a Romano-British field-system.[22] More typically, however, the shapes and sizes of minster enclosures known from topographical evidence suggest a normative range, apparent throughout England while showing a degree of regional variation.[23]

Minsters large and small seem often to have been linked in relationships of hierarchy, or of allegiance to one head, which now largely elude us. Just as hermitages or 'granges' could be dependencies of minsters,[24] so whole minsters could be subject to greater ones, or to their owners. Sites owing obedience to a great monastic ruler—St Wilfrid is the extreme case—could spread over hundreds of miles and through several kingdoms.[25] Smaller and perhaps more typical is the Middle Anglian federation comprising the head house of *Medeshamstede* (Peterborough) with its satellites at Breedon-on-the-Hill, Woking, Bermondsey, and perhaps Hoo and Brixworth.[26] Such relationships could disseminate monastic customs over great distances, as when the minster of Wenlock (Salop.) was established under the tutelage of Iken (Suffolk), 200 miles to its east.[27]

The English monastic landscape, as it had formed by *c.*750, was diverse and complex. There were huge variations in size, wealth, and character, and many channels by which communities obtained rulership, learning, cultural guidance, and economic support. The strength of the insular monastic model was that it was infinitely extendable and flexible, and could appeal in different ways to learned bishops, successful war-leaders, widowed queens, royal servants, and spiritually minded peasants.

---

[21] Below, pp. 204–20.

[22] S 65a, S 65b; Huggins and others 1978. There must, however, be an element of doubt about whether the excavated structures really are the nucleus of the minster.

[23] Below, pp. 196–8.   [24] Below, pp. 212–20.

[25] Below, pp. 95–8. A comment by Stephen (*VW* c. 64, p. 138) suggests that Wilfrid's Mercian monks were regarded as part of the Ripon community. In general terms there are parallels with the Columbanian connections linking Luxeuil, Bobbio, and Faremoutiers, though it may be going too far to say that Wilfrid's Frankish connections 'all combine to reveal Ripon and Hexham as outliers of Columbanian monasticism' (Wood 1990: 10–11). As Etchingham observes (1999: 459), Wilfrid's empire conforms as closely to the new model of Irish monastic organization as it seemed to do to the old one.

[26] Keynes 1994: 30–48; below, pp. 126, 215–16, for sculptural links. The list of Lindisfarne dependencies in the Durham 'Historia Regum' s.a. 854 points, despite its late date, to another major federation: *Symeon Op.* ii. 101–2; Craster 1954: 179–80; Hall 1984: 67–8.

[27] S 1798; Sims-Williams 1990: 98–9.

The royal and sub-royal context of monastic foundations

That the land and treasure used to endow the first English minsters came mainly from secular rulers goes without saying. It does, however, need some explanation that large-scale endowment rose so suddenly—seemingly in the years around 670—and was relatively short-lived. The first and most obvious answer is that kings were enormously rich: the construction of big kingdoms at the expense of small ones must have produced huge quantities of surplus wealth which could be recycled into religious and cultural patronage. This process had, however, been operating since at least the late sixth century, and does not immediately explain why kings should suddenly have been so generous to minsters in the late seventh. It was precisely in the decades of the monastic boom that the growth of north-west European trade, and the increased activities of Frankish and Frisian merchants in England, gave new financial opportunities to those who controlled the means of production: a mass currency in silver, and major commercial emporia on the south and east coasts, both emerged during c.670–90.[28] But again, the fact that the monastic culture blossomed most spectacularly in Bernicia, with a thoroughly old-fashioned wealth-base and essentially no coinage,[29] suggests that the financial and cultural stimulus of the new economy does not explain the phenomenon on its own.

A different kind of explanation, to do with the religious and dynastic needs of royal houses at a specific point in history, has recently been explored by Barbara Yorke. She observes that in most kingdoms there was a time-lag between the initial conversions and the kind of whole-hearted and exclusive adoption of Christianity that involved, for instance, the suppression of pagan shrines, something that only seems to have happened from the 650s.[30] This initiated a phase when, most unusually, kings vied with each other in abdicating to become monks or visit Rome. These world-renouncing gestures—which mark the point of transition from the era of conversion to that of monasticization—were unwelcome to a Church which expected other things of Christian kings, and presumably also to their followers.[31] But there was a sense in which kings could become monks by proxy by endowing minsters

---

[28] Below, pp. 256–8.

[29] Maddicott 2000: 31–40, for the view that Northumbrian prosperity rested on cattle, on established patterns of recycling treasure, and on old as well as new trading systems. Although Northumbria had a fine silver coinage from the 730s, the distribution of single finds suggests that coins did not circulate north or west of Whitby during the sceatta era.

[30] Yorke 1999a: 161–3. Bede says that Eorcenberht of Kent (640–64) was the first English king to order the destruction of idols: *HE* iii. 8 (p. 236).

[31] Yorke 1999a: 163–5; Yorke 2003a: 245–52; Yorke 2003b: 23–30; cf. Stancliffe 1983.

for their close relatives, and especially for those royal women who were the highest-ranking members of society not required for their kingdoms' urgent military needs.

This was probably one reason why the Frankish-style double house became so popular in England from about 670.[32] Another was the attraction of aristocratic but celibate havens for queens widowed in the prime of life, and for princesses whose own inclinations, or fathers' dynastic strategies, made this a preferable alternative to a royal marriage. Endowing a double minster offered an alternative to royal ladies' normal means of social and material support: a husband's household or a wergild.[33] Responsibility for providing this new career-path may likewise have mirrored traditional norms of kindred responsibility: monastic widows were provided for by their blood-relatives rather than their relatives by marriage, princesses by either their paternal or maternal kin.[34] In return, brides of Christ could weave networks of influence and cement territorial control like secular brides. Operating from a central minster, a royal abbess could be guardian of her family's history and mortuary cults and wield considerable secular power in its name: Ælfflaed at Whitby is the obvious example. Some dynasties, most conspicuously the Kentish, Northumbrian, and Mercian, founded networks of royal minsters ruled by the founders' daughters, sisters, or aunts, many of whom would be venerated in them as saints through many centuries.[35]

So English double houses, like the earlier Frankish ones, were embedded from the outset in the dynastic strategies of secular elites. The delayed but enthusiastic adoption of this fashion, and of the monastic fashion in general, may have owed much to a growing awareness that it facilitated new ways of deploying family land. The first reliable evidence that land-grants to minsters were recorded in writing comes again from around the 670 watershed (Fig. 11). The production of charters was by now well established among both Celtic and Continental neighbours, so it is not surprising that these English examples reflect a range of Italian, Gallic, and Irish models, apparently adopted and disseminated by leading minster-founding bishops such as Eorcenwald and Wilfrid.[36]

---

[32] For excellent recent work on this important topic, only treated here in passing, see: Schneider 1985; Sims-Williams 1990: 92–113; Foot 2000: 35–60; Yorke 2003*a*: 253–6; Yorke 2003*b*: 17–46; and Le Jan 2001: esp. 263–7, for the incentives for Frankish families of the previous generation to make their daughters abbesses. Below, n. 213, for some possible reasons for the decline of the fashion in the later eighth century.

[33] Examples of monastic endowments given to ladies as wergilds are Gilling (*HE* iii. 24, p. 292) and Minster-in-Thanet (Hollis 1998: 53–4).

[34] Schneider 1985: 243–52; Yorke 2003*b*: 31–6.

[35] Below, pp. 143–4.

[36] Wormald 1984 is fundamental; see also, for instance, Scharer 1999: 190–2; *Selsey*, pp. xlv–lii; *Abingdon*, i. 5–7. This is not to say that there were no English charters before the 670s (Chaplais

11. King Hlothere of Kent gives land on Thanet and at Sturry to Abbot Berhtwald and his minster of Reculver. This charter of 679, the oldest to survive as an original, is said to be issued 'in the city of Reculver' (*in civitate Reculf*), by this date an ecclesiastical *civitas* within the walls of the Roman fort (cf. Fig. 23). (British Library, MS Cotton Augustus ii.2 (S 8).)

While it cannot be disproved that earlier English charters existed, production was certainly stimulated by a boom in endowment seen also in the
narrative evidence. Before 670, we only know of Osuiu's twelve ten-hide
grants of 654/5 (an apparently unique programme of endowing a regular
network of small minsters), and the thirty-hide estate which the sub-king
Alhfrith gave to Wilfrid with Ripon in about 660.[37] Then comes the main
sequence of substantial royal gifts, often of between fifty and 100 hides: for
instance, fifty hides to Chad's *Adbaruae* and fifty to Hanbury in the early
670s, seventy to Monkwearmouth in 674, forty to Jarrow and eighty-seven
to Selsey in about 681–2, sixty to Farnham in 688.[38] Minster-in-Thanet
acquired a total of 124 hides and nine sulungs through transactions recorded
in six charters during 689–97;[39] King Ine's grant to Bradfield in north
Berkshire amounted to 120 hides.[40] Estates of 300 hides are mentioned at the
Isle of Wight, Chertsey, Gloucester, Pershore, and Eynsham.[41] The down-
turn in the decades after 700, when charters become fewer and rarely
mention large hidages, is equally striking, and emphasizes the abnormal conditions of the last three decades of the seventh century.

Expressed as pious donations by great men, charters may understate the
dynamic and commercial aspects of the transactions which they record. Land
could be bought and sold, and there are recorded cases of both male and
female founder-heads making purchases to build up estates around their minsters.[42] Money may often have changed hands, even though it is only occasionally mentioned. Unlike either charters or conventional hagiography, the
foundation-narratives for Minster-in-Sheppey and Minster-in-Thanet celebrate the building of these houses' fortunes through the wily manoeuvrings

---

1969)—they could have been written on papyrus and therefore less likely to survive—but the boom
in monastic endowment was clearly the main stimulus for charter production.

[37] Above, pp. 72–3; *VW* c. 8 (p. 16).

[38] *HE* iv. 3 (p. 336); S 1822; 'Vita Ceolfridi Anon.' c. 7 (ed. Plummer, p. 390); Bede, *HA* cc. 4,
7 (pp. 367, 370; and see Wood 1995: 3–4); *HE* iv. 13 (p. 374); S 235. Some genuine basis probably
underlies the late sources for the huge endowment of Lindisfarne, but it is very unclear how much
of it was acquired before the 670s (Craster 1954; Hall 1984: 50–71); but cf. above, p. 72 n.

[39] S 10, S 11, S 13, S 14, S 15, S 18: *St. Aug.* 139–62.

[40] S 239: *Abingdon*, i. 8–11.

[41] Caedwalla to Wilfrid, a quarter of the Isle of Wight, 686 (*HE* iv. 16 (p. 382)); Frithuwold to
Eorcenwald, for Chertsey, 672 × 4 (S 1165: there is a strong possibility that the hidage has been
tampered with); Æthelred to Osric and Oswald, for Gloucester and Pershore, 674 × 9 (S 70: 'a
corrupt text'); Eynsham is recorded later as a 300-hide estate, in about 821 (*CED* iii. 597–8). Of
these only the first and last are reliable, but the recurrence of this huge and symmetrical figure suggests that it could have been a recognized endowment for an exceptionally important minster. Other
reasonably reliable grants of between 30 and 100 hides during 670–700 are S 45/1172, S 65a–b, S
76, S 1164, S 1168, and S 1248. The 100 and 132 hides specified in two Malmesbury charters (S 231,
S 1170) could have been tampered with. For other possible cases see Roper 1974.

[42] Campbell 2000: 227–45; below, pp. 144, 254.

of their first abbesses.[43] To conceive a minster as simply 'founded' by a king may often do less than justice to his monastic relatives.

The fluid structure of kingdoms during these years, and the existence of different kinds of kings, often frustrate the clear categorization of a minster as 'royal' or 'noble', or even as 'episcopal'. The late seventh century was precisely the time when the local rulers of some regions were being defined as *subreguli* or *duces* under Mercian or West Saxon over-kings, while other regions were being put into the hands of Mercian deputies described by a similar terminology of lordship.[44] Competition within as well as between kindreds, as individuals tried to transmit resources to their immediate heirs to the detriment of a wider family, may often be an important hidden element in these political manoeuvres. Charters do not always make it clear whether the patrons were representatives of local kindreds or dynasties, attempting to reorganize their inheritances or to salvage their territorial bases in a changing world, or 'new men' recently intruded by over-kings. And, as St Wilfrid's activities illustrate, bishops with quasi-royal retinues could behave in their monastic land-strategies like territorial nobles.[45] As in Ireland, contemporary lay perspectives—unlike those of Bede or of modern historians—may have emphasized the quality of being lord over a major religious site, not whether that lord was a particular kind of ecclesiastic or layman.

The problems of definition are illustrated by two important pairs of twin minsters. In Bede's narrative his own houses of Monkwearmouth (674) and Jarrow (680/1) were founded by Benedict Biscop, 'a devout servant of Christ inspired by heavenly grace', with the help of Ceolfrith, 'sharp-minded, energetic, of mature judgement, burning with religious zeal', and the material support of King Ecgfrith.[46] What Bede avoids stressing is their dynastic and political context: Ecgfrith may have intended them as royal family minsters, and Benedict and Ceolfrith were both high aristocrats.[47] The second example concerns Eorcenwald, perhaps a member of the East Saxon royal kin, who according to Bede founded two minsters, 'one for himself and the other for his sister Æthelburh', before he became bishop of London in 675.[48] Æthelburh ruled Barking as abbess, and received land-grants by charter from King Swithfrith of Essex, from her brother, and from a sub-royal East Saxon named Œthelred. Eorcenwald, as abbot of Chertsey, obtained an endowment

---

[43] Hollis 1998: 47–8.

[44] Campbell 1986: 85–98; Yorke 1990: 157–78, for an excellent review of this area of problems.

[45] *VW* c. 24 (p. 48); below, pp. 95–7.

[46] *HA* cc. 1, 4, 7, 15 (pp. 365, 367–8, 370, 379).

[47] Wood 1995: 2–7.

[48] *HE* iv. 6 (pp. 354–6); S 1165, S 1171, S 1246, S 1248; Blair 1989; Wormald 1984: 9–11; Webster and Backhouse 1991: 44–5; Yorke 1990: 54–6; Lapidge and Herren 1979: 51–2.

from King Ecgberht of Kent; times changed, Surrey was invaded by Mercia, and in 672 × 4 we find him extracting a massive land-grant around the minster from its new sub-king Frithuwold, the charter being witnessed by the Mercian over-king and composed by Eorcenwald himself. It is typical of the times that despite these thoroughly dynastic beginnings Monkwearmouth and Jarrow would be the greatest centres of learning in the northern world, and Benedict, Ceolfrith, Eorcenwald, and Æthelburh would all be venerated as saints.

In the small surviving body of late seventh-century charters, various sub-royal and noble personages receive land from kings to establish or endow minsters, or make similar grants to minsters in their own names. The sub-kings of the Hwicce (Worcestershire and Gloucestershire) established minsters at Bath, Ripple, and Inkberrow, as well as their own family minster of Gloucester, with their Mercian overlords' consent.[49] In the 680s Malmesbury, on the West Saxon/Mercian frontier, was receiving endowments from junior members of both royal kindreds.[50] Frithuwold of Surrey and Œthelred of Essex addressed their own charters, witnessed by their respective overlords, directly to Eorcenwald and Æthelburh.[51] We can be less clear about the status of Eadfrith son of Iddi who founded the minster of Bradfield (Berks.) in the early 670s, or of Æthelmod and Wigheard who gave Oxfordshire estates to the abbess of Bath a decade later.[52] In 688 the West Saxon over-king Caedwalla, who had recently invaded the region, granted land for a minster at Farnham (Surrey) to Cedde, Cisi, and Crispa.[53] Their alliterating names suggest kinship, and although they could have been brothers in Caedwalla's invading army, it is also possible that we see here a local family group using monastic patronage to reach an accommodation with its new overlord.

Such a case as this illustrates the ambiguities of what became known (from the charter or 'book' which defined its tenure) as 'bookland'.[54] An illiterate society cannot record transactions in writing: the charter was as much an

---

[49] S 51, S 52, S 53, S 70; Sims-Williams 1990: 94, 104–5, 191–4, 122–5. Cf. the grants to Wilfrid of Ripon by the Northumbrian sub-king Alhfrith, and of an estate for a minster in Mercia by the royal *praefectus* Berhtwald (*VW* cc. 8, 40 (pp. 16–18, 80)).

[50] S 1170, S 71, S 1169; Yorke 1995: 61.

[51] Above.

[52] S 239, S 1167, S 1168; Blair 1994: 60–1; *Abingdon*, i. 5–7.

[53] S 235; Blair 1991*a*: 25, 97. Wood forthcoming: ch. 5, noting that some of this land was at *Cusanweoh*, suggests that the three recipients 'sound by their names . . . like sons or descendants of Cusa, getting his pagan holy place . . . booked to them'.

[54] This is not the place for an extended account of a highly technical problem which recent scholars have discussed at length. For these paragraphs see: Wormald 1982*a*: 97–8; Wormald 1984: 20–3; Abels 1988: 43–57; Wormald 1993: 4–6; Cubitt 1995: 69–72; Charles-Edwards 1997: 192–7; Wormald 2001*b*; and Wood forthcoming: ch. 5. Some of these arguments were foreshadowed by Faith 1966: 79–81.

import as other aspects of Christian culture, designed to record grants made to the Church on the most favourable possible terms. In origin it was thus a safeguard of specifically ecclesiastical land-rights, and so in theory it would remain for some time.[55] It conferred land (or rather the food-rent owing from that land) in perpetual possession, with unrestricted rights of alienation. This then was a situation in which minsters, founded and controlled by members of leading kindreds, received a sustained flow of endowments from those same kindreds at just the point when the advent of foreign conceptions of property gave them a privileged and immensely advantageous form of land-tenure. It does seem possible that some of the 'donors' were, in a sense, giving the land to themselves. At the least, tensions between the religious aims of some monastic promoters and the vested interests of others must have been endemic.

These tensions, which would break surface in the mid eighth century, are occasionally visible in the late seventh. Even Bede's edifying narrative of Wearmouth-Jarrow cannot quite disguise recurrent stress between aristocratic groups, including a potential claim on the communities' lands by Benedict Biscop's brother.[56] That this brother could be envisaged as achieving his ends by having himself elected abbot illustrates the obvious danger that people might take religious vows simply to benefit from monastic land-tenure. Wilfrid assigned his huge estate on the Isle of Wight to one of his clerks, Beornwine, who was also his own nephew, and since Beornwine needed in turn a priest to preach and baptize there, it seems possible that his interest in the land was more financial than evangelistic.[57] The Bradfield archive records an extremely odd series of transactions in the 690s. King Ine cancels a monastic land-grant because the beneficiaries have procrastinated over building their minster, and gives the land to one Hæha, evidently the head of a sub-royal kindred in north Berkshire. Hæha takes monastic vows under an abbess or abbot, whom he appoints to build a minster, and makes a life-grant of part of the land to his sister (perhaps the same abbess). He then changes his mind and asks for his vows to be dissolved and his land returned to him, which is solemnly agreed in the presence of no less than Bishop Hædde of Wessex and Abbot Aldhelm of Malmesbury.[58]

---

[55] For bookland and the phrase *ius ecclesiasticum* see Cubitt 1995: 69; Charles-Edwards 1997: 193.

[56] *HA* c. 11 (p. 375). Whether this refers to an actual delinquent brother (as believed by Wood 1995: 10–11), or is merely illustrative of a form of abbatial succession which the Rule forbids (as believed by Wormald 1976: 169 n. 102), is not crucial to the point that succession by a kinsman 'who has not entered on the way of truth' was a real danger to be guarded against.

[57] *HE* iv. 16 (p. 382); Wormald 1976: 169 n. 102. How valuable this property was in the seventh and eighth centuries is now underlined by metal-detected finds: Ulmschneider 2003.

[58] S 1179, S 241; *Abingdon*, i. 11–22, to whose inspired analysis of this bizarre case the following is indebted.

Such manoeuvres may have had reputable religious ends. It is possible that Hæha re-granted the land to his sister to establish a double house (as Eorcenwald had done, and some eighth-century thegns would do[59]), and that he renounced his vows in order to re-take them as abbot of his own monastic federation. Hædde and Aldhelm acquiesced in his plans; Bede and Boniface would later perceive the secular perversion of monasticism as starting no earlier than 705.[60] With hindsight, we can recognize patterns of a kind that would soon cause trouble, but leading ecclesiastics of the 680s and 690s were evidently more optimistic. Kings and nobles had to be courted on their own terms, and allowed to endow the Church in their own ways: how else could the triumphs of a Jarrow or a Malmesbury be financed? So far, the purveyors of the new spirituality and learning saw nothing to make them doubt that they could school their lay relatives along the right lines.

The episcopal context of monastic foundations

A small group of learned people, whose learning gave them a commanding status and an influence which transcended kingdom boundaries, were the channels of Christian high culture into England. Because many of these individuals were bishops, historians have tended to merge their role as magnates, landowners, and cultural mentors on the one hand into their role as prelates and diocesan administrators on the other. These are, however, potentially different kinds of identity, and the possibility of divergence between them must now be kept clearly in mind.

We can begin with two eloquent comments by members of the next generation. The first is Bede's account of Archbishop Theodore and his assistant Abbot Hadrian after 669:

Because both of them were extremely learned in sacred and secular literature . . . , they attracted a crowd of students into whose hearts they daily poured the streams of wholesome knowledge. They gave their hearers instruction not only in the books of holy Scripture but also in the art of metre, astronomy, and ecclesiastical computation. . . . Never had there been happier times since the English first came to Britain; for having such brave Christian kings they were a terror to all the barbarian nations, and the desires of everyone were set on the joys of the heavenly kingdom of which they had only lately heard; while all who wished for instruction in sacred studies had teachers ready to hand. From that time also the knowledge of sacred music, which had hitherto been known only in Kent, began to be taught in all the English churches.[61]

---

[59] S 46 (*Selsey*, 37–40).   [60] Below, pp. 102, 108.   [61] *HE* iv. 2 (pp. 332–4).

In the second passage, Stephen of Ripon describes St Wilfrid's activities during his exclusion from his Northumbrian diocese in 667–9:

He returned to an abbot's monastic seat and again lived humbly at Ripon for three years, except that King Wulfhere of the Mercians often invited him into his territory with real affection to perform various episcopal functions. The Lord raised up for himself this most kindly king, who among other good things gave for his soul's healing many tracts of land in various places to our bishop, in which he soon established minsters for servants of God. Ecgberht too, the devout king of Kent, summoned our bishop to him, and there he ordained many priests . . . and not a few deacons. . . . So he lived honourably, dear to all, and performed episcopal functions in many areas. Then he returned to his own land, with the singers Ædde and Eona and masons and craftsmen of almost every kind, and with the Rule of St Benedict he much improved the practices of God's churches [Fig. 12]. So at that time, with God's help, a great door of faith was opened in those regions to the holy bishop, as it was to the apostle Paul.[62]

The creative meeting of Roman and insular cultures, combined with patronage on a huge scale, empowered an exceptional group of individuals and enabled some of the greatest intellectual and artistic achievements of seventh- and eighth-century western Europe to occur among the recently barbarian, illiterate English.[63] If the leaders, Theodore (d. 690) and Hadrian (d. 710), came from the Mediterranean, the other key figures were English: Hild, abbess of Whitby (d. 680); Cuthbert, bishop of Lindisfarne (d. 687); Benedict Biscop, abbot of Monkwearmouth and Jarrow (d. 690); Wilfrid, abbot of Ripon and Hexham and bishop of Northumbria (d. 709); Aldhelm, abbot of Malmesbury and bishop of Sherborne (d. 709); and many other bishops, abbots, and abbesses who embraced the new learning and secured endowments to support it.

English-born men and women with claims to deference and loyalty on two counts—as members of dominant kindreds and as purveyors of Christian learning and liturgy—were uniquely well placed to promote ecclesiastical institutions among their own people.[64] Those among them who were consecrated as bishops had a special status, both because of the power and reverence due to the episcopal office in ecclesiastical theory and European practice, and because only they could satisfy the growing need for religious personnel. 'Who can count how many bishops, priests and deacons he

---

[62] *VW* c. 14 (p. 30).

[63] M. Lapidge in Webster and Backhouse 1991: 71–3; Bischoff and Lapidge 1994.

[64] Mary Helms's ethnographic model of 'culture-heroes' who derive status from their capacity to travel to exotic places, and acquire cultural goods from them, suggests another dimension to the extraordinary prestige enjoyed by Wilfrid and his contemporaries: Helms 1993: esp. 109–16.

12. *Ripon* (Yorks.), St Wilfrid's crypt: the central chamber, seen through a fish-eye lens. Probably unique in England when it was built in the 670s, and modelled on holy places in Rome, it illustrates Wilfrid's determination to re-create Rome in his own Northumbria. (York Archaeological Trust.)

ordained, and how many churches he dedicated, during his forty-six years as bishop?',[65] asks Wilfrid's biographer.

It is certain that bishops took a special interest in monastic foundations, and that this interest often centred on their own dioceses. Sometimes we can glimpse kings allowing episcopal advice or direction to mould their patronage. In Worcester diocese, King Æthelred of Mercia gave forty-four hides at Fladbury to Bishop Oftor in *c.*697 'so that just as when [the land] was first handed over, so again through his diligence the most proper life of monks living on it under an abbot may be recovered'; the minster at Old Sodbury was established on episcopal land under conditions laid down by Bishop

---

[65] *VW* c. 66 (p. 142).

Milred (*c.*744–774).[66] In Wessex, it has been suggested that the proliferation of minsters under the successive kings Caedwalla (685–8) and Ine (688–726) was guided by bishops Hædde of Winchester, Eorcenwald of London, and Aldhelm of Sherborne.[67]

Some of this activity represents the pastoral and administrative concerns of conscientious diocesans. Occasionally bishops can be seen going about their proper activities: John of Beverley visiting a nunnery and dedicating churches, Wilfrid touring his diocese and baptizing.[68] The requirement for a bishop—in theory and custom the diocesan bishop—to dedicate any new church on a monastic site must have given diocesans at least a significant moral influence over new foundations within their spheres of authority.[69] Conversely, there were circumstances in which diocesans could make nuisances of themselves: Wilfrid's monks languished under the new bishops in 678, and Wilfrid in turn vented his anger on the Lindisfarne community in 687/8.[70] Yet despite all this, what the evidence does *not* show is arguably more important: Continental bishops had powers which none of their seventh- and eighth-century English colleagues can be seen to have exercised.[71]

In the sources, bishops appear prominent in two ways: as statesmen and leading servants of their kings, and as providers of the intellectual and theological resources needed to establish correct forms of religious life in minsters. Yet despite their unique authority, they behaved in their territorial power-strategies much like their fellow-aristocrats. Wilfrid (*c.*634–709), known through his biographer Stephen of Ripon, is in both respects the extreme case. His battles to defend his huge Northumbrian diocese are so famous that he is usually seen as the supreme exponent of episcopal autonomy, but in fact Stephen tells us virtually nothing about his role as diocesan.[72] In the scale of his operations, Wilfrid was hardly typical: no other bishop except Theodore made such a contribution to the educational and liturgical maturing of the English Church; no other bishop had such a stormy political career; and it is unlikely that any other bishop exercised such extensive

[66] S 76/1252, S 1446; the Fladbury grant presumably followed a failed foundation, as in the Bradfield case above. Stratford-upon-Avon had also been given to the bishop, presumably to found a minster, by a Mercian sub-king (S 1252). See Sims-Williams 1990: 92–3, 140–1, 161–2, 156–7.

[67] Hase 1988: 47–8. Coates 1996 makes an eloquent case that the importance of bishops as sources of spiritual authority and inspiration has been understated, without, however, adducing means by which they could have exercised effective power.

[68] *HE* v. 3–5 (pp. 458–64); *VW* c. 18 (p. 38).

[69] Thus Cuthbert (*VCB* c. 34, p. 262), and Eadfrith of Lindisfarne (*DA* ll. 93 f., p. 10).

[70] *VW* c. 25 (p. 50); *VCB* c. 40 (p. 286), compared with *HE* iv. 29 (p. 442).

[71] Above, pp. 36–8; below, p. 117.

[72] The only exceptions are a reference to Wilfrid 'equitanti et pergenti ad varia officia episcopatus sui' and performing public baptisms, and another to his ordaining priests: *VW* cc. 18, 21, 66 (pp. 38, 44, 142).

power though monastic networks. Yet there is nothing to suggest that his operations differed radically from those of his colleagues except in degree, and in his embroilment in monastic politics he was a man of his times. It is worth looking again at this well-known career, but with an eye especially to its monastic dimension.

In about 660 the Deiran sub-king Alhfrith, who had aligned himself with the supporters of Roman liturgical practices, ejected Irish monks from Ripon minster and gave it with forty hides to the already formidably learned Wilfrid, then in his late twenties.[73] He was ordained priest, and in 664 defended the Roman Easter at Whitby; the election of 'Wilfrid priest and abbot' to the Northumbrian diocese quickly followed.[74] He was consecrated bishop in Gaul, but finding that the see (now re-established in York) had meanwhile been given to St Chad he returned to Ripon as abbot. It was at this stage that he founded minsters in Mercia under Wulfhere's patronage and performed episcopal functions in Kent; conceivably he prompted King Ecgberht's conversion of the Roman fort at Reculver into a minster in 669.[75] In that year he returned to his diocese, where he restored Paulinus's now-ruinous church in York; he also finished his grand Roman-style rebuilding and embellishment of Ripon (Fig. 12), culminating in a dedication ceremony at which he read out a list of endowments given by various kings.[76]

Wilfrid was becoming the ruler of an ecclesiastical empire. He ordained many priests, and 'almost all abbots and abbesses of minsters pledged themselves to him by vow, either controlling their assets themselves under his name or choosing him as their heir after their deaths'; the queen gave him the *regio* of Hexham, where he built himself another splendid minster.[77] Then luck deserted him: in 678 an alliance between Archbishop Theodore, who wanted to replace him with three bishops, and Ecgfrith, who had been persuaded that he was over-mighty, drove Wilfrid from his see. Leaving 'many thousands of his monks mourning and weeping in the power of the newly-ordained bishops', he set out for Rome to protest.[78] Returning with papal support, he was imprisoned and then exiled by Ecgfrith. A Mercian nobleman gave him refuge and offered him land to live on; Wilfrid 'at once

---

[73] *VW* c. 8 (pp. 16–18); *VCB* c. 8 (p. 180); *HE* iii. 25 (pp. 296–8). For this and his other properties see Roper 1974.

[74] *VW* cc. 10–11 (pp. 20–4); *HE* iii. 25–8 (pp. 294–316). Tuda, the first choice for bishop after the departure of the non-conformist Irish, died almost immediately.

[75] *ASC* s.a. 669 (pp. 34–5). There is no direct evidence for Wilfrid's involvement, but he would have been advising Ecgberht at about this time.

[76] *VW* cc. 16–17 (pp. 32–6); Bailey 1991; Hawkes 2003*b*: 73–5.

[77] *VW* cc. 21–2 (pp. 42–6); Bailey 1991. For ordinary minsters subjecting themselves to major federations in self-protection, cf. again Ireland: Charles-Edwards 2000: 261–2.

[78] *VW* cc. 24–25 (pp. 48–50).

13. Gold cloisonné roundel with garnet and amber inlays, mid to late seventh century. Found at Ripon, this object could be the last surviving fragment of Wilfrid's huge treasure. Actual size. (York Archaeological Trust.)

founded in that territory given for God a little minster, which his monks possess to this day'.[79] Driven out again, Wilfrid moved on to still-pagan Sussex and converted the king, who gave him his own *villa* and eighty-seven hides at Selsey to found a minster.[80] His involvement in monastic foundations in Sussex and at Bath has been proposed on the basis of distinctive charter formulations.[81]

In 686/7 Wilfrid reached a compromise with Theodore and the new Northumbrian king, Aldfrith, and was apparently reinstated at Hexham, York, and Ripon.[82] The division of his diocese was, however, maintained or quickly revived, and in 691/2 he quarrelled with Aldfrith and was again expelled. After a fruitless council at which he was pressed to surrender all his possessions in Northumbria 'whether in the bishopric or in minsters', or at least to stay quietly at Ripon within the monastic enclosure, he appealed again to Rome.[83] Finally, in 706, a compromise was reached by which Wilfrid recovered 'the two best minsters, Ripon and Hexham, with all their revenues' but the division of the see was maintained.[84] Expecting death, he appointed abbots to his minsters, distributed his treasure (Fig. 13), and nominated his kinsman, the priest Taetberht, as head (*praepositus*) of Ripon.[85] In 709 he made his last journey into Mercia, to discuss with its king the future of his minsters there. He met his Mercian abbots, repeating his last instructions and adding to their endowments. When the party reached his minster at Oundle (Northants.) he died, having named the priest Acca as his heir at Hexham.[86]

[79] *VW* c. 40 (p. 80).
[80] *VW* c. 41 (p. 82); *HE* iv. 13 (pp. 374–6). Bede is more circumspect than Stephen about whether Wilfrid established an 'episcopal seat' there.
[81] *Selsey*, pp. xlv–lii; Sims-Williams 1990: 104. S 1674 purports to be a grant by Wilfrid to Glastonbury of land in Somerset.
[82] *VW* c. 44 (p. 90); cf. Cubitt 1989: 20.   [83] *VW* c. 47 (pp. 94–8).
[84] *VW* c. 60 (p. 132).   [85] *VW* cc. 62–3 (pp. 134–8).   [86] *VW* c. 65 (p. 140).

This story opens a window onto the late seventh-century Church. In the first place Wilfrid is an extraordinarily cosmopolitan figure, both as a channel for cultural influences (Kent to Northumbria, Northumbria to Mercia and Sussex, Francia and Rome to England in general) and in his consistent success (like Eorcenwald's) in attracting monastic endowment from various and competing kings.[87] The second striking aspect is his unremitting foundation of minsters, wherever he went and through all swings of fortune, which he ruled by virtue of ownership and disposed of freely to his successors. His episcopal status clearly helped him to acquire endowments, but his empire was in no sense equivalent to his diocese: it spread far wider, but excluded major Northumbrian minsters which were not his property.[88] It was in his own minsters, not in his diocese as such, that he introduced the Benedictine rule.

Time and again, Wilfrid's monastic federation is presented as a great extended household. We read of his 'kingdom of churches' (*regnum ecclesiarum*), of his 'multitude of minsters', of his monks 'scattered in various places through the whole of Britain and grieving under alien lords'.[89] The biography ends as an arc of white light, emblem of divine protection for the embattled Wilfridians, appears over Ripon.[90] Stephen was a partisan, but the more sober and learned Aldhelm could write collectively to the exiled Wilfrid's abbots, 'sons of the same tribe':

[T]he necessity of event requires that you along with your own bishop, who has been deprived of the honour of his office, be expelled from your native land and go to any transmarine country in the wide world that is suitable. What harsh or cruel burden in existence, I ask, would separate you and hold you apart from that bishop, who like a wet-nurse gently caressed you, his beloved fosterchildren . . . , and who brought you forward in his paternal love by rearing, teaching, and castigating you from your very first exposure to the rudiments [of education]? . . . Now then, if worldly men, exiles from divine teaching, were to desert a devoted master . . . , are they not deemed worthy of the scorn of scathing laughter and the noise of mockery from all? What, then, will be said of you, if you cast into solitary exile the bishop who nourished and raised you?[91]

Here the pupils of a great master of Christian learning are also the troops of a war-captain, with whom they must stand or fall in the old heroic style. He

---

[87] Aldhelm's efforts to secure the position of Malmesbury, on the frontier between Mercia and Wessex, are a third case: Edwards 1986; Yorke 1995: 61.

[88] It may, however, have had a *cultural* impact on them, visible in the influence of Hexham and Ripon sculpture on other church sites.

[89] *VW* cc. 21, 24, 44 (pp. 42–4, 48, 90).

[90] *VW* c. 68 (p. 148).

[91] *AO* 500–2 (Lapidge and Herren 1979: 169–70). Cf. Campbell 2000: 98–100, for the 'loyalty ethic' in monastic contexts.

is their leader by virtue of being their patron, but also because he taught them Roman customs and the true monastic rule. Both Stephen and Aldhelm repeatedly call Wilfrid 'the bishop', but both concentrate on his monastic family. Aldhelm's letter displays an amalgam of Christian high culture and aristocratic values in which the federation of minsters, not the diocese, replicates the social bonds of the household.

The immunities against interference by diocesan bishops, acquired by religious houses in several parts of Europe from seventh- and early eighth-century popes,[92] offer another sidelight on attitudes to monastic autonomy. Some of these went beyond the original aim of curbing episcopal tyranny to the point of virtually excluding the diocesan altogether, putting the community directly under the Roman see's protection, and there is reason to think that privileges obtained by leading monastic rulers in late seventh-century England were of this kind.[93] This is in no sense a peculiarly English matter; but the Columbanian connections which lie in the background of all these privileges, whether in Italy, Francia, or England,[94] encourage speculation that the movement was driven by perceptions formed within insular religious culture. Some of the Frankish and English founders who sought thus to exclude diocesans from their minsters were bishops themselves—Wilfrid is an obvious case—and while it is implausible to think that they were attacking episcopal power in general, they evidently had a strong sense that within a Church governed by bishops there was an autonomous monastic sphere. So did the English episcopate's most eloquent supporter, when he lost his temper: the uninhibited anger with which Bede rebutted a slander emanating from his own diocesan's household suggests that unquestioning reverence for bishops stopped at the gates even of Jarrow.[95]

In fact, the monastic networks determined both the personnel and the seats of the episcopate. It especially incensed Wilfrid that the three bishops imposed on his diocese in 678 were 'picked up from somewhere or other (*aliunde inventos*) and not from among the subjects of that *parrochia*'.[96] The

---

[92] Levison 1946: 23–7, 187–90; Wormald 1976: 146–9; Brooks 1984: 176–7; Edwards 1986; Cubitt 1995: 196–8; Rosenwein 1999: 32–6, 52–8, 64–73. Yorke 2003*b*: 49–51 has relevant comments on the independence from bishops—indeed the sometimes quasi-episcopal functions—of leading nunneries.

[93] Wormald 1976: 146–7, for Hadrian, Wilfrid, and Benedict Biscop. The Malmesbury privilege limits but does not exclude the bishop's authority: Edwards 1986: 12.

[94] Wormald 1976: 149; Wood 1990: 18–19.

[95] See *Bedae Opera de Temporibus*, ed. C. W. Jones (Cambridge, Mass., 1943), 134–5, 307, 315, for the extraordinary letter of 708—a mixture of open anger and calculated sarcasm—in which Bede describes some of Wilfrid's feasting-companions as 'wanton boors' (*lascivientes rustici*) who have slandered him in their cups, and suggests that his attacker should read it aloud to Wilfrid and then apologize. Criticism of the bishop himself is barely veiled. Cf. Thacker 1992*a*: 150.

[96] *VW* c. 24 (p. 48). Malmesbury actually obtained papal protection against being used as an episcopal seat: Edwards 1986: 12.

point, as Catherine Cubitt has observed, was that these men did not come from his own minsters of Hexham or Ripon: the elections infringed the established convention, which even Bede would later tolerate, of choosing bishops from the communities in which their sees were sited—a convention which in itself must have tended to create a monastically orientated episcopate.[97] Again, one of Wilfrid's complaints against King Aldfrith in 691/2 was that his minster of Ripon, 'which was given to us in a privilege, was turned into an episcopal seat, thus losing the freedom which the holy [Pope] Agatho and five kings had ordained that it should firmly hold'.[98] It was normal practice, when founding a new diocese, to locate the bishop's seat in an existing minster; bishops and their households might come and go, but minsters tended to be stable.[99] This may be how we should understand Stephen's enigmatic description of Lichfield as a 'place well prepared (*locum . . . paratum*) to be an episcopal seat' for Wilfrid or anyone to whom he might give it.[100] Detached from this encompassing monastic shell, in fact, the structures of diocesan administration elude us: the English episcopate as an institution is oddly shadowy, brightly though some of its members shine for their intellectual and political prowess.

Nonetheless, there is a triumphal tone about the English hierarchy at the end of the seventh century. Problems between Irish and English had in large measure been settled, and a Christian culture which was doctrinally, liturgically, and artistically more united was looking to Rome for spiritual and material inspiration.[101] With massive royal patronage, and overseas and inland trade expanding, the Church was growing rapidly richer. Ambitiously planned and richly decorated minsters were going up across England; some of them, such as Lindisfarne and Ely, were already promoting cults of their own English saints to rival Continental neighbours. If the Lindisfarne Gospels are the supreme visual expression of these triumphs, a compelling literary expression of them is the correspondence of Aldhelm. Fine stone churches and dwellings for students stand where idols used to be coarsely worshipped; aristocratic nuns and even an English king can be addressed as fellow-students and scholars; Theodore and Hadrian are a flaming sun and moon, outshining the twinkling stars of the Irish; for the first time an Englishman can aspire to write complex Latin.[102] These letters show us a new

[97] Cubitt 1989; below, p. 110.   [98] *VW* c. 45 (p. 92).

[99] For instance, Trumwine was made bishop over the English-ruled Picts in the minster of Abercorn; when the Picts recovered their freedom he 'commended his own people to friends in minsters wherever he could', and himself retreated to Whitby (*HE* iv. 26 (p. 428)).

[100] *VW* c. 15 (p. 32). Cf. above, p. 31, for Lichfield's British background, and below, p. 110, for Bede's conception of a suitable *locus*.

[101] For instance, Cubitt 1995: 132–52.

[102] Lapidge and Herren 1979: 160–1, 59, 34, 163, etc.

community of scholarly, pious, and English-born men and women, their learning and leisure financed by the fast-growing minster endowments.

Never again, except perhaps in the twelfth century and the nineteenth, would the English Church be quite so ebulliently expansionist as it was in the years around 700. In the following decades, success would bring its inevitable penalties of institutionalization, over-expansion, failing commitment, and entanglement in secular politics. The first step along this road was taken when patronage of minsters widened beyond the narrow circle of royalty and bishops to be embraced by lesser nobles and thegns, who found that it could bring them not only spiritual rewards and cultural betterment, but also territorial and financial security.

Useless to God and man? The problem of aristocratic minsters

'Aristocratic monastery' and 'proprietary church' are deceptively easy phrases: defining an aristocratic proprietor is not straightforward.[103] If the relativities of kingship are bewildering, the distinction between fighting retinues and land-based aristocracies is equally elusive. All the Germanic peoples of northern Europe experienced, at one time or another, a stage during which the war-bands of military leaders evolved into territorial aristocrats, with some capacity to transmit lands and status to their heirs. The role of the Church in these processes is problematic (not least because it is usually the vehicle for the written evidence in which aristocracies are first recorded), but clearly often important. In parts of northern Francia, for instance, the years around 600 saw a wave of enthusiastic noble patronage of monasteries and family churches, to which commemoration and status-display would in due course shift from furnished burial in lay cemeteries.[104] It was among people such as these, as well as among royalty, that monasticism made such headway, and noble founder-abbesses in early seventh-century Francia can look very like their counterparts in early eighth-century England.

The documents which the English Church wrote to protect its own endowments are by definition our first evidence for land-tenure: they need not mark an immediate and radical change in secular inheritance practice. But the late sixth and seventh centuries were clearly a transformative time for aristocracies as well as kingships,[105] and it is hard to believe that the for-

---

[103] Reynolds 1994: 418, for the problems of this terminology; Wood forthcoming.

[104] Halsall 1992: 275–8; Burnell 1988: 194–207, 534–87.

[105] Above, p. 53, for barrow-burial; Webster 1992; Halsall 1992: 275–6, for the relationship between warrior grave-goods and aristocratic identity in the region of Metz.

tunes of both old and new elites were other than very fluid. It is in any case likely that the rewarding of faithful warriors with life-grants of land was practised throughout the seventh and eighth centuries, so that there would always have been a proportion of 'first-generation' proprietors. After the 690s there may have been fewer 'sub-royal' individuals, but more men of humbler origin who made their careers in the royal service. In the years immediately after 700, it was this expanding class who turned the flow of monastic endowment into a new channel. As top-level patronage by royal and princely families began to tail off, smaller minsters multiplied.

Bede chose to say little of these developments in his 'Ecclesiastical History'. Determined to offer his readers an English religious heritage in which they could take pride, he virtually suppressed a trend which, as he wrote, preyed deeply on his mind: the subversion of the name and culture of monasticism by lay ignorance and greed. But in 734, the last year of his life, he poured his worries out in a letter to his old friend and pupil Bishop Ecgberht of York. This is a carefully composed and literary work, but it is anything but formal in substance: it gives vent to a boiling exasperation, and to a dying man's urgency to find solutions which others would have to implement.[106] His programme for episcopal governance will be considered shortly, but one extraordinary passage must be the starting-point for any discussion of eighth-century aristocratic minsters:[107]

But others commit a more shameful offence, seeing that they are laymen neither experienced in the regular life nor attracted to it. Under the pretext of founding minsters (*monasteria*), they give money to kings and buy territories for themselves in which they can more freely indulge their lust. Furthermore, they get hereditary right over these lands ascribed to themselves in royal edicts, and have these documents of their privileges confirmed by the subscriptions of bishops, abbots and great men of the world, as though they were really worthy of God. Having thus engrossed for themselves little estates or villages (*agellulis sive vicis*) they do whatever they want on them, free from both divine and human service: laymen in charge of monks. They do not even gather monks there, but whomsoever they can find wandering around after being thrown out of real minsters for disobedience, or whom they can themselves entice out of minsters; or indeed those of their own retainers whom they can persuade to promise them a monk's obedience and receive the tonsure. They fill their

---

[106] *Ep. E.*; I am very grateful to Christopher Grocock for access to his forthcoming new edition and translation. See DeGregorio 2002 and DeGregorio 2004 for the extent to which the preoccupations of this letter also surface in Bede's exegetical works. While I accept that he was writing within a tradition of polemic (Sims-Williams 1990: 126–30), I cannot read his complaints as anything other than a straightforward statement of his own views. The rhetoric of Bede, Boniface, and the *Clofesho* canons does, however, have much in common with seventh-century attacks on abuse of the monastic name by Galician communities living a secular lifestyle (Díaz 2001: 338–59).

[107] *Ep. E.* cc. 12–13 (pp. 415–17).

little minsters (*cellae*) which they have built with these crooked gangs; and it is a most hideous and unheard-of spectacle that those same men now busy themselves with their wives and begetting children, now get out of bed and occupy themselves with zealous application in whatever needs doing within the monastic enclosures. With similar impudence they even acquire places for their wives to found (as they say) minsters, and they, with equal stupidity given that they are laywomen, allow themselves to be rulers over handmaids of Christ. The common saying suits these people: 'Wasps can make combs, but store poison in them, not honey'.

Thus for about thirty years, that is since King Aldfrith was taken from human affairs [705], our kingdom has been demented with that mad error, so that there has hardly been one of the chief nobles (*praefecti*) who has not obtained for himself a minster like this during his time in office, or involved his wife with him in the guilt of this hateful commerce; and as the worst of customs has spread, ministers and servants of the king have striven to follow suit. So, in this crazy state of affairs, one finds many people who call themselves abbots, and at the same time nobles or ministers or servants of the king. Even if they could have learnt something of the monastic life not by experience—being laymen—but by hearing about it, they are totally without the character and profession which should teach it. As you know, people like this suddenly take the tonsure on a whim, and by their own judgement are turned from laymen not merely into monks but into abbots. But since they neither know nor care about that quality, what applies to them but the curse of the Gospel where it says, 'If a blind man gives a lead to a blind man, both will fall into a pit.'

Here we have a very explicit statement that since 705 virtually every chief nobleman (*praefectus*) in Northumbria had obtained a royal charter to found a minster, that their wives had done the same, and that 'ministers and servants of the king' had followed their example. No Northumbrian charters survive, but in other kingdoms the process is illustrated by a handful of charters, dating from exactly these three decades, in which kings make grants of land to their lay followers for founding minsters. Thus in 736 King Æthelbald of Mercia gave a 'parcel of land of ten hides to my beloved *comes* Cyneberht, to build a minster in the province of which the ancient name is *Husmerae*, beside the river called Stour': a transaction which probably brought into being what is now Kidderminster (Fig. 14).[108] A few years earlier, Æthelbald had given three hides at Acton Beauchamp (Herefs.) 'to my *comes* Buca . . . so that it may forever be a dwelling of God's servants'.[109]

---

[108] S 89. The charter gives no reason to think (*contra* Sims-Williams 1990: 31 n., 376) that the minster stood near Ismere House, the modern feature which happens to preserve the folk-name *Husmerae*. On topographical, onomastic, and later parochial evidence, the obvious identification is Kidderminster.

[109] S 85; for topography and sculpture see Bailey 1996a: 109–10; Ray 2001: 134–7; Blair 2001a: 5–7. Other good examples are S 84, S 94 (Mercia), and S 46 (Sussex). The best accounts of the phenomenon are Wormald 1984, and Wood forthcoming: ch. 4.

14. The birth of a thegnly minster. In this charter of 736, King Æthelbald of Mercia gives ten hides by the Stour and in Morfe forest (Worcs.) to his 'dear old friend' (*venerando comite meo*) Cyneberht to build a minster, almost certainly identifiable with modern Kidderminster. (British Library, MS Cotton Augustus ii.3 (S 89).)

If Bede is literally correct about the extent of aristocratic participation, Northumbria at least could have acquired dozens of such minsters during these thirty years. Even in other kingdoms the known charters, preserved fortuitously in the archives of major churches, may be a minute fraction of the original total.

Bede is also explicit that these people 'usurped' the estates, and that the grants massively depleted royal assets. His statement that the *praefecti* got their charters 'during their time in office' (*in diebus suae praefecturae*) also implies that they used their special positions for gain (though this may have been to obtain the charters rather than to obtain the land). It is certainly likely that a proportion of the grantees, modest-ranking men made in the king's service (such as Buca with his mere three hides at Acton Beauchamp?), were acquiring their land for the first time. Others, though, could be representatives of long-standing local kindreds who were securing an over-king's charter to convert existing family land into monastic property which was more stable and could be more tightly controlled. Thus King Æthelbald of Mercia's charter of 716 × 37 to found a minster at Wootton Wawen (Warw.) is addressed to Æthelric, not only Æthelbald's 'most respected and dear *comes*' but also 'son of Oshere formerly king of the Hwicce': Æthelric's family had certainly once ruled the territory in which the new minster was to be built, and it is very possible that the land 'granted' to it was already in some sense theirs.[110]

So in practice, different circumstances may underlie apparently similar grants of bookland. The charter may be establishing, at the foundation of the minster, a new tenurial status for old family land (as probably at Wootton Wawen), perhaps thereby excluding kin who would otherwise have a claim;[111] or it may be establishing permanent tenure of land which the king had granted to his thegn for life only, or was now granting for the first time (as probably at Kidderminster and Acton Beauchamp). But in either case the minster-founding layman, having obtained his charter, could set himself up as a thegn-abbot 'free from both divine and human service', and pass his minster and attached bookland down through a line of abbots or abbesses chosen from his own kin.[112]

---

[110] S 94; Sims-Williams 1990: 35–6; Bassett 1989*b*: 18–19.

[111] Cf. Wormald 1984: 21; Wormald 1993: 4–6; Charles-Edwards 1997: 194. The effect of turning land—whether inherited or acquired—into bookland was to make it alienable, which inherited land normally was not. Members of a kindred who could persuade an overlord (especially a new overlord, as in the Farnham case, p. 89 above) to ratify their annexation of family land for their minster, and bar out any wider kindred, would surely take the chance to do so, replacing an old kind of hereditary right with a new one. Bede's disgusted *ius haereditarium* could therefore apply both to such cases and to new acquisitions.

[112] Charles-Edwards 1997: 194–5 n., notes the case of Old Sodbury (S 1446), where any member of the family willing and fit to take holy orders was entitled to succeed to the estate, and makes

The emergence and general acceptance of 'abbacy by descent' led to the odd situation in which land which charters had made freely alienable was in fact considered hereditary, and could descend openly through kindreds. By 734 Bede had noticed this development: he says (contemptuously and ironically?) that the charters conferred 'hereditary right', a phrase not in fact used in any that survive from before 755.[113] Before 704 two nuns, Dunne and her daughter Bucge, were granted twenty hides of bookland at Withington (Glos.) by King Æthelred and his Hwiccian sub-king to establish a minster. As Dunne lay dying she assigned the minster with its land and charter to Hrothwaru, the infant child of another daughter, entrusting guardianship to the girl's mother, a married woman. In due course Hrothwaru grew up and asked for her charter, but her mother pretended that it had been stolen. In 736/7 the matter came to a church synod, which ordered that the charter should be rewritten for Hrothwaru and vindicated her possession of the minster. The report of this judgement, written only three years after Bede's letter, condemns the thief but takes the hereditary arrangement for granted.[114] A more intimate vignette shows Bishop John of York (706–?714) visiting the small nunnery of Watton (Yorks.), where a nun named Cwenburh, daughter of Hereburh the abbess, lay dying. The bishop deplored Hereburh's incompetent doctoring, 'but the abbess entreated him still more urgently on behalf of her daughter, whom she loved greatly and had planned to make abbess in her place': the inevitable miraculous cure followed.[115]

Bede's moral strictures have sometimes been taken to mean that these establishments were *wholly* fraudulent, nothing more than profane lay households, or even that they indicate a situation in which there was no clear difference between households and minsters. When Cyneberht and Buca obtained their charters to found their minsters at Kidderminster and Acton Beauchamp, did they create establishments which a visitor would instantly recognize from their externals and lifestyles as minsters, or simply redefine their existing residences and run them much as before? Here Bede's contempt for the quality of religious life in family minsters needs to be separated from their external appearance and even, to a large extent, from their daily

the interesting comment: 'This corresponds closely to the Irish conception of the *damnae apad*, "material of an abbot", that is, a person fit and qualified to be an abbot; in order to share in the succession to the headship of a church the kindred had to provide such a person.' The complex relationship between founding families and monastic heads, and the nature of 'hereditary right', is also discussed by Wood forthcoming: ch. 4.

[113] Wormald 1984: 23.

[114] S 1429, S 1255; Sims-Williams 1990: 130–2; Charles-Edwards 1997: 185–6.

[115] *HE* v. 3 (pp. 458–62). Cf. Hollis 1998: 56–8, for mother-to-daughter succession at Minster-in-Thanet; *ECWM* 161–6, for Gloucester; Le Jan 2001 for northern Frankish precedent.

rhythms: close attention to the sources suggests that this was a world in which religious communities (however lax) were viewed by observers (however strict) as something decisively different from lay households.

For all Bede's anger at the standards in private minsters, a careful reading makes it clear that he perceives them as new and different sorts of places, not disguised households. Laymen, he says, buy estates from kings and build minsters on them which they fill with ejected or fugitive monks, or with their own followers 'whom they can persuade to promise them a monk's obedience and receive the tonsure':[116] these are not existing households but new ones, the character of which is often set by people who have experienced the religious life in *vera monasteria*. Minster-owning thegns endow their wives with separate nunneries (housing genuine nuns?[117]), but still beget children with them: we must therefore understand that these couples live together (in normal households?), even if they spend many daylight hours 'within the enclosures' of their respective minsters.[118] Bede recognizes that the founders are interested in the monastic life, and that they pursue it with 'zealous application' (*sedula intentione*). His attack is directed not so much at the fraudulent use of the monastic name for tax-evasion—deplorable though that might be—but at the lack of calling and education on the part of laymen who pick up second-hand hearsay about the monastic life, then rush to be tonsured and call themselves abbots. The nobility have thrown themselves with gusto, all the more offensive because of its moral and intellectual vacuity, into the outward forms of a new lifestyle higher and more complex than their own.

Read like this, and in the light of the gulf in education and perception between Bede and ordinary Northumbrian thegns, his comments make sense. A rapid increase in the foundation of small aristocratic minsters during the first third of the eighth century is entirely plausible. A status-conscious nobility, perceiving the huge social impact of royal minsters and their growing influence on their own lords' lifestyles, would have sought access to their reflected cultural prestige as well as their financial benefits. Bede condemns the whole institution of lay-abbacy as decadent and corrupt, but since the development of that stance began, to all intents and purposes, with

---

[116] *Ep. E.* c. 12 (pp. 415–16). Could this be a negative way of describing what may in reality have been agreements by which established minsters sent some of their personnel to new 'family' ones? In an age of rapid monastic expansion, the behaviour attacked here could simply have been the natural way of building up new communities.

[117] Bede is prepared to describe the female inmates, evidently without irony, as *famulae Christi* (c. 12).

[118] *Ep. E.* cc. 12–13 (pp. 415–16): the otherwise seemingly redundant phrase *intra septa monasteriorum* makes sense if we take Bede to be emphasizing a contrast: between the nocturnal sexual activities of the 'abbots' in their own houses and their would-be monastic duties by day within the minster enclosures.

him,[119] it is unlikely that the lay-abbots themselves thought that they had anything to be ashamed of. They would have wanted their minsters to *look* as much as possible like the great ones in layout, embellishments, and contacts with a wider world. While they would have been more interested in this than in becoming theologians or practising monks, the daily liturgical round in a luxurious minster may not have seemed an uncongenial retreat from war and politics. Many of these foundations may in fact have had a far more positive role than Bede implies, their very rootedness in secular life testifying to the Church's success in assimilating to a broad social group. The retired Northumbrian nobleman Eanmund seems precisely one of those royal *praefecti* whose foundations Bede sees as the root of the problem, but his minster as described in the poem 'De Abbatibus' was classically monastic in layout and thoroughly committed to its devotional activities.[120] The thegn Buca's minster at Acton Beauchamp might have aroused Bede's suspicions, but it was sufficiently stable and 'monastic' to acquire a magnificent stone cross around 800.[121]

It is often the fate of intellectual and cultural institutions that by accepting the patronage which they thrive on, they compromise their *raison d'être* to accommodate non-professionals who do not really understand their true purpose. This need not prevent them from maintaining their distinctive character. The colleges of Georgian Oxford mirrored the social outlook, lifestyle, and material culture of the gentry ('wasps can make combs, but store poison in them, not honey' might have been the reaction of some high-minded Victorian reformer), yet in the layout of their buildings, the make-up of their communities, the rhythms of their daily life, and their economic basis they were clearly and substantially different from country houses. But such compromises can leave establishments vulnerable, once the novelty or prestige which secured the original patronage has faded, to a potentially deadly alliance of reformers and cost-cutters. In mid eighth-century England there clearly was a principled drive for reform, but it could all too easily become a cloak for asset-stripping. To pray effectively for the souls of world-soiled nobles, a minster had to be holy: the more widely criticisms such as Bede's were disseminated, the more they played into the hands of despoilers. It was ominous for the minsters that Bede abused them to Ecgberht not merely for their decadence but also for monopolizing too large a share of public funds,

---

[119] Felten 1980 traces the Continental development of lay-abbacy, and attacks on it, from the early Carolingian period: it is easy to see how opposition to the practice in the circle of Boniface may have been stimulated by the circle of Bede. Above, pp. 47–8, for the openness of Irish sources on the subject.

[120] *DA* ll. 52–112 (pp. 7–11) and *passim*; cf. below, pp. 146–8.   [121] Above, p. 102.

and proposed that bishop and king should join forces to re-structure them for enhanced efficiency.[122] More tactful in his 'Ecclesiastical History', he still chose to end it with a cryptic parting shot at the flirtation of warriors with the monastic life: 'Another generation will see how it is all going to end.'[123]

Reaction and reform: Bede, Boniface, and the struggle for episcopal governance

It was not only Bede who thought that something had started to go wrong in the first decade of the century. For St Boniface, writing in about 747 to King Æthelbald of Mercia to protest at his fornication with nuns and violation of monastic assets, the privileges of the English churches had remained intact until the reigns of two dissolute kings, Osred in Northumbria (706–16) and Ceolred in Mercia (709–16).[124] Boniface, like Bede, stresses the immorality of kings and nobles in their dealings with monastic personnel, though he also attacks them (as Bede does not, presumably because he thought that minsters were too wealthy anyway) for stealing revenues and compromising liberties in the process. Clearly the evils recognized by Boniface were closely bound up with the 'mad error' attacked by Bede: the problems of a monastic Church which had expanded to the rhythms of elite secular life were coming to the surface.

Three urgent needs—the purification of the religious life, the extension of episcopal governance, and the protection of church property—were closely linked in the minds of the bishops who debated them in 747 at a great council held at the unidentified *Clofesho*. For the first of these needs we have very little evidence, and few grounds for thinking that it made significant or rapid headway; the third will be examined shortly in the context of the royal exactions which did, indeed, become increasingly evident and insistent from Æthelbald's time onwards. The debate on episcopal governance requires close attention, for it is one of the keys to understanding how the eighth-century Church operated at a local level. The agenda is again set by Bede's letter to Ecgberht, which uses the deplorable state of the family minsters to justify a series of radical proposals.

Bede's starting-point is that the Northumbrian dioceses are too big for bishops, however diligent, to tour them yearly as they should: remote settlements never see their bishop, even though they owe episcopal dues.[125] Some bishops are anything but diligent: they demand money from their hearers

---

[122] *Ep. E.* cc. 9–11 (pp. 412–14).   [123] *HE* v. 23 (p. 560).
[124] *Bon. Ep.* No. 73 (pp. 152–3).   [125] *Ep. E.* c. 7 (p. 410).

and then neglect to teach them, and accept charge of more people than they can possibly teach or visit in order to enrich themselves.[126] In his own diocese Ecgberht should appoint enough assistant priests and teachers to visit all hamlets and estates ('in singulis viculis atque agellis') once a year, especially to baptize, and all laity should be taught the Apostles' Creed and Lord's Prayer in English.[127]

But ideally more dioceses should be established, just as Pope Gregory first planned when he sent St Augustine, even though there have been so many stupid gifts to found minsters that it has become hard to find 'an unencumbered place (*locus vacans*) where a new episcopal seat should be made'.[128] The false minsters are indeed useless to man as well as God, for they have eaten up all the land which ought to support young warriors to defend the realm.[129] King Ceolwulf should join forces with Ecgberht (whose own see of York should be raised to metropolitan status): they should call a council and choose some place from among the minsters as a new episcopal seat. The abbot and monks there, who might otherwise resist, should be allowed to choose one of their own number 'who would be ordained bishop and take episcopal charge of as many of the attached places as belonged to the same diocese ('adiacentium locorum quotquot ad eandem diocesim pertineant'), together with that minster'.[130]

If the minster's lands and possessions need augmenting for this new role, there are 'any number of places, as we all know, given the name of minsters in a most stupid form of words', which can be 'transformed by synodal authority from luxury to chastity, from vanity to truth, from over-indulgence of the belly and palate to continence and piety of heart' and annexed in support (*in adiutorium*) of the new see: even if they have charters, it cannot be sinful to annul wrongful gifts to useless minsters and establish 'an episcopal seat in those same places if the needs of the times require it'.[131] Bishops have a habit of saying that they, not secular rulers, have oversight and governance of minsters: they should therefore accept their responsibilities by opposing wrongful land-grants rather than ratifying them, by looking closely at minsters in their dioceses, and by suppressing corruption or insubordination if they find them there.[132] The spiritual welfare of the laity also needs more attention: too few of them take communion regularly, and those who live chastely should be encouraged to do so.[133]

---

[126] cc. 7, 8 (pp. 410–12).   [127] c. 5 (pp. 408–9).
[128] c. 9 (pp. 412–13).   [129] c. 11 (pp. 414–15).
[130] cc. 9–10 (pp. 412–14). I take *adiacentium locorum* to mean 'attached places' rather than simply 'nearby places', which is consistent with Bede's usage elsewhere: 'excepta ecclesia sua et adiacentibus agellis' (*HE* iii. 17, p. 262); 'de hoc monasterio sive adiacentibus ei possessiunculis' (*HE* iv. 14, p. 378). Cf. late O. E. *licgan in to* (R. Sharpe in *ASE* 32 (2004), 268).
[131] cc. 10–11 (pp. 413–15).   [132] cc. 13–14 (pp. 416–18).   [133] c. 15 (pp. 418–19).

Bede's proposals are not entirely easy to follow, the more so because major aspects of the Northumbrian Church, common ground to these two close friends but not to us, are evidently taken for granted. Yet the letter does, in its slightly odd mixture of radicalism and compromise, provide important clues to the relationship between episcopal and monastic structures. Its strongly 'bishop-centred' stance has often been noted; what has been over-looked is the underlying assumption that administrative and pastoral structures depend on links between centres, especially monastic centres, and their dependencies. This becomes clearer when it is realized that in these passages Bede sometimes uses the nondescript word *locus* ('place') in the narrower sense of a specifically ecclesiastical place.[134] Thus when he says that no *locus vacans* for a new see can easily be found, and that Ecgberht should choose 'some place from among the minsters' and then let the abbot and convent elect their own bishop, he can scarcely mean that all topographically suitable sites have been used up. Rather, he is stating the need to set up the new see neither in a corrupt minster nor on an empty site, but in a community of appropriate standing.

Bede seems to be acknowledging the convention, the flouting of which had so annoyed Wilfrid, that bishops should be seated in minsters and chosen from their communities. He may also have thought it unlikely that any completely new foundation could attract an endowment matching that of a major minster from the previous generation. But the comment that the bishop should also take over 'as many of the attached *loca* as belonged to the same diocese' reveals another attraction of the scheme. The minster (which is evidently assumed to be large and fairly respectable) will already have a constellation of dependencies, perhaps scattered widely: those of them which lie in the new bishop's diocese could serve as ready-made local bases for his operations. He could augment them further by taking over scandalous minsters and transforming them into good-living establishments to assist him. The change being advocated is not that small minsters should be suppressed to make way for episcopal governance; rather, it is that the satellites of a large minster on the one hand, and a collection of autonomous and useless little minsters on the other, should be pulled together into a rational infrastruc-

[134] Elsewhere in the letter, Bede describes estates and peasant settlements as *territoria, possessiones, agelli,* or *viculi; locus* seems generally to mean a place in which a minster or bishopric has been or might be established (though this is not completely consistent since he complains (c. 11) 'ut omnino desit locus ubi filii nobilium aut emeritorum militum possessionem accipere possint'). Cf. Bede's report of the Synod of Hertford c. 4, forbidding monks to wander 'de loco ad locum, hoc est de monasterio ad monasterium' (*HE* iv. 5, p. 350). In the record of the 781 Synod of Brentford, a series of monastic sites are simply called *loca* (S 1257). See Davies 1978: 37–8, and Etchingham 1999: 93–4, 109, for the same convention in Welsh and Irish sources, and Dimier 1972 for early medieval Europe generally.

ture for the bishop's pastoral duties. Was Ecgberht's diocese already run on similar lines? Bede's criticism of it can indeed be read as implying that there were local centres within it, but that they were too spread out.[135] Bede had stayed the previous year in some minster of Ecgberht's which the bishop visited yearly, and this could have formed part of a system of residential centres.[136]

The really radical proposal is the appeal to King Ceolwulf to revoke charters. Bede knew that Ceolwulf (to whom he had recently dedicated the 'Ecclesiastical History') was more likely than most kings to take it seriously, and it is not hard to guess that the point about the depletion of land which should be supporting warriors was meant for his ears. Whether Ecgberht really did have any chance of turning the tide, subverting in the process what had become one of the foundations of aristocratic status, is another matter. Kings would soon start to agree that the Church monopolized all too many public resources, but they would address the problem in ways that Bede (unlike Boniface) apparently did not foresee, and certainly could not have approved.

From this analysis of a single text, two important conclusions emerge. The first is that Bede wants to reform existing structures, not destroy them: minsters, properly run and in the right hands, are the appropriate centres for pastoral care. The second is that despite Bede's general exhortation to bishops to practise what they preach and visit minsters, he offers pragmatic solutions which acknowledge that in England power flows from land. Ecgberht is not urged to make use of existing centres by exerting his due authority as bishop within his own diocese, but to take possession of a large minster with its dependencies and revoke the charters of others.

This, in essence, is what some bishops of the next two generations tried to do, though more by persuasion than by force. In the years after Bede's death bishops became increasingly worried by private minsters, and increasingly anxious to impose episcopally directed structures of discipline and pastoral care. The major expression of these concerns is the 747 *Clofesho* canons, produced at the instigation of Cuthbert, archbishop of Canterbury: a more ambitious programme for the reform of the Southumbrian Church than any attempted before or for a long time after. The canons do not, however, stand

---

[135] c. 5 (p. 408), understanding 'latiora sunt spatia locorum quae ad gubernacula tuae diocesis pertinent' to mean something like 'the areas around the centres from which your diocese is governed are wider', rather than 'the places which come under the governance of your diocese are further apart'.

[136] c. 1 (p. 405): 'I remember that you said last year, when I stayed with you in your minster in order to read for a few days, that you would like to invite me to talk to you again this year when you came to that same place.' Ian Wood (1987) has argued that the evangelistic imagery of the crosses at Otley identifies it as a regional pastoral centre of the see of York. This is quite possible; but see below, p. 165.

alone. They mirror so closely (in substance though not in language) the complaints and suggestions of Bede's letter that they are either based on it directly, or express a range of widely held and clearly articulated concerns of which Bede was merely one exponent.[137] Secondly, they are strongly influenced by ideas for Church reform which were currently being promoted by Boniface, both in a series of Frankish councils beginning with the 'Concilium Germanicum' of 742/3 and in letters which he wrote to Bede's old friend Ecgberht, now archbishop of York, and to Archbishop Cuthbert.[138] Boniface was thus the focus of a circle of would-be English reformers, and the *Clofesho* provisions for regulating the activities of priests under bishops, for suppressing a range of superstitions, and for banning gaudy clothes in religious communities are based on his formulations.[139] Especially relevant is Boniface's attack (addressed to Cuthbert and with specific reference to England) on 'any layman, whether emperor or king or one of his nobles or thegns, backed up by secular power, who violently seizes for himself a minster from the power of a bishop or abbot or abbess, and starts to rule himself in the abbot's place and have monks under him and control the money'.[140]

Thanks to Catherine Cubitt's recent work the context and substance of this material are now much better understood, even if views can differ on the extent to which episcopal governance went beyond wishful thinking.[141] More reliable than the specific prescriptions for reform may be the underlying assumptions which they reveal. Especially important is the clear assumption that religious personnel of all kinds live in communities, normally ruled by abbots or abbesses.[142] The canons sometimes distinguish, obscurely, between *ecclesiastici* and *monasteriales*, but there is no more indication that isolated clerics existed than isolated monks. Priests are to perform their high office diligently, look after the house of prayer (*oratorii domus*) and its fittings, and faithfully help their abbots and abbesses wherever necessary.[143] Nobody is to take the tonsure until 'the bishops of churches or the rulers of minsters' have satisfied themselves of his probity and vocation, to avoid the risk that he may give up and return to secular dwellings.[144] Clerics, monks,

---

[137] This point is discussed by Thacker 1983: 150–1, and Cubitt 1992: 199.

[138] I follow Cubitt 1995: 102–10, in concluding that *Clofesho* follows 'Germanicum' rather than *vice versa*.

[139] 'Concilium Germanicum', ed. A. Werminghoff, *Concilia Aevi Karolini*, i (*MGH Legum*, iii: *Concilia*, ii. 1, Hannover, 1906), 2–4; *Bon. Ep.* No. 78 (pp. 163–4).

[140] *Bon. Ep.* No. 78 (pp. 169–70).

[141] Cubitt 1992; Cubitt 1995: 99–113. These paragraphs are much indebted to Cubitt, though I am more sceptical than she is about the reality of episcopal power, and I also put more stress on the minster as the fundamental unit of local ecclesiastical organization.

[142] For earlier discussion of this point: Foot 1989*b*; Cubitt 1992; Cubitt 1995: 116.

[143] *Clof.*747 c. 8 (p. 365).

[144] *Clof.*747 c. 24 (p. 370). Thus it was at Repton minster, under the rule of Abbess Ælfthryth, that Guthlac was tonsured as a cleric: *VG* c. 20 (p. 84).

and nuns who live among the laity already must return to the houses of their first profession if they left them illicitly, though anyone who left one house for another with permission but then wandered away again must return to the second place.[145] In Ecgbert's 'Dialogue', too, it is assumed that any wandering cleric or monk must have a 'head' (*prior*) or abbot whose authority has been flouted by his departure.[146] The point is reinforced by Ecgberht's passing reference to fasts observed 'not only by the clergy in the minsters but also by the laity with their wives and families'.[147]

The 747 canons harp repetitiously on the need for good standards of life in minsters. Abbots and abbesses must set good examples, see that their subordinates live regularly, and care for their needs according to the custom of monastic life. Rulers (*praepositi* and *praepositae*) of minsters must diligently administer the monastic property, and especially avoid its expropriation. Minsters are to be quiet, peaceful places for prayer, study, and devotion, not frequented by bards and entertainers, and access by the laity is to be strictly limited. *Monasteriales* and *ecclesiastici* must dine modestly and soberly, and shun drunkenness like poison. Communities of nuns must be houses of sober living and study rather than hotbeds of scandal, drunkenness, and luxury, places for singing psalms rather than weaving gaudy clothes. Priors, clerics, and monks must wear the habits appropriate to each; nuns must dress in contempt of the world, not stylishly like secular girls.[148] Whether through the invective of Bede and Boniface or through their own experience, the bishops of 747 had become obsessed with the standards of monastic life.

Two canons give bishops a key role in this endeavour, by admonishing abbots and abbesses to enforce standards and by making vigilant inspection of the minsters in their dioceses.[149] It is not at all clear, though, how stringent a control is thought realistic, and over which minsters. It is conceded that there are so-called minsters 'which tyranny and greed currently prevent from being reformed into a proper Christian life, because secular people hold them not according to the ordinance of divine law but by the presumption of human novelty'; bishops must nonetheless visit them if need arises for the sake of the souls there, and must ensure that they are not left without the ministrations of a priest, whom the possessors should help to support.[150] A question in Ecgberht's 'Dialogue' concerns the curious but perhaps not unusual case in which the owner of a proprietary minster leaves it to two people of different sexes: should they hold it jointly, or divide it by equal lot? The solution is that the community chooses which they would prefer to be made abbot (or presumably abbess) with the bishop's advice, and when that

---

[145] *Clof.747* c. 29 (pp. 374–5).   [146] *Dialogue*, VII (p. 406).
[147] *Dialogue*, XVI (pp. 412–13).
[148] *Clof.747* cc. 4, 7, 19–21, 28 (pp. 364–5, 368–9, 374).
[149] *Clof.747* cc. 4, 20 (pp. 364, 369).   [150] *Clof.747* c. 5 (p. 364).

one dies the co-heir receives rule of the whole minster if found worthy by the bishop; if, however, the bishop disapproves the arrangement is void and liable to anathema.[151] This may well describe customary practice (a very credible amalgam of normal lay inheritance with the principle that religious communities elect their heads), but the bishop's role looks tenuous: there is an acknowledgement that he should be involved, but it is hard to believe that in such a case he could do more than protest or persuade. One has a strong sense that the texts are imposing concepts and formulations derived from universal theory, and from Boniface, on a reality in which episcopal power over minsters was much more limited and specific.

The canons relating to pastoral care say more about the bishop than those relating to minsters, and his role looks more solid. Bishops have overall responsibility, and must correct God's people well by example and teach sound doctrine.[152] They must travel through their dioceses yearly, call the laity together in suitable places (*per competentia loca*) to teach them, and must hold meetings in their own dioceses with priests, abbots, and *praepositi* to order observance of the council's decrees.[153] They must not ordain 'any of the clerics or monks' to the priesthood unless they are satisfied that they are of good life, and can preach competently and impose correct penances.[154] Priests must carefully and correctly discharge their evangelical office of preaching, baptizing, teaching, and visiting in the places and regions of the laity (*per loca et regiones laicorum*) assigned to them by the diocesan bishop, and must not set any bad example, such as in drunkenness, greed, or foul speech, to seculars or *monasteriales*.[155]

How far any of the disciplinary measures was enforceable is extremely hard to know. It is, however, worth noting that while the 747 programme is much larger in scope than Boniface's as set out in the 'Concilium Germanicum' and his letter to Cuthbert, it backs away from his outright condemnation and vigorous penalties. Where Boniface inveighs against lay abbacy and urges excommunication, *Clofesho* accepts it as an evil to be lived with; where the 'Concilium Germanicum' prescribes prison on bread and water for fornicating monks and nuns, and flogging for fornicating priests, *Clofesho* condemns monastic decadence in wordy but rather general terms, and lamely asks for lay-folk to be stopped from visiting the worst communities to avoid spreading scandal.[156] Also not adopted in 747 were the duties, laid on each priest by the Frankish provisions, to meet the bishop's yearly circuit with a group

---

[151] *Dialogue*, XI (p. 408); cf. Mayr-Harting 1976: 12.
[152] *Clof.747* c. 1 (p. 363).   [153] *Clof.747* cc. 3, 25 (pp. 363–4, 371).
[154] *Clof.747* c. 6 (p. 364).   [155] *Clof.747* c. 9 (pp. 365–6); cf. below, p. 155.
[156] *Bon. Ep.* No. 78 (pp. 169–70); 'Germanicum', c. 6 (ed. Werminghoff, p. 4); *Clof.747* cc. 5, 20 (pp. 364, 369). This point is made by Cubitt 1995: 105.

of people to be confirmed, to account to the bishop for his ministry every Lent, and (a significant omission) to receive the new chrism from the bishop every Maundy Thursday.[157] It is hard not to be left with a sense that the English canons are confronting more intractable conditions, with embedded rights interposed between minsters and reforming bishops.

There is some evidence that when later eighth- and ninth-century bishops tried to implement the *Clofesho* canons they set about it in a way which essentially followed Bede's advice to Ecgberht—by building up networks of minsters in their own possession. The evidence is too fragmentary to show that this practice was general, but traces of it surface in various contexts. Most dramatic, and at the level of high politics, was the battle over two major Kentish minsters between Archbishop Wulfred and King Coenwulf of Mercia during 817–21.[158] Perhaps more typically, small family minsters in Sussex such as Denton, Ferring, and Wittering were coming into the bishop of Selsey's hands as pious benefactions from the 770s onwards, so that substantial estates which had been given before then to endow minsters had essentially become assets of the bishopric by 1066.[159]

But it is only in Worcester diocese, with its unrivalled archive, that we can obtain anything like a rounded picture of this and other aspects of local ecclesiastical affairs. Patrick Sims-Williams's splendid study extracts much from this material, but on the matter of episcopal governance there is possibly more to be said. His view of the Hwiccian bishops' capacity to mould the institutions of their diocese is an optimistic one: 'Some monasteries . . . became episcopal estates. Over others the diocesan bishops exercised wide-ranging influence, with the evident aim of eliminating a rival source of religious authority.' Or again, '[n]umerous documents from the Worcester archive show the influence that the bishops had on the development of monasticism, overseeing abbatial succession, eliminating lay control by securing reversions to the see, and enlisting royal support for such policies.'[160]

A fundamental problem here, though, is that the documented episcopal properties covered only a small part of Worcester diocese:[161] many other probable minsters emerge in later sources,[162] and it impossible to know how

---

[157] 'Germanicum', c. 3 (ed. Werminghoff, p. 3); *Bon. Ep.* No. 78 (pp. 163–4).

[158] Below, pp. 123–4.

[159] *Selsey*, pp. lxv–lxviii; the main relevant charters are S 158, S 1435, S 1178, S 1184. It seems likely, from later evidence, that the bishops of Dorchester-on-Thames did the same: Blair 2001c.

[160] Sims-Williams 1990: 139, 140.

[161] See map in *VCH Worcs.* iii. 247.

[162] For example: in Gloucestershire, Beckford, Bisley, Cirencester, Hawkesbury, Tewkesbury; in Worcestershire, Bromsgrove, Chaddesley Corbett, Clifton-on-Teme, Halesowen, Rock, Tenbury. The point is recognized (Sims-Williams 1990: 144, 173), but its implications are not sufficiently acknowledged.

much control the bishop had over them in the eighth century. Of the documented episcopal sites, Fladbury, Stratford-upon-Avon, and Old Sodbury were minsters belonging to the bishop from their foundations:[163] thus when we find Bishop Milred insisting on priestly orders as a condition for holding Old Sodbury,[164] he was governing his own property rather than exerting episcopal control outside it. There are then some dozen family minsters which are known to have come into the bishops' hands at various dates (with one probable early eighth-century exception)[165] between the mid eighth and mid ninth centuries. The most informative case concerns Haedda, 'priest and abbot' and former pupil of the Worcester community. In 780 × 99 he promised that his 'inheritance' at Dowdeswell, either identical or contiguous with land which Hwiccian sub-kings had granted him in 759, should pass to the see of Worcester when there was no member of his family in holy orders capable of maintaining monastic rule and avoiding lay control.[166] This arrangement, in the spirit of *Clofesho*, was achieved thanks to an ordained abbot who was a member both of a minster-owning kindred and of the bishop's *familia*. Ceolfrith, the son of Æthelbald's original thegn-abbot Cyneberht, gave Kidderminster to the see in 757 × 74; his fears that 'someone of my own kindred or otherwise' might malevolently infringe the grant show vividly the speed with which monastic bookland had indeed become 'hereditary' in the eyes of kin.[167] We know little about the other gifts, though some evidently arose through links between local landowning families and the cathedral community.[168]

It would be perverse to deny that the bishops of Worcester were major figures in the religious life of at least parts of the diocese, with significant capacity to guide and persuade, and they clearly did have some success in using family connections to pull minsters and monastic estates into their sphere of influence. In the process, they took steps to see that such min-

---

[163] Above, pp. 93–4.

[164] S 1446; Sims-Williams 1990: 156–7.

[165] Withington (see p. 105), where a lease of 774 (S 1255) says that the descent of the minster had been agreed by Bishop Ecgwine (after 693–717). But both this and the synodal report of 736/7 (S 1429) are known only from the Worcester cartularies: the clauses referring to episcopal control could be interpolations.

[166] S 56, S 1413; Sims-Williams 1990: 155–6. It is not clear that Haedda's minster was at Dowdeswell, which was later part of the Withington mother-parish.

[167] S 1411; Sims-Williams 1990: 148–9.

[168] Twyning was promised to Worcester by the thegn Ælfred (S 1255; Sims-Williams 1990: 158), and something is recorded of the negotiations at Inkberrow (S 1430, S 1432; Sims-Williams 1990: 237–9, and cf. below, p. 285). The others, several of which are not known to have been in the bishop's hands before the 820s, are Bibury, Bishops Cleeve, Bredon, Daylesford, Hanbury, Kempsey, Ripple, Tetbury, and Wootton Wawen (Sims-Williams 1990: 106–7, 146–58, 166, 170–1).

sters had that capacity for a competent discharge of priestly duties which had been urged in 747. Even so, it is not self-evident that their aims were exclusively those recommended by Bede. Bishops were also aristocrats, and what is presented as diocesan reform could have contained elements of aristocratic encroachment.

What cannot be recognized is the sort of close-grained diocesan authority which bishops in Mediterranean Europe had exercised—at least at times—since the fourth century, and which Carolingian bishops would have considerable success in rebuilding and extending. The point is made by considering a Carolingian text which, in the kind of administrative power that it displays, is utterly unlike anything known from England before the twelfth century:

With our Lord Jesus Christ reigning forever, I Magnus, bishop [of Sens], wish it to be known that with the Lord's help, in the *pagus* of Melun and the *villa* called Chailly[-en-Bière], I have constructed a basilica in honour of SS. Paul and Stephen and the other saints whose relics rest there, and have dedicated it on 1 June [808]. I have further agreed . . . that the vills called Chailly, Tancouville, Fay and Barbazon ought to look there for coming to mass and for baptism or preaching, and that they ought to give their tithes to the same basilica . . .[169]

English bishops simply could not administer their dioceses in this sort of way, either before or immediately after the era of the Carolingian reforms. Bishops, Bede observed drily to Ecgberht in 734, liked saying that they had oversight of minsters; when they assembled at *Clofesho* thirteen years later they duly said it. Yet it is by no means clear that their practice matched their aspirations: so far as we can see, they operated much as Wilfrid had done nearly a century earlier. Their territorial power, like that of secular lords, was exerted through scattered estates; the main difference was that these estates contained sophisticated and literate institutions, with networks of dependencies bound to them by devotional and cultural ties, which added another layer to economic links between centres and peripheries. New sees would long continue to ride on the backs of minsters, as Edward the Elder's diocesan reorganization of 909 illustrates.[170] There is no evidence that diocesan bishops seriously involved themselves in reforming the communities, or in regulating the parochial territories, of minsters that were not their own property.[171]

---

[169] Chaume 1938: 1; cf. Fournier 1982: 535–6.
[170] Yorke 1995: 210.
[171] Except probably in the case of Wulfred: below, n. 210.

The problem of local churches

If English bishops had less power than Frankish ones, they also lacked one of the main ingredients with which Frankish bishops, at any rate by the years around 800, were seeking to build a diocese-based system of local parishes. In the age of Bede as in the previous century, a basic lack of small, aristocratically founded estate churches seems to remain an odd feature of the English ecclesiastical scene.[172] The ninth-century Frankish reforms, which sought to consolidate and extend the structures of pastoral care while protecting vested rights, operated in a world where minor local churches had long been familiar and were still being founded, and where the potential for conflict with 'public', episcopally organized structures was relatively clear-cut. French historians have seen this as the formative stage, in which Carolingian bishops forged a parochial system from the raw materials of archaic baptismal mother-churches on the one hand and uncontrolled 'private' churches on the other.[173]

The extent to which old mother-parishes gave way to local ones may have been exaggerated,[174] but it remains likely that by the 850s, when Hincmar of Rheims could picture the inclusive and undivided parish as the material expression of *Ecclesia*, the Frankish countryside contained large numbers of small churches under the supervision of bishops and priests.[175] The ubiquity of these churches, both attached to estates and owned separately, is clear from Carolingian charter evidence. To take an early instance (and the ninth century provides many more), in 791 Charlemagne confirmed property of Kremsmünster including 'at Alburg that chapel built in honour of St Martin and the things belonging to it, and at Sulzbach another church with all things belonging to it, and on the northern Vils a third church with the things belonging to it in the Donaugau'.[176] Again, an ecclesiastical capitulary of 818–19 orders that 'a whole *mansus* free of service shall be assigned to each church':[177] a prescriptive rather than descriptive statement, but one which assumes that churches are both numerous and endowed.

---

[172] Above, pp. 70–1.

[173] Imbart de la Tour 1900: 108–233; Chaume 1937, 1938; Lemarignier 1966: 470–86; Lemarignier 1982; Fournier 1982: 502–25; Aubrun 1986: 33–68; Wood forthcoming.

[174] Reynolds 1984: 81–6; cf. below, pp. 422–3, for comparisons and contrasts with England in the tenth and eleventh centuries.

[175] Lemarignier 1982; Treffort 1996a: 165–7, 188; Bullough 1999: 31–7, for a valuable survey using the case-studies of Trier diocese, France north of the Loire, and Freising; Mayr-Harting 1981: 377–8, for possible parish churches dependent on Fulda; Nelson 1987 for local and low-grade priests in the ninth-century Frankish Church.

[176] E. Mühlbacher and others (eds.), *MGH*, *Diplomatum Karolinorum*, i (Hannover, 1906), p. 227, No. 169.

[177] 'Capitulare Ecclesiasticum', c. 10 (*Capitularia*, i. 277).

On all these matters, the silence of the English sources is deafening. General statements before the 960s take it for granted that not merely monks and nuns, but also priests, will live in organized religious communities.[178] A late eighth-century English nun at Heidenheim found it necessary to comment (perhaps with Frankish readers in mind) that English nobles of a couple of generations back had been in the habit of setting up crosses, *not* churches, near their houses.[179] A century later, King Alfred's laws still assume that 'every church which a bishop has consecrated', and which is entitled to provide sanctuary, has an 'elder' and 'community'.[180] Statements like those in the Kremsmünster confirmation, or the 818–19 capitulary, are unknown in any genuine English text. Perhaps most striking, because free from documentary bias, is the total absence from English church archaeology of the little seventh- and eighth-century churches, built over elite lay cemeteries or containing 'founder-burials', which have been excavated in such large numbers on the Continent.[181]

Arguments can be advanced against all these points: that churches did proliferate, but only after the early eighth century; that Alfred implies the existence of churches *not* consecrated by bishops (though if so they were surely very small and informal); that the English charter-writing tradition, once established, was unreceptive to introducing references to new kinds of estate assets; and that seventh- to ninth-century thegnly churches existed but were so flimsy as to be invisible archaeologically. Yet taken together, the various considerations do seem to cross the line from absence of evidence to negative evidence: the English experience was clearly very different from the Continental one, even if little oratories on, say, ninth-century thegns' estates cannot be ruled out.

Yet we are left with one solid though isolated source: a pair of miracle stories involving Bishop John of York (706–?714) which Bede heard from Abbot Berhthun of Beverley.[182] In the first the bishop visits a *villa* nearly two miles from Beverley belonging to a *comes* named Puch, who has called him to dedicate a church. After the ceremony Puch invites him to eat in his house; the bishop initially declines because he has 'to return to the minster [i.e. Beverley], which was nearby', but then agrees to stay and cures his host's

---

[178] Above, pp. 112–13; cf. below, pp. 342–5, Foot 1989*b*: 48–9, and Cubitt 1995: 116. A phrase in Theodore's Penitential (*PT* II. xiv. 11, p. 333, but cf. *CED* iii. 203), 'Decimas non est legitimum dare nisi pauperibus et peregrinis, sivi laici suas ad ecclesiam/ecclesias', has been taken to refer to (presumably small) proprietary churches, but it is surely the tithes, not the church(es), which are the property of the laity; cf. Blair 1987: 267 n. 9.

[179] Below, p. 227.   [180] Below, pp. 342–3.   [181] Below, pp. 234–7.

[182] *HE* v. 4–5 (pp. 462–4). Later tradition identified the first church as Bishop Burton: Folcard, 'Vita S. Johannis', c. 6 (ed. J. Raine, *The Historians of the Church of York* (Rolls Ser. 71a, 1879), 249).

wife. In the second story, less specific, John is 'called to dedicate a church by a *comes* named Æddi' and then heals one of Æddi's retainers, who rises from his sickbed and joins the feast. In both cases the dedications of the new churches were performed at the request of lay lords who seemingly lived beside them.

There are three possible ways of interpreting these stories: that they are early references to small family minsters of the kind that Bede would later deplore; that they describe the foundation of churches that were satellites of Beverley and served by its priests, albeit on noblemen's estates; or that they are indeed evidence for small 'private' churches on the Continental pattern. None of these can be excluded, though the first is probably a rather forced reading. The common-sense approach is to remember that contrasts between England and the Continent are at all levels likely to have been a matter of gradations rather than abrupt frontiers. *Some* English landowners, especially near the east and south-east coasts, may have been able or willing to behave like Frankish ones, and perhaps Puch and Æddi were among them. This point is underlined by the fact that of the tiny handful of ostensibly free-standing small churches that do surface in pre-900 sources, most announce their Frankish pedigree by being dedicated to St Martin of Tours.[183] Small and seemingly unimportant church sites with pre-Viking sculpture fragments could represent other 'thegnly' churches, though the alternative explana-tion—that they were monastic satellites—is sometimes demonstrable and always possible.[184] These alternatives need not in fact have been mutually exclusive: a variant on the Continental pattern, including the Beverley cases, could have been co-operation between dominant minsters and landowners within their spheres of influence.[185]

Notwithstanding these important difficulties, a clear and fundamental dif-ference remains between the English and Frankish patterns. When eighth-century English noblemen and thegns embarked on religious patronage, the model available to them was not a centuries-old tradition of local church foundation by their own ancestors, but the monastic mode which their kings of the last two generations had embraced. The eventual equivalents of the Continental 'private churches' were thus Bede's 'minsters in a most stupid form of words',[186] which augmented the ranks of minsters rather than encroaching on them. As it developed through the eighth and ninth cen-

[183] Above, pp. 70–1; below, p. 220. St Mary's and possibly St Mildred's in Canterbury also existed by the early ninth century (Brooks 1984: 34–5), but these accommodated nuns who had fled min-sters attacked by Vikings, and are a special case.

[184] Below, pp. 215–16; cf. Hadley 2000*a*: 270–1, 279–83.

[185] Cf. below, pp. 383–4, for this process in the post-Viking period.

[186] Above, p. 109.

turies, the local organization of the English Church remained—still in the broad sense—overwhelmingly monastic. That is not to say that all was well with the minsters. Bede had not long been dead when the stresses which he foresaw started to show themselves.

Minsters on the defensive: external control and disendowment

Kings with their *duces* and *principes* (and then very many of the lower ranks are persuaded) are accustomed to say concerning them [i.e. churchmen]: that they not only do not love them with sincere affection but rather greatly envy their worldly wealth and too happy prosperity, that they rejoice with a hateful mind, rather than with a devout heart, and they do not cease to speak evil of their way of life with hateful slander.[187]

The prelates gathered at *Clofesho* in 747 hastened to reject such rumours, and to direct that henceforth both *ecclesiastici* and *monasteriales* should pray regularly for kings, leaders, and the whole Christian people, and deserve to live peacefully under their faithful protection. But this defensiveness seems a long way from the confidence with which an Aldhelm—or even, amidst all his troubles, a Wilfrid—could assume lay powers' respect for the Church's higher moral authority. Something had started to go badly wrong.

The long-term trend needs disentangling from the rise and fall of individual houses caught up in dynastic rivalries or power-politics. From the outset, kings had expected loyalty and support in return for their munificence to minsters,[188] and in a society of fragmented kingship and intense competition, the fall of patrons and changes in the balance of power must always have needed careful handling. In 709, Wilfrid's Mercian abbots asked him to pay a diplomatic visit to their new king: 'and they have persuaded me to agree to this', Wilfrid told the Ripon community, 'for the security of our minsters which are in his kingdom, for he has promised to order his whole life according to my judgement.'[189] Just before, he had left a quarter of his treasure to the abbots of Ripon and Hexham 'so that with these resources they may buy the friendship of kings and bishops'.[190] What might happen without such bribes or diplomacy is illustrated by the woes which a

---

[187] *Clof.747* c. 30 (*CED*, iii. 375); translation after Cubitt 1995: 111.

[188] The appropriate relationship between early minsters and their royal patrons is enunciated in the privileges issued by Wihtred of Kent and Ine of Wessex (S 20, S 245); cf. Brooks 1984: 183–4, and *St. Aug.* 41–2.

[189] *VW* c. 64 (p. 138); cf. Sims-Williams 1990: 96–7.

[190] *VW* c. 63 (p. 136).

Kentish abbess described to St Boniface in about 720: financial poverty, poor estate yields, a lack of male relatives to protect them, harassment by a king who 'has a great hatred for our line', services owed to the king, queen, bishop, reeve, princes, and nobles.[191]

So while many houses enjoyed wealth and security, there must always have been some with problems. But from the 740s, under the expansionist Mercian regime of Æthelbald and Offa (716–96), tensions started to become general rather than merely individual. Boniface lamented not just the decadence of England's minsters, but also the rapacity of its kings: 'the violent[ly exacted] service of monks on royal works and buildings', he wrote, 'is unheard of in the whole Christian world except among the English. It is not for God's priests to keep silent or consent to it: it is a wickedness unheard of through all ages.'[192] In 749, in response to such complaints, Æthelbald freed the Mercian minsters from public duties except building bridges and forts (the first reference to this important reservation), and promised not to force minsters to provide secular feasts for kings and nobles 'unless they are offered in love and free-will'.[193] Concerns about depletion of royal assets had already been expressed in Bede's letter, but now there are hints of something more: a mutual suspicion and resentment echoing the 'hateful slander' deplored at *Clofesho*, and an interference in internal affairs. Even after 749, how many Mercian minsters had the confidence to show so little 'love' as to refuse the king and his friends a feast?

King Offa's relations with minsters were formed against this background, but in a contemporary Carolingian mode. In one sense he was probably a great patron, even if the loss of charters from central Mercian houses leaves much of his patronage obscure to us. He supported his ancestral minster at Bredon (Worcs.) and also founded Winchcombe, which was to be the great Mercian royal family minster of the next two generations.[194] Offa and his Northumbrian counterpart hosted a reforming papal legatine mission in 786, the first to England since St Augustine's time; Offa's raising of the see of Lichfield to metropolitan status outraged Canterbury, but can plausibly be seen as a sensible reform of the long-obsolete Gregorian plan.[195] He obtained a papal privilege for all minsters under St Peter's patronage which he and his queen Cynethryth had built or acquired, and there is no reason to doubt that while Mercian power lasted, these favoured communities flourished.[196] But

---

[191] *Bon. Ep.* No. 14 (pp. 21–6); cf. Mayr-Harting 1991: 267–8; Yorke 2003*b*: 53.

[192] *Bon. Ep.* No. 78 (p. 171 n.).   [193] S 92.

[194] S 109, S 116; Bassett 1985; Sims-Williams 1990: 152–4, 165–8; Cubitt 1995: 210–12.

[195] Wormald 1991; Cubitt 1995: 153–90; Brooks 1984: 118–27; Cubitt 1999: 1222–3. Story 2003, a major new survey of the Carolingian context of English kingship, appeared as this book was going to press.

[196] Levison 1946: 29–31; Brooks 1984: 184–5; Cubitt 1995: 198–9, 226–7.

the privilege, which protected Offa's minsters against episcopal interference, illustrates another side to his religious policy. This also emerged in 781 when, in exchange for the important site of Bath, he 'restored' to the see of Worcester a group of minsters and other property which were apparently Worcester's already, and to which his title seems highly dubious.[197] If Offa followed Pippin III in sponsoring Church reform, and in being a liberal patron and good lord to his chosen monastic centres, it looks as though he also followed him in attacking the autonomous power of bishops and minsters.[198]

But episcopal pretensions were rising too. The Council of *Clofesho* in 803 forbade the election of laymen as lords over minsters—a more determined statement of one of the principles of 747.[199] The Chelsea canons of 816 go much further in asserting bishops' administrative power, even giving them the principal say in appointing abbots and abbesses within their dioceses.[200] There is no evidence that these initiatives built any lasting system, but their assertiveness is striking. Were expectations higher, or the threat more serious? Probably both: it looks as though English bishops, alarmed by growing secularization and encouraged by what their Frankish counterparts had recently achieved, were trying to fight off kings and nobles by re-defining their own powers along Continental rather than English lines.[201] What they were not fighting for, however, was monastic autonomy: to keep the lay world at bay, minsters were to be overseen by bishops for their own good.

The scene was set for the bitter struggle between Archbishop Wulfred of Canterbury (805–32) and King Coenwulf of Mercia (796–821).[202] This erupted immediately after the Chelsea council, and looks like a real if isolated attempt to give teeth to the canons and exert episcopal authority over a group of minsters in Canterbury diocese, especially the old and now extremely wealthy houses of Reculver and Minster-in-Thanet. Thanks to the work of Nicholas Brooks and Catherine Cubitt we can now see Wulfred's hand in the Chelsea canons, as also in the remarkable group of forgeries which he concocted to assert the same principles in his own diocese.[203] Coenwulf, for his part, pursued and extended Offa's monastic policy, to the extent of obtaining a papal privilege for his minsters which put the pope on the side

---

[197] S 1257; Sims-Williams 1990: 159–65. Below, pp. 274–5, for the probable importance of Bath.
[198] Semmler 1975; Cubitt 1995: 228–9. Cf. Hawkes 2001: 244–5, for the more Carolingian and hierarchical tone of Mercian sculptural iconography in the decades around 800. The same trend can be seen in the monetary upheaval of the mid eighth century, when many (perhaps monastic?) mints ceased functioning, and the coinage became more overtly centralized and royal under Offa: Gannon 2003: 190–3, and cf. below, p. 259.
[199] *CED* iii. 545–6.
[200] *CED* iii. 579–84.
[201] Brooks 1984: 175–7, 189–90, 194–5; Cubitt 1995: 191–203, 229.
[202] Brooks 1984: 175–206.
[203] Brooks 1984: 191–7; Wormald 1999*b*: 293–8; Cubitt 1999.

of secular resistance to episcopal reform.[204] At the end of nearly ten years' conflict, after much cost and trouble and in a new king's reign, the archbishop emerged as victor. We are left with an impression that what really mattered about these two minsters was their huge political and financial value.

The last twist in this complex affair was the accord which, after the political re-alignment of the 820s, Archbishop Ceolnoth reached at Kingston in 838 with the new masters of southern England, King Ecgberht of Wessex and his son Æthelwulf.[205] In effect, Ceolnoth handed over Wulfred's hard-won gains to Coenwulf's supplanters. An addendum to the text states that the 'free minsters' (in all territory under West Saxon lordship?) had chosen Ecgberht and Æthelwulf 'for protection and lordship on account of their own very great needs', and 'had of their own will constituted spiritual lords, that is the bishops', to protect their monastic life in alliance with the kings. The consensual tone, so different from Wulfred's, should not disguise the fact that Ceolnoth—caught between the hammer of Viking raids and the anvil of West Saxon power—had conceded effective control of the minsters to the new dynasty. But in any case they were subsidiary to the main point of the agreement, which was to recover Canterbury land and establish firm friendship between king and archbishop.

Through the century up to 838, it is as though the diffused light in which so many minsters could previously be seen functioning autonomously becomes concentrated into two spotlights, illuminating the spiritual and secular leaders but leaving everything else in shadow. The important question here is whether conditions at a local level were correspondingly gloomy. In the early 790s, Alcuin wrote to the abbot of Wearmouth-Jarrow: 'Alas, brother, alas, that almost everywhere in this land the rule of the regular life is collapsing, and the pattern of secular life is spreading. And, what is worse, the very creators have in many places become destroyers, and the builders wasters.' A few years later he urged one abbess to give alms while she still had control of her own assets, and commiserated with another over woes 'which not only your innocence suffers, but almost the whole multitude of God's servants'.[206] Is it possible to show that the century after Bede's death really did bring long-term and irreversible monastic decline, not just a natural attrition of communities left abandoned by their patrons' demise, or new forms of royal and episcopal rhetoric?

If by 'secular' Alcuin meant the life of priests as against that of nuns and

[204] Levison 1946: 30–2; Brooks 1984: 185–6; Wormald 1993: 6–7; Cubitt 1995: 198–9, 226–7.
[205] S 1438; cf. Brooks 1984: 197–203, and Cubitt 1995: 237.
[206] *Alc. Ep.* Nos. 67, 105, 300 (pp. 111, 152, 458).

monks, he was undoubtedly right: the drift from complex double and monastic communities to straightforward priestly ones was slow but inexorable. Monks and nuns retained their traditional status for a time: the old format of rule by a royal abbess was promoted by both Offa and Coenwulf (probably encouraged by the Carolingian revival of nunneries), and monastic communities in the precise sense are mentioned intermittently through the ninth century.[207] But double houses were evidently in rapid decline by the late eighth century,[208] and thereafter there is a growing tendency to stress the priestly rather than the abbatial status of monastic rulers. For instance, witnesses on behalf of the Kentish minsters in 824 and 844 were priest-abbots, a priest-provost, priests, and others 'of common grade'.[209]

One way of explaining this change might be to invoke the new Continental rules for the *vita canonicorum*, which gave priestly (as against monastic) modes of strict religious observance a clearer definition, and thus a more obvious legitimacy. Yet it is impossible to show that these rules had any impact (except arguably at Canterbury) on the pluralistic monastic culture of England.[210] If they were known at all they could have served the needs of expediency and economy, giving ammunition to those who perceived priestly communities as both cheaper and more effective than monastic ones. For pastoral ministry, priests were essential as monks and nuns were not, and it is reasonable to suppose that diligent bishops encouraged them when they could.[211] The ordained personnel of minsters, like late medieval chantry-priests, could also support demands from the laity for prayer and commemoration, as when a nobleman gave land to Lyminge in 798 in return for psalmody, masses, and alms.[212] Such priests were probably of humbler status, or at any rate less luxurious in their expectations, than the noble monks and nuns of a century earlier, and were correspondingly cheaper to support.[213] It

---

[207] Yorke 2003*b*: 53–4; below, p. 244.

[208] The last explicit reference to a double house is in an Alcuin letter of 796: *Alc. Ep.* No. 106 (pp. 152–3).

[209] Sims-Williams 1990: 170–1; Brooks 1984: 187–8; S 1434, S 1439; cf. below, p. 163.

[210] Brooks 1984: 155–64, and Brooks 1995: 12–14, as against Langefeld 1996; for further reflections see J. Barrow in *Encyc.* 86, and Story 2003: 203–8.

[211] Cf. below, pp. 155–6. For later ninth-century eastern Francia, Mayr-Harting 1981: 378 notes a shift of monastic personnel from monks to canons and speculates whether 'this was in the end found to be a preferable way of fulfilling a pastorate which such houses had always had'.

[212] S 153.

[213] Various possible reasons for the disappearance of female-ruled houses, and the decline of female religious generally, are considered by Schneider 1985: 31–7, 309, Foot 2000: 62–71, and Yorke 2003*b*: 47–63: social change giving women a more restricted role; the impact of Carolingian attacks on mixed-sex communities; and changing relationships between monasticism, land-tenure, and dynastic strategies. But the impoverishment and declining status of monastic life may be equally important.

appears that those in charge of minsters were no longer interested in financing high culture and princely magnificence, but rather in syphoning off everything that was surplus to the needs of a basic priestly staff who would work more and cost less.

We might expect such a scaling-down to be reflected in the architectural and artistic evidence. In fact, patronage of monastic buildings and ornaments at the highest level continued up to and beyond 800, in a remarkable flowering of Continental-inspired classicism. The great basilican churches of Brixworth and Cirencester (in Mercia) and Wareham (in Wessex)[214] show a concern to re-create Roman monumentality which, like the contemporary revival of interest in the ruins of Romano-British towns,[215] is likely to reflect influence from the Carolingian court circle (Fig. 15). Outstanding sculpture was produced both in Mercia, with the spectacular series at Breedon-on-the-Hill and other dependencies of *Medeshamstede*, and in Yorkshire, where classical motifs such as tiers of busts under arches copy late antique and Carolingian models.[216] Great churches still acquired gorgeous metalwork,[217] and a continuing tradition of de luxe manuscripts is attested by a small but sumptuous group, probably from midland and south-eastern centres.[218]

But two reservations—one on the scope of this patronage, the other on its chronology—suggest that the written and the physical evidence may convey the same message after all. Lavish though the buildings and sculpture of *c.*800 are, they suggest by their very modishness and uniformity something more restricted and centralized than the pluralistic minster patronage of a century earlier. These look like ideas disseminated from people and places in direct touch with European intellectual circles—Alcuin's York, Offa's Lichfield, Wulfred's Canterbury—to a few favoured sites.[219] Breedon, a great minster at the heart of the Mercian kingdom, had trained a learned arch-

---

[214] Gem 1993: 34–41; Fernie 1983: 64–73; Wilkinson and McWhirr 1998. The probably monastic hall at Northampton (below, p. 205) is of similar date, and may well have had some close connection with nearby Brixworth.

[215] Below, pp. 274–5.

[216] Wilson 1984: 77–85; Lang 1990; Webster and Backhouse 1991: 239–42; Lang 1993; Lang 1999; Lang 2000; Bailey 2000; Jewell 2001; Gannon 2003: 186; Story 2003: 174–6; Hawkes 2003*b*: 83–7. Lang, Jewell, and Gannon argue that this English classicism was derived directly from Roman and eastern models rather than passively dependent on Carolingian ones. Wessex retains one significant scheme of architectural sculpture from this period, the *porticus* arches at Britford (Gem 1993: 45–7).

[217] See for instance Alcuin's comments on the treasures of the church of York: Campbell 2000: 88.

[218] Wilson 1984: 91–6; Webster and Backhouse 1991: 195–6; M. P. Brown 1996.

[219] Cf. Lang 1993: 262. For architectural patronage at York, notably the church of the Holy Wisdom consecrated in 780 (cf. Fig. 9), see: Morris 1986 (suggesting a separate complex in the Bishophill area); Rollason and others 1998: 132–63; and Norton 1998: 11–13 (rejecting, but in my view not refuting, Morris's suggestion).

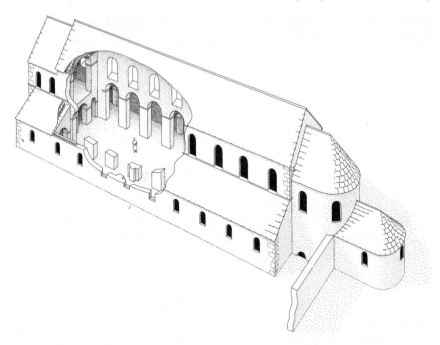

15. The minster church at *Cirencester* (Glos.): interpretation from the excavated footings. This grand building, probably of the earlier ninth century, demonstrates the continuing wealth of minsters in the late Mercian period, despite gathering troubles. (Wilkinson and McWhirr 1998: fig. 27; Richard Gem and British Museum.)

bishop of Canterbury in the 730s; Wareham received a royal burial in 802. Archbishop Wulfred's grand rebuilding of Canterbury cathedral[220] was of a piece with his magisterial assertion of his own rights. It is hard to say whether basilican churches on the scale of Brixworth and Cirencester were always exceptional, or whether large numbers have been obliterated by the intensity of later rebuilding in central and southern England, but at present they look like relative rarities. Much here is uncertain, but the physical evidence certainly admits the possibility of a shaking-out in which certain minsters continued to do well into the ninth century, but the majority languished.

There is also an impression (though the peculiar difficulties of dating ninth-century art leave it as an ill-defined one) that cultural activity in general tailed off after the 820s. For architecture, Richard Gem proposes a

---

[220] Blockley and others 1997: 100–4, III.

continuous and often innovative tradition across the period 750 to 870.[221] It is certainly no part of the present argument to suggest a hiatus. Religious life continued at hundreds of minsters, and must often have entailed extensions, alterations, and maintenance; sculpture traditions continued into and beyond the era of the Viking raids. But it must be said that only a tiny number of churches show really impressive work which can be ascribed to a post-Brixworth generation, around the middle years of the century. Repton, with its columned crypt, is exceptional, but so is its history: it was the site of three Mercian royal burials, and it may have been one of the very few double houses which survived under an abbess into the 830s.[222] The case otherwise rests on Deerhurst, and even there it remains possible that the major ninth-century phase dates from a revival under the Mercian rulers in, say, the 880s rather than earlier.[223] In this period there is only one unambiguously documented case of the addition of a new church to an existing minster, at Kempsey (Worcs.) in 868.[224] Sculpture, too, is elusive: after Breedon we find a disparate group of crosses which, though individually sumptuous, are often hard to date more closely than to c.780–880.[225] As artistic production declined, so did learning: whether or not there were fewer books,[226] there can be no doubt about the collapse both of Latinity and of scribal competence in the ninth-century Canterbury scriptorium.[227]

For David Dumville, 'it is hard to gainsay the Alfredian argument that failure to teach and consequent ignorance of Latin were what led to the Church gradually losing its way in the period from the 830s to the 880s'.[228] But perhaps the malaise lay deeper, in growing popular indifference to the cultural standards of places which were no longer the sole arbiters of

[221] Gem 1993: esp. 48–55; cf. Gittos 2002*a*: 100–6.

[222] *Encyc.* 390–2; Crook 2000: 62–3, 128–30; Gem 1993: 51; S 1624 and Yorke 2003*b*: 167. The identification of Cynewaru in S 1624 as abbess of Repton is likely but not conclusive.

[223] Gem 1993: 51–5; Rahtz and Watts 1997: 166–79, 190 (and see review by J. Blair in *EME* 7 (1998), 370–1). Wing has points in common with Deerhurst, but dating remains similarly problematic: see Crook 2000: 130–2.

[224] *JW* ii. 284. Bishop Ecgred of Lindisfarne (830–45) is also said to have built churches on some Lindisfarne estates, but the circumstances are less clear: *Symeon Op.* i. 52–3, 201 (cf. Craster 1954: 185–7, and Gem 1993: 50).

[225] Wilson 1984: 105–8; Webster and Backhouse 1991: 239–46. Jewell 2001: 262, dates the Breedon/Peterborough group c.780–810, the Breedon Virgin and Fletton friezes perhaps up to c.830. Sandbach, where the smaller cross shows innovative use of metallic models and can be dated well into the ninth century (Hawkes 2002), remained artistically vigorous: perhaps its location, at the interface between Mercia and the Irish Sea region, helped it to withstand the pressures of the time.

[226] Wilson 1984: 96, for a summary of the dating problems. Private prayer-books, a distinctive product of this period, go up to the 820s/840s: see M. P. Brown 1996, and Brown 2001, for this and for scribal activity generally.

[227] Brooks 1984: 167–74; Cubitt 1999.

[228] Dumville 1992*b*: 96–7.

civilized taste. It is suggestive that as the ninth century advances, our understanding of the English artistic repertoire rests less on manuscripts or sculpture, more on small-scale and often secular metalwork.[229] If some of the
ninth-century stone crosses are lay personal memorials, they foreshadow the
laicization of ecclesiastical culture which would be such a marked feature of
the post-Viking era.[230]

There are also growing signs of tenurial and financial problems. The vehe-
mence with which the 816 council forbade the long-term alienation of
monastic lands, except in the direst need,[231] suggests that impoverished minsters were now parting with their endowments for ready cash. Once depleted,
the land-base could no longer easily be rebuilt. By the 770s kings were issuing
charters straightforwardly to laymen, cutting the link between bookland and
monastic patronage and making obsolete the category of thegn-abbot.[232]
Charters up to the 780s, mainly from Sussex, show land still being given to
found and endow small minsters,[233] but they are the last trickle of the early
eighth-century flood: it is likely that only a tiny number of prestige
communities (most obviously Winchcombe) were actually increasing their
endowments. Otherwise, the impression is of a downwards trend. In 767 the
abbot of an unknown minster and King Offa exchanged thirty-hide estates
in Middlesex, but three decades later the abbot's portion had passed to a royal
thegn.[234] The community at St Paul's leased the ten hides of Braughing
(Herts.) in about 827 to a Mercian thegn, with reversion, if his kin should
fail, to 'the church of St Andrew Christ's apostle'. This was presumably at
Braughing, where there was still a minster in the 990s, and the ten hides
should probably be interpreted as minster land annexed to enrich first a
cathedral community, then a layman.[235] When, towards the mid-century,
Mercian minsters felt the need to buy off royal demands, they sometimes
spent land as as well as cash: Hanbury lost forty hides in such a deal in 836.[236]

And it was a matter of attitudes as well as resources: the concerns of those
in power seem more political and financial, less engaged with the minster
communities as ends in their own right. The emotional detachment of proprietors from minsters was an inevitable consequence of the replacement of
founders' dynasties by others,[237] and of the mere passage of time, but the
increasingly alienated and exploitative tone of the sources goes rather beyond

---

[229] Wilson 1984: 108–11; Webster and Backhouse 1991: 268–83.
[230] Below, pp. 321–2.
[231] Chelsea 816, c. 7 (*CED* iii. 582); cf. Brooks 1984: 175.
[232] Sims-Williams 1990: 154–5; Charles-Edwards 1997: 195.
[233] S 50, S 108, S 1178, S 1184 (Sussex); S 141 (Hwicce).
[234] S 106, S 1186*a*.   [235] S 1791; cf. *W. Æth.* 9, 30–1.   [236] S 190.
[237] Yorke 2003*b*: 52–8.

this. One pointer is the habit of referring to minsters as though they were measures of land: 'the minster called Westbury, and the bishop had that land with the charters' (824); 'the minster beside the Avon called Stratford, the quantity of which is twenty hides' (844).[238] Another is the rise of monastic pluralists, such as the Abbess Æthelburh who held life-leases of the formerly independent Hwiccian minsters of Withington, Twyning, and Fladbury in the 770s.[239] While there was nothing new about groups of minsters under one ruler, these transactions look more like a speculator assembling a port-folio: the financial control of Æthelburh's minsters was no longer in their own communities' hands, or guided primarily by their needs.

Æthelburh anticipated the behaviour of two much more powerful ladies, King Offa's widow Cynethryth and King Coenwulf's daughter Cwoenthryth, whose control of important groups of minsters in Mercia and Kent con-tributed significantly to the political tensions of the early ninth century.[240] The new tone comes through in, for instance, a settlement of 798 over the middle Thames minster of Cookham, which the see of Canterbury had just regained from Mercian royal hands. At that stage

it pleased me, Æthelheard, by the grace of God archbishop, and Abbess [and ex-Queen] Cynethryth, who at that time ruled the oft-mentioned minster [of Cookham], and the elders from both sides—namely Kent and Bedford—assembled for this purpose, that the said Cynethryth should give to me in exchange for the said minster 110 hides in Kent . . . These lands King Offa caused to be inscribed to himself while he lived and to his heirs after him, and after the course of their life he ordered them to be consigned to the church located at Bedford. And we decided in the presence of the whole synod that the abbess should receive from me the oft-men-tioned minster with its documents, and I should receive from her the lands and the deeds of the lands in Kent . . . I also concede into the possession of Abbess Cynethryth the minster located in the place called *Pectanege* for her to have, which the good King Ecgfrith gave and granted by charter for me to possess by hereditary right.[241]

The disempowerment of the communities themselves is obvious: Cookham and *Pectanege* evidently had no say in their own fates, and it is unlikely that the Bedford delegation was in a position to do more than assent. In a similar vein, the protagonists in the fight over Minster-in-Thanet and Reculver during the 820s were the archbishop, king, and queen: Coenwulf and

[238] S 1433, S 198.
[239] S 62, S 1255; Sims-Williams 1990: 37, 158; Yorke 2003*b*: 57. On female monastic proprietors in this period, see also Schneider 1985: 253–70.
[240] Brooks 1984: 180–5; Cubitt 1995: 220–6; Yorke 2003*b*: 53–63; Story 2003: 181–4. Compare the thegn Ealdberht and his sister Abbess Selethryth, who may have been put in by Mercian power as 'managers' of the Kentish minsters: Brooks 1984: 184–5; Crick 1988: 258–9.
[241] S 1258.

Cwoenthryth deprived Wulfred of the 'free minsters', and Wulfred emerged victorious as their 'lord'.[242]

Bereft of their autonomy, and reduced to pawns in political and financial strategies, minsters were not necessarily better off in bishops' than in kings' hands. If bishops were the main agents of principled reform, their administrative powers were all too easily abused: the 816 council felt it necessary to make clear that a bishop could take control of a minster when the community was in dire trouble, but not to satisfy his own greed.[243] The haziness of the boundary between reform and predation is illustrated by the grievances of a certain Abbot Forthred, who complained to the pope in 757–8 that Archbishop Ecgberht of York and King Eadberht of Northumbria had forcibly confiscated the Yorkshire minsters of Stonegrave, Coxwold, and *Donæmuthe*, given to him by a certain abbess, and conferred them on the nobleman Moll.[244] Ecgberht was none other than Bede's correspondent: did he think that he was following his old teacher by revoking grants to dubious minsters? If so, he could have had a point: Forthred, who had seemingly engrossed three nunneries or double houses, looks like an absentee monastic pluralist. But the re-grant to a lay lord, which is certainly not what Bede had envisaged, rather suggests an unholy alliance between archbishop and king to secularize monastic assets.

For bishops as for kings, minsters could be food-sources and agreeable dining-clubs. Ealhstan of Sherborne (*c.*820–867) was later accused of 'subjecting to his own purposes the minster of Malmesbury'.[245] How he might have done this is suggested by leases of the minster estates at Farnham (801 × 14) and Bromyard (840 × 52) by the bishops of Winchester and Hereford respectively.[246] Both reserve yearly food-renders: from Farnham two nights' refection and ten pots of honey, from Bromyard a barrel of clear ale, a vessel of honey or its equivalent in mead, a plough-beast, a hundred loaves, a sheep, and a piglet. In a detail which rings true enough to suggest some genuine basis, an eleventh-century forgery pictures the bishop of Worcester in 780 putting on a feast (*convivium*) for Offa and his court at Fladbury minster.[247] It is hard to avoid a sense that these bishops' interests in the minsters under their care were as much gastronomic as religious. Whether communities welcomed such self-appointed guardians against royal aggression may be doubted.

---

[242] S 1436; S 1267 for an example of Wulfred's exercise of this lordship.
[243] Chelsea 816, c. 8 (*CED* iii. 582).
[244] Letter of Pope Paul I, *CED* iii. 394–6.   [245] *GR* i. 156.
[246] S 1263, S 1270. The Bromyard list of food-renders is fragmentary, and only partly summarized here.
[247] S 118.

'After the death of Coenwulf, king of the Mercians [821]', complains a South Saxon charter, 'in various places the churches of God were greatly despoiled, in goods, lands, revenue, and all matters.'[248] That this was no short-term spasm, but a further turn of the screw on monastic assets, is suggested by a group of Mercian royal charters after 830. In return for money, precious objects, or land, they confirm to sees and minsters their own property, or exempt them from obligations to house and feed the king's followers or servants.[249] A change in charter-writing styles may heighten the novelty, but it is hard to doubt that minsters were being, in effect, blackmailed into parting with valuables to fend off arbitrary land-seizures and a ruinous escalation of hospitality demands. Thus in 840, to rid themselves of entertaining royal *fæstingmen*, Abbot Eanmund and his community at Breedon-on-the-Hill presented the king with a finely worked great silver dish, a precious ornament, and 120 gold mancuses; they were also to sing 1,200 psalters and 120 masses for the king, his dear friends, and all the Mercian people. Eight years later, fending off royal falconers and huntsmen (but not envoys from other kingdoms) cost them fifteen hides and 180 mancuses to the king, and money in a magnificent drinking-vessel decorated with gold to the local *princeps* Humberht.[250]

As he carted these treasures to the court, Eanmund may have envied the minsters in regions of West Saxon dominance whose liberties, under the Kingston accord of 838, were safeguarded by the benign joint lordship of the king of Wessex and the archbishop of Canterbury.[251] Or perhaps he did not. The 838 agreement contains no explicit protection for the minsters' financial autonomy; we know very little about them during the middle years of the ninth century, and when they re-emerge after the Viking interlude they seem not merely battered, but as heavily exploited by their royal lords as Mercian minsters had been a century earlier.[252] Kingston was a sell-out by the religious to the secular power, even if it left the house of Wessex with the moral high ground. From the point of view of ordinary minsters, it hardly mattered. Leaving them alone to run their own affairs was at the top of neither the archbishop's nor the king's agenda, and any such principle would soon collapse under external demands on their inherited assets.

Why did the tides of fortune turn against the minsters? By now it must

---

[248] S 1435 (*Selsey*, 59–65). This dates from the year of the West Saxon conquest of Sussex, but it is clear from the context that the exactions complained of were Mercian ones.

[249] Wormald 1982*a*: 138–9. S 134 sets the formula, though without specifying gifts in return. The main examples are: S 190, S 192–3, S 197–8, S 206–7, S 210, S 271, S 1271. Cf. Sims-Williams 1990: 137.

[250] S 193, S 197.

[251] One minster, probably Lyminge or Reculver, endorsed its copy: 'if anyone molests you in your election, then show this document': Brooks 1984: 199.

[252] Below, pp. 298–9.

be clear that the standard answer to this question—the Vikings—is inadequate: decline had set in well before raiding became a major destructive force. However shocking the sack of Lindisfarne in 793, and despite the temporary re-location of one or two rich minsters on the exposed Kentish coast,[253] Scandinavian attacks before 850 caused occasional tragedy and general disquiet, not total disruption. Six years after the Kingston accord, Dover, Folkestone, and Lyminge were seemingly all still functioning on their coastal sites.[254] If the Vikings did accelerate the downward trend, it was probably by putting minsters in a weak bargaining position with the secular powers who also offered their best chance of protection.

Another possibility is that society was generally poorer: that the era of the sceatta coinage which ended in the 740s—and coincided almost exactly with the era of English intellectual and artistic supremacy—saw a spectacular but transient boom which allowed the exceptional luxury of rich minsters. In the present state of knowledge, this seems unlikely. The volume of sceattas in circulation responded to flows of silver from the lower Rhineland, and while their disappearance must have meant important changes to local exchange systems, it is scarcely credible that it marked a commensurate drop in personal wealth.[255] Many metal-detected sites show a cessation of coins but an increase in other kinds of metalwork, and small-scale personal adornments in nielloed silver are a new and widespread feature of the ninth century.[256] There is in fact a strong possibility that personal wealth increased rather than decreased in England during *c*.800–60. But it is evident that a smaller proportion of that wealth was thought appropriate for luxury ecclesiastical consumption, and that the lion's share of that shrinking resource was increasingly monopolized by a few minsters at the expense of the many.

Underlying the minsters' specific problems was a deeper and more pervasive social and cultural shift. Elite establishments made wealthy in a burst of concentrated enthusiasm must justify their inherited wealth as the generations pass, or see their prestige drain away.[257] By 800 the novelty of minsters had worn off, and they no longer offered the only route to new and

---

[253] *Alc. Ep.* Nos. 19–22 (pp. 53–60); S 160; Brooks 1984: 34–5, 201–4.

[254] S 1439.

[255] Blackburn 2003: 34–5.

[256] Gabor Thomas pers. comm.; cf. Blackburn 2003: 32. To some extent we know ninth-century metalwork thanks to Viking-age hoards, but this explanation does not apply to the strap-ends and hooked tags which metal-detectors are now finding in such large numbers. See Webster 2001 for distinctively Mercian styles in eighth- and ninth-century metalwork.

[257] There are analogies for the declining prestige of English minsters. In ninth-century Tibet, anti-monastic sentiment emerged some sixty years after the initial wave of foundations; the criticisms—that monasteries encroached on royal power, enjoyed undeserved immunity from taxation, and monopolized labourers and warriors who should have been supporting and defending their country—would have been familiar to Bede and Boniface. See Tucci 1980: 11–12; Grimshaw 1983: 181.

exciting things. Few of them still supported rigorous spiritual life, their intellectual achievements had tailed away, and moral reform was now barely even an issue. All too often, they could be identified with supplanted rivals or litigious kin, or perceived as greedy, self-satisfied consumers of scarce assets. Increasingly, they were expected to justify their existence as providers of priestly ministrations rather than as centres of high culture, and to do so from fewer resources. But there is also an important sense in which they were victims of their own success: the more they developed as economic and territorial centres, the less the powers of the world could afford to leave them to their own devices, and the more tempted they were to bend them to their own needs. This largely hidden transition—which will be examined in the economic and topographical context where it belongs[258]—probably lies in the background of all the developments just considered.

As the last point illustrates, the embeddedness of minsters in the lives of their own localities was in the long run more important than the policies of kings and bishops. If their decline is striking, the survival of most of them through the middle ages as religious centres of some kind is still more so: minsters could be appropriated, impoverished, or raided, but seldom destroyed completely. In fact, from the perspective of local people (who may have cared little about the destination of surplus revenue) they very likely *grew* in importance: more pastoral care from the priests, more trading and production around the centres, the provision of Christian burial for a wider social group.[259] They must also have assumed some importance as repositories of local social memory, fixed if embattled points in a fast-changing world. To understand what the Church really meant in Anglo-Saxon society, we must turn from the relatively well-recorded political events to local relationships which can be perceived only here and there, or approached indirectly by means of later or comparative evidence.

[258] Below, Ch. 5.   [259] Below, pp. 452–6.

3

Church and People
*c.*650–850

Minsters interacted with the lay communities around them in a variety of ways. This chapter will trace four rather disparate strands linking monastic to secular life: the mutually influencing traditions of material culture; the cults of saints; the framework within which church dues were paid and pastoral care provided; and the extent to which minsters and laity participated in each others' devotional and ritual lives. What they all seem to illustrate is the inappropriateness, in the world of early Christian England, of the kind of explanatory model which sees 'clerical culture' as something inherently alienated from 'popular culture': each strand suggests areas of integration and contact between the lives of ecclesiastics and laity.

The 'minster culture' of Bede's England

The monastic culture which formed during Bede's lifetime (*c.*672–735) was a vehicle for a very distinctive fusion between the barbarian north and the Christian south: between 'interlace and icons', as Ernst Kitzinger puts it.[1] The fusion had begun two or three generations earlier, with the Anglo-Saxon aristocracy's developing taste for Byzantine and Roman artefacts.[2] As monastic networks spread under the guidance of learned men and women with far-reaching contacts, a laity wedded to its opulent and already complex material culture drank thirstily from a new, much more direct and powerful, flow of

---

[1] Kitzinger 1993, suggesting that panels of interlace (e.g. the noseguard of the Coppergate helmet or the *porticus* jamb-reliefs at Monkwearmouth) share with actionless iconic figures (e.g. St Cuthbert's coffin) a common aim of guarding and warding off adverse powers. His comparison (p. 12) between an icon from Mount Sinai and an insular Evangelist portrait, illustrating how the insular tradition 'of conveying elementary spiritual force in visual terms' transformed and intensified images from the classical world, has lessons for our understanding of other responses to Mediterranean culture. Cf. Gannon 2003: 182–8, for classical and Christian iconography in the miniature and summary medium of the early eighth-century English coinage.

[2] Above, pp. 39–40.

foreign influences.[3] The Roman civilization which was the vehicle of the Christian message became not merely more accessible to the English aristocracy, but an increasingly important part of their own lifestyles.

The interaction of monastic with secular life exposed it to charges of worldliness from within its own ranks, but also enabled it to support such high culture and scholarship as the art and learning of Wearmouth-Jarrow, or the friendship networks of Aldhelm and Boniface.[4] It is as characteristic of this world that the poem 'Beowulf', so redolent of the heroic secular past, can be interpreted as a monastic product, as that the abbess of a minor Worcestershire minster could own an Italian manuscript of St Jerome.[5] In vain might Bede, Boniface, and the *Clofesho* canons inveigh against the decadence of proprietary minsters, or Alcuin urge that 'a reader should be heard, not a harpist; patristic discourse, not pagan song'.[6] The minster culture was immune from reformers' attacks until, in the ninth century, it started to dissolve back into an aristocratic society which, having learnt so much from it, was less and less prepared to tolerate its financial and institutional autonomy.

Despite the critics, minsters were opulent not because they housed particularly self-indulgent forms of the religious life, but because gold, bright colour, and intricate ornament were integral to the society which bred them.[7] Ruled by princesses and hosting kings, they rivalled courts in extravagant display. Even the most exceptional ecclesiastics could not distance themselves: Wilfrid went around in royal state, and Cuthbert, modestly though he dressed, feasted with royal abbesses and may have worn a lavish gold and garnet cross (Fig. 30).[8] The bright, showy garments of ecclesiastics shocked Boniface, but his aristocratic contemporaries might have thought it odd if they had worn anything simpler.[9] Indeed, as well as opening English goldsmith-work and embroidery to Mediterranean styles and techniques, the Church legitimized it as a means to honour God and his saints and to stimulate devotion. Between 689 and 709, Aldhelm wrote a poem on a church recently built by a West Saxon princess:

---

[3] P. Brown 1996: 230–2, for the cosmopolitan character of what he calls this 'micro-Christendom'.

[4] Lapidge and Herren 1979: 136–51, on Aldhelm's correspondents; Yorke 1998, showing Boniface's range of contacts in West Saxon royal nunneries.

[5] Wormald 1978: 42–58; Sims-Williams 1990: 190–7.

[6] *Alc. Ep.* No. 124 (p. 183); Bullough 1993. In his commentary on 1 Samuel, Bede attacks slothful teachers who prefer to fill their minds with 'fabulis saecularibus ac doctrinis daemoniorum' rather than with the word of God (*BOE* ii. 112).

[7] For this aspect of Anglo-Saxon taste see Dodwell 1982: esp. 24–43.

[8] *VW* c. 24 (p. 48); *VCA* iv. 10 (p. 126). The cross buried with Cuthbert has seen much use, but it is of course an inference rather than certain fact that he wore it himself.

[9] *Bon. Ep.* No. 78 (p. 170). For the whole question of the secular context of monastic opulence see Campbell 2000: 85–106, esp. 98–101.

Bugga, a humble servant of Christ, built [this] new church with its lofty structure, in which holy altars gleam in twelve-fold dedication; moreover, she dedicates the apse to the Virgin. . . . The church glows within with gentle light on occasions when the sun shines through the glass windows, diffusing its clear light through the rectangular church. The new church has many ornaments: a golden cloth glistens with its twisted threads and forms a beautiful covering for the sacred altar. And a golden chalice covered with jewels gleams so that it seems to reflect the heavens with their bright stars; and there is a large paten made from silver. . . . Here glistens the metal of the Cross made from burnished gold and adorned at the same time with silver and jewels. Here too a thurible embossed on all sides hangs suspended from on high, having vaporous openings from which the Sabean frankincense emits ambrosia when the priests are asked to perform mass.[10]

This is the world of the leisured, luxurious, and (at least sometimes) learned ladies whom we meet in the hostile phrases of Bede and the councils, and more sympathetically in the treatise which Aldhelm wrote for the Barking community.[11] Excavations on monastic sites in eastern England have revealed a characteristic range of accessories: opulent dress-pins (sometimes with cruciform heads), keys, writing-styli, tweezers, fine imported pottery and glass. While some of these items are also found on secular sites, the rich assemblages occur at places which on other grounds can plausibly be considered monastic.[12] Especially striking are the styli, with their implication of literacy, and the inscribed lead plates, probably from wooden ossuaries, found at Flixborough (Lincs.) and Kirkdale (Yorks.) (Figs. 26 and 16).[13]

Other attributes of the culture would have made a bigger impact on people at large. At least on the richest monastic sites, the really revolutionary change was the revival, for the first time since the Romans left, of technologies for building and carving in stone. The permanence of sites and buildings was one of several factors which, as we will see, made monastic settlements decisively different from all others. Stone sculpture, which unlike other large-scale art-forms survives in some abundance, was a novel means of advertising the status and identity of new kinds of places. Nor can there previously have been anything like the great Northumbrian and Mercian high crosses with their complex figural iconography. Recent studies have stressed the extent to which stone crosses—sometimes with attached metal mounts and probably richly painted—imitated gold and jewelled crosses (Fig. 17). Like the idealized cross-relic pictured in the poem 'The Dream of the Rood', their ulti-

---

[10] *AO* 14–18 (Lapidge and Rosier 1985: 47–9).
[11] *AO* 226–323 (Lapidge and Herren 1979: 51–132).
[12] Below, pp. 203–8.
[13] Below, pp. 209–10 nn.

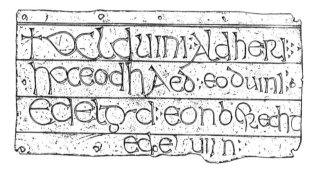

16. Inscribed lead plates from (left) the minster of *Kirkdale* (Yorks.) and (right) the high-status, probably monastic site at *Flixborough* (Lincs.). They are most convincingly interpreted as labels from wooden ossuary chests. Two-thirds actual size. (After Watts and others 1997: fig. 2, and C. Loveluck, 'A High-Status Anglo-Saxon Settlement at Flixborough', *Antiquity*, 72 (1998), 146–61, fig. 9.)

mate inspiration was the *crux gemmata* reproduced in Roman mosaics.[14] Some of these spectacular monuments stood outdoors, signalling monastic precincts and perhaps a wider range of cult sites: if they brought the cult-pillars of old beliefs reassuringly into English minds, they must surely too have overawed them as emblems of an altogether weightier civilization.[15]

Minsters were uniquely effective channels for the dissemination of ideas. Monastic federations such as Wilfrid's were like big extended families, and through them spread a social (one might almost say a domestic) culture suffused with Christianity. When the nobleman Eanmund set about founding a minster in early eighth-century Northumbria he sought advice both from the bishop of Lindisfarne and from the holy exile Ecgberht, and 'added to his family a teacher suited to the position, . . . a priest who laid down monastic laws'.[16] The rapid dissemination of charter-writing conventions from kingdom to kingdom during *c.*670–90, for instance from Northumbria to the west midlands and from both to Sussex,[17] is a trace-element which implies multiple, less visible influences. Stephen, with his Roman sympathies, stresses how such blessings as the Benedictine Rule and church music

[14] Richardson 1984; Bailey 1996*a*: 120–4; Hawkes 2001: 238. The vision in 'The Dream of the Rood' bears a most striking resemblance to the one large-scale English jewelled metal cross to survive from the period (Fig. 17): Webster and Backhouse 1991: 170–2.

[15] Flint 1991: 257–61, and below, pp. 227, 278–81, for the insular and pagan context; Hawkes 2003*b*: 76–80 argues that round-shafted and square-tapering crosses were respectively reminiscent of triumphal *columna* in Rome, and of the Egyptian obelisk re-erected by St Peter's there.

[16] *DA* ll. 93–119 (pp. 10–12).

[17] *Selsey*, pp. xlv–l; cf. Wormald 1984.

17. This English standing cross (the 'Rupertus Cross'), of gilt copper with polychrome glass inlays on a wooden core, has been preserved at Bischofshofen, Austria. It gives a glimpse of the lost brilliance of the ecclesiastical milieu in eighth-century England. (Dommuseum zu Salzburg.)

moved northwards with Wilfrid,[18] but it is also likely that the practices of Wilfrid's Ripon spread southwards through the Mercian minsters which looked to it as their head.

The variables of time, place, and patronage resulted in huge contrasts in culture, spirituality, rule, and engagement with the monastic life, and certainly there are striking differences between the complexions of, say, Whitby, Wearmouth-Jarrow, and Lindisfarne.[19] But in broader terms, and in the context of what we know of sixth- and early seventh-century secular culture, the monastic impact impresses most by its homogeneity. Minsters were a new kind of settlement, planned in accordance with conventions which, despite local variants, show a continuum across north-western Europe.[20] It is hard to see any very fundamental difference in material culture (so far as it has been recovered through admittedly very small-scale excavations) between the monastic sites at Whitby (Yorks.) and Barking (Essex). Certainly there are regional contrasts: the richness in small-finds of these and other eastern sites is conditioned by the economic precocity of eastern England, and large-scale stone sculpture was overwhelmingly a Northumbrian phenomenon. But even patterns such as these, accentuated today by the survival of certain objects and the durability of certain materials, may loom larger for us than they did for contemporaries. Crosses carved in stone or wood (assuming that the latter existed in regions without stone sculpture) would have looked much alike when painted, and churches built of stone, Roman brick, or timber could all have been plastered. The small personal objects found only in regions where that kind of 'consumer culture' existed would have been insignificant beside the major precious objects such as crosses, lamps, and altar-fittings which are now lost, but which all minsters of importance would have had. In their articulation of space, the effect of their buildings and monuments, their opulent treasures and books—in short in their public face—minsters in Kent or in central Mercia, in Northumbria or in Wessex, displayed the same distinctive organizational and cultural form.

It is useful to remember this basic homogeneity when we consider more elusive aspects of the minsters' relations with the world around them. For example, whether or not a defined network of mother-parishes could have existed before there was one authority to enforce it throughout England is, as we will see, controversial. But if cultural norms could become generalized across the kingdoms within three or four decades, it does not seem so unlikely that the first generation of English ecclesiastics guided the patronage of their

---

[18] *VW* cc. 14, 47 (pp. 30, 98).
[19] Mayr-Harting 1991: 148–67; Higgitt 1995.
[20] Below, pp. 191–204.

royal kinsmen and supporters down tracks which also basically led in the same direction. If there were also basic similarities in the ways in which kings and nobles already supported themselves from the land, and exerted authority over it, the difficulties reduce still further.

While we can get some impression of the material culture, the mental and spiritual world of the minsters (apart from a few very exceptional ones) largely eludes us. One avenue to perceiving just a little of it is by means of the evidence—formal, intractable, and often late though it is—for Anglo-Saxon saints' cults. The 'very special dead' can guide us to contacts between the ecclesiastical milieux in which they lived and the lay communities which revered them as healers and heavenly leaders, and which located episodes from their lives in the everyday landscape.

The cults of saints[21]

The late Roman and early medieval conception of a local saint was founded, to an extent often hard to comprehend today, on the physical presence of the holy. By the end of the fourth century the martyrs and other holy dead, now glorified in heaven, were identified throughout the Roman Christian world with earthly sites empowered by their bodily remains: the saint's tomb was not merely an object of devotion, but the seat of a continuing personality.[22] The constraints which in Europe led to extramural burial around martyrial tombs were scarcely a factor in seventh-century England: ecclesiastics of the conversion period were buried in or near their own churches.[23] Here as in central Gaul, a society eager to acquire the Christian heritage, but with very few late Roman martyrial sites, had strong incentives 'to seize upon contemporary or near-contemporary figures of saintly reputation as substitutes'.[24] It was this impulse, at a time when so many religious communities were coming into existence, which made the seventh and eighth centuries the English 'age of saints': after 850, saint-making was different in character and very much more restricted.

The Anglo-Saxon local saint was thus a patron in a long-standing Roman tradition. It is easy to see, however, that in secular culture such a patron might take on a more vernacular guise, as the undying leader of a kindred or

[21] This section summarizes the methodological arguments developed at greater length in Blair 2002a. See also: Cubitt 2000; Thacker 2002; Cubitt 2002; and Yorke 2003b: 118–22.

[22] Brown 1981 is fundamental here. See also Biddle 1986: 1–5; Rollason 1989a: 3–20; and Thomas 1971.

[23] Below, pp. 229, 240–1.

[24] Burnell 1988: 225; cf. Wood 2002.

folk-group. The founder or first head had a vital role in acquiring a minster's endowments and fortifying them against attack, and could do these things all the better as an 'immortal landlord' who had passed from the cut-throat company of warriors to the holy company of heaven. This mattered not only for the religious community, but for everyone associated with or dependent upon it. Centuries after St Cuthbert's death in 687, the people of the lands which his community controlled were known as the *haliwerfolc* ('holy-man's-folk'): 'so pervasive was the image', observes David Rollason, 'that County Durham seems narrowly to have escaped being called *Haliwerfolc*, rather like Norfolk or Suffolk.'[25] Stephen of Ripon describes with relish the miraculous blinding and massacre of the men who burnt Wilfrid's minster at Oundle after his death: 'with such a wonder Wilfrid, the saint of God, avenged his wrongs by his prayers.'[26]

When a church possessed its own saint's bodily relics, they were both a mark of status and a devotional focus for everyone by whom that status was recognized. The frequency and distribution of local cults, the sorts of places that possessed them, the ways in which they were presented and promoted, and the identity of the saints themselves may enlarge our understanding of how the Church interacted with a wider world. Recent scholarship has formed a more sensitive appreciation of the political, social, and psychological role of Anglo-Saxon saints' cults.[27] Even so, it is still much harder to view them through eighth-century than through eleventh-century eyes. Saints were 'made' through a combination of monastic initiatives and grass-roots veneration, and whether a revered individual was or was not a saint must often have been rather vague at the time. From the 960s, the Benedictine Reform occasioned a drastic filtering of the monastic heritage in which certain communities and saintly figures from the past were celebrated in narrative and liturgy, the rest left to oblivion.[28]

During *c.*1000–1200 the resting-places of some English saints were listed in a series of catalogues, of which the earliest (normally known from the first word of its text as the *Secgan*) incorporates what may be a brief list from the pre-Viking period.[29] But these are essentially late and post-Anglo-Saxon texts: they record a good many obscure saints, as do calendars, litanies, and hagiography from the same period, but the balance of the material is heavily influenced by post-Reform concerns. The small number of cults which the late tenth-century monastic culture chose to promote recur time and again,

[25] Rollason 1987: 56.   [26] *VW* c. 67 (p. 146).
[27] Notably Ridyard 1988, Rollason 1989*a*, and the several articles by Thacker.
[28] Below, pp. 353–4.
[29] Liebermann 1889; Rollason 1978; Blair 2002*a*: 463–7.

while many others which may have been no less important in their own day get barely a mention. From scattered references it is possible to assemble a surprisingly long list of these neglected saints, but even this has to be regarded as (at least at some levels) representative rather than in any way comprehensive: it is highly likely that many pre-Viking cults have vanished without trace. Yet through these sources we can glimpse something of the local, rather than just the metropolitan, culture of devotion.

The first conclusion must be that by 1100 many local saints were, as William of Malmesbury put it, 'bare names':[30] in their own churches they were venerated as ancient founders and patrons, but little else was known of them. Secondly, though, a very high proportion of the minor figures were thought to have lived in the late seventh or eighth centuries, the 'age of saints' attested by genuine sources. The third point is the very strong monastic association of recorded saints: at a rough count we can recognize about 120 pre-Reform English cults at places which are identifiable as minsters, about twenty at places which are not. This was evidently a world in which a saint's memory was most effectively promoted in a religious community. Indeed, if we can take the recording of saints to have been as arbitrary and incomplete as the character of the evidence implies, a situation in which virtually every religious community had its own saint does not seem inherently implausible.[31] Of course, other kinds of saint may have existed, but the very fact that we know of so few whose cults were not based at minsters carries its own message about the milieu within which ritual memory was preserved.

Where any personalities at all are ascribed to local saints, they fit into fairly clear groups. Royal males are either king-founders, honoured for their generosity (and attractive hero-figures for the laity) but usually too secular and violent personages to be wholly plausible saints, or prince-martyrs whose cults tended to be promoted for political or didactic ends.[32] An obscure category of monastic and clerical males can be understood as priest-abbots, minster-provosts, and the like. More numerous and important are the royal abbesses and the hermits. The 'holy cousinhood' of late seventh-century princesses are impressive patron-figures in early monastic culture. Respected in their own day as astute politicians who fended off royal and noble encroachers on monastic lands, they were celebrated in later hagiography for fending off royal and noble suitors. The status of these ladies as virgins and abbesses must have made them easier hagiographical material than their

---

[30] *GP* 202.

[31] These (inevitably very impressionistic) statements are based on Blair 2002*a*.

[32] Ridyard 1988; Thacker 1985; Cubitt 2000. Yorke 2003*b*: 119–20 suggests that the cults of males who died violent deaths, which is unparalleled on the Continent at the time, may have reflected older ideas about the religious importance of the violent deaths of princes.

fathers and brothers, and family solidarity was doubtless reinforced by genuine regard within communities for capable heads whose impact had been formative, and who were remembered with reverence and affection.

Yet they could earn their cults as much through connections and worldly wisdom as through personal piety, and be remembered as much for their success in secular life as for their reputation inside the monastic enclosure. Nothing illustrates this better than the foundation-legend of Minster-in-Thanet (Kent), which has a good chance of embodying an essentially pre-Viking tradition.[33] Its heroine is 'Domne Eafe'—daughter of King Eormenred of Kent, sister of three saints (Æthelred, Æthelberht, Eormengyth), mother of four others (Mildburh, Mildgyth, Mildthryth, Merefin), first abbess of Minster—who cunningly secures its eighty-hide endowment on Thanet. Her brothers are entrusted to their cousin King Ecgberht of Kent, who allows his wicked steward Thunor to murder them and bury them under the high seat in the king's hall. The bodies are marked by a miraculous column of light; the king fears God's wrath and summons a council, which advises him to pay Domne Eafe a wergild in compensation for her martyred brothers. The king takes her to Thanet, where she asks for as much land as her hind can run around in one lap—knowing secretly that the hind is trained always to run before her. The king agrees, and the hind sets off at a great pace. When they have circuited the land and reached the place called *Thunoreshlæw* ('Thunor's barrow'), the exasperated Thunor exclaims, 'Sire, how long will you pay heed to this dumb animal which will run about all this land? Will you give it all to the woman?'—whereupon the ground opens and swallows him. This strange amalgam of history and folklore, foreshadowing a good deal of later minster-based hagiography, shows how crucial to the status of minsters was the perceived status of their founder-saints: their family connections, their activities in the political arena and in the landscape, their access to divine protection.

Hermits are in a class of their own to the extent that their careers in life were by definition not based at minsters. In practice this distinction is not

---

[33] See Rollason 1982 and Hollis 1998. The three Latin sources are of *c.*1000 onwards; three Old English fragments seem to derive from an archetype which was earlier than the extant Latin versions, and which contained elements which the post-Reform hagiographers found disconcerting. The case for an early origin is cumulative and circumstantial: Hollis instances the interest in female genealogy, the acquisition of monastic land as a wergild (cf. Bede's account of Gilling: above, p. 85 n.), and Domne Eafe's purposeful guile in the matter of the hind (which the other versions sanitize as a meek surrender to providence). The complex dissemination of overlapping fragments of the story implies that it was well established at least by *c.*1000. It would go too far to claim that we have here an undiluted eighth-century source, but its assumptions and priorities are early ones, and there are decidedly odd features (for instance Eormengyth's burial in the open countryside: below, p. 232) which do not look like tenth- or eleventh-century hagiography.

so clear-cut as it seems. Hermits were often recruited from the monastic life—as, most obviously, were Cuthbert and Guthlac—and Wilfrid's monastic 'family' included anchorites.[34] Some hermitages were controlled by minsters along with other outlying chapels and holy sites, and some (again notably Guthlac's) actually became minsters.[35] But this is one area where the dominance of the monastic culture may to an extent mislead us. By the eleventh century, some of the major reformed houses had accumulated hermits' relics from obscure places. This process could have happened much earlier: relic-cults at outlying hermitages may at all periods have been perceived by minsters as alternative sites of power, to be controlled or suppressed. Whether associated with minsters or not, hermits may have enjoyed considerable spontaneous support, and are one possible link between the ecclesiastical high culture and the undisciplined, suspect world of charismatic popular religion.

From the 690s, the founder-saints of the most prestigious English minsters could be honoured by the translation of their bodies into above-ground coffins or shrines, a practice recently fashionable in Gaul. The cases which Bede has made famous are Æthelthryth at Ely (in 695) and Cuthbert at Lindisfarne (in 698), but we also know that the relics of two abbesses of Minster-in-Thanet, Mildthryth and Eadburh, had been translated into different churches, presumably for special veneration, by 748 and 804 respectively.[36] At Crowland, the hermit Guthlac (d. 714) was raised a year after his death into a monument 'which now we see built by King Æthelbald [of Mercia, 716–57] with wonderful structures of embellishments in honour of the divine power'.[37] It is likely, though, that these very opulent and well-publicized translations were in reaction to special pressures from politics or inter-monastic competition, and the practice did not become general: most Anglo-Saxon saints probably remained undisturbed for centuries in their below-ground graves.[38] The contemporary setting of more domestic—so perhaps more typical—minster-based cults may be illustrated by two examples, both in north-eastern Yorkshire, where sculpture reveals a world barely reflected in written sources.

The first concerns an Abbess Æthelburh who, according to Wilfrid's biographer, accompanied Abbess Ælfflaed of Whitby to King Aldfrith's deathbed

[34] 'All his abbots and anchorites' hastened to the ailing Wilfrid, and a member of his *familia* named Caelin left a hermit's life for administrative duties at Ripon and was then allowed to return to it: *VW* cc. 62, 64 (pp. 134, 138).

[35] Below, p. 218.

[36] *HE* iv. 19 (pp. 392–6) for Æthelthryth; *HE* iv. 30 (pp. 442–4) and *VCB* c. 42 (pp. 290–5) for Cuthbert; S 91, S 160, and Hollis 1998: 59–61, for Mildthryth and Eadburh. For the English practice of translation and its Gallic background see Thacker 2002: 45–8, 54–62.

[37] *VG* c. 51 (p. 162).   [38] Blair 2002*a*: 490–4.

in 705. Given that the minster at Hackness was a cell of Whitby, it is not hard to infer that the entry 'in Hacannessa sancta Ethelburga' in one of the twelfth-century resting-place lists refers to the same lady.[39] That would be the end of it, were it not for the lucky survival in Hackness church of fragments of an elaborate eighth- or early ninth-century memorial cross (Fig. 18). Its inscriptions include the phrases *Oedilburga beata . . . semper* ('blessed Æthelburh . . . always . . .'), *semper tenent memores olmus tu . . . te mater amantissima* ('[your community/devotees?] are always mindful [of you?], . . . most loving mother . . .') and *religiosa abbatissa Oedilburga orate pro* ('. . . religious Abbess Æthelburh pray for [them?]').[40] This eloquently inscribed memorial, probably set up several decades after her death, speaks of veneration rather than mere commemoration: in the eyes of the community, its 'most loving mother' had the status of a saint.

The second case, at Kirkdale, shows how veneration of the special dead can occasionally be inferred from physical evidence alone. This church, on the site of what seems to have been a wealthy pre-Viking minster, contains a pair of exceptionally opulent late eighth- or early ninth-century graveslabs.[41] One is carved on the surface with a long-stemmed cross, originally with an inlaid metal boss, surrounded by plant-scrolls; the treatment of the edges suggests that it formed the lid of a high tomb, with recessed panels on the sides and ends. The second is carved to imitate an elaborately decorated textile pall, the hanging tassels of which are represented around the edges of the slab. In seventh-century Francia, draped palls were used for the specific purpose of distinguishing saints' shrines from mere tombs.[42] Not only must the Kirkdale slabs have commemorated exceptionally important people; one of them may lay claim to an explicit mark of sainthood.

While this example could illustrate a status aspired to rather than a status necessarily achieved, the distinction was less meaningful in the ninth century than it would be after the twelfth. As Æthelburh's epitaph perhaps illustrates, the line between the respect due to an honoured head or founder and the veneration due to a saint was hazy. The ninth-century poem 'De Abbatibus', describing an unknown Northumbrian minster, affords some access to this conceptual world. The abbots are praised in turn for their learning, piety, and beneficence, in language appropriate to saints even though none is explicitly so described. When the founder Eanmund died 'the band of brothers placed the limbs of their revered father in a fitting tomb under the roof

[39] *VW* c. 59 (p. 128); *HE* iv. 23 (p. 412); *The Chronicle of Hugh Candidus*, ed. W. T. Mellows (Oxford, 1949), 64.

[40] Lang 1991: 135–41 and ills. 454–66.   [41] Lang 1991: 161–3 and ills. 558–67.

[42] Thacker 2002: 63–4.

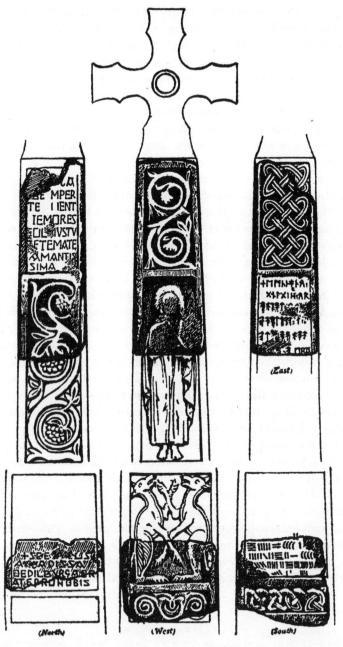

18. *Hackness* (Yorks.): the memorial cross for 'Æthelburh, most loving mother'. (Reconstruction from W. G. Collingwood, *Northumbrian Crosses of the Pre-Norman Age* (London, 1927), fig. 75.)

of the church',[43] an unusual honour which suggests high veneration. In the idealized church of the poet's vision, 'a sparkling vestment of fine linen covered the top of a tomb, which had the consecrated bones of some saint in the heart of its interior'.[44] The whole poem is charged with devotional impulses ready to focus on suitable objects: it is hard to think that any minster community which generated this kind of emotional atmosphere would have lacked its own saint for long.

As the Minster-in-Thanet story illustrates, the importance of at least some cults extended outside the monastic precincts: into dependent territories where divine power might reinforce proprietorship, and into a lay world of oral legend. The relationship between the stable (often aridly stable) idiom of saints' lives, and the kaleidoscopic fluidity of folklore, is especially hard to fathom when we can only approach it through the former. Yet the attempt is worth making: it is not impossible that genuine traces of how the seventh-to ninth-century laity perceived the cults in their local minsters may lie fossilized in hagiography. Do our sources show us episodes and motifs which students of oral history would recognize?

When great saints had to be glorified to inspire the laity, even Bede relaxed his normal reticence about anything smacking of popular superstition. Thus we know that sites and objects associated with Cuthbert's life, death, and burial drew pilgrims from far and wide; that his tomb was envisaged as attracting an 'influx of fugitives and criminals of every sort'; that people were cured by splinters from Bishop Eorcenwald's horse-litter, preserved by his 'disciples'; and that the West Saxon laity took earth from the spot where Bishop Hædde died to cure sick men and cattle.[45] On Bede's evidence, the cult of King Oswald of Northumbria (d. 642) had an extensive popular following involving dust from his death-site, splinters from the stake on which his head was transfixed, and a veneration of his dismembered body which had distinctly pagan undertones.[46] In these stories Bede recycles material that is recognizably vernacular folklore, giving it narrative coherence and moral purpose.[47]

These well-known passages are usually discussed as though they were exceptional. But probably the only exceptional thing about them is that Bede had special reasons for writing them: the sort of behaviour that they display, in which a saint's cult embodies some accommodation between ecclesiastical

---

[43] *DA* ll. 399–400 (p. 33).   [44] *DA* ll. 739–41 (p. 58).

[45] *VCB* cc. 23, 37, 41, 44–6 (pp. 230–4, 278–80, 288–90, 296–306); *HE* iv. 31–2 (pp. 444–8); Thacker 1992*a*: 166–8; *HE* iv. 6 (p. 354); *HE* v. 18 (p. 514). See also Thacker 2002: 66–71; Cubitt 2002.

[46] *HE* iii. 9–13 (pp. 240–54). Cf. Thacker 1995; Stancliffe 1995*b*; Cubitt 2000; Flint 1991: 383.

[47] McNamara 1994.

culture and popular magic, may have been perfectly normal. The gap in English hagiography between the mid eighth century and the late tenth means that the sources showing a broader base for these practices date from long after Bede's day, and they will be discussed in a later chapter.[48] But the Minster-in-Thanet story, which has more claim to be early than most, illustrates both the incorporation into monastic legend of folklore motifs—the column of light, the villain swallowed by the earth, the pitting of woman and animal against the powers of the world[49]—and its use to explain and define the local landscape. The course of the hind, divinely sanctioned by Thunor's punishment, makes the estate boundary inviolable; the existence of *Thunoreshlæw*, presumably an ancient barrow which had become associated with the pagan god Thunor, is rationalized by foisting that name on a wicked royal councillor. The sorts of landmarks that Bede's stories imply—Hædde's death-site, the place where Oswald raised his cross, the ground where the water from washing Cuthbert's body was poured away—are abundant in the eleventh- and twelfth-century texts, as is the interpenetration of hagiography and folklore: they point to intensely local kinds of popular devotion.

The model of conflicting cultures espoused by French historians of the last generation—a 'clerical' culture aggressively imposed on a 'folkloric' one[50]—seems inappropriate to this world. Anglo-Saxon society, including monastic society, was based on kinship bonds that operated vertically as well as horizontally, and bridged between ecclesiastics and laity just as they did between nobles and farmers. Minsters collaborated in assimilating folklore into the legendary lives of real people, and probably too in recycling it back, thus restructured, into oral legend. The saint-legends are one line of approach to a well-integrated Christian culture, ultimately mediated through the minsters. The geographical framework within which that culture existed is another, and we need to get some grasp on it before pursuing the more immediate and personal aspects of relations between ecclesiastics and laity.

The landscape of minsters: distribution and influences

By 750 the English kingdoms contained many minsters: to suggest a precise figure would be rash, but it must have reached the hundreds. A great deal of listing and mapping remains to be done, but it it is possible to gain at least a general sense of their geographical distribution and regional character, and also of their accessibility or otherwise from lay settlement. The following

---

[48] Below, pp. 475-7.   [49] Cf. Hollis 1998: 58.   [50] Below, n. 192.

sketch[51] is, needless to say, based on extremely incomplete written and archaeological evidence. Nonetheless, some broad patterns are so strong as to transcend the bias of the sources. They provide a useful background to the problems of territorial organization and pastoral care which will be addressed shortly.

The most striking fact is that important minsters founded before *c.*680 concentrate heavily on the east coast and its river-estuaries. This is as true of Northumbria, with its great minsters at the mouths of the Tyne, Wear, Tees, and Esk, and inland as far as the Pennines (Lastingham, York, Ripon, Hexham),[52] as it is of the south-east, with its clusters along the Kent coast (Lyminge, Folkestone, Dover, Minster-in-Thanet), on the Thames estuary (Reculver, Minster-in-Sheppey, Bradwell, Wakering, Tilbury, Barking), and up-river via London and Chertsey to the upper Thames.[53] Between these areas, a series of ill-recorded but early and important sites—Iken, Elmham, *Dommoc, Cnobheresburg*, Ely, Peterborough, Threekingham, Bardney, Caistor—were scattered along the East Anglian and Lincolnshire coasts and in their hinterlands, especially in the Middle Anglian zone on the river-routes to the Wash.[54] The visibility of this pattern is all the more striking given the lack of early charters from most of these regions. There is also an impression (but a hazy one, drawn mainly from archaeology) of a busier and more crowded monastic infrastructure in eastern England, with small monastic sites sown especially thickly in East Anglia, and dependencies of big ones (Hackness, *Osingadun*) in Northumbria.[55]

Culturally, this pattern reflects the strong orientation of early English monasticism towards north Francia. Minsters associated with well-travelled ecclesiastics (such as Iken, *Dommoc*, or Monkwearmouth-Jarrow), or with the family networks of Frankish-influenced nuns (such as Minster-in-Thanet, Ely, or Whitby), looked out across the Channel and North Sea for their inspiration, and in turn influenced communities much further inland (as both Iken and the Kentish nunneries did to Much Wenlock).[56] But there is an equally clear economic context. The regions of eastern England were wealthier than others, though for rather different reasons: the great

[51] It may be read in conjunction with the more detailed region-by-region survey of the fortunes of minsters after 850 (below, pp. 298–320). The remarkable map in Wormald 1982*a*: 71 requires only limited revision after nearly twenty years of research. There is now, however, an obvious need for a full catalogue.

[52] Roper 1974; Cambridge 1984 (cf. Blair 1995*a*: 201 n. 39); R. Morris 1989: 133–9.

[53] Rollason 1982; Brooks 1984: 180–203; Blair 1991*a*: 91–108; Blair 1996*a*.

[54] West and others 1984; Williamson 1993: 143–54; Stocker 1993; Keynes 1994; Warner 1996: 110–20, 127–33; Campbell 2000: 107–15; Sawyer 1998: 62–82; Ulmschneider 2000: 66–75; Oosthuizen 2001: 49.

[55] Below, pp. 206–12, 318–20.   [56] Above, pp. 42, 83, 85.

Northumbrian minsters were underpinned by the old, cattle-rich culture of north Britain, whereas the south-east and East Anglia were a precocious economic zone, using coinage widely and trading with Continental ports.[57]

Both economically and ecclesiastically, the south coast developed slightly later: it was only in the 680s that Sussex converted, and that Wessex adopted court-sponsored monasticism.[58] Over the next generation a network of minsters emerged in the Sussex coastal plain, separated from the lower Thames group by the great wooded common of the Weald.[59] In central Wessex, the core zone of early monastic development was around the confluence of the Test and Itchen at Southampton Water.[60] During the decades around 700, however, a series of important minsters were founded in what are now Wiltshire, Dorset, and Somerset, landmarks in a westwards expansion of the West Saxon ecclesiastical establishment seen also in the creation of the see of Sherborne around 705.[61]

This monasticization of the south-west, which extended as far as east Devon, penetrated into what had been Christian British territory.[62] No less important was the region's proximity to the Severn estuary and thus to a different nexus of contacts, with Ireland and the Irish sea. The Severn-side zone where Mercia bordered Wessex was a meeting-place of diverse influences: Malmesbury minster may have been founded by a mid seventh-century Irishman, Bath a generation later was ruled by Frankish nuns, and Congresbury bears the name of a Welsh saint.[63] Further up the Severn and into the west midlands, we enter the region documented by the Worcester archive.[64] The build-up of foundations by various kinds of patron—sub-kings of the Hwicce in the late seventh century, nobles and royal thegns in the early eighth, bishops of Worcester, King Offa—illustrates a pattern which can be glimpsed in fragments elsewhere, and is likely to be typical. Probably it extends across Gloucestershire to meet the important group of west Oxfordshire and Berkshire minsters around the head-waters of the Thames.[65] Westwards and northwards, in Herefordshire and Shropshire, the minsters seem to thin out, and we should probably envisage a few very important

[57] Above, p. 84; below, pp. 256–7.
[58] Yorke 2003*b*: 28.
[59] *Selsey*; Blair 1997; Rushton 1999.
[60] Hase 1988; Hase 1994: 52–69; Ulmschneider 2000: 66–75; Ulmschneider 2003.
[61] Aston 1986; Yorke 1995; Pitt 1999; Hall 2000.
[62] Above, pp. 31–3. Boniface was educated in a minster at Exeter: Willibald, 'Vita S. Bonifatii', c. 1 (ed. W. Levison, *MGH, SRG* (Hannover, 1905), 6–7); his association with Crediton is recorded only in the 1330s (Orme 1980).
[63] Sims-Williams 1975; Sims-Williams 1988: 165–74; Yorke 1995: 162–3.
[64] Hooke 1985; Sims-Williams 1990; Bassett 1998.
[65] Blair 1994: 56–77.

communities (notably Leominster and Much Wenlock) established in a continuing landscape of smaller and more numerous British Christian sites.[66]

In the north-west, St Cuthbert's activities around Carlisle point to the same regular trans-Pennine contacts as the Anglian-period sculptures, which overwhelmingly look to eastern Northumbria.[67] As the excavated site at Whithorn underlines,[68] this was a Northumbrian colonial church: it is characteristic that Dacre, the only minster in the region apart from Carlisle to occur in a pre-Viking written source, turns up in the context of a St Cuthbert miracle.[69] Sites with pre-Viking sculpture cluster along the coastal plain, and run up the Eden valley from Carlisle via Dacre and Lowther to Kirkby Stephen.[70] The absence of early churches from the lightly settled Pennines needs no more explanation than it does from the wooded Weald, though such river-head sites as Otley, Ripon, and Kirkby Stephen did in fact penetrate their slopes from both sides.

In most regions, the further development of the monastic map through the eighth century and beyond can be perceived in sporadic written and archaeological sources.[71] Some relatively settled areas, notably Buckinghamshire, Northamptonshire, and Leicestershire, still seem very thin,[72] and it is impossible to be certain whether they really did have fewer minsters than, say, Worcestershire or whether the contrast is simply in the surviving sources. The overall impression is of a distribution which was relatively consistent in essentials, but was moulded to the constraints of local topography, and perhaps too (though this is much harder to perceive) of local settlement patterns: thickest along coasts and river-valleys, thinnest in upland terrain and pasture zones, but providing reasonable coverage for most settled land. The experiment of drawing circles of three- to five-mile radius around the minsters of some sample areas suggests that by 800 most people who lived in England, outside the highland zone, were within what they would have considered a reasonable walking distance from a minster (see for instance Fig. 19). No view of how minsters interacted with the ordinary laity can afford to forget the scale of the impact: the sites must have become familiar features in the landscape, their communities a familiar part of rural society.

---

[66] Croom 1988; above, pp. 21, 27. Note the comment of Dark 1994*b*: 220–3, that in Wales the emergence of great monasteries such as Meifod, combined with a decline of small religious foci in the countryside, suggests evolution in the direction of mother-churches rather like the English ones.
[67] *VCA* iv. 5, 8, *VCB* c. 27 (pp. 116, 122, 242); McCarthy 1996; Bailey and Cramp 1988: 10–23.
[68] Above, p. 28; below, p. 187.
[69] *HE* iv. 32 (pp. 446–8).
[70] Bailey and Cramp 1988.
[71] Below, pp. 298–320, for more details.
[72] Bailey 1980*b*; Franklin 1982; Franklin 1985; Parsons 1996.

The territorial framework: secular and religious structures

To what extent this interaction took place within a framework of mutual obligation—pastoral care on the one side, financial support and parochial allegiance on the other—is the most controversial major strand in this book. The starting-point is the undoubted fact that when, after 1100, local sources become abundant, they reveal two tiers of parish: the familiar local ones, but also an obsolete, often near-invisible layer of older and larger parishes preserved only in the trace-elements of payments and other recurrent obligations owed by 'daughter-' to 'mother'-churches. From the late 1960s, ecclesiastical and local historians set about unpicking these tangled webs of relict rights, and reconstituting 'mother-parishes' from their fragmented components.[73] It became obvious that in many parts of England, the mother-churches of these parishes were often identical with documented or archaeologically attested pre-Viking minsters. Perhaps reflecting the general enthusiasm of local historians in these decades for W. G. Hoskins's dictum that everything in the landscape is older than we think, these studies moved with increasing confidence to the view that here was a primary and coherent parochial system, established in all the Anglo-Saxon kingdoms during the century or so after conversion, which enabled minsters to perform pastoral care and exact parochial allegiance within defined territories.

This view—which in a modified form I still hold—encountered a perhaps predictable reaction in the mid 1990s, from scholars who argued that the parishes which can be observed fragmenting from *c.*1100 onwards were themselves no older than the tenth century, the work of West Saxon kings who built order out of anarchy.[74] Subsequent and current local work has tended to take the middle position that there was indeed fundamental reorganization in the tenth century, but that it probably did make use of earlier quasi-parochial structures of some kind.[75] Until these studies have reached the point of mapping the parochial geography of all England, and correlating it with a catalogue of minsters which will trace their individual fortunes through the centuries, an extended revisiting of the debate is unprofitable. This discussion will therefore be brief, and will deal mainly with general principles rather than case-studies.[76]

[73] Notably Kemp 1968 and Hase 1975; the starting-point, though, was William Page's pioneeering survey (Page 1914–15).

[74] Cambridge and Rollason 1995; Rollason 1999 (which was available in draft in 1995); with response by Blair 1995*a*. Qualifications of other kinds were raised at the same time by Cubitt 1992 and Cubitt 1995.

[75] e.g. Pitt 1999; Hadley 2000*a*.

[76] But see below, pp. 298–320, for an outline survey of work to date on the various regions of England.

An early parochial system is plausible in direct proportion to the coherence of secular land-organization and land-lordship: just as strong governance by bishops was difficult in a society without towns, so territorial parishes would have been hard to establish in one lacking means of demarcating, assessing, and exploiting the land. It is therefore in the parochial model's favour that the seventh-century English had notably well-organized methods for doing precisely that. What is now a very large body of research, beginning with J. E. A. Jolliffe's in the 1930s, has recognized as the basic unit of Anglo-Saxon social organization the 'province', *regio*, 'lathe', or 'small shire': territories smaller than later counties and often comparable in scale and extent to hundreds, which indeed were often based on them.[77] Whether or not these entities (which often bore the names of kin-groups) were once independent 'kingdoms', or emerged within larger polities, is less important here than their role by the later seventh century as the basis of royal resource-collection. Where the system is fully visible in contemporary texts (which is only occasionally, though there is a good deal of late and indirect evidence), the territories were assessed in multiples of hides, responsible on a proportionate basis for the food-renders which supported itinerant courts.

Out of such provincial *regiones*, their assessments already established, were carved the bundles of hides which constituted the early monastic estates described in the last chapter, as for instance when King Osuiu allocated his twelve estates of ten hides each, six in Bernicia and six in Deira, or when King Æthelbald of Mercia gave Cyneberht his ten hides by the Stour.[78] These kings or their servants must have known where the lands lay, what ten hides amounted to, and how the food-renders from them could be split off from the rest and assigned to new recipients. This was 'extensive lordship', different from the more exploitative manorial regimes of later centuries,[79] but it shows a capacity to demarcate and apportion the land's resources in a fairly precise fashion. The existence of political and economic territories controlled by kings certainly does not prove the existence of parochial ones controlled by churches, but it does show that, given the will, a means existed to create

[77] See especially: Jolliffe 1933 (regular structure of Kentish lathes distinctively 'Jutish'); Barrow 1973: 7–68; Barrow 1975; Jones 1976 ('multiple estate' the archetypal land-management structure in both Welsh and Anglo-Saxon society); Campbell 1986: 95–7, 108–16 (provincial territories as a basis of royal power); Gregson 1985 and Blair 1989: 104–5 ('multiple estate' a misleading term because it confuses provincial territories with estates carved out of them); Bassett 1989*b*: 17–23 (also rejects 'multiple estates'; provincial territories as the first English kingdoms); Faith 1997: 8–14 (territories in the context of 'extensive lordship'); Hooke 1985: 75–116 and Blair 1991*a*: 12–30 (local studies).

[78] Above, pp. 72, 102; Blair 1989: 102–5, for the carving of the Chertsey monastic estate out of a putative Woking *regio*.

[79] Below, pp. 252–3, 369–71, for the early development of 'inlands' and for later Anglo-Saxon 'cellularization'.

them. The territories of regionally important churches were based in Ireland on the *túath* (folk-territory), in Brittany on the *plebs* (again folk-territory);[80] need English minsters, which were founded within the old provincial regions and often later emerged as their central places,[81] have been so different?

Kings controlled food-rents, but are unlikely to have designed structures for pastoral care: this they would surely have left to their episcopal advisers, or to their monastic siblings and children. It is easy to envisage conflicts between bishops, with an institutional and diocesan standpoint, and abbesses and abbots, with a local and territorial one, but in the circumstances of England around 700 the differences may have been less clear-cut. Bishops were aristocratic, and often trained within the monastic networks; and it was to these networks, as Bede's letter to Ecgberht illustrates, that schemes for top-downwards division of dioceses into pastoral territories almost inevitably returned. Dispute is likely to have centred on control over spiritual care to the laity and the revenues supporting it, not on the necessity of basing it at minsters.

In his letter to Ecgberht, Bede complains that remote Northumbrian villages owe tributes (*tributa*) to bishops who hardly ever visit them, and who take money (*pecunia*) from their flocks (*auditores*) while neglecting their souls.[82] The implication seems to be that it was normal for accessible as well as inaccessible places to pay episcopal 'tributes', and that these were meant to be in return for pastoral care. This duty of bishops to purvey spiritual ministry, and power to determine how it was delivered, is reiterated in the 747 *Clofesho* statutes: priests are to exercise their office by baptizing, preaching, and visiting 'through the places and regions of the laity (*per loca et regiones laicorum*) which are enjoined and committed to them by the bishops of the province'.[83] Given the amount of wishful thinking displayed at this council, the clause may not be describing actual English practice: to a large extent it could be an aspiration reflecting contemporary reforming initiatives on the Continent.[84] Bede's comments do indeed imply—at least in Northumbria— some institutionalized episcopal control, but it can be assumed that any bishops who reached the point of assigning 'places and regions' worked within existing structures.

Not all church dues in the formative period were necessarily paid to bishops. Archbishop Theodore directs that ecclesiastical tribute (*tributum ecclesiae*) should be levied 'according to the custom of the province' (in other

[80] Above, pp. 43, 47; below, p. 162.
[81] Below, p. 251.
[82] *Ep. E.* c. 7 (p. 410).   [83] *Clof.*747 c. 9 (p. 365).
[84] Cf. above, pp. 114, 117, 123. At exactly this time, the system of *pievi* in Italy was acquiring a progressively sharper territorial definition: Violante 1986: 145–82.

words on a hidage basis like food-rent?), so long as it does not burden the poor in tithes or other things;[85] unfortunately he does not specify its destination. But Bede, in his commentary on Ezra, attacks priests and ministers who demand 'a great weight and tax (*pondus et vectigal*) of secular things' and 'the payment (*sumptus*) owing to their office' without teaching their flocks or working for their salvation.[86] In the same work he rebukes 'those who build minsters with wonderful workmanship, but by no means establish teachers in them who might gather the people to God's works, but rather serve their pleasures and desires there', and in his letter to Ecgberht he reiterates the need to convert 'useless' minsters into pastorally active centres.[87] These passages, taken together, imply that early eighth-century Northumbrian minsters took obligatory payments, described in the vocabulary of secular taxation, from the ordinary laity, and that Bede at least perceived these—like the *tributa* paid to bishops—to carry a reciprocal obligation of pastoral care. He seems clear in his mind that minsters, however deficient in practice, were the normal and natural bases for this activity.

The reality may be that when kings first started to endow the Church on a large scale from the 660s onwards, they imposed new renders in kind, assessed in similar ways to the old ones, which would support minster-based priests to provide spiritual services under episcopal direction. But as monastic power was consolidated, these revenues may have been drawn inexorably into the minsters' direct control: because their local territorial power was in the end stronger, because aristocratic abbots and abbesses carried most weight, or because many bishops were themselves more attuned to monastic interests than to the rights and duties of their office. This reconstruction, tentative though it must be, is consistent with the now-familiar story of a seventh-century English Church which its founders intended to be run on Continental diocesan lines, but which in the event was fuelled by royal and aristocratic land-management strategies centred on minsters.

The problem can also be approached by looking backwards in time, from the church dues detailed in tenth- and eleventh-century laws and estate records. These are a miscellaneous and sometimes eccentric series of payments, which do not look like a programme imposed from above and suggest rather the codification of organically evolved practice.[88] The post-Viking

---

[85] *PT* II. xiv. 10 (p. 333); cf. Campbell 1986: 50, and Tinti 2003: 229–31. (In this chapter Theodore's Penitential is taken at face value: for a cautious acceptance of it as a reflection of Theodore's views at one remove, see Bischoff and Lapidge 1994: 150–3.)

[86] *BOE* iia. 359–60, 386 (and see ibid. 115, 248 for similar sentiments). This material is discussed by DeGregorio 2002 and DeGregorio 2004, and I am very grateful to Scott DeGregorio for sharing his work with me before publication.

[87] *BOE* iia. 303; above, pp. 109–11; cf. DeGregorio 2004: 50–1.   [88] Below, pp. 439–40.

sources invariably show them being paid to the local minsters (or their absentee proprietors), an arrangement which is first clearly visible in the 880s.[89] The only due for which we have explicit early evidence is churchscot, a yearly render of grain from each homestead at Martinmas which the laws of King Ine of Wessex (688–726) make obligatory, though without naming the recipients. It is possible that the widespread appearance of churchscot outside Wessex in late sources reflects the extension of Ine's law (via Alfred's) to other provinces during the formation of the English kingdom.[90] Nonetheless, Ine may be showing us, in its specifically West Saxon form, the sort of render which embedded social and economic systems would naturally generate in all English regions—levied, as Theodore says, 'according to the custom of the province'.

If the direction of such payments to minsters had become general as early as Bede's Northumbrian comments imply, it must have been as easy to know who owed churchscot to which minster as to know who owed food-rent to which royal vill. Any of the other customary payments—for burial ministrations, for repairing the church, for candles, and so on—which already existed in this period would have been allocated along similar lines; correspondingly, it would have been to the payers that the minsters owed their reciprocal duties of sacramental ministration, preaching, and pastoral care. Here is a conceptual framework—partly hypothetical, but entirely plausible—in which the idea of eighth-century minster-based parishes makes sense.

Such a system would have been built up over time rather than imposed at a stroke, and the early sources are not remotely adequate to show how consistently or comprehensively it operated. Even if Ine expected every West Saxon household to pay churchscot, there must be some possibility that minsters had a tighter grip on territories transferred directly to them than on those which remained in royal or aristocratic hands. Church dues were certainly not restricted to church tenants in the tenth century, but by then the hand of secular enforcement was heavier, and the estates belonging to at least the larger minsters had shrunk drastically. It seems most likely that the overarching provincial framework of social and economic obligation became a parochial framework in stages between the seventh century and the tenth. Around minsters we can envisage—not for the last time—circles of influence which enlarged and strengthened as the generations passed.

There is strong evidence from most parts of England that mother-parishes existed by the Norman Conquest; that they had undergone change, which usually culminated in greater or lesser degrees of fragmentation; and that the

---

[89] Below, pp. 158–60 (Bishops Cleeve and Bibury).   [90] Below, pp. 434–5.

mother-churches which controlled them included a high though not always overwhelming proportion of pre-Viking minsters (Fig. 35).[91] Proponents of late development might argue that a system created in the tenth century would naturally use the churches, new or old, which were locally important at the time: the pattern indicates continuity of churches, but not necessarily continuity of parishes. We can get a little further by asking whether mother-parishes had a symmetrical conformity to the structures of late Anglo-Saxon local government (as they most conspicuously did in Lancashire and Cheshire[92]) which might suggest relatively late origins, or whether they show a multi-layered complexity implying the re-working of older structures. For instance, Jonathan Pitt has suggested that underlying the strongly hundredal arrangement of Wiltshire's mother-parishes are anomalies pointing to an earlier, probably more variable, system.[93] Another approach is Teresa Hall's in Dorset, which reveals a strong correlation between the boundaries of mother-parishes and major geographical features.[94] These local studies carry conviction, and alongside wider patterns of regional variation and anomaly, they show that there are real difficulties with the model of late and uniform creation.

Building a circumstantial case from topographical and parochial evidence entails a level of detail inappropriate to a general book. It is, however, worth ending this section with a glance at one region which, from the wealth of its documentation and its relative stability between the ninth and twelfth centuries, offers the best chance of reconstructing early parochial developments. The Worcester archive records in exceptional detail a group of minsters on the Gloucestershire–Worcestershire border, many of which came into the bishop's hands during the eighth and ninth centuries. Correlation with the late parochial data shows that eight out of ten early minsters emerge as the mother-churches of subordinate chapels, and only two late mother-churches are not also recorded as early minsters (Fig. 19).[95] There is nothing to suggest that the region was more organized than others before 850, and the best explanation is that the lack of drastic upheaval during either the Viking or the Norman invasion has left a typical pattern unusually intact.

But even here it was not set in stone, as emerges from the evidence for churchscot payments and estate structure which, exceptionally, the Worcester charters preserve for us.[96] The fact that in 899 Ablington paid church-

---

[91] Below, pp. 298–320; cf. Blair 1995*a*: 199–203.   [92] Below, pp. 309–10.
[93] Pitt 1999, esp. 180–6.   [94] Hall 2000: 35–40.
[95] Blair 1995*a*: fig. 1, and (more accurately in some details) Bassett 1998: figs. 1–3, are the basis of the present Fig. 19.
[96] The following is indebted to Bassett 1998.

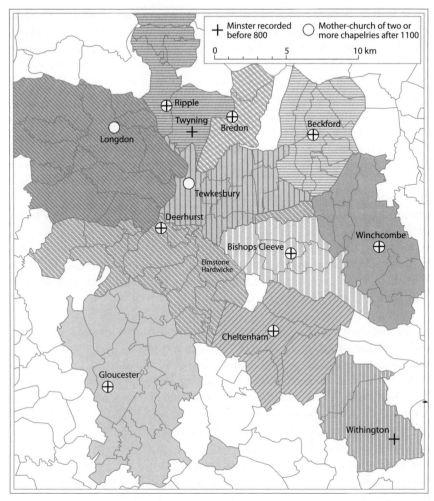

19. An area on the Gloucestershire–Worcestershire border, showing the correlation between pre-Viking minsters and post-1100 mother-churches. The different tones indicate the provable extents of the mother-parishes. (After Blair 1995*a*: fig. 1, corrected from Bassett 1998.)

scot to Bibury, only a mile away and recorded as its mother-church later, supports the model of parochial stability.[97] The same cannot be said of Elmstone Hardwicke, the churchscot from which was reserved to Bishops Cleeve in leases of 889 and *c.*900:[98] from 1283 it is recorded as a chapel of

[97] S 1279.
[98] S 1415, S 1283; see Sims-Williams 1990: 157, for the extent of the Bishops Cleeve territory.

Deerhurst.[99] Between these dates, Elmstone must have switched parochial allegiance from Cleeve minster, two miles to its east, to Deerhurst minster, four miles to its west. The explanation is probably tenurial: the 889 lease says that Elmstone had 'previously belonged to the minster of Cleeve', but in Domesday Book it figures as part of the Deerhurst minster estate.[100] Whereas Cleeve was one of several minsters that the bishops of Worcester took over, eventually absorbing their lands into those of the see,[101] Deerhurst remained independent and (at any rate in the mid eleventh century) had extremely powerful friends.[102] Another influence on the local parochial geography was Tewkesbury's mother-parish, a probable latecomer which may have been formed largely out of Deerhurst's in the tenth or eleventh century.[103] While the precise circumstances are obscure, we might envisage an exchange or re-allocation in which Deerhurst partly made up its losses at the expense of weak and fragmenting Cleeve.

So far as it goes, the later and more fragmentary evidence from other regions is consistent with the message of this one: that vested rights to parochial allegiance and church dues did exist before the tenth century, but that their stability could depend to some extent on local tenurial politics. Nor, in most regions, can we know in detail how much their final form owed to the lengthening arm of the English state from Alfred onwards. It is there-fore unrealistic to assert that a stable and regular mother-parish network was necessarily spread across the whole of England from the outset. The essen-tial point is that territorial organization did acquire an ecclesiastical dimen-sion, and that wherever this first becomes visible it seems to be constructed around minsters. To see it just as another kind of landlordly exploitation is inadequate: in this intensely reciprocal society, minsters could expect people at large to support them because they gave spiritual benefits in return. The extent to which the laity were bound into proto-parochial structures is thus inseparable from the extent to which they received pastoral ministrations.

The provision and organization of pastoral care

To examine the operations of the Church among ordinary people through limited, narrowly focused, and essentially prescriptive sources is a particu-larly challenging task. The first step is to recognize what was meant to happen

---

[99] *VCH Glos.* viii. 58. It seems likely from later evidence, and from the topography, that Uckington was attached to Elmstone.
[100] DB i. 166.   [101] Below, p. 328.   [102] Ibid.
[103] Bassett 1998: 10–18; Williams 2002: 16–18.

in theory, and it is at least a comfort that Bede, our most expansive and eloquent commentator, had a burning sense of the Church's duty to shepherd
the flocks of the unlearned with firm guidance and sound teaching. By the
740s, in the wake of his exhortations, measures for improving broad-based
pastoral care were being formulated in the same circles that were urging
monastic reform.[104]

If prescriptive sources deal mainly in aspirations, they do sometimes give
a sense of what could be taken for granted. For instance, Bede's complaint
to Bishop Ecgberht that many settlements in remote mountains and woods
had not set eyes on a bishop from one year to the next[105] implies an assumption that bishops did visit more accessible places. Around the figure of
Cuthbert, tramping between remote and scattered settlements to give his
skilled and inspiring teaching, Bede constructed what he evidently considered a realistic pastoral ideal.[106] Again, Bede's practice of handing out
English versions of the Creed and Lord's Prayer to 'many monolingual priests'
rather startlingly reveals a direct channel from the greatest scholar of the age
to Northumbrian peasants.[107] The 747 instruction that bishops should yearly
call together the people of all conditions and sexes, especially teaching those
who seldom (*raro*) heard the word of God and admonishing them to avoid
superstitions,[108] does not suggest groups untouched by Christian teaching.
From early in the eighth century, everyone was assumed to be Christian in
the formal sense that infant baptism was taken for granted.[109] One ordinary
late seventh-century Northumbrian mother was distraught when her infant
son died unbaptized, even if she held unorthodox ideas about the function
of the sacrament.[110] Reformers believed passionately that the laity should be
instructed well, and certainly thought that currently they were not instructed
well enough; it does not seem to have been on anyone's list of grievances that
they were not instructed at all.

We come now to the crux of the matter: by what means were Christian
belief and observance transmitted and fostered? The sources are few but solid,
and they permit a fairly confident answer: priests travelled around among

[104] Cf. above, pp. 108–12; for the pastoral ideals of Bede and Boniface, and their influence on
the 747 canons, see Thacker 1983, Thacker 1992*a*, Cubitt 1992, and Cubitt 1995: 99–124.
[105] *Ep. E.* c. 7 (p. 410).
[106] *VCB* cc. 9, 13, 14 (pp. 186, 198–202); cf. Thacker 1983: 139–43, and Foot 1989*b*: 46–7.
[107] *Ep. E.* c. 5 (pp. 408–9), 'multis sacerdotibus idiotis': Bede has just defined *idiotae* as those
who only know their own language. Cf. *Clof.747* cc. 10–12 (p. 366): priests are to interpret the
Creed, Lord's Prayer, mass, baptism, and the other offices in their own language, and to teach a
correct understanding of the Trinity and Creed, and the duties of baptismal sponsors.
[108] *Clof.747* c. 3 (pp. 363–4).
[109] Below, n. 139.
[110] *VW* c. 18 (p. 38); cf. Fletcher 1997: 277, and Wilson 2000: 226–7.

rural settlements, and their work was supervised by minsters.[111] The most natural conclusion, in other words, is that the territories from which minsters exacted dues, and which were unquestionably a framework for providing pastoral care to the laity by the tenth century, already had this function in the eighth.

Since this view is not universally accepted it may be useful to begin by looking at a wider context, both among the Celtic neighbours of the English and in parts of continental Europe. A large and increasing body of recent research on Ireland, Scotland, Wales, Brittany, and parts of France—the 'monastic zone' of north-western Europe as defined on pp. 75–6 above—has consistently recognized underlying structures of mother-parishes, and of pastoral mother-churches, which are essentially similar to those proposed here for England.[112] Especially useful here is south-eastern Brittany, where the unique Redon material reveals a network of regional churches staffed by groups of priests, built at the centres of the *plebes* and performing a focal, public role within them. These groups of priests were rarely more than seven miles apart (a spacing comparable to that of English minsters), and 'the density of their occurrence must suggest the existence of at least a proto-parochial structure'.[113] The head churches of the ninth-century *plebes* usually remain the parish and commune centres (and main settlements) today, though most parishes have been somewhat reduced by the foundation of lesser churches. The structure can be recognized from the 830s onwards, and must be pre-Carolingian.[114] Here then is an ancient and stable parochial system, strikingly similar in its topographical framework to the mother-parishes of English minsters, which beyond all doubt laid a foundation for spiritual and social interaction between clergy and people.

Returning to England, Willibald's 'Life of Boniface', referring to Wessex in the 680s, tells us that 'when any priests or clerics (*presbiteri sive clerici*) went out to preach to the people (*populares vel laicos*), as is the custom in those parts, and came to the settlement (*villa*) and the house of his father, ... [the child] began to converse with them on heavenly matters'.[115] That the centres from which such priests operated were minsters follows from the clear assumption of English eighth-century sources that all priests will live in religious communities, under the authority of abbots or *priores*.[116] Theodore's

---

[111] Cf. Foot 1989*b* and Foot 1999.

[112] Over-views: Blair 1995*a*: 210–12; Reynolds 1984: 81–90. Specific studies: Sharpe 1984*a*; Aubrun 1986: 11–68; Sharpe 1992; Charles-Edwards 1992; Macquarrie 1992; Pryce 1992*a*; Etchingham 1999: 239–89.

[113] Davies 1983: 191.

[114] Davies 1983, with agreement by Smith 1992: 180–1; cf. above, p. 43.

[115] Willibald, 'Vita S. Bonifatii', c. 1 (ed. W. Levison, *MGH, SRG* (Hannover, 1905), 5).

[116] Above, pp. 112–13.

ruling that anyone who moves a minster must leave behind (*dimittat*) 'a priest
for the offices of the church' at the old site implies that the minster has local
religious functions extending beyond its own community.[117] The supposed
late seventh-century foundation charter of Breedon-on-the-Hill stipulates
that the recipients of the land should 'appoint some priest of upright life and
good repute to deliver the grace of baptism and teach the Gospel to the
people assigned to him', and nominates 'Hædde, priest of marvellous
wisdom' as its first abbot.[118] This is a shaky text, but the several references
to priest-abbots of Kentish and Hwiccian minsters suggest that it may not
misrepresent contemporary expectations.[119] The lack of more references need
only worry us if we imagine that texts illuminate all areas of early medieval
life, or that writers would have been motivated to discuss rural pastoral work
whenever it took place.

The whole issue has been complicated, and perhaps clouded, by the
problem of the pastoral involvement of monks. Bede's ambivalent stance
makes it hard to see reality through his eyes: too good a clericalist to forget
that preaching and the sacraments were the preserve of ordained priests, he
was also too good a Gregorian not to set great store by the monastic example
to the laity.[120] After his death, sharper definition between the monastic and
clerical orders went hand in hand with a slow but steady rise throughout
western Europe in ordination and pastoral involvement of monks.[121] Yet the
problem may be less central than it has seemed. In the first place, we have
no real idea how many early English minsters were under the control of
monks: a high proportion were certainly in female hands, and relatively small
groups of priests ruled by priest-abbots or *praepositi* could well have been
common. Secondly, it is obvious that neither royal abbesses nor aristocratic,
highly educated monks will have passed their lives tramping the countryside:
the proposition that they exercised pastoral care is to be taken in the same
sense as the reference to an early ninth-century abbess acquiring land in

[117] *PT* II. vi. 7 (p. 320): 'Si quis vult monasterium suum in alium locum ponere, faciat cum con-
silio episcopi et fratrum suorum, et dimittat in priori loco presbiterum ad ministeria ecclesiae.'

[118] S 1803; cf. Keynes 1994: 37–43.

[119] e.g. S 12, S 23, S 1413; cf. Brooks 1984: 187–8; Sims-Williams 1990: 156–7, 170–1, 275, 356–7;
Sawyer 1998: 79–80. The point that pastoral work was mainly carried out by ordained clergy is
made by Coates 1996: 195–6.

[120] Cf. Thacker 1992*a*: 152–6. Bede's own homilies were addressed primarily but perhaps not
exclusively to fellow-monks: A. G. P. van der Walt, 'The Homiliary of the Venerable Bede and Early
Medieval Preaching' (unpublished London Ph.D. thesis, 1981), and cf. Thacker 1992*a*: 140–1.

[121] Constable 1982. Mayr-Harting 1976: 17 has useful comments on 'the process of monastic
clericalisation' during the seventh and eighth centuries. See also Rambridge 2003: esp. 373–7, for
the tradition of monastically based evangelization extending from Gregory via Bede to Alcuin; and
Mayr-Harting 1981: 377–8, for the pastoral functions of east Frankish monasteries.

Gloucestershire 'to drive her sheep there'.[122] Minsters were complex institutions, and the larger of them contained non-professed priests and subordinates of various grades.[123] The function of the rulers and core communities was surely to *provide* pastoral work rather than to *do* it, but deputy priests appear only on the edges of narratives whose frame of reference is inescapably aristocratic.

In this context, Bede's description of the Lindisfarne community before 664 deserves careful attention:

Wherever a cleric or monk (*clericus aliqui aut monachus*) came, he was joyfully received by all as God's servant. If they came across him on his travels, they ran to him and, bowing their heads, rejoiced either to be signed by his hand or to receive a blessing from his lips; they also paid diligent attention to his words of exhortation. On Sundays they flocked eagerly to the church or to minsters (*ad ecclesiam sive ad monasteria*[124]), not to refresh the body but to hear the word of God. If some priest (*siquis sacerdotum*) happened to come to a settlement (*in vicum*), the inhabitants crowded together, eager to hear from him the word of life; for the priests or clerics (*sacerdotibus aut clericis*) came to settlements for no other reason than preaching, baptizing, visiting the sick, and in short to care for their souls.[125]

As in his account of Cedd at Tilbury,[126] Bede is here describing specific arrangements which must have made sense to him. Cedd appoints priests and deacons to teach and baptize in two places where he also gathers *famuli Christi*; at Lindisfarne it is *sacerdotes* and *clerici* who preach, baptize, and visit the sick, though both *clerici* and *monachi* bless and exhort people whom they meet on their travels. In both cases Bede describes establishments containing monks and priests, and in both cases he seems to ascribe formal pastoral functions to priests only. The formulation of these passages is distinctly tentative, and it is hard to know how far the distinctions which they draw stem from Bede's own perceptions of, and worries about, monastic as against clerical functions. He does not, however, seem to be in any doubt that a minster of monks may contain ordained men for whom pastoral care is a proper activity.

How far did the minsters of Bede's own day, which he so castigated for their laziness and luxury, identify with such pastoral ideals? The subject lies

---

[122] Sims-Williams 1990: 145.

[123] Above, p. 82. Cf. Bede's story of the royal abbess Æthelhild (*HE* iii. 11, p. 248): 'aperiens ianuam monasterii, exivit ipsa cum una sanctimonialium feminarum ad locum virorum, et evocans presbyterum . . .' See below, pp. 255–6, for lower-status people at minsters.

[124] I am unable to elucidate this phrase. What difference is implied between 'church' and 'minsters'? And why is *ecclesiam* singular, *monasteria* plural (the reverse might have been more explicable)?

[125] *HE* iii. 26 (p. 310). Cf. *VCB* c. 9 (p. 186): 'Erat quippe moris eo tempore populis Anglorum, ut veniente in villam clerico vel presbytero, cuncti ad eius imperium Verbum audituri confluerent.'

[126] *HE* iii. 22 (pp. 282–4); cf. above, p. 68.

outside the range of writings—scholarly and devotional on the one hand, legal and tenurial on the other—which survive from them. But a source which does speak to us is the iconography of their lavishly carved stone crosses, and of the coins which some of them may conceivably have minted. Ian Wood has observed that the late eighth- and ninth-century crosses at Otley (Yorks.) bear strongly sacramental and evangelistic imagery—a vested mass-priest, busts and symbols of the Evangelists, an evocation of Christ's injunction to the apostles to be 'wise as serpents and innocent as doves'— and suggests that the site was a clerical out-station of the see of York.[127] The interpretation of the iconography is convincing; the inference of a specific- ally episcopal and clerical community need not necessarily follow, unless one thinks that minsters did not in general have evangelical concerns or contain ordained men. In fact the more recent work of Jane Hawkes has highlighted the rarity of those schemes, as on the Ruthwell cross and the Wirksworth slab, which depict introspective themes such as humility and obedience, or are essentially liturgical. More typically (Fig. 20), the crosses stress Christ's divine nature and ministry, the authority of his earthly Church and its sacraments, the centrality of the Evangelists and the Gospels, the terrors of judgement:[128]

such carvings, displayed on highly visible large-scale monuments in very specific set- tings, were intended, at a number of levels, to exhibit and celebrate, in permanent and public form, the function and identity of the Church in Anglo-Saxon England as the means by which each believer was able to participate in the mysteries of Christ.[129]

And commenting on the sophisticated Christian imagery of the early eighth- century sceatta coinage, Anna Gannon speculates whether their wide cur- rency among the laity offered a vehicle for preaching: 'part of pastoral commitment, as sermons in miniature for edifying meditations.'[130]

　If this material has any general message, it is of establishments confident of their standing in the outside world as appointed mentors to the Christian people. Minsters may not always have been assiduous in their pastoral role, but it provided one of the means by which they constructed their own identities. The theory, the expectations, and the structures were all in place: but what did they amount to in practice?

---

[127] Wood 1987.
[128] Hawkes 1995, Hawkes 1999; Hawkes 2001: 238–45, Hawkes 2002, Hawkes 2003*a*; cf. Lang 1999 and Lang 2000: 115–18, on apostolic imagery affirming 'the church's authority and its historic credentials'. The evangelistic emphasis is not confined to Northumbria: the probably eighth-century shaft at Lypiatt (Glos.) 'seems to represent Christ the Teacher, supported by Evangelists and by some of the trappings of a contemporary cleric' (Bryant 1990).
[129] Hawkes 2003*a*: 365.　　　[130] Gannon 2003: 190.

20. The sources of the Church's ministry and authority, as depicted on the ninth-century cross at *Sandbach* (Cheshire). Christ's Transfiguration is shown above a roundel in which he hands the Law to St Paul and the Keys to St Peter. (Hawkes 2002: fig. 6.5; Caroline Paterson and English Heritage.)

The lay practice of Christianity

'Let no man pray for them, nor God pity any of them,' jeered a group of mid seventh-century Tyneside farmers as they watched some monks drift helplessly out to sea on rafts: 'they have abolished people's old devotions (*veteres culturas*), and nobody knows how the new ones should be observed.'[131] This rare account of a negative response to pastoral care was retailed by Bede, to introduce a miracle showing the simple folk that the new ways were best after all. The story illustrates Bede's conviction that the ignorant should be taught by example, but neither he nor his readers can have been surprised that some 'rustics' at this early date remained unconvinced. This makes it all the more striking that they are presented as already invok-

[131] *VCB* c. 3 (pp. 162–4).

ing 'God' rather than 'the gods',[132] and already blaming the monks for abolishing the 'old devotions'. Is it really possible that paganism collapsed so readily?

The first distinction to be drawn—though it is one that we will almost immediately need to qualify—is between unambiguously religious practices, usually described as 'the cult of idols' or 'sacrifices to demons', and folk-magic such as charms and cures which the Anglo-Saxon Church neither suppressed nor probably, apart from a few hard-liners, seriously discouraged. Valerie Flint's sensitive study pictures a missionary church in early medieval Europe which engaged closely with popular culture, eager to reconcile the newly con-verted to the loss of their 'forbidden magic' by allowing them as much 'encouraged magic' as possible.[133] Many practices, of course, lay in a grey area, especially since the spectrum of ecclesiastical opinion was itself very broad. Priests at the coal-face could take a different view from reformers and theologians—sometimes to the point of being branded 'magicians' themselves.

In England the most remarkable fact about pagan worship is indeed how seldom it is mentioned, either in historical texts describing its survival or in prescriptive ones urging its suppression. To invoke a clerical conspiracy of silence is inadequate: sources for the conversions of Ireland, Francia, and later Scandinavia have altogether more to say about the pagan enemy. Bede merely tells us that Eorcenberht of Kent (640–64) was the first English king to order the destruction of idols, that some areas apostatized after the plagues of the 660s,[134] and that Sussex and Wight, the last pagan kingdoms, were converted in the 680s.[135] Theodore's Penitential, and the Laws of Wihtred of Kent (695), both impose penalties for making offerings to 'demons'.[136] Theodore's very severe penances for 'whoever causes grain to be burnt where there is a dead man for the wellbeing of the living and the house', and for a woman who 'places her daughter on the roof or in an oven to cure fever', suggest that these activities had pagan undertones which now elude us.[137] Eating horse-flesh had dubious resonances, perhaps because the horse was a sacrificial animal: Theodore was non-committal, but the legatine statutes of 786

---

[132] Unless this is a taunt along the lines of 'If their god is so powerful, let him save them!'

[133] Flint 1991; cf. Murray 1992: 198–205.

[134] *HE* iii. 8, iii. 30, iv. 27 (pp. 236, 322, 432); *VCB* c. 9 (p. 184).

[135] *HE* iv. 13, iv. 16 (pp. 370–6, 382–4).

[136] *PT* I. xv. 1, 5 (pp. 310–11); Wihtred, cc. 12, 13 (*Gesetze*, 13).

[137] *PT* I. xv. 2–3 (p. 310); cf. Flint 1991: 250–1, and Meaney 1989: 20–1, 30 (who makes the inter-esting speculation that putting *daughters*—not sons—in ovens or on roofs could have been to do with the transmission of magical powers from mother to daughter). Burnt grain may imply either a purification ritual or a food-offering: O'Brien 1999: 55, and cf. Wilson 2000: 301, for more recent parallels.

condemned the practice together with the ritual mutilation of horses.[138] Theodore is also the last English authority to concern himself with the problems of unbaptized adults.[139] Less than twenty years after the conversion of Sussex, it would be amazing if such issues did not arise.

Yet Bede seems to take it for granted that by his own day, two or three decades later, paganism had died out: certainly he treats the cycle of the pagan year, such as 'the month of cakes which they offered to their gods in it', as something which the English had put firmly behind them.[140] Thereafter no original English text gives any indication that worship of the old gods was a sin available to be committed, with the single exception that Ecgberht's 'Dialogue' of *c.*750 includes 'adoring idols' in a rather formulaic list of crimes barring ordination to the priesthood.[141] It is remarkable that the drafters of the otherwise comprehensive 747 canons did not include pagan worship in their list of forbidden practices, even omitting the references to it which appear in the Frankish prototype.[142] Given the range of lay shortcomings with which reformers at this time concerned themselves, it is hard to avoid the conclusion—strengthened by the extreme vagueness of even our earliest literary sources about the old religion—that paganism in the strict sense was simply not recognized as a problem.[143]

---

[138] *PT* II. xi. 4 (p. 325), as against Legatine Synod, c. 19 (*CED* iii. 458–9); Meaney 1992: 123–5. Cf. *PT* I. xv. 5 (p. 311) which forbids the eating of meat which has been sacrificed to demons. Boniface also objected to eating horse-meat: *Bon. Ep.* No. 28 (p. 50). Wormald 1991: 33–4, suggests that the horse-mutilation condemned in 786 had a Pictish context. See however Story 2003: 84–5, for the view that this and other attacks on 'pagan' practices in 786 are essentially the view of an outsider used to Mediterranean habits.

[139] *PT* II. iv. 1–3, II. xii. 18 (pp. 316–17, 328) (ibid. I. xiv. 28–30 (p. 310) imposes penances for letting children die unbaptized). The reference to baptizing the sick in Wihtred, c. 6 (*Gesetze*, 12), dating from just after Theodore, may also suggest adult baptism. Caedwalla of Wessex was unbaptized until shortly before his death in 689 (*HE* v. 7 (p. 470)), as was Guthlac's successor at Crowland (*VG* c. 48, p. 148). The Guthlac episode, located in 714, is perhaps the last explicit reference to Anglo-Saxon paganism, and Ine, c. 2 (*Gesetze*, 90), referring to Wessex c. 700, and *Clof.*747 c. 11 (p. 366), in 747, assume infant baptism. However, Bede seems to have envisaged the possibility of an adult catechumenate (Thacker 1992*a*: 141, 154). Cf. Foot 1992*a*: 186–9.

[140] Bede, 'De Temporum Ratione', c. 15 (*Bedae Opera de Temporibus*, ed. C. W. Jones (Cambridge, Mass., 1943), 211–13). Bede's account of the pagan festivals is discussed by Meaney 1985: 2–8, and (sceptically) by Page 1995. Commenting on 1 Samuel 5: 2, Bede writes: 'Et erexerunt ecclesias Christi in gentibus, manente adhuc non nullis in locis idolorum cultura' (*BOE* ii. 46–7); but this need not refer to England, and he could have been thinking of the contemporary English missions to the Continent.

[141] *Dialogue*, XV (p. 410). Other texts are discussed by Meaney 1992: 107–11, who gives reasons for discounting the Bede and Ecgberht Penitentials as original sources. For reasons given below, I do not regard Alcuin's two letters to the archbishops as referring to pagan survival.

[142] *Clof.*747 c. 3 (p. 364), compared with 'Concilium Germanicum', c. 5 (ed. Werminghoff, pp. 3–4). Practices not carried over from the 'Germanicum' to the *Clofesho* prohibitions include 'sacrifices of the dead' and 'immolations of sacrificial victims which foolish men make next to churches by pagan rite'. Cf. Meaney 1992: 112–13, and Cubitt 1995: 102–4.

[143] Cf. Wormald 1978: 66: 'the unqualified monotheism of *Beowulf* and *Waldhere* is of a piece with the Anglo-Saxon evidence as a whole. We know remarkably little about early English

But it must be admitted at once that in the area of popular belief, our sparse and one-sided texts are not remotely adequate to give us a clear picture of what was really going on. Comparative ethnography cannot make good the lack of Anglo-Saxon sources, but it can warn us that the reality was probably much more complex than we tend to assume, and suggest where some of the complexities may lie.[144] One of its messages is that the most bizarre syncretic mixtures can persist for centuries after conversion, whether in the form of indigenous belief-systems drawing in Christian theology and symbols to strengthen and legitimize themselves, or of the magical elements of paganism re-attaching themselves to a Christian core. In time the second process—what Alexander Murray calls 'swallowing up the religious core of paganism'[145]—tends to prevail, but older nature-magic and propitiatory rites can be remarkably successful in re-aligning themselves to the new power-source. Since this kind of Christianized magic survived in England in the tenth century,[146] its existence in the eighth seems certain. For the Anglo-Saxons as for the New World, 'the view of the extirpators and of too many subsequent thinkers that Christianity sat, in its purity, like a layer of oil over [indigenous] . . . magic is a highly misleading one'.[147]

How religious and magical activity is reported can be highly subjective: it is startling to find different first-hand accounts of a single Mesoamerican episode which interpret it on a spectrum ranging from unmodified shamanism to eccentric Christianity.[148] The response of educated writers can vary between over-optimism (by interpreting the superficial re-labelling of symbols as heartfelt conversion) and paranoia (by imagining scattered fragments of magic and folk-custom to reflect a pagan or satanic conspiracy). Reformers are especially prone to condemn—and even to call 'pagan'—observances which are fundamentally Christian but partake too much of indigenous culture for their liking. There is enormous scope for confusion between an observed culture's specifically religious rituals, and rituals which, however crude and distasteful the observers find them, are essentially social and secular and capable of accommodation to new belief-systems. To label customs that churchmen happened to dislike (such as eating horse-flesh?) as 'pagan survivals' is to accept a boundary drawn by critics, not by practitioners.

heathenism, and . . . the literature is among other indications that, by the eighth century at least, the Anglo-Saxon nobility was suffering from what amounts, by Celtic or Scandinavian standards, to collective religious amnesia.' Fell 1995 and Page 1995 reach very similar conclusions.

[144] Mesoamerica may be especially helpful: although the circumstances of colonization and initial enforced conversion were vastly different, the slow swallowing-up of an indigenous polytheistic system by imported Christianity since the mid sixteenth century generates some echoes of the faintly audible Anglo-Saxon debates and conflicts. In what follows I am especially influenced by Gruzinski 1989, Cervantes 1994, Vogt 1976, and Vogt 1981.

[145] Murray 1992: 199; above, p. 52.   [146] Below, pp. 473–86.

[147] Cervantes 1994: 58.   [148] Gruzinski 1989: 63–88.

Eighth-century laity, faced with the strictures of an Alcuin, might have responded as did a late sixteenth-century Mesoamerican rebuked by a friar for his superstitious ways: 'He accepted [it] with great humility and swore to me that this practice was not due to ancient belief but was simply their way of doing things, since he already believed in God and the creed of the Holy Mother Roman Church.'[149] Whether the existing 'ways of doing things', ritual, magical, and social, moulded themselves to the new belief-system and liturgical cycle, or continued to stand apart, is a better index of grass-roots Christianization than the Church's success in defining practices as illicit and stamping them out.

However much, or little, the overarching cosmological and moral framework was re-fashioned, we can take for granted the survival of magic, abundant beyond any possibility of suppression. Early medieval Europe contained hosts of diviners, soothsayers, sorcerers, seers, and wise-women, and there is no reason to think that England was any different.[150] For better or worse, the Church had to put up with them: the interesting question is whether there was mutual tolerance and influence, or a chasm between two cultures. The penetration of the repertoire of amulets and charms by relics and Christian symbols may provide some clue to the assimilation of folk-magic, in a post-pagan world, to the new religious core.[151]

The archaeological, canonical, and penitential evidence for amulets and magic has been well analysed by Audrey L. Meaney.[152] Objects of a more or less convincingly amuletic character occur regularly in graves (mainly female) through the whole time-span of furnished burial. Most early amulets are beads, notably of amber, but through the later sixth and seventh centuries the range broadens to include such items as fossils, animal teeth, and Roman coins. The waist-bags of odds and ends that occur in occasional female graves—no more one per generation in any cemetery—recall the magicians' kits described in some Continental sources, and point to a distinct category of 'wise-women'.[153] These apart, the evidence suggests a pervasive fashion for charms which developed new forms, like so much else, in the immediately pre-Christian generations, but which did not in itself mark any particular religious affiliation that we can now perceive.

The written sources, from Theodore through to the 747 canons and

---

[149] Markus 1990: 2. Ibid. 1–17 is a most illuminating critique of definitions of conversion and 'pagan survival'.

[150] Flint 1991: 59–70. In early twentieth-century north Spain there were still female 'diviners' who used cards and ribbons, or invoked the saints, to locate lost animals: Christian 1989: 195–8.

[151] Murray 1992: 192–3, 201.

[152] For this paragraph see Meaney 1981; Meaney 1985; Meaney 1992; and Geake 1997: 98–100.

[153] Flint 1991: 247–8; Meaney 1989: 10–12. Dickinson 1993.

beyond, regularly condemn amulets (*ligaturae*), phylacteries, incantations, auguries, auspices, divinations, and lot-casting—a list which shows, here as on the Continent, a particularly strong lay interest in, and clerical disapproval of, the various forms of fortune-telling.[154] Theodore gives a special penance for the 'woman who has performed incantations or diabolical divinations', corroborating the mainly female associations of amulets and amulet-bags in grave-deposits.[155] On the other hand he allows people possessed by demons to have stone or herb amulets (*petras vel holera*), so long as they do not use incantations.[156] There is in fact no reason to think that the Church took any steps against the mere carrying of amulets, as distinct from their use in magical rituals. What mattered was what the amulets were, how they were perceived, and what was done with them.

Around Theodore's time the amuletic repertoire in graves was being made in one way less threatening, in another more problematic, by the addition of new objects, of which some were explicitly Christian and others may have carried indirect Christian reference. In accordance with existing conventions, these objects were often still deposited in waist-bags, they could still be natural or animal-derived, and they were still largely confined to women. Especially intriguing are the cylindrical copper-alloy containers, none probably earlier than c.650, of which some fifty are known.[157] Many bear punched cruciform designs and one, from North Leigh (Oxon.), an unambiguous cross (Fig. 21). Occasionally they contain herbal residues and high-quality textile remains, and in one case a pair of hooked tags and a linked pin-set. It has been suggested that they are symbolic 'first-aid kits', but clothing fragments conserved in this fashion look more like Christian relics. It is fairly clear that they were ritual rather than functional, and likely—whether they were conceptually closer to amulet-bags or to reliquaries in the minds of their users—that they were made and used under Christian influence.

It is hard to know whether other new amulet types indicate conversion, availability, or simply fashion; Red Sea cowrie-shells, for instance, were popular in the seventh century but would in any case have been unobtainable earlier.[158] Teeth of horses, oxen, dogs, wolves, and boars seem to become

---

[154] Cf. Flint 1991: 117–21, 217–26.   [155] *PT* I. xv. 4 (p. 311).   [156] *PT* II. x. 5 (p. 324).
[157] Meaney 1981: 181–9; Meaney 1989: 9–10; Geake 1997: 34–5. For the analogous capsule-like containers from Frankish graves see Speake 1989: 38–9; Stiegemann and Wemhoff 1999: 440–2. These are based on Mediterranean prototypes, are sometimes associated with explicitly Christian objects, and are interpreted as personal Christian amulets; about 15% of them have been found to contain vegetable substances including camomile and henbane.
[158] Meaney 1981: 123–7; Geake 1997: 62–3. Like beaver-tooth pendants, cowries mainly accompany women and children, but with a preponderance towards women; they can occur in the same graves as beaver-teeth and metal boxes. Note that there is no contemporary evidence for their supposed sexual symbolism: it is only one of a range of meanings suggested by ethnographic parallels.

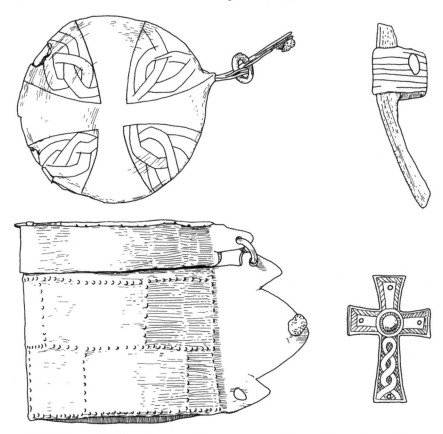

21. 'Christian amulets' from late seventh-century graves. Copper-alloy canister with cruciform decoration from *North Leigh* (Oxon.; after Meaney 1981: fig. V.*mm*); beaver-tooth mounted as pendant from *Cokethorpe* (Oxon.; after R. A. Chambers in *Oxoniensia*, 40 (1975), 192); cross-shaped silver mount from *Chartham Down* (Kent.; after C. Roach Smith, *Inventorium Sepulchrale* (London, 1856), pl. 11). Actual size.

less common in the later seventh century.[159] Instead, beaver-tooth pendants appear in relatively well-furnished burials of children and occasionally women, mostly mounted (unlike any of the other teeth) in gold or copper-alloy settings.[160] This is a deliberate new fashion, appearing at much the same

[159] Meaney 1981: 131–6; Geake 1997: 98–9. A woman in the probable nuns' cemetery at Nazeingbury (Essex) wore a shaped horse-tooth, but perhaps as a button or toggle rather than an amulet (Huggins and others 1978: 104–5). Remarkable in this context is the deposition of a boar-tusk in an *eleventh*-century grave at St Oswald's minster, Gloucester (Heighway and Bryant 1999: 214); a boar-tusk pendant was found in a ninth-century monastic occupation phase at Beverley (Armstrong and others 1991: 189 and fig. 131).

[160] Meaney 1981: 136–7; Geake 1997: 99. There is a wider context for the association of teeth with children: Wilson 2000: 280.

time as the metal boxes. It has been proposed that beaver-teeth were selected for traditional properties—strength and sharpness—as acceptable alternatives to carnivore teeth with heathen overtones.[161] A perception of beavers as good home-builders might also have encouraged the practice. But another possibility is influence from literate culture, associated with the medicinal properties of beavers or even with a word-play on *castor* (beaver) and *castitas* (chastity).[162] Given their contexts it is not inconceivable that they mark the virginal young, that group among the Christian laity whose admission to regular communion is urged by Bede.[163]

The lavish pectoral crosses occasionally found in later seventh-century graves (Figs. 21, 30) are the most direct evidence for new patterns of belief.[164] It must be accepted that these items, part of a jewellery fashion inspired by Italian and Byzantine models, had a specific religious significance for the wearers or their heirs.[165] Yet even they, Christian though on one level they obviously were, may have had ambiguous resonances. St Cuthbert's cross probably contains a relic; St Wilfrid wore a container (*chrismarium*) full of relics around his neck which Queen Eormenburh stole and 'hung beside her' for protection—though they had the reverse effect and nearly killed her.[166]

---

[161] Meaney 1981: 137. I am grateful to Christine Phillips for discussions on this problem.

[162] In the context sketched by Flint 1991: 301–19, this idea is less implausible than it may initially seem. Isidore of Seville (d. 636), whose works were well known in late seventh-century England, could have contributed another dimension to the word-play by his comment (following Pliny) that 'castores a castrando dicti sunt' because they bite off their testicles, sought-after for medicinal purposes, when hunters approach: *Isidori Hispalensis Episcopi Etymologiarum sive Originum Libri XX*, ed. W. M. Lindsay, ii (Oxford, 1911), XII. 2. 21.

[163] *Ep. E.* c. 15 (p. 419).

[164] See also below, p. 233. For the examples shown in Fig. 30 see: Webster and Backhouse 1991: 133–4, 26–9 (Durham, Ixworth, and Desborough); Speake 1989: 72–4, and Blair 1994: 71 (Standlake); Ozanne 1962–3: 26 and fig. 11, and Geake 1997: 150 (White Low). Some fifteen crosses (all pendent except Standlake and Chartham Down: see below, n. 167) are known from graves, as well as five which are apparently stray finds. For discussions of the corpus see: Hawkes and Grove 1963: 29–32; MacGregor 2000; Crawford 2004: 91–5. A catalogue (unpublished) has been prepared by Alice Chadwick, to whom I am very grateful for advice.

[165] Geake 1997: 109–13 and figs. 5.4 and 5.8, for the Continental prototypes. The distribution of crosses in Continental graves is discussed by Müller-Wille 1998, Müller-Wille 2003, Bierbrauer 2003, and Staecker 2003: 473–8. In the central Rhine and Moselle area the custom is visible only from the later seventh century (as in England), even though the region had long been Christian, whereas in Frisia and Saxony it followed soon after the Carolingian-period conversions. Cf. Burnell and James 1999: 92–6, with evidence that gold-foil crosses deterred grave-robbers. The fact that some jewellery from the pagan Migration period bears cruciform decoration (B. Ager in Collis 1983: 101–2) has led some English archaeologists to reject crosses comprehensively as evidence for Christianity (e.g. Van de Noort 1993; Geake 1997: 10); Geake does not even consider them in her account of Conversion-period artefacts. This is surely an over-reaction: the pendent crosses (as distinct from cross-shaped motifs on bracteates, composite brooches, etc.), like the cross on the Benty Grange helmet, replicate the artistic repertoire of self-evidently Christian crosses in sculpture and manuscripts (cf. Gannon 2003: 157–65).

[166] Rollason 1989a: 29; *VW* cc. 34, 39 (pp. 70, 78); Flint 1991: 304–6. The primary meaning of *chrismarium* is not 'reliquary', but a container (usually of metal) for consecrated oil: did Wilfrid wear his relics in something like the cylindrical boxes found in female graves?

A cross or relic had an utterly different meaning and power-source for Cuthbert or Wilfrid than an amulet for a sixth-century wise-woman, but the newly converted English may not have found the contrast so obvious. While most of the pendent crosses from graves were apparently on necklaces, there are three or four persuasive cases of women buried with waist- and neck-bags bearing or containing cruciform mounts.[167] This looks like the continuation of a pre-Christian tradition, illustrated by the sixth-century 'wise-woman' buried at Bidford-on-Avon with not only a waist-bag containing amulets, but also a neck-bag or bib decorated with probably amuletic bucket-pendants.[168]

So both in the late pagan and the early Christian periods, religious and amuletic grave-goods were associated almost exclusively with women. Exactly this pattern reappears in Scandinavia during its own conversion phase, two to three centuries later, when wagon-bodies, Thor's hammers, cross-marked pots, and cruciform pendants occur overwhelmingly in female graves.[169] In early medieval north-western Europe, it seems that women were very strongly associated with the display (at least the mortuary display) of religious affiliation, and perhaps of magical power. In a world where seers and magicians were often female, there could have been some continuity in perceptions of women as religious specialists: if the sixth-century 'wise-women' worked magic with their bags of trinkets, did a similar aura linger around late seventh-century Christian women who wore crosses, cross-marked pouches, and metal canisters?[170] But a broader context is also likely: the appeal of Christianity to pagan women (perhaps denied the heroic afterlife which their warrior husbands could expect), and a special female responsibility for moral and spiritual education.[171] In the pioneering stages of the English conver-

---

[167] The mount on the Swallowcliffe Down satchel has been interpreted as cruciform (Speake 1989: 77–80), but remains ambiguous. However, the undoubtedly cruciform mount from a female grave at Standlake (Oxon.) (Fig. 30; see above, n. 164), made of a tinned copper-alloy or possibly iron, was associated with a waist-bag, and has a secondary piercing in one of its two surviving arms and a cloth impression on its back: very likely it was sewn onto the front of the bag. (I am grateful to Arthur MacGregor for examining with me this object, now in the Ashmolean Museum.) At Boss Hall, Ipswich, a female grave included a leather neck-pouch containing a composite brooch and four gold disc-pendants with possibly cruciform decoration (Webster and Backhouse 1991: 51–3). In the light of this, the grave-group from Chartham Down (Kent) comprising a silver cross (Fig. 21), two wire rings, and three beads, all found at the neck of a young woman (C. Roach Smith, *Inventorium Sepulchrale* (London, 1856), 169–70 and pl. 11), should perhaps be interpreted as a neck-pouch rather than a necklace: the cross is pierced at all four terminals, so was presumably sewn onto a backing rather than suspended.

[168] Dickinson 1993. This recalls the burials of 'shamans' known from British prehistory and from other cultures: cf. N. S. Price, *The Viking Way* (Uppsala, 2002), 280–3.

[169] Staecker 2003.

[170] For female magic-workers: Meaney 1989; Nelson 1990: 70–4; Staecker 2003: 478–80. Was it part of Queen Eormenburh's sacrilege that she expected Wilfrid's relics to give her some magical power?

[171] Nelson 1990: 69–70; Staecker 2003: 478–80; Gräslund 2003: 487–94.

sion, as in some others, women may have played a dynamic role which faded when institutional structures crystallized.[172] It is thus possible that a combination of new and traditional attitudes to the female religious sphere underlies the choice of women to rule late seventh-century minsters, or the revival at the same date of furnished burial for women but not men.[173]

Alcuin's two letters on religious deviations in England, written in the 790s, give a purist's view of Christian amulets a century on.[174] He has seen, he says, people wearing amulets (*ligaturae*) as though they were something sacred; 'but it is better to imitate the examples of the saints in the heart than to carry bones in little bags (*in sacculis portare ossa*), to have gospel teachings written in the mind than to wear them around the neck scribbled on scraps of parchment (*pittaciolis exaratas*). This is the superstition of the Pharisees for which the very Truth rebuked their phylacteries.'[175] The other letter complains that 'many men in those parts' wear amulets around their necks, and 'with these most holy words of God or relics of the saints they go to their filthy acts, and even do their duty by their wives; this is a sin rather than a benefit', as St Augustine says when he condemns such things as diabolical and to be shunned by Christians.[176] The letters adopt different grounds for condemnation—hypocrisy in the first, diabolical superstition in the second—but both make it clear that the amulets are specifically Christian: the 'bones in little bags' sound thoroughly traditional, but the context shows that they were saints' relics rather than pigs' teeth. In the second letter, as in the story of Queen Eormenburh, the sin lies principally in the abuse of the holy, for instance to prevent impotence. What these letters show, like the earlier grave-goods but unambiguously, is the assimilation of overtly Christian objects into the repertoire of popular charms.[177]

---

[172] Gräslund 2003: 493. Note that Alcuin's letter (below) refers to *men* wearing amulets. Was this a change in practice during *c.*690–790?

[173] Above, pp. 181–2; below, pp. 230–3.

[174] *Alc. Ep.* Nos. 290–1 (pp. 448–9). These letters were both written in the 790s, and make the same series of points in the same order; one is addressed to Archbishop Æthelheard of Canterbury, the other to an unnamed archbishop. For advice on the context of, and relationship between, these letters I am very grateful to Mary Garrison, who suggests (pers. comm. 1997) that they were 'probably written within months of each other and reflecting first- or second-hand knowledge of the practices described; quite possibly both letters to Canterbury, one unusually emphatic and didactic; the problems described are of real concern to Alcuin'. The passages are also discussed by Flint 1991: 327, Meaney 1992: 116, and Thacker 1992*a*: 168.

[175] Matthew 23: 5 (where Christ condemns the Pharisees' big phylacteries as hypocritical ostentation).

[176] For 'ligatures', and St Augustine's views on amulets, see Flint 1991: 243–5, 301. Predictably, Bede attacked 'ligatures' and 'phylacteries' too: *VCB* c. 9 (pp. 184–6), *HE* iv. 27 (p. 432).

[177] A visitor to Spain in the 1960s noted: 'At the Dominican shrine of Las Caldas, little embroidered cloth amulets made by nuns and containing tiny snippets of paper from each of the four gospels are still sold . . . They are used to ward off evil spirits and also for cures. The bed in which

When a traditional society with participatory rituals faces destruction of its underlying belief-system, one response is to identify enthusiastically with the new religion's rituals and thereby, in some sense, to incorporate them. So, paradoxically, Christian rites and festivals can become the main vehicle for transmitting pre-Christian ones, and the converts most involved in them can also be those most strongly suspected of syncretism or deviance.[178] For eighth-century England, this model has some possibilities. The 747 canons expect a surprising amount of liturgical participation by the laity at large: they are to avoid secular business on Sundays (when they are to be invited to church), participate in Rogationtide processions with the clergy, and observe fasts.[179] This is prescriptive, but Ecgberht's 'Dialogue' asserts that the laity with their wives and families had observed fasts with the clergy since Theodore's time.[180] Historical opinion has been divided on how far such statements should be taken at face value or discounted as wishful thinking.[181] But it is precisely the practices which the *Clofesho* canons single out for disapproval, such as the singing of the liturgy like secular songs or the celebration of Rogationtide with horse-races and feasts,[182] which provide our hardest evidence that the indigenous ritual cycle had, to some extent at least, fused with the imported Christian one. By 747 it was with the overtly ecclesiastical processions and litanies of Rogationtide that at least some of the English laity celebrated, doubtless raucously and drunkenly, the spring blessing of their crops.

I slept in San Sebastian had amulets of this kind hanging on the bedstead' (Christian 1989: 197; cf. Cervantes 1994: 59–60, and Wilson 2000: 75–7, 137, 192, 366, 368–9, for the amuletic use of Christian words and objects within Christian societies). Alcuin would have despaired, but it is manifestly ludicrous to describe this context as 'pagan'.

[178] Cf. especially seventeenth-century Mexico, where Indians blamed for combining the liturgy with pre-Hispanic rites were in fact neither duplicitous nor anti-Christian, but 'engaged in an effort to reconstitute their pagan past through the appropriation and reinterpretation of Christian elements': Cervantes 1994: 51–3, 64.

[179] *Clof.747* cc. 14, 16, 18 (pp. 367–8). For the origins of litanies during solemn penitential processions at Rogationtide see Lapidge 1991: 8–13; Bazire and Cross 1982: pp. xv–xvii; Hill 2000; and below, p. 486. Adomnán's 'Vita Columbae' (ii. 44, ed. A. O. and M. O. Anderson (Oxford, 1991), 172) mentions a penitential procession in spring (so at Rogationtide?) involving the carrying of relics around the fields and reading from books. The first reference to the practice in an English monastic context is the account of Bede's death in 735 by his pupil Cuthbert; the first in an English lay context is the 747 canon.

[180] *Dialogue*, XVI. 4 (p. 413).

[181] Contrast Mayr-Harting 1991: 257–61, with Thacker 1992*a*: 160–4.

[182] *Clof.747* cc. 12, 16 (pp. 366–8): '. . . not mixed with vanities—as many are in the habit of doing—or levities, or vulgarities, that is in games and horse-races and huge feasts, but rather with fear and trembling, with the sign of Christ's passion and our eternal redemption and relics of his saints carried before.' Cf. Flint 1991: 185–7, for the assimilation of the Rogations to peasant rain-making processions. That the 747 complaint takes a context of lay Christianity for granted may be illustrated by comparing it with a late medieval one along similar lines: '. . . not to come and go in processyon talkyng of nyce talys and japis by the wey or by the feldes as ye walke . . . but ye scholde come mekely and lowly with a good devocion and follow yowre crosse and yowre bells' (quoted Pounds 2000: 78).

It is again Alcuin's two letters written in the 790s[183] that reveal something not otherwise visible before the tenth century: lay associations of a seemingly religious character, or at least operating within a Christian framework. The first letter urges Archbishop Æthelheard to ban 'those gatherings (*conventicula*) in which the people are deceived, leaving the churches and seeking hilly places where they worship (*servientes*) not with prayers but with drinking-bouts; as Christ himself said, "[Beware] if any one tells you that the things which are of Christ are in the wilderness",[184] not in the church, who gathers people together out of doors and abandons Christ's churches.' The second says that 'the curious assemblies (*conventus singulares*) which they are accustomed to have and call sworn-brotherhoods (*coniurationes*) are most certainly displeasing to God and inconsistent with the Christian religion, nor have I ever heard that the holy Doctors taught or did such things; in a Christian people there ought to be pure faith without any accretion of bad customs'. The first letter (which here as in its attack on amulets appeals to St Matthew's Gospel) implies that false prophets are misleading the laity. The sentiment of the second, that the laity are polluting Christian practice with their own bad customs, reiterates the statement a few sentences back that only the pure faith which Augustine and his colleagues had brought to the English should be allowed: 'teach whatever they taught, and hold as alien whatever they did not.'

Alcuin is not identifying these practices as pagan: if he had suspected idol-worship he would surely have said so.[185] Nor, if the 'assemblies' had been pagan or even purely secular, would the comment that the Fathers had not recommended them make any sense. The natural reading is that these were sworn-brotherhoods[186] of laity who, at the invitation of 'false' (but Christian) spiritual leaders, neglected church attendance in favour of religious if drunken open-air gatherings. The allusion to false prophets recalls a famous clash between St Boniface and a maverick Frankish bishop called Aldebert whose enterprises impinged on his German mission. According to Boniface's indignant report, Aldebert had distributed clippings of his own hair and nails as relics, offered instant absolution, set up crosses and little

---

[183] Above, n. 174.

[184] Paraphrase of Matthew 24: 26, where Christ warns against false prophets: 'If they tell you, "He is there in the wilderness", do not go out.'

[185] Here I differ from Meaney 1992: 116–17, who calls the first passage 'our only evidence that a genuine heathen cult was still being practiced at the end of the eighth century'.

[186] In Alcuin's Frankish world, a *coniuratio* had negative connotations as a potentially subversive secret society, whether secular (threatening public order and compromising the oath due to the king) or clerical (of rural clergy combining to thwart the control of their superiors): see Oexle 1982. Alcuin is probably implying that the English associations are likewise subversive, and outside the purview of (presumably episcopal) authority.

oratories in fields, at springs, or wherever he pleased, and lured the multitudes to these places so that they deserted the old churches.[187] We have only
one side of this story: the episode clearly was bizarre, but to lay devotees of
charismatics the gulf between an Aldebert and, say, a Cuthbert may not have
been self-evident. The rhetoric belongs to a very long tradition of stigmatiz-
ing as heretics, or even magicians, priests who had gone beyond acceptable
limits in assimilating their ministries to popular beliefs and practices.[188]
Alcuin's 'deceivers' of the English laity could simply have been local clergy
whom he perceived to have gone native.

A first reflection is that these 'brotherhoods' may not have been wholly
unlike the religious guilds found in association with some minsters in the
tenth and eleventh centuries.[189] A second is that the complaints simply illustrate the general suspicion with which literate reformers have always tended
to view organizations and assemblies whose theatre of activities was the
unsupervised countryside, not the controlled environment of churches.[190]
Alcuin may in fact be describing behaviour characteristic of a stage when
Christianity has largely supplanted any coherent pagan beliefs, but in doing
so has assimilated to itself the devotional and propitiatory aspects of indigenous social ritual. His is the hostile reaction of an intellectual and universalist
Christian culture to a participatory and locally embedded one, which rural
communities shared with priests who must often have been born and brought
up amongst them. Between the lines of Alcuin's laconic and alienated
words, we can possibly read a lay response resembling that of seventeenth-
century Mexicans (another society which had been officially Christian for a
hundred years or more) to a wave of new and hard-line parish priests. Serge
Gruzinski describes how a campaign to marginalize traditional ritual

managed to awaken among the Otomi the consciousness of possessing a spiritual
heritage that, although it hardly mattered, had originally been Christian, but now

[187] *Bon. Ep.* No. 59 (pp. 111–12). The episode has recently been much discussed: Gurevich 1988: 65–6; Flint 1991: 168–72; Thacker 1992*a*: 169; P. Brown 1996: 269–70; Fletcher 1997: 271–3.

[188] That priests could practice certain sorts of 'magic' with the approval of some (though not all) of their superiors is one of the central points of Flint 1991; some went too far, or fell foul of purists (ibid. 61, 67, 247, 355–6, 363–4). A traditional Catholic world in which professional magi-cians not only competed directly with the parish priests, but were often clergy themselves, survived in Spain in the 1570s: Christian 1981*a*: 29–31.

[189] Below, pp. 453–4. By then they normally seem to have met in guildhalls—perhaps one example of a general tendency for open-air assemblies to move indoors. There were lay guilds in mid ninth-century Canterbury: Brooks 1984: 28–30.

[190] See Gurevich 1988: 59–73, 98–9, for hard-liners' suspicions of autonomous charismatics and open-air sanctuaries. As he observes, penitentials are much clearer about the inherent sinfulness of gatherings in woods and fields than they are about what precisely (picnics? games? sacrifices to demons?) may have happened at them. The same reaction surfaces in sixteenth-century Mexico: Cervantes 1994: 35–7.

had to be defended even against the Church. The dividing line thus did not run, as one might think, between Christianity and indigenous paganism, but much more between what Indians considered to be in their sphere, their religious domain—confraternities and brotherhoods, holy images, churches, chapels, oratories, feasts, patron saints, springs, mountains, pre-Hispanic objects—and all the rest.[191]

To this extent we might speak of 'two cultures'—but not in the sense of two impermeable spheres, literate and Christian on the one hand, vernacular and folkloric on the other.[192] Rather, the line is drawn between the fastidious, metropolitan, temperamentally *dirigiste* moral leaders whose voices come through to us—Aldhelm, Bede, Boniface, Alcuin—and the diverse majority, clerical and lay, whose voices remain silent. Even below that line, there was a broad range between the sophisticated and the rustic. At one extreme are Wilfrid with his retinue and regal feasts, or the educated ecclesiastics who used 'Christian magic' of the kind preserved in prayer-books from the west midlands.[193] At the other are the monks and clergy who drank themselves senseless;[194] or local minster-priests who performed magic for their flocks with Christian amulets and relics, drank with the guild-brethren when they should have been saying mass in their churches, or careered tipsily on horseback between the spring crops. It is fair to suggest that thus far—unorthodox and compromised, yet broad-based and well integrated—the spiritual culture of the eighth- and ninth-century English countryside was Christian.

In the last analysis, views on how the fragmentary evidence should be interpreted will depend on how this society is thought in general to have worked: which kinds of bonds were important, by what channels ideas could be spread or social norms be modified, how far the culture and lifestyle of the great impinged on the masses. But if early Anglo-Saxon society was 'primitive' it was not anarchic, and the reciprocal obligations of followers

[191] Gruzinski 1989: 99–100. The point is developed by Cervantes 1994: 57–8, 68–73, who stresses the antipathy of the new official Catholicism towards the traditional culture of the Indians and mendicant friars, and observes that rural Spanish Catholicism had been, like Mesoamerican paganism, 'a corporate affair involving the propitiation of a host of supernatural beings who displayed benevolent and malevolent attributes'.

[192] It will be clear that I am more persuaded by the approaches of, for example, Markus 1990: 10–13, Flint 1991, Smith 1990, and Fletcher 1997: 238–9 than by those of (in a general context) Schmitt 1976 and Le Goff 1980: 153–8, or (in a specifically Anglo-Saxon one) Rollason 1999. It is worth pondering an anthropologist's study of a traditional rural Catholic culture in northern Spain (Christian 1989), which shows a complex of intermeshing social, economic, and devotional identities: anticlericalism coexists with intense devotion to images, the claims of outlying shrines compete with those of parish churches, and a 'counter-culture' of teenage groups indulging in bawdy and irreverent songs floats above the surface of underlying loyalties to church and village.

[193] Sims-Williams 1990: 273–327.

[194] *PT* I. i. 2–3 (p. 289); Wihtred, c. 6 (*Gesetze*, 12), envisaging a priest so drunk that he is incapable of performing baptisms.

with lords, kindreds with their leading members, neighbours with neighbours, must surely have meant that ideas spread quickly and that the lesser soon conformed, at least externally, to the reorientations of the great. However vague one's theology, the ingrained moral and practical imperatives to follow one's lord must have been a powerful stimulus to convert. The role of minsters in mediating ideas down the social scale is not some unlikely anomaly: embedded as it was in kinship and lordship structures, it is exactly what we should expect.

This is not to claim that the pastoral care which most of the laity received was always thorough, nor that some did not get much more of it than others. A central theme of this book is the complex of interactions, economic and tenurial as well as spiritual and social, between minsters and the rural communities around them. It is indeed likely that people who were monastic servants and tenants, who farmed and worked on monastic land, or who provided goods and services to minsters, were more bound up in this complex than were others. Ireland, where it has been argued that the *manaig* or 'monastic tenants' enjoyed more extensive spiritual services than other people, as well as being subject to a greater moral regulation, may again offer an analogy.[195] We might envisage diminishing circles of engagement, with tenants on monastic estates knowing most about their landlords' beliefs and spirituality, lying under the heaviest obligation to support the minster community with regular dues, and having the closest contact with it through the rituals of the agrarian year. The arrangements for lay burial—partly and increasingly at minsters, but partly still in kindred or neighbourhood cemeteries—are certainly consistent with this picture, and so far as they go may support it.[196]

The seventh- and eighth-century world, remote in so many ways from the later medieval west, can sometimes be illuminated by ranging further afield. I shall end with a Buddhist parallel: Anna Grimshaw's anthropological study of the monastery of Rizong in modern Ladakh.[197] Founded in the 1810s, this community has had about as long to make its mark on the local economy

---

[195] Etchingham 1991, and Etchingham 1999: 239–89, criticizing the arguments of Charles-Edwards (1992: 69–71) and Sharpe (1984a: 1992) that there were reciprocal obligations involving pastoral care between the people of a *túath* and its main church. But see the response of Charles-Edwards 2000: 118–19.

[196] Burial and grave-goods are discussed below (pp. 228–45), but it is worth noting here the recent suggestion, based on a comparison between English 'Final Phase' cemeteries and their Frankish counterparts, 'that in England the dynamics of conversion were such that from an early stage the church was able to establish an infrastructure of local pastoral care and supervision, and really could influence burial practices, in a way that the Frankish church could not': Burnell and James 1999: 90.

[197] Grimshaw 1983.

and society as had many English minsters by the 850s, and like English Christianity its Buddhism 'has had to penetrate the structure of the society's beliefs and practices and articulate them with its own perspective'.[198] The monastery's impact on the farming settlement over which it towers has been transformative, affecting almost every aspect of its inhabitants' lives. The monks are the main landlords, consumers, and employers of labour; they control the flow of commodities, establishing 'a redistributive network focusing upon Rizong monastery rather than a series of horizontal reciprocal relations between the horizontal parts of the economy'.[199] Situated 'at the core of the symbolic universe, represented by its control of the scriptures', the community provides a ritual structure for the villagers' yearly round of activities, and articulates their communal ceremonies.[200] 'The areas of economy and religious doctrine', writes Grimshaw, 'are bound together through the activity of the monks and it is this direct involvement, *thereness*, which guarantees the continued dominance of the monastery in the social organization.'[201]

Obviously, the two societies and belief-systems are in some ways very different. Yet the capacity of Rizong to intrude itself into, and transform, an undeveloped economy and settlement pattern has lessons for our view of early England, especially in the intermeshing of spiritual with social engagement to a dominant ritual and exploitative focus. Not least of the similarities are the sheer physical presence of the monastery—its scale, complexity, and permanence in a primitive and insecure world—and its role as a stimulant and regulator of economic production. These aspects of Anglo-Saxon minsters as 'central places' will now be addressed.

[198] Ibid. p. i.   [199] Ibid. 86–102.   [200] Ibid. 123–56.   [201] Ibid. 229.

4

The Church in the Landscape
c.650–850

Early English Christianity left a legacy of impressive, durable monuments in the countryside which can be seen, or at least excavated, today: monastic sites, churches, stone crosses, graveyards. Equally important, though barely visible to us, were the wider landscapes of undeveloped or unmarked cult sites, and the conceptions of sacred space which would have given them coherence and meaning for their inhabitants. Written (and thus clerical) sources stress the monumental and the architectural, emblematic of Roman civilization and orthodoxy; our own intensively built-up environments encourage us to accept that emphasis, and to forget how many Anglo-Saxon communal activities must have taken place in the natural world and the open air. In the vernacular culture of early Christian England, landscape mattered more than architecture.[1]

This chapter tries to understand ritual landscapes as contemporaries would have seen them. Although it reviews some much-discussed archaeological evidence, its concerns are less with physical remains than with the various levels of religious expression: monastic and secular, new and traditional, metropolitan and vernacular. It draws on recent anthropological perceptions of sacred landscapes,[2] from which three recurrent points seem especially useful. The first is that sacred topography often resides in memory and tradition rather than in physical monumentalization, and extends well beyond modern western definitions of 'ritual monuments' to include, for instance, routeways, mountain-ranges, or the frontiers between different land-zones. Secondly (and by extension), whole categories of sacred sites are independent of any

---

[1] Anderson 1991 describes a late Anglo-Saxon literary imagination that was 'uncarpentered' in the sense of excluding artificial structures and straight lines.

[2] The essays in Carmichael and others 1994, and in Ashmore and Knapp 1999, are a good representative range of the recent anthropological and archaeological studies. Richard Bradley's work, most recently Bradley 2000, provides the most sensitive and creative exploration of many of the issues, especially the coexistence of monuments with 'unaltered places'.

human modification: 'unaltered places' such as distinctively shaped rocks, caves, streams, or springs can be long-term sites of supernatural power, and recipients of offerings, without the patronage, investment, or control of any king, priesthood, or other central authority. The third point is that societies converted to new and more centralized religions have often shown a strong tendency to assimilate these inherited sites to the new belief-systems, however different their ideas of cosmology or sacred space may in theory be.

The physical and spatial impact of Christianity was not a simple culture-clash. When it came to re-working inherited ritual landscapes, the seventh-century English may already have had ideas and approaches in common with the people who evangelized them. In the late antique cities, Christianity had taken root by absorbing the multifarious networks of holy places: turning temples, market-halls, and houses into churches, raising basilicas over the graves of martyrs, infiltrating buildings both secular and pagan with saints' relics.[3] For their own part, the English since about 550 had shown steadily more interest in the possibilities of display and ceremony offered by monuments surviving from the past: burying their dead in Bronze Age barrows and Roman villas, constructing a monumental complex such as Yeavering between the poles afforded by two prehistoric structures.[4] When ecclesiastics, used to the Christian transformation of Mediterranean cities, solicited Roman ruins from converted English kings as sites for churches, their patrons will have understood something of the underlying psychology. The adoption of pagan cult sites and ancient monuments, an area of accommodation between the two cultures which archaeology can to some extent explore, makes a good starting-point.

Recycling the past

Anglo-Saxon churches sometimes stand on or beside prehistoric or Roman monuments. This phenomenon, once seen as evidence for long-term ritual continuity, has recently been subjected to analyses which tend rather to stress the purposeful re-adoption of abandoned sites. Ancient ruins represented, in Bonnie Effros's phrase, 'a malleable ordering principle for the reorientation of the cultural landscape', capable of being re-worked as needs changed over time.[5] But in abandoning the assumption of continuous use, we must still acknowledge that phases may have occurred which we cannot see archaeo-

---

[3] Markus 1990: 139–55.   [4] Above, pp. 51–7.
[5] Effros 2001: 118. The debate can be traced through: Bradley 1987; Bradley 1993; Williams 1997*b*; Eaton 2000; Bell 2001; Effros 2001; Hawkes 2003*b*. Further works are cited in Jong and Theuws 2001: 20 n. 34 and 214 n. 188.

logically: it is an inherent problem of the evidence that ritual activity leaves clearer traces in some periods than in others. In particular, whereas prehistoric earthworks, Roman masonry, and medieval churches have a good chance of surviving, Anglo-Saxon pagan activity is likely to be invisible to us. A church built on a stone circle, barrow, or villa which was used as a pagan shrine in the sixth or seventh century is indistinguishable from a church built on one which was not; a church built on a pagan shrine which had itself used a virgin site will probably offer no hint of its predecessor.

The extent to which places of genuine Anglo-Saxon cult were adopted is confused, at least at a superficial level, by a conventional rhetoric of purification which tended to be applied to any new Christian site. In a tradition going back to Athanasius's 'Life of St Antony', warriors for Christ such as Cuthbert and Guthlac ejected demons before taking up their solitary abodes; monastic founders followed their example.[6] Such rituals may sometimes imply that the places had been used for worshipping the pagan gods, but need not necessarily. In pagan English culture, ancient monuments and natural places are likely to have had varied and contrasting resonances: some with positive connotations (for instance as shrines, or as sites of elite burial), others negative (for instance Grendel's mere and the dragon-haunted chamber in 'Beowulf').[7] The ritual cleansing of any such places, as both a necessary and a sufficient condition for re-use, will have made sense to the English as well as to their ecclesiastical mentors. On the whole it is likely that both living pagan shrines and abandoned older monuments were used, or not used, as other requirements dictated, without anxieties about pollution posing any insuperable problem: even on his demon-infested island, Guthlac set up his hermitage in a conveniently hollowed-out barrow.[8]

It is certain that at least occasional sites of pagan cult were used for churches. A new, state-backed religion has a range of options for how to treat its predecessor's shrines: to destroy them and leave them waste; to destroy them and rebuild on the sites; or to take them over. The theatrical advantages of a dramatic burning are obvious, and thanks to Bede's account of what happened at Goodmanham in the 620s it is our normal image of

---

[6] *VCA* iii. 1 (p. 96); *VG* cc. 25–36 (pp. 88–118); Mayr-Harting 1991: 229–39; Gittos 2002*a*: 44–6. Below, p. 191, for the purification rituals at Lastingham and the 'De Abbatibus' minster. Effros 2001: 102, 115–16 shows how in Gaul such rites of exorcism were only one strand in a generally positive attitude to the re-use of 'pagan' monuments.

[7] Above, pp. 52–4; below, pp. 474–5.

[8] *VG* c. 28 (pp. 92–4); Stocker 1993: 101–6. Felix describes the structure as a 'mound built of clods of earth' (*tumulus agrestibus glaebis coacervatus*), broken open by treasure-hunters, 'in the side of which was something like a cistern' (*in cuius latere velut cisterna inesse videbatur*) which Guthlac roofed over. Megalithic chambered tombs do not occur in this region, but Guthlac could have encountered the remains of a timber-chambered long barrow, or a Roman barrow with a planked cist, preserved in peat: Meaney 2001: 34–6.

Anglo-Saxon conversion.[9] Destruction is indeed what Pope Gregory urged on King Æthelberht in June 601, but reports from Kent apparently made him change tack, and on 18 July he wrote the famous letter to Mellitus which is the ultimate statement of the case for conversion through incorporation:

If those temples are well built, they need to be converted from the cult of demons to the service of the true God. When this people see that their shrines are not destroyed they will banish error from their heart, and knowing and adoring the true God they will gather the more readily in familiar places. And since they are accustomed to slaughter many oxen as sacrifices to demons, they ought to have some other kind of ritual in exchange for this. So on the anniversary of the dedication, or on the feasts of the holy martyrs whose relics are placed there, they can make huts for themselves with branches of trees around the churches which have been converted out of shrines, and celebrate the solemnity with religious feasts. They must no longer sacrifice animals to the devil, but they can kill animals for their food to the praise of God.[10]

How many English shrines were sufficiently 'well built' to have a long-term future is debatable, but at least the strategy may (in circles where the letter was known) have encouraged on-site rebuildings. We have one explicit statement that this did sometimes happen, and that it was the origin of some minsters. Writing in the 680s, Aldhelm rejoiced that 'where once the crude pillars (*ermula cruda*) of the . . . foul snake and the stag were worshipped with coarse stupidity in profane shrines (*fana profana*), in their place dwellings for students, not to mention holy houses of prayer, are constructed skilfully by the talents of the architect':[11] language which implies substantial churches and learned communities.

Actual cases are hard to identify, but two of the more persuasive may serve to illustrate the possible modes of re-use. At Ripon (Yorks.)[12] a prominent natural hillock which could have been mistaken for a barrow, known by 1228 as *Elveshowe* ('elf's barrow'?), was used during the early seventh century for a cemetery. In the 650s King Alhfrith gave the site to the Irish

---

[9] *HE* ii. 13 (pp. 184–6); compare the account of the burning of the Nenets' shrine at Kozmin Copse, in the Arctic region, by Russian missionaries in 1837 (O. V. Ovsyannikov and N. M. Terebikhin in Carmichael and others 1994: 68–9). Bede says that the site at Goodmanham was remembered, but not whether a church was built there. It may be, though, that the probably artificial mound on which Goodmanham church now stands is the site of the shrine; compare nearby Fimber, where a church of unknown date stands on a prehistoric barrow associated with sixth-century burials (Blair 1995*b*: 22–4).

[10] *HE* i. 30 (pp. 106–8); I follow the reconstruction of Gregory's thoughts during June and July 601 proposed by Markus 1970.

[11] Letter to Heahfrith: *AO* 489 (Lapidge and Herren 1979: 160–1).

[12] Hall and Whyman 1996. It must be said, though, that the evidence for north–south burials is not conclusive. Also, the second element of *Elveshowe* (O. N. *haugr*) cannot be pre-Viking as we have it, and the first element might be a personal name.

community of Melrose as a monastic dependency, but then transferred it to St Wilfrid, who built his church west of the mound in the 670s. During *c.*700–850 the hilltop cemetery continued in use for high-status coffined burials, all adult males and presumably members of the religious community. This perpetuation of a pre-monastic and possibly pre-Christian cemetery is remarkable, as is Wilfrid's precise, deliberate alignment of his church on the 'elf's howe'.[13] At Bampton (Oxon.)[14] the main church, its associated cemetery (which on radiocarbon evidence existed by at least the ninth century), and a chapel to the west were superimposed on two Bronze Age barrows. Half a mile eastwards, at a place known as 'the Beam' on the edge of a Roman settlement, burials—one with a seventh-century bronze pin—surrounded a chapel of St Andrew, first attested in the twelfth century. This remarkable place-name, evidently the eponym of Bampton (*bēam tūn*, '*tūn* by the *bēam*'), must refer to some special tree, post, or pillar, and strongly suggests a pre-Christian cult site. Both cases, like immediately pre-Christian Yeavering, illustrate how pagan cult sites could have been incorporated into new axial alignments.

As Yeavering also illustrates, places of ritual assembly shade into places of royal residence and ceremonial, and these too could be handed over to ecclesiastics for conversion into minsters. According to the Life of St Wilfrid, King Æthelwalh of Sussex gave him 'his own vill in which he lived as an episcopal seat', probably Selsey.[15] The Kentish royal nunnery of Lyminge may also have replaced, or coexisted with, a royal estate centre, though the evidence is ambiguous.[16] Another may be Thame, a Mercian royal *villa* in 672–4 and visible as a minster in late sources.[17] Eynsham and Aylesbury, two of the four captured *tūnas* listed in the Anglo-Saxon Chronicle annal for '571', became minsters, and at Eynsham it has been shown that the eighth-century minster

[13] The axis of Wilfrid's church is established by its surviving crypt. It is of course possible that this was itself conditioned by whatever the Irish community had built, but it suggests either that Wilfrid did not perceive the mound as a problem, or that he was making a deliberate statement in Christianizing it.

[14] Blair 1994: 62–4; Blair 1995*b*: 2; Blair 1998*c*. (Note the topographical parallel with the northern Frankish case of Hordain, where the Merovingian 'founder-grave' chapel overlying a pagan-period cemetery occupies a relationship to the main church comparable to that of the 'Beam' at Bampton: Demolon 1990: figs. 18–19.) At Elstow (Beds.), a probably Bronze Age barrow underlying the east end of the church had already been used for a sixth-century cremation (Baker 1969: 28–30, 35).

[15] *VW* c. 41 (p. 82).

[16] A grant of 689 concerns land which formerly belonged to the royal estate centre (*cors*) of Lyminge, and in 838 Lyminge minster received land which had been held by a royal *colonus* and 'ad meam regiam villam ante pertinebat' (S 12, S 286: *St Aug.* 33–6). It cannot, however, be assumed that the royal centre of the lathe was necessarily on the same site as the minster to which the lathe name eventually became attached (cf. below, pp. 251, 278).

[17] S.1165; Blair 1994: 49–50, 61.

buildings overlie a sixth-century settlement, itself overlying a Bronze Age enclosure.[18] Archaeology also suggests that the great Mercian minster of Repton replaced large seventh-century timber buildings.[19] It is unlikely that such places were chosen for the sake of the structures already standing on them; probably they were perceived to have a status—whether as sites of numinous power or because they had a dynastic significance for lay patrons—which encouraged their monastic development and perpetuation.[20]

As the new monastic culture advanced, the places upon which it imposed itself were not all English or pagan. In the west and north, founders are more likely to have encountered and annexed British Christian sites, such as those which Wilfrid attached to Ripon after their clergy fled for their lives.[21] Possibly the Ripon episode was exceptionally violent, but the process may often have led to the kind of remodelling which can now, thanks to the recent excavations, be recognized at Whithorn in Galloway.[22] Here a circular shrine on the edge of the monastic enclosure, the focus of graves during the late sixth and seventh centuries, was retained after the Northumbrian takeover of *c.*730 as the western element in an otherwise totally new axial complex with an oratory and mortuary enclosure; only in the later eighth century was the oratory rebuilt as a proper church, and the shrine obliterated (Fig. 24).

Peter Hill observes that the evolution of the site at Whithorn, and the promotion of St Ninian's cult there, suggest

an unaccustomed regard for the sensibilities of the Britons . . . The absorption and re-presentation of the historical traditions is closely matched by the physical transformation of the *monasterium* . . . [*c.*730], when it was comprehensively redeveloped, while retaining and embellishing extant ritual *foci* . . . ; and the combined historical and archaeological evidence provides a compelling picture of the exploitation of tradition to achieve political control.[23]

Perhaps this regard was not so 'unaccustomed'; and if Christian sites in colonized British territory were material for such 'exploitation of tradition', so could be the traditional pagan sites of the English themselves. Different though these two contexts are, they may show a continuum in the assimilation of old ritual landscapes to the seventh- and eighth-century monastic culture. What they have in common is the imposition of radically new

[18] Hardy and others 2003: 25–52, for Eynsham; Allen and Dalwood 1983 for Aylesbury.

[19] Kjølbye-Biddle 1998: 762–4.

[20] Above, p. 57. A special case was the minster of Gilling (Yorks.), built on the site of a nobleman's house in expiation of a crime committed there: *HE* iii. 14 (p. 256).

[21] Above, p. 30.

[22] Hill 1997: 37–8, 134–50. But note that only a small, and not the central, part of the site was excavated.

[23] Ibid. 18.

architectural forms, which might not have held the same meanings for the habitual devotees of the holy places (British Christians in the one case, English pagans or converts in the other) that they held for those who transformed them (in both cases the religious advisers of Christian English kings). Different rhetorics would have been employed—of cleansing for a pagan site, of adoption into worthier hands for a British Christian one—but the main practical effect was to give an already much-frequented place a new lease of life. For Aldhelm there was all the difference in the world between a 'profane shrine' and the 'holy house of prayer' which replaced it; for local people, its survival as a locus of other-worldly power was probably more important.

Having said all this, it must still be acknowledged that the great majority of older monuments re-used for churches offer no evidence for supposing that they had any living social or cultural relevance, and that most of them are of a kind which the pre-Christian English seem not, on the whole, to have occupied. Pre-eminent here were Romano-British towns, public buildings, forts, and villas.[24] Numerous and prominent though they still were in the seventh century, decay would have largely obscured their diverse original functions: what gave them their impact in Anglo-Saxon eyes was their massive masonry and their regular planning, making them startlingly different from any non-Roman work. But the educated knew what they were; the well travelled had seen their counterparts put to new uses, mainly religious, in the re-emergent towns of Gaul; and missionaries used them to reaffirm Rome's stamp on its lost province.

The granting of deserted Roman forts and small towns by kings to monastic founders was widespread throughout the former northern provinces of the Empire. Well-attested Merovingian practice helps us to understand the many English cases known from topographical evidence (usually the presence of a later church inside the fort walls), and the gifts specifically mentioned in written sources: Dorchester-on-Thames by Cynegils of Wessex to St Birinus around 640; *Dommoc* by Sigeberht of East Anglia to St Felix, and *Cnobheresburg* (?Burgh Castle) by the same king to St Fursa, both in the 630s; Bradwell-on-Sea by Sigeberht of Essex to St Cedd; Reculver (Fig. 23) by Ecgberht of Kent to the priest Bassa in 669.[25] The churches occupy a variety of positions, sometimes roughly central (directly over the *principium* or some

---

[24] For earlier accounts: Morris and Roxan 1980; Blair 1992: 235–46; Dark 1994*a*: 93–9 (for west Britain); Bell 1998*a*; Bell 1998*b*. The fundamental study, though, is now Bell 2001, to which what follows is indebted. See Anderson 1991: 70, for late Anglo-Saxon literary praise of Roman ruins.

[25] *HE* iii. 7, ii. 15, iii. 19, iii. 22 (pp. 232, 190, 270, 282–4); *ASC* s.a. 669 (pp. 34–5); Blair 1992: 235–9, for the other Continental, British, and English cases; Hawkes 2003*b*: 79–83, for the 're-Romanization' of forts by the siting of stone crosses within or near them, Bewcastle (Cumb.) being a particularly clear case.

other major structure), sometimes set to one side or squeezed into a corner.[26] It is still unclear whether these patterns show anything more significant than a range of recurrent responses to similar remains, and they are in any case distorted by the fact that, out of the two or more churches which most minsters would have possessed, only one normally survives. At Bradwell-on-Sea, for instance, the seventh-century church, fitted into the west gateway of the fort, could have functioned as a gate-church, giving access to a precinct centred on a main church further east. 'The whole usage', as S. E. Rigold wrote of the minsters in the Saxon Shore forts, is 'not a barbarous "squatter occupation" nor a case of barbarous imitation, [but] a reclamation of Roman sites in a fairly confident, contemporary Mediterranean mood'.[27]

Major Romano-British towns offered rather different possibilities from forts.[28] The areas enclosed by their walls were much bigger than monastic precincts required: in Britain as in the sub-Roman towns of Gaul, church groups and associated buildings tended to develop within their own nuclei, such as 'Paulsbury' in London.[29] Canterbury (Fig. 9) looks like a deliberate re-creation by King Æthelberht and St Augustine of a post-Roman European town, with its cathedral group in one corner of the city and monastery outside the walls.[30] The remains of the grand public buildings associated with baths could be pressed into service, as is strikingly apparent at Leicester and Bath. For monastic founders in seventh-century England, the reclamation of civic space was both convenient and the attested good practice of their mentors: it affirmed a civilized othodoxy. The Christian topography of re-emergent Romano-British towns came almost inevitably to resemble that of Italian and Gallo-Roman towns, for the people who moulded its development had been trained in Italy and Gaul. Thus the characteristic sprawl of churches, spreading outwards from episcopal or monastic groups across the semi-abandoned town or its cemeteries, became nearly as marked a feature of Canterbury or London as it was of Paris or Limoges.[31]

The ruins of rural villas, slighter in scale and smaller in area, would generally have had less to offer, and only a handful are known to have been adopted for minsters. Some villas in south Wales and the west may plausibly be seen as post-Roman British Christian sites.[32] It is, however, unnecessary to invoke that explanation for the minsters, whose founders are likely to have been attracted to the formal settings afforded by unusually large or well-preserved villa complexes: cases are widespread, for instance Castor (Northants.), Southwell (Notts.), West Mersea (Essex), and Cheddar

---

[26] Bell 2001: 132–42.   [27] Rigold 1977: 74.
[28] Biddle 1976a; Blair 1992: 241–6; Bell 2001: 115–32.
[29] Below, p. 250.   [30] Above, p. 66.
[31] Blair 1992: fig. 10.4; see also Rodwell 1993a for London.   [32] Above, pp. 11–12.

(Somerset).[33] The idiom would flourish later, in the tenth- and eleventh-century era of local church-building, when numerous villa sites (whether or not used for unofficial religious activities) were monumentalized in this way; but that is the subject of a later chapter.[34]

The much smaller number of English minsters known to have used ancient earthwork forts likewise imply a need for enclosure and an urge to reclaim the past, but with different resonances: less the empire-wide recreation of *Romanitas*, more the high-status practices of immediately pre-Christian insular cultures. Secular re-occupation of hillforts had been common in the western and northern regions which were still beyond the English frontiers in 600,[35] and may have been one prototype for the new banked-and-ditched minster enclosures that were to become widespread among the English. Nonetheless, ecclesiastical re-use of earthwork enclosures seems to be a mainly Irish phenomenon:[36] it may not be coincidence that the hillfort-sited minsters of Hanbury (Worcs.) and Malmesbury (Wilts.) have seventh-century Irish backgrounds.[37] In some lowland areas, the founders of minsters rejected hillforts in favour of lower-lying and more accessible sites.[38]

As the last point illustrates, ancient monuments were enabling but not constraining: they could be used if they suited Anglo-Saxon locational needs, ignored if they did not. It is the essence of a monument that it is perceived to belong to the past: a past that can be remembered, adapted, forgotten, or re-invented as best suits current needs.[39] For the early Christian English the past was very important, but it could be re-created on new sites as well as revived on old ones. If Roman ruins survived, so much the better, but if not, Rome could be rebuilt from scratch: in Augustine's monastery at Canterbury, in Wilfrid's crypts (Fig. 12), in Benedict Biscop's masonry, in the stone churches of any large minster. Rome could even be moved: Wilfrid's systematic robbing of the carved and inscribed stones of Corbridge might

[33] Other certain or possible minsters on villas are Flawford (Notts.), Frocester (Glos.), Much Wenlock (Salop.), and Wimborne (Dorset): Bell 2001 for all these sites. For Southwell (where there is a reference—but perhaps not a very reliable one—to N–S burials over a mosaic pavement: Bell 2001: 193–4, 319–20), see also Dixon and Stocker 2001: 254–7. Outside towns and forts, identifiable minsters make up only a very small proportion of the total corpus of churches on Roman buildings.

[34] Below, p. 377.   [35] Below, pp. 268–70.

[36] Dark 1994a: 41–3, for the essential absence of this phenomenon from western Britain; Aitchison 1994: 239–40, for qualifications even regarding Ireland.

[37] Sims-Williams 1990: 106–7; Haslam 1984: 111–17. Other minsters in hillforts are Aylesbury (Bucks.), Tetbury (Glos.: Fig. 38), and Breedon-on-the-Hill (Leics.). Others could probably be identified, but it is clear that such sites were less commonly used than Roman ones.

[38] As in Wessex: Hase 1994: 54–7.

[39] It is again Richard Bradley who has most helpfully discussed the changing role of monuments over time (e.g. Bradley 1987, 1993). Aitchison 1994: 24–8, develops the point in the context of early medieval Ireland, as does Effros 2001 for Gaul.

almost be read as a symbolic re-location of the Roman town to Hexham minster.[40] In locational choices the perception of a human or supernatural past, to be reclaimed or tamed, was a significant factor, but only one among others.

The locations of minsters

Laying out the ground for a new minster was a solemn affair: a certain kind of place was needed, and it needed certain kinds of preparation. It seems possible that founders entertained something akin to the geomantic notions of sacred sites as *axes mundi*, or centres of a symbolic cosmos, which in other cultures have produced arcane rituals of survey, alignment, and preparation.[41] A wilderness, ruin, or site of pagan cult had resonances which could be tamed and harnessed, but in its raw state it was a polluted and dangerous spot: to turn it into a permanent earthly paradise, human action was needed.[42] In the early 650s St Cedd chose to found Lastingham minster at the foot of the North Yorkshire Moors, which Bede over-dramatically calls 'a place amid steep and remote hills which seemed more suited for haunts of robbers and for dens of wild beasts than for dwellings of men'. Anxious first

to cleanse the site by prayers and fasts from the filth of former crimes, and then lay the foundations of the minster there, he asked the king to give him the opportunity and permission to spend there the whole approaching season of Lent for the sake of prayer . . . For he said that it was the practice of those from whom he had learnt the rule of regular discipline [i.e. the Ionan Irish], that having received a site for making a minster or a church, they first consecrated it to the Lord by prayers and fasts.[43]

In Æthelwulf's poem 'De Abbatibus' the early eighth-century Northumbrian nobleman Eanmund appeals to the revered Ecgberht in Ireland, asking him to send a consecrated altar and to 'reveal which places were worthy ones in which a holy church . . . might be placed'. Ecgberht provides the altar (later installed at the heart of the main church), and replies:

[40] Eaton 2000: 111–27; ibid. 127–32 for other cases.
[41] Wheatley 1971: 414–28. Aitchison 1994: 106–22, 233–55, uses this conceptual framework to interpret early Armagh as a symbolic microcosm of Ireland; and see O'Sullivan 2001: 34–8, for the choice of the site of Lindisfarne. The locations of many English minsters, with open ground and water south-eastwards and gently rising ground north-westwards, recall the sorts of sites believed in China to generate propitious *feng-shui*. For comparative studies of Mesoamerican sacred geography arguing for a similar geomantic basis, see the contributions to Benson 1981, especially J. B. Carlson's. The possible cross-staff in an axially aligned grave at Yeavering offers one hint that expert surveyors had a special status in late pagan England: Hope-Taylor 1977: 68–9, 200–3.
[42] Cf. Gittos 2002*a*: 42–7.
[43] *HE* iii. 23 (p. 286); cf. Charles-Edwards 1974.

22. *Lastingham* (Yorks.): the carefully chosen site of Cedd's minster. Seen from the south-west (above), the church seems to nestle amid the moors; seen at close range from the east (below), it stands up imposingly on its rocky outcrop.

I confess that I never saw with bodily eye the lands which the Lord granted to thee in a great donation. There is, however, as inward vision was able to show, a small hill (*collis non magnus*) with a bending downward path, where the rising sun speeds across the face of Libra the weigher [i.e. the side of the hill with the path looked east to face the rising sun at the equinox]. This hill thorn-bushes cover on top with thick leaf. Cut these away with scythes, O brother, and remove them with all their seed from the expanse of the smooth top just mentioned, and then found in that place a fair church for God . . .[44]

Local studies and general observation reveal some very consistent patterns in the kinds of sites chosen, though also some regional variation.[45] Most minsters stood near water, whether rivers or the sea. Peninsulas enclosed by converging rivers, or sites on tributaries two or three miles above confluences, were especially popular. The main church complex was normally, to a greater or lesser extent, elevated, whether on a coastal headland, a river-side scarp or bluff, or a small local hillock (Eanmund's *collis non magnus*, or the *montes* mentioned as Welsh church sites in early Llandaf texts).[46] Minsters in river-valleys always stood slightly above the alluvium, for instance on the headlands and islands of the gravel terraces along the Thames.[47] In hilly areas (notably the north-west, where the consistency is very striking) there is a preference for sites with sheltering hills westwards and northwards, broad riverine views southwards and eastwards. In flat areas choice was more constrained, but in southern England there was a tendency to prefer clay or gravel islands in the floodplain, even when higher ground was available nearby.[48] While proximity to navigable water was important everywhere, there was possibly more emphasis on elevation in the northern and western regions which were more influenced by Irish practice, and closer to an aristocratic culture of hillforts and citadels.[49]

Because minster sites are often 'marginal' in relation to late medieval settlement patterns, there is a temptation to see in them a thoroughly monastic flight into seclusion. This may have been the ideal, but it was not usually the reality. Eighth-century rural settlements tended to be less structured and

[44] *DA* ll. 113–19, 131–7 (pp. 11–13). Æthelwulf twice identifies thorn-bushes with haunts of wickedness, and comments that Christ's suffering 'took away the thorny thickets of evil from the world': *DA* ll. 69, 134–5, 161 (pp. 9, 13, 15).

[45] This paragraph draws on: Blair 1992: 227–31; Stocker 1993: 105–6; Hase 1994: 54–60; Blair 1996a: 9–12; Blair 1996b: 98, 110; Tatton-Brown 1988: 110–13; Hall 2000: 66.

[46] Davies 1978: 37–8, 167. Cf. Hase 1994: 58: 'More often, the early West Saxon churches were built in a *locally* prominent position, on top of a hillock, such that the church is easily seen from nearby but not from any distance.'

[47] Blair 1996a: 9–10. Hase 1994 instances some low-lying sites in riverine terrain, but even these are raised above the floodplain.

[48] Hase 1994: 54–60; Blair 1996a: 8–12.   [49] Below, p. 198.

stable than high medieval ones, and dispersed settlement patterns were more general than they were to be (at any rate in lowland England) by the twelfth century. Minsters set apart in commanding locations could provide foci for terrains spread with scattered farms and homestead clusters, rather as hill-forts had done centuries earlier.[50] In England as in Ireland, minsters were often in the prime geographical zones for farming and settlement.[51] Far from being on the fringes of human activity, the rivers and coasts were the main transport arteries of early Britain; even the off-shore island of Lindisfarne was on the sea-highway of the Northumbrian coastline.[52]

None of this is to doubt that the sites, especially those encircled by water, were also valued for their topographical distinctness and boundedness, enabling the minsters to be *in* the world but not quite *of* it.[53] The rhetoric of the texts is not straightforwardly of seclusion, but rather of purifying the wilderness and making it blossom. At Lastingham Bede expounds Isaiah: '*In the habitations where once dragons lay shall be grass with reeds and rushes,* that is, the fruit of good works shall grow up there, where formerly beasts had dwelt or men had lived bestially.'[54] But the tension between the ideal of the wilderness and the reality of embeddedness in secular life required an element of make-believe. Lastingham is in fact not remote, nor a harsh place (Fig. 22): it is only three miles from a Roman road, and the east-facing outcrop on which the church stands nestles comfortably in a sheltered stream-valley at the foot of the moor.[55] Did the 'great thorn hedge' around Wilfrid's minster at Oundle help its inhabitants to imagine that they were in the Egyptian desert, not on the main river-route from the south midlands to the Wash?[56]

[50] Hamerow 1991; Blair 1992: 227–31; Blair 1995*a*: 201; Hamerow 2002: 94–9, 121–4, for settlement change—and moves towards greater organization and stability—during the seventh to ninth centuries.

[51] Hurley 1982: 310; Sims-Williams 1990: 369–71, 394–5.

[52] The monks of Tynemouth carried bulk goods on rafts across the Tyne estuary: *VCB* c. 3 (pp. 162–4). The role of the sea as highway is repeatedly obvious in Adomnán's 'Life of Columba'. Cf. Cubitt 1995: 32, for the holding of church councils on river-banks. Hill 1966 makes interesting points about the relationship of early Northumbrian religious sites to overland routes. Below, pp. 217–18, for genuinely eremitical sites.

[53] Gittos 2002*a*: 39–42. The ambiguity of monastic 'deserts' in northern Francia is brought out by Lebecq 2000: 124–9: 'It is not only because these damp and, maybe, repugnant environments encouraged asceticism that they were chosen by their founders. It is also because communications by water offered them opportunities for development.' See also Rosenwein 1999: 51.

[54] *HE* iii. 23 (p. 286).

[55] For the 'remoteness' topos cf. Hill 1966; J. M. Wallace-Hadrill, *Bede's Ecclesiastical History of the English People: A Historical Commentary* (Oxford, 1988), 120; Charles-Edwards 1974: 16–18, for moorland such as Lastingham having 'in men's ideas a position similar to that of the desert in Egypt or Palestine'.

[56] *VW* c. 67 (p. 146). Cf. the twelfth-century description of St Frideswide's refuge at Binsey (Oxon.): 'locus multigenis arboribus consitus, qui pro multitudine diversi generis spinarum lingua

We may learn something of the Anglo-Saxons' perceptions of monastic places from the names by which they called them. It is a striking and still rather puzzling fact that, whereas the place-names of Christian sites in Wales and Cornwall generally refer to saints and churches, English minster names tend (apart from the important but limited group which describe the location of some minsters at the centres of large, pre-existing folk-territories[57]) to be topographical.[58] Thus the minster 'in the Deirans' wood' where St John of York was buried in 721 was known as Beverley from the 'beaver-stream' on which it stood, not as 'Johnstow' or the like.[59] The main explanation may lie in the chronology of church-building in the English landscape: a century or so later than that of Atlantic Britain, and at a time when nomenclature had stabilized. But ecclesiastical scholars took an interest in topographical names for their own sake, bothering to note (rightly) that Selsey minster was built on a 'seal island', or (wrongly) that Wimborne meant 'wine-spring' from the clarity and flavour of its water.[60] It could be that we can see here, in a learned and monastic guise, the Anglo-Saxons' intense and fine-grained interest in the landscape, and their wide vocabulary for the natural world.[61] Like the farmers, herdsmen, and fishermen who had originally coined these and other place-names, founders and monks took a lively interest in the character and amenities of the sites where they and their colleagues lived. Rightly so: as many minsters grew into centres of economic exchange, and eventually into proto-towns, their topographical advantages would prove decisive.[62]

Saxonica Thornbiri nuncupabatur, solitarius siquidem et religioni aptissimus' (Robert of Cricklade, 'Vita S. Frideswidae', c. 15, ed. J. Blair, 'St Frideswide Reconsidered', *Oxoniensia*, 52 (1987), 71–127, at 110). In the mid eleventh century, Evesham minster was surrounded by 'altissima et maxima sepes de spinis' (Thomas of Marlborough, *History of the Abbey of Evesham*, ed. J. Sayers and L. Watkiss (Oxford, 2003), 122).

[57] Below, p. 251, for the tendency of folk-names of this type to attach themselves to the central minsters.

[58] For further discussion of this contrast see Blair 2002*a*: 469–70; cf. Gelling 1981: 4, and Padel 2002. The small number of cases where the name of an apparent founder or abbess is compounded with *burh* or *mynster* are considered above, p. 81 n.

[59] *HE* v. 6 (p. 468); Blair 2001*b*.

[60] *HE* iv. 13 (p. 374); Rudolf, 'Vita S. Leobae', c. 2 (ed. G. Waitz, *MGH Scriptores*, xv. 1 (Hannover, 1887), 123).

[61] The pioneer work was Gelling 1984: e.g. p. 6. No attempt is made here to analyse the topographical elements in the names of minsters, but the exercise might be revealing; cf. Hall 2000: 24–6, showing that river-names predominate in Dorset.

[62] Below, p. 257.

The enclosures and buildings of minsters

Enclosure was fundamental to the monastic ideal, and it is an implicit assumption of seventh- to ninth-century English sources that a minster would be contained within some physical boundary, the *vallum* or *septum monasterii*.[63] Wilfrid's minster at Oundle was surrounded by a 'great thorn hedge', for instance, and Bede took it for granted that the activities even of fraudulent minsters were contained *intra septa*.[64] One of the crimes of an early eighth-century Northumbrian tyrant was to force nobles to retire within *monasterii septis*.[65] This ideal may not invariably have been expressed physically: the enclosing boundary has only been located at a handful of English minsters, and it could be that containment was sometimes achieved by the natural topography of hills, islands, and peninsulas, or by purely notional perimeters. But it is probably right to assume, in the absence of evidence to the contrary, that a core site would have had some kind of physical definition. This is one of the many ways in which minsters differed from even the larger and more important secular sites, which seem normally to have lacked continuous and substantial boundaries.[66]

The planners of monastic sites had two 'ideal' prototypes at their disposal. One was square: the Heavenly Jerusalem of Revelation 21.[67] Where the walls of a Roman fort still stood, as at Reculver or Bradwell-on-Sea, this kind of *vallum monasterii* was provided ready-made. The possibility of square or rectilinear planning on sites without Roman remains was largely ignored until Teresa Hall's recent work, which points out that the topography of roads and boundaries around Dorset minsters is usually rectilinear rather than circular.[68] There may be regional contrasts, but it does seem likely that square or rectangular perimeters (which are harder to decipher on post-medieval maps than curvilinear ones) have been under-represented in previous work; Deerhurst, for instance, looks a possible case (Fig. 33).

---

[63] Blair 1992: 232, for the Irish and Merovingian context.

[64] *VW* c. 67 (p. 146); *Ep. E.* c. 12 (p. 416).

[65] *DA* l. 51 (p. 7). At the minster of 'De Abbatibus' there were paupers 'shut outside the gates' (*exclusi portis*), and the brethren rejoiced 'through the walls/ramparts of the minster' (*per moenia cellae*): *DA* ll. 481, 654 (pp. 39, 53).

[66] Sixth- and early seventh-century settlements were usually unenclosed. During the seventh century, groups of farmsteads often became more structured, with fenced enclosures and paddocks, and recent work is showing that small enclosed settlements were more widespread in the eighth and ninth centuries than has been thought (Richards 1999: 71–3; Hamerow 2002: 97, 154). But the few identified monastic *valla* (below, n. 74) still look more substantial, and closer in scale to serious defences, than anything normally found on secular sites. The later and smaller-scale enclosed homesteads could even have been modelled on them.

[67] Below, p. 248.

[68] Hall 2000: 49–78. Other cases may be Leominster (Hillaby 2001: 48–9) and Congresbury (Oakes and Costen 2003: 284–9).

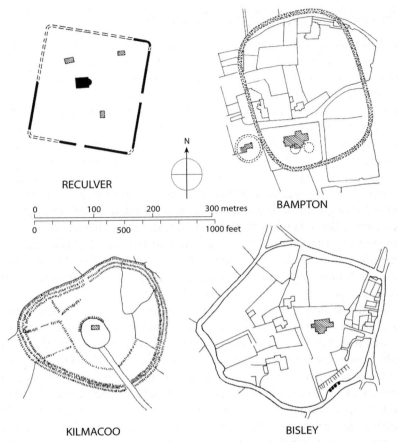

RECULVER

N

| 0 | 100 | 200 | 300 metres |
| 0 | | 500 | 1000 feet |

BAMPTON

KILMACOO

BISLEY

23. Types of minster enclosure: *Reculver* (Kent) in its ready-made Roman fort; *Bampton* (Oxon.) with its perimeter ditch confirmed by excavation; and *Bisley* (Glos.) to illustrate the perpetuation of lost boundary features in the modern topography. The Irish monastic site at *Kilmacoo*, with its surviving earthworks, is included for comparison. (After Taylor and Taylor 1965–78: ii, figs. 246–7; Blair 1998c: fig. 1; and Blair 1992: fig. 10.2.)

The second 'ideal' form—a circle—is most visible to us, as it probably was to contemporaries, in early Christian Ireland. Irish legal texts defining concentric zones of protected space, and a diagram in one manuscript showing a double circle ringed by crosses of the Evangelists and Prophets, can be understood as abstractions of the round and oval monastic sites, with concentric and radial subdivisions, known from fieldwork and aerial reconnaissance.[69] The sacred character of the boundaries (sometimes believed to have been established by founder-saints), and the solemn rituals for marking them out, are known from Irish saints' Lives and possibly carvings.[70] While an ultimate Irish source remains likely, it has become clear that the basic format of the sub-circular, banked and ditched monastic site was in no sense peculiarly 'Celtic' but occurred widely in west Britain, England, northern Gaul, and the sites of the English missions in Germany.[71] There is a range of forms and sizes, modified by regional patterns which may be culturally determined. Wales, for instance, has large, sometimes concentric enclosures resembling the more symmetrical Irish ones (Fig. 4);[72] by comparison, lowland English sites seem, so far as the inadequate evidence goes, to have been simpler and less structured, with little sign of either radial or concentric subdivision. Prototypes were probably established by the monasticization of secular ring-forts in Ireland, which retained a vernacular tradition of circular planning such as England did not, and of secular citadels in upland Britain, where the massive boundary of Coldingham reflects a fort-building idiom.[73] The more remote a site was from these cultural sources, the more second-hand and attenuated the tradition.

In England, unlike Ireland, curvilinear monastic enclosures rarely survive as earthworks, but their outlines are often reflected in boundaries or road-systems (Fig. 23). Typically they measure between 150 and 300 metres across, with perimeter ditches three to four metres wide.[74] These were not insubstantial boundaries, especially if they had commensurate internal banks, and although they can hardly be called defensive they suggest a serious wish to keep the world at bay.

Inside the enclosure, it is seldom clear how space was divided up. At Wimborne (in what is possibly an idealized description) the male and female communities were segregated by walls; at Æthelhild's minster near Partney the

---

[69] Aitchison 1994: 211–33, for this kind of Irish symbolic topography, notably at Armagh; Gittos 2002*b*: 205–8, for Irish conceptions of enclosedness; below, pp. 221–2, for the zones of sacred space; Hurley 1982, Swan 1983, Swan 1985, and Herity 1995 for the field evidence; Graham 1998: 135–42, for a sceptical view.

[70] Aitchison 1994: 235–6, 265–81.   [71] Blair 1992: 228–35, with references.

[72] James 1992*c*.   [73] Blair 1992: 233 n. 27.

[74] This statement is based on the excavated sections of ditches at the following minsters: Bampton, 4 m. (J. Blair in *South Midlands Archaeology*, 18 (1988), 89–90; Blair 1998*c*); Beverley, *c*.3 m. (Armstrong and others 1991: 7–10); Brixworth, 4–5 m. (Everson 1977: 68–72, 83); Deerhurst, *c*.4 m. or more (Rahtz and Watts 1997: 207–11); Glastonbury, ditch 4 m. plus 6-m. internal bank (Rahtz 1993: 92–3); Hoddom, 3 m. with internal fence-line (Lowe 1991: figs. 2–5). There were other kinds of boundary feature at Whitby, apparently with a 5-m. wall (Rahtz 1976: 460), and Hartlepool, with a palisade-trench (Daniels 1988: 161). An aerial photograph of Bawsey (Norfolk) shows a clear cropmark of what was probably a smallish ditched monastic enclosure, in the form of a rather angular oval (Rogerson 2003: 113).

nuns evidently lived in a gated enclosure which had the men's quarters outside it.[75] Whitby, probably one of the most complex sites, gives the impression of a big, rambling settlement with disparate activities going on in various nooks and corners.[76] Often the main church (or at least the one surviving today) is not central, but stands towards one side—usually the south—of the enclosed area. It seems likely that there was a small, densely occupied nucleus around the churches, the rest of the precinct being open, and occupied by low-level industrial and agricultural activity or kitchen gardens. Hoddom (Dumfries), where extensive survey of the ploughed site gives a better impression than elsewhere, had a scatter of industrial and agri-cultural buildings around the periphery furthest from the church.[77]

Within the core precinct, the buildings of a minster would focus on its church or, more commonly, its line or group of churches (Fig. 24).[78] In a tradition going back ultimately to the major Christian complexes of the holy land, and mediated through the 'episcopal groups' at Italian and southern Gallic cathedrals, a religious community of any importance in early medieval Francia, Britain, and probably Ireland would normally have had two or more churches. In England, starting with archetypal sites under direct foreign influence—St Augustine's monastery at Canterbury, or Hexham, Monkwear-mouth, and Jarrow in Northumbria—it became normal practice to align these churches (sometimes precisely, often very loosely) on a west–east axis. This linear configuration had been uncommon in Italy and France except, significantly, in the group of Seine valley monasteries clustered around Paris with which the first English Christian dynasties had been so closely linked.[79] But another influence must surely have been the early seventh-century

[75] Rudolf, 'Vita S. Leobae', c. 2 (ed. G. Waitz, *MGH Scriptores*, xv. 1 (Hannover, 1887), 123); *HE* iii. 11 (p. 248). For segregation of male and female communities see: Schneider 1985: 40–1; Foot 2000: 48, 53–4. The excavations at Hartlepool located traces of internal divisions defining groups of buildings (Daniels 1988: fig. 2).

[76] It could offer permanent houseroom to the exiled bishop Trumwine and his household, and included a novices' quarter 'in extremis monasterii locis' (*HE* iv. 23, iv. 26 (pp. 414, 428)). Cramp 1976: 223–9, and Cramp 1993 for the archaeological evidence; recent (unpublished) excavations strongly support the impression that seventh- to ninth-century occupation—presumably monas-tic—was spread across the Whitby headland.

[77] Lowe 1991. An interesting parallel can be drawn with the 'infield' enclosures of the Somerset Levels (Rippon 1997), where the oval, ditched agrarian nuclei of village communities resemble, and may even have been modelled on, early monastic enclosures.

[78] Blair 1992: 246–58, and Gittos 2002*a*: 75–116, for what follows; Cramp 1976 and Rodwell 1984 are earlier reviews of some of the same evidence. The phenomenon of 'double churches' through-out Christendom is now the subject of a massive collection of essays (Carrié 1996), but even this can only conclude for England that 'les "églises en file", d'interprétation d'ailleurs difficile en l'absence d'installations précises, prédominant, mais surtout en milieu monastique' (p. 226). For Gaul, see also Knight 1999: 63–84.

[79] Gittos 2002*a*: 79–85, 88–98; cf. above, pp. 42, 72, and the Gallic architectural influence on the early Kentish churches noted by Cambridge 1999: 216–18.

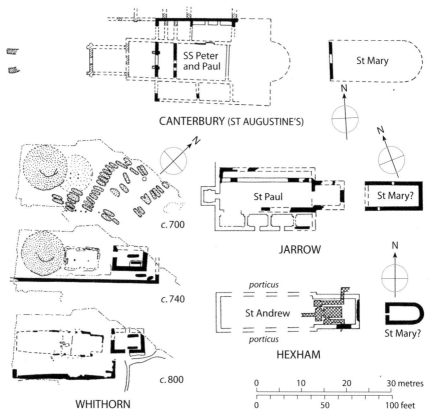

24. Aligned church groups in the seventh and eighth centuries. *Canterbury* after R. Gem in Ramsay and others 1992: figs. 4–5; *Jarrow* after Cramp 1976: fig. 5.14; *Whithorn* after Hill 1997: figs. 3.31, 3.32, 4.5, and 4.15; *Hexham* after Bailey 1991: fig. 6. Post-Roman British features are indicated by stipple; seventh- and eighth-century English features in solid black; and Wilfrid's crypt at Hexham by cross-hatching.

English practice of organizing high-status secular and ritual complexes, most strikingly Yeavering (Fig. 7), on precise axes. In the light of such cases as Ripon and Bampton, the capacity to remodel existing lines of pagan foci as Christian ones, and the familiarity of the English with this kind of formal layout, may have combined to make axiality attractive.

Again following Continental practice, recurrent groups of dedications— an apostle or martyr paired with St Mary or the Holy Saviour—became standard in England, where the lesser (St Mary's) church often stood due east of the greater (apostolic) one.[80] The alignments might also include additional

[80] Gittos 2002*a*: 84–8, 98–100.

chapels, free-standing stone mausolea,[81] and crosses. These groups tended to develop accretively, with the apostolic church built first and subsidiary churches or other liturgical foci added over generations or centuries. The Archangel Michael thus rebuked the dilatory St Wilfrid: 'You have built churches in honour of the apostles St Peter and St Andrew, but for the blessed Mary, ever-virgin, who is interceding for you, you have built nothing. You must put this right and dedicate a church in her honour.'[82] At Eanmund's minster, in eighth-century Northumbria, the founder built St Peter's but the community had to wait for the fourth abbot to build St Mary's; the fifth abbot contributed a tall cross.[83]

Defining functions within church groups is not straightforward on the Continent, and is especially hard in the insular cultures, but the basic practice of using multiple churches needs no explanation. Early medieval liturgy was characteristically performed in sequences of small compartments, and the multiplication of these compartments around holy sites was the immemorial practice of the Church. Adomnán's account of the multifarious tombs, basilicas, and oratories of the holy land, including the great line of churches on Golgotha, was known to Bede, probably to Wilfrid, and to many of their contemporaries; its descriptions of 'holy cities' presented a model for emulation.[84] The recurrent groups of dedications in seventh- and eighth-century England, symbolizing the unity of distinct sites over sometimes considerable distances, likewise affirmed the re-incorporation of a recently pagan landscape into the universal Christian one. The whole convention can be understood, in Helen Gittos's words, 'as a manifestation of the concept of the communion of saints, a unity made manifest through the Church and physically articulated in the stational ligurgy. It was an architectural reflex of a young Church in a northern outpost'.[85]

One prototype which the English conspicuously rejected was the separate baptismal church, which had been a normal component of episcopal groups in Mediterranean Christendom.[86] An octagonal tank containing a well in the north transept of the seventh-century Winchester cathedral, and an integral drain leading out of the eighth-century crypt at Repton,[87] so far constitute

[81] Below, n. 201.
[82] *VW* c. 56 (p. 122). Cf. S 22, the early ninth-century forged privilege for the Kentish minsters, referring to churches and minsters 'sanctis apostolis etiamque Maria virgine [matri] domini nostri sacrata'.
[83] *DA* ll. 143–50, 431–72, 537–9 (pp. 13–15, 35–9, 43).
[84] Adomnán, 'De Locis Sanctis', ed. D. Meehan, *Scriptores Lat. Hib.* iii (Dublin, 1958).
[85] Gittos 2002*a*: 87–8.
[86] Blair 1992: 246–9; Kjølbye-Biddle 1998: 758–62.
[87] Kjølbye-Biddle 1998. The Winchester tank contains an actual well. The chancel at Repton may have been built as a two-storey mausoleum with baptistery below, but even there the drain is not conclusive evidence: it could have been built simply because the crypt was wet. The argument for an early baptistery at Southwell (Dixon and Stocker 2001: 258–64) is speculative.

the only physical evidence for baptism in pre-Viking England. There is probably a straightforward chronological explanation: when minsters and episcopal seats were being established in England, monumental episcopal baptisteries were already becoming obsolete north of the Alps, and many of them would be demolished at the time of the Carolingian reforms.[88] In this context the only documented English example, the church of St John the Baptist which Archbishop Cuthbert (740–60) built at the east end of Canterbury cathedral,[89] must be seen as an archaism: a symbolic claim to a baptismal monopoly which Continental bishops were already abandoning, or simply a reminiscence of the Lateran baptistery in Rome.

Outside the central groups, minster precincts sometimes contained sub-sidiary chapels and oratories. When Ceolfrith departed from Monkwear-mouth in 716, mass was said in St Mary's and St Peter's and the community then processed to St Lawrence's chapel beside the monks' dormitory.[90] Barking had an oratory associated with the nuns' cemetery, on the south side of the precinct.[91] The excavations at Whithorn found a complete little axial group, comprising church and mortuary chapel, on a terrace on the edge of the precinct (Fig. 24), perhaps for the benefit of pilgrims or visitors.[92] These arrangements suggest a zoning of space, perhaps with restricted access to the core buildings but open access at the periphery.

Domestic buildings, unlike churches, never survive above ground, but written and archaeological sources indicate planning norms which show a broad continuum between Frankish, Irish, and English monastic sites.[93] Core complexes could be intensively occupied. Bede describes an approaching traveller's view of Coldingham, its 'public and private buildings' towering grandly up (*sublimiter erecta*), and notes that at Barking part of the nuns' cemetery had to be built over 'because the place in which the minster was built was so constricted'.[94] The position of the building at Oundle in which Wilfrid died, projecting against the enclosure boundary, also implies that space was tight.[95] Texts show that a big Merovingian or Irish minster would

---

[88] For example Geneva, where a grand fourth-century baptistery was scaled down and eventu-ally abandoned: Bonnet 1993. The delegation of baptism to priests, and the obsolescence of adult baptism, are the usual explanations for the phenomenon, though they clearly did not outweigh the symbolic importance of monumental baptisteries in Italy (cf. Bullough 1999: 57–60). I am grateful to Elisabeth Lorans for advice on this problem.

[89] Brooks 1984: 40–1, 51; Gittos 2002a: 95–6, 169–70.

[90] *HA* c. 17 (pp. 381–2).

[91] *HE* iv. 7 (pp. 356–8). Bede's term *oratorium* suggests that this was a subsidiary chapel, not the main church: a minster of the status of Barking would surely have had an *ecclesia* or *basilica*.

[92] Hill 1997: 40–8, 134–82.

[93] Blair 1992: 258–64, for these paragraphs. See also James 1981 for Gaul; Herity 1995: esp. 19–65, for Ireland.

[94] *HE* iv. 25, iv. 10 (pp. 424, 362).   [95] *VW* c. 67 (p. 146).

usually have a principal, multi-purpose communal building, known by such terms as the 'great house', which would be partitioned for such varied functions as eating, sleeping, cooking, reading, writing, teaching, and storage.[96] The one English example found so far (apart from the debatable case of Northampton, discussed below) is at Jarrow, where a pair of monumental stone ranges, set end to end with a narrow gap between, lay immediately south of the church.[97]

A minster's daily activities could also take place within separate small buildings. The dissolute nuns of Coldingham had 'huts' (*casae*), as well as 'little houses (*domunculae*) made for praying or reading', in all of which they misbehaved themselves.[98] The peripheral industrial or workshop buildings at Hoddom and Lindisfarne recall Bede's story of the skilful but irreligious brother who preferred to hide away in his workshop (*officina*) rather than singing and praying in the church.[99] Lesser structures on the peripheries of core precincts have been excavated at Whitby, Hartlepool, Whithorn, and Dorchester-on-Thames.[100] In all these cases rectangular 'hall'-like buildings organized in relatively dense, rectilinear groups, and demarcated at Whitby and Whithorn by paths, were maintained through a sequence of rebuildings between the late seventh century and the mid ninth. These excavated buildings belong to the English vernacular tradition known from rural settlements, where they are sometimes arranged in an orderly fashion within paddocks.[101] What does, however, set the minsters somewhat apart is the density of the groups, and their tendency to be perpetuated on the same sites over a period of up to two centuries.

Another feature of monastic excavations is the variety and quality of the small eighth- and early ninth-century objects found. Jarrow, Whitby, Hartlepool, and Barking illustrate a distinctive, recurring range: pins and other dress-fastenings, sometimes elaborately decorated; tweezers; styli for writing on wax tablets (a carved tablet-cover has been found at the probable minster site of Blythburgh); book- or shrine-mounts; coins; decorated glass vessels; and fine imported pottery.[102] Smaller-scale excavation, and stray finds, are increasingly showing that similar material occurs at other minsters. Comparing these assemblages with normal secular ones is complicated by regional

[96] Blair 1992: 260–1.   [97] Cramp 1976: fig. 5.14.
[98] *HE* iv. 25 (p. 424). Cf. ibid. iv. 8–9 (pp. 358–60) for a *domus* and a *cubiculum* occupied by nuns at Barking.
[99] *HE* iv. 14 (p. 502). Lowe 1991, for Hoddom; O'Sullivan 2001: 40–5, for Lindisfarne.
[100] Rahtz 1976; Daniels 1988; Hill 1997: 134–82; Rowley and Brown 1981.
[101] Above, n. 50.
[102] Webster and Backhouse 1991: 79–101, 132–47; Wormald 1982a: 79; Cramp 1993: 66–7. Carisbrooke may be another case: Ulmschneider 2003.

variation. Minsters participated in a consumer culture, drawing in luxury products from England, France, Germany, and Frisia, which mushroomed from the late seventh century with the growth of the coastal *wics* and the trade which they supported. This culture affected eastern and south-eastern England much more than inland regions, and it is no coincidence that the minsters which have yielded notably rich assemblages lie along the east coast from the Tyne to the Thames estuaries. Consumer goods, notably dress-items and imported pottery, are also found in these areas on secular settlements and on probable exchange sites. But it can be said with some confidence that only the *wics* show a range of imported items comparable to those from minsters, and that no sites whatever (except a few debatable ones to be discussed shortly) show the range of opulent personal belongings.[103]

Seen in a wider context, monastic settlements embody that fusion of metropolitan and vernacular which is so characteristic of their world. Their demarcated precincts and formal groups of churches reflect Mediterranean ideas of monumentality and liturgical space, expressed in the stone ranges built at Jarrow by Biscop's Gallic masons 'in the manner of the Romans which he always loved'.[104] But the shape and organization of the enclosures has much in common with Irish monastic sites, the groups of domestic buildings with the houses and settlements of English thegns and farmers. Archaeologically, the monastic settlements seem more highly developed, and sustained over longer periods, than secular ones, and they consistently produce a greater abundance of richer and more varied artefacts. It seems a reasonable conclusion that these sites, more than others so far excavated, saw prolonged and stable occupation by large groups of well-to-do people. As James Campbell wrote in 1979, before much of the relevant archaeological evidence had become available: 'A monastery such as Whitby, with its numerous buildings, its crafts and its maritime contacts must have been considerably more like a town than were most places.'[105]

Problems of identity: Northampton, Brandon, Flixborough, and the metal-detected sites

Documented minster sites therefore show a consistent set of attributes: a preference for hills, promontories, peninsulas, and confluences; enclosedness; groups of churches, often axially aligned; structured and stable settlements; and an unusually rich material culture. Some of these characteristics occur

---

[103] Below, pp. 256–61, for the economic implications of this material.
[104] *HA* c. 5 (p. 368).　　　[105] Campbell 1986: 141.

also at secular sites, but it is the minsters which recurrently combine several of them. Can we go a step further, and argue that undocumented places, known only from excavation but showing the same conjunction of attributes, are monastic too? This question is part of a larger one—were monastic settlements consistently and obviously distinct from secular settlements?—which has been posed already in relation to Bede's letter to Ecgberht:[106] would a visitor to one of his 'fraudulent' minsters have instantly recognized it as monastic? Undocumented sites force us to confront the problem of how far, by c.800, the externals of monastic culture had been assimilated into aristocratic life. It is worth considering some problematic cases, all excavated during the last thirty years and all of disputed identity.

At the heart of the town of Northampton,[107] on a promontory at the confluence of two branches of the Nene, a large eighth-century timber hall was replaced early in the ninth century by a stone hall of huge proportions, the biggest Anglo-Saxon domestic building ever found. The excavators, influenced by Carolingian parallels, interpreted this as a royal palace, but its immediate context prompts second thoughts. The hall, on a west–east axis, lies immediately east of St Peter's church, recorded in eleventh- and twelfth-century texts as the mother-church of the region. To the south-east stood the lesser church of St Gregory, associated with eighth-century burials. The immediate environs have produced evidence for a continuous spread of seventh- to ninth-century occupation. Given the location of the hall between two churches with complementary dedications, the lack of any written evidence for a palace, and the late but clear evidence for a minster, it seems most straightforward to interpret the entire complex as monastic, a (roughly) axial pair of churches encapsulating a refectory. Resistance to this view rests on the belief that so enormous a hall can only have been lived in by a king, whereas it does not conform to expectations of monastic architecture. In response it may be observed that a major early ninth-century Mercian minster under royal patronage is likely to have been very grand, and influenced by Carolingian prototypes; and that whatever the central domestic building of such a minster may have looked like, it is most unlikely to have been 'claustral' or 'monastic' in a high medieval sense. Built shortly after Alcuin found it necessary to urge that in minsters 'the reader should be heard, not the harpist',[108] the Northampton hall makes an eminently plausible setting for the social life of a royal minster under King Coenwulf or his successors.

---

[106] Above, p. 105–7.
[107] Williams 1979; Williams 1984; Williams and others 1985. The present interpretation is after Blair 1996b: 98–108.
[108] Above, p. 136.

A rather different and much larger category of sites can be introduced by the most completely excavated examples, Brandon (Suffolk) and Flixborough (Lincs.) (Fig. 25). At Brandon,[109] excavation of about a third of a sand island in the Little Ouse revealed a cluster of well-preserved rectangular timber buildings, extended and rebuilt in at least three phases between the late seventh and mid ninth centuries, which may in fact extend across the whole island. The heart of the complex (still unexcavated) was perpetuated by a later chapel surrounded by a heavily used cemetery. West of this lay the excavated half of a probable inner precinct, with dense groups of small buildings and a network of enclosure ditches. Around 800 the settlement expanded southwards to create an outer zone, containing fewer but larger buildings and focused on a timber church with its own small cemetery, which was entered from the south via a causeway. Northwards, on the river-edge, were platforms of reclaimed land used for textile manufacture, and perhaps a quay. An overlying occupation-layer produced an extraordinary assemblage of high-quality finds (Fig. 26): imported pottery, vessel- and window-glass, pins, coins, styli, and a substantial quantity of decorated and gilt metalwork. Especially notable were a large silver-gilt disc-headed pin engraved with an equal-armed cross, and a square gold plaque of the highest quality bearing the symbol of St John the Evangelist, probably from a book-cover or cross-arm. After 850 the island settlement was abandoned, but the local topography suggests the possibility of re-structuring around new foci—St Peter's parish church southwards, the town of Brandon eastwards—rather than a total hiatus (Fig. 39).[110]

The site at Flixborough (Lincs.)[111] was also on a sandy bluff, though in this case below a west-facing limestone escarpment overlooking the Trent floodplain. The excavated zone, an unknown proportion of the total, lay immediately down-slope from the disused church of All Saints, which can possibly be interpreted as the original focus of the complex.[112] Minor seventh-century occupation was succeeded around 700 by groups of

[109] Carr and others 1988; Warner 1996: 123–7; Webster and Backhouse 1991: 81–8. I am grateful to the excavator, Bob Carr, for discussing it with me.

[110] But Mr Carr observes (pers. comm. 1999): 'I do think it was abandonment, in the sense of a transfer from one focus to what was probably already a Mid Saxon secondary agricultural focus on the edge of the flood-plain.' In the late tenth century, St Æthelwold dedicated a church at Brandon at the request of its lay proprietors (*Lib. El.* 82): was this St Peter's?

[111] Webster and Backhouse 1991: 94–101; Loveluck 2001; Ulmschneider 2000: 136–7 and *passim*; Leahy 1999. I am extremely grateful to Christopher Loveluck for providing the latest results of post-excavation work and discussing them with me, the more so since my interpretation is not his.

[112] Leahy 1999: 94; Loveluck 2001: 80. In my view the nucleus of the site is likely to have been established on the stone escarpment, with peripheral settlement (the excavated area) on the sand below; Dr Loveluck prefers to envisage a gradual shift eastwards, with a relatively late church serving a deserted medieval village. Only further excavation could settle the matter.

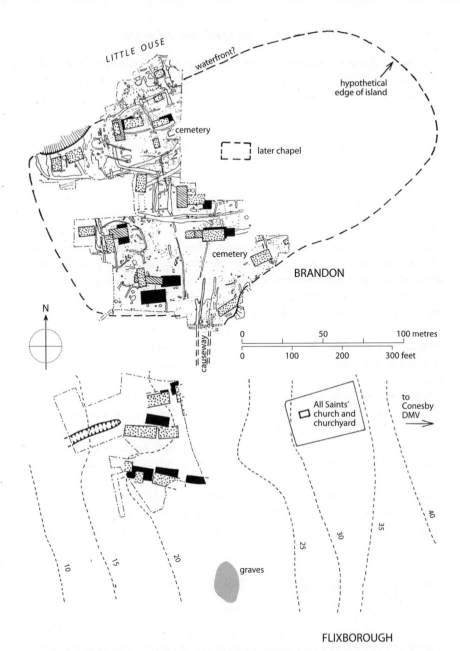

25. The mid Saxon settlements at *Brandon* (Suffolk) and *Flixborough* (Lincs.), re-drawn at the same scale. The three shading conventions (black, hatching, stipple) represent successive building phases—not necessarily contemporary on the two sites—during the seventh to ninth centuries. Contours at Flixborough are at five-metre intervals. (After data supplied by Robert Carr and Christopher Loveluck.)

rectangular timber buildings, some aligned end to end with narrow gaps between them, which persisted on much the same plots through several rebuildings up to *c.*850. (One mysterious building, heated throughout by open hearths, had graves against the outer and inner faces of its walls.) To the south was a cemetery, still largely unexcavated. Middens dumped in the late ninth and tenth centuries produced an artefact assemblage eclipsing even Brandon: window-glass, styli, opulent dress-pins, coins, loomweights, industrial waste, and tools for working cloth, timber, leather, bone, and metal. Outstanding finds were a complete set of carpenter's tools in a lead box, a ring inscribed with the first half of the alphabet, and a small lead plate, with nail-holes around the edges for attachment, engraved with seven male and female names (Fig. 16). Despite apparent Viking-age disruption this site was not abandoned: large halls were built on the old alignments in the tenth century, and occupation continued beyond the Norman Conquest.

Brandon and Flixborough show some strong similarities to known minster sites. Brandon was a bounded and tightly structured island settlement, with an outer court which a visitor entered from the causeway to see the subsidiary church and its cemetery straight ahead: an arrangement recalling the subsidiary liturgical group on the terrace at Whithorn. One and probably both sites were organized around focal churches, which survived (at a humble level) long after monastic occupation ceased. The tendency to rebuild on the same plot, and the aligned rows at Flixborough, are forms that seem characteristic of monastic settlements (though not confined to them[113]); the later Brandon buildings were exceptionally large by normal East Anglian standards.

The portable objects (Fig. 26) point in the same direction. Finds from Northampton are few (a stylus and a shrine-mount), but so far as they go they are more ecclesiastical than secular.[114] Interpreting the Brandon and Flixborough assemblages is complicated both by the unusually favourable circumstances of recovery and by the fact that both sites lie in the rich eastern zone (in the case of Flixborough on the commercially developed Humber estuary). Even allowing for this, they are exceptional in quality, in quantity, and in the association of opulent fashion accessories with a wide range of crafts and industries. Two objects, the Brandon gold plaque and the Flixborough lead inscription, are of a strongly ecclesiastical character, and for the second at least it is hard to imagine a plausible secular function: it seems best identified as a label from a wooden container for exhumed bones (the similar inscription found at Kirkdale minster (Yorks.) apparently includes the word *bancyst*, 'bone-box' (Fig. 16)), or as part of a commemorative screen or other

---

[113] Loveluck 2001: 108–10.   [114] Blair 1996*b*: 101 (incorrectly mentioning three styli).

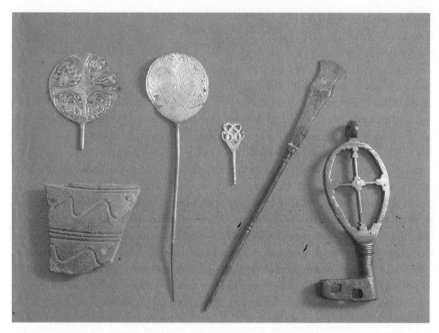

26. Typical artefacts of the eighth-century 'minster culture': three pins, a writing-stylus, a key, and a sherd of imported Frankish pottery from the probable monastic site at *Brandon* (Suffolk). (Suffolk County Council Archaeological Service.)

structure like a large-scale *liber vitae*.[115] Still more suggestive are the styli for writing on wax tablets: three from Brandon, twenty-one (nearly a quarter of the English total) from Flixborough. Almost half of the eighty-nine known styli come from places with known minsters, only thirteen (mostly single finds) from sites lacking other suggestions of a monastic past: on present showing it seems very improbable that an assemblage like Flixborough's could come from anything other than a religious community.[116]

[115] Watts and others 1997: 63–4. When part of the monastic cemetery at Barking had to be built over, the bones of male and female members of the community were exhumed, taken into the church, and gathered in one place (*HE* iv. 10 (pp. 362–4)): the container could have been labelled with just such a plate as the ones found at Flixborough and Kirkdale. In favour of the *liber vitae* interpretation, on the other hand, are the facts that the Flixborough inscription has been incised over an earlier one and that its last name seems to be an afterthought (I owe these points to Tom Pickles and Felicity Clark). The exceptionally light clay loomweights from Flixborough would be consistent with the *subtiliora indumenta* woven by the worldly nuns of Coldingham, or with the tendency of nuns, attacked in 747, 'texendis et plectendis vario colore inanis gloriae vestibus': *HE* iv. 25 (p. 424); *Clof.747* c. 20 (p. 369).

[116] Tim Pestell's recent corpus and discussion of styli is fundamental, and my own analysis is founded on his work (Pestell 1999: 57–68; Pestell 2003: 135–7). I think, though, that he pushes the

Other sites which could resemble Brandon and Flixborough are known, but only from fragments which leave their general character much less clear. Burrow Hill, Butley (Suffolk) was on an island much like Brandon, had a large eighth- to ninth-century cemetery of orientated burials (mainly adult males), and has produced vessel-glass, decorated metalwork, a cauldron-chain, and coins.[117] Again, the medieval village of Wharram Percy (Yorks.) overlies an eighth- to ninth-century settlement containing a workshop with debris from the casting of small copper-alloy mounts with interlace decoration, and has produced high-quality imported pottery, a coin, and two stone cross fragments resembling pieces at the minsters of Lastingham, Stonegrave, and Whitby.[118]

In the zone of rich material culture across eastern England, the activities of field-walkers and metal-detectorists have identified a growing category of so-called 'productive sites' (a term which has quickly outlived its usefulness) from exceptional concentrations of coins, small metal objects, and styli.[119] Some of these places, for instance Bawsey and Wormegay in Norfolk, resemble Brandon and Butley topographically; Bawsey (where there are seventh- to ninth-century burials near the later church) has produced six styli, Wormegay one.[120] The economic implications of this material will be

argument for non-monastic use too far. Thirteen of the 30 find-spots, yielding 40 (i.e. 45%) of the known styli, are documented minster-places (though this includes six styli from Winchester and five from York which were mostly found in post-Viking contexts); six 'crypto-minsters' (Bawsey, Blythburgh, Brandon, Flixborough, Northampton, Wormegay) provide another 36 (40%); and eleven places not known to be monastic contribute the remaining thirteen (15%). Furthermore, these eleven include three places in southern Suffolk near centres of St Botwulf's cult: Sudbourne near Iken, and Coddenham and Otley near Grundisburgh, where Botwulf's relics rested for a time. This is not to say that writing on wax tablets *only* happened in minsters (I find Pestell's idea that styli acquired status connotations in a wider social group quite persuasive), but in the pre-Viking period it does look like an *essentially* monastic activity which may, to some extent, have been disseminated with other attributes of the monastic culture. It is especially suggestive that the great coastal emporia have produced only one stylus between them, an abnormal grave find from Ipswich.

[117] Fenwick 1984.

[118] Milne and Richards 1992 (and see review by M. Welch in *ArchJ* 150 (1993), 532); Lang 1991: 222; Richards 1999: 74–9.

[119] The corpus of evidence is expanding rapidly, and much of it has not yet been catalogued. The essays in Pestell and Ulmschneider 2003 are now the starting-point; see also Andrews 1992 (Norfolk), Ulmschneider 2000 (Lincolnshire and Hampshire), and Pestell 1999 (East Anglia). Richards 1999 (on Yorkshire) shows that the circumstances of retrieval have often given 'productive sites' a misleading prominence, and concludes that 'the term is meaningless and should be abandoned'; he sees the Brandon and Flixborough assemblages as in a class apart, more comparable to Whitby or to the emporia. But the data from Butley, Bawsey, etc. are certainly not adequate to justify excluding them from the top category on artefactual grounds.

[120] Andrews 1992: 20–4; Rogerson 2003: 112–14, 120; Pestell 2003: 124–6. Bawsey is on a hillock in the floodplain, with a church at the centre and a perimeter ditch; Wormegay is on an island. The graves at Bawsey were revealed during excavations for a Channel Four 'Time Team' programme in 1998, and I am grateful to Margaret Cox for providing a radiocarbon date from the stratigraphically earliest burial: Wk 7057, cal. AD 668–897 at 2-sigma.

considered in the next chapter, but the point needs to be made here that Brandon and Flixborough stand at the top of a hierarchy of sites.

Clearly many or most of the lesser places must have been secular. But were the top tier marked off from the rest, in their siting, layout, and use of specialized objects, specifically because they were monastic? The current generation of archaeologists, reacting against the certainties of earlier ones, tends to resist this conclusion. For John Hines, reflecting on Bede's letter, 'it is clear that the lay and religious character of relatively high-status settlement sites could be thoroughly confused—something which leaves one wondering whether there is any point in archaeological speculations on the possible monastic character of certain fairly rich eighth-century sites that have been excavated, for instance at Flixborough . . . and Brandon'.[121] But contemporaries, to judge from their writings, were perfectly clear about the difference between minsters and lay settlements, even if they viewed some minsters as thoroughly bad ones: it is archaeologists who are 'thoroughly confused'. Close parallels for the various characteristics of the Brandon-type sites, in so far as the very patchy evidence reveals them, can be found at the places which are known from written evidence to be important minsters, and cannot at present be found at any other extensively excavated site. The styli are signatures of a culture which great minsters such as Whitby and Barking shared with these places, but not with the coastal emporia (where it looks as though they were never in normal use), nor with 'ordinary' sites producing pins, strap-ends, and coins.[122]

On present knowledge it seems fair to say that the sites which were most highly developed, lasted longest, and yield the widest and richest assemblages of finds bear a strongly monastic stamp. Or, to put it another way: if Northampton, Brandon, Flixborough, and at least some others were not themselves minsters, they were secular establishments influenced to a quite extraordinary degree by the morphological and cultural attributes of monasticism. Given the written evidence that eighth-century aristocrats founded minsters with such indiscriminate enthusiasm, and given too that these sites are mostly in a region where small minsters are most unlikely to have left surviving documentation, it seems a reasonable hypothesis that the places complained about in our texts were of like kind to those found by excavation. Not all the sites need be thegnly minsters—some could be dependencies of major communities—and their apparent concentration in the artefact-rich zone may be misleading: it may well be that similar sorts of

---

[121] Hines 1997*b*: 391. Pestell 1999: 83–7, and Pestell 2003: 135–7, take a position closer though not identical to my own.

[122] Above, n. 116.

places in the rest of England are invisible to us because they do not yield metal finds. But it is also possible (and later evidence certainly tends to support this)[123] that the economically precocious regions of East Anglia and Lindsey did in fact support unusually large numbers of small monastic sites.

Monastic centres and peripheries: cells, 'granges', hermitages, and retreats

The physical impact of Christianity on the early English landscape was largely the work of minsters, but it was not confined within their boundaries. Fragmentary clues add up to a convincing picture of dependent habitations and cult sites, scattered through the surrounding territories and associated with monastic personnel, which must have brought the religious and cultural impact of the monastic Church closer to the laity, and impinged powerfully on their ritual lives.

As in north-western Francia, where mid seventh-century communities such as Corbie and Saint-Bertin controlled scattered constellations of demesnes run from small monastic colonies,[124] important minsters had satellites on their estates. It is hard to distinguish sites with a primarily economic rationale from those which began as holy foci such as hermitages, and the distinction may have been hazy in reality. Nor is it generally possible to assess degrees of dependence, which presumably ranged from free-standing minsters within great federations to cells with no autonomous life of their own. The minster of Hackness (Yorks.), founded in 680 by St Hild of Whitby and ruled by an abbess in her name, contained an established community of nuns with permanent quarters: it must have been as substantial as many autonomous houses.[125]

An episode from the mid 680s, recounted in the two Lives of St Cuthbert, shows a rather different sort of dependency of Whitby.[126] Cuthbert sits feasting with Abbess Ælfflæd at *Osingadun*, a 'possession' of her minster[127]

---

[123] Below, pp. 318–19.   [124] Lemarignier 1966: 462–8.

[125] *HE* iv. 23 (pp. 412–14). For one abbess of Hackness, who was to be venerated as a saint there, see above, pp. 145–7.

[126] *VCA* iv. 10 (pp. 126–8); *VCB* c. 34 (pp. 262–4).

[127] 'in parrochia eius [i.e. of Ælfflæd]' (Anon.), 'ad possessionem monasterii ipsius' (Bede). Colgrave, misled by the unusual term *parrochia*, took Anon. to mean that the place was in Cuthbert's diocese; cf. Campbell 1986: 112. But the word clearly refers to the place, not to its territory, and surely follows the Gallic sense of *parrochia* as 'important but dependent (baptismal) church' (above, pp. 36–7). Cf. Cambridge 1984: 74, 84 n. 62; E. Cambridge in Stancliffe and Cambridge 1995: 140–2 (suggesting that *Osingadun* is Lythe, Yorks.). An identification with somewhere near Easington (i.e. a *dūn* and a *tūn* sharing the same first name-element) seems on the whole most plausible: Thomas Pickles pers. comm.

'equipped with no small throng of (male) servants of Christ'.[128] In a trance, he sees the soul of a holy man from her monastic household[129] carried up to heaven. She sends a messenger to 'her bigger minster'[130] (i.e. Whitby) to ask which brother has died; he finds everyone alive, but then learns that 'one of the brethren in the shepherds' dwellings'[131] has fallen from a tree and is being brought back for burial. The messenger returns next day to *Osingadun* and tells Ælfflæd; she runs to Cuthbert, who is in the process of dedicating a church there,[132] and bursts in asking him to 'remember my Hadwald in the mass'. Three points emerge from this story: that Whitby itself included male religious who lived and worked (presumably seasonally) in the sheep-pastures;[133] that *Osingadun* with its male community was thought of as a 'possession'; and that such a place would have (or at least would acquire) its own church. The male personnel are conceived in monastic terms as 'servants of Christ', but the story concerns an estate centre: if we were discussing twelfth-century Cistercians we would speak of 'granges' and 'lay-brethren'. The economic dimension of monastic estate management will be considered in the next chapter, but here we can note one way in which monastic lifestyles could have impinged on people who were not so different from ordinary peasants.

Could such a place as *Osingadun* be recognized archaeologically? This of course is one potential explanation of Brandon-type sites, though these are rarely in obvious proximity to a parent minster. We might expect something like a normal rural settlement, but maybe more concentrated and structured (because influenced by the planning conventions of minsters), and includ-ing a church. A possible candidate is the seventh-century cropmark site at Cowage Farm, Bremilham (Wilts.) (Fig. 27).[134] The core of the settlement is a cluster of rectangular timber buildings, arranged within rectilinear enclo-sures and apparently centred on a substantial hall. To the east, within its own enclosure, is a more substantial, apsidal-ended timber building which is hard to interpret as anything other than a church. Further to the west, the sur-viving parish church (though itself of unknown date) could be seen as the

[128] 'Nam et ipsa possessio non pauco famulorum Christi examine pollebat' (Bede).
[129] 'servi Dei ex familia tua' (Anon.); 'cuiusdam sancti . . . de tuo monasterio' (Bede).
[130] 'ad cenobium suum' (Anon.); 'ad maius suum monasterium' (Bede).
[131] 'unum ex fratribus eorum in pastoralibus habitaculis' (Anon.); 'corpus defuncti fratris . . . quidam de pastoribus bonae actionis vir' (Bede).
[132] 'dedicanti namque eo die ibi aecclesiam' (Anon.).
[133] Cf. Cædmon, a *frater* who looked after the cattle at Whitby though still in the secular dress: *HE* iv. 24 (pp. 414–16).
[134] Hinchcliffe 1986. The interpretation offered here is mine, not the author's. I am grateful to Mick Aston for the information that cropmarks show further rectangular buildings on the north side of the river: the site was evidently extensive.

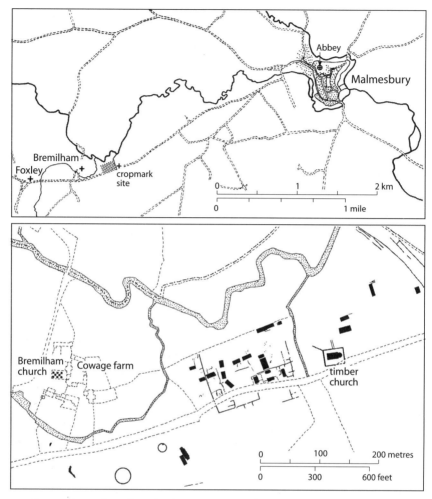

27. *Cowage Farm, Bremilham* (Wilts.): peasant settlement or monastic cell? Cropmark features are shown in solid black. (After Hinchcliffe 1986: fig. 1; wider topographical detail after OS 1st edn. 25-inch map.)

western counterpart of the timber church, forming a bi-polar axial arrangement encapsulating the settlement. But perhaps the most suggestive aspect of Bremilham is its proximity to the great minster of Malmesbury, only two miles up-river. The site must have lain within Malmesbury's seventh-century estate, and its distinctive appearance could be consistent with a semi-monastic cell with strongly agrarian functions.

Outside the range of narrative sources, links between minsters and their

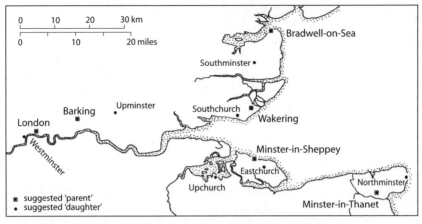

28. 'Directional' place-names in *cyric* and *mynster* around the Thames estuary.

dependencies can occasionally be inferred from place-names and from stone sculpture. 'Directional' names containing *cyric* and *mynster* (e.g. Eastchurch, Southminster) seem to be a peculiarity of the region around the Thames estuary (Fig. 28). Why these are so localized is a mystery,[135] but it seems likely that they describe ecclesiastical dependencies in the way that Norton, Sutton, Weston, and Aston names describe dependent settlements within complex estates. If 'Northminster' in Thanet (St Peter's Broadstairs) was founded in the eighth century as an offshoot of Minster-in-Thanet,[136] it may be that Eastchurch had a similar relationship to Minster-in-Sheppey, Southchurch to Wakering, Southminster to Bradwell-on-Sea, Upminster to Barking, and Westminster to St Paul's in London.[137]

Reading the sculptural evidence depends on the extent to which early pieces on small sites are held to reflect direct links between monastic centres and peripheries. A persuasive case along these lines (supported by the evidence of Bede and of place-names) has been made for parts of northern England by Eric Cambridge,[138] and it can be extended. In east Yorkshire,

---

[135] Apparently the only case outside the south-east is Westbury-upon-Trym (Glos.), *Uuestburg* in the 790s, *Wæst mynster* c.804 (S 139, S 1187). Another possible south-eastern example is Northchurch (Herts.: to the north of Chesham?).

[136] S 91 (*St. Aug.* 175–8), a charter of 748, distinguishes the original minster of St Mary from the new one of SS Peter and Paul, built by Abbess Eadburh 'non longe a predicto monasterio'. It seems likely, though not certain, that the latter should be identified with St Peter's, Broadstairs, called *North Mynstre* in 943 (S 489, with a boundary-clause defining the eastern end of Thanet); cf. Brooks 1984: 366 n. 63.

[137] Below, p. 251 n., for other kinds of 'directional' satellite.   [138] Cambridge 1984.

stylistic links between carvings at Whitby and Hackness must reflect the institutional link recorded by Bede, and it may well be that the small church of Middleton, with its fine eighth-century cross-panel, was in some way dependent on Lastingham, five miles to the north-west, which has a cross-head in the same distinctive style.[139] Lancaster, an obviously important minster in a Roman fort and with fragments of thirteen Anglian and Viking-age crosses, looks like the centre of a group including Heysham, a twin-church coastal site with high-quality sculpture and painted plaster, and a series of churches up the Lune (Halton, Hornby, and Gressingham) which have late Anglian crosses; the apparent influence of Northumbrian—and specifically Wilfridian—sculpture suggests in turn that this Lune valley group could be a trans-Pennine colony of a major centre such as Ripon.[140] Other views of isolated crosses on minor sites are of course possible, most obviously that they represent an undocumented category of small manorial churches or that they originally stood at noblemen's houses,[141] but it seems reasonable to infer that at least a proportion of these cases were monastic dependencies.

A prominent and perhaps numerous category of monastic offshoots were hermitages, though they are recorded less thickly in the English than in the Welsh and Cornish landscapes. Is this a real contrast, or a trick of the evidence? It has already been suggested that when hermit-cults were not based at minsters their chances of survival were poor, and also that holy sites did not normally generate the kind of 'Christian place-name' which we find in Wales, Cornwall, and Brittany in the form of the element *llan/lan* compounded with a saint's name.[142] Possible exceptions are a small group of place-names in *-stow*, *-ciric*, and *-burh* which denote religious sites and do sometimes include the names of saints. Their heavily western distribution shows that many of them simply reflect the Anglicization of British practice.[143] But it could be that some others, scattered lightly across England and

---

[139] Lang 1991: 141–2, 169, 187.

[140] Potter and Andrews 1994 for Heysham; Edwards 1978: 59–69 for the sculpture; Felicity Clark, work in progress, for the Ripon link.

[141] Above, pp. 119–20; below, p. 227.   [142] Above, pp. 21, 195, Padel 2002.

[143] See Gelling 1981: 5–7; Preston-Jones 1992: 109. Occasional bilingual names, such as Wonastow/*Llanwarw* (Monm.), 'St Gwnwarwy's holy site', make the point explicit; other cases are Bridestowe, Churchstow, Davidstow, Instow, Morwenstow, Padstow, Peterstow, Virginstow. Devon has two *ciric-stow* and four *ciric-tūn* names, including Cheristow, associated with St Wenn, and Cheriton, associated with St Brendan: *P-N Devon*, 59, 72, 295, 414, 427, 510. Otherwise, Somerset (Cheriton), Wiltshire (Chirton), and Hampshire (Cheriton) have one each. Nearly all of these first appear in Domesday Book. The only cases outside the south-west are Cheriton (Kent), *Ciriceton* in the Domesday Monachorûm; Cherington (Glos.), *Cerintone* in DB; Cherrington (Warw.), *Chiritone* in 1199; and the possible case of Churton (Cheshire). Woodchurch (Cheshire) first occurs as *Odecerce* c.1100, and is an alternative English name for *Landican*, 'Tegan's holy site'; see also Smith 1956: 95. Names on the pattern of Bridekirk and Kirkbride concentrate in the north-west:

compounded with Old English personal names,[144] preserve the memory of free-functioning hermits. Unfortunately, none is known to pre-date the tenth century[145] and none can be proved to record a purely local saint: if they tell us anything, it is to reiterate that while hermits may, for all we know, have been widely revered in their own day, it was minster-based cults that had a long-term future. Whereas the proliferation of Welsh and Cornish holy sites from an earlier date, and at a more localized scale, meant that they and their saints became the immediate foci of devotion, English cults developed only from the late seventh century, when the means of articulating and promoting them were largely in the hands of minsters.

Certainly the early English hermitages that are recorded tend to have strong monastic associations.[146] It is a commonplace that the symbiotic association between the cenobitic and eremitic lives, as advocated by St Benedict and realized topographically at (for instance) Lérins with its satellite hermitages, was replicated in Irish and western British monasticism.[147] This is essentially how Lindisfarne worked: the main monastery, the Lenten retreat on St Cuthbert's island, the remoter hermitage on Farne.[148] Even outside the Irish ambit, the monastic training and supervision of hermits is just as likely to have encouraged a 'centre–periphery' structure, in which minsters maintained remote spots for the use of episodic or full-time hermits among their number. Bede mentions three cases of what he calls a 'remoter house' or 'more private house' (*mansio remotior, secretior*), within a mile or two of Lichfield,

---

Fellows-Jensen 1987: 301–5. The distribution of this group of names shows that they are conditioned by British practice, and different in kind from the late Anglo-Saxon names in -*church* which are discussed below (pp. 385–7 nn.). Note in this context Bede's intriguing comment about James the Deacon, referring to an area of British survival in the north: 'the settlement (*vicus*) near Catterick in which he mainly used to live is named after his name up to the present day': *HE* ii. 20 (p. 206).

[144] Gelling 1982; Blair 2002*a*: 469–70.

[145] By the mid tenth century *stow* (cf. *locus*, above, p. 110) was a normal term for a religious establishment: e.g. Barking *c.*950, *Sancte Marie Stowe* (S 1483); Padstow 981, *Sancte Petroces stow* (*ASC* 'C' s.a. 981 (p. 124)); Burton 1002 × 4, the *stow* (S 1536); and Stow (Lincs.) 1053 × 5, *Sancte Marian stowe* (S 1478). Æthelthryth's minster (?Threekingham) is called *Ætheldreðestowe* in *Lib. El.* 30. Stow-on-the-Wold (*Eduuardestou* in Domesday Book) had a church of St Edward (S 935; Blair 2002*a*: 529–30). Ælfric regularly uses *halig stow* in the generalized sense of 'holy place'. Although at least one 'holy-*stow*' place-name existed by 840 (below, n. 155), it looks significant that whereas St Hygebald's resting-place was called *Hiboldestou* by 1086, the entry in the early part of the *Secgan* gives it a different (and topographical) name, *Cecesege* (Liebermann 1889: 11). Some minster names in -*burh* compounded with the founder's or first abbess's name are certainly early (above, p. 81 n.), but the usage continued: Malmesbury ('Maeldubh's *burh*') was also known as *Ealdelmesbyrig* ('Aldhelm's *burh*') by *c.*1000 (Liebermann 1889: 17); *Medeshamstede* became *Burh* (Peterborough) during the tenth century. It could be that most of these names are post-900 coinages, albeit referring to older saints.

[146] Above, pp. 144–5.

[147] 'Regula S. Benedicti', c. 73; Leyser 1984: 7–17; Dark 1994*a*: 46; Herity 1995: esp. 72–90; Gittos 2002*a*: 36–9, for hermitages surrounded by water.

[148] *HE* iv. 30 (pp. 442–4); O'Sullivan and Young 1995: 40–3.

Hexham, and Melrose respectively, of which the first two were used by bishops for retreats and private prayers and the third as a hermit's permanent home; the *mansio* near Hexham was surrounded by a ditch and contained a *clymiterium* (oratory?) dedicated to St Michael.[149] These were integral to their parent communities—Bede describes the Melrose hermitage as 'in' the minster even though set apart—and he writes as though this sort of appendage were something completely normal. Many of them may be perpetuated among the obscure chapels on the peripheries of minsters which turn up in sources from the late eleventh century onwards. One that happens to have been excavated, a mile west of Glastonbury minster, began as a small timber structure containing a special male burial (the founder-hermit?) around which a largely male cemetery developed during the eighth to ninth centuries; Heysham could be another.[150]

Some hermitages became minsters. An ascetic's optimum career-path was to acquire a good monastic training, graduate to the exertions of a hermit's life, and inspire enough support from the wealthy to sustain a new monastic foundation. The classic example is Guthlac: trained and tonsured at Repton, a hermit at Crowland, and finally (from 715) honoured there in a magnificent shrine, the focus of a new community under royal patronage.[151] Less spectacular, but possibly in some ways more characteristic, is the case of the Northumbrian husbandman Wilgils. The father of a family, in the 660s he entrusted his young son for training at Wilfrid's new minster at Ripon. He then embraced the monastic life himself, moving on to greater austerities in a remote oratory of St Andrew at the mouth of the Humber where he 'shone forth in signs of miracles, and his name became famous'. Kings and nobles gave him 'little possessions of land near those promontories, in perpetual gift to build a church for God', where he gathered 'a modest but distinguished congregation of God's servants'.[152] For all that this was an independently financed operation, the inspiration and perhaps the tutelage of Ripon (where Wilgils's bones were eventually taken[153]) may not be far in the background.

---

[149] *HE* iv. 3, v. 2, v. 12 (pp. 336–8, 456, 488, 496). Thomas 1971: 82–3, identifies the Hexham *mansio* as St John Lee.

[150] Rahtz and Hirst 1974: 24–39; Potter and Andrews 1994. Campbell 1987: 340 notes that Beckery means *Becc-Ériu*, 'Little Ireland'. Other likely cases are St Frideswide's retreat at Binsey near Oxford, or the Beam chapel at Bampton (above, p. 186) which was later known as the hermitage: Blair 1988*e*; Blair 1994: 64, 66.

[151] *VG*; Stocker 1993: 101–6.

[152] Alcuin, 'Vita Willibrordi', cc. 1–3 (ed. W. Levison, *MGH Scriptores Rerum Merov.* vii. 1 (Hannover, 1919), 116–18). Alcuin himself inherited this minster (c. 1: 'ego . . . eandem cellulam per successiones legitimas suscepi gubernandam').

[153] Blair 2002*a*: 560–1.

There was also a broad category of places which, initially established as hermitages or for some pre-existing ritual or symbolic reason, were developed by the building of chapels and other structures under a monastic aegis and took on a life of their own. Some may have been pre-Christian cult sites, maybe including some of the barrows and Roman villas which had acquired churches by *c*.1100. The remote *mansio* at Lichfield, dedicated to St Michael, looks as though it might have been one of the many sites across Europe where devotion to this archangel supplanted a pagan cult;[154] it recalls a charter of 840 by which King Æthelwulf grants fifteen hides at the significantly named Halstock (*Halgan stoc*, 'holy place') in Dorset to the deacon Eadberht 'for the honour of Almighty God and for the love of St Michael the Archangel whose church is in that little minster'.[155] Bede's account of a spot made holy for another reason—because St Oswald raised his timber cross there before defeating the Mercian and British forces in 634—shows how an open-air landmark might become a monastically controlled church:

That place is called in English 'Heavenfield', in Latin *Caelestis Campus*, a name which it certainly received of old as an omen of what was to come: it signified indeed that a heavenly standard would be raised there, a heavenly victory won, and that heavenly miracles would be celebrated there until today. . . . In this place the brethren of the church of Hexham, which is not far away, have long had a custom of coming yearly on the eve of the day on which Oswald was killed, to keep vigils for the welfare of his soul, to sing many psalms of praise, and in the morning to offer the sacrifice of holy oblation for him. As this good custom has developed, a church has lately been built ⟨and dedicated⟩ there to make the place more sacred and honourable in the sight of all. And rightly so: for we believe that no symbol of the Christian faith, no church, no altar had been erected among any of the Bernicians before that new leader in war, inspired by his devotion to the faith, set up that standard of the holy cross.[156]

[154] Flint 1991: 169–71; cf., for England, R. Morris 1989: 52–6. This perception of Michael begins with his appearance on Monte Gargano in 493, where he replaced a sacrificial oracle-cult and which Ælfric calls 'seo halige stow Sancte Michaelis': *Ælfric's Catholic Homilies: The First Series*, ed. P. Clemoes (EETS ss 17, 1997), 465.

[155] S 290; *Sherborne*, 5–11: 'cuius ecclesia in eodem monasteriunculo manet'. The charter is basically genuine, though probably with some interpolations. The grantee may be the same deacon Eadberht who witnesses in Æthelwulf's retinue two years earlier (S 1438). The bounds contain the modern parishes of Halstock and Closworth (now in Somerset). The site, now deserted (H. P. R. Finberg, *The Early Charters of Wessex* (Leicester, 1964), 161 n.; Hall 2000: 20), lies about five miles south of Yeovil minster. Other cases of *halig-stoc/stow* are the lost Halstow in Woodleigh (Devon), and High Halstow (Kent) on a commanding site overlooking the marshes of the Medway estuary. Cf. below, p. 377, for a 'holy place' in the charter-bounds of Fawler (Berks.) which was on a Roman villa site.

[156] *HE* iii. 2 (p. 216); see Charles-Edwards 2000: 313 n., for Wilfrid's promotion of this cult. The 'C' tradition of the text expands 'has been built' to 'has been built and dedicated' (ed. Colgrave and Mynors, p. xliii): I am grateful to Michael Lapidge for the view that this addition could be Bede's own.

Hatfield, where the same enemy forces had slain King Eadwine the previous year, provides a variant on this theme. The Whitby 'Life of Gregory' describes how a late seventh-century Mercian priest named Trimma was told in a vision to rescue Eadwine's bones from the field and take them to Whitby; afterwards he 'lived for a time at the holy site of the previous burial . . . , and he added that, if he could, he would have liked to build a minster there'.[157]

Guthlac and Wilgils won sponsorship to develop their hermitages as minsters; Trimma failed; the 'remoter mansions', and the church at Heavenfield, remained adjuncts of their parent minsters. These case-histories illustrate that sites of Christian observance, initiated within the monastic ambit, could develop in various ways, including remaining small and unimportant. This fact should condition our response to the mere four references—two in Bede, two in charters—to small chapels of unstated origin. Bede observes that Paulinus baptized in the Swale because there were not yet any *oratoria*, and tells of an Ayrshire householder in the 690s who awoke at dawn from a vision, went to the oratory of the settlement (*ad villulae oratorium*), and prayed there until the day started.[158] In the south, early eighth-century charters mention a 'church of St Martin' on an island in the Somerset Levels and an 'oratory of St Martin' near a fishery on Romney Marsh.[159] To assert that these must have been monastically founded would go beyond the evidence, but no other explanation is more convincing. Free-standing 'oratories' would fit into the broad category of sites described above; the dedications to St Martin suggest Frankish influence, perhaps via Glastonbury in the one case and the royal nunnery of Lyminge in the other.[160] Non-monastic building on this minor scale clearly remains a serious possibility, but the evidence eludes us.

[157] *WVG* cc. 18–19 (pp. 100–4).

[158] *HE* ii. 14, v. 12 (pp. 188, 488). Above, p. 70 n., for the suggestion that the phrase about Paulinus comes from a Canterbury text. The second passage refers to a region which could well have had small British churches. In his commentary on Mark 11: 11, Bede says that when we visit 'villam aut oppidum aut alium quemlibet locum in quo sit domus orationis Deo consecrata', we enter and pray: *Baedae Opera*, ii. 3 (ed. D. Hurst, CCSL 120, Turnhout, 1960), 575, and cf. Bullough 1999: 33.

[159] S 1253 (cf. Edwards 1988: 36, and Abrams 1996: 62–3, 165–6); S 24 (grant to Lyminge of land near the chapel). The Glastonbury chapel was on an island still called Marchey, 'Martin's *eig*'.

[160] Sims-Williams 1975 and Sims-Williams 1990: 110–13, for early Frankish influence on Kent and on the south-west Gloucestershire/Somerset region; cf. above, pp. 150–1. St Martin-in-the-Fields in London (within the area of the trading emporium, which would have been used by Frankish merchants) may be another case. For *oratoria* in a monastic context, cf. the narrative describing how King Ine took back a Thames valley estate previously given for religious purposes because 'nondum constructo monasterio in ea nec ullo admodum oratorio erecto': S 241 (*Abingdon*, i. 14–22).

Widening circles for the living: sacred space and the Christianization of the landscape

To return to a point made at the start of this chapter, sacredness is in the mind: purely natural sites and landmarks might have been considered holy by Christians, pagans, or both. The possible meaning of such sites, though, is usually now invisible to us. How far the ecclesiastical establishment bothered itself with such things at all is a question about which historians can take different views: was a seventh-century minster like Hrothgar's hall, a pool of light in a spiritually dark and dangerous world, or a focus in an inclusive Christian society, such as eleventh-century reformers would aspire to, marred only by isolated pools of the profane? But these may be the wrong terms in which to define the problem. Contemporaries will not have seen the matter through eleventh-century eyes, and if they took a tolerant and inclusive view of the coexistence of official with vernacular cult practices, their attitude to the sites where those practices took place was probably not so different.[161] As in other areas of life, it may be helpful to envisage widening and intensifying circles of cultural influence which radiated from minsters, and gradually imbued the 'unaltered' cult sites with perceptions that their power derived from Christ and the saints.

One clear-cut and literate idea of sacralized landscapes, as concentric zones around a holy core, was evolved in an Irish monastic context and may have had some limited impact in England. Its models were biblical, notably the temple of Ezekiel's vision:

When you divide the land by lot among the tribes for their possession, you shall set apart from it a sacred reserve for the Lord, 25,000 cubits in length and 20,000 in width; the whole enclosure shall be sacred (*sanctificatum erit in omni termino eius per circuitum*). Of this a square plot (*quadrifariam per circuitum*), 500 cubits each way, shall be devoted to the sanctuary, with 50 cubits of open land round it (*in suburbana eius per gyrum*). From this area you shall measure out a space 25,000 by 10,000 cubits, in which the sanctuary, the holiest place of all, shall stand. This space is for the priests who serve in the sanctuary and who come nearest in serving the Lord. It shall include space for their houses and a sacred plot for the sanctuary. An area of 25,000 by 10,000 cubits shall belong to the Levites, the temple servants; on this shall stand the towns in which they live . . .[162]

This biblical conception of zones around a holy centre, combined with the rather different one of 'refuge cities' for accidental killers,[163] produced an

---

[161] Above, pp. 169–70; below, pp. 473–8; the agenda is again set by Flint 1991.
[162] Ezekiel 45: 1–5 (New English Bible translation, Latin phrases from the Vulgate), referred to in *Hib.* xliv. 2 (pp. 174–5).　　　[163] Below, p. 249.

ideal image of the holy city at the heart of graded precincts, all 'holy' in the sense of being inviolable, but some accessible to the profane. A famous passage in the Irish canons prescribes two or three precincts (*termini*) around a holy place: the 'holiest' (*sanctissimus*), accessible only to holy people and clerics; the 'more holy' (*sanctior*), 'into the spaces (*plateas*) of which we allow crowds of plebeian rustics not much given to wickedness'; and the merely holy (*sanctus*), where even murderers and adulterers could go.[164] The paradigm—a magnification of the Irish cultural preference for round and concentric sites[165]—involves large and outwards-extending circles imposed on the landscape around the holy core.

Just as English monastic sites seem not to display the clear-cut zoning of Irish ones, so England offers only limited and dubious evidence, before the tenth century, for defined territorial circuits on the Irish pattern. The one potentially early text is the formula conferring 'circuits of miles' (X *milliaria in circuitu*)—three miles around Crayke (Yorks.), fifteen around Carlisle— in the purported land-grant by King Ecgfrith to St Cuthbert for the Lindisfarne community in the 680s.[166] This is a forgery, and there would be no justification for inferring any genuine basis were it not that similar formulae occur independently in early to mid seventh-century charters for Bobbio (Italy) and Stavelot-Malmedy (Francia). What Lindisfarne, Bobbio, and Stavelot-Malmedy had in common was an Irish background to their foundations: it is implausible that a late forger should have hit at random on this unusual but appropriate conception.[167] Furthermore, Crayke is sited centrally within a curvilinear parish where boundaries appear to preserve the trace of two concentric circuits.[168] Although Carlisle has no such topographical evidence, it is an odd coincidence that there was later a sanctuary zone around nearby Wetheral, which possessed an eighth- or ninth-century

---

[164] *Hib.* XLIV. 5 (p. 175, 'B' recension printed as footnote).

[165] Above, pp. 197–8; Gittos 2002*a*: 68–72 and Gittos 2002*b*: 205–8, for Irish conceptions of territorial boundedness.

[166] S 66, evidently drawing on the Lindisfarne tradition embodied in the 'Historia de Sancto Cuthberto' (*Symeon Op.* i. 199): Ecgfrith and Archbishop Theodore gave Cuthbert 'villam quae vocatur Creca, et tria milliaria in circuitu ipsius villae, ut ibi mansionem haberet . . . ; [Cuthbert] adiecit civitatem quae vocatur Luel, quae habet in circuitu quindecim milliaria, et in eadem civitate posuit congregationem sanctimonialium'.

[167] The point is made by Chaplais 1969: 537–8, and Wormald 1984: 17 and 31 n. 47. The Bobbio texts (C. Brühl (ed.), *Codice Diplomatico Longobardo*, III. i (Rome, 1973), 3–15, Nos. 1–3) use the formula 'undique fines decernimus ab omni parte per in circuitu miliaria quattuor' and variants; those from Stavelot-Malmedy (C. Brühl and others (eds.), *Die Urkunden der Merowinger*, i (*MGH, Diplomata*, Hannover, 2001), Nos. 81, 108 (pp. 207, 279)) have 'in utriusque partibus de ipsis monasteriis tam in longum quam in traversum duodecim milia dextrorum saltibus' etc.

[168] Adams 1990: 29–32; Kaner 1993. The symmetry of Crayke has a clear geographical basis, since the church stands on a hilltop affording a panorama of the landscape around. Crayke had a mid eighth-century recluse, Echa (Blair 2002*a*: 533).

stone cross.[169] It is obscure whether the original Lindisfarne formulae conferred simple possession (as at Bobbio), or a *cordon sanitaire* around the holy on the pattern of the Irish canons (as in one of the Stavelot-Malmedy texts).[170]

An essentially insoluble question is whether there is any link between these possible early zones of 'protected space' and the ones which appear, in two widely separated regions, after 900. In the north, sources of *c.*1100 onwards record circular sanctuary zones of a mile's radius at York, Hexham, Ripon, Beverley, and Tynemouth, some with penalties for breach graded on an ascending scale from periphery to centre, most of which are ascribed (in late tradition) to grants by King Æthelstan (924–39).[171] At Ripon 'St Wilfrid's league' appears in Domesday Book,[172] and we have two sources of *c.*1000–20: a legal text asserting the special status of 'St Peter's church-peace (*cyricfrið*) [York], St Wilfrid's [Ripon] and St John's [Beverley]', and a York estate memorandum listing Ripon with 'a mile's space on every side' (*æt Rypum . . . milegemet on ælcre healfe*).[173] York, Hexham, Beverley, and Southwell each had a 'peace-seat' (*friðstol*) for sanctuary-seekers, and it is remarkable that the surviving Hexham and Beverley chairs are both of the late seventh or eighth century.[174] The second group was in Cornwall, where St Buryan, Padstow, Probus, and St Keverne minsters were believed in the late middle ages to have sanctuary territories (but not circular) around them, again persistently associated with Æthelstan.[175]

[169] *The Register of the Priory of Wetherhal,* ed. J. E. Prescott (London, 1897), xxiii. 18, 371–3, 429–31, 490–2; Cox 1911: 174–6; Bailey and Cramp 1988: 153–4. The Wetheral sanctuary was small, non-circular, and recorded only in the twelfth century.

[170] As n. 167, *actum* of Sigibert III, 643 × 8: 'concessimus supradicto patre, ob cavenda pericula animarum inhabitantium et ad devitanda consortia mulierum, ut girum girando in utrorumque partibus monasteriorum mensurentur plus numeris milibus dextrorum saltibus duodecim, ut absque inpressione populi vel tumultuatione saeculari Deo soli vacarent.' The idea seems to be to make this huge zone like the *sanctissimus* of the canons, accessible only to the holy. I am grateful to Paul Fouracre for his advice on this charter.

[171] *Southwell,* 190–6; Cox 1911: 126–74; Hall 1989; Kirby 1982; RCHM(E) 1982: 2–3, 34; Palliser 1996: 210–11. Wilson 2003 has re-stated the case for an early association between Æthelstan and Beverley, citing (p. 7) a late Anglo-Saxon silver ring with inscriptions naming Æthelstan and St John. Cf. Tanguy 1984 for boundaries of Breton sanctuaries marked with crosses, especially (map p. 15) the two phases of the rectilinear *minihi* of Gouesnou.

[172] DB i. 303ᵛ: 'totum circa ecclesiam i leuga'.

[173] 'Norðhymbra Cyricgrið' (*Gesetze,* 473); *RASC* 166.

[174] Rollason and others 1998: 198, 221; Wilson 2003: 16; Cramp 1984: 192–3 and Lang 1991: 224 for the surviving seats. Southwell had a 'cathedra lapidea iuxta altare quod Angli vocant fritstol' (*Southwell,* 192). By the early eleventh century *friðstol* was being used in the general sense of 'refuge' or 'sanctuary', as in 'Grið', c. 16 (*Gesetze,* 471), or the Paris Psalter where *refugium* is glossed as *friðstol.* Cf. the earlier sacral status of the high seat in a royal hall (above, p. 57).

[175] Cox 1911: 214–26; Olson 1989: 72, 78–81; Davies 1996: 7. S 450 is a probably genuine charter of Æthelstan for St Buryan. The boundaries of the St Buryan circuit are non-geometrical, simply following natural features: Preston-Jones and Langdon 1997: 114–15.

Could some of these privileged zones represent pre-Viking arrangements? Neither group is recorded in early sources, and the association of both with Æthelstan encourages a view of them as tenth-century innovations.[176] One aspect of territorialization in the tenth and eleventh centuries was certainly the multiplication of circular territories around important churches, meeting-places, and even industrial sites;[177] Bury St Edmunds acquired a *leuca* ('league') of one-mile radius in the tenth or eleventh century, as did Battle after the Norman Conquest.[178] On the other hand, it seems odd that if Æthelstan wanted to create specially privileged sanctuaries he should create so few of them, and those only in two areas—both peripheral to the West Saxon kingdom—of which one had been under strong Irish influence in the seventh century and the other had been British.

On the whole it is likely that the two groups had different origins. Given the Lindisfarne circuit formula and the topographical evidence at Crayke, the northern group could have been genuinely early, a product of the seventh-century Irish influence. In Cornwall, where Æthelstan seems to have promoted certain established churches at the expense of others, it seems more probable that he created new protected zones on a pattern derived from the Brittonic ecclesiastical influences prominent at his court.[179] Æthelstan's involvement with both groups suggests an anxiety to consolidate a reputation for good lordship on the fringes of his power, and hence to foster an esoteric and inherited anomaly rather than suppress it.

Even if the northern circuits were indeed early, it is unlikely that they were 'chartered sanctuaries' or 'immunities' from the outset. Territorial protection had a complex history, with circuits defining a variety of distinct benefits which probably changed over time: ownership, sacred status, the right to give sanctuary, immunity from aspects of external interference. In insular cultures the Hiberno-biblical idea of sacred zones affording refuge seems to have fused with an essentially secular one, that of the protection (Old English *mund*) which any free man extended to those under his roof—in other words, of the inviolability of his homestead. The eventual result was the distinctively insular form of ecclesiastical 'protected space' described above, which included the sanctuary provisions normal in continental Europe but went much further, covering much larger physical areas and requiring violators to pay compensation.

The consensus of recent work is that this territorialization of a lay privi-

[176] Davies 1996: 9–10; cf. below, pp. 314, 348–9.
[177] Rosenwein 1999: 153, 155, 173–83 (Modena, Pozzuolo, Cluny); Davies 1996: 6 (salt-houses, 'gyrths' around Scottish churches).
[178] S 507 and Hart 1992: 57–61, 62–6; *Chron. Battle*, 46–50, 68–70.
[179] Below, p. 305.

lege in an ecclesiastical milieu, embodied in the Welsh *noddfeydd,* the Scottish gyrths, and the English chartered sanctuaries, probably did not happen before the tenth century.[180] So in origin the Northumbrian circuits may have had more to do with sacred space and refuge, and less with juris- dictional privileges, than the post-Viking sources suggest. Yet from the outset there must have been some intersection between a religious community's (literate and spatially precise) idea of the holy zone around it, and its royal patron's (less territorial?) idea of the *mund* appropriate to this large, complex, and new sort of household. Any king who acknowledged and protected these circuits of reserved space around minsters was probably agreeing to a novel kind of territorialized privilege, and the evidence suggests that early English kings only did so very rarely.

Legally defined zones of protection were not, then, an important element in the Christian topography of early England. Yet it is unlikely that a con- ception of ordinary English minsters as the centres of sacred peripheries was entirely lacking, even if it fell short of the clear-cut Irish models. The ritual integration of minsters with their dependent cult sites by means of proces- sional liturgies, and the involvement of both minster-priests and laity in Rogationtide circuitings to bless the spring crops, are likely to have encour- aged ideas of a sacred geography centred on, and articulated by, the minster and its inhabitants.[181] Like other pre-industrial societies, the pagan English probably had their own concepts of structured supernatural space within their territories, onto which the Christian model could be grafted.[182] The very fact that the great monastic estates were held by a new and specifically religious tenure—land reserved for God and his saints—may have led the peasants on them to see themselves as distinct from those whose status and obligations remained within a purely traditional framework. Minsters were embodiments of a complex, structured solemnity drawn from external sources—the Bible, formal Roman planning, the contemporary Mediter- ranean world—which can hardly have failed to have some impact on the countryside around them.

The most interesting question—how deeply Christianization penetrated

[180] Pryce 1993: 165–74; Davies 1995; Davies 1996 (but see ibid. 19 n. 12, noting feelings at the conference where this paper was given that the Irish and west Scottish developments must have been earlier). Cf. Barrow 2000a: 138–9.

[181] For the Continental background of processions between stational churches: Havercamp 1987: 131–9; Blair 1992: 257–8; Bullough 1999: 41–3, 54; Noble 2001: 83–91; Gittos 2002a: 117–21.

[182] For instance, the Keres of the Rio Grande 'conceptualise their world as a series of nested, but interrelated, regions . . . , all of which focus on a central village. The farthest, and most dan- gerous, region consists of places at the edge of the world inhabited by powerful supernatural beings' (J. E. Snead and R. W. Preucel in Ashmore and Knapp 1999: 176). The last point will not be strange to readers of 'Beowulf' (cf. Semple 1998).

into the foundations of indigenous local cult—has left virtually no impression on the written sources. But the very fact that the pre-Viking prescriptive texts are so unconcerned with activity focused on scattered cult sites such as trees, stones, and springs[183] is interesting in itself, and may point to assimilation rather than indifference. Given on the one hand the archaeological and place-name evidence for such practices in the pagan period,[184] and on the other the condemnations of them in the tenth and eleventh centuries,[185] it is most unlikely that they did not exist in the seventh and eighth. The best explanation is that 'unofficial' ritual foci were always widespread, but that until the tenth century the response of bishops and legislators was tolerant and inclusive. Gallic bishops since the fourth century had been re-sacralizing the landscape, consecrating healing springs and associating trees with the graves of saints.[186] The idiom would have come naturally to their late seventh-century colleagues in England, where the laity would have little cause to resist if acceptance of a general Christian framework did not, in practice, debar them from continuing a range of traditional rites.[187]

The general likelihood that at least some 'holy' wells, trees, ancient monuments, and natural landmarks drifted progressively into a Christian ambit during this period is thus supported both by the Continental background and by the general evidence for the interpenetration of lay society and Christian culture. Sometimes this incorporation may have been achieved at minsters,[188] but we should envisage a far greater number of humbler and less formally developed landmarks. Many such are recorded from the eleventh century in the context of traditional associations with pre-Viking saints, some of which may be early; the St Oswald sites are especially persuasive.[189]

[183] For reasons given by Meaney 1992: 110–11, I discount the references in the Pseudo-Ecgberht Penitential.

[184] Blair 1995*b*: 1–3; Meaney 1985: 15–17; Blair 1994: 18.

[185] Below, pp. 481–2.

[186] Flint 1991: 254–73. Cf. P. Brown 1996: 110, on the tolerance of Gregory of Tours: 'The [Gallic] countryside found its voice again, to speak, in an ancient spiritual vernacular, of the presence of the saints. Water became holy again. . . . All over Gaul, great trees bloomed profusely over the graves of saints.'

[187] Cf. above, p. 169. For an example of the kind of accommodation that might have been reached at these places we can go to the Kenyan coast, where spirit-inhabited pillars still coexist with mosques. In one case the traditional rituals 'take place only 10 metres away from the newly rebuilt mosque, whose imam does not approve of what goes on around the Pillar. When asked his views, he said that spirit propitiation is un-Islamic and therefore wrong. However, there seems to be a degree of tolerance, and people seem unwilling to talk about it.' (G. H. O. Abungo in Carmichael and others 1994: 158.) Valk 2003 offers some striking analogies from post-medieval Estonia.

[188] Above, pp. 185–6. Rattue 1995: 55–61 lists holy wells associated with minsters. Three suggestive cases are Southwell (Dixon and Stocker 2001: 259–60); Barton-on-Humber (Fig. 43); and Frome (Somerset)—a minster dedicated to St John the Baptist—where a 'holy' spring still issues from the north-facing slope of the churchyard.

[189] Below, pp. 475–7.

Nor could any reader of Bede's celebration of 'Heavenfield' be left in doubt about the potency of the standing cross as a sign of light victorious over darkness, the triumph of the new religion over the old. A cross must have been the normal outward and visible sign of a site's Christian status, whether freestanding like Oswald's or—as it may often have been—carved or painted on an older holy stone or tree.[190] The fact that the Old English words for 'cross' are *rōd, trēow*, and *bēam*, rather than some loan-word from *crux*, may suggest that the first crosses were perceived as of like kind to the sacred landmarks which they replaced. At Rudstone (*rōd-stān*, 'cross-stone') in east Yorkshire, a great prehistoric menhir still stands beside the church.[191]

It is especially interesting that two early texts associate crosses with aristocratic houses. In the east midlands around 674, the hand of God announced Guthlac's birth by pointing at the cross outside the door of his parents' house; in Wessex some thirty years later, the ailing infant Willibald was offered by his parents before a cross, it being 'the custom in the Saxon race' to have 'on many estates of nobles and substantial men not a church but the gracious sign of the holy cross . . . raised on high'.[192] These (presumably timber) crosses sound very like the 'guardian trees' of farms and houses in Scandinavian folk tradition,[193] and it is tempting to think that they were direct successors of cultic trees planted outside houses in the pagan period. The association of the cross with the birth of a son in these stories may suggest that in early Christian England, as in modern upland Mexico, 'a house cross erected just outside the door symbolise[d] the unity of the domestic group . . . and [wa]s the ritual entrance for the group'.[194]

Beyond this there is some rather slender evidence that stone crosses may have been set up on boundaries, at crossroads, and along routes in the eighth and ninth centuries, as they were in the tenth and eleventh, but no proof.[195] Wooden crosses would have been easy and cheap to make (it will be recalled

---

[190] As St Samson had done in north Cornwall: *VS* i. 48 (p. 144).

[191] R. Morris 1989: 81–4. In a remarkable Merovingian analogue, a seventh-century coin struck at Le Mans depicts the menhir next to the cathedral there, surmounted by a cross: E. Salin, *La Civilisation mérovingienne* (4 vols., Paris, 1949–59), iv. 356–7, fig. 166c.

[192] *VG* c. 5 (p. 74); Huneberc, 'Vita Willibaldi', c. 1 (ed. O. Holder-Egger, *MGH, Scriptores*, xv. 1 (Hannover, 1887), 88). For a later reference to a cross in a garden outside a nobleman's door, see James 1917: 234.

[193] Tolley 1995: 161–7 (usually ash, elm, or linden). For tutelary trees planted by houses or in courtyards in other societies, see Wilson 2000: 5.

[194] Vogt 1976: 51; cf. ibid. 44, 59.

[195] Below, pp. 478–80. But it is extremely hard to prove that surviving seventh- to ninth-century crosses originally occupied such locations, rather than the central church sites to which virtually all of them have now been collected. Lypiatt (below, p. 478) is suggestive, but even so not conclusive. For this reason I am reluctant to go quite so far as Flint 1991: 257–63: her picture of a cross-filled landscape could well be right, but the evidence is lacking.

that Boniface's Frankish adversary Aldebert marked his own holy sites with them[196]) and could perfectly well have stood beside most important resi-dences, many roads, and a range of old cult sites.

This is where our sources fail: virtually no specific cases of these phe-nomena can be solidly dated to the early period. Accordingly, though it is eminently arguable that the evidence is not negative but simply absent, they must be left for a later chapter: we simply do not know to what extent the indigenous magic of the English landscape had been re-moulded as Christian magic by the time of the Viking invasions. What we can perceive, at least occasionally, is the varied texture of dispersed religious landscapes re-moulded by minsters and their satellites. They give more grounds for reject-ing the view that English Christianity was a limited, exclusively aristocratic affair before the tenth-century proliferation of local churches.

Widening circles for the dead: the drift towards minster-associated burial

The same process of gradual incorporation into the ecclesiastical ambit can be seen in the development of burial practice.[197] In 650, lay burial in church or churchyard was exceptional; by 850, it was starting to become the norm. The shift was slow, and our view of it should not be too influenced by hind-sight. The appeal of *ad sanctos* burial reached an ever-widening circle, but there is still no evidence for any rigid or exclusive concept of consecrated ground, nor for pressure on the laity to abandon traditional sites or rituals.[198] Some of those buried in traditional late seventh-century cemeteries were evi-dently in some sense Christian, and it may have long remained the case that belief was signified more by the funeral ceremony than by location. The bones of the lay faithful were not yet bones of contention between compet-ing ecclesiastical jurisdictions, and minster-priests had no obvious interest in restricting last rites or funeral ceremonies to those who were buried in ground which they controlled. In some late-converted parts of northern Europe,

---

[196] Above, pp. 177–8.

[197] This section may be read in conjunction with Hadley 2000*b* and Hadley 2002*a*; 209–14, which appeared after it was drafted.

[198] The much-quoted injuction of 775 × 90 that in newly converted Saxony the bodies of the dead 'ad cimiteria ecclesiae deferantur et non ad tumulus [*sic*] paganorum' relates to the specific circumstances of forced conversion, and is irrelevant to England ('Capitulatio de Partibus Saxo-niae', c. 22: *Capitularia*, i. 69). When Jonas of Orleans (d. 843) attacks those who demand payment for allowing the dead to be buried 'in agris suis' he is condemning the greed, not the burial sites, and he goes on to praise those 'qui gratis in agris suis mortuos sepeliunt' ('De Institutione Laicali', iii. 15 (ed. J.-P. Migne, *PL* 106 (1864), 263). See Treffort 1996*a*: 154–6, 168–9, for these passages.

churchyards coexisted for centuries with traditional village burial-grounds which were accepted and sometimes even consecrated by the clergy and friars[199]—an accommodation which in an earlier age, free of canonical sanction, would have been all the easier. Before 850 (and certainly matters would soon be very different), church-associated burial was increasingly desired and available, but not imposed.

From the 680s the habit of royal burial in churches, formed by the Kentish dynasty at Canterbury and more recently by the Northumbrian at Whitby, probably became general. We still know little about royal tombs, but the (reputed) burials of the sub-kings Merewalh of the Magonsæte (d. *c*.660–70?) at Repton minster and Osric of the Hwicce (d. *c*.679) at Gloucester minster[200] may show lower kingly ranks adopting the habit. Into the eighth century, there is increasing evidence for high-status laity being buried beside minsters, sometimes in stone mausolea[201] or marked by richly carved standing crosses.[202] The latter copied a monastic idiom,[203] and it may be that lay magnates who received this kind of burial were mainly those who had opted for a monastic retirement: it was as abbots rather than as founders that King Æthelred of Mercia (d. 716), and the Northumbrian king's thegn Eanmund, were buried and honoured in the churches of their minsters.[204]

An implication of these cases is that whereas some magnates may, for all we know, have been buried in churches with traditional sets of grave-goods (a possibility suggested by the robbed grave retaining a bronze hanging-bowl in St Paul-le-Bail, Lincoln[205]), others among the secular great may now have been receiving a monastic style of burial, comparable to the late medieval

---

[199] See especially Valk 1992, on Estonia. The Estonian village cemeteries, 'usually situated on small sand or gravel hills, mostly in agricultural landscapes, not far from farms or villages', sound very like the outlying seventh- to ninth-century English ones. Although the Church sometimes went through the motions of condemning them, they were in practice tolerated between the forced conversions of the 1210s and the Lutheran reformation.

[200] Sims-Williams 1990: 60–1, 124; neither is known from a contemporary source. Note that Merewalh had married a Kentish princess. It is also a late and unreliable source that records the burials at Winchester of Cenwalh of Wessex (d. 672) and some of his successors: Yorke 1982: 80. Yorke 2003*b*: 112–18 discusses early royal burial in nunneries.

[201] Repton (Biddle and Kjølbye-Biddle 1992: 42–8; Biddle and Kjølbye-Biddle 2001*b*: 67–74); Winchcombe (Bassett 1985); Hereford cathedral or its predecessor (Sims-Williams 1990: 341–3); Hereford, St Guthlac's (Shoesmith 1980, 'Building A'); Whithorn (Hill 1997: 45–6: it is suggested that this structure is not simply a mausoleum, but a gateway-chapel or mortuary).

[202] The most convincing cases of this are the Bewcastle cross, with its probably secular figure of a hawker, and the fragment from Repton showing a mounted warrior: Karkov 1997; Biddle and Kjølbye-Biddle 1985.

[203] Above, pp. 137–9.

[204] *HE* iii. 11, v. 24 (pp. 246, 566); *DA* ll. 395–402 (p. 33); Blair 2002*a*: 507, 531; above, p. 84, for 'opting-out' kings.

[205] Jones 1994; Geake 1997: 168.

fashion for burial in friars' habits. It could be that King Sebbi of the East Saxons, buried in St Paul's cathedral in 693 × 5 in a Roman sarcophagus, was decked in his finery,[206] but given that he had just taken the religious habit it seems doubtful. The probability is that in aristocratic circles of c.670–710 there were two acceptable forms of church-related burial, the traditionally lavish and the monastically austere. This cannot be more than inference, since English church burials of this social level are lost to us; but it raises the possibility that when opulent and austere burial-rites coexisted in barrows and lay cemeteries during the same period, the context was also Christian.

Away from churches, richly furnished barrow-burial not merely continued but revived after 660.[207] In some ways—notably the even more determined re-use of prehistoric barrows[208]—it looked back to early seventh-century traditions, but in others it took a new course. The group does include a few males, of whom the warrior in the barrow at Benty Grange (Derbs.) is interesting for the unambiguous Christian cross on the nasal of his helmet,[209] but they are outnumbered by females decked in fashionable Mediterranean-style gold and silver jewellery, and often equipped with utensils, satchels, and personal items. The lady buried around 700 in a Bronze Age barrow at Swallowcliffe Down (Wilts.) lay on her bed amidst buckets, glass cups, a bronze-mounted casket, a silver sprinkler, and a satchel bearing an elaborate, possibly cruciform mount (Fig. 29).[210] The similar but poorly excavated burial at White Low (Derbs.) included a gold pectoral cross (Fig. 30).[211]

An obvious point about these opulent ladies is that they belonged to precisely the same age and class as the first generations of noble abbesses. They followed careers befitting their rank in the world rather than in the Church: just as the abbesses represented family solidarity as heads of dynastic minsters, these secular ladies may have done so in a more traditional way as transmitters of social ritual (their food-vessels perhaps symbolizing the hospitality

---

[206] Bede, *HE* iv. 11 (pp. 366–8). The difficulty of fitting Sebbi's body into the coffin suggests that it was a re-used Roman one, as does the initial response to 'look for another'; Æthelthryth's coffin was certainly Roman (*HE* iv. 19 (p. 394)).

[207] Geake 1997: 76, 124–7. The late seventh-century examples considerably outnumber the 'princely' burials of c.600–30.

[208] O'Brien 1999: *passim*, for a catalogue and discussion; Ozanne 1962–3 for the major group in the Peak District; Collis 1983 and Speake 1989 for good examples.

[209] Webster and Backhouse 1991: 59–60; Geake 1997: 148. There is no need to see the helmet as evidence of religious syncretism (as e.g. Van de Noort 1993: 70). The cross was a new and specific symbol of Christianity, the boar-crest a traditional symbol of warrior prowess; contemporary laity, and probably most ecclesiastics, are likely to have thought them entirely compatible.

[210] Speake 1989. I owe to Felicity Clark the observation that the proportion of women in early seventh-century rich burials (especially cremations) may easily have been understated. So the puzzle may be less a rise in female burials than a decline in male ones (for which see Geake 2002: 147–8).

[211] Ozanne 1962–3: 26; Geake 1997: 150. It is probable, but not quite certain, that the cross came from the barrow.

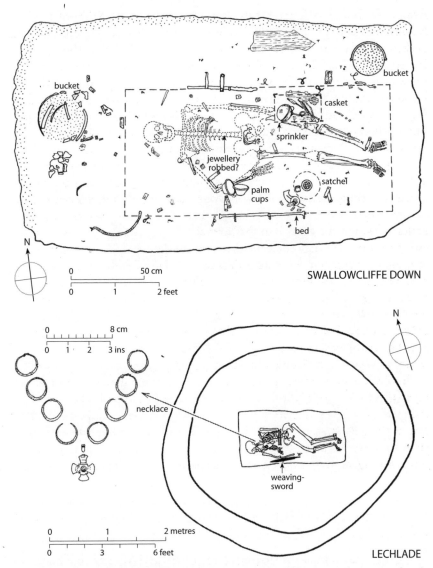

29. Contrasting—but probably both Christian—modes of late seventh-century female burial. The lady at *Swallowcliffe Down* (Wilts.) was buried in a re-used Bronze Age barrow, lying on her bed and with elaborate traditional accoutrements of wealth and hospitality. Her contemporary at *Lechlade* (Glos.) was given merely a weaving-sword, a knife, some beads, and a silver necklace with a cross pendant, even though the large size of the grave-pit, and the provision of a ring-ditch enclosing it, mark her tomb as exceptional within this cemetery. (After Speake 1989: fig. 19, and Boyle and others 1998: figs. 3.3, 5.33, and 5.105–6).

30. Crosses from late seventh-century graves. **1** *Standlake* (Oxon.); **2** *Ixworth* (Suffolk); **3** *White Low* (Derbs.); **4** *Desborough* (Northants.), detail of necklace; **5** St Cuthbert's burial, *Lindisfarne* (Northumb.). Actual size. See p. 173 n. 164 for sources.

of a great household or the sharing of a last meal).[212] Minster-in-Thanet had a tradition that the late seventh-century Kentish princess Eormengyth, sister of that same 'Domne Eafe' whose pet hind ran to such good effect,[213] chose

---

[212] Food-vessels in graves need not indicate paganism: see Young 1977: 38–40; Bullough 1983: 188; E. James 1992: 247–8; Geake 1997: 83–4, suggesting that vessels denote feasting as a symbol of power and wealth; Burnell and James 1999: 87. Above, p. 174, for the possible socio-religious role of women.

[213] Above, p. 144.

her own place of burial a mile to the east of Minster.[214] The story is too odd to be a hagiographical invention: it is tempting to conclude that Eormengyth could not quite bring herself to forsake a traditional barrow for her sister's church.

Another, more austere mode of burial, in which status could be shown by above-ground markers but not by profusion of grave-goods, was also practised in late seventh-century England. This is first apparent in Kent, where an inverse correlation seems to develop between grave-goods and annular or penannular enclosing ditches.[215] It can be illustrated by the latest grave in the long-standing cemetery at Lechlade (Glos.) (Fig. 29).[216] In an exceptionally large, deep grave-pit, surrounded by a ring-ditch and cutting into earlier graves, a woman was buried with merely a weaving-sword, a knife, and a necklace of silver hoops with a small pendent silver cross. This was not a 'poor' burial: its physical impact was exceptional, and the necklace is a luxury item. Rather, it looks like a version of the barrow-burial rite modified by self-conscious restraint, its one concession to opulence a specifically Christian symbol. This grave is making a definite statement, one which marks it out from all the older graves in the cemetery. Other graves containing pendent crosses may have been minimally furnished: Ixworth (in a coffin) with the cross and a disc-brooch, Desborough perhaps with the magnificent gold necklace and nothing else.[217] The rich pectoral cross buried with St Cuthbert in 687 makes the point that the anonymous ladies in their lay cemeteries and the miracle-working bishop in his minster were subject in death to the same fashions of mortuary symbolism.

Cuthbert's burial may in fact give us a link between Hiberno-Frankish ecclesiastical ideals and English lay practice. His Lives tell us that a cloth was wrapped around his head, a consecrated host placed on his breast, his priestly robes and his shoes ('in readiness to meet Christ') were put on him, and finally he was wrapped in a wax shroud; one of the cloths must have been that which Abbess Verca had given him, and in which he had asked to be

---

[214] Liebermann 1889: 5: 'and heo silf þar hyre licreste geceas be hire libbendre, þæt is þonne an mil be easton sancte Myldryðe mynstre.' The fifteenth-century historian Thomas of Elmham baulked at the idea of a holy virgin choosing burial 'in campo plano et loco profano', but admitted that he knew no trace of any church or chapel in the place described: *Historia Monasterii S. Augustini Cantuariensis*, ed. C. Hardwick (Rolls Ser. 8, 1858), 219–20. At grid-reference TR 325 644, a mile due east of Minster church and intervisible with it, is a south-west-facing crest resembling the sites often chosen for elite seventh-century barrows. Between this spot and the church is a known seventh-century cemetery (Meaney 1964: 129–30).

[215] O'Brien 1999: 127–41, for some of the evidence.

[216] Boyle and others 1998: 38–41, 133–4, 186, 258–9.

[217] Above, p. 173. At Desborough, however, the poor conditions of recovery make it impossible to be certain.

buried.[218] Thirty years earlier, as she lay dying in her minster at Nivelles (Belgium), St Gertrude had asked to be buried in nothing but a coarse veil which a pilgrim-nun had sent her and a hair shirt, 'for she said that superfluous things could help neither the dying nor the living'.[219] In her austere choice Gertrude was not merely breaking with an established aristocratic tradition, but purposefully adopting a Christian one.

This was one way in which membership of a 'family of believers', transcending earthly families, could be advertised; there were others, such as the host placed on the dead Cuthbert's breast, or the crosses hung around the necks of Christians.[220] It is of course possible that other burials included wooden or textile crosses, invisible to us. Just as pre-Christian grave-goods had signalled status and identity within the kindred, so the new ones claimed an identity within the framework of the institutionalized and perpetual Church: it is hardly surprising that, in England as in northern Europe, they became more limited and less expressive of life-cycle or gender.[221] The Church never condemned grave-goods as pagan, nor needed to: during the decades *c.*670–720 a new economy of salvation, a new ethic of penitential austerity, and new means of commemoration combined to make them eventually superfluous.[222]

There are thus no grounds for thinking that these English laity, whose burials away from churches observed a cosmopolitan and educated fashion, were any less Christian than their contemporaries who were buried at minsters. The main difference may be that they did not have ties of patronage, profession, or land-tenure which bound them to specific churches, obliging their kin to take them there and the religious communities to receive them. In the decades after 700, when royal *praefecti* founded minsters for themselves and their wives and lesser thegns followed them,[223] the disappearance of rich burials in barrows and lay-organized cemeteries came naturally: the children of the Swallowcliffe Down, Desborough, or Lechlade ladies would probably have been buried in their own or their lords' minsters. The late

---

[218] *VCA* iv. 13, *VCB* c. 37 (pp. 130, 272). It is worth noting that the pendent cross (not mentioned in either account) is the only item known to have formed part of the original deposit which would have survived in normal conditions: excavated in a cemetery, Cuthbert's grave would have looked much like the others.

[219] 'Vita S. Geretrudis', c. 7 (ed. B. Krusch, *MGH Script. Rerum Merov.* ii (Hannover, 1888), 461–2); probably composed *c.*670 by a priest of Nivelles. The choice of the pilgrim-nun's veil acknowledged a Christian convention: the burial clothes of St Melania the younger (d. 438/9) had included the garments of other holy people, as in turn would Cuthbert's. My interpretation is indebted to Young 1986: 379–83, Treffort 1996*a*: 73–4, and especially Effros 1996.

[220] Effros 1996: 7, suggesting that the laity used such items for the kinds of talismanic and prophylactic purposes that Caesarius and Alcuin would condemn (cf. above, p. 175).

[221] Cf. Halsall 1992: 268, on the Metz region.

[222] Treffort 1996*a*: 179–84, for a good survey of the Frankish context; Petts 2002: 44–5, for the Irish background.

[223] Above, p. 102.

seventh-century practices mark a transitional stage, both a Christianization of the princely barrow and a prelude to elite minster burial. They recall (despite cultural differences) those which Guy Halsall identifies in the region around early seventh-century Metz:

The shift from interment with a lavish display of grave-goods to burial in an expensively constructed above-ground chamber—a church—is reflected in the increased concern . . . with permanent surface-level grave-markers: sarcophagus lids visible at ground level, stone crosses, walls around graves or groups of graves, crude gravestones . . . This suggests a change in audience. From a temporary display to local people (albeit probably drawn from a number of neighbouring communities) we perceive a shift to a concern with permanent monuments, possibly, as with the urban churches, aiming at a further-flung peer-group audience.[224]

Yet this parallel highlights a fundamental and startling contrast between the Franks and the English. The Merovingian rural aristocracy had two ways of attaining church-associated burial: to desert the old cemeteries for monasteries or basilicas, or to bring Christian practice to their ancestral graves by building funerary chapels in cemeteries.[225] The English (at least sometimes) followed the first path, but not the second: they had no equivalent for the 'expensively constructed above-ground chamber' apart from those aristocratic mausolea which, in the eighth century, were sometimes built beside existing minsters.

Throughout the Merovingian world, most conspicuously in Alamannia and Bavaria but also in the Rhineland and north-western Francia, many cases are known of rich late sixth- and seventh-century burials which were either deliberately over-built with churches or deposited within them.[226] The buildings are usually small, so that the distinction between mausoleum and funerary church is not always clear, but many of them contained altars and evidently saw sustained sacramental use: sometimes they became parish churches. In England, by contrast, there is virtually no evidence that any early churches began as tomb-houses, nor even that they were built on existing cemeteries.

A comparison between a northern Frankish and a Cambridgeshire cemetery, which in other respects have some striking points in common, illustrates the contrast. At Hordain (north France) a small stone chapel was built, shortly before 600, on the south edge of a normal 'pagan' cemetery which had been in use since the fifth century.[227] The chapel contained an altar-base and a classic 'founder-grave': a richly furnished male burial in a huge rec-

---

[224] Halsall 1992: 269.   [225] Young 1986: 390–6.
[226] The fundamental study of this phenomenon is Burnell 1988: esp. 110–94, 247–52, 519–45. See also Dierkens 1981: 67–9; Young 1986: 394–401; Burnell and James 1999: 96–103, drawing the contrast with England.
[227] Demolon 1986; Young 1986: 394–6; Demolon 1990; Treffort 1996b: 58–9.

tangular pit. Around and within it, a dense cemetery of correctly orientated graves (the Christian community?) developed through the seventh century. The northern zone nonetheless continued in use, with graves on the old alignment and including cremations and horse-burials (presumably the pagan community).

What happened a century later at Shudy Camps (Cambs.) was similar in one way, yet fundamentally different in another.[228] Here a cluster of irregularly aligned graves, some two-thirds of them furnished with poor gravegoods, was succeeded by a separate zone to the north-east in which the graves, mostly unfurnished, were more-or-less correctly orientated. An empty zone within this second group looks as though it could have been occupied by a timber building. We can be much less confident than at Hordain that the north-eastern zone served a distinct Christian community, but it does not seem unlikely; the putative building could even have been a simple cemetery 'chapel' like those recognized on some sites in the Rhineland and Belgium.[229] What Shudy Camps totally lacked (at least within the excavated area) was any kind of aristocratic burial-focus for sustained ecclesiastical activity.

That timber churches over pagan burials did exist is implied by two less-than-lucid clauses in Archbishop Theodore's Penitential.[230] The first states that no altar may be sanctified in a church in which corpses of infidels are buried, but that if the church seems fit to be consecrated the corpses(?) should be ejected, and the church rebuilt once the timbers have been scraped or washed.[231] The second clause adds that if the altar was previously consecrated, 'masses may be celebrated on it if religious people are buried there, but if a pagan is [there] it is better to cleanse [the altar?] and throw [the pagan?] outside'.[232] These do sound like modest cemetery churches on the Hordain model, presumably built over ancestral graves, which were starting to be used for masses. Whether such buildings have not been found

[228] Lethbridge 1936; Boddington 1990: 184–7; Geake 1997: 147.

[229] Dierkens 1981: 67–9; Young 1986: fig. 18. I have recognized only one other possible English case, again not enclosing burials: the group of post-holes amid the graves on the Roman villa at Eccles (Kent) (Detsicas 1976: cf. Brooks 2000: 239–40, and Geake 2002: 151). The name Eccles implies a British Christian site, but it is fairly clear that this is a 'final phase' cemetery which started no earlier than *c*.600.

[230] *PT* ii. i. 4–5 (p. 312). I am grateful to Richard Sharpe for advice on these two passages, which retain irresoluble ambiguities.

[231] c. 4: 'In ecclesia in qua mortuorum cadavera infidelium sepeliuntur, sanctificare altare non licet; sed si apta videtur ad consecrandum, inde evulsa et rasis vel lotis lignis eius reaedificetur.' (See Bullough 1983: 189, for a different interpretation.)

[232] c. 5: 'Si autem consecratum prius fuit, missas in eo caelebrare licet si relegiosi ibi sepulti sunt; si vero paganus sit, mundare et iactare foras melius est.' Thomas Charles-Edwards (pers. comm.) suggests that these statements may reflect views like the Irish one that crosses should not mark graves of pagans (above, p. 59 n.). The contrast between Frankish and English practice could have been accentuated by the greater influence on England of Irish ideas about purity, penance, and the afterlife: see Petts 2002: 44–5.

because they were never common, because they were geographically confined (for instance to Frankish-influenced Kent?), or because timber structures over graves tend to be invisible archaeologically, is unclear.[233] But we can be fairly sure, from the absence of any English parish church which shows this widespread Frankish sequence, that in general the prohibition was either successful or unnecessary.

This lack of 'founder-graves' has a wider context: the resounding lack of evidence for Anglo-Saxon churches overlying pagan-period cemeteries of any kind.[234] In the few cases where minsters seem to have been built on or near earlier graves, these are seventh-century and not conclusively pre-Christian.[235] Occasional finds of seventh-century items in churchyards may point to Christian cemeteries, whether with or without churches, but tell us nothing about the adoption of pagan ones.[236] Persuasive cases of pre-Christian furnished burials from churchyards are confined to Harrietsham (Kent), with a radiate brooch, a pottery bottle, and a crystal-ball, and Wyre Piddle (Worcs.), a bizarre case of skeletons in a sitting posture, and with shields, immediately west of the church.[237] Much has been made of later churchyards near the edges of pagan-period cemeteries, which have been thought to mark a Christianizing shift of focus; this could be right (and Shudy Camps shows how such an arrangement might have begun), but there are only one or two clear cases of the phenomenon and it may be coincidental.[238] Churches occasionally adjoin Anglo-Saxon barrows, or prehistoric

[233] A grave in one of the *Hamwic* cemeteries may have been contained within a timber building, but the evidence is ambiguous and inconclusive (Morton 1992: 176–7; Scull 2001: 70).

[234] The lists in Morris 1983: 53–62 are the starting-point for any discussion of the possible perpetuation of pre-Christian cemeteries as churchyards, and I am much indebted to them. A high proportion of the examples, however, are too ambiguous or obscure to be useful: I have considered them all, but only refer to the ones where I feel that a serious case might be made.

[235] Ripon and Bampton (above, pp. 185–6); possibly Jarrow and Monkwearmouth (Geake 1997: 184–5). See above, n. 33, for possible pre-Christian burials in the Roman villa underlying Southwell minster. At Elstow (above, p. 186 n.) the determining feature may have been the probable Bronze Age barrow rather than the sixth-century cremation cut into it.

[236] Lighthorne (Warw.): hanging-bowl escutcheons (Meaney 1964: 217: there is some ambiguity about where these were found); Hilgay (Norfolk): pot, spearhead, and iron pin (Meaney 1964: 175); Skipton (Yorks.): mounted gold coin (Morris 1983: 60); Mentmore (Bucks.), Sysonby (Leics.), and Great Addington (Northants.): burials with knives and spearheads (Meaney 1964: 58, 149, 186).

[237] Meaney 1964: 123, 281. The posture of the Wyre Piddle bodies is not so improbable as it sounds: seated burials are known from conversion-period cemeteries (Geake 1997: 152, 157, 160, 167, 174). Other possibilities are a spearhead from Rochester cathedral (*MA* 5 (1961), 309) and a brooch of *c.*550 from the churchyard of Soham (Cambs.) (Meaney 1964: 69).

[238] Sancton (Yorks.) is the only convincing one (Faull 1976); there is also a find of a saucer-brooch from near the churchyard at Stone (Bucks.) (Meaney 1964: 59). The burials with knives and spears at Mentmore and Sysonby (above, n. 236) were possibly part of larger cemeteries. It is unclear why Lethbridge thought that the lost church of St Andrew at Burwell (Cambs.), parts of which survived until 1770, stood on the edge of the 'final-phase' cemetery there (Meaney 1964: 61–2; Oosthuizen 2001: 64–5): the first edition of the OS 1 : 2,500 map marks it in the same churchyard as the surviving church of St Mary, 450 m. away.

barrows with secondary Anglo-Saxon interments, but there is no solid evidence that any of the churches pre-dates the eleventh century.[239]

This is the sum total of the evidence: given the quantity of data that would survive if churches on pre-Christian cemeteries had been at all common, its slightness and fragility are striking. Were English bishops really so much more zealous or successful than Merovingian ones in keeping consecrated altars away from pagan corpses? A weightier explanation, once again, is the absence of the small proprietary church as an element in the formation of Christian England. When Franks were buried in buildings within cemeteries, these seem usually to have been their own private churches; in England, the very institution which might have perpetuated an old cemetery and eventually acquired parochial functions barely existed. It was minsters, not local lords, that determined how far the new cultic landscape would reflect the old: it is unsurprising that they showed altogether less interest than did Frankish aristocrats in giving old warrior-graves a new lease of ritual life.

Many if not most of the ordinary English laity in the generations after 670 were still buried in open-ground cemeteries, without ecclesiastical buildings, which came and went much as they had always done. New cemeteries tended to be small; distinct groups of burials appeared on the fringes of old ones (as at Shudy Camps); and graves observed a more consistent west–east orientation: in these respects the English essentially followed the contemporary practice of their neighbours.[240] Some of the new cemeteries, for instance Bromfield (Fig. 31), continue the early seventh-century habit of re-using prehistoric earthworks, barrows, and Roman buildings.[241] This time-honoured mode of giving ancestors a permanent presence in the landscape may have a retrospective quality, appealing to groups with local territorial or kin loyalties. These usages—neither pagan nor overtly Christian, but simply traditional and familial—need not have raised any clerical eyebrows.

Archaeologically the most conspicuous change, illustrated by such sites as Shudy Camps and Bromfield, is the terminal decline of furnished burial. The reduction in the number and range of non-elite grave-goods had begun early in the seventh century, and is more likely to reflect social change than conversion. Their *total* abandonment, on the other hand, may well show a

---

[239] Below, pp. 376–7.

[240] Cf. Burnell and James 1999: 89–90, comparing the English 'Final Phase' cemeteries to Frankish *Seperatfriedhöfe*. The Cannington cemetery, in British west Somerset, shows the same trend with its distinct group of orientated graves datable to *c*.650–700; several had knives in contemporary English fashion, though two richly furnished child-burials point to a different, perhaps Romano-Celtic, influence (Rahtz and others 2000: 92–8).

[241] Stanford 1995; Hadley 1995. For some other examples, Geake 1997: 159 (Thwing); Blair 1994: 32–4 (Shakenoak); Detsicas 1976 and Shaw 1994 (Eccles). The major new studies of this phenomenon are Bell 2001 and Semple 2002.

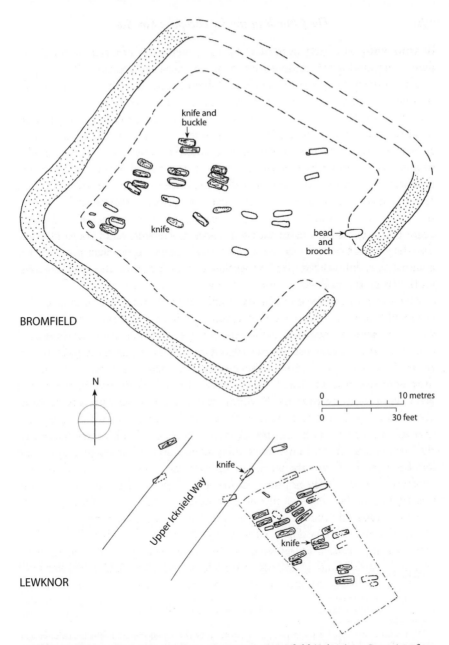

31. Two examples of small isolated cemeteries. At *Bromfield* (Salop.) an Iron Age farm enclosure was re-used during *c.*650–750 for thirty-one orientated burials, three of them with exiguous grave-goods. At *Lewknor* (Oxon.) the excavated part of a small cemetery on the line of the Icknield Way, yielding radiocarbon dates within the range *c.*750–900, included two graves with knives. (After Stanford 1995: fig. 14 and Chambers 1973: fig. 1; cf. Chambers 1976.)

dissemination of Christian modes of burial, even to lay cemeteries. But whatever it signified to contemporaries, it has a profound and potentially highly distorting impact on the evidence available to us: burials become undatable by non-scientific means, and far fewer have been recorded.

In normal lay cemeteries of *c.*670–720, some 45 per cent of burials are unfurnished and 25 per cent have knives only; even among the remaining 30 per cent, it is rare to find more than one or two complex grave-groups in any one cemetery.[242] At the extremes, proportions vary between 72 per cent furnished at Harford Farm (Norfolk), including one grave with coins of *c.*700–10, and only 10 per cent furnished at Bromfield.[243] Apart from knives, the commonest items in the residually furnished graves are buckles and beads, and occasionally the small silver coins (sceattas) which had recently come into use.[244] It is the more complex female assemblages that produce the cylindrical amulet-boxes and the beaver-tooth pendants, with their possible Christian associations.[245]

Around the 720s the deposition of all non-perishable grave-goods, except occasional knives, finally ended.[246] Had the austere mode long used by clergy and monks, and espoused by members of the Franco-English nobility a couple of generations earlier, percolated to ordinary English Christians? It seems likely enough; and it is also possible that the simple shroud, symbol of resurrection as the burial garment both of Lazarus and of Christ himself, was becoming more widely used.[247] By the early eighth century, the reasonably well-to-do could be carried to their graves in coffins.[248] If the jewellery and weapon-sets of sixth-century lay burial had expressed kin-group identity, the anonymous shroud and coffin may have done the same for those who had been received into the family of the Church.

We know essentially nothing about clerical involvement in funeral rites;

---

[242] These percentages are an average of Burwell, Chamberlain's Barn II, King Harry Lane, Shudy Camps, Thornham, and Yelford (Geake 1997: 147, 144, 157, 147, 171, 176).

[243] Geake 1997: 170, 176; Stanford 1995.

[244] Geake 1997: 19–21, 32; cf. Young 1977: 41, 49, for hand-held coins as a late Roman and early Frankish practice.

[245] Above, pp. 171–3.

[246] Perhaps the latest conventional pre-Viking furnished burial yet identified is one in the cemetery at Garton-on-the-Wolds (Yorks.) with a group of sceattas deposited after *c.*720–5 (Geake 1997: 158).

[247] O'Brien 1999: 52, for seventh- and eighth-century literary references to the burial of ecclesiastics in shrouds; cf. the Llanlleonfel inscription (above, p. 65), *in sindone muti*. For the Lazarus symbolism, including the term *lazarisatio* for the winding of a corpse, see Treffort 1996*a*: 67–70. As O'Brien notes (1999: 60), it is not impossible that knives were included with shrouded corpses.

[248] Iron mounts and locks from coffins are now known from some eighth-century sites in the north (Hall and Whyman 1996: 99–110). In a story set in *c.*710–20, Bede pictures a thegn's retainer on his deathbed with the coffin (*loculus*) in which he is to be buried set out beside him (*HE* v. 5 (p. 464)).

but it is not impossible that the new, homogeneous simplicity reflects a shift of responsibility—from the kindred to the ecclesiastical establishment—which in time would cause a shift in location—from lay cemeteries to churchyards. An especially clear mark of acceptance into the Christian family was burial *ad sanctos*: when was the ground in which ecclesiastics were laid to rest within their monastic boundaries first opened to the faithful laity?

When Bede mentions minster cemeteries it is nearly always with reference to ecclesiastical burials; at Barking the nuns killed in the plague of the 660s were buried apart from their male colleagues, and the exhumation of burials on the site a few decades later involved only 'servants and handmaids of Christ'.[249] It was monks from Cedd's minster in Essex who so prized his relics that they travelled 200 miles to 'live beside the body of their father or . . . to die and be buried there'.[250] In the first reference to the admission of a non-royal lay corpse to a minster, the late seventh-century nobleman Hildmaer asks St Cuthbert to arrange for his wife to be given the last rites and to be buried in holy ground at Lindisfarne; but here we have a saint's close friend seeking a special privilege.[251] A clue to the opening of minster cemeteries to a wider Christian 'family' may lie in the Irish canonical provision that 'if anyone should have been joined to a church he will be buried there'.[252] It is possible that a nexus of patrons, adherents, and tenants formed an intermediate group between the core community and the laity at large; and that for some time the line between burial at minsters and in lay cemeteries was drawn to include them, but few others.

Evidence is accumulating that minster cemeteries grew steadily between the late seventh and mid ninth centuries. Dating of unfurnished skeletons relies on radiocarbon determinations, and unfortunately there are technical obstacles to close accuracy within this period.[253] Radiocarbon ranges centred well back in the seventh century, and in a few cases stratigraphical or artefact evidence, nonetheless indicate minster-associated cemeteries before *c.*720

[249] Canterbury (*HE* ii. 3, p. 142); Lindisfarne (iii. 17, p. 264); Lastingham (iii. 23, p. 288); Lichfield (iv. 3, p. 344); Barking (iv. 7, iv. 10, pp. 356, 362–4); Ely (iv. 19, pp. 392–4). For France, Zadora-Rio (2003: 10) observes that a 'first separation, established during the course of the 6th century, discriminated between lay and monastic communities, not between Christians and pagans or renegades'.

[250] *HE* iii. 23 (p. 288).

[251] *VCA* ii. 8, *VCB* c. 15 (pp. 90–2, 205–7). In the anonymous version Hildmaer asks Cuthbert to afford his wife 'requiem sepulture', in Bede's that 'corpus illius hic in locis sanctis sepeliri permittas'. Both authors evidently locate the episode at Lindisfarne, even though both recount it before Cuthbert's arrival there (cf. ed. Colgrave p. 323).

[252] *Hib.* XVIII. 3 (p. 56); Charles-Edwards 1992: 76; O'Brien 1999: 53; cf. above, p. 64.

[253] Fluctuations in the calibration curve mean that more precise dates can be obtained for some parts of the period than others. Techniques for narrowing the error-terms in stratified sequences of burials are, however, described by Scull and Bayliss 1999, and will presumably be developed.

at Canterbury, Minster-in-Thanet, and Faversham in Kent,[254] at Ripon, Monkwearmouth, Jarrow, and Hartlepool (the first three perhaps starting in the pre-monastic period) in Northumbria,[255] at Nazeingbury and Waltham in Essex,[256] at Burgh Castle in East Anglia,[257] at Winchester in Wessex,[258] and at Repton and Hereford in Mercia.[259] In no case can large numbers of graves be reliably dated before c.720, and the central, insoluble problem is whether these cemeteries served lay populations or the religious communities only. The Nazeingbury skeletons were almost all female, and can presumably be identified as the nuns; the small eighth- to ninth-century cemetery around Glastonbury's cell at Beckery seems to have been used almost entirely by monks.[260] On the other hand we cannot, given the heterogeneous nature of minster communities, assume that the mixed-sex populations at Hartlepool or Burgh Castle were necessarily lay.

English minster cemeteries have produced, in total, a very small collection of relatively trivial grave-goods: glass palm-cups at Peterborough, Faversham, and Minster-in-Thanet,[261] beads at Whithorn, Jarrow, and Lichfield,[262] bone and bronze pendants at Nazeingbury and Breedon-on-the-Hill,[263] tweezers at Pontefract,[264] single coins at Canterbury (St Pancras) and Repton.[265] While the different patterns of disturbance and retrieval make comparison difficult, we probably can say that grave-goods are distinctly rarer and sparser in the excavated fragments of pre-720 minster cemeteries than in open-ground cemeteries used during the same period. It would seem either that they were more rigorously excluded from minsters,[266] or that the people buried there assimilated clerical modes a few decades earlier than others. Further speculation is hampered by ignorance of what, in practice, adopting some form of the religious life may have meant for the ordinary laity, and how wide a circle of monastic tenants and adherents may have assimilated to the outward forms of the new culture.

Radiocarbon and other evidence for burials in the range c.700–870 has

---

[254] Above, p. 61; below, n. 261.

[255] Hall and Whyman: 1996, 65–124; Geake 1997: 189, 184–5; cf. above, pp. 185–6.

[256] Huggins and others 1978: 53–4; Huggins and Bascombe 1992: 333–4; Geake 1997: 151–2.

[257] Geake 1997: 178.

[258] Kjølbye-Biddle 1992: 222; Biddle and Kjølbye-Biddle forthcoming.

[259] Geake 1997: 149, 157; Shoesmith 1980.   [260] Rahtz and Hirst 1974: 27–34.

[261] Meaney 1964: 195; *JBAA* 13 (1857), 313; letter from Mr Boys to Dr Simmons, *Archaeologia*, 8 (1787), 449; J. Douglas, *Nenia Britannica* (London, 1793), 71 and pl. XVII. A burial in a stone coffin at St Martin-in-the-Fields, London, contained two palm-cups (Vince 1990: 14–15; cf. above, n. 160). These graves probably reflect Frankish influence. The London and Peterborough finds are also discussed by Scull 2001: 69.

[262] Geake 1997: 151, 184–5; *MA*, 39 (1995), 241.

[263] Above, p. 172 n.; Geake 1997: 167.   [264] Wilmott 1986; Geake 1997: 191.

[265] Morris 1983: 61 (listing other sceattas from churchyards); Geake 1997: 149. A sceat from Wells was apparently merely in the fill of a grave, not a grave-good: Rodwell 2001: 516–17, 565.

[266] As suggested by Geake 1997: 127–8, 134–5.

been obtained at many more minsters and suggests a big expansion, in which some cemeteries grew to be very large.[267] Graves occur in groups or scatters over a wide area, often at some distance from the modern church and church-yard (for instance Addingham, Brixworth, and Pontefract). Striking ex-amples at lesser minsters are Aylesbury, where the eighth- to tenth-century cemetery spreads across the entire hilltop, and Caister-on-Sea with its ill-recorded but massive complexes of graves. Often there must have been at least two distinct cemeteries, though their extent is rarely known; what could be a common pattern is recorded on a small scale at Brandon (Fig. 25), where the southern cemetery shows the age- and sex-range of a normal lay popu-lation but the northern was seemingly more specialized.[268]

By 850, minster cemeteries were evidently serving a significant section of the laity, and their physical impact within the precincts must have increased. Perhaps they acquired more the character of public spaces, punctuated as they now were with the stone mausolea of the great and a growing range of stone crosses and markers. As the eighth and ninth centuries passed there must have been a progressive reorientation of lay mortuary interests towards the minsters, where lengthening generations of kin now lay buried and com-memorated. Dependent cells may have acquired their own small cemeteries, broadening the scope of church-associated burial.[269] There are probably resonances between ninth-century English practice and the developing Carolingian view that laity should be buried in church precincts,[270] though with the difference that ecclesiastical burial was inevitably more centralized in a society still largely without village churches.

Yet in England as in Francia,[271] burial in traditional lay cemeteries was not abandoned nor even necessarily marginalized, though after the early eighth century it becomes very hard to recognize. Apart from knives (over-

---

[267] The following is a list of examples known to me; page-references are to Geake 1997 except where otherwise stated: Addingham (191; Adams 1990); Aylesbury (145; Allen and Dalwood 1983); Bampton (Blair 1998c: 128); Brandon (177–8; Carr and others 1988); Breedon-on-the-Hill (167); Brixworth (171; Everson 1977); Butley, Burrow Hill (178; Fenwick 1984); Caister-on-Sea (169–70); Carlisle (148; McCarthy 1996); Dacre (148); Exeter (150); Flixborough (160); Hereford, St Guthlac's (157; Shoesmith 1980); Lichfield cathedral (*MA* 39 (1995), 241); Oxford cathedral (Blair 1994: 63; A. Boyle in *Oxoniensia*, 66 (2001), 350–5, 366–8); Pontefract (191; Roberts 2002); Threekingham (Meaney 1964: 165); Wells (Rodwell 2001: 571).

[268] Geake 1997: 177–8.

[269] This could explain the very occasional finds that look like late seventh-century grave-goods in churchyards of small churches (above, p. 237). Could the enigmatic site at Thwing (Geake 1997: 159) be something of the sort?

[270] Treffort 1996a: 165–7.

[271] Treffort 1996a: 168–70, Treffort 1996b: 57–8, and Zadora-Rio 2003: 2–8, for the wide occur-rence in France of scattered seventh- to tenth-century burials. Among the Lombards, too, it is unclear when burial in family cemeteries unassociated with churches ceased, and there is no evi-dence that baptismal churches controlled burial before the ninth century: Settia 1991: 10–17. I owe the last reference to Francesca Tinti.

whelmingly the commonest item in the late seventh century[272] and still occasionally deposited beyond 800) they have no grave-goods, and they are always orientated; archaeologists have often mis-dated them to the late Roman or even post-medieval periods. It is impossible to say how many such cemeteries have gone unrecognized, but recent local studies suggest that they could have been numerous.[273] Typically they contain between five and thirty bodies, can be near settlements or away from them, and occasionally continue the old habit of re-using ancient sites;[274] there are even some hints that barrow-burial continued later than is usually thought.[275] The coastal emporia, where burial arrangements do not seem radically different from those in normal rural areas, show a mixture of concentrated and dispersed burial on non-church sites.[276] Alongside the growing minster churchyards, older and more diverse arrangements clearly persisted.

On the inadequate evidence available, it may tentatively be suggested that cemeteries of this kind continued until around 900 (for example Lewknor, Fig. 31) but in general not much later.[277] The final stages may be complicated by the re-introduction of grave-goods under Viking influence,[278] but orientated burial with occasional knives perpetuated indigenous practice, and there can be little doubt that a continuous tradition of non-church burial survived. There is no reason to think that these were in any way dishonourable graves:[279] the frontiers of holy ground had yet to be defined, and there was still no obligation on the faithful to lie within them.[280] The devel-

[272] Geake 1997: 25–6, 102–3.

[273] Blair 1994: 72–3; Hadley 1995. A search of the Oxfordshire Sites and Monuments Record produced some fifty reports of finds of unaccompanied human burials, any or all of which could be Anglo-Saxon.

[274] At Yarnton (Oxon.) a small cemetery of six or more graves on the edge of an excavated settlement gave reliable radiocarbon dates between the late eighth and late ninth centuries (Hey forthcoming). Other examples are: Appleford (Hinchcliffe and Thomas 1980: 33, 66–8); Sedgeford (*MA* 3 (1959), 298); Shepperton (Canham 1979: 104); Stanmer (Gilkes 1997: 114–17, 123–4); Great Houghton (Chapman 1998: 95); Soulbury (*MA* 41 (1997), 248); Ormesby (ibid. 279).

[275] Apparent examples of very late burials in primary or secondary barrows are Alfriston, Harting Beacon, Bevis's Grave, and perhaps Kemp Howe (Geake 1997: 183, 184, 154, 158). Recent radiocarbon dates from Bevis's Grave indicate ninth- and tenth-century burials (ex inf. Annia Cherryson). A number of barrow-burials in Sussex are furnished with a knife only (O'Brien 1999: 148), and it does look as though the practice may have persisted unusually late near the south coast. See below, p. 377 n., for the probably post-750 secondary barrow-burial at Ogborne St Andrew, Wilts.

[276] Scull 2001; Scull and Bayliss 1999.

[277] Below, p. 465, for a few later cases.

[278] Instances of this would be the Borre-style necklace from a grave at Saffron Walden (Geake 1997: 152), and the little packets of coins which were sometimes deposited with the dead of the Viking 'Great Army' in the 870s (Biddle and Blair 1987).

[279] Current work by Andrew Reynolds is suggesting that special cemeteries for the executed, often on liminal sites (cf. below, pp. 465–6), were already emerging in the seventh to eighth centuries, but it is usually easy to distinguish these from regular burials in similar locations.

[280] Below, pp. 464–5.

opment of ubiquitous churchyard burial is nonetheless becoming apparent in the two trends visible by the end of the period: the apparent fading-out of the dispersed cemeteries, and the growth of those around minsters.

Burial practice offers our best hope of glimpsing religious attitudes among ordinary laity in the 'age of conversion'. Archaeologists' long-accepted equations of paganism with grave-goods, and of Christianity with churchyard burial, must be rejected: they cut across the grain of the real attitudes and the real changes. Christians could be buried by Christian heirs in traditional lay-organized cemeteries, at first with grave-goods but increasingly in a restrained mode which, precisely because it was not imposed by ecclesiastical fiat, suggests acceptance of a new spiritual economy and new ways for the living to visualize the dead.[281] Christians adopted this mode long before they necessarily expected, or were expected, to be buried near churches. This second development came more slowly, as the practice first of ecclesiastics, then of kings and minster-founding nobles, spread through a widening circle of thegns, servants, and tenants. In a trend inexorable across western Christendom, it would eventually embrace the whole family of the faithful: by 856 Hincmar of Rheims could hold that 'it is for a priest to arrange for his parishioners to be buried, according to Christian devotion, in the places which seem best to him; and that priest, remembering his order, should provide an appropriate grave for each'.[282] This kind of prescriptive parochial regime, essentially lacking in ninth-century England, would come through a combination of forces: economic growth, the rebuilding of local organization, and the extension of royal power in the aftermath of the Viking invasions.

[281] It is worth comparing the pattern of grave-good abandonment in other recently converted north European societies. In Estonia, deposition rates of knives in 20% of graves, brooches in 28%, and coins in 16%—in other words not unlike late seventh-century English practice—occur between the thirteenth and early eighteenth centuries (Valk 1992: 211).

[282] Hincmar, 'Capitula Synodica', III, c. 2 (ed. J.-P. Migne, *PL* 125 (1879), 794). Cf. Smith 1995: 672–4.

5
Monastic Towns? Minsters as Central Places
c.650–850

And who can describe in words the supreme beauty of this church, and the countless wonders of that minster (*monasterium*)—of that city (*civitas*) as we may say, if
it can rightly be called a city when it is surrounded by no circuit of walls? But because
countless peoples come together in it, it earns the name 'city' from the gathering of
crowds there. This city is supreme and metropolitan, in whose suburbs (*suburbani*),
which holy Brigit marked out with a precise boundary (*certo limite designavit*), is
feared no mortal adversary nor onslaught of enemies. But it is the safest city of refuge,
with all its external suburbs (*cum suis omnibus deforis suburbanis*), in the whole land
of the Irish for all fugitives. Treasures of kings are kept there . . . And who can count
the varied crowds and countless peoples flocking together from all provinces? Some
come because of the abundance of feasts, others to obtain healing of their ailments,
others to stare at the crowds; others bring great gifts and offerings to the celebration
of holy Brigit's birth.[1]

Thus the seventh-century Irishman Cogitosus praised Kildare. He was
writing in a tradition, suffused with biblical conceptions of cities of refuge
and the heavenly city, which presented the minsters of Ireland as places of
safety, centrality, and popular resort as well as places of cult. Both written
and physical evidence demonstrates the reality behind this idealized model.
The main centres of early Christian Ireland were indeed its monastic sites,
and several of them have now yielded archaeological evidence for complex
zoning of activities, including specialized craft production and industry,
during the seventh to ninth centuries.[2] No other insular texts are so eloquent
as the Irish ones, but the phenomenon occurs much more widely. To the
whole expanding north-western extremity of Christendom, monastic insti-

---

[1] Cogitosus, 'Vita S. Brigidae', c. 32; I am grateful to Richard Sharpe for access to his unpublished edition. Cf. Doherty 1985: 55–6.

[2] Doherty 1985 for the hagiographical and prescriptive evidence; Swan 1985 for topography;
Bradley 1999: 136–40, for a summary of recent discoveries at Clonmacnoise, Armagh, and Dunmisk.
See below, n. 78, for the reservations of B. J. Graham and M. A. Valante. Butler 1979 extends the
model to Wales.

tutions brought concepts and practices founded upon the rhythms of a more developed world: that of the still-Roman Mediterranean with its towns, its palaces, and its economic support-systems for those who lived in them. On the English, they had a physical and social impact comparable to that of Kildare on the Irish.

This impact illustrates a recurrent stage in human development. Studying societies which, in many different periods and places, evolved through pre- and proto-urban forms of organization, archaeologists, anthropologists, and sociologists have recognized the formative role of religious sites as hierarchical, economic, and eventually urban centres. During the seventh to tenth centuries, when their minsters appeared, flourished, then gradually lost status, the English may reasonably be defined as a society experiencing those stages of growth and change. It is with an eye to this model of urbanization in undeveloped cultures, rather than to modern definitions of urbanism, that we should assess whether an important pre-Viking English minster 'can rightly be called a city'.

The 'holy city' (i): symbolic urbanism

In 650 England contained no functioning places which can sensibly be called cities, or even towns. By 750 there were still no cities in any normally accepted sense, though two new types of settlement had appeared: the coastal and esturine emporia—specialized in function and apparently few in number— and complex monastic sites. In this non-urban world, how did educated ecclesiastics who used the words *civitas* and *urbs* understand the concept 'city'?

The answer must be: in a range of overlapping senses formed by their immediate environments, by their perceptions of contemporary Christendom, and by their liturgical observances and reading. They knew that the massive stone ruins in the English countryside, for which their kinsfolk had long had a special term—*ceaster*, from Latin *castrum*—had been centres of population and power under Roman rule. If they were well travelled, or had listened to travellers, they knew that similar places still flourished, and were still called *civitates*, in southern Gaul, Italy, and the Holy Land. And the Bible told them of cities with stone walls and strong gates, symbols of God's protection for the righteous.[3] If they recited the psalter, Psalm 122 was periodically on their lips:

---

[3] e.g. Isa 26: 1–2, celebrating Jerusalem as 'a strong city whose walls and ramparts are our deliverance. Open the gates to let a righteous nation in.'

> I rejoiced when they said to me,
> 'Let us go to the house of the Lord.'
> Now we stand within your gates, O Jerusalem:
> Jerusalem that is built to be a city
> where people come together in unity;
> To which the tribes resort, the tribes of the Lord . . .
> For in her are set the thrones of justice . . .
> 'May those who love you prosper;
> peace be within your ramparts
> and prosperity in your palaces.'[4]

They could also picture in their minds the heavenly Jerusalem, the ultimate paradigm of the holy city:

It had a great high wall, with twelve gates, at which were twelve angels. . . . The city was built as a square, and was as wide as it was long. . . . The wall was built of jasper, while the city itself was of pure gold, bright as clear glass. . . . The twelve gates were twelve pearls, each gate being made from a single pearl. The streets of the city were of pure gold, like translucent glass. . . . I saw no temple in the city; for its temple was the sovereign Lord God and the Lamb. And the city had no need of sun or moon to shine upon it; for the glory of God gave it light, and its lamp was the Lamb.[5]

Trade, industry, or specialized occupations were not essential to these conceptions of the *civitas*: it was not because it had a market-place, or housed a concentration of people living by non-agrarian means, that the heavenly Jerusalem was a city. The values evoked by such images were those of cultural and moral 'civilization'—in its literal sense—informed by both the biblical and the Roman worlds: the city should be stately, commodious, and populous, protected by physical boundaries and legal privileges, a place of righteousness and refuge, above all holy. No kind of settlement that was practicable in seventh- and eighth-century England could meet these requirements so well as the monastic settlement.[6]

But beyond this, the Old and New Testaments presented to the first English ecclesiastics a people evolving from the nomadic economy of Genesis to the highly urbanized one of the Gospels and Acts. They could read of

---

[4] Ps. 122: 1–7.   [5] Rev. 21: 12–24.

[6] Wood 1995: 15–16, for the various ways in which Monkwearmouth and Jarrow embodied 'the recreation of Jerusalem and Rome between the rivers Tyne and Wear'. Compare, in a Carolingian context, the resounding ninth-century text inscribed on the *Westwerk* of the monastic church at Corvey: 'Civitatem istam tu circumda, Domine, et angeli tui custodiant muros eius' ('Lord, surround this city, and may your angels guard its walls') (Stiegemann and Wemhoff 1999: 570–1). Havercamp 1987 traces ideological and political conceptions of the *civitas sancta* from the prototypes, Jerusalem and Rome, to the thirteenth century; cf. Rosenau 1983: 26–8, for square representations of the Church as Jerusalem.

cities complex, populous, and magnificent beyond their imagination, controlling groups of subordinate villages in the open countryside around[7] and acting as centres of money-based commerce. They could also learn how urban land had been held by different and more permanent tenures than rural land, and how the Lord had designated cities of refuge where accidental killers could escape vengeance.[8] As the commercial transformation of England gathered pace after 670, these hitherto alien concepts must slowly have come to make sense to the inhabitants of monastic *civitates*.

It was within the stone walls of Romano-British ruins, so enthusiastically adopted by monastic founders, that lay perceptions of special places in the landscape coalesced with literary ones of the heavenly and earthly Jerusalems. Bede could use *civitas* in the strictly physical sense of an archaeological monument,[9] and the distinction in Anglo-Latin between sites with visible Roman walls and sites with earthen fortifications mirrors an equivalent distinction, known from place-names, in pre-Christian English: *civitas* or *ceaster* as against *urbs* or *burh*.[10] But on a more conceptual level, the ecclesiastical adoption of such places conferred 'cityness'. Roman towns re-born as bishoprics or minsters embodied a transfer of meanings from old (abandoned) cities to new (revitalized and holy) ones. Thus Bede describes the gift to St Birinus of 'the city (*civitas*) called Dorchester to make his episcopal seat in it'.[11] The charter which King Hlothere of Kent issued in 679 in the 'city of Reculver' ('actum in civitate Reculf') might seem to describe a royal vill, but an earlier king had already given this Roman fort to found a minster:[12] 'built as a square . . . as wide as it was long', and with a large stone church at its centre, Reculver was a firmly monastic 'city' by 679 (Figs. 11, 23).

Stone walls were not a prerequisite for such symbolic Christian urbanism. Ireland lacked Roman ruins, so Kildare was 'surrounded by no circuit of walls', yet for Cogitosus it was still a city. Among both the Irish and the English we can recognize that extension of concepts and associations from Roman to non-Roman enclosed sites which has been described, in a European context, by Edith Ennen:

The most effective link between one historical period and another was forged by the

---

[7] Joshua 15: 20–62 lists the cities of Judah 'with their villages and hamlets' (translated by the Vulgate as '*X* cum vicis et villulis suis'; 'civitates . . . et villae'); cf. 1 Sam. 6: 18; Esther 9: 19; Ezek. 38: 11 for the contrast between walled towns and open villages.

[8] Lev. 25: 29–34; Num. 35: 9–15; Josh 20: 1–9; cf. above, pp. 221–2.

[9] As when he calls Grantchester a 'deserted little city', *civitatula desolata*: *HE* iv. 19 (p. 394); cf. 'anre westre ceastre' (i.e. Chester) in *ASC* s.a. 893 (p. 88).

[10] Campbell 1986: 99–107, 116–17, a full analysis noting some exceptions and qualifications.

[11] *HE* iii. 7 (p. 232); cf. Hunter 1974: 35–41, for Anglo-Saxon perceptions of the British and Continental Roman past.

[12] S 8; *ASC* s.a. 669 (pp. 34–5).

Christian Church. . . . The episcopal *civitates* in the Frankish period that had origi-
nated in Roman towns became the model for the defended bishops' seats east of the
Rhine. I should call this . . . continuity in the realm of ideas. The function of a town,
to be a cult site and to serve as the centre of ecclesiastical organization, is a heritage
from the ancient world. . . . [T]he fortified sites of newly founded bishoprics became
important seed-beds of medieval towns.[13]

Thus it became possible for an *urbs/burh* to attain a sacral status like that
of a *civitas/ceaster*. In 798 a Canterbury scribe wrote that King Offa had transferred 'Cookham minster and many other towns' (*coenobium Coccham et alias
urbes quamplurimas*) from Wessex to Mercia.[14] He was visualizing the *urbes*
of the middle Thames region as including, or perhaps comprising, its minsters; the English word in his mind was probably *burh*. *Burh*, as we will see,
had various and shifting meanings:[15] the point to be made here is that before
the mid eighth century it had a distinct and (in terms of elite settlements)
perhaps even dominant sense of 'minster'. English texts earlier than 750
record ten place-names in -*burh*. One is Bamburgh, two seem to denote
archaeological monuments, but the other seven are minsters: Bangor, *Cnobheresburg*, Coldingham (*Colodesburg*), Fladbury, Glastonbury, Malmesbury,
and Tilbury.[16] This is not simply a matter of minsters occupying older
forts: *burh* as a vernacular alternative to *mynster* is demonstrated by the
parallel names 'Tetta's *burh'*/*Tettan monasterium* for Tetbury (Fig. 38) and
Uuestburg/*Westmynster* for Westbury-on-Trym, or by the formulations 'the
holy church which is sited in London and . . . is called *Paulesbyri*' and 'the
minster which . . . is called *Paulesbiri*' in eighth-century charters of St
Paul's.[17] Bede seems to slip into this usage (which like Old Irish *cathir* extends
a root meaning of 'city' to include 'monastery') in his two references
to Bangor-is-Coed (Flints.): 'their most noble minster which is called

---

[13] Clarke and Simms 1985: 6–7.

[14] S 1258. In the minster of 'De Abbatibus', 'the clergy rejoiced in their citadel' ('letetur clerus
in urbe': *DA* l. 505 (p. 41)). The Llandaf texts use *urbs* to mean 'monastery' (e.g. *Tavi urbs, Guen-
tonie urbs*), sometimes perhaps with connotations of *Romanitas* or monumentality: Davies 1978:
121–2.

[15] Below, pp. 285–9, for the semantic routes leading to the rural 'burys' and urban 'boroughs'
of later England.

[16] Cox 1975: 47; cf. Campbell 1986: 107–8; below, pp. 272–3, for Canterbury and London.
Exceptionally, Boniface on one occasion calls Malmesbury (an Iron Age hillfort) *Maldubia civitas*
rather than *Maldubia urbs*, perhaps as a special compliment (*Bon. Ep.* No. 135, p. 274). Cox 1994
associates the -*burh* place-names of Lindsey with a seventh-century defensive system; but they could
have been coined at widely different dates, and their concentration along lines of communication
would be consistent with a variety of other explanations, including both the monastic and the late
manorial ones.

[17] S 71; S 139, S 1187; S 1786, S 1790, Biddle 1989: 23. St Paul's was of course within a large
Roman city, but perhaps surrounded by a new inner enclosure conceived as a *burh*.

Bancornaburg, and 'there were many of them *de monasterio Bancor*'.[18] If the *civitas/ceaster* needed Roman walls, the monastic *urbs/burh* could go some way towards replicating *Romanitas* on new sites and in new regions.

The 'holy city' (ii): economic centrality

Early minsters were sometimes spoken about in ways which recognized them as the defining foci of their regions. When minsters were founded within established territories known by the names of kin-groups, those names often attached themselves specifically to the minster sites: some cases (such as Hexham, Oundle, Barking, and Lastingham) are documented, many more (such as Woking, Godalming, Reading, and Sonning) can be inferred.[19] Some of these minsters could have been built on long-standing sites of ritual or assembly for the eponymous Bericingas, Læstingas, and so on, but the important point here is their eventual status as the sole and specific referents of these names: a modern visitor to Barking or Lastingham goes to the site of its minster. It looks as though a minster, once founded within a *regio*, might become so much its natural centre as to become synonymous with the territory.[20] Again, it seems likely that satellite place-names of the *norð-tūn*, *suð-tūn* type—and not just the specifically ecclesiastical ones—were often formed with reference to minster centres.[21] Such patterns, indelibly stamped

[18] Barrow 1973: 65; *HE* ii. 2 (pp. 138, 140).

[19] 'Inaegustaldesae, adepta regione a regina' (*VW* c. 22 (p. 44)); 'in loco qui nuncupatur Inberecingum' (*HE* iv. 6 (pp. 354–6)); 'ad monasterium eius quod in Undolum positum est' (*VW* c. 65 (p. 140)); 'fecit ibi monasterium quod nunc Laestingaeu vocatur' (*HE* iii. 23 (p. 288)). Campbell (1986: 113) notes Oundle as 'a clear example of an area name which later became a place-name. . . . Perhaps such [places] as Barking, Woking, Lastingham . . . gained their names because they were central places for areas or peoples.' It is important to stress, though, that Hexham and Barking at least were not shared with any secular power-centres, being at the hearts of estates owned by their monastic founders. Whether or not Lastingham had been a site of pagan cult, Bede explicitly describes it as an unoccupied place when Cedd took it over.

[20] This suggests a different slant on Geoffrey Barrow's comment that if southern Scottish *Eccles* names 'seem to occur in association with shires more frequently than could be dismissed as coincidence—and this seems to be true of England and southern Scotland—the reasonable inference would surely be that many of the earliest churches were deliberately founded shire by shire, and often placed close to the shire centre' (Barrow 1973: 63–4). But was it in fact the shire centres that were placed close to the churches?

[21] Above, p. 215, for Westminster, Southminster, etc. Other directional satellites are numerous, but need more study. Examples of forms in *tūn* around minsters are at Bath (Davenport 2002: 98) and Leominster (Blair 2001*a*: 8–11); examples of forms in *burh* are at (again) Leominster, which had 'Burys' in all four cardinal directions (Hillaby 1987: map 3), Westbury-sub-Mendip to the west of Wells, Astbury east of Sandbach (below, p. 309 n.), and Norbury and Sudbury (Derbs.) to the north and south of Uttoxeter. Names in *burh-tūn* combine the two elements; so many adjoin minsters as to raise the possibility that one meaning of the term could be 'the *tūn* next to the *burh*' using *burh* in its specifically monastic sense, for instance Burton Hill near Malmesbury or Black Bourton near Bampton (*P-N Wilts.* 49–50; *P-N Oxon.* 306).

on the landscape of farming and settlement as it crystallized during the eighth to eleventh centuries, suggest that minsters may have been not just religious centres, but also land-management centres of a special kind.

So far as we can tell, the dominant structures for exploiting post-Roman Britain were those of 'extensive lordship': services and renders in kind, which elites exacted by virtue of their rule over people rather than their ownership of land.[22] Where these structures first emerge into written record among the early Christian English, it is in the context of rulership and the provisioning of royal households: territories assessed in precise numbers of hides owed regular hidage-based quantities of produce to kings. As seen in our texts, the landscape was organized above all for the support of itinerant courts. A king and his retinue would move around his kingdom, living off the food-renders; the bigger the kingdom (and the retinue) the further the king travelled, up to the practical limits on the size of the circuit and therefore of the core kingdom.[23] Beyond the political and military imperatives for a king to show his face was the convenience, in an undeveloped economy, of a system which took the eaters to the food rather than the food to the eaters, reducing the need for transport and storage. Economically, therefore, the food-circuit was a cushion for established modes of aristocratic life, not a dynamic exploitation of the countryside for maximum profit.

The essence of 'extensive lordship' is that it was based on 'territories' rather than 'estates': on the exaction of episodic renders from 'free' cultivators such as feature in the laws of Ine, rather than the imposition of heavy services on tenants.[24] But it long coexisted with different and more exploitative relationships between proprietors and servile peasants, pertaining in the core zones of certain estates. The dynamically exploited *inland*, representing 'a transition between an economy based purely on tribute and the manorial system', is first apparent on the estates of seventh- and eighth-century minsters. As Rosamond Faith observes, minsters resembled other major lords in needing to command regular supplies of foodstuffs, but in one respect differed fundamentally from at least royal households: whereas kings were itinerant, ecclesiastical communities stayed in one place.[25] It thus seems possible that directly exploited core areas emerged first on the monastic estates.

A major problem in assessing how far this system was distinctively ecclesiastical is that there is one, potentially widespread, kind of land-unit about the running of which we know virtually nothing whatever: the lay aristo-

---

[22] Faith 1997: 1–14.
[23] Charles-Edwards 1989; Faith 1997: 38–41; above, p. 154 n., for systematic hidation.
[24] Wickham 1992: 232–6, for a view of the English evidence in a European context.
[25] Faith 1997: 15–16.

cratic estate. Kings and sub-kings at all levels would have had their own food-circuits, but there must have been a large class of people, whether heads of established kindreds or warriors settled on land by their lords, who lived permanently on smaller territories where they might potentially have developed inlands.[26] At the same time, the smaller minsters (at least initially) may have been content to draw the customary food-renders already due from their newly acquired estates. We should therefore be cautious in suggesting that monastic foundations created an unprecedented and rapid stimulus towards 'manorialization', in the sense of immediately imposing more exploitative and interventionist regimes on their peasants. On the other hand, their size combined with their stability must have given the major minsters very special provisioning needs: it is unlikely that sedentary thegnly households were anything like so large, while the royal fathers and brothers of the first monastic heads were always on the move. Bundles of hidated territories which had hitherto supported the food-circuit must have become subject to different pressures once they were turned into perpetual bookland estates directly controlled by great royal minsters.

It is again the more expansive Irish sources which best reveal the distinctive ecclesiastical impact on land-management, as Charles Doherty has shown. The Irish Church, he writes, 'had control of manpower that must have been the envy of kings. It had established centres that exercised a strong gravitational pull (by contrast kingship was peripatetic). It was in a position to exploit fully technical innovations such as the heavy plough and the horizontal water-mill. It was thus the only organization that could produce a surplus—particularly of grain.'[27] In the British world there are also signs that ecclesiastical institutions developed a more organized, intensive, and perhaps technologically innovative estate-management regime.[28] If Bangor-is-Coed was anything like as large a minster as Bede claims, intensive agriculture would indeed have been necessary to feed it. On the western fringes of English settlement there are some impressive cases of large enclosed inlands around monastic cores, albeit mostly mentioned in relatively late sources.[29]

As the early charters show, the greater English minsters were extremely well endowed with land, often in large, diverse tracts which, like the territories from which they were carved, contained a range of resources.[30]

---

[26] An example of this might be the residence (*villa, domus*) of Hildmaer, King Ecgfrith's *praefectus*: *VCA* ii. 8, *VCB* c. 15 (pp. 92, 206).

[27] Doherty 1985: 55. Cf. Doherty 1982: 318, for evidence suggesting 'that the church had the power to redistribute land to tenants or to redeploy her resources for more efficient exploitation of the soil'. Cf. Rahtz and Meeson 1992: 156, for early mills in Ireland and elsewhere.

[28] Pryce 1992*b*: 28–31; Faith 1997: 16–17.

[29] Faith 1997: 18–27.   [30] Above, pp. 87, 154.

Medeshamstede (Peterborough) may have had from the outset a large compact estate including peat and silt fens as well as extensive uplands, and in 852 it was drawing timber, fuel, and food-renders from Lincolnshire properties thirty miles away.[31] The minsters of the well-documented west midlands provide several examples, such as Fladbury and Wootton Wawen.[32] Other founders and heads can be seen amalgamating scattered acquisitions to form concentrations of land which could be run more efficiently. At late seventh-century Jarrow, Ceolfrith acquired eight hides in exchange for a rich manuscript, then traded them together with some money for twenty hides 'because this seemed to be nearer to the minster'; in 686 St Augustine's paid £10 for land adjoining their own at Stodmarsh.[33] In a charter of 811 for Eastry (Kent), Archbishop Wulfred states that he has gathered small land-units together and formed them into one estate enclosed by a single boundary fence, so that they will be easier to administer and cultivate.[34] On the other hand, minsters also acquired outlying upland, woodland, or marshland pastures when these were needed to build up a healthy range and diversity of resources.[35] Aldhelm, amid his literary exertions, negotiated astutely for 'a becoming place especially suitable for the catching of fish'.[36]

The subsistence economy was not, of course, peculiar to monastic estates: peasant communities would have used the same diverse resources, for instance in transhumant pastoralism. Where the minsters probably scored was in the scale of their endowments, the coherence of their estate organization, and in the special needs which drove them to intensify production and generate surpluses. The networks of cells and 'granges' such as *Osingadun* may have been established to manage properties that were too scattered or too extensive to run from one centre, and as stopping-points on journeys which had economic as well as religious purposes.[37] As would be true of the Cistercians centuries later, the more austere aspects of the monastic ethic did not sit badly with the exploitation of large and diverse estates in undeveloped terrain.

---

[31] Biddick 1989: 9–12; S 1440. Potts 1974 argues that the original estate was of 600 hides and essentially comprised the land of the North Gyrwe; cf. Keynes 1994: 33–5.

[32] Hooke 1985: 132–9.

[33] *HA* c. 15 (p. 380); S 9 (*St. Aug.* 30–3); cf. Faith 1997: 35.

[34] S 1264; Brooks 1984: 138, for this and other amalgamations by Wulfred. Cf. the Bexhill minster inland: Faith 1997: 30–1.

[35] Faith 1997: 30–1, for Lyminge. Upland sheep-pastures occur in two dubious texts: S 1782 (twenty hides at Pinswell on top of the Cotswolds for an early eighth-century abbess of Gloucester 'ovibus suis illic adhabendas'), and S 254 (four hides in the Brendon Hills 'ad pecora alenda' to Taunton in '737').

[36] *AO* 502–3 (Lapidge and Herren 1979: 170).

[37] Above, pp. 212–14. Cf. the contemporary arrangements for specialized production and distribution on the great monastic estates of northern France: Lemarignier 1966: 462–7; Doehaerd 1982: 98–9; Lebecq 2000: 129–39.

The manpower of great minsters was considerable, especially the relatively humble 'brethren' (*fratres*) who appear sometimes to have supplied labour. In 716 the twin communities of Wearmouth and Jarrow had nearly 600 *fratres*, who cannot all have been 'choir monks' as later defined.[38] While the working brethren of Whitby and its cell are presented as servants of Christ and holy men,[39] the context is one in which the monastic round of work and prayer might in practice have assumed a character not wholly unlike labour-rent; it is conceivable that some people acquired the obligation of performing it not through their own choosing.[40] The 747 canons enjoining abbots and abbesses to treat their *familiae* as their children rather than as their servants, and restraining proprietors of *congregationes* from violently exacting work before they could feed and clothe them, suggest that some religious personnel were seen more as economic than as spiritual assets.[41] These passages recall the Irish 'monastic tenants' (*manaig*), people of mostly peasant status who lived on church property under special tenurial conditions, or their apparent equivalents the *hereditarii* of Welsh charters.[42] The 'monks' whom King Æthelbald forced to labour on royal works and buildings in the 740s[43] were surely men of this kind: his perception of them as a resource to be tapped is our first glimpse of a secular exploitation which was to have dire consequences later.

It cannot be known what proportion of the manpower on minster estates comprised such semi-monastic personnel, or how quickly this distinctive form of lordship influenced the lives and settlement patterns of the rest. Archaeological evidence for mid Saxon rural settlements clustering densely around minsters (Brixworth, Northants.), or being replanned at around the likely time of a transfer to monastic control (Yarnton, Oxon.),[44] might point in that direction. A particularly clear case is a planned settlement of *c.*730–50 which extended westwards from the monastic core of Ely: the inhabitants did not use high-quality pottery, and were probably peasants producing meat,

[38] *HA* c. 17 (p. 382). At least one *frater* at the Northumbrian minster of 'De Abbatibus' had a wife and children (*DA* ll. 321–94, pp. 27–33).

[39] Above, p. 213.

[40] Doherty 1982: 316, for an Irish mother who gives her infant son to a monastery in time of famine as an alternative to killing him. Wilfrid restored a child to life, but ruthlessly claimed him into his service at the age of 7 (*VW* c. 18, pp. 38–40). When Wilfrid baptized and freed the slaves of Selsey (*HE* iv. 13, pp. 374–6), did they become a workforce of 'monastic tenants'?

[41] *Clof.*747 cc. 4, 28 (pp. 364, 374).

[42] Doherty 1982: 315–16; Etchingham 1991; Charles-Edwards 1992: 67; Faith 1997: 17; Etchingham 1999: 394–454. There were different categories of *manaig*, including free clients, but 'the predominantly labouring class is most commonly portrayed as engaged in the toil proper to monks in the true sense, although the lower orders of ecclesiastical dependents are also sometimes cast simply as semi-servile tenants or serfs' (Etchingham 1999: 454). Cf. the 'monasticization' of peasant communities in seventh-century Galicia (Díaz 2001: 352–9).

[43] Above, p. 122.   [44] Hall and Martin 1979; Hey forthcoming.

grain, and textiles for consumption in the minster or for sale.[45] It is also possible that eighth-century minsters, sited as they so often were near running water, may had an impact on one central aspect of economic growth: the spread of watermill technology.[46] Two of the earliest English mills so far excavated (the status of the other three is unclear) were near minsters, at Wareham (between 664 and 709) and Barking (shortly after 705).[47] In 762 the Kentish king negotiated with St Augustine's to acquire a half-share of its mill near Chart for the use of the royal vill at Wye—the king needing recourse to the monks' mill rather than vice versa.[48]

There are thus three important respects in which minsters may have had the edge on other kinds of proprietor: in the scale of their landholdings and the control over them which charters conferred; in the ability to exploit low-status quasi-monastic personnel, and perhaps a broader range of the peasantry, in ways going beyond the mere extraction of food-rents; and in the ability to invest in new kinds of infrastructure and equipment. It seems likely that the operation of major monastic estates was, by 800, significantly and visibly different from that of territories run in more traditional ways.

The minsters' conspicuous consumption of imports and other expensive luxuries must have been paid for: organized estate management is likely to have been directed to the creation of surpluses. At Eanmund's Northumbrian minster in the eighth century 'wealth increased everywhere, and the crops piled up with fat ears under cultivation, and all kinds of beasts, though taken from the pastor's stock, were not able to cause a loss in number to the flocks'.[49] Such stockpiles could now generate income. The rise of monastic endowment after 670 coincided with a critical change in English commercial activity, most evident in the major coastal emporia (*wics*) of Southampton, London, Ipswich, and York, the counterparts of emporia on the north-west European coastline, and in the inland dissemination of the low-value silver

---

[45] This site at West Fen Road, Ely, is not yet published, and I am very grateful to Richard Mortimer for providing information. It must have been laid out on land belonging to the royal nunnery. The settlement contracted in the later ninth century, but the southern half had a continuous existence thereafter.

[46] For which see Rahtz and Meeson 1992: 156; Holt 1988.

[47] Hinton 1998: 49–50; MacGowan 1996: 174–5. The Wareham mill was at Worgret, about a mile west of St Mary's minster. A mill at Old Windsor, a site of ambiguous status, produced a late seventh-century radiocarbon date (Holt 1988: 3–5; below, p. 278). Seventh- to eighth-century mills have recently been excavated at Northfleet (Kent) and Wellington (Herefs.), places of unknown status (ex inf. Stuart Foreman). Early monastic mills have been found in Ireland, notably the seventh-century tide-mill at the important monastic site of Nendrum (Crothers 2000).

[48] S 25 (*St. Aug.* 44–7). Cf. the exchange of property at Droitwich between Æthelbald of Mercia and the Worcester community (S 102), whereby the king acquires salt-houses already built by the community.

[49] *DA* ll. 490–4 (pp. 39–41).

coins known today as 'sceattas'.[50] The emporia were primarily entrepôts for overseas trade, and the nature of their integration into regional economies is debatable. While a high proportion of export and import trade was probably channelled through them, they are unlikely to have had a monopoly. Sceatta distributions show a tide of monetary activity spreading into Deira, Lindsey, East Anglia, the south-east, and the south midlands during *c*.680–740, perhaps stimulated by coastal activities of Frisian and Frankish merchants but in turn stimulating local exchange; it is an astonishing fact that the volume of the English currency in these decades was greater than it would ever be again before 1200.[51] Large, well-organized monastic estates stood to gain from this boom, and the minsters themselves had some strong ready-made advantages. On their coastal and riverine headlands, many of them were well placed to concentrate production and distribution and to profit from a developing commercial traffic which must have relied heavily on water-transport. They often stood on running water, and waterfronts have been found at Jarrow and Brandon.[52]

A useful illustration of a widespread pattern is the series of major minsters built, often at confluences, along the upper and lower stretches of the River Thames, the main artery between the productive midland regions and the commercially advanced south-east.[53] At such upper Thames minsters as Bampton, Eynsham, and Oxford, hides, minerals, and salt from inner Mercia, wool from the Cotswolds, and grain from the developing agrarian regions of the south midlands could have been loaded onto the river. Integrated road and water communications surely lie behind a privilege of the 740s which remits the bishop of Worcester's tolls from two ships at the port of London.[54] Down-river from *Lundenwic*, the pivotal point of exchange systems in the south-east, contacts were directed outwards towards the Continental ports. In the eighth century the great minsters which had been built by Kentish and East Saxon kings along the Thames estuary and adjoining coasts were participating in overseas trade, and taking advantage of a

---

[50] The *wics* now have an extensive literature; see especially Hodges and Hobley 1988, Anderton 1999, Hansen and Wickham 2000, Hill and Cowie 2001, Palmer 2002, and Palmer 2003; Scull 1997 is a stimulating critical review of some of the main issues. For the sceatta coinage: Metcalf 1993–4; Blackburn 2003; Metcalf 2003. Maddicott 2002 is a new review of economic growth.

[51] Metcalf 2003: 42–5; Blackburn 2003: 27–31.

[52] Cramp 1976: 240–1; Carr and others 1988: 374–5; Blair 1996*a*: 10–12. Artificial water management associated with minsters is a potentially important but still under-explored topic: see Blair 1994: 121, and *Encyc.* 81.

[53] Blair 1996*a*: 16–18; Blair 1994: 80–7. Palmer 2002 and 2003 survey the evidence for *Lundenwic*'s hinterland, including the Thames corridor. Metcalf 2003: 42–5 provides strong numismatic support for discrete economic 'hot spots' in the upper Thames region and the Thames estuary, the former representing 'the long arm of international trade' stimulated by Cotswold wool production.

[54] S 98; Kelly 1992: 5, 12–13.

privileged status. This emerges most clearly from the five extant toll privileges granted by kings to Minster-in-Thanet.[55] By the 760s this royal
nunnery had accumulated a small fleet of ships, including one bought from
a Frank and another built locally. Minster-in-Thanet's biggest commercial
ventures seem to have involved trade between London and the northern
Frankish ports, for which it was exceptionally well sited; but one of the privileges grants toll-remission through the whole Mercian realm, and the community's interests may have extended inland. The commercial activities of
the Thames estuary minsters look like those of their better-documented
Frankish counterparts along the Seine.[56]

The surpluses sold by minsters would mainly have comprised agrarian bulk
goods, but some, again like their Frankish counterparts,[57] dealt in more specialized commodities. Late seventh- and eighth-century minsters can be seen
participating in lead-mining in Derbyshire, in iron-mining in the Weald, in
salt-making at Droitwich (where some of them had their own salt-houses)
and on the coast, in freestone quarrying, and perhaps in the carving of sculpture for other religious sites.[58] When Hanbury minster (Worcs.) obtained a
royal exemption in 836, it was 'with all utensils and with salt-pits and leaden
furnaces'.[59] The archaeological evidence which reveals minsters as prodigous
consumers shows also that the normal range of industries—working of iron
and copper-alloys, carpentry, weaving, leather-working—was practised in
zones on several monastic sites.[60] Such activity cannot really be quantified,
and it could have happened on secular sites in a less concentrated and therefore less archaeologically visible fashion. But concentration in itself suggests

[55] Kelly 1992: 5–7, 9–10.
[56] Doehaerd 1982: 244–64 and Lebecq 1989: 409–28 (both noting monastic acquisitions of
coastal and riverine properties to facilitate transport and exchange); Johanek 1987; Kelly 1992: 13–16;
Lebecq 2000: 136–48. In 704 × 9 the abbess of Inkberrow (Worcs.) acquired an outlying five-hide
property at Ingon (Warw.) on the Avon (S 1177): was this as a riverine entrepôt?
[57] Doehaerd 1982: 207; Lebecq 2000: 130–9.
[58] Lead: S 1624, a render of lead provided by Wirksworth in 835 (cf. Stafford 1985: 56). Iron: S
12 (*St. Aug.* 33–6), a grant of 689 to St Augustine's of a Wealden iron-mine, adjoining Reculver
property which may also have produced iron. Salt: S 97, S 102, S 1824, Evesham, Worcester, and
perhaps Gloucester with Droitwich salt-houses in Æthelbald's reign; S 23, S 254, Lyminge (732) and
Taunton (dubious: 737) with salt-pans on tidal marshes. Stone-quarrying is suggested by the place-
name of the Yorkshire minster Stonegrave, and stone-carving by the various 'schools' of sculpture
which appear to be centred on important minsters.
[59] S 190; 'cum fornacibus plumbis' probably means that the salt-pits had leaden vats for evapo-
rating the brine.
[60] Haslam 1980 (Ramsbury); Armstrong and others 1991: 13, 239 (Beverley); Carr and others
1988: 374–5 (Brandon); Leahy 1999 and Loveluck 2001 (Flixborough); Hill 1997: 402–4 (Whithorn);
Blinkhorn 1999: 18–19, for these cases and others. Cf. the processing activities grouped around some
better-documented Frankish communities, showing 'how the monasteries, even the relatively isolated ones, could become foci of new towns, thanks to their numerous peripheral activities': Lebecq
2000: 136–9.

32. Industry at *Hartlepool* (co. Durham): fragments of seventh- to eighth-century clay moulds for making an Evangelist's symbol, an equal-armed cross, and a trapezoidal mount, found in the minster boundary ditch. Actual size. (Hartlepool Museum Service.)

intensification, and the fact remains that—assuming the monastic character of Brandon and Flixborough—no other contemporary sites outside the emporia have produced evidence for production on quite this scale.

The making of luxury ecclesiastical items, indicated by millefiori and reticella glass rods (Jarrow and Barking) and moulds for casting decorative plaques (Hartlepool) (Fig. 32), is likely to have been a monastic speciality.[61] It was perhaps because he could make such things that a skilled but dissolute monk who stayed day and night in his workshop was tolerated by his colleagues; brother Cwicwine of Eanmund's minster, a skilful worker in iron, beat out vessels for the community's meals.[62] While items of this kind must often or usually have been for internal consumption, they could also have been made in larger numbers to supply a lay market.[63] This line of thought is encouraged by Anna Gannon's recent argument that some of the early to mid eighth-century silver coins, with their sophisticated religious iconography, may actually have been minted at monastic sites.[64]

The commercial activities of the great Frankish monasteries often took

[61] Cramp 1976: 239–40; MacGowan 1996: 175–6; Daniels 1988: 186–9; Webster and Backhouse 1991: 140–1.

[62] *HE* v. 14 (p. 502); *DA* ll. 278–320 (pp. 25–7).

[63] One of the Hartlepool moulds (Fig. 32), for an expanded-armed cross not unlike the pectoral crosses from female graves (above, pp. 232–3), raises the interesting possibility that some of these may have been made in monastic workshops. Items of ecclesiastical decoration or equipment could have been recycled as lay ornaments. One possible candidate is the 'sprinkler' from Swallowcliffe Down (Speake 1989: 30–43); another is the Standlake tinned-metal cross (Fig. 30: above, p. 174 n.), where the perforation (for attachment to a waist-bag?) is secondary.

[64] Gannon 2003: 188–92; see also Newman 1999: 42–4, for the suggestion that 'Series Q' sceattas were minted at Ely minster.

place near their own premises.[65] In Ireland and England too, many minsters were the sites of permanent markets by the tenth or eleventh centuries.[66] For earlier periods this is harder to demonstrate, though a long-established tendency for exchange to occur at places of public resort and ritual seems likely.[67] What is becoming increasingly clear, though, is that a high proportion of inland coin finds occur at or near minsters.[68] Whithorn is especially remarkable not only for its sixty-two eighth- and early ninth-century coins within the excavated area, but also for the concentration of most of them in an open zone between the domestic buildings and the terrace in the 'outer precinct'.[69] These casual losses can hardly be interpreted as offerings: the best explanation may be that merchandise was sold from stalls backing against the terrace.

In eastern and southern England, the sites which have produced metal-detected material may tell us something about the role of minsters in distribution and marketing structures. Probably no body of evidence relevant to this book is growing so quickly: clear-cut conclusions would still be premature, but a picture is starting to emerge.[70] The sites are not homogeneous but show a wide range, from the large, putatively monastic ones down to coin scatters (in places such as old hillforts) which look like periodic trading sites or fairgrounds. Most seem to have had some involvement in exchange, and most were well sited in relation to water and road transport, for instance at fords on navigable rivers. Pottery, small-finds, and especially coins indicate catchment zones on different scales: rather as late medieval England had hierarchies of markets, so the bigger sites may constitute a layer between the long-range trade of the emporia and the inter-regional and local trade of the lesser ones.

In her study of Lincolnshire and Hampshire, Katharina Ulmschneider argues that the most important centres of inland consumption and exchange were principally monastic, and indeed that the expansion of sites during the earlier eighth century was stimulated by the superior organization, productive capacity, provisioning needs, and perhaps trading privileges of the minsters.[71] This conclusion, which current work seems on the whole to be

---

[65] Doehaerd 1982: 244–5, 262–4.

[66] Doherty 1980: 81–2; below, pp. 335–6.

[67] Morris 1991: 22–4. Doherty 1980: 81, suggests that in Ireland the ceremonial tribal fair held on the borders of territories was sometimes being taken over by minsters by the early ninth century.

[68] For instance: Blair 1994: 82–4 (upper Thames); Ulmschneider 2000: 31 (Flixborough, Stow, Caistor, Louth); Newman 1996 (near Walton Castle, *?Dommoc*); Darling and Gurney 1993 (Caister-on-Sea, *?Cnobheresburg*); Carr and others 1988: 375–6 (Brandon); Cramp 1976: 454–7 (Whitby); Ulmschneider 2003 (Carisbrooke).

[69] Hill 1997: 351–5, suggesting that this 'may have been a contact zone between the individual wealth of guests and pilgrims and the corporate wealth of the minster'.

[70] Above, pp. 203–4, 208–11.

[71] Ulmschneider 2000: 95–9, 105, etc.; cf. Andrews 1992: 14–19, 26–7.

supporting,[72] underlines the role of monastic sites in the most extensive system for regional and local distribution of commodities that can be perceived in non-Atlantic Britain since the Roman period. It is important not to lose sight of the limitations. This was probably a much less developed market economy than would exist by the tenth century, and the role of the minsters in it was most conspicuously as centres of consumption. The economic concerns of the inhabitants of Whitby, Barking, and Flixborough are likely to have focused on keeping consumables flowing in from their estates, on maintaining their supplies of imported glasses and pots (and presumably imported wine to go in them), and on replacing the gaudy silver pins which they mislaid so recklessly. But consumption, as we will shortly see, is likely to have been in itself a prime stimulus of economic growth.

Beyond their wealth and physical presence, it is hard to doubt that the minsters' functions as estate and production centres, markets, protected zones, shrines, mausolea of the great, and sources of charity made them very exceptional places of resort for the laity. To turn again to Ireland, the canons focus on the tension between reserving holy precincts and offering sanctuary to society's dregs: 'a place cannot be called holy in which murderers with their plunder and thieves with their loot and adulterers and perjurors and hawkers and conjurors and prostitutes are accustomed to enter, because every holy place ought to be cleaned not only at its core but also at its peripheries, which, consecrated by the holy ones, ought to be clean.'[73] If English minsters were also refuges, they would have encountered similar problems. The dying St Cuthbert, in words put into his mouth by Bede, urges his monks not to take his body back to Lindisfarne 'on account of the influx of fugitives and guilty men of every sort who will perhaps flee to my body'.[74] Religious communities and relics also brought the sick and destitute: in 'De Abbatibus' Abbot Sigwine gives 'gifts to the wretched paupers who, being shut out of the gates, laid their very cold limbs in the rubbish to warm them'.[75] All this suggests, if it does not prove, that by 850 some English minsters may already have been attracting more-or-less transient populations of craftsmen, traders, pilgrims, and undesirables on their fringes.

---

[72] See for instance the recent emphasis by a pottery specialist on the role of ecclesiastical communities in the consumption and redistribution of Ipswich Ware and imported wares (Blinkhorn 1999: 18–19). Moreland 2000, emphasizing production (as against consumption) in eighth-century England, reaches similar conclusions, as do Palmer 2003: 52–4 and Newman 2003: 108–9.

[73] *Hib.* XLIV. 8 (p. 176, recension 'B' printed as footnote); Doherty 1982: 301–2; Doherty 1985: 57–9. Cf. above, pp. 221–3.

[74] *VCB* c. 37 (p. 278); cf. Hall 1989.

[75] *DA* ll. 478–81 (p. 39).

Minsters and urbanization: problems of definition and hierarchy

So the 'monastic town' can be defined in two ways: as the physical expression of a late seventh-century sacred ideal realized in topography, architecture, and art; or as an economic centre which changed through time with the changing world around it. It is an observable fact that, as the centuries passed, the one tended to become more and more like the other, with the eventual result that a high proportion of minsters are now urban, at least in the broad sense of being locally important market towns. Not only did minsters look more like towns than any other kind of pre-Viking settlement; they also showed a strong tendency to become real towns as the economy developed between the ninth and twelfth centuries.

What is a town? Asked without chronological reference, this tends to be a metaphysical rather than an empirical question. One way of focusing it is to define a bundle of criteria and require any place, in any time or culture, to fulfil at least some of them before it can be called a town. This approach permits urbanism to be assessed cross-culturally on a relatively consistent basis; for instance, it enables some societies to be defined as completely non-urban. It will, however, be very misleading if it imposes modern conceptions of urbanism to the exclusion of conceptions—however inappropriate to us—which people entertained in the past. Societies convinced that they have contained towns and cities have identified them using varied criteria—privileges, populations, seats of government, palaces, fortresses, walls, gymnasia, baths, market-places, temples, mosques, churches—which are culturally relative.[76] Since we are much more inclined than inhabitants of England in, say, 750 to privilege economic over ritual and hierarchical criteria, we will tend to conceive of a place as urban at a later stage than they might have done themselves.

In a survey of urban origins in non-Roman Europe, H. B. Clarke and A. Simms emphasized the importance in urbanizing societies of 'proto-towns': places with a variety of incipiently urban features which were often (though not necessarily always) destined to become towns at the requisite stage of economic development. They proposed a classification of such places as trading settlements, cult settlements, stronghold settlements, and market settlements.[77] If this model is accepted, many English minsters as they existed by c.850 were clearly 'proto-towns'. The model has in fact come in for some

[76] Redfield and Singer 1954: 55–6, 75–6; Adams 1966: 10–12; Wheatley 1971: 371–88, commenting on the criteria proposed by Weber and Childe; Wheatley 1972. Biddle 1976a: 100 suggests a bundle of criteria for Anglo-Saxon towns.

[77] Clarke and Simms 1985: esp. 672–6; Bradley 1999 for a re-statement.

criticism, principally on the grounds that it tends to be self-fulfilling and to rely on teleological perceptions derived from later stages of development.[78] The problem with such objections is that they admit only the synchronic, 'bundle-of-criteria' approach and exclude valid questions involving change over time: if we admit that urbanism is a quality relative to the societies supporting it, the observation that special places of one kind consistently evolved into special places of another kind becomes more than just a teleological construct. The facts remain that England between the late seventh and late ninth centuries was experiencing profound social and economic changes which presaged urbanization; that certain focal places (in addition to the *wics*) played a special part in these changes; and that when such places can be identified from written and archaeological sources they were—as will shortly appear—to a large extent ecclesiastical.

A promising approach is to examine the secular functions of ritual centres in other cultures, however distant in time and space, as they developed towards social and economic complexity and urbanization. A series of comparative studies, notably R. Redfield and M. B. Singer's article on the cultural role of cities (1954), Robert Adams's survey of urbanization in early Mesopotamia and pre-Hispanic Mexico (1966), and Paul Wheatley's monumental work on the early Chinese city (1971), have sought to establish a processual model for the 'urban revolution' which gives ceremonial sites a major role. All these works identify recurrent evolutionary stages in which the foci of social organization were in the first instance autonomously religious and ceremonial, then politico-religious, and eventually economic, expressing an evolving idea of 'cityness' from a period well before urbanization in the full modern sense. In Wheatley's words:

---

[78] For instance Scull 1997: esp. 272, 291–2. The debate on Ireland (Graham 1987*a*; Clarke and Simms 1987; Graham 1987*b*) has generated more heat than light. Graham's latest contribution (1998) sets out a model of later royal and defensive encroachment which is very consistent with the one proposed here for England (below, pp. 287–9), but produces nothing to refute the view that the major Irish centres *before the tenth century* were predominantly ecclesiastical. The most sustained recent attack is Valante 1998, but it seems to me that this still does not (despite citing much of the relevant sociology) allow for the relativity of 'town-ness' to different social and economic contexts, and still gets bogged down in semantics. Nobody, surely, has proposed that monasteries in otherwise unviable economic contexts became urban (pp. 4, 6); the distinction between 'cities and towns developing around monasteries' and 'monasteries themselves developing into cities' (p. 5) seems unhelpful; and the treatment of Kells and Kildare (pp. 15–16) falls into the trap of confusing constitutional manifestations of towns with economic ones. Valante accepts that some monastic sites engaged in specialized manufacture, that suburban zones around monasteries did sometimes become urban, and that some monasteries had fairs and eventually market-places (pp. 12–15, 17–18). Since none of this shows Ireland as essentially different—gradations in economic development apart—from the other societies discussed in this chapter, the 'Irish monastic town' can still stand as a paradigm of the process.

Whenever, in any of the seven regions of primary urban generation . . . , we trace back the characteristic urban form to its beginnings we arrive not at a settlement that is dominated by commercial relations, a primordial market, or at one that is focused on a citadel, an archetypal fortress, but rather at a ceremonial complex. . . . Naturally this does not imply that the ceremonial centers did not exercise secular functions as well, but rather that these were subsumed into an all-pervading religious context.[79]

The English minsters' attributes of higher civilization, wider networks, and legitimacy transcending local kingship look typical of this developmental stage, when the most extended and sophisticated modes of organization are characteristically in religious hands.[80] In comparable societies, 'cities' have often been marked by a high sacred culture involving the extension and codification of received values by a priestly elite, and expressed in monumental building and a flowering of sculpture, metallurgy, and the decorative arts.[81] They have also acted as foci for scattered rural communities whose members have visited them episodically—at festivals, to obtain spiritual benefits, or to provide service—and have accepted them as intermediaries with the divine. Sometimes they have attracted permanent lay settlement, as artisans and other workers have gathered around the ceremonial core with its high-status resident consumers.[82]

These were 'cities' as Cogitosus understood them; were they also what historical geographers, using the model first formulated by Walther Christaller in 1933, would call 'central places'? 'Central place theory', at least in its original form, has a severely economic rationale, ascribing the size, number, and distribution of towns to the organization of space within market zones for the maximum convenience of consumers needing goods and services; lower-order centres and their territories 'nest' within the territories of high-order ones, which offer the same services plus a range of more specialized ones that consumers will travel further to obtain.[83] It has been obvious to archaeolo-

[79] Wheatley 1971: 225.
[80] Adams 1966: 124: 'Powerless as man might be before the major disasters, the emphasis on the building of temples and the formation of priesthoods undoubtedly also reflects a more "rational", economic aspect. In the absence of widely extended political controls, offerings brought to a sanctuary in aggregate would have constituted a larger reserve than otherwise could be attained, a reserve transcending the environmental limitations of its parent community and reflecting the advantages of complementarity to be derived from establishing a network of permanently related communities in adjacent ecological zones.'
[81] Redfield and Singer 1954: 56–7, 60–1; Adams 1966: 125–30 (Mesopotamia); Wheatley 1971: 257–67.
[82] Wheatley 1971: 257, 305–8, 324, 389–91. Cf. Horden and Purcell 2000: 434–8, for the ceremonial genesis of the Mediterranean town.
[83] Christaller 1933. Useful critiques, especially with reference to the ancient and early medieval worlds, are: Hodder and Orton 1976; P. Salway, *Roman Britain* (Oxford, 1981), 540–2; Grant 1986;

gists and landscape historians that this ahistorical, free-market model gives too little weight to political, administrative, and religious factors in the initial siting of foci, and so understates the impact on market zones of existing elite centres: to apply it in any simple form to the hierarchically dominated economy of seventh- to ninth-century England is anachronistic. Still, it can give us some pointers. 'Central places' in the Christaller model do not have to be fully urban in the modern sense, so long as they provide economic services that people within a given range—depending on the centre's place in the hierarchy—will go to a given amount of trouble and expense to obtain.[84] If the definition of 'service provision' is broadened from the strictly economic to the social, cultural, and religious, then many minsters had strong in-built advantages conferring centrality. It is clear (setting aside for the moment the question whether other types of centre were similarly placed) that minsters often had the capacity, which for geographers is one of the functional definitions of urbanism, of organizing dependent territories and binding them to the central point. To quote Wheatley again on other cultures:

In this context 'organization' implies a reorientation of the social, political, and economic activities of a tract of territory, not merely its exploitation . . . By this yardstick the ceremonial complexes . . . qualify as urban forms, for the transformation that they symbolized from a primarily reciprocative to a dominantly superordinate redistributive mode of economic integration did indeed result in the generation of effective economic space. And, as economic processes were mediated by essentially non-economic institutions, the economic space generated by the ceremonial city was at the same time effective social, political, and administrative space. Above all, it was sacred space, the sanctified *habitabilis* of a group integrated politically, socially and economically by the reallocative functions of the central shrine.[85]

Coming though they do from very different cultures, such perceptions have points of contact with some historians' views on economic re-growth and urbanization in post-Roman continental Europe. Pirenne wrote: 'The prestige of the bishops naturally lent to their places of residence—that is to say, to the old Roman cities—considerable importance. It is highly probable that this is what saved them. . . . [In the ninth century] the towns were

Wood 1998: 403–7, 414–18; Horden and Purcell 2000: 102–3. M. Millett (Grant 1986: 45–7) observes that the political and administrative factors behind the siting of *civitas* capitals in Roman Britain, and the decisions to wall some small towns but not others, means that the distribution of walled towns is better explained by a socio-political model than by central place theory. Cf. Thomas Charles-Edwards's comment (Scull 1997: 301): 'Approaching Middle-Saxon towns from the Roman Empire going forwards in time, rather than from the later medieval or modern periods going back, one would not set up criteria of urban status that privileged the economic sphere as against the political.'

[84] Christaller 1933: 138–40.   [85] Wheatley 1971: 388–9.

entirely under their control. In them were to be found, in fact, practically only inhabitants dependent more or less directly upon the Church.'[86] More recently, Janet Nelson observed that 'in the early middle ages it was churches, episcopal and monastic, which provided the major, if not quite the only, *foci* for town life', and she characterizes the impact of Christianity as follows: 'institutional continuity of the church in old urban centres; the transformation of those old centres and the growth of new ones under ecclesiastical direction or at least strong influence; the disappearance or attenuation of certain urban functions in these centres as barbarian lay political power was established in the countryside; and a spacial dislocation between lay and ecclesiastical power which meant that kings, though based in the countryside, had to find some mode of access to the towns through relations with the church.'[87]

Yet this is not, on the whole, how the beginnings of English urbanism have been envisaged. Monastic sites have been allowed some part in the process, but a secondary one in relation to royal power-centres. There seem to be two reasons for this. First, the belief that early English minsters largely perished in the Viking period, leaving a hiatus in ecclesiastical geography until new monasteries were founded in the (already urban) late tenth century, has proved hard to dislodge. Secondly, the work of a series of scholars since the 1930s has taught us to see early England as a very orderly world, in which stable and well-defined territories were governed and exploited from royal vills.[88] Given the power of the post-Viking English state, these centres of administration, law, and food-collection have seemed the obvious nuclei for growth in the expanding late Anglo-Saxon economy, especially since a high proportion of our twelfth- and thirteenth-century small towns stood on manors which Domesday Book lists as royal. Since the 1960s many studies of local territorial organization have sought for—indeed have assumed—a recurrent pattern of royal vills paired with minsters, the secular sites and systems being inevitably prior to, and formative of, the ecclesiastical ones.[89]

This approach has been reinforced by two non-ecclesiastical models of how urbanization began elsewhere in Europe. One is the growth of commercial and artisan suburbs around princely strongholds, especially prominent in

[86] Pirenne n.d.: 43, 46; cf. Damminger 1998: 73–4, for the economic role of the Church in Rhineland towns.

[87] Nelson 1979: 103–5.   [88] Above, p. 154.

[89] An important influence on this genre of local and landscape history has been William Page's pioneering article (Page 1914–15), where the starting-point is an assumed dependence of ecclesiastical sites and territories on secular ones. I am as guilty here as any other (Blair 1988*c*: 40–7; Blair 1991*a*: 12–14, 19–21, 104), and have only slowly become convinced that the model is fatally flawed because it projects an eleventh-century pattern back to the seventh.

Viking and Slavic regions between the ninth and twelfth centuries.[90] More influential has been a particular tradition of work on ex-Roman Europe which has stressed the survival of secular urban power-centres. Carlrichard Brühl's argument that the *praetoria* of Gallic towns had a continuous administrative existence, through the palaces of barbarian kings down to modern *Palais de Justice*,[91] has conditioned thinking on the fate of Romano-British towns. Even for places with no Roman past, the Brühl model has formed an expectation of stable, firmly established royal residences to which the major churches were attached. Thus John Williams interprets the eighth- and ninth-century buildings found in Northampton from the premiss that 'it would be reasonable in England to expect minsters to be established at important existing administrative centres' and suggests that 'with the erection of the timber "palace" . . . [Northampton] can be identified as a major seat of royal power, and the subsequent construction of the stone hall and adjacent minster serves to confirm its pre-eminent position'.[92] Again, Jeremy Haslam believes that Wiltshire small towns began with 'proto-urban development around royal *villae*, which acted as re-distributive and administrative centres; as loci for industrial activity . . . ; as ceremonial ecclesiastical centres'.[93]

This conception of minsters as secondary to royal *villae* sits uneasily with their apparent independence, social importance, and topographical centrality. Nor, before the tenth century, is there any good evidence for the attachment of important English churches to important residences on the Carolingian model.[94] By the eleventh century it certainly was common for minsters and royal vills to be juxtaposed, but which came first is another matter: the models of Williams and Haslam depend on a sequence of cases where the primacy of the secular centre is assumed, not demonstrated. Preconceptions about the general character both of 'palaces' and of minsters have been taken too much for granted.

[90] Clarke and Simms 1985: ii. 681–4. Graham 1998: 142–7 is an example of the 'citadel/suburb' model used synchronously and set up in opposition to the 'monastic core' model, rather than recognizing both as stages in a process of transformation over time.

[91] Brühl 1977 (synthesizing the case-studies in Brühl 1975–).

[92] Williams 1984: 127–8, 134; the first comment follows directly from a citation of Brühl. Above, p. 205, and Blair 1996*b* for the problems of interpreting Northampton. Cf. recent work on Glamorgan: 'Where we find a royal centre in close proximity to an early episcopal or monastic site, it is reasonable to speculate whether the religious settlement was located there because of established secular importance'—even though in some regions 'locating religious centres is easier than finding any attendant [*sic*] royal sites' (Jenkins 1988: 44, 48); or Barrow's comment on *eclēs* names (above, n. 20). This is not to say that the primacy of secular sites is never possible—in west and north Britain it is often likely (cf. Dark 1994*a*: 15, 43–4)—but to urge that it should not be assumed when, as in the English case, the evidence points in a different direction.

[93] Haslam 1984: 137.

[94] Above, pp. 69–71, for reasons for thinking the small churches attached to early seventh-century Northumbrian royal vills as peculiar to their generation and context, and p. 205 for reasons for discounting Northampton.

At this point, then, we will digress to examine the various kinds of places from which secular power and exploitation were organized in the English kingdoms. To anticipate, the survey will find remarkably little evidence that such places had much physical or institutional permanence before the mid ninth century, and will call in question the whole idea of 'palaces' as long-term centres of territorial organization in early Christian England. Against this background, the economic centrality of minsters should make more sense.

Hierarchical centres (i): princely citadels

Among the indigenous peoples of post-Roman Britain and Ireland, the construction or reoccupation of enclosed or defended residential sites was widespread. This pattern contained much regional variety. In Ireland a large number of new circular enclosures ('ring-forts') were built, ranging in size from major sites to very small ones. In west and south-west Britain, Iron Age hillforts were re-occupied and re-fortified, the apex of a still ill-defined miscellany of elite centres and strongholds. In the north, a cattle-rich warrior society with an opulent material culture adopted old defended sites and also built new ones.[95] Yet there is enough broad homogeneity to suggest that 'a common pattern of specific site-types, and indeed of landscape organization, existed throughout the fifth- to seventh-century Celtic-speaking world'.[96] Sites of this kind were major consumers, and those near the Atlantic coasts were involved to a greater or lesser extent in continuing Mediterranean and Continental trading activity.[97] In South Cadbury, Tintagel, or Dunadd we have the kind of 'princely' centres which, in Scandinavian and Slavic contexts, were to be among the prime generators of economic activity a few centuries later on the other side of Europe.

Given the broad resemblances between insular cultures, one might have expected princely citadels (which could in turn have attracted both religious communities and lay settlements) among the early English too. The silence of Anglo-Saxon sources, both written and physical, is therefore startling. Elizabeth Alcock's map of 'enclosed places AD 500–800' shows heavy concentrations in lowland Scotland and west Cornwall, a scatter across Wales and Devon, but a total blank in areas which had experienced English coloniza-

---

[95] Among a large literature, see especially: Ireland: Warner 1988; Edwards 1990: 6–48. Wales and the south-west: Dark 1994*a*; Jenkins 1988: 44–50; Yorke 1995: 19–24, 26–7; Longley 1997. The north and west compared: Alcock 1988*a*; Alcock 1988*b*; Maddicott 2000.

[96] Dark 1994*a*: 54–5.

[97] For recent surveys see: Alcock 1988*b*; Thomas 1993; Dark 1994*a*; Dark 1994*b*; Campbell 1996.

tion by 600.[98] Negative archaeological evidence is always a dangerous basis for argument, but here it is supported by an extraordinary lack of written evidence that fortifications played any part in English life or warfare before the mid eighth century. The only exceptions are in the context of transfers of territorial power from British to English rulers. The four *tūnas* believed in ninth-century legend to have been captured by the West Saxon pioneers in '571' included the hillforts of Limbury (Beds.) and Aylesbury (Bucks.).[99] Neither is known to have continued as a royal centre (though Aylesbury did eventually become a minster); nor is there evidence that any hillforts used by south-western British potentates were occupied in turn by their West Saxon successors.[100] The northern Angles clearly did to some extent adopt the hill-fort culture of the British whose territory they annexed. Bamburgh, their major royal stronghold, was inherited from British rulers; Bede calls it an *urbs*, a word which he otherwise reserves for London and Canterbury, for the British strongholds of *Alcluith* and *Urbs Giudi*, and for minsters.[101] Bamburgh, like Edinburgh, Dunbar, and the unlocated *Broninis* which are also mentioned in English hands,[102] tells the same story as the Anglian material culture excavated on fortified sites in south-western Scotland.[103] But the phenomenon is specific to the world of cultural interchange between Bernician Angles and northern British, and it is only in this context that Bede envisages military strongholds: it is a British 'city' that he calls 'most strongly defended' (*civitas Brettonum munitissima*), a Welsh potentate whom he pictures being besieged 'in a fortress-town' (*in oppido municipio*).[104]

Terminology points in the same direction. The standard word for an Irish or Scottish citadel is *dūn*, as in Dunottar, Dunollie, Dunadd, and many others.[105] Its direct and obvious English equivalent is *burh*, but it is extremely difficult to find evidence before the late ninth century that this word was used in a similar way.[106] Apart from the sites, already considered, where *burh*

---

[98] In Alcock 1988*b*: 40–6.

[99] *ASC* s.a. 571 (pp. 18–19). This is neither contemporary nor reliable evidence, though it does suggest that at some point in the eighth or ninth century they were considered ancient and important places. For the Aylesbury hillfort, and earthworks near Limbury, see Allen and Dalwood 1983; *VCH Beds.* i. 268–9, 280. A similar context is probably to be envisaged for *Mons Badonicus*, wherever that was.

[100] Maddicott 2000: 42–3.

[101] *HE* iii. 6, 16 (pp. 230, 262); Campbell 1986: 100; Alcock 1988*b*: 32–3.

[102] Alcock 1988*a*: 4–9; *VW* cc. 36, 38 (pp. 72, 76). Cf. King Ecgfrith's Bernician itinerary 'per civitates et castellos vicosque', ending at Coldingham: *VW* c. 39 (p. 78).

[103] Campbell and Lane 1993; Dark 1994*a*: 8; Maddicott 2000: 37–8. See Proudfoot and Aliaga-Kelly 1997 for the Anglian adoption of defended sites in south-east Scotland.

[104] *HE* i. 1, iii. 1 (pp. 20, 212).   [105] Alcock 1988*b*: 31; Warner 1988: 58–9.

[106] The one suggestion that this term was used at an early date to describe enclosed residences comes in Ine's law-code (*c.*700), which imposes penalties for '*burh*-breaking' (*burhbryce*), gradated according to the status of the injured party from a king or bishop to a lesser landholding thegn

is used in a monastic sense, the term only rarely occurs in the names of places associated with English royal activity before the rise of Wessex.[107] This is certainly a very odd contrast with the British world, and argues against the existence of a comparable category of major royal strongholds which either re-used, or physically resembled, Iron Age forts. It is only with the reservation of fortress-work in Mercian royal charters from the 740s that we start to find the language of fortification applied to royal sites, and archaeological evidence for defended citadels such as Tamworth and Winchcombe.[108]

This contrast between the English and their neighbours is hard to ascribe merely to different cultural traditions. Nor does it seem plausible that levels of endemic violence differed so greatly that fortification and enclosure were necessary in upland but not lowland Britain. Different *conventions* of violence, making the destruction of homesteads more likely in the one society than the other, might suggest one kind of explanation.[109] But there could be another kind, to do with the difference between economic regimes based on food-collection sites controlled by great kings, and those based on autonomous citadels occupied by small ones. Thomas Charles-Edwards has contrasted Anglo-Saxon kingdoms, where kings ruled large areas by travelling between food-render collection-points, and Ireland where the typical king ruled a small, confined territory centred on a residence owing hospitality to an over-king, and speculates that Irish dynastic segmentation could have been 'the effect of the lack of a network of royal centres such as the *villae regis* of Bede'.[110] It may be that a local king's permanent power-base was more likely to become developed, both militarily and economically, than a mere staging-post in a great king's circuit. But whatever the reason, it is impossible—except in semi-British Bernicia—to perceive a category of Anglo-Saxon royal and princely citadels which can be regarded as 'parent' foci for seventh- and eighth-century monastic foundations.

(Ine, c. 45 (*Gesetze*, 108–9)). Since a broad range of sites could evidently be affected by *burhbryce* it seems best understood as a term of art, describing an offence with the symbolic quality of modern 'breaking and entering', rather than the slighting of real fortifications. Patrick Wormald (1999a: 267) translates it as 'enclosure penetration'.

[107] This statement excludes: Canterbury and London (below, pp. 272–3); Aylesbury, Limbury, and Bamburgh; possible royal assemblies at the minsters of Malmesbury and Glastonbury (S 256, S 356, S 152); and Irthlingborough and Salmonsbury (below, n. 149).

[108] Below, pp. 287–9.

[109] The northern British, who had the most developed hillfort culture in this period, also had a tradition of siege warfare, whereas the Irish and seemingly the Anglo-Saxons did not: fortresses of which sieges were reported in the Irish Annals were almost wholly in Scotland (Bannerman 1966–8: 156–7). Apart from Yeavering (again in Bernicia), excavated Anglo-Saxon settlements of the period seem very rarely to have perished by fire. The burning of the West Saxon atheling Mul with his twelve companions (*ASC* s.a. 687, pp. 38–9), presumably in their hall, was perhaps a particularly heinous breach of convention, meriting a drastic response and special mention. I am grateful to Thomas Charles-Edwards and John Maddicott for discussions on this difficult problem.

[110] Charles-Edwards 1989: 39; cf. Bhreathnach 1998, and Charles-Edwards 2000: 527–30.

Hierarchical centres (ii): Roman towns and forts

How relevant to England is the Brühl model of administration based in Roman towns? For present purposes the issue is not whether towns had any continuous (or indeed intermittent) existence as settlement sites through the fifth to seventh centuries,[111] but rather how much evidence we have for royal residence in them, during the seventh and eighth centuries, to set alongside the very clear evidence for monastic residence. The belief that Roman towns served as royal headquarters is now so deep-rooted that it tends to be taken for granted (as for instance in the reiterated but unsupported assertion that Northumbrian kings had a palace in York).[112] The retrospective and symbolic overtones of the description of an ex-Roman place as a *civitas* mean that we can draw no conclusions from it about any current secular use. Even the issuing of royal charters from *civitates* is ambiguous, given that kings (as in the Reculver case) sometimes attested charters in minsters.[113] No excavation in any Romano-British town has yet identified an Anglo-Saxon palace, but the small scale of the excavations means that this fact is useless as negative evidence. We are therefore forced back upon the written sources.

Only a few Roman sites are explicitly named as royal centres before 750. Like the defended citadels, these are in contexts—again mainly Bernician—where the background of British territorial power is extremely close. Catterick (Yorks.), presented by Bede as a *vicus* in the 630s, and much later by Simeon of Durham as a site of eighth-century royal marriages, was probably a British stronghold which passed into Anglian control around the late sixth century.[114] Catterick was one of five Roman places in Deira, Lindsey, and Elmet (the others being York, Lincoln, probably Littleborough, and the unlocated *Campodunum*) where Paulinus preached under King Eadwine's aegis between *c.*626 and 633, and this may suggest (though only *Campodunum* is

[111] Biddle 1976*a* is the classic statement of the problem, which has set the agenda for more than two decades; Loseby 2000 is a recent review of the archaeological data. In summary, there is evidence for continued occupation in *Verulamium* through the fifth century and in Wroxeter even into the seventh, but both in British hands; the same could be true of some other western towns, for instance Bath (Davenport 2002: 16–28). Elsewhere, most clearly at Winchester, Dorchester-on-Thames, and Canterbury (Biddle 1973: 232–41; Biddle and Kjølbye-Biddle forthcoming; Blair 1994: 1–6; below, p. 272), archaeological evidence for at least sporadic Anglo-Saxon settlement within the walls during the fifth and sixth centuries can plausibly be associated with clusters of cemeteries outside them. Proof of continuity from British to Anglo-Saxon occupation remains, however, elusive.

[112] A recent comprehensive survey of written sources (Rollason and others 1998) demonstrates the lack of evidence for a royal residence in York before (perhaps) the 930s (pp. 166–70). Sources relating to Eadwine's reign (pp. 125–9) are silent (cf. above, p. 69 n.).

[113] Above, pp. 85–6, 249.

[114] *HE* ii. 14, iii. 14 (pp. 188, 256); *Symeon Op.* ii. 42, 44, 54. For some striking archaeological evidence see Wilson and others 1996.

actually called a *villa regia*) that Eadwine and his British predecessors used them as bases; in Lincoln Paulinus's patron was the 'ruler (*praefectus*) of the city (*civitas*)'.[115] Carlisle, another Roman city in territory recently colonized by the Northumbrians, had a reeve (*civitatis praepositus*) in the 680s.[116] Finally, the Anglo-Saxon Chronicle reports the capture of the British 'chesters' of Gloucester, Cirencester, and Bath in 577.[117] Cumulatively, this evidence shows that Roman walled places were important in the process of the absorption of British polities by English war-leaders, probably because British rulers were using them already: in this respect their history recalls Bamburgh's. But it is important to stress that whereas York, Lincoln, Carlisle, Gloucester, Cirencester, and Bath were all perpetuated as major minsters, only Bath provides any further evidence for royal activity before *c.*900.

This leaves two special cases: Canterbury and London.[118] Bede, presumably influenced by the local pride of his informants there, calls Canterbury the *metropolis* of Æthelberht's *imperium*.[119] It is reasonable enough to think that the king had a residence in or near it, though the fact that his queen used St Martin's church, half a mile outside the walls, might rather suggest an extramural site. A charter confirmed by the archbishop and king in 738 'in metropolitano urbe' is surely thinking of Canterbury's status as seat of the metropolitan archbishop; those of the 760s onwards given 'in the *civitas* of Canterbury' could as well have been issued in Christ Church as in an intramural palace.[120] That said, Canterbury yields more archaeological evidence for early Anglo-Saxon intramural settlement than any other Romano-British town, and by the later eighth century it shows signs of a precocious urban landscape.[121] Perhaps what this chiefly underlines, like so much else about Canterbury and east Kent generally, is their essential alignment with the Frankish rather than the English culture-province.[122]

The only other place which Bede calls a *metropolis* is London.[123] The Kentish king's 'hall' (*sele*) there is mentioned in the 670s, but in a commercial context which indicates a customs-house in *Lundenwic* rather than a royal

---

[115] *HE* ii. 14, ii. 16 (pp. 186–8, 190–2); Yorke 1993: 141–2. Another may be *Ad Murum* (Wallbottle?) (*HE* iii. 21–2, pp. 278, 282).

[116] *VCA* iv. 8 (p. 122).

[117] *ASC* s.a. 577 (pp. 18–19), a counterpart to the '571' annal (above, p. 269).

[118] Note the forms *Cantwaraburg* and *Lundenburh*, which break the normal rule that ex-Roman places do not have names in *burh* (above, p. 249). Were their physical and symbolic status as *ceasters* overridden by some social and practical status as *burhs*?

[119] *HE* i. 25–6 (pp. 74, 78); cf. Campbell 1986: 103, and Loseby 2000: 350.

[120] S 27 (and cf. S 286); S 28, S 105, S 35.

[121] Blockley and others 1995: esp. 19–21, 463–5; Brooks 1984: 16–30; *St. Aug.* 47–51. But see above, pp. 66–8, for the lack even here of any clear evidence for continuity.

[122] Above, pp. 69, 236–7.

[123] *HE* ii. 3 (p. 142).

palace within the Roman walls.[124] Bede tells us that King Sebbi of the East Saxons (d. *c.*694) summoned to his deathbed the bishop of London, the city 'in which he then lived'. But Sebbi had just paid Bishop Wealdhere for the privilege of the religious habit: Bede says that he was buried in the church of St Paul 'through whose teaching he had learned to aspire to heavenly things', and the likelihood is that he was living in the cathedral precincts.[125]

We might, for the sake of argument, concede the possibility that the Brühl model has some relevance to Canterbury and London.[126] Even so, the total list of ex-Roman centres is tiny compared with more than fifty non-Roman sites where royal vills are mentioned, or where charters are attested, in pre-Viking England. Set beside the many Roman walled places where bishoprics and minsters were founded in the same period, its brevity is equally striking. The message of later urban topography tends in the same direction: when central public buildings were so commonly assigned for religious use, they can hardly have been in high demand as seats of government. Given how many places of other kinds are associated with royal activities, this is not simply *absence* of evidence but persuasive *negative* evidence.

Roman walled places clearly played a part in the transfer of power from British to English rulers, but the view that seventh- and eighth-century kings habitually set up home within them is not sustained by the sources. The emergence of that view is understandable given the recurrent correspondence between Romano-British towns and medieval ones—which demanded an explanation—and the availability of the Brühl model—which seemed to provide one. But it has gained too much the status of an orthodoxy,

[124] Hlothere and Eadric 16-16. 1 (*Gesetze*, 11): transactions are to be witnessed by the king's *wicgerefa*. For the possibility of a 'palace' see Vince 1990: 54–5; Biddle 1989: 22–3. It needs stressing (since the example is sometimes cited as though it were solid fact) that the tradition that Offa had a palace in the Cripplegate fort is recorded only from the later middle ages, and its status as a piece of independent evidence is extremely low.

[125] *HE* iv. 11 (pp. 366–8). An attestation of 748 'in the *civitas* of London' (S 91) could likewise have been made at St Paul's.

[126] Winchester, however, has been presented as the type-site. The argument will be set out in Biddle and Kjølbye-Biddle forthcoming: pt. I, ch. 6 (meanwhile see Biddle 1973: 237–47 and Biddle 1983: 116–17), and I am extremely grateful to the authors for allowing me to debate it with them in advance. It is proposed that the channelling of traffic between the west and east gates, and the blocking of the south gate with a ditch and then wall, points to the use of the city by a secular power during the fifth to seventh century. But the blocking could post-date the foundation of the Old Minster in (probably) the 640s, and one might conceive the whole walled area as an outer precinct or 'inland' for the religious community (cf. above, p. 252). The excavated seventh- to ninth-century material (including the Lower Brook Street complex discussed by Kjølbye-Biddle 1992: 219–22) seems as compatible with the activities of a major religious community as it does with the hypothetical royal focus; the palace site first mentioned in the late tenth century remains unexcavated, and its origins are undated. There is no historical evidence that Winchester was a centre of royal administration in this period, nor even that late seventh- and eighth-century kings took a notable interest in it (Yorke 1982).

bypassing the (in fact much more obvious) role of major churches in re-adoption and then re-urbanizatioñ, and begging the question whether sixth- and seventh-century English rulers can necessarily be assumed to have behaved like Italian and Frankish ones.[127]

Between Bede and the Vikings there is clearer evidence for royal vills in Canterbury, where there was a reeve 'in this royal vill in this[?] city' around 780, and London, where charters of 811–12 were issued in the royal *oppidum/vicus*.[128] Dorchester (Dorset) was later identified as the 'king's *tūn*' to which an ill-fated reeve tried to force the first shipload of Vikings in 789;[129] a series of charter attestations there between 833 and 868 includes one of 864 given in the royal residence (*in þam cynelican setle*) there.[130] Rochester is a possible case, but inconclusive.[131] Bath is both problematic and suggestive: it already contained an important nunnery, and the earliest charter issued in it, in 796, exists in two versions of which one describes the place as 'the famous vill' and the other as 'the famous minster'.[132] A charter of 864 is dated in Latin and English 'in that famous town (*urbs*) which is called "at the hot baths"', a formulation striking for its emphasis on the enduring natural pecu-liarity of the place.[133]

The clustering of these references in the years *c.*780–820 should probably signal to us that they are not describing long-standing practice, but rather the current preoccupation of English rulers with Frankish culture. We can detect here a modish and Carolingian-inspired *Romanitas*, such as a great king might express by setting up residences in one or two pre-eminent 'chesters' within his realm.[134] The royal assembly at Bath in 796, perhaps the

---

[127] Loseby 2000, which appeared after this section was drafted, reaches a similar conclusion.

[128] S 1259 (a text of 805 referring back to Aldhun 'qui in hac regali villa [huius?] civitatis [Canterbury] praefectus fuit', cf. Brooks 1984: 33, 158); S 168 ('in loco praeclaro oppidoque regali Lundaniae vicu'); S 170 ('in vico regis Lundon').

[129] ASC s.a. 789 (pp. 54–5); *Æthelweard*, 27.

[130] S 277, S 298, S 336, S 333, S 340.

[131] In *c.*750 the *Cæstruuara*, or inhabitants of the region named after Rochester, had a reeve, but we meet him supervising pig-pastures and there is no evidence that he lived in Rochester itself (S 30); a grant to the bishop of Rochester in 779, issued 'in civitate supradicta', is ambiguous for reasons already given (S 36). However, a series of late eighth-century grants of blocks of land within the walls of Rochester (S 32, S 34, S 131, S 266) could point to a precocious revival of activity resem-bling Canterbury's.

[132] S 148 :'in celebri vico qui Saxonice vocatur æt Baðum', as against 'in celebre monasterio quod Saxonice nominatur æt Baðun'. Above, p. 151, for the nunnery.

[133] S 210. The possibility that other Roman places (Cambridge, Godmanchester, Leicester, Lincoln, Worcester) were re-fortified in Offa's time is suggested, on topographical and archaeolog-ical grounds, by Haslam 1987: 81–3.

[134] Such sentiments led the drafter of the 803 *Clofesho* canons to distinguish bishops of *civitates* from those of mere *ecclesiae*, and that of a ninth-century episcopal profession to call London an 'illustrious place built by the skill of the ancient Romans' (*CED* iii. 546–7; Cubitt 1995: 207). Cf. above, p. 126, for classicism in English art of the period; and Story 2003: 169–211, for the political context.

first in the brief reign of Offa's successor Ecgfrith, is particularly intriguing. Two years previously, Charlemagne had begun to adopt a more sedentary life by the hot springs of Aachen, where his great stone palace was now rising. For an English Aachen the only possible choice was Bath, where hot water still welled up from its holy spring through the stupendous ruins of the great bath, flanked northwards by the churches of the minster overlying the temple of Sulis Minerva.[135] Ecgfrith may not necessarily have shared Charlemagne's taste for holding court in the bath,[136] but he must have been alive to the current resonances of assemblies at hot springs, as well as to the generally Roman and imperial connotations of recycling monumental ruins.

As we have seen already in the choice of episcopal and monastic sites, the *Romanitas* of Christian English kings was European and contemporary rather than indigenous and archaic. It followed ecclesiastical practice rather than determining it, and in no case can it be shown that a royal vill in a Romano-British town or fort preceded the cathedral or minster there.

Hierarchical centres (iii): open-ground royal vills

Since the 1950s several seventh- and eighth-century sites with large timber halls have been identified by aerial photography, and in a few cases excavated. Archaeologists usually call them 'palaces', or (more soberly but still begging a question) 'royal sites',[137] though in fact the only ones which can be identified as royal on historical evidence are Yeavering, probably originally a ritual site,[138] and its successor at *Maelmin* (Milfield). Again we cannot argue from silence—royal sites of a totally different and unexpected type may yet come to light—but for the time being we must base our models on what we have.

The timber architecture of these establishments—no doubt lavishly decorated—was designed to impress, and their halls were remarkable achievements of structural carpentry. Nonetheless, their functional limitations, and their undeveloped character compared with anything that might have been called a 'palace' in Europe, have been too often disregarded. They were largely

[135] For the topography and likely state of the bath: Cunliffe 1984; Blair 1992: 243–6; Davenport 2002: 31–8.

[136] Einhard, 'Vita Karoli Magni', c. 22 (ed. Halphen, p. 68). See Nelson 2001 for Charlemagne's development of Aachen into a grand capital, genuinely urban and firmly royal, of an essentially new kind.

[137] For a summary with bibliography see P. Rahtz in *Encyc.* 399–401; cf. Hamerow 2002: 97–9. I am also very grateful to Steven Bassett for showing me an unpublished paper on these sites, with conclusions pointing in much the same direction as mine.

[138] Above, pp. 56–7.

or wholly unenclosed;[139] they represent a low density of settlement (if perhaps sometimes with a penumbra of subsidiary accommodation which has not been recognized); and despite frequent on-site rebuildings their lives were short, to be measured in decades rather than centuries. Nor can we perceive a clear-cut category of *villae regiae*, but rather a range in size and complexity embracing the monumental and undoubtedly royal (Yeavering, Milfield), the ambiguous but still evidently high-status (Hatton Rock, Atcham, Cowderys Down), and ordinary settlements which lack the larger and more imposing halls but show signs of planning (Chalton). In terms of density and capital investment, these secular sites simply do not compare with the ecclesiastical sites described in the last chapter. They have also, when excavated, produced remarkably few small-finds compared with such slightly later and probably ecclesiastical sites as Flixborough and Brandon, though it remains possible that certain 'productive' sites will eventually be identified as royal or aristocratic dwellings.[140]

While it seems fair to assume that these sites do illustrate for us the kind of food-collection and residential bases which itinerant kings used, 'royal vills', as a distinct and formal category of places, are curiously elusive in historical sources. (An account of an episode in 757 describes the unidentified West Saxon royal residence of *Meretun* as a *burh* with defensible gates, but is non-contemporary.[141]) Nor—significantly—is there any category of place-name or element which is peculiar to royal sites.[142] What we do have are several narrative references to places called *villae regiae*, *vici regales*, and so forth, and many more statements in charters that the king and his court attested them in named places.[143] It must be stressed that this is a highly incomplete (and geographically biased) selection of sites which were known

---

[139] Milfield, known only from cropmark evidence, looks like an exception, but it should be noted (i) that this site is in the Bernician zone of Anglo-British contact; and (ii) that although more recent aerial photographs confirm the Yeavering-type hall 'it is no longer so clear that the double palisade was intended to enclose it; indeed, the palisade no longer looks so complete and embracing as it formerly did' (Alcock 1988*a*: 9).

[140] Cf. Ulmschneider 2000: 75–80.

[141] *ASC* s.a. 757 (pp. 48–9): '7 þone æþeling on þære byrig metton þær se cyning ofslægen læg, 7 þa gatu him to belocen hæfdon.' This annal is late ninth-century as we have it. Whether it is based on an earlier source, for instance a verse epic, has been much debated: for a recent review see Kleinschmidt 1996, concluding (p. 219) that the annal is a piece of later criticsm of the West Saxon dynasty and cannot be taken as a contemporary record.

[142] Campbell 1986: 115, shows that the element *tūn* was used in the names of royal sites, but clearly it was in no way confined to them. Even places called Kingston (apart from Kingston-upon-Thames) were subsidiary rather than central places (Bourne 1987–8; current work by Duncan Probert), and there is no reason to think that such names are early. For Kingsbury names see below, p. 326. Cf. the perception of Pohl 2001: 458–9, that the generally vague nomenclature for barbarian residences suggests that they were 'not, as might be expected, knots in the net of political geography of barbarian countries'.

[143] A first attempt to list this material was made by Sawyer 1983. Susan Kelly's revised *Handlist* of Anglo-Saxon charters (currently available in typescript, or on-line as the 'electronic Sawyer') pro-

as royal houses, and as places where kings held assemblies. We cannot assume that these were identical categories, nor can we expect to have more than a sample of either. But if the Domesday network of royal vills were really of pre-Viking origin, we might reasonably expect the sample that we do have from that period to be consistent: it should make sense in terms of the later pattern, and should mostly comprise places which are visible as royal centres later. This is conspicuously not the case.

The period before 750 gives twenty-seven places (excluding Roman sites and hillforts) which are described as royal vills in contemporary or reasonably trustworthy sources, or where reliable charters are attested. Of these, thirteen are unidentified and seven have no known royal or monastic association later. Of the remaining seven, Benson and Eynsham are among the *tūnas* listed in the problematic '571' annal in the Anglo-Saxon Chronicle.[144] Benson is one of the very few genuinely stable and long-standing rural *villae regiae*;[145] Lyminge, Eynsham, and Thame, which are mentioned as royal places in this period, seem soon to have become minsters.[146] The *vicus* called *Tomtun* (where King Æthelred of Mercia attested a charter in his *cubiculum* in 675 × 92)[147] may be Tamworth, which was to emerge as a stable residence a century later. Finally, Somerton (Somerset) and Driffield (Yorks.) are said to have been royal vills in this period, but only in much later sources.[148]

During 750–820, twenty-six non-Roman royal vills or attestation sites occur for the first time: fourteen unidentified, five of no visible later importance, one Iron Age hillfort (an isolated attestation),[149] and six which can reasonably be regarded as stable royal centres thereafter. Pre-eminent is Tamworth, which emerges from 799 as a major Mercian royal centre, more like a 'capital' than any other English place before the tenth century.[150] Given the date this looks very much like another reaction to Aachen, an attempt by

vides more references, and I am deeply grateful to her for early access to this material. The following analysis omits the sites of church councils (*Clofesho*, Chelsea, Brentford, etc.). For the connotations of the term *villa* see Campbell 1986: 110–12.

[144] Above, p. 269.   [145] Holmes 1999.   [146] Above, pp. 186–7; S 12; S 1165.   [147] S 1804.

[148] The *ASC* s.a. 733 (pp. 44–5) says that King Æthelbald captured Somerton in 733, but only the much later Æthelweard calls it a royal vill (*Æthelweard*, 21), which indeed it was by his day; below, p. 325, for its emergence as a shire eponym (along with Wilton and Southampton) in the early ninth century. Driffield is called a royal vill in *ASC* 'D', 'E' s.a. 705 (p. 41), and (like Catterick) is a comital estate in Domesday Book.

[149] S 1184, a confirmation issued by Offa at Irthlingborough (Northants.) where the hillfort has produced some evidence for early Anglo-Saxon settlement (*South Midlands Archaeology*, 19 (1989), 27–8). Cf. S 114, a grant by Offa of land 'attinens urbi illi qui nominatur Sulmonnes burg', i.e. the hillfort of Salmonsbury (Glos.): the formulation recalls that of the Faversham and Rainham charters (below), and suggests that this too may have been adopted as a royal centre.

[150] Attestations in 780 (S 120–1) and 790 (S 133) may be spurious; a series of genuine attestations beginning in 799 (S 155) are listed by Sawyer 1983: 296. Below, p. 287, for the archaeology of Tamworth. One other Mercian royal place is Wychbold, recorded from 815 (S 178, S 188) and comital in Domesday Book; its industrial character makes it a special case.

King Coenwulf to copy Charlemagne's recent move to a more sedentary court life.[151] It is scarcely coincidence that the regular cycle of Christmas, Easter, and Pentecost courts, hinting at festal court-holdings of the kind recorded in the eleventh century, began under Coenwulf:[152] the appropriate theatre for a new and Carolingian-style ritual would have been a Carolingian-style *palatium*. As a secular residence developed for regular and intensive use, Tamworth represents a new kind of place which we will consider shortly.

A possible further case is the site at Old Windsor (Berks.) on the lower Thames, where excavations found an early Anglo-Saxon settlement replaced, from the beginning of the ninth century, by a high-status complex including a stone building with glazed windows and a tiled roof; an elaborate water-mill apparently dated from the seventh century. There was a royal house at Windsor by the 1060s, and if this was the site's original function it can be regarded as a counterpart to the Mercian centres. As we will see, though, numerous royal residences were added to existing minsters during the ninth to eleventh centuries, and Old Windsor might be explained in that light rather than as a West Saxon version of Tamworth; it could be significant that the now-isolated parish church stands on the edge of the site.[153]

East Kent is the only region in which something like the Domesday network of royal centres is evident by around 800. Wye was a royal vill by 762, Eastry had a reeve in the early ninth century, and in 811 Coenwulf granted land in the *regiones suburbanae* of the *oppida regis* Faversham and Rainham.[154] To this can be added persuasive archaeological evidence that Faversham, Milton Regis, and Eastry were important high-status centres from the pre-Christian period.[155] It is quite possible that east Kent (different once again) really was more coherently organized at an earlier date than other areas of English settlement; but we should be cautious about pushing the Kentish evidence too far,[156] and still more cautious about assuming that all the provincial territories necessarily had stable centres within them.

[151] Cf. Bullough 1985: esp. 294–5, 300–1; Nelson 2001.

[152] Hare 1997: 44–8; Wormald 1999*a*: 445–6. As Wormald points out, the earliest extant English king-making liturgy is likely to date from just this time.

[153] Astill 1978: 69–73; P. A. Rahtz in Wilson 1976: 433; J. Fletcher in *Current Archaeology*, 76 (1981), 150–2. The field was called 'Kingsbury': below, p. 326, for cases of this term associated with minsters. Windsor was later one of the regular crown-wearing sites (Hare 1997: 55–7) and might conceivably have had this role from the outset, though if so the lack of charter-attestations is strange.

[154] S 25, S 287, S 296–7; S 1500; S 168, and cf. S 169–70, S 178, S 286a. S 328 lists complex dependencies of Wye and other Kentish royal centres.

[155] T. Tatton-Brown in Haslam 1984: 1–36, at 28–32; above, p. 57, for the possible pre-Christian religious context of some of these places.

[156] For reservations about the coherence and stability of the lathe structure in Kent see N. Brooks in Bassett 1989*b*: 70–3. Nonetheless, it may be that the arguments of Jolliffe 1933 for the singularity of Kentish arrangements were nearer the mark than recent commentary has tended to believe.

With these few and rather special exceptions, it is hard to recognize a category of royal places during the seventh to early ninth centuries which were inherently deep-rooted and stable. We may have underestimated the extent to which the theatres of royal activity were provided by nature, equipped with relatively few and simple (even if sometimes large and formal) timber buildings which could be supplemented by temporary or portable accommodation and facilities as need required. Some phrases are redolent of impermanence. An attestation of 691 by Æthelred of Mercia 'in this place (*locus*) . . . which is called Marefield and Stapleford'[157] seems to be topographically vague, for these two Leicestershire places are eight miles apart. Surrey charters issued *iuxta* ('next to') a sub-king's vill (672 × 4) and *iuxta* a minster (809)[158] imply open-ground assemblies beside establishments which lacked space to house them; a Sussex assembly in 791(?) on an unidentified hilltop[159] may not have been near any established centre at all. Gumley (Leics.), which was an important place for Mercian royal assemblies in the eighth century, has 'a small natural amphitheatre near a mound'.[160] These sound like the sorts of places where hundred courts and shire courts met, as did major church councils: not in great churches or concentrations of settlement, but on open-ground sites which were near road and water transport,[161] and provided plenty of space for the participants with their retinues, tents, and field-kitchens. This makes more sense of the initially surprising fact that the names of so many royal vills and assembly points, like those of council sites, are now unidentified.

Secular residence, itineration, and encroachment on minsters

Some general statements can now be made about royal sites before the early ninth century. First, a very small number of major and stable centres emerge during the period of the Mercian supremacy, or occasionally (and more doubtfully) before that: Canterbury, London, Tamworth, Dorchester (Dorset), Benson, possibly Bath, some of the royal vills in east Kent. Secondly, these are only a small minority among the recorded places which were called *villae regiae*, or where assemblies were held, between the early seventh and early ninth centuries: of the others a good half are completely lost, some

---

[157] S 10.   [158] S 1165, S 164.

[159] S 1178, 'in monte qui vocatur Biohtchandoune'; see *Selsey*, 56–8.

[160] S 92, S 109, S 114; *VCH Leics.* v. 117; Stenton 1970: 1–2.

[161] Cubitt 1995: 32–9. For open-air sites of assembly, generally at mounds, trees, or natural landmarks, see Pantos 2002: 61–175.

look more like camp-sites than permanent settlements, and none was demonstrably used by kings for more than a generation or two. Thirdly (to recall a point made earlier), a few very early royal vills or assembly-places appear to have attached themselves to sites of pagan cult, while others survived specifically because they were turned into minsters.[162]

To project ideas of 'palaces' backwards from later centuries, or northwards from southern Europe or even Francia,[163] are temptations to be resisted: our view of seventh- and eighth-century royal life must be informed by what we know of contemporary society. Residence, food-render collection, and formal assembly need not have occurred at the same sorts of places. Some of these activities were peculiar to kings; others may have been pursued by kings and aristocrats in much the same kinds of ways. It is possible that there were linked sites—the court housed at one place, food-renders collected at a second, and consumables prepared at a third—but none of them necessarily required stable manpower or large-scale capital investment.[164] Gathering-in of renders needs a minimal staff; a moving body of people—including high-status people—can live in tents;[165] and even very large and important assemblies can be held on open ground. Even the erecting and dismantling of halls was not necessarily a daunting investment for rulers with timber and manpower at their disposal.[166]

---

[162] Above, pp. 56–7, 186–7.

[163] A message of Dierkens and Périn 2000 and Liebeschuetz 2000 is that Continental *sedes regiae*, even north of the Seine, tended to be attached to continuing cities; as Liebeschuetz says (p. 29), the success of this 'depended both on the Romanization of the barbarians and on the health of the cities', and in these respects 'the Anglo-Saxons were the odd men out'. The same contrast between Francia and (except east Kent) England is well made by Charles-Edwards 2000: 474–6. England was perhaps closer to early Scandinavia, where high-status activities took place in multi-functional 'central areas' rather than in monumentally permanent complexes: Brink 1996; Hedeager 2001. See also Pohl 2001 for the elusiveness and, at least sometimes, impermanence of barbarian royal residences.

[164] Here I differ from Foard 1985 and Hase 1994: 52–4: it seems to me that they describe a tenth- and eleventh-century system rather than a seventh- and eighth-century one.

[165] For references to tents see Cubitt 1995: 35 n. 71; cf. Bullough 1985: 273 n. 1. A site on the middle Thames, where multiple pits of *c.*750–75 contained rubbish including luxury glass and pottery but were not associated with any permanent buildings, may illustrate this kind of place: Foreman and others 2002. Irish royal and assembly sites had a combination of 'permanent' structures (though known to us only from highly fanciful descriptions) and ephemeral ones: Bhreathnach 1998.

[166] Experiments have shown that the building of a seventh-century hall would have required a large team, especially to prepare the timber (Mills 1999: 69), but given the likely resources at his disposal it is unlikely that a seventh-century king would have thought this very onerous. In 836 the minster of Hanbury (Worcs.) was released 'ab omni constructione regalis ville' (S 190). In the late twelfth century the tenants of West Auckland (co. Durham) had to make a hall and other structures in the forest for the bishop's hunting (*Boldon Book*, ed. D. Austin (Chichester, 1982), 36): an illustration of the kind of episodic, limited-life facilities which by this date were presumably confined to hunting-lodges, but which could have been the normal equipment of earlier royal vills.

However stable the *regiones* of early England may have been, and however effectively exploited through hidage-based assessment, there is no real reason, except possibly in Kent, to suppose that their central places were stable too. The essential mutability of ordinary rural settlements between the fifth and ninth centuries is one of the clearest messages of recent archaeology.[167] Sites of royal residence may have moved for rather different reasons than did peasant villages: specific decisions to build or abandon, rather than a gradual drift across the landscape as the generations passed. But there is no sign that the royal sites were any more permanent until the point came—which by 750 or even 800 it generally had not—when capital investment in buildings, fixed equipment, and earthworks was on a scale to encourage long-term use.[168] To reiterate a point made already, it may be that a food-render regime supporting a great king's court militated against this kind of sustained development: where the court visited occasionally, and only a skeleton staff was maintained in between, the stimuli would have been too spasmodic. So far at least, English high-status secular sites have yielded little trace of the specialized, high-grade craft production which we find at Celtic citadels and (rather later) at English minsters.[169]

It must again be acknowledged that there are unanswerable problems of scale and context. The intensity of activity must have varied with the size of households and the extent of circuits. Sub-kings, nobles, queens, and princes had their own itinerant courts, which were presumably supported by food-render regimes similar in kind to those which maintained kings.[170] The residences of small proprietors, stationary on single estates, could have been rather different from residences of their social superiors which were only used episodically. When the land could be exploited and occupied in such different ways, there was probably no simple relationship between the size of land-units and the character of their central places. Archaeologically, though, we are left with a vacuum: whether that vacuum is eventually filled, or assumes the status of negative evidence, remains to be seen.

The minster sites, by contrast, stand out as a group, both for their developed character and because such a high proportion of them, unlike nearly all the secular sites that we can perceive, came through into the high middle

---

[167] Hamerow 1991; Hamerow 2002: 93–9. To reiterate: we are not in a position to *deny* the archaeological existence of developed and stable high-status secular sites, but if they do exist they have not been found yet.

[168] On a human time-scale, of course, a residence that lasts for, say, fifty years is 'permanent'. A critical threshold is nonetheless crossed when capital investment in a place and its immediate environs reaches such a level as to militate strongly in favour of long-term modification and repair, and against complete re-location.

[169] See for instance R. Cramp in Driscoll and Nieke 1988: 75.

[170] Charles-Edwards 1989: 28–32.

ages and afterwards as stable central places. This becomes less puzzling when
we remember the contrasts within the aristocratic culture of England between
650 and 750. Kings and noblemen still belonged to an undeveloped social
system with—notwithstanding the production of spectacular prestige
items—a restricted material culture, and their domestic habits and environment still looked more to Scandinavia than to Italy or Gaul.[171] Minsters, like
the charters which safeguarded their lands, were ready-made imports from
an urban and bureaucratic Mediterranean world. It was inevitable that they
should bring lifestyles radically different from those of the insular aristocracies which first patronized them, and in turn that those aristocracies should
become aware of the opportunities which the minsters offered for transforming their own lives. Hence the close relations between minsters and the
laity which ecclesiastical writers from the 730s onwards viewed with such
dismay; hence too the signs, slowly visible after 750, that kings were starting
to develop a few special places as royal centres on a Continental pattern. The
political and tenurial factors in secularization and lay encroachment have
been touched on already,[172] but now the enquiry must be extended to the
wider context of social and economic interaction.

'Secularization' is a vague word: there may have been a big difference
between influences which purists thought morally suspect, and interference
which minsters themselves perceived as threatening. In the earlier stages,
when communities were often ruled by the founders' close kin, the relationship between monastic households and visiting secular households could be
cosy and unproblematic. Kings recovered in lavish hospitality a fraction of
the surpluses which they had given away by charter, and few can have thought
this unfair. Bede, noting that kings ate frugally when they visited Lindisfarne
before 664, implies (and deplores) that minsters which entertained their royal
lords more lavishly did so because they were worldly and luxurious, not
because they were under duress.[173] When Ecgfrith of Northumbria and his
court took in Coldingham nunnery (ruled by his aunt and certainly not
noted for austerity) on their festive progress around royal centres in 681, only
the queen's illness spoiled the jollifications.[174] Kings or thegns who came to
seem more like exploiters, less like good lords and kindred, would presum-

---

[171] Cf. the interesting comments of Wickham 1992: 240–3, comparing what he calls the 'peasant-based' societies of Iceland and England: 'This weakness in English material culture, even by Merovingian standards, I would associate with the economic logic of the "peasant-based" social system. What English kings and aristocrats got from their dependents in 700 or so (and they got a good deal) . . . they largely had to hand out again, to gain support and power; the systematic demand necessary for artisanal development suffered as a result.'

[172] Above, pp. 121–4.   [173] *HE* iii. 26 (p. 310).

[174] *VW* c. 39 (p. 78); cf. *HE* iv. 25 (pp. 420–6).

ably have been less welcome guests, especially if their visits became longer and more frequent: Æthelbald's promise in 749 to take monastic hospitality only when freely offered suggests that the reverse was all too common.[175] Worst of all, they might move in and take up permanent residence, annexing the space and assets of the community for their own households.

The eventual working-through of this process left the minsters the losers, but in the eighth century the relationship was more ambivalent. Its earlier and more positive aspects may be illustrated by an analogy, the relationship between itinerant kingship and royal monasteries in tenth-century Germany. In some ways the territorial constraints on Ottonian rule seem more comparable to eighth-century than to tenth-century England, so the two episodes of monastic expansion may have something in common. In Germany it was a relationship of mutual advantage: the Ottonians endowed monasteries on a princely scale, but expected commensurate hospitality when their huge households were in transit. In some of the greatest monasteries, special premises were set aside for the court. Quedlinburg nunnery was founded by Otto I in 936 in a royal hilltop fort; when the court visited, the men were accommodated in a new residence at the foot of the hill while the women stayed with the nuns inside the convent.[176] J.W. Bernhardt writes: 'it appears that where monasteries and royal residences, and sometimes royal fortresses, stood side by side, the functions and the use of the two were integrated and cannot be separated: rather, one has to think of a double proprietary right or at least of a double function of the various buildings and property.'[177]

Yet there was a fundamental difference, both in tenth-century Germany and in eighth-century England, between a palace with an associated church, and a monastery owing hospitality services. A secular residential complex which is self-sufficient and in continuous operation—something which we have found hard to recognize in England—was not the same thing as a monastery with an infrastructure to keep a community of ecclesiastical ladies and gentlemen in food, wine, and the other good things of life from day to day and month to month, and to enable it to host lay visitors when the need arose.[178] A countryside still far from fully exploited could bear the extra demands; the losers, if there were any, were the peasants who now had to support intensified demands of lordship.

In short, there was a mutually advantageous relationship between a

---

[175] Above, p. 122.
[176] Bernhardt 1993: 138–42, developing a point made by Leyser 1979: 103–4.
[177] Bernhardt 1993: 138.
[178] The kind of regular provisioning arrangements that might have developed on minster estates are illustrated by a mid eleventh-century rota of twelve manors which each supplied a month's food-rent to Bury: *RASC* 194–6.

monastery endowed with estates which it could develop 'manorially' to create fine buildings and a rich lifestyle, and its patron and his household who could now expect an altogether higher grade of bed and breakfast. The Ottonians used monasteries as theatres for solemn display[179] and English kings may have done the same, but the great buildings and formal ritual spaces also went naturally with monastic rhythms of life. In eighth- and ninth-century England these rhythms, now well established, may have been setting up novel reverberations in estate management and surplus-extraction which the secular great began to notice, and to harness creatively. In such terms Janet Nelson explains the move of the Emperor Charles the Bald (838–77) towards residence in urban monasteries: 'the main reason surely was that the *civitates* and monastic urban centres were becoming wealthier, and the churches which could tap that wealth by controlling markets were therefore in a good position to sustain the new royal demands—sustain, and perhaps also to benefit from them.'[180]

These developments, however attractive in the short term, were far from being in the minsters' long-term interests: here is a major background cause of the troubles deplored by Bede, Boniface, and Alcuin. Boniface's lurid image of the depraved King Osred (706–16), fornicating his way through the Northumbrian nunneries,[181] illustrates in extreme form the problems of an itinerant court which expected monastic hospitality. Beyond the anecdotal, we cannot know how burdensome on eighth- and early ninth-century monastic resources the duty to entertain kings really was. Kings occasionally issued charters at minsters, such as Offa at Peterborough in the abbot's presence in 765, Ecgfrith at Bath in 796, or Coenwulf 'next to' Croydon minster in 809;[182] Selsey and Repton, of which the first and perhaps the second had originally been founded on royal vills, were the sites of royal attestations in 780 and 844 respectively.[183] As we have seen, kings from Offa onwards were increasingly hard-nosed in their attitudes to minsters, and increasingly inclined to use them as pawns in political and dynastic power-games.

How the innumerable lesser minsters interacted with their aristocratic patrons is still harder to perceive. Smaller and more obscure than the royal

---

[179] Bernhardt 1993: 45–7, 50, 290, 296. It is easy to imagine, for instance, Coenwulf of Mercia holding court in the great stone hall at Northampton, even if it was primarily a monastic building.

[180] Nelson 1979: 113; cf. Février and others 1980: 506–9.

[181] *Bon. Ep.* No. 73 (p. 153): 'Osredum quoque spiritus luxoriae, fornicantem et per monasteria nonnarum sacratas virgines stuprantem et furentem, agitavit.'

[182] S 34, 'in monasterio quod appellatus est Medy[s]haemstede praesidente abbate Botuuino'; S 148 (above, p. 274); S 164, 'iuxta monasterium quod dicitur Crogedena'. Attestations at Malmesbury (S 256, S 356) and Glastonbury (S 152) are in unreliable charters but could have an authentic basis.

[183] S 1184 (*Selsey*, 47); S 197.

foundations, they were also in the hands of people whose sphere of operations and range of economic resources must have been narrower, and who
are likely to have imposed a correspondingly heavier burden on their family
minsters. I have argued that such places were new and different kinds of communities, not households spuriously redefined as minsters.[184] Nonetheless,
the assimilation of monastic to lay culture is likely to have proceeded at the
level of noble as well as royal households, perhaps more quickly in cases when
the former were sedentary already. Access to that 'special kind of nobleman's
club' which was a well-endowed minster must have grown in demand during
the eighth century. Even Bede's patron King Ceolwulf retired to Lindisfarne,
where he was later remembered for introducing alcohol, and the prospect of
luxurious monastic retirement must have appealed to such time-expired vet-
erans as Cyneberht and Buca.[185] Minsters had been imbued with secular
culture from the outset; but whereas the secular great of the late seventh
century had interacted with monastic culture by patronizing it, their descendants of the late eighth and ninth were increasingly prone to bend its economic and material assets to their own ends. Thus there gradually evolved a
new conception of minsters: places which kings and nobles could not merely
support, control, bestow on their kin, or use for episodic hospitality, but actually annex as sites of permanent residence.

A minster where we can glimpse thegnly residence in the making is
Inkberrow (Worcs.), the subject of some complex transactions in 822–3.[186]
One Wulfheard, who apparently already had a life-interest in the minster,
asks to be found 'some estate'—which from the context is evidently to be
Inkberrow itself—where he can 'live honourably and have his dwelling in the
burh there (*his wic þære in byrig*) during his life'. At Inkberrow the sub-oval
minster precinct, with the village on its periphery but containing a moated
site as well as the church, stands out clearly on modern maps (Fig. 33).
Whether or not the moated site is a direct successor of Wulfheard's house, it
seems that he expected a permanent residence within the enclosure and that
this was not thought unacceptable. This text marks a stage in the extension
of *burh*'s earlier sense, 'enclosed or defended (monastic) place', to one of the
senses in which it was being used by the tenth century: 'manor-house'.[187]

---

[184] Above, pp. 105–7, 211.
[185] Above, pp. 102–4; cf. Campbell 2000: 96–9.
[186] S 1432 (*RASC*, 6); Sims-Williams 1990: 96, 191–4, 237–9 for background.
[187] Williams 1992: 223, uses this text as her one specific pre-Alfredian case of *burh* meaning
'manor-house' (in other words in the kind of sense implied by Ine's *burhbryce*). In that light it is
interesting that the context should in fact be monastic.

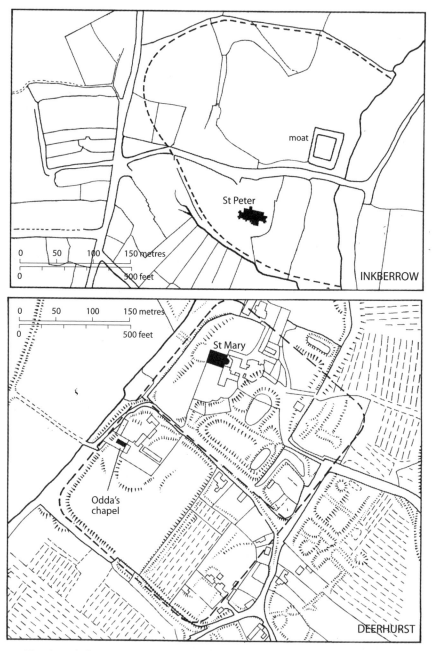

33. Two 'invaded' minster precincts in Worcester diocese. At *Inkberrow* (upper) field boundaries suggest the outline of a precinct, presumably where Wulfheard claimed his 'dwelling in the *burh*' in 822–3. At *Deerhurst* (lower, using data from Rahtz and Watts 1997: fig. 1 and field survey by Mick Aston) it is possible to conjecture a rectangular precinct divided in half, one half perhaps retained by the minster and the other annexed by Earl Odda.

Fortress-work, citadels, and minsters

Another strand in the semantic development of *burh* leads to modern English
'borough'. Archaeologists have a habit of using the word in a very narrow
sense, for the defended sites of Alfredian Wessex. These places were indeed
crucial, both in the transformation of West Saxon royal power and in the
growth of urbanized England. Yet to treat them as an exclusively West Saxon
and post-Viking phenomenon is to obscure an earlier phase of urbanization,
in which monastic 'towns' and royal fortresses show similar and sometimes
common roots. From the mid eighth century, English kings seem to have
become rapidly more successful in marshalling resources for capital investment in their power-centres: the emergence of Roman towns and Kentish
lathe centres as royal *villae* in the years around 800 is part of a larger process.

Insistence on the duty to build or maintain fortresses, first explicitly
reserved in a Mercian royal privilege of 749 and gradually more frequent (as
one of the 'three common burdens') thereafter,[188] suggests not only that kings
were becoming warier about alienating their assets, but also that they were
becoming keener to build fortresses. An obvious recipient of these newly
directed resources must have been Tamworth, which is now known to have
been enclosed by a pre-Viking palisade and to have possessed an elaborate
ninth-century watermill.[189] The spread of the system to Kent, where Offa
imposed the 'common burdens' in 792, precedes the reference in 811 to *oppida
regis* at Faversham and Rainham, the first of which retains evidence for
rectilinear planning.[190] Apparently for the first time since the migrations,
fortresses gained a major role in English political life.

The status of the churches at Tamworth and Faversham is unclear,[191] but
two further places of this kind within the Mercian ambit contained major
minsters. At Winchcombe, a Mercian royal minster in Coenwulf's and probably Offa's reign, the aligned churches stood at the centre of a large enclave
enclosed by a ninth-century or earlier bank (Fig. 34); royal documents were
kept there, as was a political prisoner in 796–8.[192] The second case is
Hereford, where excavations have found eighth-century timber buildings
aligned on a street, overlying slightly earlier grain-drying ovens; by the mid
ninth century a rectilinear area at the head of the river-crossing, containing
the cathedral, had been enclosed by a bank and ditch.[193] If Offa did indeed

188 Brooks 1971: 76–8, 82–3; Abels 1988: 52–6; Williams 2001.
189 Rahtz and Meeson 1992; Gelling 1992: 149; Cubitt 1995: 312–13.
190 Brooks 1971: 79; Abels 1988: 54; S 168.
191 But see above, p. 242 n., for an early eighth-century grave from Faversham churchyard.
192 Bassett 1985; Ellis 1986; Sims-Williams 1990: 165–8; S 1436.
193 Shoesmith 1982; Gelling 1992: 160–2.

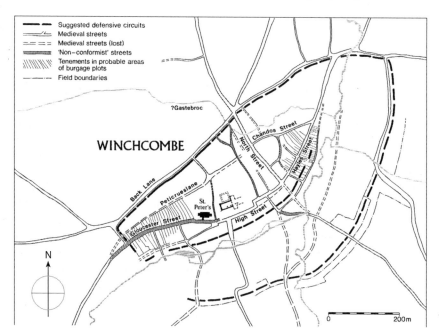

34. *Winchcombe* (Glos.): fortified minster, royal fortress, or proto-town? Reconstruction by Steven Bassett of the late medieval town, showing the defences, and the sites of the paired churches, probably dating from the late Mercian period. (Bassett 1985: fig. 1.)

transfer the Magonsætan see from *Lideberi* (Lydbury North or Ledbury) to the defended frontier site at Hereford, it was probably in the context of a defensive and administrative reorganization connected with the building of his Dyke.[194] Winchcombe's link with Offa and Coenwulf is clear, but Hereford was an episcopal seat: archaeology cannot tell us whether its roads and banks were laid out by its bishop, by the Mercian king, or by both of them using public levies. It may be compared with North Elmham (Norfolk), a well-excavated episcopal site in another kingdom, where the presumed cathedral stood in an undefended eighth- and ninth-century settlement of small dwellings articulated by a street-grid.[195]

[194] See Sims-Williams 1990: 90–1. The early twelfth-century Life of St Æthelberht contains some intriguing glimpses of the region in Offa's time (James 1917; Blair 2001*a*: 8–11). The murder of Æthelberht in 794 is located at Offa's 'palace' of Sutton St Michael, which, though twelve miles south of the minster at Leominster and only four miles north of Hereford, is suggested by its place-name (*suð-tūn*) to have been a satellite of the former. The martyr's body is carried to the place 'once called *Fernlage*, now Hereford', where the minster is built over his grave. Late though it is, this tradition could recall the insertion of Hereford into an older religious landscape dominated by minsters such as *Lidebiri* and Leominster.

[195] Wade-Martins 1980: 37–124.

As a group, these are places of a new kind, directly descended from earlier monastic sites but less exclusively ecclesiastical. There are differences between them, on a spectrum extending from the clearly royal Tamworth, Winchcombe, and Faversham via Hereford to North Elmham; but in all cases there are indications that secular interests of some kind were involved, and in no case (except probably North Elmham) does the church have clear primacy in date or status. Here we can recognize new initiatives in settlement planning, sometimes associated with royal fortress policy, which would soon set a pattern for the encapsulation of minsters within royal forts in Wessex.[196]

Once again, it seems more useful to locate such places on a scale of topographical and socio-political evolution than to argue about whether they were towns. To return to the anthropologists' comparative models, societies have characteristically reached a stage in the growth of secular organization when palaces and administrative headquarters were added to the major ceremonial centres, beginning a process which transformed them into royal and political citadels, fortresses, and eventually towns.[197] Lowland Britain, on its slow build-back after the fifth-century collapse, was reaching by 800 a stage comparable in some respects to the late Iron Age, when the major construction projects were primarily defensive and economic, only ritual in their secondary aspects. It is at this point that we encounter a group of sites, of which we may take Winchcombe as the paradigm, where the residences or citadels of rulers (kings and bishops, perhaps aristocrats) were associated with important churches, with defences, and with systematic planning, and which possessed a physical permanence and capital assets hitherto seen only at minsters. These features would recur a century later—and in the face of Viking attacks—in the *burgi* of Charles the Bald's France and the *burhs* of Alfred's Wessex, when the hemming-in of old religious sites and the erosion of their autonomy would intensify.[198] But the basic link between increasingly ambitious residences and fortresses and growing pressure on minster assets is already evident under Offa—indeed under Æthelbald, for the wider context of the complaint that he made monks labour on royal works must now be obvious.

---

[196] Up to a point, this argument is along similar lines to that of Haslam 1987, which proposes that a series of Roman and non-Roman bridgehead sites were fortified by Offa and served thereafter as administrative and market centres. The difference is that whereas Haslam's emphasis is on the creation *de novo* of central-place functions as an act of royal policy, my own is on the harnessing by kings of functions which had developed organically, in many cases around minsters.

[197] Cf. Adams 1966: 148–9, on Mesopotamia and Mexico: 'In both areas . . . the principal temple of a town became identified as the key redoubt of its political autonomy and military resistance.' Wheatley 1971: 311–16 describes the transfer of power from theocracies to kings in several societies, with the consequent rise of palaces as centres of ceremony and display rivalling temples.

[198] Below, pp. 330–4.

As the English landscape became more organized through the late eighth and ninth centuries, the minsters' natural role as its central places—its 'cities' in a sense that Cogitosus would have acknowledged—grew more marked. In weak or fragmented states they might have preserved their autonomy (as the theocracy of post-medieval Tibet illustrates), but it was impossible that the expansionist kingdoms of Mercia and Wessex could forgo the political and economic power residing in these crucial sites, or that ecclesiastical and lay magnates could resist milking them for their own social, territorial, and financial ends. England once again mirrors the parallel cultures where, as power-politics and market economics became stronger determinants of social change, the religious institutions which had once been the main articulators of living-space and its routines were forced into an altogether humbler role.[199] In 850 the golden age of Anglo-Saxon minsters was nearly over, and their coming tribulations would be at the hands of friends as well as enemies. Minsters were becoming so much the foci of secular life that the pressures against their remaining privileged centres of elite religious culture would in the end prove inexorable. Monastic towns were to become progressively more urban, progressively less monastic.

[199] This is the transition which has been variously defined as from mechanical to organic or from orthogenetic to heterogenetic, and in which the claims of hierarchy, tradition, and sacred space have been seen to give way to market forces and commercial space: Redfield and Singer 1954; Adams 1966: 136–8, 170–2; Wheatley 1971: 267, 390–3. Ibid. 396 observes 'a phase when a mechanically organized society . . . structured centripetally about a cult center and directed to the achievement of traditional, sacrally sanctioned goals, was—if the process continued for long enough—succeeded by one in which both society and economy were subject to increasing differentiation, and in which both new and old institutions were concerned with patently secular achievements'.

6

Minsters in a Changing World
*c.*850–1100

We have King Alfred's word for it that in the 860s, 'before everything was ravaged and burnt, the churches throughout England stood filled with treasures and books, and likewise there was a great multitude of the servants of God'.[1] Yet the growing pressure on minsters, and their growing insecurity, can be traced from the disputes of the 740s, through the encroachments and exactions of Offa and his successors in Mercia, to the ostensibly benign but ultimately exploitative lordship of Ecgberht's family in ninth-century Wessex.[2] The erosion of autonomy, and the appropriation of estates and sites for defence, administration, and land-lordship, were long-term trends spanning the mid eighth to late eleventh centuries. Alfred was focusing, naturally enough, on the destruction which he had seen with his own eyes, but minsters were also victims of longer-term political, social, and economic processes.

It is no aim of this book to question the destructive force of Viking attacks. Alfred's comments are to be taken seriously: eastern sees lost their bishops; minsters were raided and burnt; books and treasures were destroyed and looted; and it can hardly be doubted (though there is actually very little explicit evidence) that monks, nuns, and priests were massacred.[3] Production of manuscripts, which had declined progressively through the previous decades, virtually ceased.[4] It is likely that the experience of English minsters was part of a general depletion of ecclesiastical settlements throughout the British Isles during the Viking age.[5] But the rhetorical accounts of devastation and abandonment that have so moulded historians' views of the English monastic Church from Alfred to Eadgar are late, of a conventionalized

---

[1] *King Alfred's West-Saxon Version of Gregory's Pastoral Care*, ed. H. Sweet, i (EETS Orig. Ser. 45, 1871), 4–5.

[2] Above, pp. 121–34.

[3] Wormald 1982*b*: 139–41; Dumville 1997: 1–10. Yorke 2003*b*: 58–9 is sceptical of the 'rape and pillage' topos.

[4] Dumville 1992*b*: 96–7; cf. above, pp. 127–9.   [5] Dumville 1997: 17–18; cf. Etchingham 1996.

character, and emanate from strict monastic circles eager to maximize their own achievements: they cannot be read quite at face value.[6]

The Scandinavian impact

After seventy years of sporadic raiding, the English faced from the mid 860s a wave of far heavier attacks. In some regions these culminated in short-term military domination and long-term cultural influence, which can broadly be characterized as Danish in East Anglia and east of the Pennines, and Norwegian in the north-west. There is now a consensus that the armies were relatively large, and that the invasion involved not merely plunder and subjection, but the settlement of large areas by significant immigrant populations.[7] In the continuity or disruption of their religious life, these areas are likely to have fared very differently from those further west, which suffered raids but were not settled. The distinctiveness of Danish eastern England has been much debated, and bears on the chances of ecclesiastical structures surviving within it.

If the argument for numbers and impact was won in the early 1980s, local studies and comparative approaches are suggesting more sensitive ways, not demanding a choice between continuity and cataclysm, of envisaging contacts between Danish and English peoples.[8] To an extent, scholars have reached different conclusions because they have addressed different issues. While students of learning and literature have been persuaded that the 'evaporation of almost the entire literate culture of the pre-Viking Danelaw can only be the responsibility of the Vikings themselves',[9] archaeologists and topographers have stressed the tendency for old sites to re-emerge in new forms. It is characteristic that the recent discoveries at Repton have been used as evidence both for the violent destruction of minsters and for their continuity. But it is possible to accommodate both approaches, and in a sense both conclusions.

If the impact of warrior invasions on militarily weaker but culturally more developed societies has characteristically been violent and exploitative, incoming aristocracies have also seized extremely quickly on elements in the

---

[6] Fleming 1985: 247–9, tends to accept the narrative evidence; Dumville 1992*a*: 31–6 is more sceptical but agrees that destruction and abandonment were real and widespread.

[7] Hadley 1997: 70–1 nn. 6–10 gives a convenient bibliography for this long debate. For definitions of the Danelaw see: K. Holman in Graham-Campbell and others 2001: 1–11; L. Abrams in Higham and Hill 2001: 128–43.

[8] A great deal appeared in print while this chapter was being drafted: Hadley 1997; Hadley 2000*a*; Hadley 2002*b*; Hadley and Richards 2000; Graham-Campbell and others 2001.

[9] Wormald 1982*b*: 139.

old cultures—including religious ones—which conferred legitimacy and status. It may have been a relatively short period during which ethnicity was the main determinant of relations, and before the leaders' self-perception as elites like their English counterparts became more important to them than the differences.[10] Supposedly Danish features of organization and land-tenure in the Danelaw may in fact have taken shape during the tenth century, as Danes and English alike experienced re-conquest, urbanization, and accel-erating economic change.[11] Indications that some Scandinavian leaders quickly embraced traditional status-markers such as Christian memorial sculpture are therefore not surprising; in Dawn Hadley's words, 'Christian-ity may, in the long run, have been less a factor which distinguished the native population from the Scandinavian settlers, than a force for their integra-tion.'[12] It would not have needed much more than the formal conversion of individual landowning magnates—nor much literacy or learning on the part of either patrons or priests—for low-level corporate religious life and Christian ritual to have continued at many of the old minsters.[13]

Viking raiders, however unsavoury, came for captives and booty: murder and destruction were by-products and not inevitable. Total obliteration was not an inherently likely outcome, and might have been deliberately avoided so that the communities could survive to be raided again.[14] That even invad-ing pagans recognized the cultic and symbolic prestige of their victims' holy sites is suggested by the extraordinary discoveries at Repton, the great Mercian royal minster where the Viking army settled during the winter of 873–4.[15] Grouped close around the chancel, with its relic-crypt of St Wigstan (d. 849), lay Scandinavian-type graves of the 870s; one mature warrior, killed by a sword-blow, was buried with his sword, amuletic boar's-tusk, and Thor's

---

[10] Hadley 1997 and Hadley 2002*b* for this line of argument.

[11] Hadley 1997: 80–1, 93–6; Hadley 1996: 119–26.

[12] Hadley 1997: 92.

[13] Lesley Abrams takes a rather more sceptical view of such continuity, as also of the speed and depth of conversion: Abrams 1995*a*: 215–16; Abrams 1998: 122–3; Abrams 2000; Abrams 2001.

[14] Etchingham 1996: 35–47, 54–7, argues that the main objective of raids on Irish religious sites was to take captives, and that after *c*.850 the raids were more selectively targeted on major sites, perhaps with 'a more calculating attitude, which discouraged random destruction of church settle-ments, whose human resources in particular might be repeatedly exploited'. The impact on Gaelic Scotland was probably more extensive than on Ireland; see Dumville 1997: 10–12, for attacks on hermits around the Scottish coast.

[15] Biddle and Kjølbye-Biddle 1992; Biddle and Kjølbye-Biddle 2001*b*. Especially intriguing is the apparent contrast between the Viking warriors who buried their dead at Repton church, and their colleagues who cremated their dead nearby at Heath Wood, Ingleby (Richards 2002: 165–70). Julian Richards proposes an ideological split in the ranks: 'The Mercian landscape and even the royal church and mausoleum were appropriated by one section of the Great Army in order to legit-imate their political control. However, on a side stage 4 km away a more traditional ideology of cre-mation, ship burial and sacrifice were being practiced on the hilltop at Heath Wood' (ibid. 169–70).

hammer pendant. To the west, a stone mortuary building was re-used for disarticulated bones, perhaps including those of Vikings,[16] and was then sealed by a barrow, which in turn became a focus for graves of wealthy Scandinavians in the early tenth century. The pre-Viking church stood, though much battered;[17] St Wigstan's relics were being venerated there when Cnut removed them in 1019; and even in 1086 there were still 'a church and two priests with one plough'[18] to hint at what Repton had been. Here as in many other cases, the steady decline of the minster continued well after the Vikings, and in a Christian milieu.

At most of the smaller minsters in eastern England, we simply cannot see what happened. But abandonment is not necessarily a more reasonable assumption than low-level continuity: it is salutary at this point to read one exceptional text, a narrative of a place (and indeed of a type of place) that is otherwise largely undocumented in this period:

Before the fury of the pagans who devastated East Anglia had raged through Cambridgeshire, and consigned the land to waste and desolation [874–5?], there existed at Horningsea a minster of royal dignity, in which was a substantial community of clergy (*non parva congregatio clericorum*). At the very time that the army was rampaging in that place, Cenwold the priest discharged the sacerdotal office there. Then those who flocked together there from paganism to the grace of baptism gave that minster five hides at Horningsea and two at Eye. Cenwold died, and Herewulf the priest succeeded in his place; he made suit to King Æthelstan [924–39], who took that place under his care and protection. In those days Wulfric the provost (*prepositus*), who was Cenwold's kinsman, unjustly took away the two hides at Eye by force from the minster. Then in King Eadgar's days [957–75], Æthelstan the priest, Herewulf's kinsman, obtained as his deputy the sacerdotal office which he exercised in that minster. . . . [Æthelstan was implicated in a burglary, but Herewulf bribed the authorities with] treasures of the church, which good men devoted to God had given to the minster for their souls in ancient times . . . , on the understanding that mercy would be shown to him and that he might possess his minster for the rest of his life; and he gave the bishop certain ornaments so that Æthelstan the priest might be neither executed nor degraded. After a certain time Herewulf the priest passed away, and Æthelstan succeeded him. After these events, St Æthelwold went forthwith to King Eadgar and bought Horningsea from him for 50 gold [coins] . . .[19]

This is an unusual departure from the standard narratives and the stan-

---

[16] This is controversial: compare Biddle and Kjølbye-Biddle 2001*b*: 78–80 with Halsall 2000: 263, Hadley 2002*a*: 214–16, and Richards 2002: 167.

[17] Biddle and Kjølbye-Biddle 2001*b*: 84–5, stress this dereliction, but perhaps go a little too far in seeing it as 'a ruthless assertion by the Vikings of their own ancient religion': contrast Richards, n. 15 above.

[18] DB i. 272ᵛ.

[19] *Lib. El.* 105–6. Cf. Whitelock 1941: 169; Pestell 2003: 130–1; and below, pp. 319, 453.

dard rhetoric: late tenth-century monastic writers portrayed an obliterated religious landscape awaiting reclamation. But specific local evidence rarely supports such a view, except in some easterly regions where the old order may have been effaced as much by transformative growth after 950 as by violence a century earlier. The reliable facts that some individual minsters were raided, and that most minsters were drastically reduced in wealth and status by the time of Domesday Book, cannot sustain a generalized model of pillage followed by long years of abandonment. An approach which gives more weight to local evidence and to factors other than the Vikings, and which stands back from the polemical texts produced in a small and atypical group of houses, shows instead a gradual but inexorable trend towards secularization which nonetheless left a high proportion of minsters as functioning religious sites. In this process, the Viking attacks played an important but not all-determining part.

Continuity, disruption, and development: regional variation in the experience of minsters

Beyond this point, generalization runs the risk of obscuring fundamental regional diversity. The difference in experience between western regions which suffered only sporadic attacks, and eastern ones which were ruled by Scandinavians for forty years, must have been immense, and pressures which were not directly of the Vikings' making seem on the whole to have heightened this contrast. Raiding and colonization, royal and ecclesiastical lordship, the competition of newer and smaller churches, all took a heavier toll on minsters in eastern and southern England than in the west, and it is unrealistic to propose a single model. Our picture must be based on the diversity of local experience, which will be explored here by means of a clockwise tour of England from Kent to Essex, focusing on monastic survival across the ninth to eleventh centuries (Fig. 35).

First, a few words on the evidence and how it can legitimately be used.[20] The most obvious sources are contemporary or near-contemporary charters and other texts which describe the fortunes of individual religious communities through the Viking age. The preservation of older charters in a minster's archive should indicate that its whole community did not meet a violent end, or at least that the site was not abandoned long-term. Conversely, the widespread absence of charters most probably indicates disruption: their almost total non-survival in northern and eastern England strongly suggests

[20] Cf. Blair 1995a: 199–203.

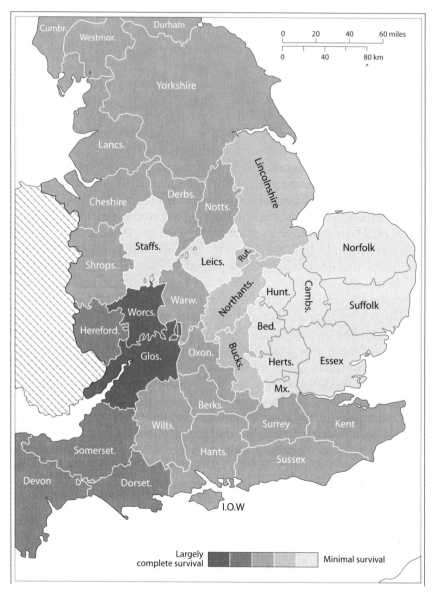

35. The incidence of identifiable continuity between pre-Viking minsters and parochial mother-churches of *c*.950–1200: an impressionistic depiction. The denser the shading, the higher the visible survival of early organization into the later period. Contrast Fig. 50.

that minsters in these regions suffered greater, or more violent, disruption than those in the west and south. But it need not mean that they were totally destroyed. One may envisage a religious community returning to its burnt-out buildings after a raid, or sinking to a level of illiteracy which militated against the survival of documents, while still preserving some corporate life and remaining pastorally active. It heightens our sense of disaster that the areas in which literacy, art, and material culture had developed most brilliantly were precisely those in which they were most brutally destroyed.

Here a different source, monumental stone sculpture, complements the written evidence, being most prolific in precisely those Anglo-Scandinavian regions (except East Anglia) which have lost their early charters. Sculpture can show the degree of continuity in workshop styles and techniques, and is sometimes evidence for the burial of new warrior-aristocrats at old ecclesiastical sites. The last point is to an extent ambiguous, since burial could have continued around abandoned church ruins (as many Irish sites illustrate today), but a correlation between major early minsters and Viking-age monuments would at least suggest a continued perception of holiness and status. In a minority of cases, surviving stone churches or excavated occupation-deposits point to continued religious use; more often, the layout of precincts, boundaries, and church groups remains visible in the modern topography. Such evidence offers the best means of measuring whether or not a substantial proportion of the locally important churches persisted on the same sites. Inevitably it is also less eloquent than documents, and harder to read unambiguously.

Religious continuities can also be traced in patterns of devotion to saints, whether expressed in church dedications or in local cults. Paired dedications, characteristically to an apostle and St Mary, may often reflect pre-Viking practice.[21] More helpful are the cults of very minor local saints, where these are known or inferred to be of pre-Viking origin and are attested in post-Viking sources.[22] Cults which had spread outside their regions via liturgical texts could have been revived after a hiatus, and cults of local notables (especially if mentioned by Bede) are sometimes of late creation. The more obscure the saint, therefore, the stronger the likelihood of genuine continuity: it is hard to believe that regions in which several such cults survived into the

[21] Above, pp. 200–1. As noted below (p. 399), paired dedications in East Anglia can result from the relatively late foundation of adjoining churches by different lords, but there is no evidence for this practice in other regions.

[22] Above, pp. 142–3, and Blair 2002*a*, for a fuller discussion of this evidence in its pre-Viking context. For respectively sceptical and positive views of cult continuity, see Cambridge and Rollason 1995: 103, and Blair 1995*a*: 202–3. Cf. below, p. 353, for the translation of relics from obscure minsters, which had preserved them through the Viking age, to reformed abbeys.

eleventh century or later had suffered complete dislocation of their devotional lives.

Territorial continuity, in the sense of the survival of pre-Viking parochial territories centred on minsters, does not necessarily follow from the continuity of monastic sites. Even where it can be shown—as it often can—that mother-churches recorded in post-Conquest sources had been pre-Viking minsters, the possibility remains that these ancient sites were adopted in the tenth century to build a new parish organization. Recurrent and symmetrical correspondences between mother-parishes and hundreds might be pointers in that direction, suggesting a tenth-century remoulding of the parochial geography to fit the new administrative geography of West Saxon government.[23] It may well be that where kingship weighed most heavily, or where post-Viking reconstruction was most necessary, old patterns were most thoroughly overlain by new ones. Topographical historians can be guilty of over-rigidity, and a flexible approach is required to what must have been a regionally diverse and evolving system.

(i) *Southern England.* The appropriate starting-point is the peninsula of east Kent: the birthplace of English Christianity, and also one of the first regions to suffer Viking raids. Canterbury was attacked in 851, though Christ Church and St Augustine's essentially weathered the storm.[24] Coastal minsters were probably less fortunate; late (and not necessarily reliable) traditions describe the sack of Minster-in-Thanet, Lyminge, and Folkestone by Vikings.[25] There are, however, fragments of evidence suggesting that disruption was not long-term. Asser, describing the 855 landing at Sheppey forty years after the event, could write in the present tense that 'an excellent minster is established on the island'; its great seventh-century church still stands to eaves level.[26] Boundary clauses of 946 and 948 mention land of the Folkestone and Minster-in-Thanet communities, and Reculver with its twenty-six hides passed to Christ Church during the tenth century.[27] There is also a fair correlation between early minsters and mother-parishes. Dover, Folkestone, and Lyminge emerge in the 1080s with groups of chapels, as do

---

[23] Correlation of hundreds with minsters is the central interest of Page 1914–15, a pioneer work which remains remarkably useful. Cf. above, p. 158.

[24] *St. Aug.* p. xvii; Dumville 1992*b*: 99.

[25] Rollason 1982: 22–4, 79–80; Brooks 1984: 201–4 and 367 n. 82; *St Aug.* pp. xxviii–xxx; S 398 (with comment by Dumville 1992*a*: 51); Yorke 2003*b*: 58–60.

[26] *Asser*, c. 3 (pp. 4–5, trans. p. 68); Taylor and Taylor 1965–78: i. 429–30; work by Richard Gem in progress.

[27] S 510, 'æt þara hina lande to Folces stane'; S 535, 'þæs hiredes mearc to sancte Mildryþe'; S 546 (but a problematic text: cf. Brooks 1984: 232–6). Gough 1992 and below, pp. 513–14, for the Reculver estate.

Reculver and Minster-in-Thanet in later sources; Minster-in-Sheppey was a dependency of Milton Regis, but a late tradition held that that was what it had always been.[28] Other mother-churches—Lympne, Wingham, Wye, Teynham, Maidstone, Newington—may or may not be post-Viking additions. It would be surprising if so traumatized a region did not need reconstruction, but enough remained of the old monastic culture to preserve, for instance, the body of tradition encapsulated in the Minster-in-Thanet foundation-legend.[29] Indeed, if the minsters' monopoly on archiepiscopal chrism is really a survival from the seventh century, the eastern Kentish Church preserved its primary, idiosyncratically European character against all the odds.[30]

The regions around the Weald are less well documented, and their fortunes less visible. The will of Ealdorman Alfred (made between 871 and 889, and therefore either in the thick of Viking raiding or in its aftermath) makes bequests to Christ Church (Canterbury), Rochester, and Chertsey, and directs that 'the surplus is to be divided among the minster-houses of God's churches in Surrey and Kent as long as they wish to perform [their religious duties]'.[31] Chertsey preserved traditions of a Viking slaughter, but there was still a religious community in 964 which retained both its relics and its earliest charter.[32] By 1086 the manorial and parochial landscape of the zone around London was fragmented to a point that makes reconstruction difficult, but in western Surrey the pre-Viking minsters of Chertsey, Woking, Godalming, and Farnham come through with large mother-parishes almost identical to the hundreds.[33] The early minsters of the Sussex coastal plain survived as parish churches, and in several cases (such as Bosham, Pagham, and Steyning) with mother-parishes; Steyning preserved the relics and traditions of St Cuthmann.[34] With relatively poor charter survival and virtually no sculpture, we cannot even guess whether the several mother-churches first mentioned in the eleventh century were early or late foundations. Mother-parishes often correspond with hundreds, but here this may not imply late reorganization: boundaries radiating into the Weald were determined by strong and persistent geographical and economic factors, and may have existed in their main lines for centuries or even millennia.[35]

---

[28] Tatton-Brown 1988: 107–10; Rollason 1982: 87.   [29] Above, p. 144.   [30] Above, p. 69.
[31] S 1508: 'gind mynsterhamas to Godes ciricum in Suþregum ond in Cent, þa hwile þe hio lestan willen.' The phrase later in the will 'þa hwile þe fulwiht sio', 'so long as baptism [i.e. Christianity] may last', underlines the uncertainty; cf. Foot 1992*a*: 191.
[32] Blair 1989: 231–6.
[33] Blair 1991*a*: 91–108; one eastern Surrey minster, at Croydon, can now also be identified as pre-Viking (S 164).
[34] *Selsey*; Blair 1997; Rushton 1999; detailed parochial evidence in *VCH Sussex*. Masters 2001 argues for regional variation within Sussex, some areas having unusually high densities of minsters with small and rather ill-defined mother-parishes.
[35] Page 1914–15: 79–83; Everitt 1986; Blair 1989: 98–100.

Hampshire, Wiltshire, and Berkshire were the core of the West Saxon kingdom, which emerged triumphant from the Viking wars. The cathedral and community at Winchester survived without known disruption, as did the great minster of Malmesbury.[36] Britford (Wilts.) and Titchfield (Hants.), with architecturally ambitious pre-Viking churches, are visible as minsters in the tenth to eleventh centuries.[37] Ramsbury (Wilts.), a bishop's seat from 909, retains a cross fragment of (probably) *c.*800.[38] Abingdon and Cookham, on the Berkshire bank of the Thames, also survived after a fashion, though Bradfield declined to a mere parish church.[39] All except the last emerge in post-Conquest records as the centres of mother-parishes; Malmesbury's in particular was enormous. In Hampshire, Patrick Hase has shown that mother-parishes around the Solent—Titchfield, Bishops Waltham, Romsey (replacing Nursling), Southampton, and Eling—were probably all based on pre-Viking minsters.[40]

These elements of an early system were much changed, but less by disruption in the ninth century than by royal, aristocratic, and monastic intervention in the tenth and eleventh. At the Domesday survey, churches with marks of superior status clustered more densely in Hampshire and Wiltshire than in any other region,[41] and the congruence of mother-parishes with hundreds was clearer and more persistent in Hampshire, Wiltshire, and Berkshire than anywhere else outside the north-west.[42] In Wiltshire, Jonathan Pitt's detailed work suggests a tenth-century re-moulding of old minster territories into a system of hundredal mother-parishes, which diversified during the late tenth and eleventh centuries as major landlords carved out parishes for new 'secondary minsters'.[43] This is more plausible than to suppose that the pre-Viking West Saxon heartland had so many more

[36] There is little sign of physical damage in Winchester or elsewhere in Hampshire, though the need to raise heavy tributes caused some stress: Yorke 1995: 122. The '*familia* of the Holy Saviour at Malmesbury' was probably engaging in land-transactions in around the 890s (S 356, S 1205, but neither above suspicion), and William of Malmesbury (*GP* 385 ff.) tells a narrative of continuous religious life there.

[37] Gem 1993: 45–7; Hare 1991. The witnesses to a charter of 982 (S 842; *NMW* 123) include 'þara hina on Ticcefelda', and one of its boundary-clauses 'on þara hina mearce to Ticcan felda'; the Domesday entry for Britford church (DB i. 65) is of the kind which normally indicates a small minster.

[38] Bailey 1996*a*: 20–2, vindicating this earlier dating; note also the important eighth-century ironworking site near Ramsbury church (Haslam 1980).

[39] Blair 1994: 64–5, 113–14, *Abingdon*, pp. cxcvi–cciii, 3–22, and *Encyc.* 3–4, for the problems of Abingdon and Bradfield; below, p. 327, for Cookham.

[40] Hase 1975: 44–181; Hase 1988: 45–7; Yorke 1995: 182–5. Excavations at Romsey (Phases 5–8) imply continuous ecclesiastical activity through the ninth to eleventh centuries (Scott 1996: 5–43).

[41] Blair 1985*a*: 108, 112, 116; Hase 1994: 53, for map of Hampshire and Wiltshire minsters.

[42] Page 1914–15: 72–8; Kemp 1967–8: 18–19 gives qualified support with the example of Thatcham.

[43] Pitt 1999.

churches than the Mercian heartland, or (especially given the political and tenurial pressures on the hundredal organization of Hampshire) that the very regular parish system had stood unchanged for centuries. Rather, the concentration of court life and royal landholding in these shires after 900, not to mention the wealth and influence of the Winchester minsters, created abnormal conditions in which small religious communities could still be founded and endowed; their mother-parishes seem to have been moulded to a hundredal framework which was in the process of modification, and to have evolved with it as many of the great estates became hundreds in their own right.[44]

Which individual minsters were new, and which old but undocumented, is rarely clear. One exception is the church on the Old Minster estate at Hurstbourne Priors (Hants.), consecrated in 902: this probably marked the splitting of the mother-parish of Hurstbourne Tarrant into two parishes, royal and monastic, represented by the interlocked Domesday hundreds of Hurstbourne and Evingar.[45] Shortly afterwards, a tantalizingly laconic text directs that tithes from two neighbouring but not contiguous hundredal mother-parishes, Great Bedwyn (Wilts.) and Lambourn (Berks.), are to be assigned to 'God's servants for provisions at Bedwyn'.[46] Why one group of priests should have controlled two minsters is obscure, but the episode shows that apparently simple topographical arrangements may conceal financial and parochial arrangements that were complex and changed over time: Lambourn had an autonomous mother-church a century later.[47] The will of Wulfgar (931 × 9) reserves food-rents to the 'servants of God' in 'the holy foundation' at Kintbury (Berks.), while Wynflaed (*c.*950) makes small bequests to the

[44] Cf. Hill 1984: 87–91, 101; Hase 1988: 48–9, 63 n. 27, 64 n. 33; Yorke 1995: 123–9, 185; below, p. 371.

[45] S 1285, dated 'ða man þa cyricean halgode æt Hysseburnan' in the presence of the bishop, nineteen priests, and a deacon. Since the agreement concerns an Old Minster estate it can probably be assumed that this church was at Hurstbourne Priors, where Leofwine held the church and one hide from the bishop in 1086 (DB i. 41); Hurstbourne Tarrant church, held from the king by a royal priest and entitled to churchscot (DB i. 39), could have been an older minster, and may have been the recipient of the churchscot payments (*cyricmittan*) stipulated in 900 (S 359). Cf. Hase 1988: 64 n. 33.

[46] Meritt 1934: 344; below, p. 440, for date and wider context. The phrase 'þam godes þeowum to fostre æt Bedewindam' indicates that the provisions are to be at Bedwyn, but the priests could have been based at both Bedwyn and Lambourn.

[47] *RASC* 240; cf. below, p. 449. The complex relationship between Great Bedwyn, Kintbury, and Lambourn could be interpreted in a number of ways, as emerges from the careful but inevitably inconclusive analysis of Pitt 1999: 127–42. Estates at both Bedwyn and Lambourn appear in King Alfred's will, the first left to Edward the Elder and the second to Alfred's wife; could the arrangements for parochial finance have been temporarily linked after the latter's death in 902, when Lambourn would presumably have reverted to Edward (cf. Wormald 2001*b*: 273)? Or was Lambourn simply a parochial outlier of Bedwyn, with no church of its own, at the time of the tithe memorandum?

communities at Kintbury, Shrivenham, Coleshill, Childrey, and Wantage (Berks.), and Wilton (Wilts.).[48] What was possibly the mother-church of Basing (though oddly described as 'a monastic mansion called king's-horse-croft') was sold by King Eadmund to a royal priest in 945.[49] There are royal grants in 963 of eight hides to the servants of God in St Andrew's church at ?Meonstoke (one of three endowed churches in the Meons),[50] and in 990 of ten hides to St Peter's at South Stoneham.[51]

These references support the Domesday picture of a local religious culture which, though formed in several layers, was still based on minsters. This is not to deny the impact of the great Winchester monasteries, which with their power and wealth must have tended to monopolize ecclesiastical culture, and to privilege the centre over the localities. Yet if the old order was transformed, the new order was a replication of traditional modes within a regulated mother-parish framework, quite unlike the uncontrolled free-for-all of church-building that was currently happening in East Anglia.

Further west, in Dorset, Somerset, and east Devon, early arrangements seem more visible:[52] we perceive, as we will in western Mercia, an eighth-century institutional base which came through largely intact. Several minsters for which there is good pre-Viking evidence, such as Wimborne, Wareham, Sherborne, Bath, Taunton, Exeter, Axminster, and Braunton, were still significant in the eleventh century.[53] At Glastonbury the charter evidence

---

[48] S 1533, S 1539 (*RASC* 52; *Wills*, 10–14); Blair 1988*b*: 5.

[49] S 505 (*NMW* 67): 'aliquantulam terre partiunculam, hoc est mansionem monasticam ad Basyngum que nostro dicitur famine cyninges hors croft', and two hides at Lickpit (Hants.). See the commentary in *NMW* 70–1, suggesting that the *mansio monastica* was intended to be a dependency of New Minster. The recipient transferred it shortly afterwards to New Minster (S 1418; *NMW* 72); in 1086 Mont-Saint-Michel held a church with one hide and the tithes of Basingstoke manor (DB i. 43).

[50] S 718: 'aecclesiae beato Andreae apostolo dicate loco qui cælebri æt Meone nuncupatur onomate ad usus servorum Dei inibi degentium.' Meonstoke is the only one of the Meon churches later dedicated to St Andrew (*VCH Hants*. iii. 256). In 1086 the bishop of Winchester held West Meon church with one hide, East Meon church with six hides and one yardland, and received 20*s*. from Meonstoke church (DB i. 40ᵛ).

[51] S 942. In 1086 Richer the clerk held South Stoneham church from the bishop, with two dependent churches, a hide, and all tithe (DB i. 41ᵛ).

[52] Aston 1986 for Somerset; Hall 2000 for Dorset; Hase 1994: 53, for map of Dorset and Somerset minsters; Orme 1991: 7–12, for Devon.

[53] *Encyc.* 480, 467–8, 418–19, 54, 177. Wimborne: Coulstock 1993. Wareham: architectural evidence (Gem 1993: 39–42), and the burial of King Beorhtric in 802 (*ASC* s.a. 786 (pp. 52–3)). Sherborne: it kept its early charters, though no new ones are recorded between 864 and 933 (*Sherborne*). Bath: Sims-Williams 1975; Cunliffe 1984: 347–53; Davenport 2002. Taunton: archaeological evidence for the minster cemetery, with one ninth-century radiocarbon date (Leach 1984: 11, 26–31); below, pp. 446–8, for later mother-church status. Exeter: above, p. 151 n.; Henderson and Bidwell 1982. Axminster: royal burial in 757 (*ASC* s.a. 757 (pp. 48–9)), writ of Edward the Confessor (S 1161). Braunton: recorded as *Brannocminster* in 839 × 55 (S 1695); Ælfgar the priest and the priests of Braunton in Domesday Book (DB Exon. 66, 194ᵛ). Two Somerset minsters without early references, Yeovil and Milborne Port, occur *c*.950 in the will of Wynflæd (S 1539; *Wills*, 10–14).

is just about good enough to show that the community had a continuous existence, and identity as a landholding corporation, between the mid ninth century and the revival of royal patronage under Eadmund.[54] King Alfred and his heirs took an interest, though a somewhat predatory one, in the prosperous minsters of this region. Alfred's will refers to some kind of agreement between the Cheddar community and the royal family—a relationship that would prove much to the community's detriment—and indicates (by restoring them) that the Damerham community had been deprived of its charters.[55] On his favourite Asser—a shameless pluralist by later standards—he bestowed Banwell, Congresbury, and Exeter minsters; Edward the Elder may have added Plympton.[56] Asser could have been thinking of the south-west, which he knew so well and where he may have felt in need of some self-justification, when he observed that 'quite a number of minsters (*perplurima monasteria*) which had been built in that area still remain but do not maintain the rule of monastic life in any consistent way'.[57]

There are also grounds for envisaging an early parochial geography which was subdivided and modified, but not obscured. In her study of Dorset, Teresa Hall has found a significant difference between the boundaries of mother-parishes controlled by known early minsters, which tend to follow major natural features, and the more complex, artificial boundaries of lesser parishes.[58] In Dorset, Somerset, and east Devon, mother-parishes and hundreds often but by no means always coincide, and the relationship looks less artificially symmetrical than in Hampshire.[59] Various conclusions might be drawn, but it seems possible that the major mother-parishes preserve a reflection of early territorial organization before the imposition of hundreds.[60]

[54] Abrams 1996: 7, 337–45.

[55] S 1507; below, pp. 326–7. Many of Alfred's bequests to his younger son were at west-country sites known to have had minsters then or later (below, pp. 325–6).

[56] Below, pp. 324–5; S 380 (a dubious charter). Cf. Oakes and Costen 2003 for the continued importance of Congresbury.

[57] Below, p. 347.   [58] Hall 2000: 31–40.

[59] Somerset: Aston 1986, fig. 7.4 compared with fig. 7.5. Dorset: Hall 2000: 41–8. Devon: Orme 1991: 9, 13 (illustrating the examples of Tiverton, Hartland, Plympton, and Crediton); Probert 2002: 60–240, a detailed reconstruction of tenth- to twelfth-century mother-parishes around Exeter concluding (pp. 238–40) that they represent pre-hundredal units of some kind. Cf. Page 1914–15: 68–72. Studies of individual mother-parishes which correlate with hundreds are Dunning 1976 (Crewkerne) and Leach 1984: 29–30 (Taunton). Of the three counties, hundredal correlation seems weakest in Dorset and strongest in parts of Devon, though there the pattern breaks down to the west. The iconoclastic analysis of Reichel 1939, which starts from the assumption that connections between hundreds and parishes are inherently implausible, modifies some of Page's conclusions; but it remains true that there were several one-minster hundreds in north and east Devon.

[60] Hall 2000: 44–7, prefers to envisage in Dorset an early tenth-century correlation of mother-parishes and hundreds, after which the latter were progressively modified. In either case there is a definite contrast with Hampshire, and probably with Wiltshire and Berkshire.

Many mother-churches, by no means all of which need be of pre-Viking origin, are visible after the Conquest, and adjustments to accommodate new ones can sometimes be suspected; but the tenth-century contribution was evidently to fill gaps in an old system rather than to build a new one.[61]

The lands west of Dartmoor are a case apart: the last zone of English colonization, they were only exposed directly to English ecclesiastical culture for a few decades before the Viking age began.[62] The impact of Scandinavian raiding was sharp but short. Change came when West Saxon kings and their clients took control of the major religious sites, as Asser did of 'Exeter with all the *parochia* pertaining to it in Saxon territory and in Cornwall'.[63] Sources pre-dating these developments convey a different impression from later ones. The early hagiographies, and the Vatican list of Cornish parochial saints written *c.*900, indicate a landscape thick with small religious sites focused on local saints' cults, in some areas of a density more comparable with later English parish churches than with minsters.[64] In Domesday Book and other tenth- to twelfth-century texts, by contrast, a handful of clerical minsters stand out with unusual clarity, notably Bodmin, Padstow, St Buryan, St Germans, Launceston, Hartland, and Plympton, and the smaller communities of priests at Constantine, Crantock, Probus, St Keverne, St Neot, and St Piran.[65]

In fact there seems—much more than in zones of older English settlement—to have been a basic remodelling of the ecclesiastical landscape. Some pre-English religious sites would have been larger and more important than others, but there is no clear correlation between these and the major centres of the tenth century onwards. Of the *monasteria* mentioned in early texts,[66] only St Kew (*Landochou*) can also be recognized as a significant site in the tenth and eleventh centuries. Others could of course have escaped record, but the lack of written, sculptural, or topographical evidence for a distinct category of pre-eminent sites across the seventh to eleventh centuries is striking.[67] Nor, except very occasionally, are minster-based territorial structures visible. There is no tidy correlation of minsters with hundreds or even with the larger parishes; documented links between mother- and daughter-churches are rare; and numerous small parishes contain their own indigenous

[61] Reorganization is especially likely around Wareham: Hinton and Webster 1987: 51–3; Hall 2000: 34–5. In Dorset, Hall 2000: 79, proposes a progressive filling-in of blank areas.
[62] Cf. Todd 1987: 270–5.
[63] Below, pp. 324–5; cf. Todd 1987: 275–89.
[64] Above, p. 21; Olson and Padel 1986.
[65] DB Exon. 86, 199ᵛ–200, 202–7, 456–456ᵛ; Olson 1989: 86–97, for the Cornish sites; Orme 1991: 7–12.
[66] Above, p. 19.   [67] Here I differ from Olson 1989: 95–6.

saint-cults.[68] Where mother-parishes do exist they look artificial, and less centralized than in England. St Buryan's included Sennen and St Levan, the sites of their eponymous saint-cults; Hartland's contained cult foci of St Wenn and St Heligan as well as its own St Nectan; and St Kew parish boundary bisected a long-cist cemetery beside St Endellion church.[69]

It seems most likely that the minsters of Cornwall and west Devon did develop out of typical early British religious sites, housing small communities centred on their own saints' relics, but only rose above the normal run of such places after 800, and mainly under English influence. At Bodmin and Padstow (*Dinuurrin* and *Languihenoc*), the hagiographical sources suggest a takeover by the community of St Petroc, perhaps in the early to mid ninth century, which displaced the local cults of St Uuron and St Wethinoc.[70] St Germans, identified by its earlier name (*Lanalet*) as another British cult site and probably represented by 'Gernun' in the Vatican list, was an important community and bishop's seat from the early tenth century.[71] Hartland (*Nectanstoc*) in north-west Devon was a major English minster by the eleventh century, but was centred on the cult of a local hermit, Nectan.[72]

Most suggestively, there is evidence that several of the prominent eleventh-century sites—St Buryan, St Germans, St Kew, and perhaps Padstow and Bodmin—received lands and privileges from Æthelstan and other tenth-century kings.[73] The effect of such patronage would have been to build up certain favoured churches, selected from the multitude of small ones spread across the Cornish landscape, to the point that in Domesday Book and later sources they look like English minsters. Mother-parishes were assembled around some of them, though the density of existing religious settlement may often have made this difficult or unnecessary. It is interesting to find a Cornish nobleman, Maenchi *comes*, giving land to St Hyldren's of Lansallos in a charter issued 'in the land of the Saxons in the island of Athelney in the reign of King Æthelstan'.[74] Here is one instance of the kind of endowment by nobles (whether native or immigrant), under the royal aegis, which could have helped some establishments to rise above the majority. This Anglo-Cornish culture of patronage is also represented by the series of late ninth-

---

[68] Orme 1991: 9–10. For medieval parishes see N. Orme's maps in R. Kain and W. Ravenhill (eds.), *Historical Atlas of South-West England* (Exeter, 1999), 212–15; the most convincing mother-parishes in Cornwall are Perranzabuloe, St Neot, St Keverne, and St Buryan.

[69] Pearce 1985: 268–9; Trudgian 1987; Picken 1973–7, and below, p. 522, for St Kew's parochial rights.

[70] Olson 1989: 66–78; Dark 1994*b*: 233; Jankulak 2000: 41–71. The young Alfred's devotions at the church housing the relics of SS *Gueriir* and Neot illustrate elite West Saxon interest in this kind of place: *Asser*, c. 74 (p. 55; trans. p. 89).

[71] Olson 1989: 60–6.   [72] *Nectan*.

[73] S 450, S 810; Olson 1989: 63–5, 72, 78–84; cf. above, pp. 223–4, for Æthelstan and the sanctuary zones.

[74] S 1207; Padel 1978–9.

to tenth-century crosses, carved in relief in an English-influenced style, which centre on the more prominent monastic sites such as Bodmin and St Buryan.[75] A minster system along lines long familiar to the English, using but transforming the region's ancient ecclesiastical sub-structure, was a natural product of Cornwall's assimilation into Wessex.

In southern England as a whole, the effects of Viking-age disruption lessen steadily from east to west, and in all the counties (except Cornwall with its different basic system) a substantial number of minsters can be seen surviving across the Viking age. More significant—in a zone equivalent to the kingdom of Wessex after 825—was royal and aristocratic intervention, which modified and extended the old pattern but did not efface it.

(ii) *The west midlands.* The old territories of the Hwicce and Magonsæte—Gloucestershire, Worcestershire, Warwickshire, Herefordshire, and Shropshire—remained an abnormally stable region, neither overrun by the Vikings nor subjected to undue pressure from the West Saxon court. Worcester has a greater claim than any other English centre to preserving some liturgical and intellectual continuity across the ninth and tenth centuries.[76] After the 870s, Worcester and Gloucester became the centres of a revived Mercia which preserved its identity under the semi-autonomous rule of Æthelred and Æthelflæd, who in the next decades extended their grip over more peripheral and disrupted areas such as Staffordshire and Cheshire.

The unusually rich sources for the core region show both continuity and innovation. Many minster communities survived without interruption, and charters show the lord and lady in a generous and constructive light: freeing the Berkeley community from their remaining obligations to the king's *feorm* (883); confirming land and transferring manpower to Worcester's minster of Pyrton (Oxon.) (887); restoring land to keep the Much Wenlock community in food and giving them a gold chalice in St Midburh's honour (901).[77] In *c.*903 they negotiated a settlement over an ex-monastic estate at Old Sodbury (Glos.) which the bishops of Worcester had been trying to recover since the 840s: as Bishop Wærferth put it with apparent feeling, 'we could never get anywhere until Æthelred became lord of the Mercians'.[78]

---

[75] Thomas 1978; Preston-Jones and Rose 1986: 159; Todd 1987: 294–300. Note the especially fine cross at St Neot, and the pair at Sancreed which, like the Lansallos charter, may indicate an incipiently important site that failed to develop later. 'Runhol', the craftsman who signed crosses at Sancreed and St Gwinear, and 'Ægured', who gave an altar-slab at Treslothan, had English names.

[76] Dumville 1992*b*: 99–101.

[77] S 218 (though this is in return for land and money, and bears some resemblances to the 'exploitative' early ninth-century Mercian charters); S 217; S 221 (in exchange for a smaller land-holding). Cf. S 1442, which shows that early ninth-century provisions for the leasing of a Winchcombe estate were still in force in the 890s.

[78] S 1446.

Thanks to the Worcester archive, monastic geography is more thoroughly documented in north-east Gloucestershire and south Worcestershire than in any other part of England.[79] The charters reveal an almost perfect correlation between minsters recorded before 800 and mother-churches recorded after 1100 (Fig. 19). At Deerhurst, complex enlargements and embellishments of the church through the ninth to eleventh centuries can be traced in the standing fabric.[80] There is explicit evidence that Bishops Cleeve and Bibury enjoyed the rights of parochial mother-churches by the 890s.[81] Here it is hard even for the most sceptical to deny that in Alfred's time a group of early minsters survived intact, and were the basis of a parochial geography which persisted thereafter.

Did minsters fare notably worse outside the pool of light cast by the Worcester archive? There is no obvious reason why this should be so. Eastwards and southwards, several of the most prominent mother-churches can be recognized as pre-Viking minsters, for example Wootton Wawen, Berkeley, and the cluster in west Oxfordshire comprising Charlbury, Minster Lovell, Bampton, Eynsham, and Oxford.[82] Excavation has revealed sequential rebuildings within the precinct at Eynsham between the eighth century and 1005, and obscure cults survived at Oxford, Bampton, and Coln St Aldwyn.[83] Northwards, Leominster and Much Wenlock preserved both their early saints' cults and their huge mother-parishes.[84] Although pre-900 references become rarer the further we move from Worcester, substantial parts of all these regions can be reconstituted into mother-parishes. This in itself suggests that the problem is more one of archival loss than of institutional disruption: it may be largely because the Worcester charters have survived, whereas those of Hereford, Lichfield, and Dorchester-on-Thames have not, that Worcestershire and Gloucestershire demonstrate such strong continuity.

Again there was development as well as survival. A peculiarity of western Mercian towns—Gloucester, Hereford, Shrewsbury, Chester, Oxford—is that by the eleventh century they contained dual or even multiple minsters. It is certain at Gloucester, and likely at some of the others, that the second minster was founded around 900 by Æthelflæd, as part of a drive to restore

---

[79] Blair 1995*a*: 199–200; Bassett 1998 (which makes more thorough use of the later parochial evidence); cf. Bassett 1996.

[80] Rahtz and Watts 1997. The precise dates of the individual phases are open to dispute, but their number and extent make it implausible that the church suffered any significant period of neglect.

[81] Above, pp. 158–60.

[82] S 94 and Bassett 1989*b*: 18–19; S 1433 and Kemp 1968; Blair 1994: 69–70, 111–16.

[83] Hardy and others 2003: 46–69, 472–87; Blair 2002*a*: 536, 517, 509.

[84] Blair 2002*a*: 507, 527, 537, 544–5; Hillaby 1987; Kemp 1988; Croom 1988. Cf. Hillaby 2001: 59–70, for Ledbury, Bromyard, etc.

the prestige and efficacy of the Mercian Church.[85] Outside the boroughs, there were probably some post-Viking foundations for which new mother-parishes were carved out of old ones (Tewkesbury from Deerhurst is a strong possibility), as well as adjustments in mother-parish boundaries in response to late Anglo-Saxon tenurial changes.[86] But there are no persuasive signs that parishes were re-formed from scratch. Across the west midlands there is a significant, but variable and by no means exact, correlation between mother-parishes and hundreds, and in Worcester diocese Steven Bassett may well be right to read the mother-parishes as fossils of early secular territories which were manipulated into the Domesday hundreds during the tenth and eleventh centuries.[87] The pattern is markedly less clear and symmetrical than in the regions to the north, which Æthelflæd and her successors would annexe from Scandinavian rule and may have had to re-plan comprehensively.

The west midlands saw steady development rather than hiatus, and in the eleventh century the pre-Viking minsters still dominated its religious landscape. Thanks partly to this late resilience, partly to the exceptional early sources, the case can be made more strongly here than anywhere else. Whether or not the region was typical is open to debate, but at the very least it proves that continuity was possible, a clean slate not inevitable.

(iii) *The north midlands and the north-west.* The mainly Norse-settled zone of Staffordshire, Cheshire, Lancashire, and Cumbria is virtually undocumented territory, but there are compensations. Where texts fade out, stone sculpture becomes more common. It is also in the sparsely settled terrain of the north-west that a mother-parish system survived essentially intact until the nineteenth century, with huge parishes containing multiple townships dependent on the central church and its graveyard. The late Anglo-Saxon parochial structure is thus remarkably visible, and can be interpreted in the light of the occasional written references and, more importantly, of a considerable body of sculpture from both before and after the Viking invasions.

[85] Hare 1993 and Heighway and Bryant 1999 for the Gloucester minster, to which Æthelflæd moved St Oswald's relics from Bardney. For the others: Barrow 1992: 80–8; Thacker 1982 (Chester and Gloucester); Pearn 1988 and Bassett 1991 (Shrewsbury); Blair 1994: 112–13 (Oxford). See also *Encyc.* for all these places. In the cases of Hereford (Shoesmith 1980, Pearn 1988) and Shrewsbury (Bassett 1991) it seems likely that two minsters already existed before the time of Æthelflæd. A Hereford agreement of 1043 × 6 (S 1469) is witnessed by 'the two communities at St Æthelberht's minster and St Guthlac's'.

[86] Bassett 1998: 10–19, 6–7; above, p. 160.

[87] Bassett 1996: 157–72; cf. Page 1914–15: 93, and Croom 1988: 69–71, for negative conclusions regarding hundredal correlation in parts of the region. Oddly enough, in about 1130 Pershore was called the 'mother-church of the hundred', apparently the only known explicit use of the term: Kemp 1967–8: 19.

This is least true of Staffordshire, where the minsters remain very obscure. Lichfield at least survived, as an episcopal seat which in due course generated a town.[88] Eccleshall, with its British ecclesiastical place-name and huge mother-parish, looks like a striking case of continuity.[89] Hanbury, the early site of St Wærburh's cult, lost her relics but remained the mother-church of a large parish.[90] By 1066, Staffordshire would be notable for its group of wealthy clerical minsters, later to have the peculiar legal status of 'royal free chapels': Gnoshall, Penkridge, Stafford, Tamworth, Tettenhall, Wolverhampton.[91] Their origins are uncertain, but some of them appear among the Herefordshire, Shropshire, and Staffordshire minsters in the will of Wulfgeat of Donington (*c.*1000).[92]

Cheshire and Lancashire show an exceptionally strong correlation between mother-parishes and hundreds, each hundred usually comprising two or three interlocking parishes.[93] It may be that post-Viking reorganization, perhaps begun by Æthelflæd and developed through the tenth century, created this exceptional symmetry. Some of the mother-churches are certainly older, notably Sandbach and Lancaster, which have major groups of eighth- to ninth-century crosses and emerge in late sources as the heads of large mother-parishes.[94] There is strong though circumstantial evidence that the mother-churches of West Kirby and St John's Chester were also early minsters,[95] and the same could be true of other complex centres of huge parishes, notably Prestbury with what may have been the largest mother-parish in England. But we can probably see the hand of Æthelflæd in the foundation of Chester's second minster, which acquired the relics of St Wærburh, and in the dedications to St 'Bertelin' (Beorhthelm) and St Oswald at Runcorn

---

[88] *Encyc.* 286–7.   [89] Spufford and Spufford 1964: 5–25.

[90] Thacker 1985: 4; Blair 2002*a*: 557. The other saints' cults in Staffordshire, at Ilam, Stafford, and Stone, are late-recorded: Blair 2002*a*: 515–16, 561.

[91] Styles 1936; Styles 1954; Denton 1970. The lavish, probably ninth-century carved cross-shaft at Wolverhampton (Wilson 1984: 105–6) points to a high-status church. At Stafford, crop-processing was occurring next to the church in the mid ninth century, well before Æthelflaed fortified the site in 913: Moffett 1994.

[92] S 1534 (*Wills*, 54–6; Blair 1988*b*: 5): bequests to St Æthelberht's and St Guthlac's at Hereford and to Leominster, Bromyard, Clifton-on-Teme, Wolverhampton, Penkridge, Tong, and Donington.

[93] Cheshire: Higham 1993: 126–81 (with synthesis p. 176); *VCH Cheshire*, i. 268–73. Lancashire: detailed data in *VCH Lancs.*, indicating the following interlocking groups: Blackburn, Whalley; Leyland, Croston; Eccles, Manchester, Prestwich; Lancaster, Halton, Heysham, Melling; Preston, Kirkham, St Michael's; Warrington, Winwick, Wigan, Prescot.

[94] Sandbach: Hawkes 2002; *VCH Cheshire*, i. 276–7; note the implication of the name Astbury ('the east *burh*'), to the east of Sandbach and with an interlocking parish. Lancaster and its satellite sites: above, p. 216.

[95] West Kirby (a *kirkjubý* name): *VCH Cheshire*, i. 256, 269. Chester: Thacker 1982; Higham 1993. See also Griffiths 2001: 183–4, for Farndon as a possible minster.

and Winwick.[96] In both shires, Viking-age sculpture tends to concentrate, though by no means exclusively, at the mother-churches; one workshop, probably associated with St John's at Chester, made a distinctive group of crosses.[97] The impression is of older ecclesiastical structures re-worked after the 870s, and of an economic context which allowed them to survive.

Westmorland and Cumberland were never organized in hundreds, but the large parishes bear some relationship to the estates and territorial divisions thought to underlie the Norman baronies.[98] In the 880s the region was stable enough for St Cuthbert's community to settle there, and Carlisle and Heversham still had abbots; power only passed to Norse rulers after *c.*910.[99] The fate of minsters in this region may be exemplified by the excavations at Whithorn, a major (and exposed) religious centre on its north-western periphery: after a probable Viking sack in the 840s it not merely survived but flourished in its new Hiberno-Norse milieu, becoming both a centre for stone cross production and an incipient town.[100] All three Cumbrian minsters known from early sources had some kind of afterlife. Carlisle's cemetery continued to receive high-status burials through the ninth and tenth centuries;[101] Dacre, mentioned by Bede, preserves both a fine Anglian cross and an iconographically elaborate post-Viking one;[102] and Heversham remained the mother-church of three chapelries.

For undocumented sites we have sculpture and parochial evidence, as well as the distinctive Scandinavian place-name *kirkjubý* (Kirkby or Kirby, literally 'church-settlement').[103] A high proportion of the twelve Kirkbys in Lancashire, Cheshire, and Cumbria were important churches, with early sculpture or mother-parishes, and it looks as though the term was a standard Norse one for an established minster centre.[104] St Bees (*Cherchebi c.*1125),

---

[96] Thacker 1982; Thacker 1985; Pearn 1988; Higham 1993: 111, 128–30; *VCH Cheshire*, i. 253; Freke and others 1987: 34–5; Thacker 1995: 121–3. In a charter of 958 (S 667), a rare survival of a royal grant to a minster in northern Mercia, Eadgar gave seventeen hides to the community of St Wærburh at Chester.

[97] Cheshire: *VCH Cheshire*, i. 277–81; Bailey 1996b: 30–1. Lancashire: Eccles, Halton, Melling, Walton-on-the-Hill, Whalley, Winwick (Edwards 1978: 58–60, 67–9, 72–6; Bailey 1980a: 81, 102, 157–61, 181–2, 231–2).

[98] Barrow 1975; Winchester 1985: 90–3; Winchester 1987: 22–7.

[99] Bailey and Cramp 1988: 5; *Symeon Op.* i. 203, 208.

[100] Hill 1997: 48–55.

[101] McCarthy 1996: 36–8: excavations under the cathedral found a burial with a radiocarbon date of cal. AD 680–820, and three phases of graves associated with both Anglian and tenth- to eleventh-century artefacts.

[102] *HE* iv. 32 (pp. 446–8); Bailey and Cramp 1988: 90–3. The configuration of parish boundaries suggests that the huge mother-parish of Greystoke may once have belonged to Dacre.

[103] Fellows-Jensen 1985: 34; Fellows-Jensen 1987: 299.

[104] This conclusion is modified, but probably not overthrown, by the current work of Thomas Pickles suggesting that some of the 'Kirkbys' in Yorkshire were *satellite* settlements to minsters rather than actual minster sites.

Kirkby Lonsdale, Kirkby Kendal, and Kirkby Stephen have huge mother-parishes, and the last retains both eighth- and tenth-century crosses.[105] In the north-west as a whole, 63 per cent of sites with pre-Viking sculpture also have post-Viking sculpture,[106] and some though not all sites with early pieces controlled large parishes.[107]

The types of evidence for this region are miscellaneous, and less robust than those previously examined, but they suggest broadly similar conclusions. While it would go too far to argue for full institutional continuity, total abandonment and dislocation are implausible. After 900 the region strengthened its westwards orientation, towards the Norse culture of the Irish Sea,[108] but the milieu was one in which the old Northumbrian religious sites could survive and succeed.

(iv) *The Northumbrian heartlands.* To cross the Pennines is to move from a backwater of pre-Viking religious culture to its heart. The catastrophic end of Northumbria's intellectual and artistic golden age has so dominated scholars' thinking that they have seen it as total. But if the fall was from a greater height, it was not necessarily to a lower depth: Lindisfarne or Jarrow in 950 should be compared with minsters elsewhere at the same date, not with what they had been. Admittedly the shadow of the past created a stronger impetus to revival than in other regions, and the foundation of Benedictine cells at Lindisfarne, Monkwearmouth, Jarrow, Whitby, and Lastingham after the Norman Conquest was consciously retrospective and reverential.[109] This dictates caution in the case of any site mentioned by Bede, which could potentially have been revived after a hiatus of centuries. Such *pietas* can hardly,

---

[105] Bailey and Cramp 1988: 120–5.

[106] Fellows-Jensen 1985: 402–3, 408: 'the evidence of the sculpture shows continuing cultural well-being in the Viking-period for most of the areas where Anglian-period sculpture is found.' There are local variations, notably the absence of late sculpture from the lower Kent valley (Bailey 1985: 57; Bailey and Cramp 1988: 27–8), but the apparent long-term stability of Carlisle, Kendal, and Heversham should warn against using this negative evidence as evidence of discontinuity.

[107] Bailey and Cramp 1988: *passim*. Brigham and Bewcastle have large parishes, but Addingham, Beckermet, Irton, Lowther, Penrith, and Workington do not. The thick concentration of apparently early church sites along the Cumbrian coastal strip probably owes something to British survival or to Irish influence.

[108] Bailey 1985: 58–9; Bailey 1996*b*: 31–2. However, Bailey's suggestion that cross-Pennine contacts became unimportant is at variance with some economic evidence, for example in links between York and Dublin (current work by Fiona Edmonds, pers. comm.).

[109] *Symeon Lib.* 200–10, 234–6; Piper 1986; Burton 1994. The narratives include the topoi, familiar from late tenth-century monastic sources, of re-colonizers finding ruinous, abandoned churches. There are several reasons, some of them very recent, why churches along the Northumbrian coast could have been ruinous in the 1080s, but the evidence set out below is against long periods of abandonment. The minster at Jarrow still housed the relics of Bede in the 1030s or 1040s (*Symeon Lib.* 164–6).

however, explain tenth-century sculpture, and is unlikely to have extended to re-establishing churches as the heads of large parishes when they were no longer important or convenient. Here as elsewhere, physical and parochial evidence supplements the scattered fragments of tradition.[110]

A good starting-point is the community of St Cuthbert, always a spotlight on the ecclesiastical fortunes of the north. Its migrations with its patron's corpse during 875–83, from Lindisfarne to Norham, Cumbria, Crayke, and eventually Chester-le-Street, are too famous to need repeating here. This was no band of ragged exiles clinging desperately to their precious burden, but rather a prosperous religious corporation responding to political change by making a series of planned moves between estates which they already owned.[111] During 883–95 the bishop and community were settled peacefully and prosperously at Chester-le-Street, basking in the favour of West Saxon kings.[112] If the northern Church was now dependent on political and economic support from the south, this community at least had adjusted to new realities. A further point is worth making. Even though Cuthbert's relics moved on from Lindisfarne and in turn from Norham, prestigious sculpture-marked burial continued in both places: they must have retained groups of priests, presumably affiliated in some way to the main community.

Of the many sites in the region with pre- or post-Viking sculpture, only a minority have both, but these include several of the major early minsters. Lindisfarne and Hexham, those ancient rivals, stand out for their big collections of crosses, grave-markers, and slabs covering the whole chronological range through the ninth to eleventh centuries.[113] There can have been no time in the Christian Anglo-Saxon period when these were not important burial places, and other evidence—the surviving paired churches at Lindisfarne, the saints' cults maintained at Hexham, and the priests recorded there from c.1000—reinforces the impression that they had an unbroken or almost unbroken existence.[114] Auckland St Andrew, Billingham, Hart, Jarrow, and Monkwearmouth have at least one post-Viking grave monument each, and all but the first retain parts of their pre-Viking churches to eaves level.[115] Virtually all sites with early sculpture were functioning churches in the later middle ages.

[110] Sawyer 1978 provides a useful summary of written evidence for the ecclesiastical fortunes of the north-east during the ninth and tenth centuries.

[111] *Symeon Op.* i. 234–7; *Symeon Lib.* 86–126; Hall 1984: 72–93; Rollason 1987.

[112] *Symeon Op.* i. 207–13; Bonner 1989; below, p. 348.

[113] Cramp 1984: 194–208, 174–83.

[114] Blair 1991*b*; Raine 1863–4, i. 34–40, 49, 208–10; Blair 1995*a*: 200–1; below, p. 361.

[115] Cramp 1984: 41, 48–53, 93–7, 108–9, 123; Taylor and Taylor 1965–78, i. 66–70, 287–9, 338–49, 432–46. Cf. Cambridge 1984: 66–71. In the absence of the final report, it would be premature to comment here on the excavated post-850 phases at Jarrow and Monkwearmouth; Rosemary Cramp informs me that there is evidence for dereliction of the main buildings, but also for continued use of the sites for burial.

The late parochial evidence highlights some of the same places. Lindisfarne and Hexham again stand out with their huge, multi-chapelry parishes;[116] the parishes of Jarrow, Tynemouth, Rothbury, Auckland St Andrew, and Bywell were smaller, but still above average size.[117] This is not to say that all late mother-parishes had pre-Viking monastic centres. Norham and Chester-le-Street, where in both cases the extant sculpture begins in the mid to late ninth century and continues through the tenth,[118] could have acquired status with the migrations of the Cuthbert community. A dozen or so other mother-churches, some with tenth- to eleventh-century sculpture, are of unknown origin and may have been new foundations of that period.[119] Clearly there is likely to have been some post-Viking reconstruction, which may have included the extension of ecclesiastical structures into the western, Pennine parts of the region, but the most straightforward interpretation of the evidence is that this happened within an established framework.

In Yorkshire, despite forty years of Danish rule and a virtual lack of charters, evidence for continuity or revival is remarkably frequent. As generally in the north and the east midlands, ecclesiastical asset-stripping from the late ninth century onwards reduced a once-plutocratic Church to near poverty, though the practice of holding the sees of York and Worcester in plurality from 971 was probably an instrument of southern control rather than evidence that York was incapable of supporting an archbishop.[120] The Vikings sacked York in 866 and, in the view of a later chronicler, 'destroyed minsters and churches far and wide with sword and fire', but their king Guthfrith was buried in 895 'in the city of York in the high church (*in basilica summa*)'; Æthelstan gave Amounderness to the cathedral community in 934.[121] It is

---

[116] Lindisfarne: chapelries of Ancroft, Kyloe, Lowick, and Tweedmouth (Durham Cathedral Muniments, 3.1.Spec.67a, 3.1.Spec.72, 4.1.Spec.52, and cf. Fig. 54; *Feodarium*, 220–30, 302–5; Jones 1992: 79–81, for the secular territory of 'Islandshire'); Hexham: chapels of Allendale, Bringfield, St John Lee and St Oswald Lee (Raine 1863–4, ii. 121–4; Bateson and others 1893–1940, iv (1897); Wrench 2003: 137–55).

[117] Jarrow: chapelries of Heworth, Wallsend, and Willington (Durham Cathedral Muniments 2.4.Spec.23; *Feodarium*, 104–15, 208, 329; Piper 1986); Tynemouth: chapelry of Earsdon (Bateson and others 1893–1940, viii–ix (1907–9)); Bywell: Bateson and others 1893–1940, vi (1902).

[118] Cramp 1984: 208–14, 53–9.

[119] Cambridge 1984: 78–82, for examples in co. Durham and various possible explanations for the existence or non-existence of early fabric and sculpture; cf. Cambridge and Rollason 1995: 96. The distinction between 'monasteries' and 'secular minsters' is in my view invalid, but I agree that the parochial structure of the region is likely to reflect a range of variables, both functional and chronological.

[120] Fleming 1985: 250, with substantial agreement by Dumville 1992*a*: 37, for the view that more monastic land was alienated in the north and east midlands than in Wessex, East Anglia, or the west midlands; cf. Bailey 1996*a*: 78–9. Barrow 1994: 27–8, for the sees held in plurality.

[121] Rollason and others 1998: 64, 71–3, 173; the Æthelstan charter (S 407) is corrupt but probably has an authentic basis.

evident, not least from the forty-eight excavated pieces of funerary sculpture of all periods between the late seventh century and the eleventh,[122] that the cathedral remained a religious centre throughout.

Survival of community and cult is also likely at two of the greatest minsters, St Wilfrid's at Ripon and St John's at Beverley. On both sites, excavation tells the usual story of a rich monastic culture petering out around 850, but also demonstrates continuing activity—funerary at Ripon, domestic and industrial at Beverley—through the tenth and eleventh centuries.[123] There is hard evidence that St John's cult was active at Beverley in the mid to late ninth century.[124] Æthelstan's visit to the two communities is a legend, but Ripon at least was functioning in 948, when King Eadred burnt the minster and Archbishop Oda stole Wilfrid's relics.[125] Both minsters were still important at the Conquest, when Archbishop Ealdred was promoting Beverley and its cult.[126] Two other important sites, Whitby and its dependency at Hackness, suffered dire impoverishment but apparently retained their early church groups and some memory of their cults and communities.[127]

In and around Yorkshire, at least 60 per cent of sites with pre-Viking sculpture also have sculpture of the ninth to eleventh centuries.[128] Coherent local patterns sometimes start to emerge, as in Ryedale and the vale of Pickering,

---

[122] Lang 1991: 53–78.

[123] Hall and Whyman 1996; Armstrong and others 1991. At Ripon the excavated monastic cemetery, with iron-bound coffins, ceases around 850, but burials (some with combs) in a subsidiary chapel seem to continue to the eleventh century; there are two Anglo-Scandinavian cross-heads, one showing the Sigurd story (Bailey 1980*a*: 120–1). At Beverley, the excavation on the boundary ditch found a coin-hoard of *c*.851, followed by tenth- to eleventh-century timber buildings, glass-working, and industrial debris; note the comment in R. A. Hall's review (*Yorkshire Archaeological Journal*, 65 (1993), 182–3) that 'the evidence for Viking raids is nil' and that there is no definite evidence for destruction in this part of the precinct.

[124] Blair 2001*b*.

[125] Above, pp. 223–4, for Æthelstan and the sanctuary zones; Brooks 1984: 227–30; Wrench 2003: 80–114.

[126] DB i. 303ᵛ, 304. For Beverley see: Morris and Cambridge 1989; Love 1996: pp. xliv–xlv; Palliser 1996: 209–14.

[127] At Whitby, Peers found little evidence that the excavated area was occupied after the ninth century (Rahtz 1976). However, the dual churches of St Peter and St Mary which existed *c*.1100 look like a survival of early monastic topography, and the second of the two names recorded in 1072, *Witebi* and *Prestebi* (Cramp 1976: 223), shows that the hilltop site was known in the Anglo-Scandinavian period as the 'priests' settlement'. Hild's relics survived at Whitby until they were supposedly taken to Glastonbury in the 940s (Blair 2002*a*: 538). Hackness also retained dual churches of St Peter and St Mary, and the cult of Æthelburh was remembered (above, pp. 145–7). The main texts for both sites during and after the Norman re-colonization are in J. C. Atkinson (ed.), *Cartularium Abbathiae de Whiteby*, i–ii (Surtees Soc. lxix and lxxii, 1879); see also Wrench 2003: 115–36.

[128] Bailey 1980*a*: 80; Lang 1991. In addition to the sites discussed here, Otley and Dewsbury stand out for their notable collections of both pre-Viking and post-Viking sculpture. Stocker 2000: 198 observes that the later material does not noticeably concentrate at the minsters, but he surely goes much too far in claiming that 'the pattern of Deiran sculpture suggests that the new Hiberno-Norse ecclesiastical regime largely ignored the former centres of Deiran monasticism'.

where the known minsters of Lastingham, Kirkdale, and Stonegrave, and the undocumented churches at Kirkbymoorside, Hovingham, and Middleton, all have assemblages of both pre-Viking and post-Viking sculpture.[129] Whatever the original status of these sites[130] it is clear that they were the enduring focal points of a religious landscape, into which the mother-church of Pickering, and Sinnington parish church with its large collection of tenth-century crosses, may have been post-Viking insertions.[131] This area may be representative of Yorkshire as a whole: Dawn Hadley shows that the most prominent mother-churches after 1100 included many of the major early sites, such as Ripon, Beverley, Otley, Gilling, Whitby, and Dewsbury, as well as others of unknown origins.[132]

This story is becoming familiar. The experience of most of the communities must have been more or less traumatic during *c.*870–930; few can have preserved more than exiguous liturgical life, and some may have been temporarily abandoned. But enough remained for the basic fabric of ecclesiastical centres and cult sites to emerge in recognizable form, if modified and extended, in an era of reconstruction.

(v) *The east midlands and East Anglia.* The north-east midlands, comprising Derbyshire, Nottinghamshire, Leicestershire, and Lincolnshire, are a poorly documented Danelaw region, and one which provides a good deal less pre-Viking literary and sculptural evidence than Northumbria.[133] This need not necessarily mean that it was more disrupted: the archaeological narrative of attack, pagan adoption, and Christian revival at Repton illustrates how minsters in the region could have weathered the Vikings. Another good case is Bakewell (Derbs.), a minster (*coenubium*) which King Eadred gave with its lands to Uhtred *dux* in 949: it retains fragments of rich late eighth- and ninth-century crosses and sarcophagi, as well as an astonishing accumulation of tenth- and eleventh-century funerary sculpture (Fig. 53).[134] There is good evidence for continuing cults at Repton (St Wigstan), Derby

---

[129] Lastingham is mentioned by Bede, Stonegrave in a papal letter of 757–8, and Kirkdale in an eleventh-century inscription (above, pp. 191, 131; below, pp. 358–9). Lang 1991: 144–8, 154–74, 181–7, 215–20 for the sculpture in all these churches; Rahtz and Watts 2003 for continuity at Kirkdale. Jones 1992: 81–4 discusses the secular estates centred on Hovingham and Kirkbymoorside.

[130] Above, pp. 215–16.

[131] Lang 1991: 199–201, 207–13. For the later status of Pickering church see W. Farrer, *Early Yorkshire Charters*, i (Edinburgh, 1914), 311, 333–6.

[132] Hadley 2000*a*: 216–97; cf. Palliser 1996; work by Thomas Pickles in progress.

[133] Hadley 2000*a*: 216–97.

[134] S 548; below, p. 469. The minster is not mentioned explicitly in the body of the charter, but an addendum (perhaps an endorsement on the original) describes the property granted as a *coenubium*.

(St Alchmund), Louth (St Herefrith), and Hibaldstow (St Hygebald); St Oswald's relics survived at Bardney until they were removed to Gloucester in 909.[135] The excavated site at Flixborough displays the usual decline in material culture after 850, but also a continuity in building-plots and alignments through the eighth to eleventh centuries which in a normal domestic context would be highly exceptional.[136] Dawn Hadley's analysis of evidence for mother-parishes in Derbyshire and Nottinghamshire suggests that some of them, most clearly Ashbourne and Bakewell, were formed before components broke away as independent estates, but not independent parishes, during the tenth century.[137] Some of the mother-parishes (such as Repton and Bakewell) centre on known pre-Viking minsters, many do not: once again we can recognize areas of probable continuity, areas of probable change, and a large number of cases where there is simply no evidence.

Parochial continuity is hardest to recognize in the southern and eastern parts of the region. The Leicestershire mother-churches mostly lack evidence before the eleventh century, though they include (on the Derbyshire border) the great Mercian minster of Breedon-on-the-Hill, which retained its saints' cults.[138] Of the early Lincolnshire minsters which survived as churches or market centres, only a minority, notably Caistor and Edenham, are also visible as the heads of mother-parishes.[139] In other cases the churches or mother-parishes, or both, may be post-Viking creations. Grantham and Wragby, like Conisbrough (Yorks.), received tithes from bundles of scattered sokelands which are unlikely to have been assembled before the tenth or eleventh century.[140] Although late funerary sculpture is plentiful in Lincolnshire, it does not concentrate at minsters.[141] Moving southwards, in fact, we come closer to an East Anglian pattern in which early religious sites were often perpetuated, but their mother-parishes (assuming such to have existed) were largely effaced by a greater intensity of tenurial change and local church-building.[142]

It is indeed in East Anglia, the south-east midlands, and Essex that the

---

[135] Blair 2002*a*: 558–9, 511, 537–8, 539–40, 549–50.

[136] Loveluck 2001; above, pp. 206–8. Barton-on-Humber is likely to be another continuing minster: below, p. 360.

[137] Hadley 1996: 114–15; Hadley 2000*a*: 131–3.

[138] Parsons 1996: 19–32; *Encyc.* 73–4; Blair 2002*a*: 515, 521, 531–2, 535–6.

[139] Hadley 2000*a*: 253, 271; Everson and Stocker 1999: 73, 121–5. Cf. Ulmschneider 2000, and the largely negative conclusions of Sawyer 1998: 62–3, 99–100, 144–6.

[140] Hadley 1996: 122–3.

[141] Stocker 2000: 186: Stow is the exception.

[142] Hadley 2000*a*: 279–95 proposes patchy coverage from the outset, rather than Viking depredation, as the main reason for the elusiveness of mother-parishes in the more southerly parts of her region. Parochial fragmentation *after* 950 is, however, a third possibility (below, pp. 320, 423).

search for monastic and parochial continuity is least rewarding.[143] The region was under Danish rule until 917, and no bishops of the East Angles are recorded between the 860s and the 940s.[144] The charter evidence is limited, there is little sculpture, and mother-parish structures are thoroughly submerged. Here as further north, the speed of conversion is debatable, and there clearly was a period, even if a short one, when Danish proprietors were pagan. Pagan or Christian, it is likely that they seized monastic estates: so, after all, did their English contemporaries. But it is no clearer here than anywhere else that the minsters were obliterated, or disendowed to the point of extinction. One at least of the Elmhams must have been episcopal land before as well as after the invasion.[145] The St Eadmund memorial coinage shows that by the 890s the Danes acknowledged, even if they did not share, the cult of the king whom they had so recently murdered, and his relics were soon installed in what may have been a pre-Viking minster.[146] Scrutiny of other individual sites suggests widespread continuity, or at least re-occupation.

At North Elmham (Norfolk), a likely site of the pre-Viking as well as post-Viking East Anglian see,[147] excavation has revealed phases of domestic and industrial buildings spanning the ninth and tenth centuries, with a probable break or temporary contraction during *c.*850–75; the site then assumed a more vernacular character, but still evolved within the existing framework of boundaries.[148] After 950, when there were bishops once more, the cemetery expanded across the settlement from its presumed nucleus around the church.[149] This sequence points to the same conclusion as the disruption in the line of bishops, but it also shows how quickly and precisely the pieces could be put together again.

The great fenland minsters of Peterborough (*Medeshamstede*) and Ely were re-founded as abbeys late in the tenth century, so shared a historiography stressing their dire fate at the hands of the Danes. Yet their relics and

---

[143] Problems of continuity and disruption are also discussed, with essentially similar conclusions, by Pestell 1999: 88–135, 282–361, and Pestell 2003 for East Anglia, and by Oosthuizen 2001 for Cambridgeshire.

[144] Whitelock 1941: 171–2; Hart 1992: 29–33; Campbell 2000: 116–19; Barrow 1994: 28–9.

[145] Campbell 2000: 117.

[146] Abrams 2000: 147. For Edmund's cult and the tenth-century clerical minster at Bury, see Whitelock 1941: 173; Gransden 1985; Ridyard 1988: 211–26; Hart 1992: 30–1; Warner 1996: 136–9; Blair 2002*a*: 528. A late source, an interlineation in the *Liber Eliensis*, identifies Bury (*Betrichesuurthe*) as the minster founded by King Sigeberht (d. *c.*640): *Lib. El.* 11.

[147] Wade-Martins 1980; Pestell 1999: 306–12; Campbell 2000: 110–12, on the location of the see.

[148] Wade-Martins 1980: 125–52, 629–31; it is observed (p. 139) that a tenth-century building 'and the underlying Middle Saxon ditch followed almost exactly the same orientation; this is good evidence for continuity of orientation in the settlement plan despite a possible period of abandonment in the ninth century.'

[149] Ibid. 185–9.

traditions survived; Peterborough kept its charters, and at Ely at least there was a group of priests.[150] These houses should not be seen as essentially different, before the 960s, from the majority that were never reformed. For example, Aylesbury, Northampton, and Oundle preserved their local saints, their mother-parishes, and their burial functions: the evidence is exiguous, but enough to show that they must have been important religious sites throughout.[151] Bedford, by tradition King Offa's foundation and burial-place, had an abbot in 971.[152] Barking (Essex) preserved pre-Viking charters, was operating a glass-furnace in the early tenth century, and housed a community in the 940s.[153]

In East Anglia small minsters do in fact seem remarkably numerous in both the pre- and post-Viking periods. Assessing the overlap between the two chronological groups is not straightforward, given that the earlier are known mainly from archaeology, the later from texts of the 940s onwards. It is a recurrent feature of putative minster sites indicated by eighth- to ninth-century metal finds, such as Brandon, Bawsey, and Wormegay, and of occasional documented but 'failed' sites such as Iken, that a church or chapel survived through the middle ages; in a remarkable number of cases, post-Conquest priories were built on or near the sites.[154] Such places are comparable in scale to the small minsters which seem numerous in the region when written sources start again from the 940s. Bishop Theodred's will (942 × 51) mentions communities at Bury, Hoxne, and Mendham, while Ealdorman Ælfgar (946 × 51) and his daughters leave bequests to Barking, Bury, Mersea, Hadleigh, Sudbury, Ely, and above all Stoke-by-Nayland, the 'holy foundation at Stoke where my ancestors lie buried' for which one of the daughters begs royal protection.[155] Not all of these need have been ancient, but some

---

[150] Ely: Whitelock 1941: 173–5; *Lib. El.*, pp. xii. 52–62; *Encyc.* 166–7; Love 2004. Peterborough: Stenton 1970: 179–92; *The Chronicle of Hugh Candidus*, ed. W. T. Mellows (London, 1949); Potts 1974, arguing for territorial continuity.

[151] Allen and Dalwood 1983, and *VCH Bucks.* iii. 1–19; Blair 1996*b*; Hart 1992: 148–9, and Johnston 1993/4.

[152] Matthew Paris, *Chronica Maiora*, i (ed. H. R. Luard, Rolls Ser. 57, 1872), 363; *ASC* 'B', 'C' s.a. 971 (p. 119); *Lib. El.* 105.

[153] MacGowan 1996 for the excavated glass-house. There is a bequest of 946 × *c.*951 to 'St Mary's *stow* at Berking' (S 1483, *Wills*, 6), and a grant of 950 to the 'monastice conversationis familia in Bercingum' (S 552a).

[154] This point has now been brought out strongly by Pestell 2003; see especially pp. 135–7 for a judicious assessment of the likelihood of religious continuity. Cf. above, pp. 206–12.

[155] S 1526, S 1483, S 1486, S 1494 (*Wills*, 2–4, 6–8, 34–40); Whitelock 1941: 172–3; Blair 1988*b*: 3–5 (with map plotting the bequests). Bury, and St Gregory's at Sudbury, also have bequests before 995 from Æthelric (S 1501; *Wills*, 42); Bishop Ælfric's will (S 1489; *Wills*, 70–2) has bequests to communities of priests at Elmham and Hoxne. For small minsters in the region see also Hart 1992: 471; Williamson 1993: 143–7; Barrow 2000*b*: 165–7; and below, p. 359, for Godmanchester, Huntingdon, and Little Shelford.

of them have a documented or archaeologically visible pre-Viking past; the Horningsea narrative describes unambiguously the survival of a clerical minster in Cambridgeshire through the raids of the 870s, its patronage by converted Danes, and its fortunes during the next century.[156]

Saints' cults and legends in the region reinforce the sense of a populous, polyfocal monastic culture, spanning the Viking interlude. Around the coast, cults at Blythburgh (Hiurmine), Iken (Botwulf and Athwulf), Chich (Osgyth), and Wakering (Æthelred and Æthelberht) are attested across the ninth to tenth centuries, while the fens were a veritable landscape of saints ranging from the eminent (Æthelthryth at Ely, Guthlac at Crowland) to the utterly obscure (Æthelberht at Bedford, Cett at Oundle, 'Inicium' at Boxworth).[157] The richness of fenland and East Anglian hagiographical tradition reflects partly the interest of the great abbeys during the tenth to twelfth centuries, partly the region's eloquent religious culture in the later middle ages.[158] Yet it was clearly believed in the late tenth century that many of these cults had persisted across the Viking interlude, albeit in unworthy settings, and the correlation with early ecclesiastical sites is impressive. Given that there must have been far more early minsters than our sources tell us, archaeology may yet support even the most unpromising legends. For instance, the story that King Anna was buried at Blythburgh in 654 looks like, and may be, fantasy; yet an eighth-century writing-tablet and styli have been found near the church.[159]

The later sources for the south-east midlands and East Anglia convey a vivid sense of the past, stemming partly from the nostalgic tinge in reformed monasticism[160] but also heightened by genuine perceptions of loss and change. Their authors knew, and we should not doubt, that the region's religious culture had been shattered during and after the Viking age. Certainly the identification of mother-parishes seems to be largely impossible, though a plausible case has been made for a system of tenth-century hundredal minsters in Northamptonshire.[161] On the other hand, the correlation between identifiable pre-Viking and post-Viking minsters is not noticeably worse than

---

[156] Above, p. 294. The story implies remarkably long-lived incumbents: Cenwold *c.*875–920, Herewulf *c.*920–965? (cf. Abrams 2001: 38). This is surprising but not impossible: the post-medieval clergy lists of many parish churches could show the same. It is unclear how long the author thought the army was 'rampaging', so Cenwold could have become priest slightly later than the mid 870s.

[157] Blair 2002*a*, under the relevant names; Hart 1992: 32–3.

[158] Below, pp. 353, 399; Warner 1996: 139–43.

[159] *Lib. El.* 18; Webster and Backhouse 1991: 81; Campbell 2000: 110; Warner 1996: 120.

[160] Below, pp. 347, 353.

[161] Williamson 1993: 150–4, Warner 1996: 133–6, Bassett 1997, and Oosthuizen 2001 for exiguous traces of mother-church arrangements in Norfolk, Suffolk, Essex, and Cambridgeshire respectively; Franklin 1982: 11–13, 179–96, 313–33, Franklin 1985, and Franklin 1988 for Northamptonshire.

in other regions. Assuming that mother-parishes had ever existed, it must be a serious question whether they were obliterated by Vikings in the late ninth century, or swamped by the exceptional proliferation of local churches during the late tenth to eleventh (compare Fig. 35 with Fig. 50). The two may be linked in the sense that dissolution of old structures would have left new ones to grow unfettered, but economic growth and social diversification offer more convincing solutions.

The region illustrates how thin the line of continuity might wear while still not breaking completely. Only a tiny proportion of sites have early documentation, and visible mother-parish structures shade from the patchy in the north to the virtually non-existent in the south. But the saints' cults show a widespread later awareness, if not survival, of devotional sites, while the material traces of pre-Viking ecclesiastical status (here small-finds rather than sculptures) show a recurrent correspondence between early sites and later churches. While individual cases could be seen as re-use rather than continuity, it is the broad base of this correlation between the pre-Viking and post-Viking patterns which makes re-use implausible as a general and exclusive explanation.

Standing back from so many case-studies, we can see beneath the substantial regional variation a basic homogeneity. Out of a series of variables (pre-Viking charter references, sculpture, mother-church rights, complex planning, local saints, residual staffs of clergy), two or more tend to recur in relation to the same churches. While most obvious in the relatively undisrupted west midlands and south-west, such churches can be perceived both beneath the overlying layers of later ecclesiastical development, as in central Wessex, and through Viking-age traumas and archival lacunae, as in Yorkshire and Lincolnshire. As a category, a high proportion of the pre-Viking minsters remained in some sense in existence.

To assert this is not to deny that they grew poorer and less diverse with the passage of time, and that in several respects they suffered fundamental and traumatic change in the Viking age and after. The most obvious sign of this is material impoverishment. The rich 'minster culture' of eastern and south-eastern England, expressed in sculpture, metalwork, de luxe manuscripts, and personal adornments, did not survive beyond the mid ninth century; at the same time, the large and complex monastic settlements began to contract. The excavations at Carlisle, Monkwearmouth, Jarrow, Hartlepool, Whitby, Beverley, Ripon, Flixborough, Brandon, North Elmham, and Barking, and metal-detecting on other potentially monastic sites, all show rich small-finds assemblages petering out around 850. This was clearly part of the same story as the disasters that Alfred would deplore, the ending of book production and the scattering of libraries.

But impoverishment did not necessarily extend to long-term abandon-ment: churches remained at all the excavated sites, burial continued on at least some of them, and Flixborough and Eynsham show a continuity of buildings across the ninth to eleventh centuries which would be exceptional in a normal domestic context. Minsters survived: but they lost that distinc-tive and luxurious culture which, in some regions at least, had made them so different from other places. Never (so far as we know) actually suppressed, they were increasingly forced to share their assets and premises with a range of lay activities. This, in a sense, was a key to their survival: new demands on them, which forced them to become useful in new ways, gave them a continuing public role.

After the 870s, stone sculpture opens a window on patterns of continuity and change in the minsters' lay audience. We have seen that in some regions sculpture tends to concentrate at important and often pre-existing religious sites. Mortuary crosses and slabs would soon appear in a fast-growing category of local churchyards,[162] but there was probably a phase during *c.*880–940 when Anglo-Scandinavian elites tended to be buried at the min-sters of their English predecessors. Furthermore, the decoration and format of memorial sculpture show continuities across the Viking age which suggest that established (monastic?) workshops simply went on working for new patrons.[163] For the patrons themselves, sculpture—at least the higher-grade sculpture—could affirm their links with the ancient monastic past as well as their membership of the new Anglo-Scandinavian Christian culture.[164]

But there is another side: the workshops which had once served an elite monastic market now catered for a broad-based lay one.[165] Sculpture was pro-duced in much larger quantities, and was generally of a more summary and 'vernacular' quality. It also acquired a repertoire of imagery which reflected the self-perceptions of the laity: heavily armed warriors, groups of horsemen, hunting scenes. As Richard Bailey observes, such secular themes had usually been excluded from pre-Viking sculpture: 'the change in patronage has removed that conventional taboo and given us access to the manner in which this society thought it most appropriate to express its ideals and achieve-ments, through the symbolism of the hunt and warfare'.[166] The scenes from

[162] Below, pp. 467–71.

[163] Lang 1978: 145, arguing 'that the emergence of Anglo-Scandinavian styles enjoyed an unin-terrupted transition, that an Anglian conservatism continued through the tenth century even in thoroughly Scandinavianized areas, and that many of the features hitherto regarded as Scandina-vian can be traced to English, insular origins'. For arguments along similar lines: Bailey 1985: 54–5; Lang 1993: 266–7; Bailey 1996*a*: 80–4; Hawkes 2002: 139–41. Stocker 2000: 193 raises some doubts.

[164] Cf. Hadley 1997: 91–2, 94.

[165] Bailey 1980*a*: 76–84; Bailey 1996*a*: 78–80; Hadley 1996: 126–7.

[166] Bailey 1996*a*: 84–5. An interesting parallel might be pursued with the earlier Pictish stones and their similar iconographical tastes.

36. English and Scandinavian cultures in contact: a Viking-age cross-shaft at *Halton* (Lancs.). Plant and animal motifs and Christian iconography, drawn from earlier Anglian traditions, are here associated with a scene from the Norse legend of Sigurd the Volsung. (W. G. Collingwood, *Northumbrian Crosses of the Pre-Viking Age* (London, 1927), fig. 191.)

Scandinavian mythology carved at Gosforth and elsewhere (Fig. 36) have been taken to show continuing paganism, but they should perhaps rather be seen (as Bailey again argues) as an assimilation of secular cultural material into Christian iconography: a folkloric manifestation of successful conversion.[167]

It is only in Cumbria, Northumbria, and the east midlands that we have sculpture to reveal these secular influences, but apart from the Norse mythology it is unlikely that they were peculiarly Viking. Recent work on Anglo-Scandinavian society has tended to qualify its distinctiveness, and to stress the common development of the various societies of England after the late ninth century.[168] In all regions, to a greater or lesser extent, minsters became

---

[167] Bailey 1996a: 85–94; cf. Bailey 1985: 59–61. In contrast, Stocker 2000: 194–7 argues for 'a hybrid religion which had characteristics of both paganism and Christianity'.

[168] Above, pp. 292–3.

poorer and weaker, and we will see ample evidence for their vulnerability to secular greed. English elites had not, like Scandinavian ones, been recently pagan, but they may have enjoyed a similarly heightened self-confidence in the face of traditional monastic culture. And from Alfred onwards the greatest laymen of all, the kings of Wessex, were developing an agenda which involved bending ecclesiastical institutions to their service.

This intervention cut both ways. The activities of a strong, centralizing monarchy, concerned both to establish systematic structures of authority and to rebuild learning and Christian culture, were coherent and creative.[169] If a re-definition of old minsters as hundredal churches did in fact occur during territorial re-structuring by Edward the Elder, Æthelflæd, and Æthelstan, it was the natural extension, one tier down, of Edward's radical reform of West Saxon episcopal provision and foundation of new sees.[170] The systematic legislative backing which these kings gave to mother-church revenues will be considered later.[171] But it was also in this period that proprietorship—royal, episcopal, and lordly—started to escalate into full-scale annexation and absorption, leaving tenth- and eleventh- century minsters, apart from the reformed abbeys, mere shadows of their pre-Viking selves.

The secularization of minsters (i): annexation by kings, lords, and religious corporations

Involvement of lords and patrons in the activities of religious communities was of course nothing new, either in England or on the Continent; elite society accepted it, and it could be both supportive and creative. But the comprehensive running-down of assets, going beyond the worst fears of observers before 850, signals something altogether more radical: a progressive takeover of the minster sites themselves, which left few communities (except, from the 960s, the reformed ones) in autonomous control of big endowments. By the Domesday survey, most of them were adjuncts of secular territorial centres, and possessed modest enclaves of land embedded in much larger secular estates. The mid ninth to late eleventh centuries thus saw a transformation: places which were minsters—if perhaps with lay residential functions—at the start of the period appear by the end of it as secular places containing residually important churches.

The decline of monastic landholdings, the tale of narratives and charters, has been more discussed than the decline of monastic sites. In an important

---

[169] A point developed especially by Dumville 1992*a*: e.g. 147–8, 161–3, 170–1, 190–205.
[170] Yorke 1995: 210; Rumble 2001: 238–44.   [171] Below, pp. 440–4.

paper of 1985, Robin Fleming argued that kings from Alfred onwards took advantage of the minsters' decay and vulnerability to deprive them of strategically important estates, especially in the east midlands and the north, by seizure or exchange; this policy, essential for the unity and defence of the West Saxon state, meant that by 1066 many estates of the king and his great secular officials were ex-monastic.[172] David Dumville has criticized several aspects of Fleming's argument, notably its reliance on late sources, but accepts the basic case that 'the circumstances of the First Viking-Age drove much ecclesiastical property into lay hands'.[173]

Both writers neglect one central point: not merely the estates but the minsters themselves were being more and more thoroughly absorbed into secular public life, as royal and noble residences, land-management centres, fortresses, and towns. These developments in ninth- and tenth-century England followed naturally from those described at the end of the last chapter; they also mirrored contemporary changes in France where, in the context of *la mutation féodale*, they have received more attention.[174] The growing importance of French towns in political life brought tensions between the religious corporations, which had controlled them since the fifth century, and secular powers. In such towns as Angers, Tours, and Nantes the building of large comital residences, sometimes jostling for prime space with cathedrals and monasteries, symbolized the rising power of the count at the expense of the Church. At the same time, the rise of the artisanal *burgus/bourg*—often, in this more Romanized townscape, around a surburban monastery—created zones which were of commercial as well as religious importance, and which by the late ninth century needed defending against the Viking threat. The same three strands—residential encroachment, urbanization, and defence—can be traced in the treatment of English minsters by the West Saxon kings, their nobles, and their bishops.

A good starting-point is the remarkable autobiographical passage in Asser's 'Life of King Alfred' which has been mentioned already:

I was summoned to him [i.e. Alfred] at daybreak on Christmas Eve, and he presented me with two documents in which there was a lengthy list of everything which was in the two minsters named Congresbury and Banwell in English. On that same day he granted those two minsters to me, with all the things which were in them, as well as an extremely valuable silk cloak and a quantity of incense weighing as much as a stout man. He added that the giving of these trifles would not prevent him from giving me greater gifts at a future time. Indeed, with the passage of time he unexpectedly granted me Exeter with all the jurisdiction (*parochia*) pertaining to

---

[172] Fleming 1985.   [173] Dumville 1992*a*: 29–54, esp. 53–4.
[174] Février and others 1980: 506–22, for a good summary; below, pp. 369–70, for the 'feudal revolution'.

it in Saxon territory and in Cornwall . . . He then immediately gave me permission to ride out to those two minsters so well provided with goods of all sorts, and from there to return home.[175]

While there is no suggestion that the minsters ceased to function ecclesiastically, Alfred had no compunction about using these 'trifles' as a Christmas present for a valued adviser. The inventories, and Asser's prompt visit to take stock, evoke a proprietorship which did not depend in any serious way on his clerical status: if he chose to reside at Congresbury or Banwell with his retinue, the religious communities there could presumably do nothing to stop him.[176] The affair lends plausibility to the late-recorded accusation that Alfred himself turned the minster of Abingdon (Berks.) into a royal house, also supported by Æthelstan's reception of a Frankish embassy there and by a meeting of the witan in 950 at 'the royal vill of Abingdon'.[177]

Does the fate of these minsters illustrate a trend? Here we resume the analysis of royal vills which the last chapter pursued up to the 820s. From that point a change becomes evident, first in the context of the West Saxon rise to supremacy and eventually throughout England. The most conspicuous new factor is stability. After 830, rapidly more West Saxon royal centres of long-term importance become visible: Kingston-upon-Thames and Wilton (838), Southampton (840), Wantage (849), Chippenham (853), Amesbury (858), Somerton (860), Sutton Courtenay (868).[178] As we go forward in time through King Alfred's will (c.880 × 88) and tenth-century charters, the network of royal vills and hundred centres recorded by Domesday Book comes into focus.[179]

This could be just one facet of the stabilization of settlement and the emergence of manor-houses which is a feature of these centuries, but it has an important additional dimension: it becomes common to find sites with documented or archaeologically visible monastic pasts, or with place-names in -*mynster*, treated straightforwardly as royal estate centres. At least nine places in King Alfred's will are of this kind: Aldingbourne, Beddingham, Damerham, Exminster, Godalming, Hartland, Lyminster, Steyning, and

---

[175] *Asser*, c. 81 (pp. 67–8; trans. p. 97).

[176] These two minsters would have made stopping-off points on Asser's regular itinerary between Wessex and St Davids. He could have crossed the Severn there or slightly further north, perhaps towards the minster at Caerwent where he was taken ill: *Asser*, c. 79 (p. 65, trans. pp. 94, 261 n. 175). Cf. below, n. 217.

[177] *Chronicon Monasterii de Abingdon*, ed. J. Stevenson, i (Rolls Ser. i, 1858), 50; *GR* i. 218; S 552a; *Abingdon*, pp. ccviii–ccix, 209; Thacker 1988: 45–6. For Alfred and Edward the Elder as despoilers of church property, see also Brooks 1984: 149–50; Thacker 2001: 252–3.

[178] S 1438, S 288, *Asser*, cc. 8, 9 (pp. 1, 8; trans. pp. 67, 69), S 1274, S 329, S 338a (= S 539).

[179] These later assembly-sites are listed by S. Keynes, *The Diplomas of King Æthelred 'the Unready'* (Cambridge, 1980), 269–73.

Sturminster.[180] Others occur during the next few decades: Warminster (899 × 924), Axminster (901), Thatcham (951 × 5), Cheddar (956).[181] Many more are identified as minsters on textual, hagiographical, or archaeological grounds well before they appear in their new guise of royal vills in the late tenth or eleventh centuries, and a list of examples drawn from Domesday Book would be lengthy. To a significant extent, the royal administration had achieved territorial stability by battening onto minsters. Well might late tenth-century polemicists blame kings of Wessex and their magnates, even more than the Vikings, for despoiling the Church's resources.[182] The scars of Viking raids had healed, but the secularization of minsters continued on its slow, consistent course.

The topographical result of the process just described should be a recurrent juxtaposition of ninth- to eleventh-century royal houses with earlier minsters. Only excavation, on a scale not yet undertaken, could provide hard evidence, but persuasive reflections of this pattern can sometimes be seen in late and post-medieval arrangements. One obvious example is Westminster itself, where the eleventh-century palace is crammed awkwardly along the eastern edge of the monastic enclosure formed by Thorney island.[183] The relationship of minsters to sites called 'Kingsbury' (*cyninges burh*) or its Danelaw equivalents deserves more attention. At St Albans and Aylesbury the 'Kingsburys' are down-slope from, and clearly peripheral to, the crest-sited minsters, and it is interesting that a village called Conesby adjoined the rich mid Saxon ecclesiastical site at Flixborough (Fig. 25).[184]

Two eloquent illustrations of how royal encroachment impacted on and transformed monastic sites are Cheddar (Somerset) and Cookham (Berks.) At Cheddar, Philip Rahtz's excavation gives a unique glimpse of a minster interacting through this period with a royal hunting-lodge.[185] The minster, built on a Roman villa, stands in the angle of a canalized river which would

---

[180] S 1507; Keynes and Lapidge 1983: 173–8, 313–26. Several other places listed occur as minsters later, for instance Bedwyn, Crewkerne, Cullompton, Leatherhead, and Yeovil. For the history of the estates bequeathed by Alfred see Wormald 2001*b*: 268–74: his conclusion that these were acquired (and therefore disposable) properties, not some official 'royal demesne', is consistent with identifying many of them as recently annexed minsters.

[181] S 1445, S 364, S 1515, S 611.

[182] Dumville 1992*a*: 39, citing for instance Æthelwold's view that proper monastic observance had been impaired 'through the robbery of evil men and through the consent of kings who had little fear of God'.

[183] Blair 1996*a*: 9, 12–13, 25.

[184] Slater 1998: 162–3; Allen and Dalwood 1983: fig. 1; Loveluck 2001: 80–1. In the Wiltshire cases discussed by Haslam 1984: 103–4, 122–9, and 132–6, the relationship between the churches and the 'Kingsburys' is topographically ambiguous. Cf. the 'Earlsburys' in eleventh-century Exeter and York: Fleming 1993: 23–4.

[185] Rahtz 1979. The present account summarizes the re-dating and reassessment suggested by Blair 1996*b*: 108–20.

have bounded the precinct on the south and east. North-westwards, probably just inside the periphery of the precinct, lay the excavated group of
timber buildings centred on the king's hall. The dating of the earlier phases
is disputed, but on the evidence available it can be suggested that the house
was established in the late ninth or early tenth century, in other words in the
reign of Alfred or Edward the Elder. Alfred's will mentions 'the community
at Cheddar' as a seemingly autonomous body which is asked to 'choose'
Alfred's son 'on the terms which we have previously agreed'. Cheddar next
appears as a double minster engaged in land-transactions with Edward the
Elder. Thirty or forty years later, matters were different. Assemblies were held
in about 940 at the *villa* of Cheddar and in 956 at the *palatium regis* there,
while King Eadmund's celebrated near-accident in the Gorge occurred
during a hunting expedition from his Cheddar residence. Domesday Book
presents Cheddar as a royal manor, without even mentioning the church.
Here archaeology and documents tell a similar story: the hunting-lodge was
the cuckoo in the nest, founded on the edge of the Cheddar community's
precinct in about Alfred's reign and effectively absorbing it over the next two
centuries.

For Cookham,[186] in the middle Thames valley, a Canterbury memorandum records that King Æthelbald (716–57) gave this minster to Christ
Church, but that Offa later transferred it with 'many other towns (*urbes*)'
from Wessex to Mercia; in 798 the archbishop of Canterbury was compen-
sated for its loss with 110 hides in Kent. Here then was a major religious site,
fit to be called an *urbs* and commensurate in value to a huge landholding.
Yet in 1086 we find Cookham as a royal manor of eighteen hides, attached
to which was a church with a mere two hides held by Regenbald the chancellor and two clerks. This Domesday entry (which is a very typical one)
ostensibly shows a royal centre served by a modest mother-church; only the
survival of the Canterbury text tells us that in origin the place was a rich
minster.

Aristocrats, so far as the limited evidence goes, exploited minster sites and
lands much as did kings. It seems possible that, as monastic estates were progressively absorbed into royal hands, shares were allocated on a more-or-less
systematic basis to the local ealdorman;[187] in other cases the ealdorman

---

[186] S 1258; Blair 1996*a*: 13–14, 23; DB i. 56ʳ; above, p. 250. Cookham was a royal centre in the
990s: *Wills*, 44; *JW* ii. 458.
[187] This possibility, suggested by Stephen Baxter's recent work, may for instance explain how
Ealdorman Ælfheah (*c.*971) could bequeath land at a series of minster-places—Cookham,
Thatcham, and Faringdon (Berks.), Aylesbury and Wendover (Bucks.), and Godstone (Surrey)—
to the king, queen, athelings, and his own brother: S 1485 (*Wills*, 22–4, 121–5). Langford (Oxon.)
may be an example of a relatively important church founded on one of these split-off comital portions: Blair 1994: 107, 111, 136.

acquired the minster itself. The impact of such aristocratic annexation, fore-shadowed at early ninth-century Inkberrow,[188] is illustrated for the eleventh century by Deerhurst (Fig. 33). Here a partition of the estate between the minster and Earl Odda (d. 1056) seems to have involved a physical division of the precinct itself, with the northern half retained by the community but the southern half developed as the earl's residence. Odda and his brother Ælfric (d. 1053) both died at Deerhurst, and the chapel which Odda built for Ælfric's soul (Fig. 48) stands apart from the church, built into the late medieval manor-house on Odda's share.[189] A comparable partition, between the king and the Godwinessons, had occurred by the 1050s at the hugely wealthy Sussex minster at Bosham, where the Bayeux Tapestry's scene of Earl Harold riding and feasting is our most powerful visual image of late Anglo-Saxon lordship over minsters (Fig. 37).[190] At a humbler level, the Hwiccian minster of Wootton Wawen ('Vagn's Wootton') became the chief manor of Vagn, a rich thegn in Earl Leofric's following in the 1050s.[191] There must have been many others.

Bishops, like kings and nobles, continued and extended ninth-century modes of exploiting minster estates. During *c.*870–900 the bishops of Worcester leased small hidages from the minster-lands of Stratford-upon-Avon, Bibury, and Bishops Cleeve, reserving church dues payable to the see via the original minster centres.[192] A much later Worcester text, of the 1050s, implies heavy demands made on dependent land by the estate administration at Bredon, once an important minster of Offa's kindred but here called merely an 'episcopal vill'.[193] In 904 the bishop of Winchester paid massively to free the great Taunton minster estate from accommodating royal hunting-parties and provisioning royal vills.[194] In 1053 × 5 Bishop Wulfwig of

---

[188] Above, pp. 285–6.

[189] Rahtz and Watts 1997 for the topography around Deerhurst church; *VCH Glos.* viii. 34–41, Williams 1997*a*: 7–9, and Williams 2002: 15–18, for the division of the manor. The manor-house incorporating Odda's chapel served Westminster Abbey's (i.e. Odda's) half.

[190] Gem 1985. Bosham is twice mentioned as a port used by Godwine: *ASC* 'C' s.a. 1049, 'E' s.a. 1051 (pp. 168, 176).

[191] A. Williams 1997: 29 n. 73; Williams 2002: 9–10; Baxter 2003: 271–4; above, p. 104, for this minster's earlier history. There are remains of a large late Anglo-Saxon church with a central tower and *porticus* (Taylor and Taylor 1965–78: ii. 685–8); research by S. Bassett (in progress) suggests that this is probably rather earlier than the time of Vagn.

[192] S 1278, S 1415, S 1279, S 1283. The Stratford land was to revert to Stratford itself; in the other cases, reversion is to the see but churchscot is payable to the minsters.

[193] S 1408: three hides in Teddington and Alstone are to be free of all service to Bredon, including sake and soke, churchscot, tithe, and rent, so that neither future bishops nor their reeves at Bredon can claim anything from it.

[194] S 373, S 1286: these much-mistrusted texts have recently been said to 'make a good impression' (S. Keynes in *EHR* 109 (1994), 1144–5), though it remains possible that some of the detail was interpolated later at Winchester.

MILITES : EQVI TANT: AD BOS : HA(M) ECCLESIA : HIC

37. 'Harold, earl of the English, and his knights ride to Bosham church': the Bayeux Tapestry illustrates the relationship between the leading magnate and the richest unreformed minster remaining in southern England in the 1060s. (Re-drawn.)

Dorchester, while co-operating in the revival of the old minster at Stow (Lincs.) on his estate, was careful to keep his established food-rents: 'two-thirds of everything that comes into the minster, and the priests shall have the remaining third except at the two festivals. The bishop, however, shall have everything that accrues to it for eight days at the earlier festival of St Mary, and for eight days at the later festival of St Mary, except for food alone. The priests, however, shall have the third part of the food which accrues to it.'[195]

Wulfwig, like Asser nearly two centuries earlier, saw no conflict between maintaining an appropriate religious life at old minsters and syphoning off much of their revenue for his own household. Food-renders, which still remained important in the economies of the large, complex estates of kings, great nobles, and bishops, would in such cases have been transferred directly from the minsters to the provisioning requirements of their lords. This process of re-allocation began before the Viking invasions, and continued independently of individual kings' political or religious policies. It was not, as we will see, incompatible with creative support for religious communities at the minsters; but in the broad scheme of things the financing of those communities was given an ever lower priority.

---

[195] S 1478 (*RASC* 212–16). A copy of the agreement was to remain 'in the possession of the bishop at the holy foundation' (i.e. Stow), a phrase which underlines its continued role, even after the re-foundation, as an episcopal centre. See Baxter 2003: 199–207, for the context of this text. Susan Wood observes (pers. comm.): 'The variations for patronal festivals make it look rather like countless French arrangements for dividing a church's tithes and offerings between its priest and its lord (lay or ecclesiastical).' For the annexation of other minsters by bishops of Dorchester, see Blair 2001c.

The secularization of minsters (ii): urbanization

At the end of the ninth century, a Mercian at King Alfred's court translated Bede's phrase 'per cuncta et urbana et rustica loca' ('throughout both town and countryside', as we would say today) as 'þurh mynsterstowe ge þurh folc-stowe', literally 'through minster-places and through people-places'.[196] This phrase was written in the same generation and milieu as the Burghal Hidage, yet for its author the principal characteristic of an 'urban place' was that it contained a minster. Alfred's reign initiated an age in which the role of minsters was to change, and in political and religious terms to diminish, but it was also an urbanizing age: the sites which declined as religious centres gained a new lease of life as urban ones.

Most of the major Domesday towns were royal fortresses in the late ninth or tenth centuries, and many of them contained minsters: defensive policy makes one important link between royal minsters and urbanization. Alfred and his heirs not merely acquired monastic lands for strategic purposes,[197] but also made strongholds of the minsters themselves. In fact, the rise of Wessex greatly extended the association of minsters with fortified sites seen already in later eighth-century Mercia, where it seems to have been announced by the earliest reservations of fortress-work from bookland estates.[198] The 840s, when the same public burden first consistently appears in West Saxon charters,[199] may mark the serious beginnings of the militarization of southern English minsters.

The forts of Alfred's Wessex are known to us above all from a brief but crucial text, the Burghal Hidage, which lists thirty-three places together with the hidage assessments of the territories obliged to support them.[200] Many of the sites are now recognized as remarkable products of early medieval town planning, with formal street-grids and a consistent technology of rampart construction and road-metalling.[201] But the very fact that the Burghal Hidage defines these places as parts of a whole—a royal, centrally planned defensive system—has deflected attention from their very diverse origins. The Hidage is not a complete list of one kind of place but a selective list of varied places, ranging in size and importance from big towns such as Winchester

---

[196] *OEB* i. 160; Campbell 1986: 141.

[197] Fleming 1985: 253–65; Dumville 1992*a*: 46, 54.   [198] Above, p. 287.

[199] Brooks 1971: 81–2; Abels 1988: 54; Brooks 1996: 129. A single earlier instance in a West Saxon charter of the 790s (S 267) should probably be seen against the background of strong Mercian influence.

[200] The essays in Hill and Rumble 1996 survey the textual and historical problems, and are the starting-point for future work.

[201] Biddle 1976*a* remains the best survey of the archaeological evidence.

to garrison-posts such as Shaftsey; their one common feature is that they had been chosen as strategic strongholds to be supported from hidage-based levies.[202] In fact many of the Burghal Hidage sites, like others of a similar general kind, were ecclesiastical when first recorded: some two-thirds of them either contained or adjoined minsters.

This point can be illustrated by three examples. The first is the old and important Dorset minster which Asser, in the context of the Viking campaign of 876, revealingly describes as 'a fortified site called Wareham, a convent of nuns situated . . . between the two rivers Frome and Tarrant, in a very secure position except on the west'.[203] The other two are Wimborne (Dorset), an eighth-century royal nunnery, and Christchurch at Twynham (Hants.), a minster after the Conquest (below, pp. 514–19). Both had defensive potential: Wimborne had originally had 'high and strong walls' segregating the male and female communities, while Twynham occupied a river-confluence spur cut off by a ditch.[204] The Anglo-Saxon Chronicle tells that in 900 the atheling Æthelwold seized the 'residences' (*hām*) at Wimborne and Twynham; the king encamped near Wimborne, and Æthelwold (who had abducted a nun there) 'stayed inside the residence with the men who had submitted to him, and he had barricaded all the gates against him, and said that he would either live there or die there'.[205] Burials of kings (Beohtric at Wareham in 802, Æthelred I at Wimborne in 871) gave two of these places a symbolic importance for the royal house; Wareham (Fig. 38) and Twynham have archaeological evidence for banks and planned streets, and occur in the Burghal Hidage.[206] All three are now small towns.

At Wareham, as at some slightly later West Saxon burghal places such as Oxford and Cricklade, the forts encapsulated the minsters; in other cases they were built on strategically preferable but adjoining sites, for instance Shaftsey island in the Thames beside Cookham (a juxtaposition which may reflect the earlier interest of Mercian kings in this minster).[207] Later, the sites fortified by Alfred's children, Edward in the east midlands and Æthelflæd in Mercia, included such minsters as Bedford, Bakewell, Gloucester, and Worcester. The predilection for attaching new forts to existing minster-places

---

[202] See especially Brooks 1996, the most historically convincing analysis of the underlying system, which interprets the assessments as 'a series of piecemeal compromises in different local and political circumstances by hard-pressed officials' (p. 132). The text as we have it has probably been updated, and it may well have been modified with changing needs (for example by the addition of Worcester: below, pp. 333–4). Dyer 1988 makes a strong and refreshing case for seeing the burghal towns in a broad economic context rather than a narrow and political one.

[203] *Asser*, c. 49 (pp. 36–7; trans. p. 82).

[204] Above, pp. 198–9; Coulstock 1993; Hase 1988: 51.

[205] *ASC* s.a. 900 (pp. 92–3); Keynes and Lapidge 1983: 120.

[206] Haslam 1984: 224–7; Hill and Rumble 1996: 198–9, 221–2.

[207] Hill and Rumble 1996: 213–14; above, pp. 250, 327 for Cookham.

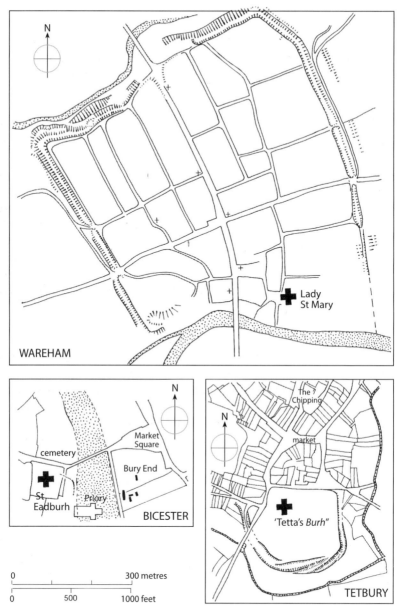

38. The urbanization of minsters: planned and accretive. *Wareham* (Dorset) illustrates the encapsulation of a minster within formal burghal defenses in mid to late ninth-century Wessex. At *Bicester* (Oxon.) excavation has revealed a late Anglo-Saxon settlement—linked to the minster by a causeway across an intervening stream—which acquired a triangular market area. *Tetbury* (Glos.) shows, in its post-medieval topography, the eventual result of this kind of development: a market area ('The Chipping') and formal streets, on the north edge of the minster in its Iron Age hillfort. The minster churches are indicated schematically by the large black crosses. (After L. Keen in Haslam 1984: fig. 78; Blair 2002*b*: fig. 1; OS 25-inch 1st edn.)

was clearly strong, and the exceptions may reflect specific local factors: for instance, we cannot know why the Burghal Hidage fort which is now Axbridge was not built two miles away at Cheddar minster, but the reservation of the hunting-lodge at Cheddar for courtly recreation is one possible explanation.[208]

Archaeologists have been eager to define these places as royal planned towns; contemporaries, inhabiting an un-urbanized landscape in which minsters remained the visually dominant centres, might have seen them differently. Would a visitor to, say, Oxford in 900 have thought of it primarily as a fortified minster, a royal fortress, or a town? On the Continent, where *burgi* were forming around monasteries such as Saint-Denis[209] and where kings were allowing major churches to be fortified, the religious communities often took the initiative. In 891, for example, King Guy of Italy authorized the church of Modena to 'dig moats, construct mills, build gates, and fortify the territory within the radius of a mile around the church for its safety and defense and that of its canons'; ten years later, Charles the Simple conceded to the monks of Corbie that no public agent should 'have any right to judge or administer or command anything as if by force within the *castellum* constructed at the monks' own expense and initiative within the very walls of their monastery'.[210] Linked to this process of enclosure was the emergence of commercial *vici*: thus in 867 a charter of Charles the Bald for Arras mentions a *vicus monasterii* and a '*vicus* called New Town (*nova villa*) sited next to that monastery'.[211] These documents may be compared with an English one of the 890s by which the Mercian rulers established the fortifications of Worcester, soon to be incorporated into the assessment system of the Burghal Hidage:

To Almighty God, the True Unity and the Holy Trinity in heaven, be praise and honour and thanksgiving for all the benefits which he has granted us. For whose love in the first place, and for that of St Peter and the church of Worcester, and also at the request of Bishop Wærferth their friend, Ealdorman Æthelred and Æthelflæd ordered the fortress (*burh*) of Worcester to be built for the protection of all the people, and also to exalt the praise of God therein. And they now make known, with the witness of God, in this charter, that they will grant to God and St Peter and to the lord of that church half of all the rights which belong to their lordship, whether

---

[208] Blair 1996*b*: 119–20; cf. Hill and Rumble 1996: 189–91.

[209] *Un village au temps de Charlemagne*: cat. of exhibition, Musée national des arts et traditions populaires, 1988–9 (Paris, 1988), 60–9.

[210] Quoted Rosenwein 1999: 153, 138; cf. Settia 1991: 81–94. A recent attempt to apply the *bourg* model to Ireland (Graham 1998: 142–9) has points of contact with the present argument.

[211] *Recueil des actes de Charles II le Chauve*, ed. G. Tessier, ii (Paris, 1952), 170–6. Verhulst 2000: 115–19, stresses the role of pre-Carolingian ecclesiastical sites in the revival of economic life after 850.

in the market or in the street, both within the fortress (*burh*) and outside; that things may be more honourably maintained in that foundation (*stow*) and also that they may more easily help the community to some extent; and that their memory may be the more firmly observed in that place for ever, as long as obedience to God shall continue in that minster.[212]

We can recognize here a more interventionist approach than in the Frankish texts, and a bishop with a compelling need to co-operate with his lord and lady. Yet both the initiative for the works and the economic benefits are associated, at least ostensibly, as much with the church as with the rulers.

This was a rather different balance of interests and influences than would be normal a century later. The shift was not just a matter of rulers' powers growing and churches' declining, but also of a sharpening contrast between urban and rural places. When the Worcester text was written, urbanization in a sense that a geographer would recognize was still to come.[213] Even the large burghal places with planned street-grids, which were clearly meant from the start to acquire settled populations, did not attain urban densities or levels of craft activity until after 950. When this happened, it was in the context of an altogether broader and more organic wave of economic growth, involving increased industrial and commercial activity at a multitude of small sites rather than simply a few large ones, which percolated southwards and westwards from the northern Danelaw during the tenth century.[214]

This process affected far more minsters than the small minority which had been fortified by kings. Nor was there any simple relationship between general economic growth and urbanization. As in the pre-Viking period, we should probably envisage a multiplicity of informal and ill-recorded production and exchange sites spread across the countryside. During the tenth to twelfth centuries, their functions were controlled and concentrated through a process of settlement formation culminating in the high medieval landscape of market towns and villages.[215] The planning and nucleation of settlement, both urban and rural and both before and after the Conquest, involved the manipulation of existing assets as well as speculative entrepreneurship. On the pre-nucleated landscape, with its centres of authority

---

[212] S 223; trans. from D. Whitelock, *English Historical Documents*, i (2nd edn., London, 1979), 540. See N. Baker and R. Holt, *Urban Growth and the Medieval Church* (2004), 133–4, 174–6, 297.

[213] For this reason I cannot really agree with Barrow 1994: 29, and Barrow 2000*a*: 130–1, that Edward the Elder's new episcopal seats were deliberately marginalized by being located 'in grossly unsuitable sites, far away from burgeoning urban centres', rather than in boroughs. Which urban centres would burgeon still remained to be seen (some boroughs such as Cricklade conspicuously failed to do so), and in the 900s a major church would still have seemed likely to prove as much a cause as a beneficiary of urban growth.

[214] Astill 1991: 103–13; Hinton 1990: 82–105.

[215] For ideas along these lines see: Astill 1991; Britnell 1981; Dyer 1988; Dyer 1992; Blair 2000.

on the one hand and its open-ground markets on the other, was overlaid a new organizational layer.

Minster-places were one special kind of potential nucleus. The broad context for their urban development was a steadily growing economy, but their individual experiences must have been moulded by local patterns of set-tlement and communication, or by competition with other regional centres. In this competition, they had in-built strengths for their commercial (if perhaps not for their spiritual) growth. Their original topographical advan-tages remained; so did their role as estate centres, as places of resort for sacra-mental and social rituals, and as refuges for sanctuary-seekers who could continue to practise their trades there.[216]

This centrality explains the very widespread association of minsters with markets. One such case surfaces in 904, when the lord of Taunton minster (Somerset) bought exemption from providing 'whatever the king wished to take thence to Curry or Williton by wagon and horse' and from escorting travellers, and secured control over 'the market of the vill' (*þæs tunes cyping*).[217] Again, the reform of the minster at Stow (Lincs.) in 1053 × 5 was done with the cognizance 'of all the citizens of Lincoln and of all the men who attend the yearly market at Stow (*7 on eallra þæra manna þe seceað gear-markett to Stowe*)'.[218] Peter Sawyer and others have emphasized both the correlation of markets with minsters in Domesday Book, and the later prevalence of Sunday or feast-day assemblies at major churches where goods could be bought and sold.[219] These churchyard markets and 'wakes'—often unmentioned until twelfth- or thirteenth-century authorities tried to sup-press them—give a last glimpse of activities which may have been going on for centuries. It is surely such centres for coming and going, for provision-ing and hospitality, for gossiping and bargaining, that the Alfredian transla-tor knew as *mynsterstowe*.

---

[216] Above, pp. 221–5, for the major sanctuaries; but it could have occurred elsewhere. Parallels can also be drawn with the Welsh sources (Pryce 1993: 163–203), and with the influence on settle-ment formation of 'inhabited churchyards' and sanctuaries in France and Catalonia (essays in Fixot and Zadora-Rio 1990; Bonnassie 1994), which were stimulated by sanctuary and refuge requirements.

[217] S 373 (n. 194 above for its authenticity). Goods were presumably transported via Taunton to the port of Watchet, which adjoins Williton; cf. Asser's use of Somerset minsters on his route to the Severn estuary, n. 176 above.

[218] S 1478 (*RASC* 212–16).

[219] Sawyer 1981; Morris 1991; Dyer 1992: 145; Sawyer 1998: 174–7; Ulmschneider 2000: 1–2, 81–2, 87–100, 105–6. Sunday markets were opposed on religious grounds, and there is very little pre-Conquest evidence for them (pers. comm. Patrick Wormald); Domesday Book mentions Saturday markets in King Edward's time at Hoxne and Wallingford (DB ii. 379, i. 56ᵛ), and in 1086 at St Germans and Otterton (DB i. 20ᵛ, Exon. 194ᵛ). It may be that Sunday markets were illicit, but in practice widespread. Cf. Fry 1999: 47–65, for the multifarious social, commercial, and legal uses of churchyards in Ireland.

Somewhere around half of all Domesday markets and boroughs can be recognized as minster sites, as can some two-thirds of the places where coins were struck during *c.*870–1070.[220] Since much of the evidence for small minsters remains to be assembled, these will be underestimates. Studies of different areas suggest that 30 to 40 per cent of known minsters had urban or quasi-urban attributes by 1300, and that maybe 50 to 60 per cent of medieval small towns have minster origins.[221] Given that the secularization of minsters and the establishment of lay residences near them gathered momentum only slightly earlier than urbanization, it must sometimes be doubtful whether the church or the secular centre provided the main stimulus. Nonetheless, the specifically monastic context of much of the earliest economic evidence is supported by the topography of some small towns which are grouped around ex-minsters (Fig. 38), sometimes leaving secular manorial centres on their fringes.[222] The churches remained the natural foci for growth, however much of the revenue thus generated was syphoned off by proprietors.

These broad patterns disguise complexities in the experience of individual sites which are not yet properly understood, and which can only be explored through archaeology. Hitherto, while we have learnt a good deal about the origins of large planned towns before 1000 and about the layout of small ones after 1100, proto-urban settlements of the tenth and eleventh centuries remain remarkably obscure. A few excavations, notably at Northampton, Beverley, Steyning, Bampton, North Elmham, St Neots, Warminster, and Bicester, are just beginning to show the accretion of relatively low-density occupation, sometimes in the form of enclosed farmstead-type dwellings and sometimes associated with limited industrial activity, around and eventually inside religious precincts.[223] At North Elmham, writes Peter Wade-Martins, early eleventh-century villagers 'moved onto the area which during the tenth century seems to have been reserved exclusively for the use of the large halls and their outbuildings. The site now took on quite a different character, with

---

[220] These calculations are based on the lists in Darby 1977: 364–70, and Hill 1984: 131–2.

[221] Cumbria: Winchester 1987: 122–7. The south midlands and upper Thames region: Blair 2000: map 11.1; Blair 1994: 57, 117–21 (and cf. Blair 1996*a* for the Thames valley). Dorset: Hall 2000: 7 compared with 102. Somerset: Aston 1986: 62 compared with 74–6. Such calculations obviously require defining both minsters and towns, and in using these data I have had no choice but to adopt criteria of my own. A nation-wide analysis is needed.

[222] The examples in Blair 1988*c*: figs. 2.1–2, 2.3, and 2.5 support this proposition, though the argument which they illustrate there needs radical revision. Bampton is a clear case of a manorial centre left on the margin of a small town which developed around a minster focus: Blair 1998*c*.

[223] Williams and others 1985: 43–4; Armstrong and others 1991: 9–22; Gardiner and Greatorex 1997; Blair 1998*c*; Wade-Martins 1980: 125–95; Addyman 1973; Haslam 1984: 118–21; Blair 2002*b*. For Stafford see above, n. 91.

peasant dwellings with their outbuildings, sheds and animal pens set within fenced enclosures.'[224] The discovery of simple sunken-floored timber buildings at the incipient minster-towns of Northampton, Steyning, and Bampton[225] underlines the distinctive character of such places: larger versions are characteristic of major towns in the late tenth and eleventh centuries, and at this date (in contrast to the early Anglo-Saxon period) they seem to be unknown in ordinary rural settlements.

In the mid tenth century, the proto-urban landscape may have had a homogeneity which it would have lost by 1066. Even the big towns were mainly divided into large, open-ground tenements (*hagae*), resembling farm-yards and still supporting relatively low populations, which were not unlike the homesteads grouped around a minster such as Steyning. It may have been chiefly this precocious clustering which marked out some minsters, along with the boroughs, from peasant settlements which were barely starting to coalesce into something like later medieval villages. It was only from the 970s that the townscape of the major boroughs intensified, with subdivision of plots and building-up of street frontages. The late tenth and eleventh centuries apparently saw a concentration of production, exchange, legislation, and other formal business into the rapidly growing shire towns, perhaps rather to the detriment of, for example, small-scale industry on manorial sites.[226]

It is unsurprising that some minsters, but not others, became urbanized during these stages in the growth of the market economy, for locational factors must have operated with growing force. This is the point at which 'central place theory', as modified by historical geographers and anthropologists, becomes more relevant to the English case: a hierarchy of regional and local commercial centres was crystallizing, their catchments determined by criteria such as range of goods and services, or accessibility.[227] The minsters' inherited advantages will have operated powerfully on these market forces, but by no means have overridden them. The actual outcome, in which many of the potentially urban minster sites forged ahead while others stagnated, is therefore exactly what might have been predicted.

The clearest victims of this winnowing-out were those cathedrals which

---

[224] Wade-Martins 1980: 151.

[225] Williams 1979: 92–5; Gardiner and Greatorex 1997: 159–61; Blair 1998*c*: 127–8. Manchester may provide another example: Griffiths 2001: 173, 177–8.

[226] Astill 1991: 104–9, 112–13; Biddle 1976*b*: 340–2, 382–5, 453; Blair 1994: 149–52, 161–3; Wormald 1999*a*: 430–8.

[227] Above, pp. 264–5. Austin 1986: 101–3, is a stimulating attempt to chart the emergence of a Christaller-type urban hierarchy in north-east England from a landscape of pre-urban foci. But the evidence does not support its starting assumption that the region had a network of stable royal centres by the ninth century.

by 1050 had been left absurdly stranded in 'villages',[228] but the experience of many ordinary minsters was similar. Some developed into proper towns, especially in regions where the extension of the shire system gave them a chance to acquire official functions, whereas in other cases the early promise of growth atrophied: Northampton illustrates the first experience, Steyning the second. At the less successful sites, small-scale industry and hospitality functions will have declined as people turned to the major centres to buy their goods, and lodged there to transact their business. It may often have been at this stage that the old minsters which are now isolated or attached only to villages—more than half the known total—failed as settlement nuclei. Marketing functions, especially at minsters which stood at nodal points or on through-routes, may have been more resilient in what was probably already a distributive economy with hierarchies of markets. It is interesting that at least nineteen of the eighty-seven mints recorded between 973 and 1066 (albeit mostly small ones) were at minster sites which were neither Alfredian boroughs nor eleventh-century shire towns.[229] Potential for development may often have been delayed rather than suppressed.

After 1050 the tide of settlement planning and town foundation flowed across the face of England, creating completely new settlements but also re-structuring old ones: a broad range of minster-orientated settlements now acquired a coherent and stable topography which has survived to appear on Ordnance Survey maps.[230] Among the earliest are small towns developed by reformed Benedictine monasteries at their own gates. A recent study of St Albans suggests that deliberate urban development by the community on the edge of its precinct may have begun as early as the tenth century.[231] Other cases are Bury St Edmunds, where a new town 'within a greater perimeter' was laid out at the abbey gate between 1066 and 1086; Abingdon, with its 'ten merchants dwelling before the gate of the church' in Domesday Book; and Evesham, where the growth of a complex settlement, occupational diversity, and a cloth trade can be traced through the late eleventh and twelfth

---

[228] For this reason several cathedrals moved site, for instance Crediton to Exeter (*C&S* 524–33), and Dorchester-on-Thames, commercially overshadowed by Oxford and Wallingford, to Lincoln (Blair 1994: 117–19).

[229] Hill 1984: 131–2. My list (probably conservative and certainly not definitive) is: Aylesbury, Bedwyn, Berkeley, Bury, Caistor, Dover, Frome, Horncastle, Launceston, Milborne Port, Newark, Pershore, Peterborough, Reading, Rochester, Steyning, Sudbury, Taunton, Warminster.

[230] It is again French historians and archaeologists who have been more alive to church-generated settlements in this period: see for instance Fournier 1962: 127–90, 539–76, or the essays in Fixot and Zadora-Rio 1994.

[231] Slater 1998; it must be said, though, that the supposed urbanizing activities of a mid tenth-century abbot are known only from a late source, which locates them well before the earliest reliable evidence for a reformed community at St Albans.

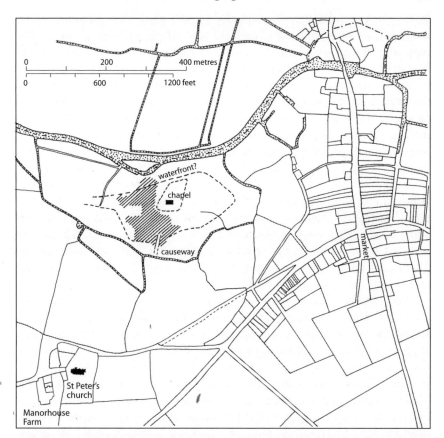

39. Minster to town at *Brandon* (Suffolk): the rich ecclesiastical site abandoned around 850 (shown hatched; cf. Fig. 25), and the parish church of St Peter, represent a settlement nucleus perpetuated after the Conquest as a typical small town with main street and burgage-plots.

centuries.[232] These are merely the top of a pyramid: a much larger number of unreformed minsters appear in Domesday Book with 'messuages' (*hagae*) and burgesses, or have quasi-urban attributes visible by 1300.[233] Typically, planned streets and burgage-plots survive from this period, but have obliterated any organic pre-Conquest settlement growth.

Even so, the former minster precincts can often be traced, sometimes with

---

[232] DB ii. 372; DB i. 58ᵛ; Hart 1992: 57–9; Hilton 1982; Astill 1991: 113; Slater 1996; Barrow 2000*a*: 133–4, 138–9. For other cases indicated by topography see Aston and Bond 1987: 68–77.

[233] Blair 2000: 256–61, 268–9. Cf. Waltham, where the settlement which grew beside the minster could be called a *burgus*: *Walt. Chron.* 74.

the outlines of triangular market areas at their gates; burgage-plots tend to lie in distinct blocks, added around the edge of the precinct or encroaching within it.[234] Today the zone around an English ex-minster, like its equivalent the French or Breton *bourg*, can retain the detached and slightly sleepy atmosphere of a precinct or close, adjoining the market-place or high street but set somehow apart.[235] Such places (Figs. 38–9), with their more complex accretive layouts, look obviously different from ordinary twelfth- and thirteenth-century planned settlements.

In less immediately visible ways, even the smaller minster settlements tended to keep a distinct character. In religious terms the survival in their midst of clerical communities, with long histories behind them and with an important pastoral role in rural hinterlands, must have made them special. Parish guilds, which sometimes had a continuous life between at least the eleventh and fourteenth centuries, formed a bridge from the religious life of minsters to the social life of towns and mother-parishes; more complex patterns of liturgical and guild activity marked out many former minsters into the later middle ages.[236]

Economically, they had a strong tendency to retain their old character as the centres of complex estates. Christopher Dyer has noted the tendency in Domesday Book for groups of 'inland-orientated' peasants such as cottars to concentrate around incipient towns,[237] a point which can be taken further by observing that many such places were minster centres, and that sometimes the cottars were specifically linked to the minster in 1086 or even later. The minsters of the Thames valley provide four illustrations.[238] Two of them involve the provisioning of developed urban communities in 1086: forty-one cottars at Westminster paying rent for their gardens, and twenty-three 'men with little gardens' living beside Oxford's secondary minster of St Peter.[239] Bampton, with a market worth 50*s.* in 1086, was surrounded by satellite

---

[234] Slater 1982: 188–90, and Blair 2000: 250–8, for market-places. Hall 2000: 49–78, for a survey of minster settlements in Dorset and their development into lay settlements.

[235] G. I. Meirion-Jones, *The Vernacular Architecture of Brittany* (Edinburgh, 1982), 35, gives an evocative description of the *bourgs* at Breton *plou* centres which recalls many of the more rural English minsters: 'Essentially a non-agricultural nucleated settlement developed around the parish church, it comes to life on Sundays and market days, but for the rest of the week gives the impression of being lifeless. . . . Roads radiate to outlying farms and hamlets on the parish boundary and often go no further. A *placître*, a triangular space, usually lies on the periphery and is often lined with farms. Other modern essentials of a *bourg* are its *mairie*, post-office, a school, shops, cafés, agricultural tradesmen and a weekly market on the *place*.' Cf. ibid. 26–8 and Davies 1988: 36, 65–6, for the equivalence of *bourgs* with *plebs* churches.

[236] Below, pp. 453–5, 509–10; cf. Rosser 1988*a*; Rosser 1992; Blair 1998*a*.

[237] Dyer 1985; cf. Faith 1997: 70–4, and above, p. 252.

[238] Blair 1996*a*: 13–14, for references.

[239] DB i. 128, 158ᵛ. Cf. the eighteen gardens at Steyning which were in contention between St Cuthmann's minster and William de Briouze in 1086: *Lawsuits*, 129 (No. 163).

settlements with names in -*cot*, and as late as 1317 a rental of the rectory manor reveals some fifty cottage tenements grouped around the church. The fourth case is Cookham, where in 1086 the minster's two remaining hides housed ten cottars, as against only twenty-one on the king's eighteen hides.[240] It says much for the minsters' economic role that they still, after three centuries of attrition to their wealth and independence, remained linked to service provision and the creation of surpluses.

Tenth- and eleventh-century churchmen mourned the golden age of Bede and railed against the more obvious agents of its destruction. But if minsters were victims of Vikings and of rapacious kings, they were more fundamentally victims of their own success. They had become so important as economic and strategic centres that the great men of the world had an overwhelming self-interest in absorbing them completely. And the patterns of life, the estate-management regimes, and the central-place functions which the minsters had pioneered were progressively assumed by secular manorial centres, both royal and aristocratic, and by towns. The minsters persisted as adjuncts to developed secular places, merely one element in a more complex late Anglo-Saxon world.

Communities, patronage, and reform (i): from Alfred to Eadgar

To qualify that rather negative conclusion, it must be stressed that minsters were still numerous and still of great local importance. At King Eadgar's death in 975, most of them probably remained a good deal more wealthy than they would be a century later, and competition from local churches was barely a cloud on their horizon. Kings and other owners took an active interest in minsters' religious lives, and the tenth and eleventh centuries saw several initiatives to rebuild and reorganize communities. The reform and re-endowment of some sites as Benedictine abbeys has dominated the literature, contemporary and modern, to the point of consigning all other kinds of intervention to oblivion. Thanks to the last generation of research, we can now hope for a more balanced view of how religious communities, in all their diversity, fitted into the political, financial, and devotional aspirations of those who controlled them and lived near them.

It can occasionally be seen that individual minsters not only escaped destruction by the Vikings, but must also have enjoyed a measure of support and protection from rulers and local magnates. The level of patronage cannot be quantified from the stray references collected above, and church buildings

---

[240] DB i. 56ᵛ.

between the mid ninth and mid tenth centuries are peculiarly hard to date. But if we can judge from Deerhurst (perhaps more an exceptional survival than exceptional in its own day), at least some minsters were capable of relatively ambitious modernization.[241] Minster patronage in the early tenth century seems to have initiated the east midlands fashion for sumptuous west towers, notably Barnack with its elaborate decoration in a style looking back to ninth-century Mercia, and its ceremonial seat (for an archpriest or 'elder'?) in the internal west wall.[242]

While some communities may have financed buildings and fittings from inherited resources, it is hard to doubt that lay patrons had a role. The minsters founded by Edward the Elder and Æthelflæd at Winchester and Gloucester were built and embellished on a princely scale (Fig. 40).[243] Admittedly these were prestige court projects; but Æthelflæd's minsters in other western Mercian towns could be part of a broader programme of investment, possibly connected with development of the hundredal system. One of these more obscure sites, Winwick (Cheshire) with its probably Æthelwoldian cult of St Oswald, acquired a stupendous stone cross, its head nearly six feet across, which must have been one of the largest in Britain.[244] The accumulations of sculpture at such sites as Gosforth, Bakewell, or Sancreed[245] suggest active involvement by new local aristocracies, perhaps especially incoming Scandinavian aristocracies in the north and English ones in the south-west.

It is much harder to see what kinds of religious life the minsters supported than to see how they were controlled or endowed, but we can start with a broad generalization. Between the reigns of Alfred and William II, most minsters except the greatest approximated to a flexible but widely accepted norm. This was the 'secular' community of men in priest's orders: living at a central site, associated in the service of one central church and (probably) the pastoral care of one mother-parish, but not necessarily holding assets in common, sleeping in a dormitory, or bound to any strict liturgical round. The clerics in such communities were often married: it was a running sore for reformers (echoing Bede long before) that their endowments could be passed on to lay or priestly heirs, enmeshing monastic assets in family strategies. Thus Alfred's laws seem to assume clerical minsters in which priests held shares. If a criminal takes refuge in 'any church which a bishop has consecrated' he is to be moved into another building 'if the community (*hiwan*)

[241] Above, pp. 128, 307.

[242] Taylor and Taylor 1965–78: i. 43–7; Fernie 1983: 139–41 (sceptical on date); Gem 1991: 817–19 (more confident of an early tenth-century date). Cf. Brigstock (Fernie 1983: 138–9).

[243] Biddle and Kjølbye-Biddle forthcoming; Heighway and Bryant 1999. See Rumble 2001: 235–7, and Thacker 2001: 253–4, for the likelihood that Edward's enthusiasm for the New Minster at Winchester was to the detriment of the Old Minster.

[244] Bailey 1980a: 159–61, 231–2, pl. 56; Thacker 1995: 121–2; Bailey 1996b: 29.

[245] Above, pp. 316, 306 n.

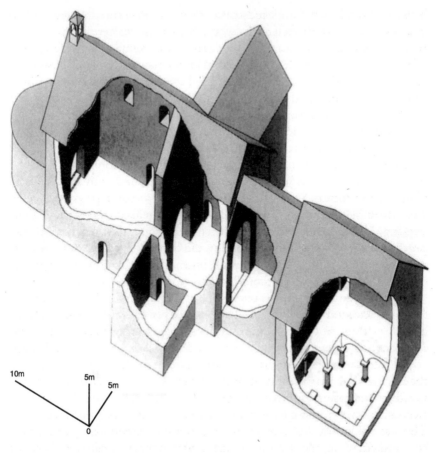

40. Royal patronage in late ninth-century *Gloucester*: St Peter's 'golden minster' as built by Æthelred and Æthelflaed, with the crypted mausoleum or shrine-chapel added shortly afterwards. (Heighway and Bryant 1999: fig. 1.9.)

have more need of their church', and the 'elder' (*ðære cirican ealdor*) is to supervise him. A priest who kills another man 'is to be handed over, and all of the monastic[?] property which he bought for himself, and the bishop is to unfrock him, and he is to be delivered up out of the minster'.[246]

---

[246] Af. 5–5. 2, 21 (*Gesetze*, 50–2, 62; *C&S* 24–5, 29–30). *Mynstres ealdor*, as a generic term for the head of a minster, occurs in 695 (Wihtred, c. 17, *Gesetze*, 13), and in a late tenth-century Benedictine context (S 1449; *RASC* 102). The heads of tenth- and eleventh-century unreformed minsters were known by various terms, but 'elder' recurs; at Christchurch (Hants.), for instance, the clergy in the 1090s treated their leader 'not as dean—for they were ignorant of the name—but as elder and patron' (below, p. 516). The Chester colleges in 1086 were headed respectively by a *custos* and a *matricularius* (DB i. 263).

There is unlikely to have been uniformity, and old ways will have lingered in conservative regions such as the west midlands. A charter of 883 addresses 'the abbot and the community at Berkeley'; Winchcombe had recently had abbesses in 897; and St Milburh's double house at Much Wenlock, though now under a male 'elder', may have retained some female members in 901.[247] In Wessex, Wareham had nuns in the 870s, Wimborne possibly in 900, while Cheddar may have been a double house in Edward the Elder's reign.[248] Alfred's laws envisage monks, though ones who borrow property and have lords.[249] But it is evident that the sites reviewed in the first part of this chapter were now occupied mainly by priests, as were the new communities in the cathedrals and minsters founded by Edward, Æthelflæd, and their heirs in the wake of territorial re-structuring. Although wills and other texts often use phrases like 'the servants of God' and 'the holy foundation', the old terminology of monks, nuns, 'monastic conversation', and 'regular life' had largely vanished. The priests of Horningsea (Cambs.),[250] with their financial dealings and family loyalties, were probably more typical of English minsters through the period than any conventional monastic model.

Large, diverse communities were thus reduced to establishments altogether more modest and less complex. In a sense this levelling-down stemmed inevitably from the diminution of their resources and status, but it was also a response to other pressures. Minsters would always have contained *some* priests, and the proportion in orders may have gradually increased with the general rise in monastic ordination.[251] Ninth-century episcopal attempts to maximize the pastoral utility of minsters could (ironically, given the attitude of Eadgar's bishops) have hastened clericalization.[252] Even if the priests were originally subject to abbots and abbesses, their role in pastoral care may have helped them to seem indispensable while the monastic high culture of the eighth century eroded away. The courtly abbesses and nuns were integral to that culture and never likely to outlast it; their world was fading well before the Vikings came, and even perhaps before Carolingian-inspired suspicion of double houses reached England.[253] It was the clergy who had become embedded in local life, and that was why they survived.

---

[247] S 218, S 1442, S 221. The witnesses to the second include three women. The third is addressed to the *congregatio* of Wenlock, and says that the land is to be 'sub dominio senioris illius eclæsiæ'; the witnesses include four women. Cf. Foot 2000, ii. 207–9; Yorke 2003*b*: 47–71.

[248] *Asser*, c. 49 (pp. 36–7; trans. p. 82); *ASC* s.a. 900 (pp. 92–3); S 806. Cf. Foot 2000: ii. 197–204, 233–7, 59–61.

[249] Af. 20 (*Gesetze*, 60; *C&S* 29).   [250] Above, p. 294.

[251] For which see Constable 1982.   [252] Above, p. 125.

[253] Schneider 1985: 24–6, 36–7, 309; Sims-Williams 1990: 118; Foot 2000, i. 61–84; Yorke 2003*b*: 47–58.

In a wider context the clericalization of English minsters is no surprise whatever, for it was exactly what happened elsewhere. In post-Carolingian Europe, reform both monastic and canonical was directed so regularly against the decadence and laxity of 'clerics' as to suggest that their way of life was ubiquitous, as it certainly was in the numerous *collégiales* of tenth- and eleventh-century France and Normandy.[254] In Wales and Cornwall there is a fairly clear contrast between the monastic communities mentioned in early sources and the groups of priests, as involved in land-strategies as their English counterparts, who appear during the tenth to twelfth centuries;[255] the Welsh *clas* communities, as they emerge in late sources, are directly comparable in character and organization to English clerical minsters of the eleventh and early twelfth centuries.[256] Irish 'monasteries' became secular collegiate communities despite retaining the terminology of abbots and monks, while several of the Scottish religious centres are known to have housed groups of clergy well integrated with local aristocratic life.[257] In Brittany the exceptionally well-documented groups of clergy who served regional churches seem much as one might imagine English minster-priests: literate and articulate, with a hereditary interest in their office and properties, central to the life of the localities in which they were firmly rooted.[258]

The pattern and the *raison d'être* for this mode of religious life had been set long before, by the groups of priests serving the *vici* of late and post-Roman Europe under episcopally appointed archpriests.[259] The Rule of Chrodegang of Metz (*c.*755) and the Rule of Aachen (816) sought to revive this tradition, in a pure and strict form which borrowed extensively from monastic rules. Even on the Continent their impact was limited, however, and in the tenth century the clerical life in a laxer form prevailed, flourishing uncontrolled under lay patronage. In England, where minsters were so bound up with local territorial interests and episcopal authority was so weak, it could hardly fail to succeed. It ran along the grain of late Anglo-Saxon society, providing lords with clerical personnel free from restrictive rules, and

---

[254] Wormald 1988: 27–8, for an illustration; Hubert 1977 and Musset 1961 for the *collégiales*.

[255] Davies 1978: 124–8, on south Wales: 'the tenor of the evidence, with its later stress on priests, is to suggest an increasing preponderance of houses of secular clergy, but it is far from conclusive'. Olson 1989: 106: 'the early monasteries of Cornwall clearly ended up as groups of priests serving and sharing the lands and revenues of a church'. For Wales see also Pryce 1992*a*: 52–5 and Pryce 1992*b*: 28 (suggesting that appropriation of church lands by kindreds happened relatively late in the period); Davies 1994: 93–6, for an over-view of religious communities in the Brittonic world at this date.

[256] Evans 1992; Pryce 1993: 184–8.

[257] Sharpe 1992: 101–3, 107–8; Macquarrie 1992 (e.g. Deer, p. 130, where a local aristocrat gave a feast for a hundred people at the central church every Christmas and Easter); Davies 1994: 97–101.

[258] Davies 1983: 191–2, 195–6; Davies 1988: 100–2; above, p. 162.

[259] Above, p. 37.

local communities with priests who could relate to them on their own terms, socially as well as spiritually. Ecclesiastical historians' distaste for the lifestyle of secular minsters, which has become less explicit but can even now seem virtually instinctive, reflects contemporary partisanship absorbed into a historiographical tradition which has privileged the centre over the localities, and the ideals of reformers over the realities and needs of grass-roots religious life.[260]

Nonetheless, a major alternative to the clerical mode, and one which had a decisive impact on elite religion and culture, did become available in the mid to late tenth century. The reform of many important minsters as communities of regular Benedictine monks was made possible by King Eadgar's sponsorship; at its centre, a small but powerful group enunciated high ideals so strongly felt, and rhetoric of such dramatic intensity, that they have held the attention of scholars to the neglect of other possible viewpoints. Recently, a series of important studies has thrown new light on the reform and its proponents, and helps us to see the whole phenomenon in a wider context.[261] Lengthy discussion of the reformed houses, especially of their political, devotional, cultural, and liturgical achievements, would be inappropriate here. Reform does, however, have a central place within the continuum of intervention in the affairs of minsters by kings, lords, and bishops.

The recent work, setting the English reform in its European context, has drawn attention to ways in which its indigenous background and effects were decidedly singular. One is the isolation, compared with both earlier and later centuries, of the ninth-century English Church. There is no evidence, except rather equivocally at Canterbury under Archbishop Wulfred, that the Frankish rules for canons, let alone Benedict of Aniane's monastic rule, had any impact.[262] This meant that while England retained many religious communities, no clear prescriptive norms of the religious life remained embedded in its culture to be taken up by tenth-century reformers. Rules and models therefore had to be drawn from the distant past, or from outside; and since grass-roots enthusiasm for reform—whether monastic or canonical—was at best lukewarm, they had to be imposed from above if they were to succeed. Formidably powerful, the West Saxon kings assumed the Carolingians' mantle in this as in so much else: in seeking to impose monastic uniformity as a matter of political principle, Eadgar at Winchester was following Louis the Pious at Aachen.[263] From these circumstances emerged ideals that were

---

[260] As astutely observed by Wormald 1988: 35: 'our assessment of reform may be too much affected by our instinctive sympathy for royal and central, rather than aristocratic and local, power.'
[261] Below, n. 281.   [262] Above, p. 125.
[263] Wormald 1988: 18–19, 31–5; Cubitt 1997: 79, 82–3.

clear-cut and uncompromising but also rather narrow-based, and that were formed by a very few committed protagonists. For some of these protagonists, the guiding light was the glorious English monastic past portrayed by the greatest English historian: a large dose of nostalgia informed their efforts.

Nostalgia in fact begins with Alfred. In his celebrated preface to his translation of Gregory's 'Regula Pastoralis', he remembered 'what wise men there were in former times throughout England, of both spiritual and lay orders; and how happy times then were throughout England . . . ; and also how zealous the spiritual orders were both about teaching and learning and about all the services which they should do for God; and how foreigners came hither to this land in search of knowledge and instruction, and we now would have to get them from abroad, if we were to have them'. Before the recent disasters, the king recalled, there had been 'a great multitude of the servants of God', even though they no longer had the learning to understand the wisdom of the past.[264]

Alfred does not define the 'wise men in former times', but the saintly monks of Bede's 'Ecclesiastical History' (a translation of which he probably commissioned) were surely in his mind. His principal religious foundations, for monks at Athelney and for nuns at Shaftesbury, were both monastic in a strict sense,[265] and it was evidently the official stance of his court that the 'true' monastic life, as practised on the Continent and formerly in England, was more virtuous than that lived in contemporary English minsters. He had to people Athelney with foreign monks, says Asser, because

at first, he had no noble or free-born man of his own race who would of his own accord undertake the monastic life . . . —not surprisingly, since for many years past the desire for the monastic life had been totally lacking in that entire race (and in a good many other peoples as well!), even though quite a number of minsters which had been built in that area still remain but do not maintain the rule of monastic life in any consistent way. I am not sure why: either it is because of the depredations of foreign enemies . . . , or else because of the people's enormous abundance of riches of every kind, as a result of which (I suspect) this kind of monastic life came all the more into disrepect.[266]

Such views in Alfred's circle, doubtless genuinely felt, began a broadening of horizons that was to culminate in monastic reform under Eadgar. What

---

[264] Above, n. 1; cf. Dumville 1992*a*: 185–98.

[265] *Asser*, cc. 92–8 (pp. 79–85; trans. pp. 102–5). The Athelney community, headed by a Continental Saxon abbot and including Franks and Vikings, was an odd and not entirely happy mix: as Asser relates, two members tried to murder their abbot as he prayed in the church. As Yorke observes (1995: 202), Asser's conception of a strict monastic rule could have been a Welsh rather than necessarily a Carolingian one.

[266] *Asser*, c. 93 (pp. 80–1; trans. p. 103).

must on no account be supposed is that they were incompatible with continued patronage of secular minsters, or with manipulation of their assets when convenient: it will be recalled that the 'trifles' which Alfred gave to Asser included two west-country minsters, and that Asser possessed himself of them with all speed. Economic realities may have dictated that only a small minority of royal minsters could be exempted from this kind of patronage. If Alfred preferred the regulars he was keen to present himself as a good lord to the seculars, assigning an eighth of his income to 'neighbouring minsters throughout the Saxon land and Mercia'.[267] It is striking that neither of Alfred's principal heirs, Edward in Wessex and Æthelflæd in Mercia, is known to have founded a single Benedictine house. The new minsters at Winchester and Gloucester were apparently clerical, and there is no real evidence that even the nunneries at Winchester, Romsey, and Wilton, probably founded by Edward and his mother, matched the Benedictine image later projected back on them.[268]

Kings from Æthelstan to Eadwig (924–59) were similarly eclectic and inclusive. Æthelstan's reign saw a considerable opening-up of court and Church to foreign influences, most notably from Brittany, and a determined reconstruction, visible to us especially through the circulation and production of books, of the shattered ecclesiastical culture.[269] He also founded (or re-founded) two minsters, at Milton Abbas (Dorset) and Muchelney (Somerset), though there is no reason to think that they were anything other than clerical, and we know them only from late and dubious sources.[270] These waters are muddied by Æthelstan's almost folkloric reputation as a founder, which made him a favourite hero of later origin-myths. It is likely that the reputation was in general terms well founded, and more-or-less reliable charters show him patronizing Sherborne, St Augustine's at Canterbury, St Peter's at York, and Selsey.[271] He gave lavishly to the Cuthbert community at Chester-le-Street (now apparently clerical under a provost): a relationship of mutual advantage in which books and treasure were transferred from Wessex to the impoverished north, while the north contributed a great national saint to shed lustre on the house of Wessex.[272] Æthelstan's association with the

---

[267] *Asser*, c. 102 (p. 89; trans. p. 107). These were perhaps the same privileged group of minsters 'to which the king's food-rent belongs' that had special sanctuary privileges: Af. 2 (*Gesetze*, 48; *C&S* 23).

[268] Yorke 1995: 203–6; cf. Dumville 1992*a*: 198–9, 202; Foot 2000: ii. 152–3, 221–31, 243–52.

[269] Dumville 1992*a*: 154–63, 179–82, 200–1; Dumville 1992*b*: 97–8, 111–26.

[270] Dumville 1992*a*: 163; Yorke 1995: 204–5.

[271] S 422–3; S 394; S 407; S 403.

[272] Bonner 1989: 390–4; Rollason 1989*b*; Simpson 1989; Dumville 1992*b*: 106–10. Aldred *presbiter indignus*, who added his famous colophon to the Lindisfarne Gospels, is probably identical with Aldred *se provast* who was in Wessex in the bishop of Chester-le-Street's company in 970 (*Rituale*, pp. xiv–xv, xix; Bonner 1989: 391–3).

zones of 'protected space' around some Cornish and Yorkshire minsters is problematic but intriguing; Brittonic influence provides one possible explanation.[273] The acquisition of a Welsh or Cornish gospel-book by the minster-priests of Great Bedwyn (Wilts.), probably in Æthelstan's reign, illustrates how quickly this Brittonic culture at court could have percolated to ordinary West Saxon minsters.[274]

The cosmopolitan religious cross-currents under Æthelstan and his successors naturally included the strict monastic. The group of abbots who witness some of his charters are evidence for (unidentifiable) houses of monks in England, whether surviving or reformed.[275] Bishops who identify themselves as *monachi* may have had confraternity with Continental houses, and by the 930s we find a generation of bishops, notably Oda of Ramsbury and (from 941) Canterbury, whose monastic interests led directly into the reforms of Eadgar's reign.[276] There are signs of growing interest in monasticism among the aristocracy, most intriguingly the series of thirteen grants of land during 939–55 to 'religious women', probably bent on pursuing their vocations in their own households.[277] The rising tide of monastic reform in continental Europe, and in particular the intellectual developments at Fleury on the Loire and in Lotharingia, was at last beginning to have a major impact on English culture.

Yet these kings and their advisers did not hold the view, so soon to develop in the circle of Bishop Æthelwold of Winchester, that Benedictine monasticism was the only worthwhile form of the religious life. It is anachronistic to see contradictions in the career of Eadmund (939–46), who gave Glastonbury to St Dunstan, welcomed refugees from monastic reforms on the Continent to the old minster at Bath, and may have granted privileges to the unreformed community of Bury St Edmunds.[278] Eadwig gave land to the minster-priests of Bampton (955 × 7), as did the young Eadgar, before his accession in Wessex, to those of St Wærburh's at Chester (958).[279] Archbishop Oda was interested in reform, but his 'constitutions' (942 × 6) describe

---

[273] Above, p. 223; cf. S 1207, the grant to Lansallos by a Cornish *comes* which may have been issued under Æthelstan's aegis (above, p. 305).

[274] Dumville 1992a: 79–82.

[275] Ibid. 164 n. 153. I cannot see any particular reason for identifying Evesham, Glastonbury, or Malmesbury as strictly monastic in this period.

[276] Ibid. 164–6, 176, 193, 203, arguing for a continuum of reforming interests from Alfred's advisers to the generation of the 940s.

[277] Ibid. 165–6, 177–8. Foot 2000 argues that large numbers of women may have pursued vocations as *nunnan* (as distinct from *mynecenas*) outside the established female houses. See Yorke 2003b: 72–85, for royal patronage of nunneries before Eadgar.

[278] Dumville 1992a: 176; Nightingale 1996: 25–7 (arguing that Bath may have received exiles from Fleury as well as Saint-Bertin); S 507 (a disputed but possibly genuine text).

[279] *Regesta W. I,* 464; S 667.

the duties of priests, clerics, and monks in traditional terms, drawn mainly from pre-Viking insular sources.[280]

The English monastic reform has been so often described, and so ably re-interpreted since the early 1980s, that it need not be dwelt on here.[281] Briefly, its protagonists were three aristocratic churchmen: Dunstan, archbishop of Canterbury 959–88; Æthelwold, bishop of Winchester 963–84; and Oswald, bishop of Worcester 961–92 and archbishop of York from 971. After reaching maturity in Æthelstan's court circle, where they must have absorbed the intellectual currents of the 930s, Dunstan and Æthelwold spent much of the next decade developing monastic life, and studying Benedictine texts, at the old minster of Glastonbury, the first centre from which reformed monasticism would be disseminated in southern England; the second was Abingdon, a decayed minster which King Eadred gave to Æthelwold in about 954. Oswald, a nephew of Archbishop Oda, was introduced by his uncle to the reformed Fleury, where he was ordained and where he spent most of the 950s. Meanwhile, during 956–8, Dunstan was exiled in Flanders, observing the Benedictine practices of St Peter's, Ghent.

Thus the accession in 959 of Eadgar, the first king prepared to identify wholeheartedly with reform, was an opportunity for two learned men with direct experience of Continental monasticism, and a third with a vision of England's own monastic past. What was special about the English reform of the 960s and 970s was that it was court-driven: occasionally imposed by royal fiat, and always backed by strong royal encouragement. Not surprisingly, monks from Glastonbury, Abingdon, and Oswald's Westbury-on-Trym rapidly colonized a considerable group of other old minsters (hardly any of the reformed houses were completely new foundations), taking rules derived from a mixture of European sources; a small but important group of nunneries, closely connected with the royal house, was established in Wiltshire

---

[280] *C&S* 67–74. Oda principally uses the legatine statutes of 786, with elements (e.g. on wandering monks, c. 6) from the *Hibernensis.* The injunctions for priests and *clerici* (cc. 4–5) are his own, but like other tenth-century English sources they show no trace of interest in continental rules for canons (cf. Barrow 1994: 29–33).

[281] The classic account—concerned specifically with reformed monasticism and in strong sympathy with the reformers—is that of Knowles 1949: 31–66. Growing awareness of the singularity of the English reform, and of the possibility of other points of view, can be traced through Darlington 1936, Fisher 1958, and John 1959–60. The collections of millenary essays for Æthelwold, Dunstan, and Oswald are now the starting-point: Yorke 1988*a* (especially Wormald, Lapidge, Thacker, and Yorke); Ramsay and others 1992 (especially Brooks, Lapidge, and Thacker); and Brooks and Cubitt 1996 (especially Barrow, Bullough, Lapidge, Nightingale, Thacker, and Wareham); Cubitt 1997 takes stock of all three. Other useful contributions are: Williams 1982; Brooks 1984: 243–56; Gransden 1989; Stafford 1989: 184–93; Yorke 1995: 210–25; Cownie 1998: 14–18; and Foot 2000. The reformed houses are listed by Knowles, and mapped by Hill 1994: 150–4 and Cownie 1998: 27. Many of the main texts on the reform and 'reaction' are printed in *C&S* 113–65.

and Hampshire. The English houses received a uniform rule, the 'Regularis Concordia', and a notable feature of the whole movement was its *dirigiste* tone: there was to be one acceptable mode of the religious life, and the king and his advisers were to decide it.

The narratives of the reform present Eadgar's reign as a golden age which transformed the English Church. So it did, in terms of what it added; its impact on what existed already is another matter. Geographically, it was restricted to old Wessex and to the zones in the west and east midlands where Oswald and Æthelwold held property; female houses were virtually confined to the West Saxon heartland. The secular communities were expelled from Winchester on royal and papal authority,[282] but in general Eadgar's bishops reformed minsters in the time-honoured tradition of their eighth- and ninth-century predecessors: by acquiring them as personal property from patrons or kindred. By 975, up to thirty male houses (many of them quite small) and seven or eight nunneries had been re-founded. Given that some hundreds of secular minsters were probably still functioning, it is unlikely that the reformed communities ever comprised much more than 10 per cent of the total. This numerical measure is in a way misleading (the richest reformed houses probably each had assets worth those of dozens of ordinary minsters), but it puts the local impact of the reform into perspective.

In England, as on the Continent, the fundamental aim of the Benedictine movement was to establish and disseminate high liturgical, spiritual, and pastoral standards. To generalize from the highly coloured and polemical texts written and inspired by St Æthelwold, the sternest and most uncompromising of the reformers, distorts the picture. Recent work has stressed the extent to which Dunstan, Æthelwold, and Oswald pursued their separate political, dynastic, and ecclesiastical strategies, which sometimes left them in different camps.[283] Discarding the image of three monastic heroes standing shoulder to shoulder, we can see that their attitudes to reform were not identical, and in particular that Æthelwold's rejection of all forms of religious life but the monastic was decidedly odd. The lurid stigmatizations of clerics as foul, lazy, and lascivious come mainly from his circle,[284] and it was he who

---

[282] *C&S* 109–18; Rumble 2002: 65–97, 233–7 (though the authenticity of the papal letter has been contested). There is no reason to think that many other clerical communities were forced to leave: we have evidence for Milton and Chertsey (*ASC* 'A' s.a. 964 (p. 116)), but otherwise only general (and not strictly contemporary) statements in sources concerned to emphasize government support for the movement. Wormald 2001*a*: 140 suggests a specific political context for the 'unique ferocity' of the Winchester episode.

[283] Yorke 1988*b*; Stafford 1989: 190–1; Brooks 1992; Wareham 1996; Cubitt 1997: 85–6, 93; Barrow 2000*b*: 163–5.

[284] *C&S* 125, 136, 150; Rumble 2002: 17–18, 67–9, 81–4, 131, 236. For example (S 818; Rumble 2002: 18, 131): 'Undoubtedly, the canons, disfigured by every blemish of vices, exalted with vain

stage-managed the expulsion of the unreformed communities from both Winchester minsters on 21 February 964.

Æthelwold's determination to have monks and monks only, even in his cathedral, must have looked anomalous from the Continent (where the normal model for a bishop's *familia* was the Aachen Rule for canons), and Dunstan and Oswald were not whole-hearted in following it.[285] The distinctly low-key and hesitant drift of the Canterbury cathedral community towards reformed monasticism during Dunstan's pontificate carries its own message.[286] Oswald did establish a Benedictine cathedral chapter at Worcester (as would Bishop Wulfsige at Sherborne); but he was altogether less heavy-handed than Æthelwold, building a new church for his monks alongside the clerics' church and treating the two groups as colleagues in a single episcopal *familia*.[287]

Supplementation of clerics with monks, not substitution, may in fact have been normal: at other reformed houses (including the nunneries), it is likely that the groups of priests serving parochial altars who appear in later sources had a continuous existence from the pre-Reform clerical minsters.[288] A complex religious establishment simply could not function without several priests, who would naturally organize themselves as a community along familiar and accepted lines. It is possible that Eadgar did avoid patronizing unreformed minsters, but there is no evidence that he tried to suppress them; indeed, he legislated to protect their parochial revenues.[289] Rich and prominent unreformed communities such as Chester-le-Street or Bury flourished unopposed through the reform period and beyond.[290] The polemic may belie a religious culture in Eadgar's reign which, when we probe beneath the surface, starts to look less exclusive and more like that of Æthelstan's and Eadmund's.

glory, putrifying with the malice of envy, blinded by the blemishes of avarice, taking pleasure in the fires of wantonness, entirely devoted to gluttony, subject to the earthly king not to the bishop, were wont to feast themselves by ancient custom in modern time on the food of the aforementioned land. Since indeed, following drunkenness with murder, and embracing their wives in an unseemly manner with an excessive and uncommon lust, very few wished to visit God's church, and rarely, they did not deign to keep the canonical hours.'

[285] Wormald 1988: 25, 37–8 (and cf. Darlington 1936: 403–4).

[286] Brooks 1984: 255–66; Thacker 1992*b*; Brooks 1995: 25–8.

[287] The most convincing analysis of the Worcester sources (as usual the best) is Barrow 1996. It is notable that Worcester monks were content to be referred to as *clerici*, which Winchester ones were not; that Worcester's books show a lack of interest, again in contrast to Æthelwold's houses, in Continental monastic texts; and that Worcester displayed a strong interest in pastoral care (ibid. 88, 92–3, 96).

[288] Hase 1988: 46; Rosser 1992: 270–3; Yorke 1995: 206; Blair 1998*a*: 281–2.

[289] Below, p. 442. Apart from the pre-reform Chester charter (S 667), Eadgar's only known gifts to seculars are very minor ones to ?Meonstoke (S 718) and Plympton/St Kew (S 810).

[290] *Symeon Op.* i. 211–14; *Symeon Lib.* 140–54; Aird 1998: 112–22; Ridyard 1988: 211–26; Gransden 1989: 173–9.

Yet in the narrative and liturgical sources, Æthelwold's voice remains the loudest. His vision of an all-monastic church was retrospective and nostalgic—inspired by the golden age portrayed by Bede—and was projected the more easily because England lacked coherent models for the religious life in his own day: the reform could reject the recent insular past but embrace a more distant one.[291] But history was not merely studied: as Æthelwold showed when he constructed dubious pedigrees for his houses, it could be appropriated and rewritten to inflate the former status of places which the new tides of fortune had favoured.[292] The best possible way of bringing the past under control was to obtain physical possession of the early English saints. In an age when they were believed to remain both present and active in their earthly remains, and when grants of land could be addressed to the saint in person, possession of relics meant land and power as well as prestige. Thus a feature of the reform—one in which Æthelwold showed characteristic energy—was the transfer of many saints' bones from obscure minsters and hermitages to the new communities, notably the fenland abbeys of Ramsey, Thorney, Peterborough, and Ely.[293]

This appropriation of the English Church's historical and spiritual heritage to the Benedictines was at the expense of the seculars, who risked losing both their relics and their reputations, and lacked scholars of standing to celebrate their past glories or present virtues: no response to Æthelwold has come down to us.[294] In turn, the re-handling of the material by early twelfth-century Benedictine historians, notably John of Worcester and William of Malmesbury, reinforced the stereotypes. So the reform determined not only which minsters would dominate in the future, but also which would be perceived as ancient and venerable. The reality of early Christian England, with its multiplicity of minsters and diversity of religious types, was remodelled to fit the more authoritarian perceptions of a small number of houses which followed a common observance, claimed the moral high ground, and possessed a virtual monopoly of record. The reformers used their considerable powers of communication and dissemination to form a homogeneous national religious

---

[291] Wormald 1988: 38–41; Gransden 1989; Foot 1989*a*: 318–20; Cubitt 1997: 82, 88.

[292] Wormald 1988: 39; Thacker 1988: 52–5, 63; *Abingdon*, pp. cxciii–cxciv.

[293] Thacker 1988: 60–3; Rollason 1989*a*: 177–82; Thacker 1992*b*: 232–6; Thacker 1996. Unreformed churches from which relics were stolen, such as Dereham and Wakering (*Lib. El.* 120–3; Love 2004: 66–72; Rollason 1982: 102–4), had to be presented as so disrespectful and negligent that their saints wanted to desert them. Thus the *passio* of the Wakering saints says of them: 'They were buried in the church of the vill called Wakering, which was lazily served by a few careless priests, on account of whose sloth, and the infrequency of adequate ministration by those who should have honoured them with due service, [the saints] were exasperated and unwilling to dwell there further.'

[294] Thomas Charles-Edwards observes (pers. comm.): 'This is what strikes me as different about the English minsters as opposed to their Welsh and Irish counterparts: the standard offices in the latter included a teacher, the *scholasticus* of Llandeilo, the *fer léigind* of Irish and Scottish houses.'

culture, embodying carefully selected elements from the past, beneath which the religious culture of the localities sank to near-invisibility. A lasting consequence of reform polemic has been to make the Anglo-Saxon Church seem more uniform, hierarchical, and centralized than it ever really was.

Communities, patronage, and reform (ii): from Æthelred II to William II

For all their great and continuing achievements, the reformed houses after the 970s lived more on inherited capital than on dynamic growth. There were periods when the monks enjoyed a measure of royal backing; there was a small crop of new foundations, and patronage and rebuilding at a range of others; under a series of able eleventh-century abbots the fenland houses did well.[295] But the general depletion of resources and enthusiasm is obvious, not least in an architectural and cultural recession which only lifted in the 1040s;[296] one gets a distinct sense that the dire effects of renewed Viking attacks and escalating taxation bore more heavily, relatively speaking, on the monks than on either the small minsters or the emergent local churches. This is not to say that there was a grass-roots movement against them, but merely that they now had to make their own way in a society drained of cash, and in a pluralistic religious culture of which they were no longer the unquestioned leaders. Exposed to these realities, monastic writers railed against what they saw as a malevolent conspiracy. After 975, wrote Byrhtferth of Ramsey, 'monks were smitten with fear, the people trembled; and clerics were filled with joy, for their time had come. Abbots were expelled with their monks, clerics were installed with their wives, and the error was worse than before.'[297]

It is doubtful if such stark categorizations meant much to the laity at large. It is now agreed that politics, not antipathy to monasticism, lay behind the 'anti-monastic reaction' associated with Ealdorman Ælfhere of Mercia.[298] Ælfflæd, whose will expresses such eloquent devotion to her ancestral minster at Stoke-by-Nayland, was married to the 'pro-monastic' Ealdorman Byrhtnoth.[299] Certainly by the end of the century we find aristocrats cheerfully

---

[295] Knowles 1949: 58–66; Cownie 1998: 18–22; Stafford 1989: 189, 192. The main new monastic communities were at Sherborne, Burton, Eynsham, Bury, and St Benet's; see Gransden 1985 for the re-foundation of Bury.

[296] Gem 1975.

[297] Byrhtferth, 'Vita Sancti Oswaldi' (ed. J. Raine, *The Historians of the Church of York*, i (Rolls Ser. 71. 1, 1879), 443, and (extract) *C&S* 161)).

[298] *C&S* 155–65; Fisher 1958; Williams 1982; Wormald 1988: 36–7; Wormald 1999*a*: 156.

[299] Above, p. 318; Blair 1985*a*: 119–20; Stafford 1989: 190–1.

supporting both the regulars and the seculars. Æthelgifu (*c.*990 × 1001) left substantial property to the reformed St Albans, where she hoped to be buried, and Bedford, but also stock and food-rents to what seem to be nearly all her local minsters: Ashwell, Braughing, Flitton, Henlow, Hertingfordbury, Hitchin, and Welwyn.[300] Ealdorman Æthelmaer (971 × 83) made bequests to reformed monasteries, but also to the (presumably) unreformed Cricklade and Bourne; Leofwine (998) remembered God's servants at Notley (Essex);[301] a Kentish couple, Brihtric and Ælfswith (973 × 87), left land to Godstone minster (Surrey).[302]

It is hard to know how such minor and conventional support intermeshed with the long-term decline. We can see when minsters were under external control, but rarely trace the atrophy of their local economic base or religious life. There are signs that the collapse of the communities and the ways of life that they supported was more a matter of the eleventh century than of the tenth,[303] and some of Domesday Book's impoverished minsters may have been prosperous a century earlier. Nor was it only the seculars who proved vulnerable: some of the smaller reformed houses, such as Cholsey, Bedford, and Eynsham, had reverted to the status of ordinary clerical minsters by the Conquest,[304] and Æthelred II found it necessary to provide for monks whose monasteries had been taken over by canons or nuns.[305] While the broad trend was downwards, the forces bearing on religious communities cut in more than one direction: through the eleventh century they variously experienced endowment or loss, reform or relaxation, in accordance with their proprietors' religious, political, or economic aspirations.

A few secular minsters—but perhaps only a few—were patronized by kings. The most impressive in terms of surviving evidence is probably St Mary's at Dover, with its great axial-towered church of *c.*1000, where a community of priests flourished up to the Conquest.[306] In 1004 Æthelred II con-

---

[300] S 1497 (*W. Æth.*).

[301] S 1498 (*Wills*, 24; *NMW* 117–21); S 1522. Cf. Stafford 1989: 191.

[302] S 1511 (*Wills*, 28): 'into þæm mynstre to Wolcnesstede'. This minster is otherwise unknown; it is perhaps Godstone parish church (Blair 1991*a*: 103).

[303] For instance, the several estates given by Ælfgar's family to Stoke-by-Nayland up to *c.*1000 seem to have leached away quickly thereafter (Blair 1988*b*: 3–4; Hart 1992: 501–3).

[304] Bedford and Cholsey were both Benedictine houses with abbots at the end of the tenth century (*ASC* 'B', 'C' s.a. 971 (p. 119); *NMW* 153), but both appear as secular minsters in 1086 (DB i. 211, 217ᵛ, 56ᵛ–57). Eynsham: Hardy and others 2003: 10–11. Evesham passed through a clerical phase before being reformed again (Thomas of Marlborough, *History of the Abbey of Evesham*, ed. J. Sayers and L. Watkiss (Oxford, 2003), 142–54).

[305] VI Atr. (Latin) 3. 1 (*Gesetze*, 249; *C&S* 364–5).

[306] Taylor and Taylor 1965–78: i. 214–17; Fernie 1983: 115–16; S 1461, S 1472–3, S 1400 (*RASC* 150, 190, 192, 204) for Leofwine the priest and the community of Dover; DB i. 1ᵛ; Tatton-Brown 1988: 110. Given its later history, it is highly likely that this minster was in royal hands *c.*1000, though Williams 2002: 8 prefers Earl Godwine as the re-founder.

firmed the endowments of the minster-priests at St Frideswide's, Oxford, after the burning of their buildings and charters, and apparently rebuilt the church on a larger plan.[307] Æthelred may also have endowed a small minster at Stow-on-the-Wold (Glos.), possibly in honour of his murdered brother, though the evidence is problematic.[308] In 1016 Edmund Ironside gave one-and-a-half hides to the 'new minster of the Holy Trinity, Our Lord's mother and all saints' at Peakirk (Northants.), and by 1020 Cnut had built a small minster on the site of his victory at Ashingdon (Essex).[309] After these modest benefactions, we have nothing until four writs from Edward the Confessor's last years giving rights to the cathedral chapters at Hereford and St Paul's and the minster-priests at (possibly) Wolverhampton (Staffs.) and Bromfield (Salop.), with the injunction in the case of St Paul's that they must not 'receive into their minster any more priests than their estates can bear or they themselves desire'.[310] Given Edward's Lotharingian links it is tempting to ascribe to him the remarkable cruciform aisled church, probably the work of a Lotharingian architect, on the royal manor of Great Paxton (Hunts.).[311]

This cannot be a complete picture. Nonetheless, there is rather a striking contrast between such exiguous evidence for royal patronage and the growing signs, from Cnut's reign onwards, of noble patronage. For English kings, with their distinctive and central role as protectors of the reformed abbeys, secular minsters were small fry except as a means of supporting clerical dependants. For nobles great and small, on the other hand, they offered an avenue, in the context of wider land-strategies, to building power-bases and acquiring the dignity of patrons. Until 975 the monastic party's hold at court may have discouraged the laity from major, transformative patronage of the seculars, but the re-endowment and probable rebuilding of the old minster at Wolverhampton by the Mercian noblewoman Wulfrun around 990 suggests a revived confidence in traditional forms.[312]

[307] S 909; Gem 1975: 32; Blair 1988*d*: 226, 235, 247.

[308] Blair 2002*a*: 529–30.

[309] S 947; *A-SC* 'C', 'D' s.a. 1020 (p. 154); Gem 1975: 33–4; Hart 1992: 553–65; Rodwell 1993*b*. The nave at Peakirk could be early eleventh century: Taylor and Taylor 1965–78: ii. 488–9.

[310] S 1101, S 1104, S 1155, S 1162; the Wolverhampton writ is spurious but could have some genuine basis. For Bromfield cf. Blair 1985*a*: 128–31.

[311] Taylor and Taylor 1965–78: ii. 484–8; Fernie 1983: 129–34. In 1086 Great Paxton, which had belonged to King Edward, had a church and priest with one hide (DB i. 207). Given the archi-tectural evidence this entry almost certainly disguises a college of clergy, for a charter of 1124 × 8 enjoins that 'prior et clerici eiusdem ecclesie in religione canonice eidem ecclesie serviant' (Parsons 1916–17).

[312] S 1380, a spurious privilege of Archbishop Sigeric with genuine elements, confirms Wulfrun's land-grants and her building of a new church in honour of God, St Mary, and all saints in the ven-erable minster of *Hamtune*, where masses are to be performed and which is to be ruled by a reli-gious provost. The appearance of the name as *Wlurenehamtona* (i.e. 'Wulfrun's *hām-tūn*') by *c*.1080

Such initiatives did not, however, become prominent until the 1030s, as the stature of the highest magnates grew and territorial power became more entrenched.[313] It was Tofig the Proud, one of Cnut's chief thegns, who transferred a wonder-working stone crucifix from Somerset to Waltham (Essex), where he installed it with great treasures in a new church served by two priests and other clergy.[314] The rise of the great earldoms coincided with growing prosperity and a revival of interest in European models, both institutional and architectural. Earl Leofric of Mercia (d. 1057) and his wife Godgifu were noted patrons of the seculars as well as the regulars, a relationship of mutual advantage which, while revitalizing several Mercian minsters, may also have enhanced their own status.[315] John of Worcester wrote that they rebuilt the minster at Coventry

from the foundations out of their own patrimony, and endowed it adequately with lands and made it so rich in various ornaments that in no minster in England might be found the abundance of gold, silver, gems and precious stones that was at that time in its possession. They enriched with precious ornaments the minsters of Leominster and Wenlock too, and the minsters at Chester of St. John the Baptist and of St. Werburg the virgin, and the church which bishop Eadnoth of Lincoln [i.e. of Dorchester, 1009–16 or 1034–49] founded in the famous place which is called Stow St Mary [Lincs].[316]

In the case of Stow, an agreement of 1053 × 5 records Leofric and Godgifu's patronage; the massive crossing-piers of the church which they or Eadnoth built there still stand, a landmark in the beginnings of English Romanesque.[317]

In Wessex, known patronage of minsters is associated less with Earl Godwine (d. 1053) than with his widow and son, Gytha and Harold. At Hartland (Devon), according to its twelfth-century 'Miracula', Gytha greatly

---

corroborates the underlying tradition (*Regesta W. I*, 796). The minster was royal by Edward the Confessor's time, if his writ for 'my priests at *Hampton*' (S 1155) has any authentic basis. Cf. *VCH Staffs.* iii. 321; Denton 1970: 41–4; *Charters of Burton Abbey*, ed. P. H. Sawyer (*Anglo-Saxon Charters*, ii, Oxford, 1979), pp. xl–xli; Hooke and Slater 1986.

[313] Cf. Brett 1995: 290–2, who observes: 'Since in Normandy these [collegiate] churches often provided the nucleus of a later, more elaborate, enterprise, it may well be that it is here we should look for the germ of magnate great churches beyond the king's control, though the development was checked by the destruction [in and after 1066] of the families that created them.' See also Cownie 1998: 23–6.

[314] *Walt. Chron.*, pp. xv–xix, 16–24. The chronicler's belief that Tofig built his church on an empty site is contradicted by archaeological evidence: Huggins and Bascombe 1992.

[315] Baxter 2003: 156–223, arguing that Leofric's family patronized minsters in regions where they were themselves tenurially weak, as a means of bolstering their power, while at the same time using minster resources to support their own commended men.

[316] *JW* ii. 582–3.

[317] S 1478; Sawyer 1998: 151–3, 246–52; Fernie 1983: 124–7.

honoured St Nectan's church, gave it lands and precious objects, and installed the clerks Æthelmann and Leofmann whose posterity held it thereafter; in 1066 there were twelve canons, each holding a ploughland.[318] Her other minster at Nether Wallop (Hants.), where Domesday records tithe and churchscot payments, was rebuilt in the early to mid eleventh century and adorned with a large 'Winchester School' wallpainting over the chancel arch.[319]

The best-recorded work of Godwine's family was at Waltham Holy Cross, which Earl Harold acquired in the late 1050s and transformed into a lavishly equipped and thoroughly up-to-date secular college. It was later remembered that he increased Tofig's two priests to a community of thirteen, provided for all their needs, and

> rejoicing that he had been able to confer upon it such remarkable prosperity that there was no church in the kingdom which approached Waltham in its fine performance of ecclesiastical offices, or in the honourable behaviour of the brethren, he began to adorn the inside of the church with many beautiful gifts. He employed the finest workmanship in the building of the church from its very foundations, using bronze plate and gold inlay everywhere; he had the capitals of the columns, the bases, and the twists of the arches adorned with a marvellous quality of workmanship. Twelve statues of the apostles were also cast to support the front of the golden altar . . . He provided in sufficient quantity the vessels necessary for service of the altar, golden for special days, silver for ordinary days. In addition there were four golden, and nine silver, reliquaries, candlesticks of gold and silver, censers, ewers, and basins, three golden, and six silver crosses; there were three large golden gospel-books, and five of silver-gilt. . . . In addition he provided the church with a large quantity of vestments, some made of unembroidered cloth and others woven with gold thread; there were copes, chasubles, dalmatics, tunics and other garments ornamented with gold and pearls.[320]

Lesser lords could not match such princely magnificence, but there is occasional evidence that small minsters were rebuilt or re-endowed as mid eleventh-century local magnates consolidated their lands and residences. A peculiarly clear case is Kirkdale (Yorks.), where Orm Gamalsson's proud inscription still adorns his modest but architecturally innovative church (Fig. 41).[321] Also probably in the 1050s, the rich East Anglian thegn Ælfric

---

[318] *Nectan*, 406–8; Pearce 1985: 265; DB Exon. 456–456ᵛ.

[319] DB i. 38ᵛ; Gem and Tudor-Craig 1981. Gytha sometimes resided at Berkeley minster (Glos.), where Godwine bought her a nearby manor so that she would not need to use up the minster's assets (DB i. 164: I owe this reference to Ann Williams).

[320] *Walt. Chron.* 26–33; ibid., pp. xix–xxv, and Huggins and Bascombe 1992 for possible remains of Harold's church. Cf. Williams 2002: 14–15.

[321] Watts and others 1997: 75–92; Williams 2002: 10–11. It is not conclusively demonstrated, though it seems on balance most probable, that the Romanesque details are contemporary with the sundial (Watts and others 1997: 89 and n. 165); cf. Taylor and Taylor 1965–78: i. 357–61; Fernie 1983: 159–60.

41. *Kirkdale* (Yorks.): 'Orm Gamalsson bought St Gregory's minster when it was completely broken and fallen, and he had it newly built from the ground for Christ and St Gregory in the days of Edward the king and in the days of Tostig the earl [1055 × 65]'. The uniquely informative inscription on this sundial records what may have been a common kind of mid eleventh-century patronage by minor aristocrats.

Wihtgarsson gave the manor of Clare (Suffolk), worth £40, to St John's church there and installed a group of clergy under the priest Leodmær.[322] For Orm and Ælfric, as for their contemporaries Odda and Vagn,[323] to be open-handed patrons and lords need not have been incompatible with setting up home in the minsters and drawing on their resources and manpower. It was a relationship from which religious communities could both gain and lose; although the overall trend was downwards, some individual communities of priests must have felt secure and well befriended.

Minsters in the hands of reformed abbeys may have missed some of the positive aspects of lay lordship and were particularly exposed to confiscation of their relics, but if they bore the brunt of Æthelwoldian distaste in other ways we have no sign of it. Breedon-on-the-Hill, Huntingdon, Godmanchester, and Little Shelford, given to the reformers in Eadgar's time, seem no different from many other worn-down secular minsters by 1086 and later.[324]

---

[322] DB ii. 389ᵛ; *RASC* 425; *ECEE* 71; *Stoke Cart.* iii. 2; Williams 2002: 6. The Domesday entry is evidently based on a written agreement endowing the community, assigning it to the care of Abbot Leofstan of Bury and Ælfric's son, and forbidding the clergy to alienate land from St John's; it was probably formulated along similar lines to the Dickleburgh agreement (S 1608: below, n. 329), which also involved Leofstan and forbade alienation. A later source claims that Ælfric endowed seven prebends with churches, land, and tithes from his estates in Suffolk and Essex (*Stoke Cart.* i. 54–8). But was this really a pre-Conquest arrangement? Ælfric gave his priests the entire manor, and its annexation by William I (according to DB) may have occasioned reorganization to provide them with alternative finance. DB offers two indications that the later arrangements did not exist in the 1080s: four of the later prebendal churches are listed there as ordinary manorial churches, with no indication that they had already been annexed to prebends; and the head-priest Leodmær is stated to have held two properties before 1066 (Bendysh and Gestingthorpe: DB ii. 34, 39) which do not appear as prebendal lands after 1090.

[323] Above, p. 328.

[324] In 972 Eadgar gave Æthelwold thirteen hides in and near Breedon which were never to be alienated 'ab ecclesia Dei que in Breodune sita est' (S 749; Dornier 1977*b*: 159–60), but this minster

Eadgar's grant of Barrow-on-Humber to Æthelwold in 971 may have included the nearby minster complex at Barton, and may account for its sumptuous late tenth-century tower-nave church, but there is no evidence that strict monastic life was revived on either site.[325] In 1001 Æthelred II gave the minster (*cenobium*) of Bradford-on-Avon (Wilts.) to the nuns of Shaftesbury, as a temporary refuge from Vikings and to remain a cell thereafter; once again a lavishly decorated little church seems to have resulted, and once again there is no further trace of regular life.[326] Wrangles between rapacious minster-priests and acquisitive abbots and bishops, illustrated by the tortuous history of Horningsea and its assets,[327] can hardly have improved local religious life, but there is no evidence that in this respect religious proprietors behaved very differently from lay ones.

In the eleventh century, the attitude of regulars to seculars could be not merely neutral but supportive. Ælfric Wihtgarsson entrusted his re-founded clerical minster at Clare to the supervision of Abbot Leofstan of Bury (1044–65).[328] Leofstan also had guardianship of what was effectively a chantry of four priests at Dickleburgh (Norfolk), set up by Osulf and Leofrun in the late 1050s to provide twelve weekly masses for their souls.[329] Monks no longer had scope or need to strike belligerent anticlerical attitudes, and

followed a normal later course culminating in reform as an Augustinian cell in 1122. For the others see *ECEE* 171, 181–2, 232–3; *Chron. Ram.* 47–9; Hart 1992: 221–8; Hart 1995: note that these sources are post-Conquest. Ramsey evidently regarded Godmanchester church as mere property, for the monks almost immediately returned it to the king in an exchange. Domesday Book mentions a *monasterium* of the demesne farm of Ely at Little Shelford, describes the transfer from hand to hand of Huntingdon minster, and merely notes a priest and church at Godmanchester: DB i. 191, 198, 208, 203ᵛ.

[325] S 782, describing the estate as 'a portion of land *Æt Bearuwe* which St Chad once possessed before the devastation of the pagans'; Everson and Knowles 1993, arguing that the charter-bounds probably include Barton as well as Barrow; Rodwell and Rodwell 1982: 292–9; Gem 1991: 827–8.

[326] S 899 (S. E. Kelly (ed.), *Charters of Shaftesbury Abbey* (Anglo-Saxon Charters, v, Oxford, 1996), 114–22); Taylor and Taylor 1965–78: i. 86–9; Fernie 1983: 145–9; Gem 1991: 831–2. Note the continuance here, as at Barton-on-Humber, of two separate churches into the later middle ages.

[327] *Lib. El.* 106–8, 420–1; above, p. 294.

[328] Above, n. 322. Mid eleventh-century Bury may have had a particular interest in colleges of clergy; cf. the late tradition that the priests from the pre-reform minster there were re-constituted by Cnut as a 'guild of twelve', and provided with a church by Abbot Baldwin (1065–97): Gransden 1985: 14–16.

[329] S 1608; *ECEE* 86–91 for text and commentary. The four priests, 'two after Osulf's day and two after Leofrun's day', were Godric, Ælfric, and two to be chosen by Leofstan and Leofrun; as in the Clare agreement (above, n. 322), they were not to alienate the property. The land was at Dickleburgh and Semer, and the priests were evidently to sing in a minster: in the Middle English version (the Latin is hopelessly garbled) Leofstan was to be 'þis minstres mund', which is parallelled by S 1047 ('ic eom þæs mynstres mund 7 upheald', 'I am the guardian and upholder of the minster'). In 1086 Dickleburgh had a church and was held by two priests, whereas Semer had no recorded church then or later (DB ii. 211ʳ⁻ᵛ). Given that Dickleburgh church was still held in four portions in the twelfth century (*The Chronicle of Jocelin of Brakelond*, ed. H. E. Butler (London, 1949), 60, 64), it can be confidently identified with the minster.

minsters could be re-moulded in so many useful and profitable ways. In about 1030 the ancient Kentish minster of Reculver, now Archbishop Æthelnoth's property, housed some kind of Flemish religious community under a dean named Giuchard, though part of its demesne was leased to archiepiscopal thegns.[330] This curious arrangement, only recorded by chance, reminds us that the premises and lands of decayed minsters could have accommodated a range of more-or-less ephemeral establishments at their lords' whims and enthusiasms. All in all, the attitudes of proprietors were opportunistic and diverse, and elude rigid definition.

Hardly anything is known about the regimes in these clerical minsters, but such hints as we do have suggest that they were relaxed, with little enthusiasm for forcing minster-priests to order their lives as strict-living canons on the Continental pattern. As Julia Barrow has shown, there are no grounds for thinking that either of the main Carolingian rules for canons—the Rule of Aachen and the Enlarged Rule of Chrodegang—was applied or even widely read in England before the 1050s.[331] Laws drafted by Archbishop Wulfstan in 1008 enjoined canons to live chastely in their minsters, to eat in refectories, and to sleep in dormitories; in 1014 the oaths of priests 'who live by a rule' were to be valued above those of secular priests. Like so many of Wulfstan's enthusiasms this may be wishful thinking, and the threats of ejection and dispossession had little effect on the many minsters of married and hereditary prebendal clergy which survived through this period.[332] When the Cuthbert community arrived at Durham in 995, their first action after clearing the site was to cast lots for their sepatate house-plots.[333] The hardy clerical dynasty of minster-provosts at Hexham, considerable local lords in their own right, perpetuated themselves by hereditary succession from c.1000 until the late eleventh century.[334] At a more modest level, an exceptional source tells the doubtless common story of the descent of a prebend at Plympton (Devon) from the priest Ælfheah (c.1040) to his son Sladda, the priest Ælfnoth, and then Ælfnoth's son Dunprust.[335] Annotating one of Wulfstan's

---

[330] S 1390 (below, pp. 513–14). The members were called *monachi*, but were headed by a *decanus*. I am grateful to Nicholas Brooks, Simon Keynes, and Teresa Webber for their views on this text.

[331] Barrow 1986: 552–5; Barrow 1994: 30–3. The extracts from the first which circulated in England were inadequate to make a structured daily timetable; the second was known from the mid tenth century, but textual evidence suggests that this was essentially in a monastic context until Leofric took it up at Exeter.

[332] V Atr. 7; VI Atr. 4; VIII Atr. 19–21 (*Gesetze*, 238–9, 248–9, 265–6; *C&S* 365, 394–5). In the light of Barrow's work, I was too ready in Blair 1985a: 123, to take these laws as evidence for a rule in action.

[333] *Symeon Lib.* 148.

[334] Raine 1863–4: i. pp. l–lxiii, appendix pp. vii–viii; Bateson and others 1893–1940: iii (1896), 118–26; Aird 1998: 116–22; *Symeon Lib.*, p. lxxxix.

[335] Below, p. 521.

exhortations, a (presumably priestly) contemporary said exactly what he thought about the celibacy rule: 'It is right that a priest love a decent woman as a bedmate.'[336]

It is again under Edward the Confessor, with the opening of England to influences from Europe in general and Lorraine in particular, that some limited application of the rules to English minsters can at last be recognized. The prime movers were Bishop Leofric (1050–72) in his new cathedral chapter of Exeter, and Archbishop Ealdred (1061–9) at York and its satellites Beverley and Southwell, followed slightly later in the century by Lotharingian and Lotharingian-inspired bishops at other sees, for instance Giso at Wells.[337] At these prestige sites a common life with refectory and dormitory (fragments of which may have been found at Wells),[338] and limitations on the canons' control of revenues, seem to have been imposed in the short term with some success.

How widely the Chrodegang or Aachen rules influenced ordinary minsters is virtually impossible to say. The two documented cases (albeit in post-Conquest texts) are Earl Harold's Waltham, which he re-constituted around 1060 along Aachen lines and with a Lotharingian master, and Christchurch (Hants.) where twenty-four canons under an 'elder' celebrated the round of liturgical offices.[339] There are occasional hints elsewhere, such as the statement in 1053 × 5 that when Leofric and Godgifu re-endowed Stow they 'settled it with priests, and desire to have service (*þeowdom*) there exactly as one has at St Paul's in London',[340] or the late and enigmatic reference to the 'institution of canons' at St Frideswide's, Oxford, in 1049.[341] It is fair to say

---

[336] Wormald 1999*a*: 203, citing Cotton MS Nero A.i (B) fo. 72ᵛ: 'Riht is þæt preost him lufie clænlicne wimman to gebeddan.' The author of this comment was probably a priest in either the Worcester or the York community.

[337] Barrow 1986: 553–6; Barrow 1994: 32–4, with references. Both Leofric and Ealdred had strong support from King Edward. A royal writ of the early 1060s (S 1161) grants Ealdred's deacon the minster of Axminster (Devon), with all possessions and with sake and soke as fully as any priest had it before, as a pious benefaction for St Peter's minster at York. Another (S 1067) allows Ealdred to draw up a privilege for all lands pertaining to St John's minster at Beverley, which is to be as free as any other minster, to be protected by the bishop under the king, and to maintain 'minster-life and assembly' (*mynsterlif 7 samnung*) forever. The canons of St John's had another writ from King Edward, for land which Drogo claimed in 1086: DB i. 374. Cf. Morris and Cambridge 1989. For Ealdred's intervention at Gloucester see Hare 1993: 17–27.

[338] Rodwell 2001: 98–105.

[339] *Walt. Chron.*, pp. xix–xxiii. 26–30, 64–6; below, p. 516; Hase 1988: 51–2.

[340] S 1478 (*RASC* 212–14; *C&S* 538–43); the description of the community of priests as 'the brethren' reinforces the impression that it was intended to be relatively strict.

[341] BL, MS Cotton Nero D 2, fo. 98 (printed *Flores Historiarum*, ed. H. R. Luard, i (Rolls Ser. 95a, 1890), 568): 'Eodem etiam anno institutio canonicorum Sancte Fredeswide de Oxonia.' This fourteenth-century Rochester MS is a version of the standard *Flores*, but the only one to contain this entry. Cf. Blair 1988*d*: 226–7.

that the Waltham and Christchurch narratives are exceptional survivals, and that such initiatives need not have been uncommon in the climate of the 1050s.

Strict regimes, then, were sometimes followed. But they were fragile, and ultimately doomed to relaxation. If Harold was inspired by the old Carolingian rules, their rigour soon lapsed at Waltham: the canons had their own houses, could marry (the original Lotharingian master was succeeded by his son), and enjoyed gargantuan allowances of food and drink.[342] In her will of 1035 × 44, the East Anglian lady Leofgifu may (though the phrase is slightly ambiguous) be appointing to prebends: 'And I desire that Æthelric the priest and Ælfric the priest and Æthelsige the deacon shall have the minster at Colne as their lord granted it to them. And it is my wish that Ælfric the priest shall be in the same position in which Æthelnoth was.'[343] The evidence that canons at Waltham, Clare, Christchurch, Hartland, Plympton, and Cullompton had individual prebends is all post-Conquest, but consistent.[344] By the early twelfth century the Waltham and Christchurch canons seem to have lived among the laity in the neighbouring towns, as did those of Chester and Clare in the late eleventh.[345] The ideals of Aachen were unlikely to withstand the pressures of kinship, patronage, and a social milieu in which so many clergy lived like thegns.

An apparently growing expectation that clerics thus endowed would continue in their lords' active service was detrimental to community life of any kind. Hence the most characteristic fate of minster endowments as seen in Domesday Book: to be annexed to the support of royal, noble, or episcopal clerks. Here we are not even dealing with self-indulgent communities, but with absentees who only in the most tenuous sense were members of the communities at all. This must have impacted pre-eminently, as the central bureaucracy grew, on the many once-important minsters still in royal hands. Pluralism and absenteeism were nothing new, as the case of Asser shows; more than a century later his minsters of Congresbury and Banwell were

[342] *Walt. Chron.*, pp. xxii–xxv, 28–30 and n. 3. The author complains about declining standards, and some of these luxuries may have developed after the Conquest, but it is at least clear that Master Adelard was non-celibate. Cf. Hase 1988: 52–4, for the prebendal system at Christchurch.

[343] S 1521 (*Wills*, 76).

[344] Waltham: *Walt. Chron.*, pp. xxiv, 28–30. Clare: *Stoke Cart.* i. 56 (but see n. 322 above). Christchurch: Hase 1988: 52–4, and below, pp. 516–17. Hartland: above, pp. 357–8. Plympton: below, p. 521. Cullompton: *Chron. Battle*, 80–4. At Dover, however, Domesday Book comments: 'T.R.E. erant prebende communes . . . ; modo sunt divise per singulos per episcopum Baiocensem' (DB i. 1ᵛ).

[345] *Walt. Chron.* 78; below, p. 517; DB i. 263; *Stoke Cart.* i. 57. The Christchurch narrative (which unfortunately is obscure or corrupt at this point) appears to say that Ranulf Flambard moved the canons from houses around the cemetery to houses in the town while he was rebuilding the minster and its offices. Cf. Blair 1992: 264 n. 161, and Blair 1996c: 10, for other cases of canons' houses in France and England.

pressed into service once again by Cnut, who gave them, together with one of the Gloucester minsters, to his priest Duduc.[346]

It is with Edward the Confessor, however, that the practice becomes marked, at least in surviving sources. By 1066, as Domesday Book makes clear, a high proportion of the king's more valuable churches had been pressed into service to support his clerks. The important men, such as Spirites in Shropshire and Herefordshire, Ernuin in Lincolnshire, and above all the chancellor Regenbald, tended to have whole minsters of ordinary size or shares in the very big ones: Regenbald alone held five minsters.[347] St Martin-le-Grand in London may have been founded or re-founded under Edward by the priest Ingelric as a college for royal clerks.[348] Edward's shares in the great collegiate churches of Dover, where at least five of his clerks held canonries, and Bosham, which supported the royal clerks Osbern (later bishop of Exeter) and Godwine, must also have been central to financing this part of the royal entourage.[349] Such assets could be negotiable: at Huntingdon Edward gave St Mary's church and its lands—former property of Thorney Abbey—to two of his clerks, who sold it to a royal chamberlain, who sold it in turn to two local priests.[350]

After the Norman Conquest, minsters were probably exploited more heavily but along similar lines.[351] The new elites had just as much need for endowed clerks as the old ones, and less respect for ancient English institutions. The movement of sees, the reform of abbeys, and the foundation of alien priories all put new pressure on what were clearly seen as transferable resources: it was the fate of many old minsters to be annexed to Lincoln, Salisbury, and other chapters as prebends for their canons. William I's clerical and court personnel often succeeded to the minsters which had supported Edward's. Sometimes Norman ecclesiastics were interposed between the king and locally based clergy, as at Hartland (Devon), where in 1086 Gerald the chaplain held two hides 'which the canons of that house used to hold: . . . the same twelve canons . . . now hold them of Gerald and pay him 40s. yearly'.[352] Still worse, the Conquest must have seriously undermined the financial base of minsters by speeding up the diversion of mother-church dues to other religious purposes.[353]

[346] Above, p. 324; 'Historiola de Primordiis Episcopatus Somersetensis', in J. Hunter (ed.), *Ecclesiastical Documents* (Camden Soc. [8], 1840), 15; *Sherborne*, p. xlvi; Hare 1993: 9–11. However, someone paid for a lavish stone shrine at Congresbury at about this date: Oakes and Costen 2003.

[347] Barlow 1979: 129–36, 156–8, 190–1; Campbell 1986: 149–51.

[348] Davis 1972: 24–5.

[349] Dover: DB i. 1ᵛ; Barlow 1979: 131, 133, 156–8. Bosham: DB i. 17a–b, 27a, 43a; Barlow 1979: 190–1; Gem 1985.

[350] DB i. 208.

[351] Blair 1985a: 125–7, for a fuller account with references; cf. Barrow 1986: 555–60.

[352] DB Exon. 456–456ᵛ.   [353] Below, pp. 449–51.

The pressure of noble residence on old ecclesiastical sites reached its logical conclusion after the Conquest: several of the new royal and baronial castles engulfed minsters, which were re-cast as castle colleges or chapels, extruded out to new sites, or suppressed completely.[354] Norman magnates also had their own household clerks, for whom minsters continued to provide rich pickings. No lord had more clerical mouths to feed than Roger earl of Shrewsbury, whose Domesday holdings included twelve 'superior' churches in Shropshire and six in Sussex. He exploited the Shropshire churches systematically, annexing six to his abbey in Shrewsbury and giving Wenlock's manor of Stoke St Milburgh to his chaplains; at Morville he depleted the once-prosperous minster for both purposes:

The church of this manor is in honour of St Gregory, which in King Edward's day had eight hides of this land, and eight canons served there. St Peter's church [Shrewsbury Abbey now] holds this church with five hides from the earl. . . . There are three priests there . . . The earl's chaplains hold the other three hides, and five men from them . . .[355]

The count of Mortain's seizures, on a comparable scale, from Cornish minsters are also prominent in Domesday Book. Well might an adherent of Launceston minster rebuke its patron saint: 'O blessed Stephen, Stephen, for long I have laboured faithfully in your service, but now it would seem in vain. If I had served the Count of Mortain, who is now lord of Cornwall, as much as I have long served you, he would have enriched me with many gifts.'[356]

As in earlier periods, the local effect of such fiscal and tenurial pressures is hard to assess, but in general they must have marked another big step on the downward path. Some minsters may have dissolved totally into groups of benefices for non-resident clergy, whether absent on their lords' business or devolved to chapels,[357] destroying even the last semblance of community

[354] Examples are: Dover: the canons were probably moved after 1066 from St Mary-de-Castro into the new Romanesque church of St Martin-le-Grand in the town (Tatton-Brown 1988: 110). Clare: the college of priests was first encapsulated within the Norman castle, then moved to Stoke-by-Clare (*Stoke Cart.* i. 54–8). Taunton: the castle overlies the presumed minster cemetery (Leach 1984: 11, 26–32). Pontefract: the castle chapel overlies part of a pre-Norman complex of churches and cemeteries, presumably a minster associated with the royal vill of Tanshelf (Roberts 2002: 73–4, 401–4). Newark: the castle overlies an Anglo-Saxon cemetery 200 m. west of the church (Dixon and others 1994), presumably again part of the minster. Hereford: the castle bailey encapsulates St Guthlac's and its mid Saxon cemetery (Shoesmith 1980). The social importance of honorial centres meant that old minsters now associated with castles could attract patronage from their proprietors' tenants, though for the same reason they tended to be replaced by something grander: see Cownie 1998: 172–84.

[355] DB i. 253. For Earl Roger's treatment of his English churches see Mason 1963.

[356] Hull and Sharpe 1985: 20–1. For the count of Mortain's depredations see ibid. 37–8; Croom 1988: 74–5; Olson 1989: 90–6.

[357] Blair 1985*a*: 127–31, for some possible Domesday cases of this; below, p. 384, for devolution to chapels.

life. On the other hand, the idea of the clerical college was familiar to the new lords, both ecclesiastical and lay, coming as they did from Normandy where some twenty-four secular *collégiales* are known to have existed during the period 990–1066.[358] England over the next half-century provides fragmentary but persuasive evidence for many such communities on royal and episcopal manors or associated with baronial castles, some new, others re-foundations of old minsters.[359] Sometimes the survival of community life is suggested by architectural evidence, notably a large aisleless nave with north and south *porticus* on what was by now an old-fashioned proto-cruciform plan, but one which would have accommodated the liturgical activities of more than one priest.[360] Regenbald the chancellor, that hardy survivor from Edward's reign into William's, rebuilt his minster at Milborne Port (Somerset) in a sumptuous hybrid style where, in Richard Gem's words, Anglo-Saxon and Romanesque features 'are welded together into an articulate and satisfying whole: a truly Anglo-Norman fusion has been achieved'.[361] A bureaucrat of the next generation, Ranulf Flambard, transformed both the internal life and the buildings of the community at Christchurch.[362] Harassed though they may have been by the count of Mortain, the canons of Launceston were building themselves an ambitious stone tower in the 1090s.[363]

In 1086 a church of any status, unless it was one of the reformed minority, was still assumed in the normal course of things to house a group of priests. A map of Domesday Book's 'superior' churches—defined as those stated to have multiple priests, distinct landholdings and values, and other miscellaneous marks of status—shows them spread thickly but unevenly across the landscape, with clusters in the Wessex heartland, western Mercia, and the south-west.[364] Such a map is a complex palimpsest, built up in many

---

[358] Musset 1961.

[359] Blair 1985*a*: 131–7, for a fuller treatment with examples; Franklin 1988 and Gardiner 1989 for the cases of Daventry and Hastings; Masters 2001: 175–7, for collegiate foundation and re-foundation in Anglo-Norman Sussex; Cownie 1998: 30–3 for patronage of seculars and regulars in Anglo-Norman England, showing how enthusiasm for the reformed orders rapidly caught up with, and eclipsed, the initial enthusiasm for secular colleges in the early post-Conquest years.

[360] Blair 1985*a*: 121–2, 137.

[361] Gem 1988: 27.

[362] Below, p. 517; Hase 1988: 49–51.

[363] Hull and Sharpe 1985: 16–18, 36, 40–1.

[364] Blair 1985*a*: 105–14, for maps and a discussion of these criteria, including the problems of divergent presentation between the Domesday circuits. See below, pp. 514–15, for a typical example of DB's portrayal of an unreformed minster. There is an (inevitably slightly subjective) map of the more important secular colleges at the Conquest in Cownie 1998: 29. To recognize minsters as still a distinct category in 1086 is not of course to deny that there was by then a substantial grey area, between very worn-down or modestly endowed minsters and the more substantial tenth- and eleventh-century estate churches: below, pp. 371–4.

layers since the seventh century and distorted by many local vicissitudes, and it can be nothing like complete; but it still shows an evolving system.

Yet that system was on the verge of succumbing to a combination of new assumptions and definitions by the Church, the withdrawal of legal protection by the state, and the release of pent-up pressures from below. As a distinct group, standing out above the ordinary run of local churches, the minsters which have been the main theme of this book make their last appearance in 1086. Locally they would often remain important, but after *c.*1100 their significance must be teased out of sources which acknowledge no formal category between regular monastery and parish church.[365] The college of secular clergy would soon be an obsolete form of the religious life, disreputable and friendless. Meanwhile, the late eleventh century was seeing the collapse of the legislative restraints with which, since Æthelstan's time, kings had maintained the financial integrity of the minster-based parochial system. Hastened though it undoubtedly was by the Conquest, this collapse was the culmination of a larger process. The shift from mother-churches to local churches happened in different ways in different regions, but its background was the tenth- and eleventh-century restructuring of the English landscape, which eroded the minsters' pastoral *raison d'être* just as social and political change had eroded their wealth and status. It is to this new world of local churches that we must now turn.

---

[365] The only exceptions to this statement are a small group of prebendal colleges which survived into the later middle ages, either because they were royal free chapels (Denton 1970) or for special local reasons, cf. below, p. 509.

7

The Birth and Growth of Local Churches
c.850–1100

When Bishop Hereman of Ramsbury visited the pope in 1050 he told him, says Goscelin of Saint-Bertin, about 'England being filled everywhere with churches which daily were being added anew in new places, about the distribution of innumerable ornaments and bells in oratories, and about the most ample liberality of kings and rich men for the inheritance of Christ'.[1] Probably Hereman was thinking mainly of great churches, but a national, transformative boom in building and patronage is just as obvious at a local level. By the Norman Conquest, the religious landscape in at least the more easterly parts of England looked very different from the minster-centred world which this book has considered so far. It was gradually filling up with solidly built little churches with their own priests, landholdings, and rights to burial and tithe.

The critical shift from mother-parishes to local parishes was disguised, and to some extent retarded, by the remarkable institutional tenacity of the former, which remained into William I's reign the only units of parochial authority that officialdom would recognize. Even so, a law-code of 1014 acknowledges new realities by setting a scale of fines for breaking the sanctuaries of a 'head minster', a 'rather smaller minster', 'one still smaller', and a 'field-church'; by 1020/1 the last two could be defined more precisely as 'one still smaller where there is little [parochial?] service but there is a graveyard' ('þær lytel þeowdom sig 7 legerstow þeah sig') and 'a field-church where there is no graveyard'.[2] Presumably the 'head minster' is a cathedral, the 'rather smaller' one a normal clerical minster, and the 'field-church' a chapel without rights. The 'still smaller minster' can hardly be other than the thegn's semi-autonomous estate church, equipped with the graveyard which in a

---

[1] Goscelin, 'Historia Translationis S. Augustini', iii. 3 (ed. Migne, *PL* 155 (1880), col. 32); cf. Gem 1988: 21.
[2] VIII Atr. 5. 1, I Cn 3. 2 (*Gesetze*, 264, 282; *C&S* 390); below, p. 429, for the meaning of *þeowdom*.

slightly earlier law had given it tithe-worthy status: the definition of this new group as little minsters is evocative both of their current transformation into permanent stone buildings and of their incipient parochial status. The 'field-churches' can be dimly perceived as a humbler and more amorphous group of which some, as we will see, may have given new leases of life to old but informal cult sites.

During *c.*1070–1120, the pressures which had been mounting from below burst the old order apart and became overt in the written record. Domesday Book lists over 2,000 'churches', 'priests', and 'priests with churches'—an undoubtedly incomplete list even so.[3] The apparent equation of church and priest implies that the country parson was already a familiar figure by 1086, and it was assumed, at least in eastern England, that every village would be able to provide a priest to serve on the Domesday jury.[4] From this volatile material—a multitude of new ecclesiastical entities jostling for space among the decaying old ones—twelfth-century bishops built a framework of rural parishes, destined to survive in essentials until the twentieth-century unions of benefices.

The background to this shift was the complex of transformative changes, experienced by much of western Europe at both a political and a local level during the ninth to eleventh centuries, which some historians have charac-terized as a 'feudal revolution'. At their heart was the growth and consolida-tion of magnate power, expressed in the building of lordly strongholds, the formation of military retinues, the privatization of public authority, and the exertion of legal, fiscal, and economic power by lords over local communi-ties.[5] A strong historiographical tradition in France argues for a multi-layered 'cellularization' of society, the local dimension of which was the grouping of populations into more clearly defined units of organization and exploitation; settlement nucleation, and the formation of local parishes, are seen as inte-gral parts of this process.[6]

---

[3] Below, p. 418–20.   [4] Below, p. 502.

[5] The formative studies are Duby 1953 and Fossier 1982. A debate in the mid 1990s, rounded off by Reuter and others 1997 (where references to earlier work may be found), focused on power and violence; but note Reuter's reservations about English 'sophistication' (pp. 191–2) and Wickham's support for *encellulement* in local communities (pp. 205–7). The debate has now been revisited by Bates 2000, who endorses the model of *encellulement* in England at a local rather than national level. Here, however, I have chosen to render *encellulement* into English ('cellularization'), to dis-tance it from the connotations of a breakdown in public authority which the word carries in French writing.

[6] Thus Georges Duby, on the Mâconnais: 'la chevalerie . . . est au XIIᵉ s. une collection de familles; de même, la société rurale devient progressivement une collection de communautés d'habi-tants, les paroisses' (Duby 1953: 290); Robert Fossier: 'la fixation du cadre paroissial est un des phénomènes liés à la "révolution" du XIᵉ siècle: elle accompagne à la fois les démembrements et remembrements fonciers dont la campagne est le lieu' (Fossier 1982: i. 346).

The power of the late Anglo-Saxon state meant that England was abnormal in jurisdictional and military terms: no princely states emerged, thegns and even earls did not dispense autonomous justice, and their houses were not strongholds of feudal power.[7] But in the impact of economic growth on the structure and obligations of local communities, England followed European trends. Big, multi-vill estates broke up into smaller, more tightly focused ones; intensified manorial exploitation gradually replaced food-render regimes; farmsteads coalesced into villages; systems of common agriculture developed; and peasants felt a heavier hand of lordship.[8] The connections between these variables remain poorly understood, and there is scope for debate on whether agrarian and demographic growth made smaller-scale and more intensive lordship viable or whether they were themselves stimulated by its demands. What cannot be doubted is increasing pressure on resources from a growing population and a more developed economy. It is symptomatic that by the mid tenth century, charters routinely described the detailed course of estate boundaries through a minutely demarcated landscape. From the 970s, the rapid growth of towns and of the coinage are signs of a take-off which, as we will see, can also be traced in the rising tide of church-building.

As several local studies have shown, these new manorial structures fostered a closer link between minor royal servants and small estates, and thus contributed to a growing and broad-based class of local proprietors rooted in their communities: the original 'English country gentry'.[9] Whether or not the impact of their lordship explains the more systematic apportionment of peasant settlements and field-systems, it can certainly be seen in the growth of complex manor-house sites. And the aristocratic urge to own a church, ubiquitous across early medieval Europe, was now focused at a much more local level. Parvenu elites often try to buttress their status by building ritual monuments: seventh-century 'princely' barrows and tenth-century manorial churches resulted from not dissimilar impulses. In the tenth- and eleventh-century east midlands, for instance, Pauline Stafford identifies 'a group of small-scale landowners, whose only record is that left in the place-names,

---

[7] For instance: Campbell 1986: 155–89; Campbell 2000: 179–99; Wormald 1999*b*: esp. 313–57; Williams 1992.

[8] The many national and local studies can be approached through Faith 1997 (who tends towards a rather later chronology for aspects of the process than would some other scholars). Hadley 2000*a* reminds us that England was geographically and socially diverse, and that a monolithic model of re-structuring from large to small land-units is over-simple.

[9] For instance: Gelling 1978: 162–90 (place-names); Hooke 1985: 106–13 (west midlands); Stafford 1985: 29–39 (east midlands); Blair 1991*a*: 30–4 (Surrey); Williams 1992 (manor-houses); Blair 1994: 132–40 (Oxfordshire); Yorke 1995: 245–55 (Wessex). Gillingham 1995 vindicates the use of the term 'gentry' in such contexts.

[who] gave concentrated attention to their new lands; their pride in them was expressed in building activity, in churches and in memorial building'.[10] By the first half of the eleventh century, a freeman had the outward and visible signs of thegnly rank once he had acquired 'five hides of land of his own, a church and a kitchen, a bell-house and a fortress-gate, a seat and special office in the king's hall'.[11]

Relativities of scale in a changing parochial culture

These diverse and fluid tenurial and social structures determined when and where churches were built during 850–1100, and ultimately the form taken by rural parishes. New foundations must be understood in the context not only of these structural changes, but also of the slow but fundamental conceptual change in how people viewed 'their' churches.

At the top of the scale—and especially in regions, such as the West Saxon heartland, which saw exceptional levels of lay patronage after the mid ninth century[12]—developments were an organic extension of traditional parochial culture, in the sense that the new churches of kings and great nobles look very like small minsters. Several local studies have identified a mid-way category of churches, often on royal or comital manors of between twenty and fifty hides, which have some of the recurrent characteristics of minsters: multi-vill parishes and sometimes chapels, glebes of a hide or two in post-Conquest sources, and buildings of more than average architectural pretension from the mid eleventh century onwards. An important group in this category are the new 'hundredal minsters', characteristic of areas where local government structures were rearranged after 900.[13]

The possession of significant land-endowments from the outset may set some such cases apart from ordinary manorial churches. At Wotton-under-Edge (Glos.), for instance, 'the church hide and all that belongs to it' is men-

---

[10] Stafford 1985: 39.

[11] The Wulfstan text of *c.*1000 known as 'Geþyncðo' or the 'Promotion Law' (*Gesetze*, 456–7); cf. Stenton 1970: 383–93, Faith 1997: 126–7, 164, and Williams 1992. A complication is that the words *cirican 7 kycenan* do not occur in the earliest manuscript (*D*), but only in the Textus Roffensis version (*H*). They may therefore be a mid eleventh-century Kentish interpolation (which would be interesting evidence for the growing prominence of local churches as marks of rank), but since *D* has a tendency to drop words and phrases this cannot be considered certain. I am grateful to Patrick Wormald for his advice.

[12] Above, pp. 300–2.

[13] For examples see Blair 1991*a*: 113–14 (with specific reference to 'hundredal minsters'); Blair 1994: 136, 138; Pitt 1999; cf. Patrick Hase's comment in Blair 1988*b*: 18 n. 40. See also above, p. 342. A similar category can be recognized in ninth- and tenth-century Wales (Davies 1978: 123).

tioned casually in a boundary-clause of 940; in 961×95 Æthelric made a bequest of land at Bocking (Essex) but reserved 'one hide which I give to the church for the priest who serves God there'.[14] One slightly enigmatic, but consistent, pointer is the expression 'white church' ('stone-built church',[15] or perhaps 'plastered church'?): in the later ninth and tenth centuries it seems to have been applied to churches which, while not necessarily ancient minsters, had a degree of special local status. It occurs at Whitchurch Canonicorum, Dorset (*æt Hwitancyrican* in King Alfred's will), evidently a minster; at Whitchurch, Hants. (*Hwitan cyrice* in 909), which has a fine ninth-century headstone; at Whitchurch, Oxon., where a local thegn was called Leofric *æt Hwitecyrcan* in 990;[16] and several times in post-Conquest sources.[17] It seems best to regard the churches in this category as small, late minsters (which is probably how contemporaries would have seen them), built at a time when humbler churches were still generally of unplastered timber.

At the other extreme, the bottom of the 'gentry' spectrum, advanced manorial fission bred lordship and lordly church-building on a very small scale: a process seen in extreme form in East Anglia, where a landscape still thickly spread with churches is the legacy of a complex mix of small manors and sokeland. We should not be dogmatic about whether churches were founded by 'lords' or 'peasants' when many regions had substantial groups of freeholding farmers not readily pigeonholed as either, and when groups of tenants could sometimes have played an important but unrecorded part in the process.[18] But what distinguishes the multitude of purely local churches from minsters, and even from the relatively high-status tenth-century churches just considered, is their lack of recorded endowments or of any independent public status before the critical changes of the eleventh century.

Nonetheless, perceptions of how the local Church should function did gradually change in response to social and topographical realities. In the tenth century the clerical minster remained the normal form of religious life, and

---

[14] S 467; S 1501 (*Wills*, 42).

[15] As explicitly in Bede's etymology of Whithorn: 'commonly called At the White House (*Ad Candidam Casam*), because [Ninian] built a church of stone there': *HE* iii. 4 (p. 222). Roman masonry could also have been considered 'white': at a number of places with names in *hwit-*, including Whitchurch Canonicorum, the church overlies a Roman building (Bell 2001: 20–1).

[16] S 1507, and Hall 2000: 13; S 378, and Tweddle and others 1995: 271–3; S 1454, and Wormald 1999*a*: 148–53.

[17] The Whitchurch in Somerset is mentioned in S 1042; those in Devon, Warwickshire, and Buckinghamshire in DB. A cluster of Whitchurch names in Herefordshire, Shropshire, and Wales share with Whiteparish (Hants.) the curious characteristic of being translated into Latin or French (*Album Monasterium, Blancmuster*, etc.) in twelfth- and thirteenth-century sources (*P-N Salop.* i. 310–11; Stancliffe 1995*b*: 87). See the fuller discussion of this problem in Pitt 1999: 32–4, 193–5, and the comment by Fellows-Jensen 1987: 201.

[18] Hadley 2000*a*, 72–84, 180–96; below, pp. 399–400, 409–10.

contemporaries had no experience of a parish church system with which to contrast it. A landowner with fifty hides might found a church hard to distinguish from a continuing pre-Viking minster; even if he only had five, his church might still most naturally be conceived by contemporaries, as by the drafter of Æthelred's law on compensation, as a 'minster still smaller'. But it was the re-structuring of the countryside into more local, self-contained units in the five-hide to ten-hide range which, as well as creating a land-base for the lowest tier of church-owning thegns, gradually encouraged even great landowners to found multiple small churches rather than single large ones, suggesting some expectation that not just lords but *places* should have their own churches. A peasant community, too, reorientated away from the old, extensive systems of pastoral care towards expectations of local provision, might acquire a taste for 'its own' church, even if jurisdictionally this had to remain dependent on a minster. And in a more demarcated landscape, where it was increasingly likely that everything belonged to someone, informal cult sites may have become more and more vulnerable to annexation by seigneurial interests.

The great differences in internal manorial organization will have produced largely irrecoverable contrasts in peasants' obligations and attitudes to their lords' churches. Did a manor with a large workforce on the 'inland' have a bigger ready-made congregation for its new church than one mainly inhabited by autonomous 'warland' farmers? Were dwellers in villages, and cultivators in common fields, readier to re-direct their devotional loyalties than the inhabitants of farmsteads?[19] The 'lord-driven' processes of foundation and endowment which are inevitably, by the nature of the sources, the focus of this chapter should not obscure the likely communal element, to be pursued in Chapter 8, in the formation of parochial loyalties and communities.

'Local' churches are thus a broad and diverse category, made all the harder to pin down by their lack of clearly defined status. If they can be equated formally with the 'still smaller minsters' and 'field-churches' of the 1014 law, the distinction implied there (possession or non-possession of a graveyard?) is only one of several criteria that we might want to use. For purposes of this discussion, churches will be grouped according to their various kinds of origin. There is an element of artificiality in these criteria, both because they merge into each other (a church could be both a lay lord's foundation and an offshoot of a minster, for instance), and because direct and specific evidence for the origins of most English parish churches is simply not available. One fundamental distinction can, however, be drawn: between churches

---

[19] These questions are framed within the terms of reference, and especially the contrast between 'inland' and 'warland', set out by Faith 1997. Cf. Hadley 2000a: 210–13.

which stand where they do because their sites had some prior sacred significance, and those which grew from the contemporary locational needs of manorial or peasant settlement and had no roots in any ritual past.

Origins (i): the privatization of 'undeveloped' sacred sites

In Cornwall and Wales, parish churches seem often to have emerged by a winnowing-out process: from the multitude of 'undeveloped' religious sites which existed by the ninth century, a minority acquired parochial status and buildings, while the others remained static and sometimes eventually vanished.[20] This model has not, on the whole, been applied to England, where parish churches are normally seen as offshoots of manor-houses. There is also once again the ingrained assumption that 'Celtic' ecclesiastical developments were necessarily earlier than whatever may have happened in England. Yet it does seem likely that some English churches, and more chapels, developed during the tenth to twelfth centuries from sites of long-standing religious cult; and moreover that this process may not have been so far removed in time from what happened, more visibly to us, at numerous sites in Wales, Cornwall, and the north-west.

Quantitively, it may remain true that most English parish churches began on manorial sites which had no religious significance before the tenth century, whereas Christian sites capable of 'development' were more common in the west. Yet the landscape of pre-Viking England contained a wide range of open-ground cult places, their fate generally unknown. The impulse to control and privatize sacred space by re-fashioning it in an architectural form would be consistent with the whole thrust of western European seigneurialization during the tenth and eleventh centuries, and with the drive by religious corporations to regulate popular cult activity. To view it as an essentially post-950 phenomenon, alike among the English and their neighbours, is made easier by a recent shift in perceptions of the chronology of churches and chapels built over the cemeteries, *llans*, and holy wells of Atlantic Britain.

The first serious research in this field, during the 1950s to 1970s, tended to date both the establishment and the 'development' of sites very early: cemeteries in the sixth century, simple stone-built chapels in the seventh or eighth.[21] Contributions of the last fifteen years have been more sceptical, pointing out the difficulty of dating sites of all kinds, the lack of any really

---

[20] Thomas 1971: 50–1; Preston-Jones and Rose 1986: 160; Thomas 1989: 24–6; Edwards 1996: 51–3.

[21] This is the 'enclosed developed cemetery' model of Thomas 1971: 48–90.

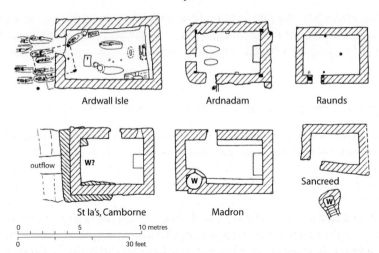

42. Cemetery- and well-chapels in Atlantic Britain, compared with a tenth-century thegn's church in the east midlands. *Ardwall Isle* (Kirkub.) after Thomas 1967*b*: figs. 23 and 26; *Ardnam* (Argyll) after Rennie 1984: fig. 15; *St Ia's, Camborne* (Cornwall) after Thomas 1967*a*: fig. 15; *Madron* and *Sancreed* (Cornwall) from the author's sketch surveys. The church at *Raunds* (Northants.; after Boddington 1996: fig. 24) is included for comparison; cf. Figs. 45–6. **W** = holy well.

reliable evidence for stone buildings in Wales and Cornwall before the eleventh century, and the likelihood that some Cornish churchyards based on Iron Age 'rounds' began no earlier than the tenth century.[22] Two recently published Welsh cemeteries show why caution may be needed. At Llanelen a group of graves over a sixth- to seventh-century settlement were associated with a frail timber structure, which seemingly stood until a stone chapel was superimposed in the eleventh or twelfth century; at Capel Maelog a probably eleventh- or twelfth-century cemetery, again overlying an older settlement, acquired a two-cell stone chapel no earlier than *c*.1150– 1250.[23]

Thus in western Britain it now seems possible to recognize a broad category of very small single-cell chapels, some perhaps tenth-century but mostly

[22] Edwards 1996: 51–5; Preston-Jones 1992: 114–15. Similar conclusions have been drawn for Orkney and Shetland (C. Morris 1989: 9–17, 20–8: rather than 'early Celtic monasteries', a landscape of chapels built during the tenth to twelfth centuries in a Norse milieu). Since this section was drafted, the appearance of Petts 2002 and Turner 2003 has strengthened the case that enclosed cemeteries in Wales and Cornwall developed at a relatively late date; cf. above, p. 21.
[23] Schlesinger and Walls 1996; Britnell 1990.

from the eleventh and twelfth, of which representative examples are shown in Fig. 42.[24] Some of them are shown by excavation, or by visible remains, to be 'developments' of older cemeteries and wells, suggesting the possibility that others perpetuate different sorts of ritual feature—such as trees, posts, or standing stones—which have left no trace. Cornish well-chapels surviving as ruins (sometimes with Romanesque constructional details and therefore unlikely to pre-date *c.*1100) can be enlargements or adaptations of older well-structures; the excavation of St Ia's chapel at Camborne showed that what may have been an open enclosure around the holy well was replaced by a chapel only in the twelfth century.[25]

This emerging picture gives cause for comparing, rather than perpetually contrasting, English developments with Welsh and Cornish ones. Across England generally, it is an important but totally unanswerable question how often, if at all, dispersed seventh- and eighth-century cemeteries evolved into later churches or chapels. The known examples did not, but it is of course precisely for that reason that they are known: twenty or thirty unaccompanied burials under a normal parish graveyard would have no chance of detection. The half-dozen cases where knife-burials or seventh-century dress items have been found in later churchyards[26] could indicate small family or community cemeteries, functioning maybe during *c.*650–900, which were 'developed' in the tenth century by the addition of a church.

Small churches built on older ritual monuments have slightly more to offer: sites of this kind may have been selected for reasons beyond the purely practical, including long-standing perceptions of sacredness. The potentially large number of churches on or beside Bronze Age barrows may thus reflect the late 'development' of a category of vernacular cult-sites in which the early minster-builders seem to have shown little interest.[27] Especially intriguing cases are Taplow (Bucks.), High Wycombe (Bucks.), and Ogborne St Andrew (Wilts.), where the churches adjoin elite barrow-burials of respectively the early seventh, the late seventh, and perhaps the eighth or ninth century: were

---

[24] The Ardwall Isle chapel has been dated much earlier (Thomas 1967*b*: 174–7); but the small-finds are undiagnostic, there is no early non-funerary sculpture (except for a small gable-finial which could be from a cross or shrine rather than a building), and dating is essentially by parallels which must now themselves be considered dubious. At Ardnadam (Rennie 1984: 37–8) the chronology is vague, amounting to little more than a conjecture that the religious site was suppressed around 1100. None of this is to deny that very small chapels existed in the seventh to ninth centuries (e.g. St Patrick's at Heysham: Potter and Andrews 1994), but simply to question the chronology of 'developed cemetery' chapels. Cf. Arnold and Davies 2000: 180–94, for a recent survey of the Welsh evidence suggesting a continuum between structures over special graves and the cemetery chapels which, though apparently later, are sometimes very similar in shape and size.

[25] Thomas 1967*a*: 75–85. The evidence that the tenth- or eleventh-century altar-slab came from here is inconclusive: see Okasha 1993: 82.

[26] But above, 243 n., for another possibility.   [27] Semple 2002: 497–528.

they founded in the late Anglo-Saxon period to Christianize tombs to which folk-legends attached, and which were identified with ancestors or local worthies?[28]

In the same way, nearly 200 English churches and chapels of ordinary parochial status or lower are known to overlie or adjoin Roman villas, and the widespread background pattern of sixth- to eighth-century graves in villas makes it plausible that at least some of these are 'developments' of perceived ancestral burial sites or shrines.[29] It is frustratingly difficult to find a clear case of a villa with early burials which also attracted a church, but the usual problems of detecting exiguous archaeological phases under heavily used graveyards could be to blame.[30] We are on firmer ground at Fawler (Berks.), where charter-bounds of 931 and 953 mention a 'holy place' (*to þære halgan stowe*): this spot has not only produced remains of a Roman tessellated pavement, but was also by the late middle ages the site of a chapel of St James.[31] Here there can be no doubt that a Roman villa thought 'holy' by the tenth century was later 'developed' by the addition of a chapel.

A larger and more visible category (natural water-sources are not easily suppressed or concealed) are churches and chapels on or beside holy wells. In the high middle ages these could have been almost as thick on the ground in England as in Wales and Cornwall, though their more recent folkloric aspects are less frequently recorded.[32] A possibly early case (though its curative well is not mentioned before the eighteenth century) is Cokethorpe (Oxon.), called the 'old church' in charter-bounds of 958.[33] Sub-parochial

---

[28] Geake 1997: 146, 186; Stocker 1995. In my view, Stocker's argument for a pre-Viking church at Taplow cannot be sustained from the parch-mark evidence. The Ogborne St Andrew burial (currently being investigated by Sarah Semple) was secondary in a Bronze Age barrow, and had a coffin with scroll-ended iron brackets such as were used in England in the ninth to tenth centuries, and perhaps the eighth; the type may be Carolingian-inspired (cf. Heighway and Bryant 1999: 208–15; Stiegemann and Wemhoff 1999: 339–40). See Speake 1989: 120–3, for the possibility that an exceptional barrow-burial of *c.*700 was still remembered in the tenth century.

[29] Bell 2001 for catalogue; see above, p. 54, for the burials, and pp. 189–90 for minsters on Roman buildings.

[30] A much-cited case was Rivenhall (Essex), where excavations found burial zones moving across a Roman villa platform towards the tenth- and eleventh-century churches, and a grave from one of the earliest phases was initially dated on radiocarbon evidence to the early ninth century (Rodwell and Rodwell 1985–93: i. 83–4). Calibration, however, puts this and associated dates into the tenth to twelfth centuries: Bell 2001: 314–15, 366–70. More promising cases may be Scampton (Lincs.), where a villa containing numerous burials was associated with a chapel and well of St Pancras; and Huntington, where a cemetery of unaccompanied orientated burials overlying a villa apparently contained a late Anglo-Saxon chapel: Bell 2001: 254–5, 297.

[31] S 1208, S 561; Hooke 1987.

[32] See the statistics and comments in Rattue 1995: 67–8. He is surely right to envisage 'an incoming system of parish churches adapting itself to a more primitive religious landscape', though I doubt whether the separate well-chapel beside a church 'is almost universally Celtic and displays . . . how thoroughly different Cornwall is from the rest of the country': different patterns of late medieval development and post-Reformation destruction are a more likely explanation for the seeming contrast.   [33] S 678; *VCH Oxon.* xiii. 146.

well-chapels are generally undatable,[34] but others come through as parish churches, and in these cases the wells occasionally gave their names to the parishes or townships. The church of Holywell (Hunts.), which is dedicated (significantly) to St John the Baptist and which stands on a south-facing bluff above the well, existed by 1007.[35] There are other parish churches, such as Berkswell (Warw.), Bisley (Surrey), and Throapham (Yorks.), which combine holy wells with dedications to the Baptist.[36] In the eleventh century St Bride's church, just outside London, was aligned axially on an artificial well or cistern, cut through the remains of a Roman building on the bank of the Fleet.[37] The late twelfth-century Life of St Frideswide claims that in her refuge at Binsey (Oxon.) 'she obtained by her prayers a well which remains to this day, and performs healing works for many who drink from it'; a twelfth-century chapel stands due east of the well.[38] Of the spot at Romsley (Worcs.) where the murdered St Cynehelm's body lay (supposedly *c*.821), his late eleventh-century Life says that 'a holy spring burst forth, which to this day flows into the stream and gives healing to the many who drink from it'; another version adds that 'there is now an oratory there', and a twelfth-century chapel, with a chamber under its chancel from which the spring flowed eastwards, still marks the spot today.[39] This version of a common Cornish pattern—the chapel built physically over the water-source—may be exemplified in Anglo-Saxon guise at Stevington (Beds.) (Fig. 43).[40]

As these cases suggest, 'development' pulled wells which were 'holy' in a miscellany of ways—through association with saints, possibly through baptismal use, or for reasons not visibly Christian at all—into the category of incipient parish churches.[41] The process could have been facilitated and rationalized by some fusion of vernacular and Christian folklore, for instance the adoption of so many wells and well-chapels under St Mary's patronage.

---

[34] Unless by archaeology: for instance, the chapel excavated beside St Katharine's Well at Nafford (Worcs.) was apparently twelfth-century, overlying older footings (Bond 1988: 141). Work of this kind is much needed.

[35] *Chron. Ram.* 85 (and cf. *VCH Hunts.* ii. 175 and *ECEE* 234).

[36] *VCH Warw.* iv. 27–34; Blair 1991*a*: 111–12; Jones 1986: 64. At Berkswell (*Berchewelle* in DB) the eponymous well survives as a large stone-lined tank near the churchyard gate. The well at Bisley, near a possible *eclēs* place-name, was used for baptism into recent times; Rattue 1995: 67, notes other cases.   [37] Milne 1997: 26 and figs. 23–4, 99–102.

[38] Blair 1988*e*.   [39] Love 1996: 68, 129.

[40] The surviving early fabric, at the west end of the nave, has late Anglo-Saxon structural features but no trace of Romanesque ones: Taylor and Taylor 1965–78: ii. 571–2. Here and in several other cases, it seems possible that the inconvenience of an internal spring has been eliminated at a later date by culverting and embanking; an archaeological approach to this question might be fruitful. At Kirkoswald (Cumb.) the spring feeding 'St Oswald's Well' flows westwards from under the church. For some other wells inside chapels, and cases of wells perpetuated as small local churches, see Rattue 1995: 76, and Everitt 1986: 296–300.

[41] Below, pp. 476–8, for the much larger number of wells which remained 'undeveloped'.

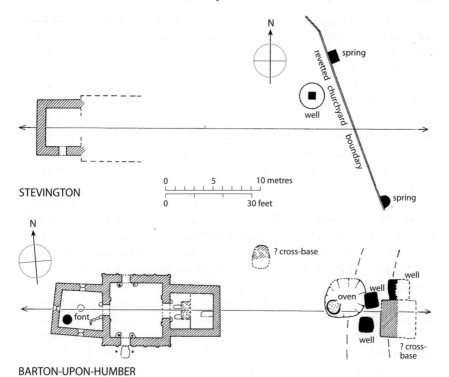

43. Late Anglo-Saxon churches associated with ritual wells. At *Stevington* (Beds.) the small tenth- or eleventh-century church lies west of holy springs now issuing from the base of the revetted churchyard wall (see n. 40). At *Barton-on-Humber* (Lincs.; after Rodwell and Rodwell 1982: fig. 6) the church of *c.*1000 is aligned on a group of wells around a monument-base, and the west *porticus* contains the impression of a contemporary font.

The cult of St Helen, and its strong association with wells in parts of Britain, may be a particularly intriguing case of the interplay of literate and oral culture. The Continental and insular legends foisted on the Emperor Constantine's mother were tortuous, folkloric, and widespread among the Welsh and English by the tenth century.[42] In England the sites of her cult

---

[42] See Matthews 1982–3, Jones 1986, and the sources cited there. Matthews shows that the Welsh folk-myths of (H)elen embodied in the 'Dream of Macsen Wledig' and later works must have existed by the late tenth century. The story of Helen's expedition to Jerusalem and successful excavation for the True Cross was well known in England by the late tenth century: Bodden 1987 is a guide to this tradition, which has nothing to say about holy wells.

have strong associations with dedications to the Holy Cross,[43] with Roman antiquities, and with wells: the first obvious (Helen was believed to have rediscovered the True Cross), the second consistent with the Welsh legend,[44] the third puzzling. The formulation, or at any rate the diffusion, of these links could have happened at a relatively late date. The churches of St Helen at Worcester and Abingdon were important and probably ancient, but it is notable that the *dedications* (as distinct from the sites) are unattested before the late Anglo-Saxon period, and that both were then regarded as antiquities: one at the gate of Roman Worcester and linked with a dedication to the Romano-British martyr St Alban, the other the legendary focus of Abingdon's early minster and Cross-cult.[45] Churches dedicated to St Helen in York (where Constantine was proclaimed emperor in 306) and in Colchester overlay Roman buildings; the latter was believed in the fourteenth century to have been built by Helen herself.[46] If in towns (H)elen stood for the heritage of Christian Rome, it seems possible that in the countryside she became a folkloric personification of conversion, assimilating to herself the superficially similar, but pre-Christian, terms *Alauna* (the recurrent Celtic stream- and deity-name) and *ellern* (Old English 'elder-tree').[47] The holy wells in her name could thus have had very different origins, for instance as 'elder-wells'. In their kaleidoscopic incoherence, these manifestations look more folkloric than hagiographical.

It is rarely clear who was responsible for such reclamation of folk-cult sites, and the practice should probably be seen as a continuum from the earlier

[43] For instance, Chesterfield (Derbs.) had a Holy Cross guild, and a chapel of St Helen in the street called Haliwellgate, i.e. 'holy-well-street' (Riden and Blair 1980: 100, 181–3). However, dedications to St Helen and to the Holy Cross have completely different core zones, the one in Lincolnshire and Yorkshire and the other in the west midlands (Jones 1986: 59), as though they were regionally articulated variants of the same phenomenon.

[44] Matthews 1982–3: 432, 436–8, 447, for her association with Roman Caernarfon, and for the term *Sarn Elen* ('Elen's Causeway') applied to Roman roads.

[45] For Worcester this line of thought results in a rather different emphasis (less on continuity, more on later perceptions) from that in Bassett 1989*a*: 243–6 and Bassett 1992. For Abingdon see *Abingdon*, p. cc.

[46] Magilton 1980; Crummy 1981: 26, 47–8. At York, where the pottery evidence makes a pre-tenth-century date for the church unlikely, it was built directly over a battered Roman mosaic showing a female head: in fact Medusa, but was she mistaken for Helen?

[47] Jones 1986: 69–70; E. Ekwall, *English River-Names* (Oxford, 1928), 5–8, and A. L. F. Rivet and C. Smith, *The Place-Names of Roman Britain* (London, 1979), 243–7, for *Alauna*. Elder-trees were considered magical (Blair 1997: 178; Wilson 2000: 156), and 'elder-wells' are plausible pre-Christian cult sites. At Wroughton, Wilts. (*Ellendun*, 'elder-tree down', folk-etymologized to *mons Ealle* by John of Worcester), the church occurs in charter-bounds of 956 and is dedicated to St John the Baptist and St Helen (S 585; *P-N Wilts.* 278; *VCH Wilts.* xi. 235, 249). Again, the dedication to St Helen at Elstow (Beds.) is presumably a folk-etymology from the name; this is usually interpreted as 'Ællen's *stow*', but its early forms (*Elnestou*, *Alnesto*) can be compared with e.g. Alnwick (*Alnewyk*, from Ptolomy's Αλαυνα): was it a *stow* at a (lost) *Alauna*?

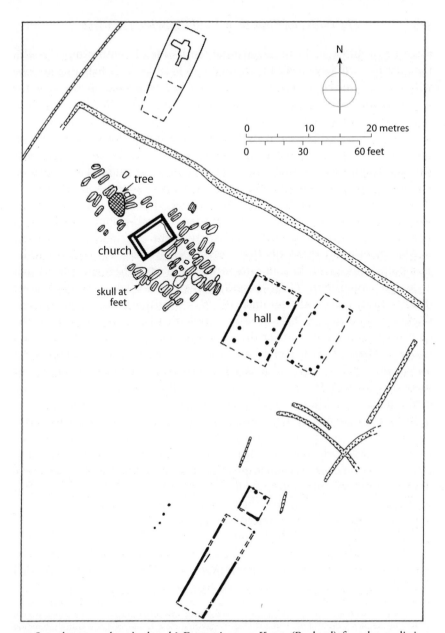

44. Sacred tree or thegn's church? Excavations at *Ketton* (Rutland) found two distinct groups of graves, one clustered around a large tree and the other around a small church; it is currently uncertain which came first. By the eleventh century these features formed part of a manor-house complex, but whether the ritual nucleus attracted the domestic one, or vice versa, is again unclear. The head of one of the burials near the church had been cut off and placed by its feet, presumably to lay a troublesome ghost. (Northamptonshire Archaeology; from data provided by Ian Meadows. Some minor features are omitted in the interests of clarity.)

activities of minsters. In the seigneurial tenth- and eleventh-century world, the initiative will have passed increasingly to local lords. It may therefore be wrong to assume, in cases of churches attached to manor-houses, that the church is always the secondary element: a lord eager to establish control over a source of traditional power such as a holy well, tree, or lay cemetery could sometimes have 'developed' it by building his church there and setting up home next to it.[48] At Ketton Quarry (Rutland)[49] a tiny one-cell timber church, surrounded by graves, adjoined a complex of timber halls dated by pottery to c.900–1100; a group of graves clustered around a very large tree immediately north-west of the church (Fig. 44). It is tempting to see this as a holy tree, already a focus of burial, Christianized by the building of a chapel which in turn attracted manorial-status settlement.

This is not to say that lords always saw precisely eye to eye with the ecclesiastical establishment. In about the 1070s the thegn Ælfsige built his church at Longney-on-Severn (Glos.) beside a huge nut-tree where he liked to sit dicing and feasting in the summer. When St Wulfstan objected to the overshadowing branches, Ælfsige retorted angrily that he would rather leave the church unconsecrated than cut the tree down; Wulfstan cursed the tree, and it duly withered.[50] This could have been no more than a clash between a bishop in a bad temper and a thegn addicted to relaxing after lunch, but there is a distinct echo of the stage-managed fellings of holy trees beloved by earlier missionary bishops. Richard Morris points out that nut-trees, especially hazels, have often been considered sacred and that their nuts and twigs are found in ritual deposits of widely different dates.[51] Alliance with seigneurial power could help the Church to tighten its grip on popular ritual and raise its threshold of acceptable practice, but the relationship could break down: as this story illustrates, if a lord chose to reject episcopal discipline it is unclear (miracles apart) that the bishop could do much about it.

Churches of the sort just described represent one way in which 'undeveloped' cult sites could be adopted into a more demarcated, hierarchical, and explicitly Christian landscape. A place of popular cult could not easily be suppressed, but by building a church over it it could be controlled; if a well

[48] Cf., in Cornwall, Thomas 1967a: 52–4, 57–62, for a 'manorial practice . . . of appropriating disused or defunct Celtic (pre-Conquest) chapels standing close to manor-houses, and rebuilding them as private ones'.

[49] Interim note in *Medieval Settlement Research Group Annual Report*, 13 (1998), 46–7. I am grateful to the excavator, Ian Meadows, for further information.

[50] *Vita Wulf.* ii. 17 (pp. 94–6); *VCH Glos.* x. 197–204. A slight mound on the south side of the church, between it and the pond which divides the churchyard from Manor Farm further south, is a possible site for the nut-tree. It is intriguing that the dedication of Longney church is first recorded (c.1708) as St Helen: could the tree have stood above a holy spring feeding the pond?

[51] R. Morris 1989: 79–81; cf. Jolly 1996: 110, 160.

dedicated to St John the Baptist was already used for baptism or cures, adding a chapel was a step towards bringing Christian initiation within a framework of local parochial observance. If the builders were minster-priests or local lords, they had an interest in defining and perhaps directing the devotions of the ordinary laity.

These cases therefore contributed to parish church origins; but there is an important reservation. Minsters apart, many of the churches and chapels associated with Roman villas and holy wells were never parochial, but were of a kind that the drafter of the 1014 law would probably have perceived as mere 'field-churches'. The sample contains a high proportion of dependent sites and an abnormal number of deserted and abandoned ones. The locations of these churches were pre-determined by factors unconnected with eleventh-century social reorganization and economic growth: they were part of a traditional but increasingly marginalized culture of open-air ritual and assembly at boundaries, hills, confluences, and the like.[52] This is not to deny that churches which developed older sites could sometimes also be manorial, as the Ketton and Longney cases perhaps illustrate. But although they played an important continuing role in local religion, it was at a subordinate (and to us very obscure) level.

Origins (ii): devolution from clerical communities

Some substantial tenth-century aristocrats controlled groups of priests, either by establishing them within their households or by acquiring patronage rights over prebends in minsters.[53] Thus Æthelflaed (962 × 991) leaves two hides each to her priests Ælfwold and Æthelmaer, and Ælfhelm's will (975 × 1016) reserves 'that which I grant to my priest'.[54] Æthelgifu, the rich Hertfordshire widow of the 990s, had a group of priests in her household and stipulates that one of them, Eadwine, is to be given a church and freed; as the editors of her will observe, 'one fair conclusion seems to be that the priests, of whom Edwin was one, served the estates of Langford, Clifton, and Stondon as one ecclesiastical institution'.[55] The gradual re-location of such priests from households to dispersed manors suggests one potential context for the building of estate churches.

These aristocrats were evidently free to direct the pastoral activities of priests under their control. But there must have been cases where the local minster clergy had their own ideas about how new churches should be served,

---

[52] Above, p. 280; below, p. 475; Pantos 2002 for open-air meetings.   [53] Above, p. 363.
[54] S 1494, S 1487 (*Wills*, 36, 32).   [55] W. *Æth*. 8, 74.

and the autonomy or influence to enforce them: who said mass in a church built on a thegn's estate when all tithes still went to the minster?[56] Two answers seem possible: either the church was served by the lord's own priest under a strict understanding about vested financial rights, or one of the minster-priests was appointed to it. The second has the plausibility that it would simply extend to the new church the existing practice of serving out-lying cult sites from the centre. There is no explicit pre-Conquest evidence, but a narrative from Christchurch (Hants.) shows such an arrangement being set up in the 1090s. A witness later recalled how Ælfric the Small, lord of Milford, obtained consent from the dean of Christchurch minster to build a chapel on his manor and endow it with half a yardland. The chapel was financially subject to the canons of Christchurch, who appointed one of their own priests to serve it, perhaps travelling out from the minster whenever he needed to say mass.[57]

There is a hazy line between this kind of devolved service, to a chapel built for a lay lord's convenience, and service devolved to a chapel founded at the minster's own initiative, whether or not on an ancient cult site. A twelfth-century statement that the chapel of St Martin at Meddon, five miles from St Nectan's minster at Hartland (Devon), 'was from of old time endowed with a certain little meadow, which was reserved for the use of the clerks of St Nectan who used to celebrate divine service in the same chapel several times yearly',[58] points to the latter process. Devolution also occurred on royal land in south-west Devon, where by the 1030s a canon of Plympton was holding the dependent timber chapel of St Andrew in Plymouth as part of his prebend.[59] It is unclear, on the other hand, by what means the preben-daries of Bromfield minster (Salop.) had assumed by the 1150s the role of locally based priests at chapels scattered through the mother-parish.[60] It is unrealistic to think that 'proprietary church' and 'field-chapel' were exclusive categories: probably various kinds of deal could be worked out between a minster careful of its rights, peasants feeling neglected by their priests, and a lord attracted to the idea of hearing mass at home in his 'own' church. This becomes clearer after 1100, when bishops licensed manorial chapels to remain

[56] Below, p. 442.
[57] Below, p. 518. I am grateful to Susan Wood for her comments on this text. She observes that Hase 1988: 54–6 and Blair 1988*b*: 8 may have been too definite in assuming that the priest was sent episodically to serve the chapel but continued to reside at Christchurch: *mittere* can mean 'put in' as well as 'send'. If the priest shared his time flexibly between the two places, this could be more a matter of degree than of clear alternatives; his loyalties must have been to some extent divided between Ælfric and the canons.   [58] *Nectan*, 409; cf. Pearce 1985: 266–9.   [59] Below, p. 521.
[60] Blair 1985*a*: 128–31 (with map), which also notes some possible Domesday cases of the same process. Chapels in the Leominster mother-parish were served from the centre as late as the 1180s: Kemp 1988: 90.

parochially subordinate and to be used exclusively by the local lords and their men.[61] In about 1080 a chapel at Whistley (Berks.) was built (at the request of the locals?) to obviate the three-mile journey to Sonning mother-church.[62] Whether such cases represent pre-Conquest practice remains imponderable.

Origins (iii): foundation by estate proprietors

When small churches appear in late tenth- and eleventh-century texts, it is generally as the property of landowners. By the 960s, King Eadgar and his advisers saw need to legislate against churches on thegns' bookland (with or without graveyards) encroaching on minster tithe.[63] In 1086 the Domesday commissioners could list hundreds of churches as manorial assets along with the meadows, woods, and mills. In the Domesday satellite text from Canterbury, the east Kent churches of Blackmanstone, Dymchurch, Eastbridge, and Orgarswick appear as *Blacemannescirce, Demancirce, Aelsiescirce,* and *Ordgarescirce,* and Blacmann and Ælfsige duly figure as landowners in 1066; a Norfolk will made just before the Conquest mentions 'the church which Thurweard owned'.[64] It was above all with such churches, in the hands of locally influential people concerned to build up their independence and tithe-revenue, that the parochial future lay: they were integral components of the new local power-centres, and prospered with them.

It would be surprising if Eadgar's tithe-law did not reflect a growth of minor thegnly churches in the West Saxon heartland, and indeed we glimpse them there in a series of charter-boundary terms meaning 'church site' or 'church enclosure' which can be identified more or less plausibly with existing parish churches: Wroughton (Wilts.) and Bleadon (Somerset) in 956, East Kennett (Wilts.) and Dyrham (on the Gloucestershire/Wiltshire border) in 972, Wonston (near Winchester) in the eleventh century.[65] These stray

---

[61] Blair 1988*b*: 11. Good examples are Alvescot, Oxon. (the chapel to remain subject to the mother-church, only the founding lord's tenants to hear mass in it), and Ashtead, Surrey (no priest to sing mass in the chapel without consent of the priest of the mother-church): F. Barlow (ed.), *EEA* xi: *Exeter 1046–1184* (Oxford, 1996), 24–6 (No. 25), and *Winch. Acta*, 4 (No. 6).

[62] *Hist. Abb.* ii. 22; Lennard 1959: 297–8, 302–3; this was probably the present church of Hurst, recorded as an undedicated chapel in 1220 (Blair 1988*b*: 18 n. 57).   [63] Below, p. 442.

[64] Tatton-Brown 1988: 108; S 1516 (*Wills*, 88). Alswick ('Ælfflaed's *wic*'), Herts., became Layston ('Leofstan's church'): *VCH Herts.* iv. 77.

[65] S 585, S 606, S 784, S 786, S 360 (the last an eleventh-century forgery of a charter of '900': *NMW* 18–26). The terms are *ciricean heow wah* ('church-enclosure-wall'?) at Wroughton, *ciricstede* in the other cases. The identifications are explicit at Wonston ('ðone cyricstede on Wynsiges tune') and convincing at Wroughton (above, n. 47); at Bleadon, East Kennett, and Dyrham the bounds do not allow a solution which is anywhere near conclusive, but are compatible with the existing church sites. These names are discussed, with similar conclusions, by Sandred 1963: 59–60. A similar term occurs in the unattached bounds of Oundle (Northants.), where *on ciricfeld* can be identified with the chapel of *Chirchefeld* mentioned in 1189 (S 1566; Hart 1992: 142, 173; *Cal. Charter Rolls*, iv. 274).

references are a useful counterweight to the otherwise largely eastern evidence, while their absence from Mercian charter-bounds heightens the impression that local churches appeared more slowly in that region.[66]

The next written evidence for local manorial churches—if it can be trusted—survives in late memoranda recording gifts to Ramsey Abbey of four churches in Cambridgeshire and Huntingdonshire in the 970s and 1000s.[67] Beyond that, we are confined to a small handful of wills of which only one is appreciably earlier than the mid eleventh century. This is the long and elaborate will of the noblewoman Æthelgifu (990 × 1001), who leaves land to 'the church', apparently on one of her Essex manors, and the church itself to a slave-priest who must maintain it. This case is complicated by the fact that Æthelgifu could have built it in the first instance for her household of quasi-monastic ladies rather than for any wider use; the language at all events suggests something very private and informal, even if the bequest was meant to secure the church a more independent future.[68] The other wills, which start to give an impression that local churches were common, are all closer to 1050 and all from the eastern part of the country.[69] Given the silence of the several tenth-century wills surviving from other regions, it is hard not to conclude that manorial churches which anyone thought worth mentioning were still a localized and relatively new phenomenon in 1000.

Finally, a small number of place-names, in which personal names and descriptive terms are compounded with the suffix *-ciric* ('church'), contribute mainly to tracing the spread of private churches during the eleventh and twelfth centuries.[70] As noted above, names in the form 'Ælfsige's church' are

---

[66] Below, pp. 418–20. The only 'church-way/path' boundary term before 1000 is also in Wessex, at Manningford Abbots (Wilts.) in 987: below, p. 459 n.

[67] *Chron. Ram.* 51, 74, 84–5 (*ECEE* 48, 233–4, 238); the churches are Burwell, Wilbraham, Elsworth, and Holywell. A handful of gross post-Conquest forgeries (S 68, S 189, S 213, S 370, S 538, S 746, S 1189; see *NMW* 39–40) grant manors with their appendent churches or chapels; the total absence of such formulae from genuine Anglo-Saxon charters underlines the contrast with the Frankish world (above, pp. 118–19).

[68] *W. Æth.*; Foot 2000: i. 139–40; above, p. 383.   [69] Below, pp. 408–9.

[70] What seems to be the earliest clear case, Thorpe Achurch (Northants.), occurs as *(æt) Asencircan*, 'Asi's/Asa's church', in about 980 (*RASC* 74, 78). Offchurch (Warw.), first mentioned as *Offechirch* in 1139, occurs in the hagiography of St Freomund (Blair 1994: 75) and may have had some folkloric association with King Offa. Pucklechurch (Glos.), *Puclancyrcan* (*ASC* 'D' s.a. 946 (p. 112); S 553), is problematic because of the implausibility of the personal name *Pucela, 'little goblin', or alternatively of the description 'little goblin's church'. In this case and perhaps others, it is conceivable that *-ciric* was used figuratively or ironically to describe some inappropriate or natural feature. Cf. the 'Green Chapel' in 'Sir Gawain and the Green Knight', which has been identified with the natural hill-cleft of Ludchurch, 'Lud's church', Staffs. (R. Elliott, 'Language and Topography', in D. Brewer and J. Gibson (eds.), *A Companion to the Gawain-Poet* (Woodbridge, 1997), 105–17, at 111–17; for alternative ideas see M. W. Thompson, 'The Green Knight's Castle', in C. Harper-Bill and others (eds.), *Studies in Medieval History Presented to R. Allen Brown* (Woodbridge, 1989), 317–25, and M. W. Twomey, 'Morgan le Fay at Hautdesert', in B. Wheeler and F. Tolhurst

especially prominent in Kent, where it is suggestive of their relative informality that most of them are attested in local sources rather than in Domesday Book.[71] Names describing the church building (such as 'stave-built',
'boarded', 'variegated', 'horned') are rarely recorded until after 1100, perhaps
because they tended to be used for the humblest churches.[72]

For a process of such fundamental importance, this is indeed a meagre
record; topographical analysis and archaeology take us a good deal further.
The number of excavations to modern standards remains small, but they
support the impression of later tenth- and eleventh-century origins, and
suggest that patterns still widely visible in the landscape reflect arrangements
of that date.

Of these the most important is the juxtaposition of churches with lay residences. A characteristic English rural scene is the cluster of buildings including both manor-house and church: the physical expression of a world, which
lasted for almost a millennium, in which squire and parson lived and worked
as neighbours. Local studies show that this pattern is widespread, and that
the church (usually) and the manor-house (sometimes) demonstrably existed
by the twelfth or thirteenth century.[73] However, the full integration of
churches into residences, in the sense that they were contained within the
domestic enclosure, seems to be an exceptional and essentially elite practice.
Three known cases belonged to high-status residences—one royal, one
comital, one episcopal—intruded into minster precincts: Cheddar, where
the fully excavated royal domestic complex included a tenth- or early eleventh-

---

(eds.), *On Arthurian Women: Essays in Memory of Maureen Fries* (Dallas, 2001), 103–19, at 117 n. 14;
I owe these references to Carolyne Larrington).

[71] In Kent, in addition to the Domesday Monachorum examples on p. 385 above, Textus Roffensis gives Dowdeschurch (Dud) and Lillechurch (Lilla); note also Dymchurch (*Demancirce*,
'judge's church'?) in Domesday Monachorum. Examples from other counties in DB are: Alvechurch,
Worcs. (Ælfgyth); Bonchurch, IOW (Buna); Colkirk, Norfolk (Cola); Dunchurch, Warw. (Duna);
Gosberton (*Gosebertechirche*), Lincs. (Gosbert); and Litchurch, Derbs. (Luda). Cases like this should
be distinguished from the western British names (Cheriton etc.) which reflect earlier British practice: above, pp. 216–17. See Gelling 1981: 7, for an earlier discussion.

[72] However, the *windcirice* ('wattle-church'?) in Winchester and *gerschereche* ('turf-roofed
church'?) in London occur in charters of 901 and 1054 (S 1443, S 1234; *NMW* 12, 16; *RASC* 216);
the probable minster of St Alchmund in Derby is called *Wythechirche*—a spelling which suggests
'withy-church' rather than 'white-church'—in a late source ('Vita S. Aelkmundi', c. 8, ed. P. Gros-
jean, *Analecta Bollandiana*, 58 (1940), 182). In Domesday Monachorum: Ivychurch, Newchurch,
Woodchurch, all Kent. In twelfth- and thirteenth-century sources (references in relevant EPNS
volumes or E. Ekwall, *The Oxford Dictionary of English Place-Names* (4th edn., Oxford, 1960)):
Berechurch, Essex ('boarded'), Felkirk, Yorks. WR ('plank-built'), Frome Vauchurch, Dorset ('variegated'), Hawkchurch and Honeychurch, Devon ('hawk' and 'honey' or people called Heafoc and
Huna), Hornchurch, Essex ('horned'), Stokenchurch, Bucks. ('stave-built'), Vowchurch, Herefs.
('variegated'). At Hornchurch, the remains of a hart's horns built into the wall of the church were
reported in 1647 (Aubrey 1972: 198). See Gelling 1981: 7–8, for an earlier discussion.

[73] e.g. Blair 1991a: 134–6; Blair 1994: 133–6.

century chapel; Deerhurst, where the manor-house of what had been Earl Odda's portion was later rebuilt to engulf his chapel (Figs. 33, 48); and Winchester, where a small chapel served the episcopal residence formed in the late tenth century.[74] The *oratorium* in Æthelred II's vill at Gillingham, where he heard mass in 993, was presumably analogous to Cheddar; so perhaps was Colchester, where an apparently tenth-century timber chapel with elaborate wallpaintings was built alongside the podium of the Roman temple, later the castle site.[75] These seem to be a small and specialized group confined to the highest social level, though presumably reflecting a wider and growing expectation that any lord should have access to private religious space.

Much more typically, the church was peripheral to the manor-house, and in a number of cases can now be shown to have been built on, or just outside, the bank or ditch enclosing the curial site. The best example so far is the completely excavated complex at Raunds (Northants.), where the tiny tenth-century church was built right on the north-eastern edge of a rectilinear ditched enclosure containing the manorial buildings, its west end actually overlying the boundary (Fig. 45).[76] A tenth- to eleventh-century site at Trowbridge (Wilts.) shows an almost identical relationship: a church in a rectangular graveyard just touches the north-eastern perimeter of a ditched manorial enclosure.[77] The surviving parish churches at Goltho (Lincs.) and Sulgrave (Northants.) also stand immediately outside the perimeter banks and ditches of the excavated tenth- to eleventh-century manor-houses (Fig. 45).[78] In many other cases, neither the house nor the church has been excavated but a similar juxtaposition is evident from the later topography.[79] At Studham (Beds.), where the church adjoins a moated manor-house (Fig. 47), an agreement of *c*.1060 records the construction of 'a church and all the buildings in that manor' with timber supplied by the landlord to the resident lay couple.[80]

[74] Above, pp. 326–7; Biddle 1976*b*: 324; *AntJ* 55 (1975), 327.

[75] S 876; Drury 1990.   [76] Cadman 1983; Boddington 1996: 5–7, 11.

[77] Graham and Davies 1993: 21–56. Tenth-century pottery provides a *terminus post quem* for the church and graveyard, which continued until a castle was built in 1139. The excavators are sure that the churchyard boundary ditch (880) pre-dated the manorial enclosure ditch (1554), which slightly clipped its corner. But there must be a slight doubt about such a relationship between two converging ditches, both of which would have been scoured at intervals during their lives: since ditch 1554 was the deeper its primary fills lay at a lower level than the base of ditch 880, and at one point were directly overlain by clay from the castle bank. The stone church resembled the *second* church at Raunds in form and scale, and there are no architectural grounds for dating it earlier than *c*.1050 (below, pp. 412–15).

[78] Beresford 1987; Davison 1977; Sawyer 1998: 7, asserting a tenth-century date for Goltho.

[79] R. Morris 1989: 263–74; Hall 2000: 49; Everson and others 1991: 44–6 (some slightly different speculations based on Lincolnshire field evidence).

[80] S 1235 (*Charters of St Albans*, ed. J. Crick (*Anglo-Saxon Charters*, forthcoming), No. 16): Oswulf and Æthelgyth give Studham to St Albans but retain a life-interest. In the English version the donors

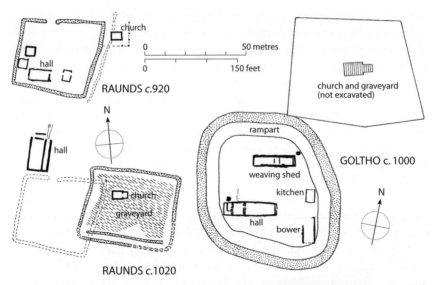

45. Manor-house and church. At *Raunds* (Northants.) the manorial enclosure, the addition of a tiny church to its north-east corner, and the subsequent formation of the churchyard are revealed in their entirety by excavation. At *Goltho* (Lincs.) the church and graveyard, known only from their post-medieval layout, can be seen to have a similar relationship to the excavated early eleventh-century house-enclosure. (After Cadman 1983, Boddington 1996, and Beresford 1987.)

How should we read these oddly liminal church sites: not inside manorial enclosures, but also barely outside them? The answer is surely that such a church had to be accessible not only to inhabitants of the manor-house, but also to people from outside it whose presence in the domestic zone was not necessarily expected or welcomed.[81] This is important, for it implies that a church such as Raunds, however much a thegnly status-symbol, was envisaged from the outset (in contrast to the Cheddar palace chapel) as serving a wider community than the manorial family and resident staff. As we will see, the services provided for this community soon came to include burial. This

ask the abbot 'þæt he heom geafe tymber to anre cyrican 7 to eallum gebytlum on þam ilcan tune' to demonstrate that the land is St Alban's own property; the Latin version reads '. . . ut dedisset eis ligna ad edificandam in eadem villa ecclesiam in honore domini nostri Ihesu Christi et sancti Albani, ut et hec ecclesia sibi in specialissimum fieret proprietatis signum . . .'.

[81] At Raunds, access into the manorial enclosure was always from the east, the side on which the church stood, and during the tenth to early fourteenth centuries this eastern access led directly to the hall.

locational pattern is the earliest evidence that English local churches had functions which can meaningfully be called 'parochial'.

Yet their physical appearance was not that of later parish churches. Fragments of several tenth- to eleventh-century manorial churches have now been excavated, a few of them with reasonably coherent plans (Fig. 48).[82] The timber churches at Rivenhall, Wharram, and Burnham need not have looked rough: Anglo-Saxon carpentry was expert and could be elaborately decorated, and it may be that their walls were plastered and even painted. Nonetheless, they shared the impermanent technology of normal domestic buildings. They were also slightly smaller than the tiniest eleventh-century churches still standing today.[83]

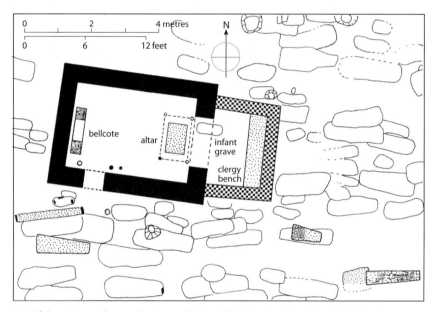

46. 'If there is any thegn who has on his bookland a church with which there is a graveyard . . .' The manorial church at *Raunds* in its mature state of *c.*1000, after the addition of the chancel and establishment of the graveyard. Some of the graves near the church, very likely those of the founder and his family, were marked with slabs and other structures. (After Boddington 1996: fig. 11.)

[82] Wharram Percy (Yorks.): Bell and Beresford 1987: 55–61; Rivenhall (Essex): Rodwell and Rodwell 1985–93: i. 85–90 (with comparative plans); Burnham (Lincs.): Coppack 1986. For dating of Rivenhall and Burnham see below, n. 189. Reports on the important excavations of late Anglo-Saxon timber churches with graveyards at Cherry Hinton and Gamlingay (both Cambs.) are not available at the time of writing: for brief accounts, with a plan of Cherry Hinton, see Taylor 2001: 165–6, 175. So far as can currently be seen, they support the present argument.

[83] Cf. table in Taylor and Taylor 1965–78: iii. 1033.

The only Anglo-Saxon church and graveyard which has been totally excavated and published to modern standards is at Raunds (Figs. 45, 46, 48).[84] This was one of those townships in which each half of a divided manor had its own church;[85] it is because one church was abandoned in the twelfth century that its tenth- and eleventh-century phases survived almost intact, undisturbed by later enlargements or burials. There is no reason, though, to think that it was abnormal in any way other than its arrested development, and it is a time-capsule from the beginnings of manor-centred parochial life.

Soon after 950, the proprietors of Raunds cleared a plot of waste ground on the edge of their manor-house enclosure, filled in a section of the boundary ditch and built a tiny church. It was a simple rectangle, with rubble walls and a timber-framed doorway; up to twenty people, standing and rather crowded, could have heard mass in it. Projecting from the clay floor, and probably covered by an altar set away from the east wall, was a pot which had been used first for boiling honey or making wax, then as a receptacle for ashes, and finally probably as a piscina drain.[86] At this stage the church had no graveyard, though a small area around it was marked out by posts possibly supporting a fence.

Around 1000, the church's status seems to have risen. A tiny eastern annexe with a clergy-bench was added, the nave altar was re-located under a canopy, the nave floor was paved, and a probable bellcote was built at the west end. At much this time a graveyard started to develop around the church, and remained in use for a century or more.[87] Demographic analysis suggests a total burying population of around forty individuals at any one time, which would be consistent with the estimate from the floor area that about half this number (in other words all the adults) could stand inside the church.[88]

The sequence at Raunds recalls Eadgar's law of the 960s: what began as a 'thegn's church without a graveyard' acquired, thirty or forty years later, the graveyard which gave it limited tithe rights, and a bellcote for the bell which an aspirant thegn needed.[89] Even the tiny first phase was distinguished from the manorial hall and chambers by being built of stone. The eastern extension, though hardly more than a place for the priest to sit, gave the building something of the aspect of the larger two-cell churches of the next century. The size of the burying population supports inferences already drawn from the church's site: this community of perhaps eight to ten households did not

---

[84] The following summary is based on Boddington 1996. However, it uses the important revisions in the chronology, moving the later Anglo-Saxon phases forwards by up to a century, which will be published in the forthcoming report on the manor-house.

[85] Below, pp. 397–8.

[86] D. Parsons considers the liturgical aspects in Boddington 1996: 58–66.

[87] Below, p. 471.   [88] Boddington 1996: 28–31, 67.   [89] Below, p. 442; above, p. 371.

live inside the manor-house and must have comprised at least some section of the wider manorial inhabitants.

How commonly tenth-century thegns built anything more ambitious than Raunds is unclear, but the evidence for small stone churches of a quality to last is remarkably slight until well into the eleventh century. Indeed, the very fragmentary evidence from other excavations suggests that timber churches, not necessarily unimposing but inevitably short-lived, remained the norm in many if not most regions at the Conquest and beyond. An ambitious timber church with north, south, and east *porticus* and an attached baptistery, probably of the mid to late eleventh century, has been excavated at Potterne (Wilts.) (Fig. 52), and the Studham church envisaged in the agreement of *c.*1060 was to be of timber.[90] Five out of six recent excavations at Essex churches, and one in Oxfordshire, located timber phases replaced by post-Conquest rebuildings.[91] The one 'Anglo-Saxon' timber building still standing above ground, the two-cell stave-church built of split logs at Greensted (Essex), is now dated by dendrochronology between 1063 and *c.*1100.[92]

In the counties where Domesday Book gives something approaching a useful picture, there is an impression that the manors of the wealthier lay proprietors were better provided with churches, and that a modest lord of three or four scattered manors might typically have a church on one only.[93] It is clear, on the other hand, that the downwards diffusion of the practice was continuing, and that churches were starting to be built on holdings even smaller than the upwardly mobile freeman's five hides.[94] This must have been stimulated by the post-Conquest loosening of tithe obligations to old minsters, though it is hard to believe that the great multitude of Domesday churches in East Anglia (where, as we will see, there was the special stimulus of collective foundation) were all less than twenty years old in 1086. Especially in Suffolk, churches and fractions of churches were attached to minute holdings of no more than a few acres.[95]

Outside East Anglia, 'manor-houses' at this microscopic level were rarely equipped with churches until after the Conquest. An excavated example,

[90] Below, pp. 460–1; above, p. 388.

[91] Essex CC 1984; Rodwell and Rodwell 1985–93; Drury and Rodwell 1978: 138–40 and fig. 5 (the dating of all the first stone phases to post-1066 is mine, not the authors'). Blair 1998*b*: 228–32, for Woodeaton (Oxon.), where the walls of the eleventh-century church were of close-spaced vertical timbers with daub infill. See James 1917: 233, for an early post-Conquest reference to a timber church in Essex.

[92] Christie and others 1979; I. Tyers, 'Tree-Ring Analysis of Timbers from the Stave Church of Greensted, Essex', unpublished Ancient Monuments Laboratory Report 14/1996.

[93] Blair 1991*a*: 115–19, for Surrey; but cf. below, n. 99.

[94] In Surrey, for instance, Chaldon (two hides) and Tatsfield (half a hide): Blair 1991*a*: 122, 124, and fig. 34; above, p. 371, for the 'five hides'.	[95] Below, pp. 399–400.

Hatch Warren (Hants.), acquired a standard two-cell stone church beside a timber house shortly before 1086, when it was recorded as a one-hide farm with two villans and eleven slaves.[96] Growth of the settlement, and an apparent vacuum in parochial authority, allowed Hatch to emerge during the twelfth century as a tiny independent parish with its own churchyard.[97] In terms of pastoral and practical utility to patrons and congregations, it is unlikely in practice to have been much different from the larger number of late foundations which were formally no more than chapels—in other words dependent on parish churches rather than autonomous—in the Continental terminology introduced to England from the 1070s. The hardening of this canon-law boundary after 1100 tends to disguise the continuum in lay foundation, which extended through the late eleventh into the twelfth and even thirteenth centuries in areas of late and expanding settlement, and within which no clear line can be drawn between provision for lordly households and for peasant communities.[98]

The proprietary church as a mark of status and influence was ubiquitous through the early medieval west: the relationship between a resident English thegn and the church which he built outside his house, staffed with his own priest, and heard mass in is clear enough. When a great aristocrat owned several churches on numerous scattered manors,[99] the nature of the relationship is less clear-cut. Why did lords bother to build churches in places which they only visited episodically? Does the fact that they did so imply overriding concerns for the pastoral care (or parochial obedience) of their tenants, rather than for their own liturgical needs? Was it a response to demands from tenants on outlying manors to be as well served as those on core ones? Did such churches necessarily have their own priests, or did priests go to them from a central or itinerant household? Exactly when, in the two centuries between 900 and 1100, the clerical group gave way to the one-church priest as the dominant agent of pastoral care remains very obscure.

Churches on manors of non-resident religious corporations raise the same questions and others: the reformed monasteries held great constellations of

---

[96] Fasham and others 1995: 76–91, 146–50. The church, which is mentioned in 1086 (DB i. 49), was architecturally typical of the 'rebuilding' stereotype (below, pp. 412–16).

[97] Fasham and others 1995: 149. The parish was, however, barely viable, and succumbed quickly after the Black Death: a 'last in, first out' mechanism which probably means that such late and marginal foundations, like the multiple and tiny churches of Domesday East Anglia, are heavily over-represented among abandoned churches.

[98] Everitt 1986: 205–22, and Blair 1991*a*: 152–7, for the continuing foundation and pastoral role of chapels in the Wealden areas of Kent and Surrey. Cf. Rosser 1991.

[99] As in Surrey, especially the several churches of Æthelnoth of Canterbury and Beorhtsige: Blair 1991*a*: 115–19. Lennard 1959: 290–1 refutes the suggestion of Page 1914–15: 92–3 that a thegn would necessarily have only one church.

scattered manors from the 970s onwards, and any churches which they built on them cannot have been primarily for their own use. And if any group among the late tenth- and eleventh-century aristocracy had an active concern to build churches for the laity at large, it should have been the monks and the bishops.[100] Certainly there are hints. There is no reason to doubt the Canterbury tradition that St Dunstan built churches on rural estates of the see, though even these may have been mainly at archiepiscopal residences.[101] Three generations on but in the same tradition, it could be said of St Wulfstan of Worcester that 'many were the churches throughout the diocese that he began with vigour and completed to an excellent standard', and that 'through all his diocese he built churches on lands that were in his jurisdiction, and pressed for such building on the lands of others'.[102] Yet the most striking thing about this kind of evidence is its rarity. For whatever reason, bishops and monasteries in England had nothing like the dynamic and formative role in building and controlling local churches that they were currently assuming in France.[103]

The church-founding of religious landlords should be visible in Domesday Book, but even this gives no clear picture. Some great ecclesiastical estates seem abnormally well stocked with churches,[104] others abnormally *under*-provided, as though their proprietors were trying to preserve some central monopoly.[105] Vagaries in estate-based returns to the Domesday commissioners may partly explain these patterns, but in Surrey it is interesting that manors of Chertsey Abbey and the see of Canterbury were, by local standards, unusually well supplied with churches, with the notable exception of the great block of land around Chertsey itself.[106] Here it seems reasonable to

---

[100] Darlington 1936, Deanesly 1962: 104–36, and Rosser 1992: 270–84, for earlier discussions of the practical pastoral concerns of the reformed monks. Any such activity is in any case likely to have centred on demesne manors, since the tenants of manors on long leases are likely to have behaved like other minor lay lords.

[101] Eadmer, 'Vita S. Dunstani', c. 28 (ed. W. Stubbs, *Memorials of Saint Dunstan* (Rolls Ser. 63, 1874), 204–5). In the one specific instance given, Dunstan is said to have built a timber church at *Magavelda* (Sussex) 'as also in the other places of his hospices (*hospitii*)'. This apparently refers to Mayfield, later an archiepiscopal palace but not recorded as the archbishop's property in either DB or the Domesday Monachorum (as noted in the edition currently in preparation by A. J. Turner and B. Muir).

[102] *Vita Wulf.* i. 15, iii. 10 (pp. 52, 120). Wulfstan is of course being presented as a model (so not necessarily typical) bishop.   [103] Below, p. 422.

[104] For instance, the Suffolk manors of Bury St Edmunds look particularly well supplied, especially in Thedwestry hundred which has a recurrent formula 'ecclesie huius ville *x* acre de libera terra pertinent pro elemosina' (DB ii. 361ᵛ–3ᵛ). This example is, however, in the context of an abnormally well-churched county. In the area around Winchester there are some grounds for thinking that the bishops founded churches systematically: Hase 1994: 68–9.

[105] Page 1914–15: 62, for St Albans, Coventry, Glastonbury, Muchelney, Athelney, Bath, and London; Yorke 1995: 230, for Wells.   [106] Blair 1991a: 114–15.

suggest that the Chertsey monks had taken a coherent decision to build churches on the outlying manors, while keeping an old-fashioned pastoral system, centred on the abbey and its priests, in the core estate.

The Chertsey case also reminds us of an alternative topographical context for church-building. Several of Chertsey's villages in Surrey (for instance Great Bookham, Fig. 47) are laid out in regular and clearly deliberate house-plots along a street, with the churchyard comprising a larger-than-average plot fitted in among the others. This pattern, obviously, is widespread throughout England: if thousands of churches were adjuncts to manor-houses, thousands more were components of structured peasant settlements. The huge diversity of English nucleated settlement, ranging from the organic and diffuse to the planned and tightly structured, excludes any simple contrast between churches which were contained within villages and those which were not, and in some regions villages have themselves often grown around manor/church nuclei.[107] Nonetheless, we can probably sometimes see in these village-sited churches a pattern of origins orientated more towards the identities, obligations, and pastoral needs of villagers, less towards the convenience and status-claims of resident lords.

To an extent this is a chronological distinction as well as a social one, for the row-plan village is a relative latecomer. The first specific reference to an English village with its church dates only from *c.*1000, when a nobleman surrendered the manor of Snodland (Kent) together with 'all the house-plots which he had west of the church' ('7 þa hagan ealle þe he bewestan þære cyrcan hæfde'):[108] an accurate description of Snodland village today (Fig. 47). There is no archaeological evidence that normal row-plan villages are any earlier than this, and scholars are increasingly tending to date most of them after 1050. So just as one wave of church foundations followed manor-house foundation in the tenth century, so another seems to have followed village foundation in the eleventh and twelfth. In this world, local identity was becoming more clearly marked: certainly in the physical setting of life and work, perhaps too in perceptions. Here we could be edging a little closer to the local church as an expression of community. These hints become stronger in the special circumstances of divided lordship.

---

[107] Hadley 2000*a*: 197–207, for a review of recent work on village origins which emphasizes regional diversity and a broad range of causes; Blair 1991*a*: 59, 135, 140–2, for an argument associating churches integrated into village plans (in contrast to those adjoining manor-houses) with absentee—and especially monastic—lordship.   [108] S 1456 (*RASC* 140–2).

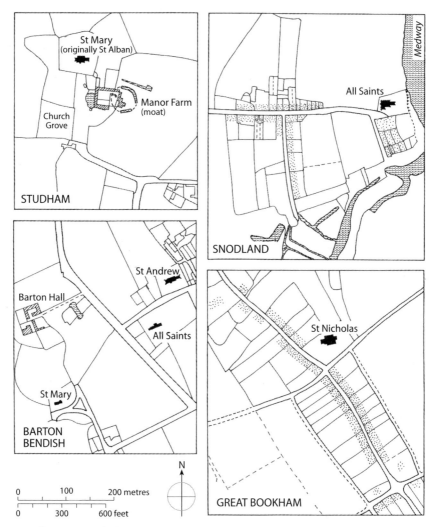

47. The settings of eleventh-century local churches: four examples. *Studham* (Beds.), where Oswulf and Æthelgyth were given timber to build the first church in about 1060 (after OS 1880); *Snodland* (Kent), where Leofwine relinquished 'all the messuages which he had west of the church' in about 1000 (after tithe map, 1845); *Barton Bendish* (Norfolk), illustrating the grouping of three churches at the core of a township (after OS 1884, and Rogerson and others 1987: fig. 2); *Great Bookham* (Surrey), a row-plan village on a Chertsey Abbey manor (in 1618: after Blair 1991*a*: fig. 18).

Origins (iv): divided townships, joint founders, and shared churchyards

Single villages, or even single churchyards, containing two or more churches remain an enigmatic feature of the Norfolk landscape. The temptation to regard this phenomenon as a local oddity should be resisted: it was the extreme manifestation of pressures, exerted by the breaking-up and intermixture of lordships within economically coherent townships, which occurred to a lesser degree throughout England. It is of great interest nonetheless, for it may have created—or at least focused and brought to the surface—ideas of common ritual co-operation and parochial identity which elsewhere are hard to detect at the level of the local parish before the twelfth century.[109]

The splitting-up of manors, for example by royal grant or between heirs, was a continuing process—in the context of steady economic and demographic growth—through the ninth to thirteenth centuries. The impact of such tenurial changes on the agrarian lives of peasants varied between regions, but could be complex, especially when they cut across existing open-field townships. On one model, fission might involve the reorganization of an open-field village into two separate ones, or fragmentation into long, progressively narrow territories to share out diverse soil types. When each share had its own manorial/village nucleus, that is where any church would be built. This mechanism does not normally produce clusters of churches; where the strip-like manors were strung out in a line (as on the Surrey Downs) the churches could be close together, but within their distinct territories.[110]

Alternatively, tenurial division might leave the village and its fields physically undivided, so that demesnes, tenant holdings, and house-plots belonging to two or more lords lay intermixed, perhaps on a regular share-by-share basis.[111] Decisions on church provision—whether each tenurial share needed its own church, or one church might serve the whole township—must have been taken through processes which were presumably the more complicated the more landowners were involved. One possible outcome, the building of two or more churches on separate sites in one settlement, may have been a response to particularly complex tenurial arrangements, which perhaps explains why it was so common in East Anglia. To take one example among many, the village of Barton Bendish (Norfolk) contained separate churches of St Mary, All Saints, and St Andrew, of which two had eleventh-century

---

[109] The present analysis owes much to Peter Warner's stimulating study: Warner 1986. See also Batcock 1991; Williamson 1993: 154–61.

[110] Blair 1991a: 32–4, 66–9.   [111] Dodgshon 1980 expounds the mechanics of the process.

stone phases and one is known to overlie a tenth-century cultivation horizon (Fig. 47).[112] Likewise, when in about 1050 the Norfolk thegn Eadwine bequeathed 'ten acres south of the street to Bergh church and ten acres north of the street to Apton church', he was endowing two churches in what is today the single village of Bergh Apton.[113] The arrangement may have been more widespread than it seems: examples have been noted in Lincolnshire, Essex, Northamptonshire, and Gloucestershire,[114] and it is suggestive that the long-forgotten church excavated at Raunds was originally one of two churches, on either side of the village street.

Thirdly, there are the cases where two or three churches stood in one churchyard. The great majority of recorded examples are in Norfolk (thirty-six, as against four in Suffolk, three in Cambridgeshire, and one in Essex), though the figures may be distorted by the particular interest of Norfolk antiquaries in the phenomenon.[115] These churches too, it seems, normally served the interspersed manors (and therefore eventually parishes) of townships which were tenurially divided but had common agrarian organization.[116] In status terms they were normally independent churches controlling distinct parishes, but it is sometimes apparent that one was 'senior', set squarely in the churchyard, the other 'junior' and built on its edge.[117] The Domesday entry for Stowmarket (Suffolk), describes such an arrangement created between 1066 and 1086:

In the time of King Edward [there was] a church with one carucate of free land. But Hugh de Montfort has 23 acres of that carucate and claims them [as belonging] to a certain chapel which four brothers, freemen under Hugh, built on their own land adjoining the cemetery of the mother-church—and they were inhabitants of the parish of the mother-church (*manentes de parrochia matris ecclesiae*)—because [the mother-church] could not accommodate the whole parish (*non poterat capere totam parrochiam*). This mother-church had by purchase (*per emptionem*) half of the burial [fees] for all time, and a quarter of the other alms that were made. And the hundred does not know whether or not this chapel was dedicated.[118]

Given that the brothers and their lord won independent rights for their chapel, it is all the more striking that they built it next to the existing church,

---

[112] Rogerson and others 1987: 1–66.

[113] Below, pp. 408–9. The modern village has St Martin's church (demolished) on its eastern edge, SS Peter and Paul some way to the south beside Bergh Apton Hall.

[114] R. Morris 1989: 232, 458–9 n. 13; Everson and others 1991: 20 (with comments by Hadley 2000*a*: 210–15) for two Lincolnshire cases.   [115] Warner 1986: 39–41.

[116] Ibid. 45–50, showing that discrete parishes, sometimes with a tortuous common boundary laid out in such a way as to bisect the churchyard, are likely to be post-medieval rationalizations of earlier intermixed arrangements.   [117] Ibid. 41.

[118] DB ii. 281ᵛ. Whether or not the chapel was dedicated may have had implications for its status: below, p. 496.

and that the hundred jurors could seemingly regard it as a parochial asset. It is hard to fault Peter Warner's suggestions that 'the pull of a pre-established graveyard and an ancient sacred site may have seemed more attractive and more equitable than locating the new church on lands belonging to one or other of the partners', and that 'there may well have been a common sense of community shared between worshippers in the new church and the loose association of landholders resident within the mother-parish'.[119] One other fact reinforces this view. Among the 'lesser' churches in the contiguous pairs and threes, a high proportion (including Stowmarket) were dedicated to St Mary.[120] While this might partly have a chronological explanation,[121] the pairing of a 'major' dedication (often to an apostle) with a 'minor' one to the Virgin would have had widely understood resonances: it was the long-established practice of minsters.[122] It looks as though these freemen were helping their local churches to assume the outward form of older and grander establishments by giving them (to use a later term) their own 'lady chapels': they foreshadow the pretentious chapels, screens, and images provided by East Anglian parish guilds of later centuries.

Domesday Book gives some overall impression of divided church owner-ship in eastern England, especially in Suffolk where the exceptional data reveal a bewildering abundance of churches, attached to portions of tenurially fragmented townships and often themselves fractionalized. It is clear that two separate processes were at work—co-operative foundation as at Stowmarket, and the division of churches along with other assets when manors were divided between heirs—which can sometimes but not always be distin-guished.[123] The complexity of the data may be illustrated by examples, in which the components of two Suffolk townships are reconstructed from their scattered entries. Wantisden (Table 1) looks like a straightforward case of fragmentation, with a church divided into a half and two quarters and its land divided proportionately. Coddenham (Table 2), on the other hand, gives the extraordinary total of five-and-three-quarter churches and 'a part of three churches', including a church endowed with an acre which ostensibly served the two acres cultivated by the freemen Ælfric and Wihtric.[124] Common sense

---

[119] Warner 1986: 50.   [120] Ibid. 41-5.

[121] Ibid. 44; cf. Aubrun 1986: 76, for the prevalence of Marian dedications among French local churches founded after 950.   [122] Above, pp. 200-1.

[123] For analyses of the Domesday data: Page 1914-15: 86-8, 92-3; Boehmer 1921: 317-19; Darby 1971: 75-6, 138-9, 190-2, 249-51, 310. For Lincolnshire: F. M. Stenton in Foster and Longney 1924: pp. xxi-xxii; Sawyer 1998: 157-67. In three Suffolk entries it is said of the church that 'many have shares in it' (DB ii. 326, 388ᵛ, 400ᵛ).

[124] This bizarrely complex case should, however, be seen against the background of rich mid Saxon metalwork finds which may identify Coddenham as a minster (Newman 2003: 106; Pestell 2003: 132-3). It suggests that one cause of the East Anglian pattern could sometimes be the extreme fragmentation of earlier ecclesiastical entities.

Table 1. *Wantisden (Suffolk) in Domesday Book*

TRE tenant	TRW tenant	Size (acres)	Churches
16 freemen	Count Alan	60	—
Eadwine, a freeman	Count Alan	14	—
Oslac, a freeman	Count Alan	3	—
Eadhild, a free [wo]man	Count Alan	8	—
22 freemen	Robert Malet	121	$^1/_2$ church + 20 ac. free land
—	Robert Malet	16	—
Ælfwine and 'Alflet', freemen	Robert Malet	7	$^1/_4$ church + 10 ac.
Ælfric, a freeman	Robert Malet	4	—
Ælfric, Brihtric, and Eadhild, freemen	Roger Bigot	11	—
a commended man	Roger Bigot	—	$^1/_4$ church + 10 ac.
14 freemen	Roger of Poitou	40	—
—	Ely Abbey	12	—
Morwine, a freeman	Ely Abbey	2	—
		298	**1 church, 40 ac.**

Sources: DB ii. 296, 296^v, 306^v, 307, 344, 353, 384.

suggests that there must have been co-operation in which such churches were open to tenants of churchless holdings, but practical puzzles remain, not least as regards service: did one priest say mass in all the churches in turn?

Cases like Coddenham illustrate the intensely individualistic instincts which operated at even this level of proprietorship: a Suffolk freeman, however humble, wanted a share in his own church, however tiny. Whether the founders were kinsmen, like the Stowmarket brothers, or simply groups of neighbours, they regarded their shares as property. Many of these churches can have made no pastoral or financial sense, and it is hard not to see them to some extent as manifestations of social climbing, or even of attempts to divert tithes. Nonetheless, a society in which church-building can be a joint enterprise, and in which separate owners build their churches at a common township focus, looks like one in which some conception of the local parish, as a devotional entity over and above the manorial contexts of churches, may be emerging.

Table 2. *Coddenham (Suffolk) in Domesday Book*

TRE tenant	TRW tenant	Size (acres)	Churches
Ælfmar, a freeman	the king	8	—
3 freemen	Count Alan	4	—
1 freeman	Robert Malet	10	—
Wigwulf, a freeman	Roger Bigot	76	$^1/_2$ church + $2^1/_2$ ac.
Wigwulf	Roger Bigot	—	1 church + $12^1/_2$ ac.
Wigwulf	Roger Bigot	—	1 church + 8 ac.
'Wailoffus', a freeman	Roger Bigot	36	—
27 freemen	Roger Bigot	75	—
Leofric, a freeman	Roger of Poitou	3	—
Godwine, a freeman	Roger of Poitou	10	—
2 freemen	Roger of Poitou	18	—
Ælfmar, a freeman	Odo of Bayeux	60	1 church + 3 ac.
Ælfric and Wulfric, freemen	Odo of Bayeux	60	
Ælfric and Wihtric, freemen	Odo of Bayeux	2	1 church + 1 ac.
Harold, a freeman	Odo of Bayeux	30	2 ac. belonging to the church
3 freemen	Odo of Bayeux	7.5	—
Leofgifu, a free woman	Odo of Bayeux	10	—
15 freemen	Odo of Bayeux	79	—
Ely Abbey	Ely Abbey	16	—
Leofric, a freeman	Ranulf Peverel	60	a part of 3 churches; 1 church + 3 ac.
3 freemen	Roger of Rames	30	$^1/_4$ church and $^1/_4$ of what belongs to it
Ælfwine, a freeman	Roger of Rames	1	—
—	Roger of Rames	4	—
6 freemen	Roger of Rames	26	—
Ælfric and Boti, freemen	Roger of Rames	9.5	—
Saeric, a freeman	Eudes son of Spirwic	5	—
11 freemen	Humfrey son of Aubrey	78	—
Ælfric, a freeman	Humfrey son of Aubrey	8	—
1 freeman	Humfrey son of Aubrey	4	—
—	Frieb', a priest	0.5 ac. in alms	—
		730.5	$5^3/_4$ churches, 'part of 3 churches', 32 ac.+

Sources: DB ii. 285, 294^v, 304^v, 338, 352, 352^v, 375, 383, 417, 422, 422^v, 423, 434^v, 436, 447.

Origins (v): small urban churches[125]

The role of minsters in framing urban topography, and in generating a network of small towns and markets, was considered above. By the time of Domesday Book, a century of sustained economic growth had created a top tier of developed towns in something more like the modern sense, with large populations and built-up frontages.[126] Where minster precincts with their clusters of churches underlay such towns, they tended to be absorbed into an increasingly dense streetscape. It is arguable that some late Anglo-Saxon bishops and other proprietors founded symmetrical groups of churches to extend liturgical practice and to reinforce—in the face of increasing commercial and demographic pressures—the extent to which even towns could be regarded as 'sacred space'. Thus a late source claims that Abbot 'Wulsin' of St Albans (mid tenth century?) built churches around his minster at the cardinal points of the town, reminiscent of the 'cross of churches' which Bishop Bernold (1027–54) laid out around Utrecht cathedral.[127] The evidence, however, is negligible compared with episcopal cities in Germany,[128] and attempts to identify a special category of gate and crossroads churches as elements in the original layouts of Alfredian-period planned towns are hardly more successful.[129]

In town as in countryside, churches multiplied through individual initiatives rather than grand schemes. London churches with such names as St Nicholas Haakon, St Mary Wulfnoth, St Mary Ailward, and St Martin Orgar, proclaiming their thegnly owners as clearly as did the churches of east Kent, illustrate that eleventh-century towns were no islands of civic freedom in the seigneurial sea.[130] The 'courts' (*hagae*) of the great, often attached to rural manors, were much bigger than later urban tenements and tended to develop groups of dependent houses, operating through the late tenth and eleventh centuries as manors in miniature. The churches built on them were as much

[125] This subject has been particularly well served by recent studies, where more detailed information will be found: Brooke 1970; Barlow 1979: 192–3; Haslam 1984; Campbell 1986: 139–54; R. Morris 1989: 168–226; Barrow 1992; Barrow 2000*a*. There are useful summaries of statistics in Pounds 2000: 116–28.   [126] Above, pp. 337–40; Astill 1991; essays in Palliser 2000.

[127] Matthew Paris, *Gesta Abbatum Monasterii S. Albani*, i (ed. H. T. Riley, Rolls Ser. 28. iva, 1867), 22; Rosser 1992: 275; Hoekstra 1988. Cf. Parsons 1992, suggesting that a similar arrangement may have developed in Northampton using All Saints' church as the focus.

[128] Barrow 1992: 80.

[129] e.g. Haslam 1984: 96, 125; R. Morris 1989: 197–204, 214–19, is more cautious. There is no written or archaeological evidence that such churches are generally earlier than 1000, except at Winchester where the church at the West Gate was founded in the 930s, and that at the East Gate probably existed by *c.*994 (Biddle 1976*b*: 329–30, 333).

[130] Fleming 1993: 31–2, and generally for aristocratic property and power in late Anglo-Saxon towns.

property as any rural church, sometimes on secluded sites set back from the street-frontages.[131] In 1055 Earl Siward was buried 'in *Galmanho* [in York, the earls' residence] in the church which he himself had built and consecrated in the name of God and [St] Olaf'.[132] Its West Saxon counterpart, St Olaf's in Exeter near the street called *Irlesbyri* ('earl's *burh*'), received small endowments in its own right from Earl Harold's mother and the king in the early 1060s.[133]

Lesser churches of this sort sometimes appear in grants of the properties on which they stood. In about 1005 Ealdorman Æthelmaer gave Eynsham Abbey his *curia* in Oxford including St Ebbe's church; in 1012 a *praedium* in Winchester, including St Peter's church built by the reeve Æthelwine, was in royal hands; before 1032 another Æthelwine left to Abingdon Abbey a rural manor with his *haga* in Oxford and the 'little minster' of St Martin; and in 1054 Brihtmaer of Gracechurch gave to Christ Church Canterbury 'the homestead which he occupies and the church of All Hallows [Gracechurch Street, London] with all the endowments which they [his family] have bestowed upon it', on condition 'that the service which belongs to the church neither ceases(?) nor falls off in view of the endowments of the church'.[134] All this is simply the natural extension of lordly church-building from countryside to town: at least before the 980s, when even the big towns were still relatively unpopulous and retained the aspect of groups of farmsteads, 'proprietary' churches must have been the norm. In fact, as Brihtmaer's endowments illustrate, seigneurial patronage remained central through the eleventh century; Domesday Book lists many urban churches as property of rural magnates.

In the eleventh century as later, the activities of social, occupational, and religious brotherhoods in town and countryside seem often to have focused on churches.[135] Historians have been much attracted by the idea that groups of urban neighbours or craftsmen clubbed together to found them,[136] a proposition in which there is nothing inherently unlikely, and for which we should perhaps not expect to find clear evidence. Too much weight, however, may have been placed on data that would bear other interpretations. Christopher Brooke sees poor endowments and informal ownership as suggesting

---

[131] This pattern is best documented, and was first recognized, at Winchester: Biddle 1976*b*: 340–2, 382–5, 453; cf. R. Morris 1989: 204–7.

[132] *ASC* 'C', 'D' s.a. 1055 (pp. 184–5); cf. R. Morris 1989: 171.

[133] S 1037, S 1236; Fleming 1993: 23.

[134] Blair 1994: 151; S 964 (*Abingdon*, 540–3); S 925 (and cf. Biddle 1976*b*: 37–8 n., 342, and Rumble 2002: 217); S 1234 (*RASC* 216).   [135] Below, pp. 453–5.

[136] Brooke 1970: 77–8; Campbell 1986: 147; Rosser 1988*a*: 32; Rosser 1992: 274. This perception has been much influenced by north-west European scholarship, but note the scepticism expressed in a recent study of Danish towns: Andrén 1985: 33–49, 250–1.

churches which began with low-status, communal, and perhaps ephemeral initiatives, sometimes perhaps merely 'the passing mood of piety of a group of neighbours'.[137] Yet lords could be guilty of such improvidence: in Lincoln in 1086 the great thegn Colswein had 'two churches to which nothing belongs which he has built on waste land that the king gave him'.[138] Joint ownership of churches in Domesday Norwich and Lincoln has been perceived as corporate burgess tenure, but was it necessarily so different from the fragmented lordship of the surrounding countryside?[139] In this as in constitutional matters, we should beware of picturing late Anglo-Saxon towns too much in the image of late medieval ones.

Turning to problems of incidence and chronology, there is great variety in the numbers of churches recorded in different towns by *c.*1200—a variety which mirrors the geographical diversity in the distribution of rural churches.[140] The five biggest cities are put in a class of their own by their multitudes of churches: over a hundred in London, fifty-seven in Norwich and Winchester, over forty in Lincoln and York. As Richard Morris observes, there is a correlation in these places between estimated population size in 1086 and incidence of churches, suggesting that above a certain demographic level, churches would multiply when there were people to fill them.[141] Lesser ranks of towns drop to a markedly lower level of church provision: between sixteen and twenty-two in Exeter, Oxford, Bristol, and Huntingdon, between nine and eleven in Gloucester, Worcester, Chester, and Northampton. These places seem to have ratios of churches to people significantly lower than in the great cities, perhaps indicating qualitative differences in wealth, social diversity, or patterns of lordship.[142] What such calculations do not tell us is when the churches were founded: earlier growth-rates need to be approached through individual cases.

It is appropriate to begin in Winchester, though in some ways it was the least typical of major cities. Not only did it contain the greatest and richest monastic complex in the kingdom, with its own penumbra of small churches

---

[137] Brooke 1970: 78.   [138] DB i. 336[v].

[139] The restraint on a Lincoln church being alienated outside the borough without the king's consent (DB i. 336) seems to be more to do with royal rights and burghal customs than with any special status of churches. The statement at Norwich that the burgesses hold fifteen churches with 181 acres, and forty-one chapels in the borough (DB ii. 116[v], 117) is more explicit than any other such in DB, but does not look wholly different in kind from entries describing the tenure of rural assets by groups of freemen.

[140] Brooke 1970: 64–7; R. Morris 1989: 176–92; Barrow 2000*a*: 134–8, revising earlier estimates. Below, pp. 417–22, for regional variation.

[141] R. Morris 1989: 177. As Campbell points out (1986: 146), 'people needed space to go to church in': when the buildings were individually so small, proliferation was necessary in a major town to make church attendance possible.   [142] R. Morris 1989: 177.

developing through the tenth and eleventh centuries; it was also set amid an exceptional concentration of rural manors belonging to rich proprietors, which generated abnormal levels of patronage for the small minsters and large estate churches of rural Hampshire and Wiltshire.[143] A record of negotiations for building Edward the Elder's new minster in 901 suggests a clutter of ecclesiastical buildings (St Gregory's, the 'wattle(?)-church', the stone dormitory) north of the old one, and mentions the king's church of St Andrew with its enclosure (*worðig*).[144] A further five small churches are mentioned between the 930s and 1010s, and excavation has shown three more to be pre-Conquest, two of them (St Pancras and St Mary Tanner Street) established by the tenth century.[145] Beyond this, it can only be said that most of the fifty-seven later parish churches existed by *c.*1150.[146] So while Winchester clearly had several small churches by 1000, the evidence admits the possibility of an eleventh-century boom.

Elsewhere, tenth-century provision is clearest in the two major towns of the northern Danelaw. In York the picture is confused by the presence of two old monastic groups (around the cathedral and on Bishophill), but several small churches additional to these complexes have produced fragments of tenth-century sculpture; excavation has shown that St Helen-on-the-Walls was founded in the tenth or early eleventh century.[147] Lincoln had at least thirty-two churches by *c.*1100, and four of them have produced sculpture fragments in the range *c.*950–1050;[148] the one church so far fully excavated, St Mark's in Wigford, was established together with its graveyard around the mid tenth century.[149]

London has now seen more church excavations than any other English town.[150] There is currently good evidence that some twenty-four churches (less than a quarter of those known a century later) existed by *c.*1100. The sources are fragmentary and this could be a big underestimate, but three other facts are striking. The first is that the written references to minor London churches are exclusively post-1050.[151] Secondly, although several churches in

---

[143] Above, pp. 300–2.

[144] S 1443 (*NMW* 12–17; Rumble 2001: 233–4; Rumble 2002: 52 and fig. 8).

[145] Biddle 1976*b*: 329–30; Keene 1985: 741–4, 761–3.

[146] Biddle 1976*b*: 329.

[147] Lang 1991: 79–114; Magilton 1980. Cf. Hall 1994: 37–8, 49–54, for the archaeological and (essentially eleventh-century) architectural evidence. Domesday Book mentions six churches by name (DB i. 298). Above, pp. 68 n., 126 n., for the early groups.

[148] DB i. 336; Sawyer 1998: 184–8; Everson and Stocker 1999: 194–221. St Benedict, St Mary-le-Wigford, and St Peter-at-Gowts have 'overlap' towers (Taylor and Taylor 1965–78: i. 390–8).

[149] Gilmour and Stocker 1986.

[150] Schofield 1994: 42–5; the following comments are based on his gazetteer (pp. 81–133).

[151] This statement excludes the 'old wooden church' of St Andrew Holborn mentioned *c.*959 (S 670), which was extramural.

the city have been excavated to their earliest levels, the first phase is invariably a standard rubble-walled building datable more or less convincingly to the eleventh century.[152] Thirdly, the various fragments of late Anglo-Saxon and 'Saxo-Norman' sculpture found on London church sites can all be dated in the same range.[153] There is in fact no indication that any of the city churches (unless surviving from the early monastic group aligned on St Paul's)[154] existed in 1000. This does not prove that none of them did, but it does suggest a very marked expansion during the eleventh and early twelfth centuries.

At Norwich Domesday Book lists fifty or more churches, several of them said to have existed in King Edward's day, in the hands of various magnates, priests, and burgesses.[155] Two others, Christ Church and St Mary, received bequests in about 1050;[156] St John de Sepulchre, St John Timberhill, St Julian, and St Martin-at-Palace retain eleventh-century architectural remains;[157] and excavations have found two timber churches of *c*.950–1050.[158] But the pattern resembles London in its strong weighting towards the eleventh century: not one in this multitude of churches can be dated with confidence to much before 1000.

A full survey of church provision in middle-rank towns is beyond the present scope, and only two points need be made here. The first is geographical: in line with the broader contrasts in the incidence of rural churches, East Anglian and east midland towns seem already by 1100 to have had many more churches than their counterparts further west. The second is chronological: the typical pattern is that of London and Norwich rather than that of Winchester and York, with the churches (other than continuing minsters) not known to be earlier than the eleventh century, or specifically shown not to be by excavation.[159] A considerably higher proportion of

---

[152] This applies even to the supposedly early walling at All Hallows Barking, and is self-evident in such cases as St Nicholas Acon (overlying a pit containing an eleventh-century coin) or St Benet Sherehog (the construction dated by associated pottery to *c*.1080): Schofield 1994: 43–6, 123, 94.

[153] Schofield 1994: 44, 49; Tweddle and others 1995: 218–31.

[154] Tatton-Brown 1986; Rodwell 1993*a*.

[155] DB ii. 116–17ᵛ; Barlow 1979: 192; Campbell 1986: 146.   [156] *Wills*, 94.

[157] Taylor and Taylor 1965–78: i. 471–5 (also including St Mary-at-Coslany, which is in an 'overlap' style).

[158] St Martin-at-Palace had a standard tenth- to eleventh-century 'timber-to-stone' sequence (though one underlying burial with a mid Saxon radiocarbon date offers a tantalizing hint at something more unusual): Beazley and Ayers 2001: 4–21, 54–7. The other timber church was sealed by the late eleventh-century castle: Ayers 1985. See also Ayers 1994: 33–40.

[159] For example: Haslam 1984 (several towns); Davenport 2002: 65–6, 73 (Bath); Brooke 1985, Taylor and Taylor 1965–78: i. 129–34, and Everson and Stocker 1999: 49, 90 (Cambridge); Tatton-Brown 1998: 236–45 (Canterbury); Blair 1994: 163 (Oxford); Batcock 1988: 184–8, and Dallas 1993: 208–17 (Thetford); Baker 1980 (Worcester). At Worcester the suburban church of St Peter, just

urban than of rural churches have been investigated archaeologically, and the negative evidence is starting to build a strong case.

Architecturally, minor urban churches are not essentially different from rural ones: timber in the tenth to eleventh centuries, small but solid two-cell and one-cell stone buildings in the eleventh to twelfth.[160] Occasional irregularities of plan reflect cramped sites, and All Saints in Oxford may have been converted from a domestic building.[161] Regional variation in architecture is apparent in towns as in the countryside (most obviously, round towers in East Anglia). But there seems no reason to think that town churches looked, or were meant to look, any different from their rural counterparts.

All this suggests that in trying to understand the spread of churches in towns we should lay the stress not on models of urban distinctiveness projected back from later periods, but on individualistic parochial mentalities, bred by high population levels and fragmented land-tenure, which may have been as evident in the most developed rural areas as in towns, and shared by lords, peasants, and tradesmen. When small rural churches started to proliferate, so did urban ones, a process that can be detected rather earlier in the northern Danelaw (Lincoln and York from *c*.950) than in East Anglia and the south-east (London and Norwich from *c*.1000). And the numerical weighting of rural churches towards eastern England is simply reinforced— more sharply, as the evidence is easier to quantify—by adding those in towns. Richard Morris calculates that eastern and south-eastern England contained about 60 per cent of all urban churches, the midlands (with nearly as many towns) only 22 per cent; the remaining 18 per cent, in central-south and south-west England, were mostly in Exeter and Winchester.[162] Multiple church ownership is most striking in Domesday Norwich, just as it is most prominent in rural Norfolk.[163] In 1100, such social and topographical patterning was still more important than conceptions of distinct civic status.

Endowment and the 'Great Rebuilding'

Manorial churches were property, but the point came when they had property of their own. The listing of so many small churches in Domesday Book underlines their status as assets, which derived partly (though not wholly)

---

outside the city wall, existed by 969 when a lease included 'þa circan 7 þone circ stall' (S 1327; Hooke 1990: 284).

[160] See Dallas 1993: 79–92, and nn. 157–9 above, for this sequence in Thetford and Norwich; Schofield 1994: 42–5, for London.

[161] Blair 1994: 163.   [162] R. Morris 1989: 176–7.   [163] Campbell 1986: 146.

from their landholdings.[164] In 1102 an English church council forbade the founding of a new church without adequate support for both priest and church, which to one contemporary meant at least a ploughland.[165] This expectation—no church without land to support it—was the product of an evolutionary process spanning the previous century: around 1000, assumptions about the status and financial basis of local churches may have been very different.

The beginnings of endowment can again be traced in the wills. In the 990s, Æthelgifu directs that 'the half-hide which Wineman possessed [is to be given] to the church, and Eadwine the priest is to be freed, and he is to have the church for his lifetime on condition that he keep it in repair, and he is to be given a man'.[166] Sifflaed's second will leaves 'to the *tunkirke* ('township church') in Marlingford [near Norwich] five acres and one homestead and two acres of meadow and two wagonloads of wood'.[167] Thurketil of Palgrave (before 1038) leaves 'the middle furlong at Roydon hill free to the church, and *Scortland* and the priest's homestead (*toft*) all free to the church', while Eadwine of Caddington (*c*.1050) wishes land held by two tenants 'to belong to my church at Sundon [Beds.] as a privilege forever'.[168] Between them the East Anglian wills of Thurstan (1043 × 5), Wulfgyth (1046), Eadwine (*c*.1050), and Ketel (1052 × 66)[169] give modest landholdings and other assets to more than twenty rural churches scattered across Norfolk, Suffolk, and Essex. The endowments, varying from two acres to half a hide (notionally sixty acres), but mostly in the range of eight to ten acres, are reserved out of estates (left to heirs or religious corporations) in or near the townships where the churches stood. Thus Thurstan leaves his land at Weston to Æthelswith and after her death to Ely, except what Saewine holds for service which is to go *into tunkirke*. Ketel leaves Stisted to Christ Church but grants 'to the church the land which Wihtric had in his possession . . . to where the fence reaches Leofric's hedge', and Harling to Archbishop Stigand 'except that the men shall be free and that I grant ten acres to the church'. Eadwine's will is remarkable:

I grant the estate at Algarsthorpe to St Edmund's, except ten acres which I give to the church there. . . . And I grant the estate at Little Melton to St Benedict's, and ten acres to the church . . . And ten acres south of the street to Bergh church, and

---

[164] Occasional entries for unendowed churches (e.g. Cornard (Suffolk), 'ecclesia sine terra': DB ii. 286ᵛ) suggest that they were worth listing for their tithes and other church dues.
[165] Westminster (1102) c. 17 (*C&S* 676); Brett 1975: 127, 130.
[166] W. *Æth.* 8–9.   [167] S 1525 (*Wills*, 94).
[168] S 1527 (*Wills*, 68); S 1517 (ed. S. Keynes in *ASE* 22 (1993), 275–9).
[169] S 1531, S 1535, S 1516, S 1519 (*Wills*, 80–90).

ten acres north of the street to Apton church. And four acres to Holverstone church, and four acres to Blyford church, and ten acres to Sparham church . . . And after Ketel's death, the estate [at Thorpe] is to go to St Edmund's without controversy; and [that] at Melton to the church which Thurweard owned; and the land which Eadwine, Ecgferth's son, had, free to the church; and eight acres from the estate at Thorpe to Ashwell church, and eight acres from the estate at Wremingham to the old church, and two acres to Fundenhall church, and two to Nayland church.

If bequests on this scale were at all common in eastern England, it is easy to see how, by 1086, so many small private churches in the region had become worth the Domesday commissioners' notice. In Suffolk, where uniquely Little Domesday itemizes glebes, and in Surrey, where they have been analysed from later evidence, they were often equivalent to standard peasant holdings of their districts, conditioned by local tenurial and land-measurement customs, but very variable in size.[170] In the range between sixty acres and five or six, it is hard to see any rationale in the scale of endowment. To return to the Suffolk examples used above (Tables 1–2), the single church at Wantisden had forty acres comprising 12 per cent of the total land listed, whereas the several churches at Coddenham had on average some five acres each, their combined endowments making only 4 per cent of the land listed. But for a local church to gain any permanent holding, however small, must have been a big step on its long road from informality to autonomous status.

Joint endowment could have happened in a variety of ways. The wills, especially Eadwine's, imply gifts in free alms—with no strings attached—to churches not necessarily in the donors' control. On the other hand, the lords of divided manors who co-operated to found churches also co-operated to endow them, as is implicit in many Domesday entries, and explicit at Clopton (Suffolk) where the church held its land 'from four lordships (*de quattuor dominationibus*)'.[171] The cases of Stonham (Suffolk), with twenty acres given by nine freemen for the good of their souls, and Stifford (Essex), with thirty acres given by the locals (*vicini*) in alms,[172] point towards a third possible process, the creation of glebes by a systematic allocation of strips from peasant smallholdings. There is no unambiguous evidence for this until the twelfth century, when Worcestershire and Northamptonshire churches were maintained from smallholdings of 'peasants' and 'cottagers' (*rustici, cotmanni*), and a Warwickshire church was endowed by a group of local 'good

[170] Boehmer 1921: 312–13; Lennard 1959: 306–9, 314–15; Blair 1991a: 135–42; cf. Bond 1988: 134 (Worcestershire) and Masters 2001: 89–90 (Sussex).   [171] DB ii. 417ᵛ.
[172] DB ii. 438, 24ᵛ. The idea of tenure in alms was recent: J. Hudson, *Land, Law and Lordship in Anglo-Norman England* (Oxford, 1994), 90–1.

men' (*probi homines*).[173] Tenants whose lords invited such contributions may of course have had little choice,[174] but there are no grounds for ruling out autonomous and perhaps earlier peasant initiatives, fuelled by a rising popular concern for mass to be devolved to local sites. It is certainly possible that a higher proportion of glebe-land than we can ever know was given by the relatively humble, and that such gifts were one strand in the silent formation of parochial identities.

The sources give us little impression of collectively endowed churches outside East Anglia, but it is fairly clear that the principle of endowment had become, or was becoming, more widely established by the mid-century. Reform-minded bishops in Edward the Confessor's reign may have tried to steer proprietors in this direction. A yardland, a cotland, and eight acres were given to Lower Heyford church (Oxon.) when it was dedicated by Bishop Wulfwig of Dorchester (1053–67).[175] This points forward to the administrative measures of Henry I's bishops, and to the innumerable post-1100 grants of churches together with small specified endowments.[176] By contrast, the silence of sources before the 1040s is striking.

The relationship between foundation and endowment is hard to discern. Were tenth-century manorial churches initially landless? Did the East Anglian churches mentioned in the mid eleventh-century wills already have any land before they were endowed through these bequests? Does the growth of endowment represent a shift from priests maintained in thegnly households to priests controlling earmarked lands and expected to support themselves? The buying and selling of churches (by implication relatively small ones) was already being perceived as a problem around 1000,[177] which hints that they were acquiring value as independent property rather earlier than our specific sources demonstrate. At all events it looks as though a great deal of small-scale patronage must have been going into the endowment of local churches in the course of the eleventh century.

---

[173] Lennard 1952; Brett 1975: 130; other cases in Stenton 1920: pp. lxx–lxxi, lxxvii, 342–3. See Davidson 1998: 79–107, for a spirited argument (perhaps pushed a little too far) for the communal element in church foundation and endowment.

[174] Cf. the language of an archdeacon's *actum* of *c.*1150: 'my peasants of Walton, at the dedication of St Giles's church [Oxford], . . . have given their tithes to the same church with my assent and will': B. R. Kemp (ed.), *Twelfth-Century English Archidiaconal and Vice-Archidiaconal Acta* (Canterbury and York Soc. xcii, 2001), 104–5.

[175] H. E. Salter (ed.), *The Cartulary of the Abbey of Eynsham*, i (Oxford Hist. Soc. 49, 1906–7), 109.

[176] Brett 1975: 141–8, 223–4. For one typical example: soon after 1100, William son of Wibert confirmed Westfield church (Sussex) to Battle Abbey 'with one wist of land belonging to that church in perpetual right, which my man Wening gave them with my permission' (British Library, Add. Ch. 20161). [177] Below, pp. 494–5.

Into their buildings too: physical evidence shows fundamental and accelerating change during just this period. The rebuilding of low-grade churches using specialized technology and permanent materials was a process which became evident around 1000, gathered pace in the immediately pre-Conquest decades, and continued—architecturally enriched by the Norman regime but not thrown off course—through the later eleventh century. Thus it became possible for local churches to be emancipated from the physical transience which they had shared with domestic buildings, and to take on the longevity of the minsters. The chronological and geographical congruence between endowment and rebuilding suggests that an impulse towards permanence underlies both: churches were becoming 'established' in both the financial and the physical senses. To borrow phrases from the vocabulary of vernacular architecture, this was a 'Great Rebuilding' in which a high proportion of English churches crossed the 'vernacular threshold', the line above which a structure is sufficiently well built for future generations to maintain, adapt, or enlarge it rather than simply replace it.[178]

The starting-point for any study of Anglo-Saxon architecture is the great corpus compiled by H. M. and Joan Taylor, which lists a total of some 400 churches (including over 100 more-or-less undiagnostic fragments).[179] To set the chronology of Anglo-Saxon architecture on a rigorous footing, the Taylors classified their churches where possible into periods: 'A' (600–800), 'B' (800–950), and 'C' (950–1100). Although 'C', which comprises about four-fifths of the total number, runs well beyond the Conquest, the aim was to include work by English masons, the underlying assumption being that any building can be classified on architectural criteria as *either* Anglo-Saxon *or* Norman. Archaic technology, and decoration handled in primitive ways, were taken as hallmarks of Anglo-Saxon work because they seemed retarded in relation to the mature Norman Romanesque style.

Applied to a period when English and Norman masons coexisted in an expanding market, this approach causes problems.[180] There is no reason to think that Romanesque masonry technology was widely used in minor English churches for decades after the Conquest, while crude versions of Romanesque decorative motifs are likely to be later than their prototypes, not earlier. Careful analysis, principally by Richard Gem and Eric Fernie, has

[178] Gem 1988 for the application of the term 'Great Rebuilding'.

[179] Taylor and Taylor 1965–78. These and subsequent comments are based on my own provisional re-sorting of the entire corpus into 'pre-950', 'late Anglo-Saxon', and 'overlap'. There have been many minor discoveries and excavations since 1978, and I recognize that no two attempts to re-work the Taylors' data are likely to produce exactly the same result (cf. Fernie 1983: 171–2): proper new lists are needed. Keynes 1985 remains a useful critique.

[180] Fernie 1983: 162–73, and Gem 1988, for much of what follows.

defined a broad category of churches where English masonry techniques coexist with moulding forms borrowed from the Romanesque repertoire, or where stylistically English forms are realized by means of techniques probably learnt on major Anglo-Norman building projects. Fernie is surely right to recognize a 'school of minor churches, inhabiting the hundred years from the second quarter of the eleventh century to the second quarter of the twelfth, which is neither simply "Saxon" nor simply "Norman"'.[181] When this phase began is open to debate, since few of the key English buildings are well dated, but the underlying architectural developments on the Continent were not under way until the 1040s and 1050s.[182] 'Anglo-Saxon' and 'Norman' are singularly bad labels for such churches, and it seems best to characterize them as products of an 'overlap'.

Returning to the Taylors' 400-odd churches, about half of them, including the majority in 'period C', have features which push them into this 'overlap' category.[183] If the small minority (nearly all minsters) with standing fabric likely to date from before 900 are also eliminated, we are left with some 150 churches which potentially constitute the surviving corpus of post-Alfred, pre-Conquest building activity. Even so, a high proportion of these are fragments which might have been recognized as 'overlap' cases had they been more complete. There also remain some important chronological questions. In most of these buildings the diagnostic features are corners built of dressed stones in the 'long-and-short' technique, 'double-splayed' windows (i.e. with equal splays from the inner and outer faces of the wall), and decorative stripwork. Not only were all three traits still current at the Conquest; neither of the first two occurs in any English building which can be dated at all securely before about 1000.[184] It is also at around this time that two different (and more datable) artefact types associated with stone churches, dedication inscriptions and inscribed sundials, start to become common.[185]

The stylistic arguments do now seem to be pushing all but a small minority of our standing 'Anglo-Saxon' local churches into and beyond the last eighty or so years of Anglo-Saxon history. The sumptuous tower-nave of *c*.1000–50 at Earls Barton (Northants.), emulating a group of slightly earlier minster towers, probably marks the beginning of the drive for architecturally imposing manorial churches, as well as introducing an apparent thegnly fashion for towers combining ecclesiastical, residential, and defensive

---

[181] Fernie 1983: 171.   [182] Cf. ibid. 112–53; Gem 1988: 26–7.   [183] See below, n. 205.

[184] Fernie 1983: 145, 169. Of 'long-and-short' work he writes: 'if the earliest German examples appear to belong to the late tenth century, then it is no more than prudent to accept a broadly similar date for the English equivalents, none of which have any documentary anchors.'

[185] Higgitt 1979: of twelve surviving dedication inscriptions, four are pre-Viking and associated with minsters, the other eight of the late tenth century onwards.

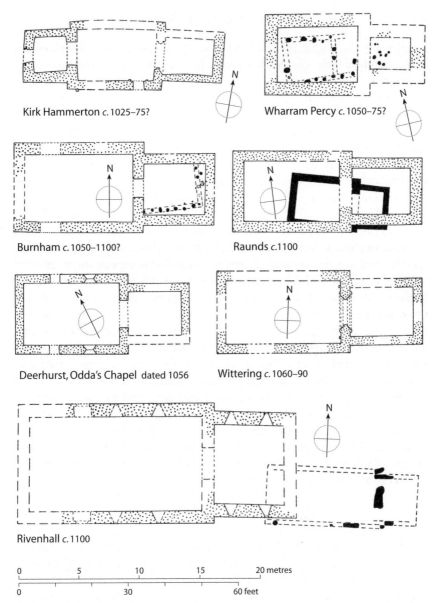

Kirk Hammerton c. 1025–75?

Wharram Percy c. 1050–75?

Burnham c. 1050–1100?

Raunds c.1100

Deerhurst, Odda's Chapel dated 1056

Wittering c. 1060–90

Rivenhall c. 1100

| 0 | 5 | 10 | 15 | 20 metres |
| 0 | | 30 | | 60 feet |

48. Small churches from the eleventh-century 'Great Rebuilding': seven examples (plans of underlying earlier churches shown in black): *Kirk Hammerton* (Yorks.) after R. Morris 1976: fig. 3; *Wharram Percy* (Yorks.) after Bell and Beresford 1987: fig. 11; *Deerhurst* (Glos.) after Taylor and Taylor 1965–78: i, fig. 90; *Raunds* (Northants.) after Boddington 1996: fig. 6; *Burnham* (Lincs.) after Coppack 1986: figs. 4–5; *Wittering* (Northants.) after Taylor and Taylor 1965–78: ii, fig. 347; *Rivenhall* (Essex) after Rodwell and Rodwell 1985–93: i, figs. 59–64.

functions.[186] At a more modest level, it certainly remains possible that some of the standard little 'late Anglo-Saxon' churches of which fragments survive were built before 1000; but the evidence is much more fragile than has generally been realized.

All this may seem less surprising when we remember not only the documented chronology of endowment, but also the nature of the tenth-century manorial churches so far excavated. These, as we have seen, were either of timber or (at Raunds) of rudimentary stonework. The typical 'Rebuilding' church was built of mortared rubble, with properly arched doorways, windows, and chancel arch; its corners, openings, and arches were often built of dressed stone; and it was set out within a range of standardized plan-forms (Figs. 48, 49). It seems likely that this rising demand for consistent ashlar blocks, coinciding with the final exhaustion of re-usable Roman rubble, stimulated the first systematic freestone quarrying since Roman times.[187]

A key example—both because it is well preserved and because, uniquely, its dated dedication-stone survives—is the chapel which Earl Odda built near Deerhurst minster for the soul of his brother Ælfric, and which Archbishop Ealdred dedicated on 12 April 1056.[188] The context is unusual but the building type is standard, replicated in scores of parish churches with late Anglo-Saxon or 'overlap' details. As Fig. 48 shows, the 'Odda's chapel' stereotype was employed to replace the non-permanent churches at Burnham, Raunds, Wharram Percy, and (on a rather larger scale) Rivenhall, as also at Wittering (Northants.) which has lavish Romanesque mouldings and was clearly built towards the end of the century.[189] Standardized modules and building techniques imply that in the late eleventh century, the level of demand sustained groups of masons who could provide 'off-the-peg' one-cell and two-cell churches.[190]

---

[186] Fernie 1983: 137–53; Audouy and others 1995; Renn 1994; Blair 1994: 163–7; Blair 1998*b*: 233–5; above, pp. 342, 360, for the prototypes at Barnack, Brigstock, and Barton-on-Humber. In about the 1060s Wihtgar son of Ælfric, a benefactor of Bury St Edmunds, 'dwelt in a certain tower where the hospital now is' (*ECEE* 71); a drunken and lecherous chaplain slept under the church tower at Tynemouth ('Vita Oswini Regis Deirorum', c. 7, ed. *Miscellanea Biographica* (Surtees Soc. viii, 1838), 20).

[187] Fernie 1983: 156–7, 165; Morris 1988: 192–5; Parsons 1991: 4–17; Eaton 2000: 10–30.

[188] Taylor and Taylor 1965–78: i. 209–11. For the inscription see Parsons 2000, which concludes that its expression *regia aula* can be translated straightforwardly as 'church'.

[189] Coppack 1986; Boddington 1996: 22–5; Bell and Beresford 1987: 57–61, 99–109; Rodwell and Rodwell 1985–93: i. 90–1, 130–1; Fernie 1983: 164–5. I believe that Coppack dates the first two phases at Burnham a century too early (Coppack 1986: 39–42, 51–2). His dating depends on 'tenth-century' pottery, but this was in dump-layers and in any case has a broad date-span; and note his reservations about some of the architectural features (ibid. 51). At Rivenhall, reliance on uncalibrated radiocarbon readings caused the excavators to date the phases unnecessarily early (cf. above, p. 377 n.). For urban examples of the same sequence see above, pp. 405–7.

[190] Rodwell and Rodwell 1985–93: i. 135–6; Blair 1991*a*: 122 and fig. 31.

49. *Kirk Hammerton* (Yorks.): a small 'Rebuilding-period' church comprising nave, chancel, and west tower. The doorway outlined in stripwork and the belfry opening are standard features.

In archaeological terms these replacements mark a cultural horizon, rather as does the replacement of an Iron Age native farm by a Roman villa, or of an Anglo-Saxon manor-house by a motte-and-bailey castle. At Raunds, again uniquely informative, this is emphasized by the ruthless obliteration not only of the original church but also of all the grave-mounds and grave-markers around it: a determined new start around the beginning of the twelfth century which never, in the event, went further.[191] A miracle-story describes a similar scene at Lytham (Lancs.): the site of the crude old timber church marked only by remnants of its altar, the fine new stone one standing alongside.[192] These buildings of the mid eleventh to early twelfth centuries reflect

---

[191] Boddington 1996: 70.
[192] *Reginaldi Monachi Dunelmensis Libellus*, c. 133 (ed. Surtees Soc. i. 1835, pp. 281–2); cf. *VCH Lancs.* vii. 216–18. The stone church had been built by the late twelfth-century lord's grandfather.

at a modest level the Romanesque ethic of clearing away, and starting again on a more accurately orientated alignment, which had been spreading across western Europe.[193]

The rise of church endowment and rebuilding in the English countryside also coincided with the trauma of the Conquest: those 'overlap' churches—probably the large majority—which were built after 1066 are collectively a most impressive monument to the creative fusion which was one aspect of early Norman England. The momentum of rebuilding continued through the 1070s, 1080s, and 1090s, and it was in this period that church towers started to become common in eastern regions at the level of village and small-town churches.[194] In Domesday Book we can occasionally glimpse the dynamics: Wilcot (Wilts.) had a 'new church' along with its other amenities, 'an excellent house and a good vineyard'; Bretforton (Worcs.) had 'oxen for one plough but they are dragging stone to the church'; and the church at Netheravon (Wilts.) (about to be replaced by the 'overlap' building which partly survives) was 'ruined, unroofed and on the verge of collapse'.[195]

Norman entrepreneurship may have provided considerable economic stimulus for church-building,[196] but it is worth noting that two of the most lavish 'overlap' churches—Milborne Port (Somerset) and Langford (Oxon.)—were commissioned by lucky English survivors, Regenbald and Ælfsige of Faringdon.[197] The lay church-builders with whom St Wulfstan of Worcester had dealings in the post-Conquest decades had English names: Swerting, Ælfsige, Saewig.[198] The sundials and dedication inscriptions asso-

---

[193] Cf. Gem 1988: 23. One likely reason for the *tabula rasa* approach was the greater importance now attached, for small churches as for large ones, to orientation: see Ali and Cunich 2001 for the latest discussion of this difficult topic, with bibliography. The Canterbury legend (above, n. 101) of Dunstan dedicating a timber church at *Magavelda* (Sussex) and observing it to be poorly orientated ('ad aequinoctialem solis ortum minime versam') reflects this, though on that occasion the saint avoided demolition and rebuilding by miraculously nudging the church into line with his shoulder.

[194] Below, p. 420. Towers in Lincoln, York, and Norwich are contemporary, and of a piece, with the late eleventh-century rural fashion: Taylor and Taylor 1965–78: i. 390–8, 471–5, and ii. 697–9; Wenham and others 1987. For the explosion of stone church-building in late eleventh-century London see Schofield 1994.

[195] DB i. 69, 175ᵛ, 65; Blair 1987: 273–4.

[196] Another kind of stimulus could have come from the Penitential Ordinance of 1067 × 70 (*C&S* 583), which gave a Norman who did not know how many Englishmen he had slain at Hastings the choice between doing penance for one day per week for life, or building or endowing a church. Intriguingly, though, this commutation of penance by church-building may come from the English rather than the Norman tradition. A group of early eleventh-century English penitential texts allow a penitent 'to build a church in praise of God' if he 'has the resources' (R. Fowler, 'A Late Old English Handbook for the Use of a Confessor', *Anglia*, 83 (1965), 1–34, at 29), whereas the closest Norman precedent for the Penitential Ordinance (Archbishop John of Rouen's tariff of penances for homicide, Oxford, Bodleian, MS Barlow 37 fo. 50) does not. I owe these points to Felicity Clark and Victoria Thompson.

[197] Blair 1988*b*: 6; Blair 1994: 178–80.   [198] *Vita Wulf.* ii. 9, ii. 17, ii. 22 (pp. 78, 94, 104).

ciated with 'Rebuilding-period' churches bear English and Danish names: 'Ulf ordered the church to be erected for himself and for Gunwaru's soul' (Aldbrough, Yorks.); 'Sumarleði's housecarl made me' (Old Byland, Yorks.); 'Eirtig had me made and endowed with possessions to the glory of Christ and St Mary' (St Mary-le-Wigford, Lincoln); '. . . ard and Grim and Æse raised [this] church in the name of the holy Lord Christ, and to St Mary and St Martin and St C[uthbert?] and All Saints' (St Mary Castlegate, York).[199] It is unlikely that all of these are actually pre-Conquest, and it looks as though their production continued in an indigenous milieu. First-generation Norman proprietors could often have left church-building, along with other aspects of local management, to English tenants, a reduced survivor class who may have felt a particularly compelling need to build permanent and public monuments. It could be that most of the 'overlap' churches, even where Domesday Book names Norman lords, were the work of English patrons as well as English builders, and that Norman patronage at a local level was only widespread after 1100 when architectural styles changed more clearly.[200]

Regional variation

The move towards permanent, endowed churches is treated above as a national phenomenon, but the heavy regional bias of the sources will have been obvious. The Ramsey memoranda refer to Cambridgeshire and Huntingdonshire, the wills mentioning small churches are all East Anglian, and the buildings for which a date before 1050 can reasonably be suggested lie almost exclusively in the east, the south, and the east midlands. So do the sites (Asheldham, Burnham, Raunds, Rivenhall, Wharram Percy)[201] where tenth-century manorial churches have been excavated. To generalize from these areas, and to conclude that minster-based parochial organization was collapsing everywhere in England by 1050 or even by 1100, is clearly wrong: in the north-west, to take an extreme case, a landscape of mother-parishes has survived to modern times. Overriding the multiplicity of local variations in church provision, which reflected geography, settlement zones,

---

[199] Okasha 1971: 47, 104–5, 92–3, 131 (and see 63–4 for the inscription at Odda's chapel, Deerhurst); Williams 2002: 11–12, for Aldborough; Eaton 2000: 82–3, for St Mary-le-Wigford, arguing that Eirtig deliberately associated his own inscription with a Romano-British one. Herbert of Winchester's inscription at Weaverthorpe (Yorks.) dates from well after 1100.

[200] For Orderic Vitalis, the peaceful conditions in England after 1101 bore fruit in the 'novae basilicae et multa oratoria nuper condita per vicos Angliae': 'Historia Æcclesiastica', x. 19 (ed. M. Chibnall, *The Ecclesiastical History of Orderic Vitalis*, v (1975), 320).

[201] An exception is Trowbridge, but I am unconvinced that this church is tenth-century rather than eleventh (above, n. 77).

mother-church authority, and landlord policy,[202] were some broad patterns at a regional level. It is worth trying to establish how far the chronology and extent of church provision varied in response to wider economic and cultural factors.

The most direct approaches are through Domesday Book and the architectural evidence. The problems of using the Domesday record of churches are immense, and it must be axiomatic that omission is never proof of a specific church's non-existence in 1086. Two particularly obvious deficiencies are the under-recording of Norfolk compared with Suffolk, and the under-recording of Kent revealed by the 'Domesday Monachorum' lists. Some counties omit churches completely.[203] Nonetheless, plotting the gross statistics by county shows a very clear pattern, which the obvious gaps in the data do not obscure (Fig. 50). In 1086 churches were thickest on the ground in Lincolnshire, East Anglia, and the south-east, and thinned out markedly to the north and west of a line drawn from the Humber to the Severn. This is hardly a surprising pattern, given that it matches both the incidence of population in 1086 and the density of parishes after the parochial system crystallized in the twelfth century,[204] but it is a useful vantage-point from which to look backwards at growth over the previous century or so.

Architecturally, a rough over-view of building activity up to *c.*1050 may be obtained by plotting the churches in the Taylors' corpus, having first elimi-nated the minsters on the one hand and churches with 'overlap' features on the other.[205] This exercise suggests that well-financed building campaigns on local church sites had only become common within five discrete zones: (*a*) Norfolk and Suffolk; (*b*) easternmost Kent; (*c*) Hampshire and Wiltshire; (*d*) Surrey and west Kent north of the Weald; and (*e*) the east midlands, extend-ing northwards in a belt through Northamptonshire into central Lincolnshire and Yorkshire. The upper and middle Thames region,[206] and the zone east-wards into Hertfordshire, Essex, Cambridgeshire, and up to the fens,[207] contain only occasional examples. West of the Pennines,[208] the Fosse Way,

---

[202] e.g. Hase 1994: 63–9, for local variation within Hampshire.

[203] See Lennard 1959: 288–94, Darby 1977: 52–6, Keynes 1985, and Blair 1987: 275–6, for the general problems of the DB data for churches; Blair 1991*a*: 120–7, for Surrey as a case-study.

[204] Darby 1977: 93; Pounds 2000: 87.

[205] Taylor and Taylor 1965–78: i–ii, with the addenda in iii. 1071–7. For this exercise I have excluded (*a*) churches with Romanesque mouldings or other decorative details, including tympana; (*b*) Lincolnshire and east Yorkshire towers of the standard 'overlap' types; and (*c*) East Anglian round towers.   [206] Inglesham, Waterperry, and South Moreton are candidates.

[207] Little Bardfield, Boreham, Chickney, and Walkern are candidates. At Widdington (Essex) a convincingly pre-Romanesque chapel has been converted into a house (Smith 1989), though this is aligned on the parish church to its east and could have been a component within a more impor-tant ecclesiastical complex.   [208] Crosby Garrett is a candidate.

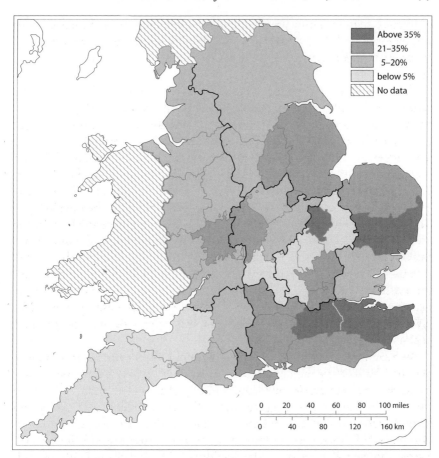

50. The Domesday Book (1086) data for local churches: percentages (by shire), out of all places mentioned, of places where churches and/or priests are mentioned. Shire boundaries which were also circuit boundaries are shown in thick line. (Based on Darby 1977: fig. 17 and statistics on p. 346.) Contrast Fig. 35.

the Cotswolds,[209] and the east borders of Somerset and Dorset,[210] there is no sign that the fashion had penetrated to any significant extent. The sample is obviously small and may have been distorted by later patterns of destruction, but its message cannot be wholly wrong.[211] Essentially, it confirms

[209] Barrow is a candidate; the data at Kilpeck and Peterstow are inconclusive. In Herefordshire the pattern of small church foundation may be complicated by the survival of much older British sites: Blair 2001a: 11–12, and above, pp. 27, 151–2.

[210] Winterbourne Steepleton with its stone angel is an exception; the stone chamber at Sidbury is anomalous. St George's in Exeter had long-and-short quoins.

[211] Thus Norfolk as well as Devon experienced a late medieval building boom, but it retains many eleventh-century churches, which Devon does not.

Domesday's emphasis on East Anglia, Kent, and the east coastline generally; the only slight surprise is the gap in Essex, which may then, as later, have had a particularly rich tradition of timber building.

The distribution of small churches with 'overlap' features, or features in a simple Norman Romanesque style without Anglo-Saxon influence, gives some idea of expansion during the next phase, *c.*1050–1120; more precise definition within that period is probably impracticable on architectural criteria alone, given that even in a single church 'Anglo-Saxon' elements can postdate 'Norman' ones.[212] Rebuildings intensified in the eastern zones, where west towers were now often provided: usually round in East Anglia, square with two-light belfry openings in east Yorkshire and Lincolnshire.[213] The fashion percolated northwards into Durham and Northumberland, and gaps in south-central and south-eastern England were now filled in: notably Essex, which acquired standardized groups of two-cell churches with details in re-used Roman brick, and of one-cell apsidal churches.[214] There were striking expansions in Surrey, where building (often probably *ab initio*) and replacement followed settlement growth along the Downs-edge and in the colonizing Wealden commons;[215] in the Sussex coastal plain;[216] and into the southern Cotswolds.[217] The zone of rebuilding activity also now spread westwards into Shropshire, Herefordshire, and Worcestershire, including the notable 'overlap' churches at Stanton Lacy and Diddlebury.[218] But Somerset, Devon, Cornwall, and the trans-Pennine counties still apparently lay beyond the frontier of rebuilding: nothing in the architectural evidence contradicts the view that in these regions, as in Wales, small churches were still mostly non-permanent structures in 1100.

The institutional and physical transformation of local churches can be conceived as a tide which rose in eastern and southern England around 1000, rolled slowly but steadily westwards and northwards through the eleventh

---

[212] Heywood 1988: 170.

[213] Heywood 1988; Morris 1988; Gem 1988: 28–9; Everson and Stocker 1999: 64–5.

[214] Rodwell and Rodwell 1985–93: i. 133–8; Essex CC 1984: 58–60. Again the dating is mine.

[215] Blair 1991*a*: 120–6.

[216] Masters 2001: 149–50, 180–3, arguing for a boom in church-building after 1070 in this previously retarded area.

[217] Ampney Crucis, Ampney St Peter, Coln Rogers, Daglingworth, Duntisbourne Rouse, Edgeworth, Miserden, Leonard Stanley, Somerford Keynes, Winstone, all in Taylor and Taylor 1965–78. The region contains several simple 'early Norman' churches which the Taylors discounted, but which probably belong to much the same phase.

[218] Taylor and Taylor 1965–78; Parsons 1995; Bond 1988. This is consistent with the Life of St Wulfstan, which implies that his drive to build good-quality local churches (above, p. 394) occurred mainly in the post-Conquest part of his episcopate: *Vita Wulf.* i. 14 (pp. 52–3 and n. 5). The five specific occasions on which he is shown consecrating new churches are all in this period: ibid. ii. 9, ii. 15, ii. 17, ii. 22, iii. 15 (pp. 78, 88, 94, 104, 128).

century, but failed to spread far into the highland zone until after our period. If the detail is often obscure or unreliable, the broad pattern seems beyond question: local churches would surely have figured in the rich Worcester archive, for instance, if they had been anywhere near as important in that region as they were in Norfolk. These contrasts warn against the temptation to assume a developed system of local churches unless the sources actually show one: in Oxfordshire, for instance, it is completely imponderable whether three-quarters, a half, or a quarter or less of the thirteenth-century parish churches had crossed the threshold of rebuilding and endowment, or even existed, by 1100.[219]

Rebuilding marked the consolidation of the new parochial order in the countryside: the zones where it did not occur retained more of a mother-parish structure, and probably more too of the old-style substratum of unendowed chapels and cult sites. While on the whole it remains likely that there were always more undeveloped cult sites in the western than in the eastern parts of Britain, it is also clear that this contrast was heightened during the tenth to twelfth centuries: in local religious culture, Cornwall and Gloucestershire were probably more different from each other in 1150 than they had been in 950. Likewise, it is striking how little the broad trend seems to have owed to the Norman Conquest, except probably as a stimulant to processes already in train, and in the purely technical sense that masons were trained in the technology and ornamental repertoire of Norman Romanesque.

In terms of settlement patterns, the early proliferation of churches in eastern and south-eastern England took place in a landscape where small villages and hamlets coexisted with countless dispersed farms. It was by comparison slightly later, and in a more controlled fashion, that local churches came to the midland belt, with its strongly nucleated villages and homogeneous farming communities.[220] East Anglia was very highly developed economically and commercially (as it had been in the seventh century and would be again in the fifteenth), and supported a mass of middle-range to small proprietors with the will and the means to express their individual piety and status. The forebears of those countless late medieval patrons whose brasses strew the floors of Norfolk churches may have exerted enough upwards pressure on the mother-parishes to explain, in itself, their dissolution. The strong, unitary manorial regimes of the midlands built estate churches and often managed to break free from minster control, but it was the unregulated, minutely fragmented societies of the eastern areas which bred churches in luxuriant profusion. Although the roots of this pluralistic culture lie in earlier

---

[219] Blair 1994: 137–8.
[220] Compare the present Fig. 50 with Roberts and Wrathmell 2000: figs. 3, 9, 10, and 15.

periods, its church-building habits need to be seen in the wider, contemporary context of eleventh-century northern Europe.

How different was England?

Historians of parochialization in France see the period 950–1100 as a marginal 'third stage', when a last wave of usually small and sometimes unsuccessful local parishes was fitted into the interstices of a framework first set out by late Gallo-Roman bishops, and then extended and systematized by their Carolingian successors.[221] England was obviously not like this. The first stage had differed fundamentally, the second had never happened; such 'local' churches as existed in 950 had no independent status and could be annexed or bypassed, leaving a larger scope for private initiatives than the Frankish world had known for two centuries.[222] Nor was there any Hincmar of Rheims for lords to contend with: they had to respect the vested rights of minsters enshrined in Eadgar's code, but not (at least so far as we can see) any serious efforts to enforce episcopal control. Here there is a most striking contrast with central and northern France, where from the late tenth century bishops and rulers encouraged a massive transfer of private churches into monastic hands, splitting them off from their estates and forming local ecclesiastical networks which in due course assumed a role in the Peace of God movement.[223] England, with its stronger kings and weaker bishops, would only see such a transfer after the 1080s, in a Norman and a Gregorian context.

Although in England the post-950 phase of church-founding was more fundamentally transformative than in France, the course that it took was not

---

[221] Imbart de la Tour 1900: 234–99; Fournier 1982: 532–4; Aubrun 1986: 69–76.

[222] Up to a point I accept the view of Reynolds 1984: 82–7, that the contrast between England and Italy on the one hand, and Francia and Germany on the other, has been over-drawn, although recent work on the chronology of English settlement formation makes me dubious about her explanation that 'the real contrast with Italy and England derives from the apparently small number of completely new villages founded in either of those countries after 900 compared with the large number founded in France and Germany'. It is also likely that the diversion of tithes to local churches was under way much earlier in the Carolingian realms, leaving more scope for this in England after 950. It does, however, appear that in some parts of France there may have been more church foundation in the later period (especially in the context of southern *incastellamento*) than the general works imply: in Lodève diocese, for instance, over half of the churches could have been founded after 1100 and only a quarter are known to have existed before 1000 (Alzieu 1998: 8–10 and my calculations from the catalogue).

[223] Lemarignier 1977; Aubrun 1986: 71–3, 81–5, 102–5; Chibnall 1958: 104–9; Bates 1982: 193–4. In England it is unusual before *c.*1080 to find grants of local churches separate from their parent manors; the two conspicuous cases (S 1055; *Stoke Cart.* i. 54–8, iii. 16–18, 29) are only recorded in later sources, and are both East Anglian.

in fact so very different. On both sides of the Channel, new churches were linked principally to the emergence of residences as local territorial centres, even if in England these centres did not embody the privatization of public jurisdiction and powers. Minsters re-founded to serve English earls' houses,[224] or even tiny estate churches such as those at Goltho and Raunds, echo the *collégiales* of magnate headquarters and the churches of knightly castles; groups of local inhabitants were zealous to have their own churches in Normandy, and around Narbonne, as in East Anglia.[225] Normandy, where tenth-century disruption left more scope for re-structuring than in many parts of France, shows during *c.*990–1030 a development very similar to contemporary East Anglia, with small estate churches proliferating and being fractionalized into halves and thirds.[226]

If we are to define a frontier between contrasting zones of late tenth- and eleventh-century church provision, it should perhaps be the English midlands rather than the North Sea. The region of rapid growth comprised East Anglia, south-east England, Normandy, and—from the early eleventh century—Scandinavia. Indeed, it is worth recalling that if small timber churches were becoming common in England by 1000, there is virtually no evidence for their endowment or rebuilding in stone before the Danish invasion of 1013–16. The dynamics of the shift from minsters to local churches were working through, in what were both the most economically developed and the most Scandinavianized areas, when England formed part of Cnut's North Sea empire. During these years the foundations of Scandinavian Christianity were being laid by English churchmen,[227] but at a local level the provision of churches in the two zones was not far from contemporaneous. Studies of Skåne (southern Sweden) show that churches were being added to local farmsteads and manor-houses with the infiltration of seigneurial power-structures during the eleventh century, and that the oldest surviving stone churches, like the 'overlap' churches in England, date from *c.*1060–1100.[228] Further north, in Norway, northern Sweden, and Iceland, society was still based on settlement districts rather than lordship, and the new churches tended to be built at the sites of central assemblies (*things*).[229] Sometimes there are even signs of a mother-parish system on the English model, with

---

[224] Above, pp. 328–9.   [225] Aubrun 1986: 74.

[226] Lemarignier 1977: 384–91; cf. Bates 1982: 193–5, for ducal reconstruction of the local church after 990 and the possible survival of older churches. Ducal charters from *c.*1000 grant estates with such formulae as *et in supradictis villis* x *ecclesias,* y *molendinos,* or *villam totam cum ecclesia* (*Actes Norm.* 79 f., Nos. 9, 11, 15, 18, etc.); fractions of churches occur from the 1020s (e.g. ibid. 124–31, 254–5, Nos. 34, 99).   [227] Abrams 1995*a*; Abrams 1998; Brink 1998: 20–1, 28–32.

[228] Andersson and Anglert 1989: 148, 208–9, 241, 286; Anglert 1995: 206–8; cf. Brink 1998: 24, 26.

[229] Brink 1998: 22–8. Cf. Abrams 1995*b*: 34–40, for the likely influence of landowners, and the territorial structures which supported them, on the formation of the Scandinavian local church.

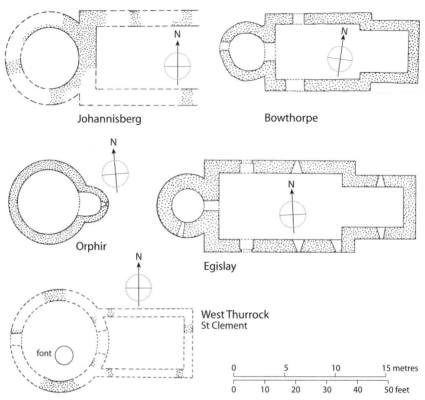

51. The church-building culture of the eleventh- to early twelfth-century North Sea region: round west towers and tower-naves. *Johannisberg* (Hessen) after Fernie 1988: fig. 21; *Orphir* (Orkney) after Fisher 1993: fig. 22.1; *West Thurrock* (Essex) after Essex CC 1984: fig. 9; *Bowthorpe* (Norfolk) after Beazley and Ayers 2001: fig. 38; *Egilsay* (Orkney) after Fernie 1988: fig. 16a.

groups of clergy at central churches.[230] Writing some fifteen years before Domesday Book, Adam of Bremen could measure provinces of Denmark by their churches: 300 in Skåne, 150 in Zealand, 100 in Fünen.[231] If England was catching up with France, Scandinavia came hard on its heels.

Interchange with Scandinavia underpinned the distinctiveness of eleventh-century eastern England. Its enduring monuments are the round west towers

---

[230] Brink 1998: 26–8, 32.

[231] 'Gesta Hammaburgensis Ecclesiae Pontificum', iv. 7 (ed. B. Schmeidler, *Adam von Bremen, Hamburgische Kirchengeschichte, MGH* (Hannover, 1917), 234–5; cf. Campbell 1986: 146, and Brink 1998: 32.

of East Anglian parish churches, which (as Eric Fernie and Stephen Heywood have shown) belong to a North Sea architectural tradition embracing Schleswig-Holstein and Orkney;[232] round naves, and the thegnly tower-naves of central and eastern England exemplified by Earls Barton, may also reflect distinctive tastes of the Norse and Anglo-Danish nobility (Fig. 51).[233] In its teeming towns with their many churches, eastern England belongs to the same world as Denmark and southern Sweden,[234] and the many eastern English dedications to St Clement and St Olaf can be located in the early to mid eleventh-century Anglo-Scandinavian context.[235] By the same token, some East Anglian saints' cults, notably Botwulf's, had an impact on Scandinavian liturgical commemoration.[236] On both sides of the North Sea, urban church life merely reflected, in intensified form, a rural context in which multiple proprietorship interacted with the communal identities of neighbours. If the co-tenants of divided East Anglian townships were lords in miniature, their habit of grouping their churches in one nucleus recalls the Scandinavian folk-district with its central *thing*.[237]

In the eleventh century, therefore, there was a strong cultural affinity between the two regions which were acquiring local churches more rapidly than any other part of contemporary western Europe. This same North Sea culture displays an interweaving of religious affiliation, social obligation, and group identity, apparently even a common terminology for parochial allegiance, which points the way in tackling our last and most intractable topic: the emergence of the local parish.

[232] Fernie 1988; Heywood 1988.

[233] Blair 1996c: 14; Fisher 1993 and C. Morris 1989: 20–8, for Norse homestead chapels in Orkney including the round-naved one at Orphir. It is interesting that the round-naved church at West Thurrock (Fig. 51) is dedicated to St Clement. Cf. Blair 1998b for rectangular tower-naves.

[234] Andrén 1985: 33–49, 250–1, noting that the chronology of churches in Lund (one founded by c.990, most during c.1050–1150) is much as in the countryside around; R. Morris 1989: 190–2.

[235] Crawford 1992; R. Morris 1989: 171, 175–6; Brooke 1970: 75.

[236] Toy 1983: esp. 95; R. Morris 1989: 217–19; Toy 2003.

[237] Cf. Brink 1998: 22–8.

8

From *Hyrness* to Parish: The Formation of Parochial Identities
*c.*850–1100

To what extent had the English landscape been organized into local parishes by 1100? Later in the middle ages, a good working definition of a parish would be: 'a self-contained local ecclesiastical territorial unit which controls pastoral provision to its inhabitants and claims their religious allegiance'. But in a society with two competing tiers of parishes, there will be degrees of self-containedness and allegiance. There will also be big differences of scale, and it is these that most clearly distinguish the new from the old structures. Whereas mother-parishes had been complex federations of sub-districts, served from one centre but stretching across large and diverse territories, the parishes of midland England were often unitary entities with strong internal foci, characteristically containing a single agrarian community, village, or manorial centre. Even in the regions—most obviously East Anglia—where parishes were tenurially and economically more fragmented, their smaller scale still enabled the forging of a sharper parochial identity and firmer discipline. The model of 'cellularization'[1] does not explain everything, but it provides a social and land-management context for the new parochial order, just as the world of provincial *regiones*, itinerant courts, and food-renders had done for the old one.

In the broad picture the reality of the transition from bigger to smaller parishes is obvious, but when we try to pin it down it proves strangely slippery. There is a big discrepancy between the architectural and archaeological sources, which show fast-growing numbers of small but permanent churches set in graveyards serving ordinary lay communities, and the written sources, which barely recognize a tier below mother-parish level. Were it not for the physical evidence, the world of local parishes and parish churches might seem to spring fully formed into being when it emerges in twelfth-century epis-

---

[1] Above, p. 369.

copal documents. Faced with this gap between reality and official recognition, we must approach the problem sideways and from various directions. In asking how and when the new parishes were defined in relation to the old ones, and what prompted their emergence, this chapter will look at a series of connected themes: the vocabulary for parishes and parishioners; the jurisdictional and pastoral relations between mother- and daughter-churches; the emergence of local churches and local priests as foci of spiritual and social identity; the assimilation of a wider vernacular sacred landscape into an 'official' Christian one; and the interconnections between the main kinds of local collectivity—township, manor, parish—that existed by *c.*1100.

The language of parochial allegiance

To begin with the words used for parishes is certainly not to suggest that a local community's self-perception as a parish depended on vocabulary. As Susan Reynolds observes of western Europe generally, collective nouns for parishioners were 'just a convenient way of describing the local community when it was acting together. "Acting together" was, moreover, just that. . . . [T]he records show that parishioners, like other groups, could engage in much the same sort of activities whether they were described explicitly as a collectivity or simply as the inhabitants, named or unnamed, of a parish.'[2] It will indeed emerge that late Anglo-Saxon parochial vocabulary was a blunt and old-fashioned tool, inadequate to describe the grass-roots changes that were happening by 1050. Nonetheless, the two tiers of English parish first become visible to us through successive phases of definition by superior authority: mother-parishes in the tenth century with the protection of their revenues in secular law, local parishes in the twelfth with the definition of their rights and obligations by the ecclesiastical hierarchy. Terminology may be a poor guide to how things worked on the ground, but it does help us to see how they were perceived from above.

First and most obviously, *parochia* had been the standard term for 'parish', in the sense of a sub-diocesan ecclesiastical territory, in the prescriptive Latin texts of continental Europe since the early ninth century.[3] Remarkably, no genuine surviving Anglo-Saxon document uses the word in this way.[4] One

---

[2] Reynolds 1984: 97–8; ibid. 79–100 is the best general discussion of the problem.

[3] This is amply clear from the Carolingian and later texts cited by *Novum Glossarium Mediae Latinitatis: Fasc. Paniscardus–Parrula* (ed. J. Monfrin, Copenhagen, 1987), cols. 385–400, for instance 'possessionem ecclesie vel parochiam' (802?), 'presbiter illius parochie' (806–9), 'ut presbyteri per parochias suas . . .' (810–13). This is of course a different matter from the word's older and more general sense of 'diocese', which is common in insular texts from the seventh century.

[4] Bullough 1999: 32, cites as an exception a letter of 797 in which Alcuin urges Archbishop Æthelheard to supervise pastoral care 'per singulas aecclesias atque parochias' (*Alc. Ep.* No. 128

reason for this may be that English bishops lacked the will and the means of their Continental colleagues to define parochial hierarchies from above (the tariff in VIII Æthelred ranks churches in terms of their status as sanctuaries, not in terms of mother–daughter relations between them); another may be that such things were normally written about in English. But even the Normans, who had been referring to the *parochiae* of local churches in Normandy since the 1020s,[5] were reluctant to do so in England, and the rare appearances of *parochia* (in its sub-diocesan sense) in Anglo-Norman texts before 1100 all seem to refer to minsters and mother-parishes.[6] Domesday Book describes how Nigel, a servant of Count Robert, encroached on Stowmarket mother-parish for the benefit of his own church at Combs, so that twelve sokemen who 'used to be parishioners (*parrochiani*) in Stow[market] church . . . are now in Combs church', but even this avoids a direct acknowledgement that the new, small church was capable of having its own *parrochiani*.[7] When references to local parishes become common during the twelfth century, it is through the assimilation of Continental definitions by English diocesan officials.

The earliest known vernacular term, which in Eadgar's tithe-law of the 960s describes the parochial obligation due to an old minster, is *hyrness*.[8] Its

(p. 190)). But Alcuin would have followed Carolingian usage (cf. above, p. 177 n.), and in any case the phrase may refer to Æthelheard's metropolitan authority over other bishops' dioceses.

[5] A ducal *actum* of 1015 × 25 mentions the *parrociae* of St Remi and St George in Breteuil; from the 1050s the term becomes more frequent, as do phrases like 'duas partes decime totius parrochie': *Actes Norm.* Nos. 29, 120, 126, 128, 140, 214, 222 (pp. 117, 285, 296–7, 301, 316–18, 402–8, 423). William I's English *acta* offer a single comparable example, and that in a possibly 'improved' transcript: a confirmation of Count Alan's grant of Linton church (Cambs.) 'cum terra que eidem pertinet et decima parrochie et partem decime eiusdem manerii': *Regesta W. I*, 1008 (No. 258a).

[6] The Somerset geld accounts mention 5½ geld-free hides on Bishop Giso's estate in Somerset held by six 'presbiteri parrochiani' (DB Exon. 78ᵛ); but these look over-endowed for ordinary manorial priests, and perhaps served episcopal mother-churches such as Banwell, Chew Magna, or Wedmore. In Shrewsbury, Domesday Book says that Earl Roger has given the 'monasterium Sancti Petri ubi erat parochia civitatis' to his new abbey (DB i. 252ᵛ). In the 1090s, during the long-running dispute over St Cuthmann's minster at Steyning, its proprietors claimed the 'parochiam que ad Sanctum Cuthmannum pertinet' (*Lawsuits*, No. 163B (p. 130)). Two uses of the word by Goscelin of Saint-Bertin are a case apart. Of Much Wenlock he says that 'in plebeiam parrochiam monasterium deinceps destituitur' by the eleventh century, and that 'duorum aut trium clericorum plebeia erat parrochia'; the 'parochianus presbiter' witnesses a miracle: 'Translatio S. Mildrethe Virginis', capitula, c. 5, c. 27 (ed. D. W. Rollason, *Mediaeval Studies*, 48 (1986), 139–210, at 154, 162, 195). Likewise, he reports that the old minster of East Dereham 'in vulgarem parrochiam est destitutum': 'Vita S. Withburge', c. 8 (ed. Love 2004: 66). In contemptuously contrasting a proper monastery with a *plebeia/vulgaris parrochia*, Goscelin is using the word in its archaic Gallic sense of 'clerical [baptismal] church' (above, pp. 36–7, 212 n.), not to mean an area of jurisdiction. I am grateful to David Howlett and Theodore Christchev for checking the unpublished slips of the *Dictionary of Medieval Latin from British Sources*.

[7] DB ii. 291ᵛ: twelve sokemen in Combs 'solebant esse parrochiani in ecclesia Stou, sed modo sunt in ecclesia Cambas: idem Nigellus abstulit'. [8] Below, p. 442.

root meaning was simply 'lordship', 'obedience' (or perhaps 'belongingness', 'togetherness'?) in their secular sense, but before 1000 it seems to have been the normal word for 'parish': thus where Theodulf of Orleans forbids a priest to entice people from 'another priest's parish' (*de alterius presbiteri parrochia*) to his church, his late tenth-century English translator has 'of oðre cyrcean hyrnysse . . . ne of oðre preostscyre'.[9] After the Conquest, it reappears in connection with three major minsters in the west midlands. The Anglo-Saxon Chronicle for 1087 reports the ravaging of 'the whole lordship of Berkeley' (*Beorclea hyrnesse*); a charter of Henry II gives Gloucester Abbey the prebends which various priests 'held in the lordship of Bromfield (*Bromfeldehernesse*) in the time of King Henry my grandfather'; and the four bailiwicks of the demesne of Leominster Priory were known by the 1160s as the *hernesii*.[10] All three places were the centres of large and valuable west midland lordships, and one might be tempted to translate *hyrness* as *simply* lordship were it not that all three were also minsters which preserved their mother-church rights into the twelfth century with conspicuous success. At Bromfield and Leominster the contexts are specifically ecclesiastical, which suggests that in the third case this formulation may have been chosen because Berkeley had been an exceptionally rich and powerful minster.

With one exception, other vernacular terms for parishes and parishioners also come from the vocabulary of lordship and attachment. Ælfric exhorts a priest to look after his own *hyrnysse* and keep out of any other priest's *folgoþe*,[11] the second synonym elsewhere denoting 'authority' or 'office'. Likewise, I Cnut's version of the law on breaking the sanctuary of a 'still smaller minster' defines it as one with 'little service' (*lytel þeowdom*).[12] For both the Theodulf translator and Ælfric, the laity under a priest's pastoral care, in other words his parishioners, are his *hyrimen* or subjects.[13] *Scriftscir*, literally 'absolution-district', is only recorded in the Ælfric–Wulfstan circle and is unique among these vernacular terms in signalling the spiritual quality of parochial jurisdiction. Ælfric may have coined it to make a point—that priests have responsibilities as well as rights—in the face of an otherwise

---

[9] *Theodulf*, c. 14 (pp. 320–1).

[10] *ASC* 'E' s.a. 1087 (p. 223); Kemp 1968: 98; Blair 1985*a*: 128–30; Hillaby 1987: 594–6.

[11] Ælfric, 'First O.E. Letter for Wulfstan', cc. 183–4 (*C&S* 296).

[12] Above, p. 368. In the light of the use of *þeowdom* in the Stow agreement (above, p. 362), the phrase in I Cn. 3. 2 could be translated 'where there is [only] a little [regular] service [of God]'. But in the light of the other service-related terms, 'where there is a small parish' remains possible; the 'Quadripartitus' translator who rendered it 'ubi parva parrochia sit' (*Gesetze*, 282) certainly thought so.

[13] Below, p. 497; *Theodulf*, 341, 347, 377. Cf. the uses of *folgoþe* and *hyrimen* in II As. 25. 1, VI As. 11, 'Gerefa', c. 7 (*Gesetze*, 164, 182, 454).

secular vocabulary reflecting secular conceptions of how people were bound together.[14]

The final term, *ciricsocn*, is altogether more complex and difficult. Its root sense is simply 'church-seeking', as in the Alfredian rubric *be ciricsocnum* to Ine's law on fleeing to a church for sanctuary.[15] Tenth- and early eleventh-century homilists enjoined the observation of Rogationtide with church attendance (*mid ciricena socnum*) and other spiritual disciplines.[16] From 'church-seeking' as a moral duty—something that all Christians are obliged to do regularly—could have emerged the idea of *a* 'church-seeking' as a collective noun—a group of people whose common identity lies in the fact that they regularly 'seek' the same church. This hypothetical semantic development, not explicitly attested by any Anglo-Saxon source, surfaces in a late twelfth-century reference to the 'custom that each *chirchsocne* goeth this day [Palm Sunday] a procession'.[17]

A second and distinct thread, its starting-point again *socn* 'seeking', runs through the jurisdictional senses of the term which give us the 'sake and soke', the 'sokes' and 'sokemen', of late Anglo-Saxon England. To enjoy sokeright was to be able to require those subject to it to 'seek' or attend one, for a variety of purposes, as their lord.[18] Hence complex lordships, which included the dependent holdings of people under soke, are often called 'sokes' in Domesday Book and other late sources. Uniquely, Domesday defines the lordships of the three Rutland mother-churches as 'churchsokes', using the formula 'in Ocheham cherchesoch cum v bereuuitis habebat Eddidd Regina iiii car[ucatas] terre . . .' etc.[19] Like the Chronicle's *Beorclea hyrnesse*, these would seem to be secular lordships which had a special character through being based around major churches.

---

[14] Wormald forthcoming: ch. 8 shows that *rihtscriftscir* is very probably a Wulfstan neologism. Even *scriftscir* seems only to be used by Ælfric ('Zwei Homilien der Ælfric', ed. in R. Brotanek, *Texte und Untersuchungen zur altenglischen Literatur und Kirchengeschichte* (Halle, 1913), 3–27, at 26), by Wulfstan himself (in homilies and laws), and in the Wulfstan-inspired *NPL* c. 42. The occurrence in II As 26 (*Gesetze*, 164) is non-contemporary (*scir* meaning 'diocese', with *scrift* interlineated in *Textus Roffensis*). Compare Ælfric's replacement of *gangdagas*, the normal vernacular term for the Rogations, with the more explicitly religious *gebeddagas*: Bedingfield 2002: 194.

[15] Ine, c. 5 (*Gesetze*, 91); Joy 1972: 38–40.

[16] Below, p. 486; Joy 1972: 37–8, 41–2. For Wulfstan, *ciricsocn* was to be undertaken frequently, regularly, and in the right frame of mind (*Hom. Wulf.* 229, 248). This sense of 'churchgoing' survives in a late twelfth-century homily which enjoins people not to work on Sunday but to go to church (*chirche bisocnie*): R. Morris (ed.), *Old English Homilies and Homiletic Treatises* (EETS 29, 34, 1867–8), 45.

[17] R. Morris (ed.), *Old English Homilies of the Twelfth Century* (EETS 53, 1873), 89.

[18] Among the large literature on this complex subject, Joy 1972 is a valuable (and neglected) survey; see also Hadley 2000*a*: 167–76.

[19] DB i. 293ᵛ: the churches are Oakham, Hambledon, and Ridlington.

Ciricsocn, still in the sense of a church-based jurisdiction but at the local manor/parish level, also figures in two supposed writs of Edward the Confessor for Westminster Abbey, each granting an ordinary manor with rights including 'the church and the churchsoke'.[20] Alas, one of these writs is a post-Conquest forgery, the other heavily interpolated; their value may amount to little more than telling us that this kind of usage seemed plausible by the early twelfth century. Tantalizingly, a Latin term which looks as though it could translate 'churchsoke' in this sense—*sequela parochialis,* literally 'parochial suit'—occurs in a single late twelfth-century text as due from a peasant holding to Bodenham church (Herefs.).[21] This kind of 'church-suit' looks analogous to late Old English *fyrdsocn* (army-service), or Middle English and Latin compounds with *soken* and *secta* such as mill-suit, fold-suit, or hundred-suit: legal duties to attend or participate in specific places or activities.

These two strands of *ciricsocn*—obligation to attend the same church regularly as a good Christian, and to do so as a manorial tenant—are not only hopelessly entangled for us, with our exiguous sources, but are also likely to have been entangled for contemporaries. What matters here is whether the fusion of meanings betokens an idea of territorially defined churchgoing communities, and on this an illuminating sidelight shines from across the North Sea. The medieval word for 'parish' in most Scandinavian languages was *sókn,* in West Frisian even *kercsoekinge.* Current specialist opinion favours the view that this term did not develop independently from a primitive Scandinavian sense of 'seeking', but was imported in its specifically ecclesiastical sense from eleventh-century England.[22] This interpretation, eminently plausible given the very strong English influence on the incipient ecclesias-

[20] S 1117, S 1148 (*Writs,* 301, 340, 492–4; 336–7, 368–9, 522–3). These writs purport to give the *burh* at Wennington (Essex) 'mid þære cyrice [7] mid þære cyricsocne', and land at Islip and Marston (Oxon.) with rights including 'mid ciricen 7 mid ciricsocnen'. The supposed original of S 1117 was demonstrably post-Conquest, while it seems likely that S 1148 conflates genuine and spurious material.

[21] J. Barrow (ed.), *EEA* vii: *Hereford 1079–1234* (Oxford, 1993), 106 (No. 153). This *actum* of 1179 × 83 settles a dispute between the priors of Hereford and Brecon 'super sepultura et sequela parochiali' from a half-hide at Dudales Hope: the tithes of corn are to go to the prior of Hereford, whereas the 'sepultura colonorum terram tenentium virorum ac mulierum cum eorum divisa, sequela parochiali, et sepultura familiarum ibi servientium et etiam puerorum, et omnes alii proventus' are to go to Bodenham church. The most familiar sense of *sequela* denotes villeinage, but it is also used for suit/soke in the legal sense (e.g. *sequela molendini,* 'mill-soke'). I owe this reference to Julia Barrow.

[22] Especially the work of Stefan Brink, summarized for English readers in Brink 1998: 33–7. For alternative views: Stenton 1970: 145 n. 1 (*sokn* not from an English root but from a primitive Scandinavian sense of 'seeking'); Sawyer 1988: 41 (*sókn* referring to the district within which a church's tithe was 'sought'). I am grateful to Alexandra Sanmark for access to an unpublished paper synthesizing recent Scandinavian historiography.

tical structures of Scandinavia,[23] points towards the same hypothetical Old English usage that might underlie the Westminster forgeries, or the late twelfth-century *chirchsocnes* with their Palm Sunday processions. On the whole, a conception of the local parish defined by reference to the obligations, spiritual and secular, of 'church-seeking' does seem likely to have emerged in eleventh-century England.

This survey of terminology suggests two main conclusions. The first is that late Anglo-Saxons called (mother-)parishes by a range of secular terms for lordship or belongingness—*hyrness, socn, folgoþe*, perhaps *þeowdom*. This vocabulary looks somewhat fluid, and perhaps regional: West Saxon/Mercian *hyrness* (Berkeley, Leominster, Bromfield), as against east midland/Danelaw *socn* (*Ocheham cherchesoch*)? The 'lordship' could be parochial (as in II Eadgar's 'to þam ealdan mynstre þe seo hernes to hyrð') or territorial (as in the ravaging of *Beorclea hyrnesse*): what mattered was that it was centred on a locally superior church. Clerics translating such terms into Latin would presumably have used *parochia*, but contemporaries seem generally less interested than modern historians in distinguishing spiritual from temporal lordship; the exception proving the rule is *scriftscir*, an explicitly pastoral term probably coined because none other did the job. The second conclusion is that English administrative vocabulary was reluctant to concede, either before or for some time after 1066, that ordinary village churches could control anything so formal as a 'parish' or 'parishioners'. If the *lytel þeowdom* of I Cnut is an exception its very tentativeness makes the point, and if a group of villagers worshipping regularly in a manorial church was starting to call itself a *ciricsocn* we can only guess so from later evidence.

The failure of written language to describe an emerging reality reflects the same conservative stance as the prescriptive sources to be considered next: support for the fiscal and jurisdictional integrity of mother-parishes, only grudging and indirect acknowledgement of parochial identities and activities at a lower level. At the grass roots, a coalescing group of worshippers in a new manorial church would have taken their time, in a world in which parishes were assumed to be mother-parishes, to work towards a new vocabulary. A more general point about late Anglo-Saxon ideas of lordship and territory must, however, be made. If there was no exclusive word for any kind of parish, the same must be said of the kind of secular unit of lordship which since the twelfth century has normally been known in England as the manor. Not all late Anglo-Saxon manors, of course, were compact or clearly bounded, but there were undoubtedly moves towards cellularity and boundedness which the vocabulary does not reflect. The many tenth-century char-

<hr>

[23] Above, p. 423, and see especially Abrams 1995*a*: 247–8.

ters which trace in minute detail the boundaries of land-units, later to emerge virtually unaltered as manors, parishes, or both, call them by such clumsy formulations as 'a certain little parcel of land containing *x* hides in the place known to the locals as *y*'.[24] The vernacular ecclesiastical vocabulary followed a secular vocabulary which described obligations and membership of groups of people within complex entities—'the *hyrnes* of Berkeley' and the like— rather than units of land. In the eleventh century it is therefore not very useful as a guide to the dynamic rather than the traditional strands in local organization.

The background and context of mother-church dues

During a century beginning in the 920s, English kings and their advisers gradually brought the various fiscal rights of minsters under the protection of law-codes.[25] The context is a notably powerful and interventionist state, and the seeming paradox—that kings who milked so many minsters to support themselves and their clerks should provide legal underpinning for their parochial finance—is in fact typical of a regime which was eager for systematic and closely regulated local structures, but suspicious of autonomous power-bases such as the great minsters had once been. The campaign to rebuild institutions at grass-roots level runs through the activities of kings from Alfred to Eadgar: in a local religious context the minsters, however slimmed down, were its natural foundation.[26] To these kings and their advisers, mother-parishes would have made sense as ecclesiastical counterparts to hundreds.[27]

New aspirations of kings to organize their kingdoms were perhaps not the only stimulus; the new pressures from below may have prompted the definition of what had hitherto needed no defining. Local churches appeared hard on the heels of the first legislative measures under Æthelstan and Eadmund; Eadgar made the first formal acknowledgement in England of the private local church with its own priest, already familiar in the Frankish world for

[24] Below, pp. 501-2, for *tūn/villa* meaning in the first instance township, not manor. *Manerium* is a Norman word, emphasizing in its etymology the central buildings rather than the land-unit.

[25] References to church dues in the tenth- and early eleventh-century laws are exhaustively discussed by Wormald forthcoming: ch. 8, which may be read in conjunction with this section and the next. I am deeply grateful to Patrick Wormald for sharing his work with me before publication, especially the crucial observation that some ostensible references in tenth-century codes are in fact interpolations by Wulfstan.

[26] Cf. Dumville 1992*a*: 202-3, on 'the largely unsung but fundamentally necessary reintroduction of the Church in all its aspects to rural England'.

[27] Most obviously where, through the deliberate intervention of Alfred's heirs, the two did in fact coincide: above, pp. 300, 309.

two centuries and more. Minsters and their patrons may have started to see that they had to assert their rights or risk losing them. Extracting church dues from recalcitrant noblemen must always have been a struggle, which doubtless grew harder as the land-market developed and minsters became less independent; but the prospect that low-ranking thegns might transfer their dues to priests and churches of their own was new and more alarming.

In revealing the West Saxon kings' legislative debt to their Frankish predecessors, recent work has highlighted the extent to which English laws on church dues followed the formulations of Carolingian capitularies issued between the 770s and 820s.[28] This realization has prompted two very different hypotheses: that tenth-century kings established a mother-parish system from scratch under Frankish influence, and that they used the vehicle of Carolingian-inspired legislation to bolster an ancient system under stress.[29] This book has argued that a distinctively English nexus of lay obligations to minsters was in place before the first Viking age, and was the foundation of developments thereafter. The evidence will now be considered in more detail.

One payment had almost certainly been enforced, at least in Wessex, since the great age of monastic foundation. Churchscot, a render of grain, is ordered in the laws of King Ine of Wessex (688–726) to be paid from each homestead at Martinmas on pain of a severe fine.[30] This obligation is not only reiterated through the tenth-century codes but also, more significantly, appears in a series of leases, two of them from before 900. In 871 × 7 the bishop of Winchester leased eight hides in Hampshire 'free of everything except bridge-work and army-service and eight churchscots [i.e., presumably, one churchscot per hide] and the priest's dues and soulscots', and in 899 a Worcester lease reserved 'the bishop's due which is customarily called churchscot and soulscot'.[31] Churchscot turns up in several tenth- and eleventh-century leases and estate records from Mercia and Wessex, and in Domesday Book and later sources it can be recognized yet more widely.

That the two crucial leases date from when they do, rather than only a few years earlier or later, is tantalizing. It is chronologically possible that Winchester's churchscot in the 870s stemmed from an Alfredian application of Ine's law, and that Worcester's in 899 was in turn an innovation of Bishop

<hr/>

[28] Wormald 1999*a*; Wormald 1999*b*.

[29] Cambridge and Rollason 1995: 97–103, as against Blair 1995*a*: 196–8.

[30] Ine, cc. 4 and 61 (*Gesetze*, 90, 116); the first of these clauses specifies Martinmas (11 November), which agrees with later sources, the second 'midwinter', which may mean the same. The grain was perhaps to be taken at the time of winter threshing. We can be confident that Ine's code as we have it dates substantially from his time, though enactments could have been 'added to an original core over years or decades': Wormald 1999*a*: 103–5. Cf. Tinti 2003: 221–2.

[31] S 1275 (*RASC* 26), S 1279; see Tinti 2003: 222–9.

Wærferth, Alfred's old friend and adviser, informed by West Saxon practice.[32] Against this may be balanced an impression that these were established arrangements at the time of the leases rather than ones being worked out experimentally: in a slightly earlier lease (889), Wærferth had already stipulated that 'every year *censum aecclesiae* [presumably churchscot] is to be rendered justly to [the minster of Bishops] Cleeve'.[33] These relatively early references at both Winchester and Worcester, combined with the near-ubiquity of churchscot later, do on the whole suggest that such renders were, in general terms, a known means by which laity were required to support their local minsters in the pre-Viking kingdoms. A levy in kind, taken from each household's (that is, notionally, each hide's) grain stored over winter, was an obvious and natural extension of the ubiquitous English practice of assessing food-rent on the hide: was this what Archbishop Theodore had meant by 'ecclesiastical tribute' levied 'according to the custom of the province'?[34]

Whereas churchscot was distinctively English, the due that one might have thought the most fundamental of all the Christian community's material obligations is conspicuous by its absence. The payment of tithe—a tenth of all produce or revenue—has the clearest possible scriptural authority, yet before the Carolingians it seems to have been regarded both in continental Europe and in England as a voluntary pious act.[35] On the Continent the landmark is Charlemagne's Herstal Capitulary of 779, decreeing that tithes must be paid by everyone and dispensed on the bishop's instructions,[36] and it was against this background that the legatine delegation to England in 786 enjoined that 'all are to take care to give tithes from all they possess—because that is reserved for the Lord God—and to live and pay alms from the nine parts'.[37] But whereas tithe-payment enforced by king and bishop became firmly established in the Carolingian world,[38] the legates' decree seems to

---

[32] This is Patrick Wormald's view, and I am grateful to him for debates which have shifted my position some though not all of the way. As he observes, the reflection in the Domesday Book entry for Pershore (DB i. 175ᵛ) of Ine's severe sanction for non-payment of churchscot (Ine, c. 4) does imply the extension of West Saxon law to Mercia. It is entirely possible that an organic but variable system of renders in kind was systematized along West Saxon lines during the unification of the kingdom. Cf. Tinti 2003: 228.

[33] S 1415: 'nisi tantum ut omni anno censum aecclesiae saecundum rectitudinem to Clife reddantur [*sic*]'. Cf. above, pp. 159–60.   [34] Above, pp. 155–6.

[35] Constable 1964: 9–31; Wormald forthcoming: ch. 8. Thus Theodore's Penitential *allows* the giving of tithes to paupers, pilgrims, and churches (*PT* II. xiv. 11 (p. 333)), and Bede presents Bishop Eadberht of Lindisfarne's gift of a tithe to the poor as an act of piety (*HE* iv. 29 (p. 443)). Irish texts imply that tithes were compulsory from an early date, though whether more than a small group paid them is debated (Etchingham 1999: 240–5, 267–71).

[36] c. 7 (*Capitularia*, i. 48); Constable 1964: 28–36; Wormald forthcoming: ch. 8. Charlemagne was following a first move by Pippin in the 760s.

[37] *CED* iii. 456–7; cf. Tinti 2003: 230–6, and Story 2003: 85–6, for the likely non-relevance of this to English conditions.   [38] Constable 1964: 31–56; Wormald forthcoming: ch. 8.

have been a dead letter in England: the leases of c.870–910 which reserve churchscot and soulscot have nothing to say about tithe, and only in the 920s does it emerge, rather suddenly, as an important and compulsory render.[39] Tithe is the one English church due which (as an obligation) seems to have had no indigenous roots, and the one major innovative strand in the tenth-century reconstruction of the local Church: it constituted a new basis for parochial finance.[40]

Between the 770s and the 920s, therefore, there was a sense in which Continental tithe and English churchscot were direct alternatives. How then did they compare in profitability? There is post-Conquest evidence that the customary 'load' of churchscot from each hide contained forty or forty-eight sheaves,[41] and if this was representative the question becomes whether the yearly produce of a hide was greater or less than 400–80 sheaves. By the thirteenth century, when manorial accounts become available, it was hugely greater, by a factor of ten or more.[42] Whether the discrepancy was anything like so big in the eighth century is a very different matter, but clearly it must have increased proportionately as grain-production per hide rose. After the 920s, English landowners were in the unenviable position of paying a new and heavier render on top of the one which they already owed by ancient custom.

So there is little mystery why tithe should have appealed increasingly to potential recipients from the early tenth century—a period when the economy grew and more intensive field-systems spread—nor why it should have been resented by proprietors who must often have felt that their traditional obligations went far enough. By Continental standards, they were arguably wrong: it looks as though the average ninth-century English minster receiving churchscot was disadvantaged, hide for hide, in comparison with a Carolingian mother-church receiving tithe. If on the other hand we look back still further, to the late seventh to late eighth centuries, we find the position reversed: English minsters (at least in Wessex) had a form of systematic guaranteed revenue from the laity, whereas Frankish churches did not. This is one strand in a pattern which historians of Anglo-Saxon territorial organization have learnt to recognize: idiosyncratic but oddly effective structures in the societies of sixth- to eighth-century Britain; the enunciation of normative fiscal and administrative modes in late eighth- and early ninth-century

---

[39] Below, p. 440.   [40] Michael Franklin's phrase: Franklin 1982: 11 f.

[41] Below, p. 445 n. The Winchester 'eight churchscots' from eight hides (above, p. 434) implies that there was already a hidage-based assessment by the 870s.

[42] Thirteenth-century accounts suggest a yield of 200–24 bushels from a yardland. At Cuxham six sheaves produced a bushel, suggesting 1,200 sheaves or more per yardland, in other words 4,800 or more per hide. I am very grateful to Rosamond Faith and Ralph Evans for these calculations.

Frankish capitularies; and a re-structuring of local England by its tenth-century kings which, while influenced by these Carolingian methods and definitions, was rooted in old insular practice.[43]

The mortuary (in English 'soulscot'), a payment for the privilege of burial with priestly ministrations or in a holy place, had a controversial European history behind it.[44] Gregory the Great forbade priests to claim money for land in which corpses would rot or to profit from survivors' grief, a view echoed by some Carolingian and post-Carolingian canonists who condemned mortuaries as simoniac. The opposite view, which could cite the fact that Abraham had bought land on which to bury his family (Genesis 23), was inevitably more attractive to religious establishments and gained ground through the ninth and tenth centuries,[45] perhaps as a perception that the payment was for funerary ministrations shifted to one that it was for the grave-plot. The Church had effectively accepted the obligation of laity to pay mortuaries by *c.*1000, and it was one of the 'abuses' which the heretics of Arras attacked in 1024.

Against this background, soulscot occurs remarkably early in England, in the same two late ninth-century leases which reserve churchscot.[46] At that date it cannot, as a compulsory payment, be a European import, and it may be seen as an established and distinctively English custom which allowed at least some churches to demand the soulscots of those who lived and died in their territories. This looks rather at variance with the indications, to be discussed presently, that the English laity before the tenth century had wide freedom in choosing their places of burial. One solution is to interpret the soulscot of these leases as a payment for last rites and funerary ministrations, not for a grave-plot in a specific place: people living on the leased lands could be buried where they chose, but were obliged to employ the Winchester or Worcester priests if they wanted Christian rites. It is, on the other hand, possible that the piecemeal extension of ecclesiastical control over land had produced local variation: whereas tenants on certain monastic estates were tied to the head churches, other people still had freedom to pay their soulscots to burial churches of their choice.

The obligation to maintain the church building ('churchbot') appears, well before the main legislative programme, in a Wiltshire lease of 902 which

---

[43] e.g. Campbell 1986: 109–16, 159–66.

[44] Treffort 1996*a*: 172–4, and Wormald forthcoming: ch. 8, for what follows. See also Costambeys 2001: 187–8, for the equivocal attitudes to burial fees in sixth-century Rome.

[45] A red herring which misled Aubrun 1986: 67 and Treffort 1996*a*: 173 is a supposed decretal of Leo III (795–816) allowing people to choose their own places of burial but reserving the due mortuaries to their parish churches (A. Friedberg (ed.), *Corpus Iuris Canonici*, ii (Leipzig, 1881), cols. 548–9); this should clearly be ascribed to some much later Pope Leo. See Wormald forthcoming; I am again grateful to Patrick Wormald for his advice.   [46] Above, p. 434.

stipulates that the lessee 'is to contribute every year to the repair of the church to which the land pertains (*to ðære cyrican bote þe ðet land to hyrð*) in the proportion that the rest of the people do, each according to the extent of his property'.[47] One striking feature of this passage is its resemblance to the legislation which, nearly seventy years later, would enforce tithe-payment 'to the old minster to which the jurisdiction pertains' (*to þam ealdan mynstre þe seo hernes to hyrð*).[48] Another is its explicit statement that churchbot was assessed on land, on a pro rata (presumably hidage) basis. This is intriguing evidence for church maintenance as a systematically apportioned public duty, though it is odd that this relatively early and seemingly important obligation is so seldom mentioned again.[49]

The principle behind churchscot, soulscot, and churchbot is of reciprocity: they are payments in return for priestly ministrations, a Christian passage to the next world, and the use of a church building. At Leominster the local name for churchscot, 'shrift-corn', recalls its primary justification as a payment to support spiritual care, perhaps especially 'shriving' or penitential arrangements.[50] The render to Lambourn minster in the eleventh century of the crop from two 'shrift-acres' on the king's land must have a similar origin.[51] These terms remind us that contemporaries would have recognized an exchange between the pastoral services which they received and the grain and pennies which they handed over, perhaps to the individual priests serving communities within the mother-parishes.

Such personal relationships must also underlie a range of miscellaneous and sometimes rather obscure alms and oblations, some but not all afforced by legislation. The Winchester lease of the 870s also reserves the 'mass-priest's dues' (*mæsseprestes gereohta*)—whatever they may have been—payable from an estate three miles from the cathedral.[52] Alms-money, Romescot (hearth-penny), plough-alms, and lightscot crop up in the later laws.[53] Lightscot, like soulscot, does not appear in genuine legislation until 1008; yet it is foreshadowed by a provision in 847 that the lessee of the land of Bredon minster (Worcs.) must provide oil for the minster's lamps.[54] How should we understand the yearly 'gift and aid' which the twelfth-century freemen of seven

---

[47] S 1285. The recipient church is not stated, but the land was at Ebbesbourne, which later parochial evidence places in the mother-parish of Broad Chalke (Pitt 1999: 42–5).

[48] Below, p. 442.

[49] The 'churchscot-work' of S 1287 may be the same obligation. The other (laconic) references to *cyricbote* are in VI Atr. 51, VIII Atr. 6, and II Cn. 65. 1 (*Gesetze*, 258, 264, 352). I Em. 5 (*Gesetze*, 186), essentially an ecclesiastical synod, orders that all churches are to be well maintained, including bishops' on their own property.

[50] Kemp 1988: 87–8.   [51] Below, p. 449.   [52] S 1275 (*RASC* 26).

[53] Below, pp. 441, 444.

[54] Sims-Williams 1990: 170. See Fouracre 1995 for the Frankish arrangements by which kings, and then from the ninth century tenants called *luminarii* or *cerarii*, were responsible for providing

Cornish vills owed to the minster-priests of St Kew?[55] In the unique texts describing the internal life of the late eleventh-century minster at Christchurch (Hants.), it is striking to see the importance of purely voluntary offerings, carefully divided into gifts made at a mass to the individual canon celebrating it, and other offerings shared between the canons equally.[56] All this looks much more like a web of custom than an imposed system of finance; the need to pay soulscot 'at the open grave' is a vivid glimpse of entrenched social ritual.[57] Legislation merely contributed a partial—and often late—ratification: charters show that soulscot and churchbot, at least, were being paid long before the first references in the law-codes.

Both in this sweeping-up of a selection from a ragbag of miscellaneous and sometimes eccentric dues, and in its late introduction of tithe, the English legislation on parochial finance differs radically from its Continental prototypes. The Carolingian capitularies had imposed tithe—which needed no precedent or justification beyond scripture—to support mother-churches and to protect them from encroaching *oratoriae*. In England the first requirement was met by churchscot and other indigenous customs, while the second was not an issue before Eadgar's time. The Continental preoccupation with threefold and fourfold divisions of tithe between the clergy, the bishop, the poor, the fabric, and the lights barely appears:[58] it looks as though such allocations were unnecessary in England precisely because customary renders—levied, in traditional English fashion, on the household or hide—catered for most of these needs already. It remains true that the Frankish provisions are recorded from the late eighth century, the English ones (except churchscot) only from the late ninth and tenth. But where the whole essence of the former is to found a system of ecclesiastical finance on a 10 per cent

oil and wax for lighting churches. As he observes (p. 75 and n.), these arrangements, and the assignment of fractions of tithes for lights, look different in kind from the separate due which occurs in England.

[55] Below, p. 522.   [56] Below, p. 516; Hase 1988: 53.

[57] V Atr. 12 (*Gesetze*, 240; *C&S* 352). Recent traditional practice in north Wales was exactly this: 'Outside the church, at the porch or at the graveside, a second contribution was made, this time to the parish clerk. This was commonly known as *arian rhaw* (spade money) because it was collected on a shovel held over the open grave by the clerk himself' (J. Geraint Jenkins, *Life and Tradition in Rural Wales* (Stroud, 1976), 139–40).

[58] Constable 1964, and Wood forthcoming, on these divisions in Francia. Wood doubts whether in practice they were active over much of the Continent either, but at least drafters bothered to enunciate them. Reserving a share for the bishop scarcely features in England. For the very few English references to division, see Tinti 2003: 238 n. 51. Ælfric, followed by the 'Canons of Eadgar' and the 1014 code, says that tithes should be divided between the poor, the church fabric, and the priests, in other words a Continental-type scheme, though one that excludes the bishop ('Pastoral Letter for Wulfsige III', c. 68; 'Canons of Eadgar', c. 56; VIII Atr. 6: *C&S* 209–10, 333, 390–1). This is based, via Wulfstan's canon law collection, on Ghaerbald's Capitulary (c. 7), and its relevance to actual English practice is imponderable.

tax, the latter define and enforce an organic web of relationships. In requiring English landowners to pay both the traditional churchscot and the imported tithe, Alfred's heirs managed to have the best of both worlds, but they did so because support for minsters was already deeply rooted in English local custom. If they had started with a clean sheet, they would surely have come up with a simpler and more conventionally Frankish package.

The enforcement and erosion of mother-church dues

Between the 920s and the 1020s, a mixture of customary practices and new injunctions acquired the status of legislation, building the formal written framework which would define mother-parishes into at least the middle years of the eleventh century. King Æthelstan's ordinance of 926 × c.930[59] not only reiterates Ine's churchscot law, but also for the first time insists on compulsory tithes. With the advice of his bishops, he directs the reeves of every borough to 'give tithes from my own property both in livestock and in the yearly fruits of the earth'. His bishops, reeves, aldermen, and everyone subject to them are to do likewise, and the duty to pay tithe is emphasized by an appropriate scriptural passage. The king's reeves are further to bring it about 'that churchscot shall be paid to that place to which it rightly belongs; and they shall rejoice therein in those places who want to deserve it more worthily of God and us'. With its insistence that the recipient minsters do their own duty in return, this measure is in line with Æthelstan's drive to rebuild the institutions and moral standing of the English Church,[60] but it also suggests negligence by the laity.

It may not be coincidence that this law is almost exactly contemporary with the first archival reference to local tithes, an instruction that two-thirds of the tithes from Great Bedwyn (Wilts.) and Lambourn (Berks.) are to go to 'God's servants for provisions at Bedwyn'.[61] It is impossible to say whether this memorandum illustrates a fashion for voluntary tithe-giving which encouraged Æthelstan to make his law, or was a direct response to it, but it suggests that the principle of the minster taking two-thirds of the tithe—later to be enshrined in Eadgar's laws—was already in operation. References to tithe become common from mid century, for instance a Huntingdonshire

---

[59] I Æthelstan (*Gesetze*, 146-8; *C&S* 43-7); I follow Wormald forthcoming: ch. 8, in taking the references to soulscot and plough-alms as an interpolation by Wulfstan.

[60] See for instance Dumville 1992a: 161-6.

[61] Meritt 1934: 344; Dumville 1992a: 82, for the date; Pitt 1999: 130-45. Given the normal usage of *dæl*, 'þa twegen dælas þære teoðunge' can confidently be translated as 'the two-thirds of the tithe'.

grant of 955 which observes that 'a prudent landowner [will make himself responsible for?] churchscot, soulscot and tithe'; in the same year, Pennard minster (Somerset) was receiving what looks like a tithe, the produce of two out of twenty hides.[62]

Eadmund's only original contribution was to give legal backing to the enigmatic 'alms-money' (*ælmesfeoh*),[63] but it was probably around the mid tenth century that a brief statement was added to a manuscript of Alfred's laws ordaining, with penalties, that 'Romescot is to be given before mid-day on St Peter's Day after midsummer'.[64] Romescot (*Romfeoh*, later 'Peter's Pence') was an English oddity: a yearly lump sum payment to the papacy, apparently a formalization of gifts of alms by ninth-century and perhaps earlier kings.[65] In theory, it was not a church due like the others because the money left the kingdom. In practice, though, there are grounds for thinking that the pennies raised from individual householders totalled far more than the traditional lump sum, and that the balance might be retained by collectors. Who these were is rarely clear; in each Northumbrian wapentake two thegns and a priest were sworn to collect the money and deliver it to the bishop's see, and in east Kent, where it was paid directly to the archbishop, there are signs of lathe-based assessment.[66] In this kind of framework the natural collecting-points for an ecclesiastical tax would have been minsters, and it may be that some laws mention Romescot in the same breath as tithe and churchscot because it was, in effect, a minster asset. That this could have applied especially to minsters controlled by bishops is suggested by the intriguing fact that two ex-minsters which were still collection-points for

[62] S 566 (*RASC* 56); S 563, a grant of twenty hides to a nun of Wilton, on condition 'ut ex his binarum usus vernantibus ad eius oracula monasterii prout antiquitus destinabatur'. The *monasterium* was presumably (East) Pennard itself. The name (*Pengeard mynster* in the charter, *Pennarminstre* in DB) clearly belongs to the distinctive south-western group of *-minster* place-names (but for a different view see Abrams 1996: 195–8).

[63] I Edm. 2 (*Gesetze*, 184; *C&S* 62; again, it was probably Wulfstan who substituted Rome-money and plough-alms for alms-money). There may be a direct link between this enactment and a charter of 946 (S 509) in which Eadmund reserves to Glastonbury, from each household on the land, almsgiving as well as churchscot and churchbot ('omne sacrificium quod nos dicimus munus ecclesiasticum et opus ecclesiasticum et munus rogificum ab omni familia illius terre reddatur'). On the Tidenham estate, every yardland owed four *ælmespeneg* (S 1555).

[64] *Gesetze*, 474; Wormald 1999a: 227, 368–9, for date and context.

[65] Keynes and Lapidge 1983: 99, 268; Neilson 1910: 197–201; Barlow 1979: 145, 295–7; Wormald forthcoming: ch. 8. Later laws show that it was levied, apparently normally at the rate of 1*d.* per household, at midsummer.

[66] *NPL* c. 57. 1–2 (*Gesetze*, 384; *C&S* 464); Barlow 1979: 296. Brett 1975: 168–73, shows what a small fraction of the Romescot raised in the twelfth century actually reached the pope. The 'hearth-penny' of Eadgar's code is unambiguously identified there with Romescot (below); if the *heorðpenegas* of eleventh-century estate records were also Romescot (which cannot be taken as certain: *C&S* 100 n.), they seem to be treated there as an ordinary manorial render.

Peter's Pence in the twelfth century are also, and equally exceptionally, known to have distributed the bishop's chrism.[67]

It was Eadgar who, after a legislative gap of at least thirteen years, over-hauled the legal basis of church finance and—crucially—updated it to meet new conditions. The relevant sections of his code (959 × 72) are worth quoting in full:[68]

[1. 1] And all tithe is to be given to the old minster to which the jurisdiction pertains (*to þam ealdan mynstre þe seo hernes to hyrð*), and it is to be rendered both from the thegn's inland and from the tenanted land (*geneatlande*), according as it is brought under the plough.
[1. 2] But if there is any thegn who has on his bookland a church with which there is a graveyard, he is to pay the third part of his own tithe into his church.
[2. 1] If anyone has a church with which there is no graveyard, he is then to pay to his priest from the [remaining] nine parts what he chooses.
[2. 2] And all churchscot is to go to the old minster, from every free hearth.[69]
[3] And the tithe of all young stock is to be rendered by Pentecost and of the fruits of the earth by the Equinox; and all churchscot is to be rendered by Martinmas, under pain of the full fine which the lawbook prescribes [i.e. Ine c. 4].
[3. 1] And if then anyone will not render the tithe as we have decreed, the king's reeve is to go there, and the bishop's reeve, and the mass-priest of the minster, and they are to seize without his consent the tenth part for the minster to which it belongs, and to assign to him the next tenth; and the remaining eight parts are to be divided into two, and the lord of the land (*landhlaford*) is to succeed to half, and the bishop to half, whether it be a king's man or a thegn's.
[4] And every hearth-penny is to be paid by St Peter's Day.
[4. 1] And he who has not rendered it by that appointed day is to take it to Rome, and thirty pence in addition . . .

The explicit penalty for withholding tithes is new, as is the incorporation, under the name hearth-penny, of Romescot (backed by a singularly improbable sanction). More important for present purposes are the apportionment of demesne tithes in fractions, and the assertion that *hyrness* over any thegn's land can be expected to lie with an existing 'old minster' and must be respected if the thegn builds a church. The first recalls the Continental practice of splitting tithes between various destinations, though Eadgar's

---

[67] Leominster (Herefs.) and Bishops Waltham (Hants.): Kemp 1988: 93 n. 9, and *Winch. Acta*, 36 (No. 52). The latter was an episcopal minster, but there is no evidence that this had applied to Leominster (unless it had been the Magonsætan bishop's seat before Hereford). In east Kent, where Peter's Pence was collected under archiepiscopal control, some of the archbishop's chrism was distributed through the minsters (above, p. 69).
[68] II Eadgar 1. 1–3. 1 (*Gesetze*, 196–8; *C&S* 97–9); Wormald 1999a: 313–17 for context.
[69] Here Wulfstan adds plough-alms.

formulation—at least two-thirds of inland tithe always reserved for the minster, one-third allowable to certain kinds of bookland church—is purely English and new as a general principle.[70] The assignment of two-thirds of a Wiltshire nobleman's tithes to Bedwyn minster, some forty years earlier,[71] suggests that it could have been a principle based on English custom. The clause about bookland churches probably echoes a Carolingian one of 803, which allows people to build churches on their own land with episcopal consent, but safeguards older churches against loss of tithes or other rights: the English input is to specify the demesne tithe fraction and (characteristically) to delete the bishop's involvement.[72]

Eadgar and his advisers may have been encouraged to acknowledge the existence of small estate churches because the Carolingian exemplars had done the same. In a more intensively exploited England, it may also have impressed them that the Carolingians had allowed colonizers of waste land, four or five miles from mother-churches, to give the tithes to their own new churches.[73] It was presumably this kind of sentiment—that the satisfying of new public needs deserves a measure of freedom from vested interests—which prompted a tithe concession specifically to churches with graveyards. But that the borrowing should come so late, and at precisely the time when small English estate churches become visible archaeologically, shows that it was also a genuine reaction to new circumstances. English minsters, alarmed

---

[70] For the bewildering variety of tithe fractions in Carolingian and later Europe see Constable 1964: 43–83; see also Wood forthcoming for versions of the one-third/two-thirds division. The abbey of Prüm's division of the tithes from an outlying estate in 893, two-thirds for itself and one-third for the priest resident there (Constable 1964: 69), illustrates a common formulation of a kind that might have guided Eadgar's drafters. Eleventh-century councils asserted that one-third of the tithes from an estate should be reserved for the local church and its priest: Councils of Toulouse (1056), cc. 10–11, Tours (1060), c. 8, Lillebonne (1080), Rouen (1096) (J. D. Mansi (ed.), *Sacrorum Conciliorum Nova et Amplissima Collectio*, xix (Venice, 1774), cols. 849, 928; Orderic Vitalis, 'Historia Æcclesiastica', v. 4, ix. 3 (ed. M. Chibnall, *The Ecclesiastical History of Orderic Vitalis*, iii (1972), 28, v (1975), 22)). There is, however, a basic difference between these Continental arrangements, which asserted the *right* of a local church to its one-third portion while tacitly accepting that the lord of the estate might take the rest, and Eadgar's scheme, which enforces payment of most of the tithes to the minster and *allows* a small fraction to a new local church. I am very grateful to Susan Wood for her advice. See also Tinti 2003: 237–8.   [71] Above, p. 440.

[72] Salz (803), c. 3 (*Capitularia*, i. 119): 'Quicumque voluerit in sua proprietate ecclesiam aedificare, una cum consensu et voluntate episcopi in cuius parrochia fuerit licentiam habeat; verumtamen omnino praevidendum est, ut aliae ecclesiae antiquiores propter hanc occasionem nullatenus suam iustitiam aut decimam perdant, sed semper ad antiquiores ecclesias persolvantur.' The same principle is stated in Mainz (813), c. 41 (A. Werminghoff (ed.), *MGH Legum, sec. iii, Concilia*, ii. 1 (Hannover, 1906), 271): 'Ecclesiae antiquitus constitutae nec decimis nec aliis possessionibus priventur, ita ut novis oratoriis tribuantur', followed by 'Capitula e Conciliis Excerpta' (826), c. 4, and 'Ansegisi Capitularium' (827), ii. 34 (*Capitularia*, i. 312, 422); this passage was known and used by Wulfstan (Wormald forthcoming: ch. 8). But again, such models may have influenced Eadgar's drafters more in the general principles enunciated, and in the modes of expression, than in the specific outcome envisaged.

[73] 'Capitulare Ecclesiasticum' (818–19), c. 12; Tribur (895), c. 14 (*Capitularia*, i. 277, ii. 221).

by a new threat to their status and assets which had long been all too familiar to their Frankish counterparts, may have regarded Eadgar's law as a satisfactory modus vivendi, as indeed it probably remained for up to a century after.

In his law-codes for Æthelred II and Cnut, Archbishop Wulfstan re-formulated the existing legislation on church dues but made only small additions.[74] Plough-alms (fifteen days after Easter) and lightscot (three times yearly) make their first genuine appearance in or soon after 1008.[75] The same code's insistence that soulscot is to be paid to 'the minster to which it belonged', even if the body is buried elsewhere, reflects both the growing prescriptiveness of burial arrangements and the rising competition of manorial churchyards.[76] The mis-named 'Canons of Eadgar' (1005 × 8) provide some more specific directions for payment dates.[77] The notable contribution from Æthelred's reign (1014) is the tariff of penalties for breaking the sanctuaries of a 'head minster', a 'rather smaller minster', 'one still smaller', and a 'field-church': the first and only official acknowledgement of a multi-layered hierarchy of churches. Wulfstan repeated it in 1020/1 but added another criterion: the 'still smaller' minster has a graveyard, the 'field-church' none.[78]

This body of legislation was accretive: injunctions to pay dues were repeated from code to code, with only two admissions—the bookland church in 959 × 72, the fourfold hierarchy in 1014—that the ecclesiastical landscape was changing. Ostensibly, Cnut in the 1020s was protecting exactly the same category of churches as had Æthelstan a century earlier. This inherent conservatism, combined with the absence of law-codes after the 1020s, means that legislation cannot really be used to show whether the rise in local church-building and endowment during *c.*1000–60 caused any significant diversion of dues from the minsters. What we know in general about late Anglo-Saxon law-enforcement might suggest that the legislative dam could have held the tide back until the Conquest.[79] A minster community seeking redress against

[74] Wormald 1999*a*: 330–66 for context; Wormald forthcoming: ch. 8, for details. As already noted, Wulfstan made it appear that plough-alms and lightscot already had legal protection by writing them into MSS of earlier laws.

[75] V Atr. 11. 1 (*Gesetze*, 240–1; *C&S* 351; cf. Wormald 1999*a*: 330–45, for dating problems); Wulfstan adds in 1020/1 that lightscot is levied at a halfpenny-worth of wax per hide (I Cn. 12: *Gesetze*, 294–5; *C&S* 477). Lightscot is presumably the origin of the wax-renders which chapels often owed to their mother-churches in the late middle ages, though by then it had often merged into other manorial dues, or been devolved to small churches: Neilson 1910: 192. Cf. p. 438 above.

[76] V Atr. 12. 1 (*Gesetze*, 240–1; *C&S* 352). On the other hand, it also reinforces the idea that soulscot was basically a payment for funerary ministrations rather than for a grave-plot.

[77] 'Canons of Eadgar', c. 54 (*C&S* 331–2).   [78] Above, p. 368.

[79] Thus Wormald forthcoming: ch. 8: 'We face . . . the possibility that the Old English kingdom's structures were in good order up to first light on 14 October 1066, thereafter falling into the hands of a ruling-class that subverted because it did not understand them.'

non-payers or encroachers would presumably have gone to the hundred court, where its own members are likely to have constituted a heavy presence, or the shire court, where the bishop was co-president.[80] But the archaeological, architectural, and sculptural evidence for small churches gives reason to think that the legislation, like the parochial vocabulary, describes a world of unified mother-parishes which in reality was ceasing to exist: by the 1060s this embattled system of restraints may have been ready to fall when pushed. We may learn more about what happened in practice from some of the more specific local evidence, such as estate records and wills, which increase in number just as the legislative programme reaches its climax.

Churchscot was widely rendered to local minsters through the later Anglo-Saxon period.[81] It was always paid at Martinmas,[82] was usually assessed on the hide, and always took the form of a quantity of grain. This quantity was expressed in a variety of ways, for instance a *mitta* of wheat per hide at Bishops Cleeve *c.*900, or forty-eight sheaves of 'shrift-corn' at Leominster in the twelfth century, but in the absence of precise measurements it is impossible to know the real extent of local variation.[83] In 1086 the shire testified that Pershore minster (Worcs.) should have churchscot at the rate of one load of grain at Martinmas from every hide where a free man lives, but 'if they have more hides they shall be free'; in the eight hundreds of Aylesbury 'each sokeman that has one hide or more renders one load of grain to this church'.[84] Where minsters remained parochially strong into the twelfth century, the churchscot revenues from hidated land within a defined mother-parish were perhaps the clearest sign of maternal status (even if it was not

---

[80] The first witnesses named in the Lambourn minster document, which was promulgated both in the shire court and in Lambourn hundred, are the priests Croc, Heardyng, Werman, Walter, and Theodoric and the deacon Walter, perhaps Lambourn minster-priests: *RASC* 240. (I read 'innan þare scire 7 innan þan hundred on Lambourne' as 'in the shire [i.e. Berkshire] and in Lambourn hundred', not 'within the parish and within the hundred of Lambourn'.)

[81] Wormald forthcoming: ch. 8, and Barlow 1979: 160–2, for the following references and others; Kemble 1849: ii. 490–4, 559–62, and Round 1890, are still useful.

[82] This is reiterated in the laws, and is also specified in the Lambourn document (below, p. 449). and in the Domesday statement that from every hide of free or unfree land belonging to the church of Worcester, the bishop has at Martinmas one load (*summa*) of the best grain growing there (DB i. 174).

[83] S 1283 (*RASC* 28–30, and note, ibid. 290–1, for other leases reserving churchscot; cf. *cyricmittan* in the Hurstbourne survey of 900, S 359); Kemp 1988: 87–8 (calculating from the stated levy of twelve sheaves per yardland). The bishop of Winchester reserved 'eight churchscots' from eight hides at Easton (Hants.) in 871 × 7: S 1275 (*RASC* 26). However, Taunton in the mid to late eleventh century levied a total of seventeen churchscots from some twenty-three hides, apportioned rather irregularly (*RASC* 236–8). Late ninth- and tenth-century Worcester tenants could also be made responsible for 'churchscot-work' (cf. above, n. 49) and for sowing and harvesting the grain and bringing it in: S 1287, S 1303 (*RASC* 28, 64, and note ibid. 289). In the 1090s, tenants on Abingdon Abbey estates traditionally rendered forty sheaves per hide or the tenth acre of the cultivated land, an odd formulation suggesting that here churchscot and tithe were alternatives: *Hist. Abb.* ii. 34–6.   [84] DB i. 175, 143ᵛ.

necessarily still the minster-priests who received them).[85] But where minster assets were absorbed into the nexus of secular manorial lordship, churchscot was eventually absorbed too, and divided up as manors were divided, so that from the twelfth century onwards it occurs widely as an ordinary manorial due.[86] The tenth- to eleventh-century lists of the obligations of tenants at Hurstbourne Priors (Hants.) and Tidenham (Glos.) might, on one interpretation, suggest that this devolution started before the Conquest, for what seem to be subdivided churchscot obligations are lumped in with other manorial dues.[87] Both estates, though, were in ecclesiastical hands and both probably centred on old mother-churches: it is likely that these churchscots were still in theory paid to the minsters, but in practice pocketed by the minsters' proprietors as though they were secular estate revenues.[88]

Soulscot surfaces in the less formal context of testamentary instructions. Around 1000 the Staffordshire thegn Wulfgeat of Donington left land, money, and men as soulscot to an unnamed destination, presumably self-evident to his executors.[89] Wynflaed's will (c.950) treats 'soulscots' as free gifts to several churches, not as one obligatory payment to her burial church.[90] The amount could range from precious plate and whole manors for nobles and archbishops to a penny for a Devon guild-brother.[91] In post-Conquest texts, soulscot sometimes (though less frequently) appears alongside churchscot as an attribute of minster status,[92] notionally indicating the right to take

[85] A good example is the Taunton survey (*RASC* 236–8). The Domesday entry for Nether Wallop (Hants.) shows tithe partitioned between mother- and daughter-churches, but churchscot reserved wholly to the former: 'Ibi ecclesia cui pertinet una hida et medietas decime m[anerii] et totum cirset, et de decima villanorum xlvi den. et medietas ag<n>orum. Ibi est adhuc ecclesiola ad quam pertinet viii acras de decima' (DB i. 38ᵛ).

[86] Neilson 1910: 193–6; Barlow 1979: 195. In Coventry and Lichfield diocese, *cherchambre* (cf. *RASC* 455) occurs in the later twelfth century as a separable revenue, though one episcopal *actum* lists in some detail the renders of it owing to the mother-church of Marton (Warw.) from named vills and tenements: M. J. Franklin (ed.), *EEA* xvi: *Coventry and Lichfield 1160–82* (Oxford, 1998), 7, 64, 74–5 (Nos. 8, 69, 80).

[87] S 1555, S 359 (*RASC* 204–6). The Hurstbourne *ceorlas* render from each hide '40 pence at the autumn equinox, and six "church-measures" (*ciricmittan*) of ale, and three sesters of wheat for bread'—an eccentric version of churchscot if that is what it is. At Tidenham each *gebur* (but not the other people) must cultivate an acre sown with seed from his own barn as churchscot.

[88] Above, p. 328, for this process; above, p. 301 n., for Hurstbourne; Faith 1994 for the background to the Tidenham estate. See Tinti 2003: 239–51 (which appeared as this book was going to press), for a rather stronger argument that after 900 churchscot was widely transformed into an essentially seigneurial revenue, tithe taking its place as the prime church due.

[89] S 1534 (*Wills*, 54). There is no evidence that Donington was a minster, but nor is there any indication in the will that that is where he expected to be buried.

[90] S 1539 (*Wills*, 10–14). Soulscots go to 'every servant of God' in an unnamed, probably monastic community, and to the minsters of Milborne, Yeovil, and Wantage.

[91] S 1505, S 1486, S 1488, S 1534 (*Wills*, 30, 40, 52, 54); below, p. 454 nn., for Exeter.

[92] For some examples: below, p. 518 (Christchurch); Kemp 1988: 88–9 (Leominster); Bond 1988: 133 (Pershore); Neilson 1910: 192–3 (Durham and Abingdon). In late texts soulscot usually appears as 'mortuaries' or 'sepulture'.

all corpses within the mother-parish for burial. It may be that the dominant sense of the word shifted, during the eleventh century, from the broad one of a pious gift for priestly and funerary ministrations, towards the narrow one of a due owing to a specific church.

Tithe would remain the central church due of the laity down to the mid nineteenth century, but collection in late Anglo-Saxon England seems to have varied with local custom and landlords' commutation strategies. At Peterborough in the late tenth century, tithes from the two core hundreds were paid to the minster in the ratio of a fother of corn for every plough 'as was always done', whereas the two hundreds of Norman Cross and a long list of *tūnas* rendered fixed acreages of crops; on the great minster estate of Taunton the tenants paid 'a tithe of eightpence from every hide'.[93] An Evesham lease of land at nearby Norton in the early 1020s specifies that 'both churchscot and tithe shall go to the holy minster'.[94] It is notable that although limited diversion of demesne tithe to small churches had been allowed by law since Eadgar's day, surviving Anglo-Saxon documents make no reference to anything other than minster tithes.[95] In the 1050s Ælfric Wihtgarsson supposedly endowed his foundation at Clare with a collection of small churches and detached tithe-portions in Suffolk, but the source is third-hand and nearly a century later.[96]

The main indication that many local churches had indeed acquired their one-third portions emerges after 1066, when many Norman magnates granted away, usually to monasteries in Normandy, two-thirds of the demesne tithes from long lists of their English manors.[97] Eadgar's principle had in effect been inverted: whereas the one-third portions of tithes became increasingly closely associated with local churches, the new lords (familiar with French rather that English practice) felt entirely free to withdraw the two-thirds portions from the minsters.[98] The extent of the minsters' revenue loss, though obviously severe, is obscured by the uncertain history in this period of peasant (as distinct from demesne) tithes. These

---

[93] *RASC* 72–4, 236–8.   [94] S 1423 (*RASC* 156).

[95] The Domesday entry for Nether Wallop (above, n. 85) illustrates division of tithe between a mother-church and chapel, but half and half rather than as prescribed by Eadgar. See Wormald forthcoming: ch. 8, for post-Conquest references to mother-churches continuing to receive their two-thirds portions.

[96] *Stoke Cart.* i. 54–8, iii. 16–18, 29. The source is a text of 1136 × 43, rehearsing one of 1090 which supposedly listed Ælfric's gifts of forty years earlier. Similarly, twelfth-century Abingdon tradition vaguely ascribed a grant of demesne tithes in East Hendred to 'the time of the Danes': *Hist. Abb.* ii. 48.

[97] For examples see Wormald forthcoming: ch. 8; Wood forthcoming; Blair 1991*a*: 148.

[98] Lennard 1959: 300, 316; Blair 1988*b*: 12–13; Blair 1991*a*: 148–9; Kemp 1988: 84–5, for an example of the complexities that these divisions could cause in the twelfth century. Above, n. 70, for the French councils which simply reserved a third to the local church.

were rarely if ever alienated to absentee owners from their local destinations,[99] which unambiguously, under Eadgar's law, should have been
the minsters. But tithe-payment was ultimately a fundamental duty of
parishioners to their own churches, and from soon after 1100 charters defining the rights of local churches use formulae such as 'all tithes both of the
demesne and of the rustics'.[100] How far eleventh-century lords managed to
re-direct their tenants' tithes to estate churches, along with their burials
and routine churchgoing duties, thus remains an important unanswered
question.

Some minsters had one further privilege, though none of the laws mentions it. Judicial ordeals, whether by hot iron, hot water, or cold water, were
administered in many parts of eleventh- and twelfth-century Europe by the
clergy of major churches. The right to conduct the ordeal, sometimes evidently within the church itself, enhanced communities' dignity and prestige
and gave them a central role in determining innocence or guilt.[101] It was
a monopoly which, not surprisingly, old minsters defended vigorously, as
is apparent (from post-Conquest evidence) at Taunton, Northampton, St
Albans, and Llandaf.[102] The right to hold ordeals is so rarely mentioned that
it is impossible to say how far, if at all, it devolved to lesser churches; oddly
isolated claims to it were being made in the early twelfth century for the ordinary manorial churches of Westfield (Sussex) and Feering and Ockendon
(Essex).[103] On the whole it is likely to have remained closely linked to the
sites of hundredal justice, and therefore perhaps to the main churches of the
hundreds; it may have been one of the essentially unrecorded aspects of life
that maintained minsters' local standing despite the post-Conquest decline
in their regular income.

Our most complete picture of how mother-church rights were asserted at
the end of the period (albeit at a modest and perhaps rather late minster)

---

[99] Brett 1975: 225–7. Lennard's doubts (1959: 317 n. 1) centre on Cirencester Abbey's possession of 'duas partes decimae de toto dominio Cirencestriae et totam decimam totius parrochiae'; but Cirencester had been a well-protected minster (one of Regenbald's), and this must be a case where the two-thirds fraction was *not* alienated, but remained payable to the mother-church along with the peasant tithes. There may, however, have been some freedom in the disposition of substantial freeholders' tithes up to the mid twelfth century (Blair 1991a: 149–50). For peasant tithes in Normandy see Wood forthcoming.

[100] As at Ashtead (Surrey): *Winch. Acta*, 4 (No. 6) (which should surely read 'cum omnibus decimis de dominico et de rusticis', not 'et de iustitiis'). Cf. Brett 1975: 128–30.

[101] Bartlett 1986: 90–4 for the wider context; Rollason 1988: 12–17, and Reynolds 1998: 78–81, for the ritual.

[102] *RASC* 238 (Taunton); Blair 1996b: 107–8 (Northampton); Bartlett 1986: 47–8, 93 (Llandaf and St Albans).

[103] Westfield: *Chron. Battle*, 120 and n.; the ordeal is not, however, mentioned in the lay lord's confirmation of this grant in 1107 × 24 (BL, Add. Ch. 20161). Feering and Ockendon: *Regesta W. I*, 950 (No. 324) (a mid twelfth-century Westminster forgery).

comes from Lambourn (Berks.), in a memorandum which may have been drafted in Cnut's reign but was re-worked, as we have it, near the time of the Domesday survey.[104] After listing the church's own land, a geld-free hide, the document itemizes what was due from 'the king's land' (on Lambourn royal manor): tithes of grain, lambs, and piglets, two 'shrift-acres' at harvest, cheese at Michaelmas, corn and a pig at Martinmas, and 15 pence at Easter. The priest could pasture ten oxen and two cows with the king's, his bullocks with the inhabitants'(?), his sheep after the king's, forty pigs in wood and open country, and two horses with the reeve's; every day his firewood was brought to him from the king's wood. Dues from tenanted land are then listed. Every hide of *geneat*-land at the two Lambourn settlements owed an acre's crop or a hundred sheaves as tithe, whereas every *geneat*, and every *gebur* at Eastbury, owed a sester of corn as churchscot. This looks rather like a distinction between tithe from land and churchscot from people, but if so it is not applied consistently: every hide above Coppington owed 12 pence as churchscot; the thegnland *upe tun* owed two acres as tithe and two sesters of corn as churchscot, as did Ralph's estate at Brockhampton; Eastbury and Edward's estate at Brockhampton each owed two acres as tithe, but otherwise only 'one churchscot' from Eastbury. Normally all of this would be hidden from us apart from the land, which is mentioned in Domesday Book as in scores of other cases. Lambourn mother-parish was relatively small and straightforward:[105] it illustrates how potentially complex might be the deals worked out between minsters and their individual tenants to reconcile archaic and simply expressed obligations with an increasingly intensive economy.

The archival evidence is on the whole consistent with a rapid collapse in the authority of mother-churches after 1066, most visible initially in the widespread diversion of tithes. The pressure on vested interests presumably varied across England with the variation in church-building patterns, and it seems doubtful if minsters could (or wanted to) actually stop churches from being built; but nowhere except perhaps in East Anglia is it likely that the builders had much freedom to annex major dues beyond their one-third demesne tithe-portions. The Domesday jurors' rather striking statement that one Stori, a landowner in Nottinghamshire and Derbyshire in King Edward's day, could 'make himself a church in his land and his soke without anyone's leave, and send his tithe where he would', is placed prominently on the first

---

[104] *RASC* 236-8; for the origin and date of this text (which had been preserved in a Lambourn missal) see the notes, ibid. 490-1. Cf. above, p. 301, for Lambourn and Great Bedwyn.

[105] East Garston, though clearly carved out of Lambourn hundred and mother-parish, seems already to have gone its own way by the time of the survey and is not mentioned there.

Nottinghamshire folio as though an unusual anomaly needing special mention.[106]

Obviously minsters' rights did not simply melt away at the Conquest: if they had, the reconstruction of Anglo-Saxon arrangements from late medieval evidence would be impossible. Most ex-minsters kept unusually large parishes—the rumps of still larger ones—the continued subdivision of which can often be traced from the twelfth century onwards. But for two generations or more, the vested interests which mother-churches had enjoyed under the late Anglo-Saxon laws were extremely vulnerable, and had to be asserted and defended on an individual basis. If some minsters could safely be ignored by church-building magnates, others were under the strong protection of the king, bishops, or abbeys. William I's charter confirming Bampton minster (Oxon.) to the chapter of Exeter cathedral in 1069 includes the crucial little phrase 'and all the king's tithes', which helps to explain why this mother-parish remained so exceptionally intact through the next four centuries.[107] An equally unusual notification by William I (or possibly II) confirms Andover church (Hants.) with its tithes and possessions to the abbey of Saint-Florent at Saumur as in King Edward's time, and orders that churches built under the mother-church are to be destroyed or held by the monks.[108] In 1086 the Conqueror vindicated the burial and other rights of St Cuthmann's minster at Steyning (Sussex), then in the hands of Fécamp abbey, against encroachment by William de Briouze, with the result that 'the bodies which had been buried at William's church were dug up by William's own men and taken back to St Cuthmann's church for lawful burial'.[109] And a writ of Henry I (probably 1114) orders that the churches of five royal manors in Yorkshire 'are not to lose their parishes (*parochiae*) which they had in the

---

[106] DB i. 280: 'De Stori antecessore Walterii de Aincurt, dicunt quod sine alicuius licencia potuit facere \sibi/ ecclesiam in sua terra et in sua soca, et suam decimam mittere quo vellet.' This comes at the end of the description of Derby (which follows that of Nottingham), immediately after a note about royal dues 'on the witness of both shires'; the 'dicunt' therefore refers to the shire courts of Nottinghamshire and Derbyshire. Another DB entry implying a need for consent to build and endow a church, though in this case royal, is that for St Nicholas outside Norwich: 'fecit Colebernus [presbiter] quandam ecclesiam Sancti Nicholai concessu regis, et si rex concedit dabit xx acras, et ideo cantat missam unaquaque ebdomada et psalterium pro rege': DB ii. 263ᵛ.

[107] *Regesta W. I*, 465 (No. 138). Later, and perhaps originally as an interpretation of this phrase, the parishioners of Bampton mother-church were defined as the 'ancient demesne' tenants of the royal manor there: Blair 1985*b*.

[108] *Regesta W. I*, 814 (No. 270): 'precepit ut ecclesie ille que sub matre ecclesia Andeure constructe erant, vel omnino destruerentur aut monachi Sancti Florentii eas haberent.' The Domesday entry for the bishop of Winchester's manor of South Stoneham (Hants.) contains an unusually explicit statement of mother-church rights: 'Huius manerii ecclesiam tenet Richerius clericus cum duabus aliis ecclesiis iuxta Hantone que ad hanc ecclesiam matrem pertinent, et ibi adiacet i hida terre, et om[ni]s decim[a] eiusdem ville et etiam de terra regis' (DB i. 41ᵛ).

[109] *Lawsuits*, i. 128–33 (No. 163); *Regesta W. I*, 482–4 (No. 146); Wormald forthcoming: ch. 8.

time of King Edward on account of sokes which I gave thence to certain of my barons, but each mother church is to have these [parochial rights], and its chapels and tithes, through all the sokes which pertained to these manors in King Edward's day'.[110]

But these are exceptions (at least in the written record), on behalf of unusually well-protected churches. To maintain its position through the hazardous years of endemic encroachment and *ad hoc* bargaining, a minster needed powerful and professional allies. Nor can it be assumed that the Anglo-Norman kings acknowledged old minster rights as a system of general obligation in the way that the late Anglo-Saxon kings had done, or took seriously the tenth- and eleventh-century legislation on the subject. The influx of canon law to England from the 1070s brought a new raft of provisions which, though often pointing in the same direction as the old English laws, derive from the Carolingian exemplars by a completely different route. Anglo-Norman Church councils of 1076 and 1102 prohibited 'supplantings' of churches, the building of new chapels without episcopal consent, and the burial of the dead or diversion of their mortuary dues outside their proper parishes.[111] All of these provisions could, and the second certainly does, derive purely from Continental practice, and on their own they establish adequate grounds for the recorded defences of minster rights in Norman England. Furthermore, these were grounds on which *any* established church could defend its rights: perhaps minsters could put up a stronger case than most, but the privileged status which the old laws gave them had largely vanished. In practice the situation may have been yet more anarchic, except in the islands of stability that were the mother-parishes of unusually well-protected minsters. It says much that a Hampshire lord thought it sensible to claim in 1114 that 'the men of his fee were not ascribed either to the [old minster] church of Carisbrooke or anywhere else but that, by ancient custom, alive they could go to whatever church they wished, and they could bury the bodies of their dead wherever they wished'.[112] The relaxation of tithe obligations, and surely too a serious weakening of many minsters' capacity to withstand encroachment, must have facilitated the building and endowment of manorial churches through the late eleventh and early twelfth centuries. This loosening-up was the most important (and perhaps the only really fundamental) change to the English local Church which was a direct result of the Norman Conquest.

[110] W. Farrer (ed.), *Early Yorkshire Charters*, i (Edinburgh, 1914), 335 (No. 428).
[111] Winchester 1076, c. 7, Westminster 1102, cc. 16, 26 (*C&S* 620, 676, 678).
[112] *Winch. Acta*, 2-3 (No. 3).

The mother-church as spiritual and social focus

If the legal basis of churches' parochial authority was important, their moral and social standing within their own local communities may ultimately have been more so. Manorial church-builders wishing to compete with minsters which not only received nearly all the traditional parochial revenues, but also claimed the devotional loyalties of society at large, faced an uphill struggle. A thegn's priest was of little use if people ignored his ministrations, nor his graveyard if they refused to bury their dead in it. The founder with ambitions for his church needed at his disposal, whether by persuasion or duress, a potential congregation and a body of due-payers. And however much the nexus of lordship moulded perceptions of identity, lords' aspirations could not afford to cut across peasant communities' own ideas about their religious allegiances. Ultimately, the new churches succeeded because people at large were prepared to identify with them. By 1150, this tug-of-war between minsters and local churches for parishioners' allegiance had been won hands down, except in under-developed zones and a few privileged pockets, by the new order; a century earlier, this outcome would not have looked at all certain. Because the minsters ultimately went under, and at a point when our sources improve sharply, their continuing importance in the eleventh and even early twelfth centuries tends to be forgotten. In analysing change, we should start with the status quo.

However controversial earlier arrangements may be, there can be no serious doubt that the ordained priests who staffed tenth- and eleventh-century minsters performed pastoral care. The very names of some of the renders paid to minsters—'shrift-corn', 'light-dues', 'the mass-priest's dues'— are redolent of pastoral and liturgical contact between minster-priests and parishioners. Except where new churches were available as alternatives, the tenth- and eleventh-century English looked to minsters for their religious needs. Even in the twelfth century, when local records become numerous, the priests and owners of many ex-minsters were still struggling against the devolution to autonomous local sites of mass-performance, burial, and church dues.

If monastically and episcopally centred sources tell us extremely little about routine pastoral care, this may be because it was taken for granted. Even in the reformed houses, groups of priests coexisted with the monks and the laity had access to the monastic churches.[113] In the secular colleges of Christchurch (*c.*1090) and Waltham (*c.*1130), ordinary people made offerings

---

[113] Hase 1988: 62 n. 23; Rosser 1992: 270–1; Barrow 1996; Blair 1998*a*: 281; Yorke 2003*b*: 127–9, for the continuing public and pastoral role of nunneries.

on feasts and at normal masses; pots containing the laity's herbal remedies seem to have cluttered the altars of tenth-century minsters.[114] The impact of reform, disendowment, and pluralism on the pastoral efficacy (as distinct from the community life) of minsters is in fact very unclear. The problem is still much as for the pre-Viking period: texts focus on the status and assets of an elite, whether monks or prebend-holding priests, whereas day-to-day duties may always have fallen largely on a humbler and undocumented clerical stratum, the kinds of people who eventually emerge in the twelfth-century guise of vicars and chaplains.[115] Old ways of operating may have persisted much more successfully in local arrangements than at the level of formal tenure.

Like the other strands followed in this chapter, the fragments of evidence for pastoral care and social functions suggest that the transition from the 'age of minsters' to the 'age of local churches' was slow and tentative. Often up to 1100, and sometimes well beyond it, minster communities remained wealthy and parochially dominant, and their members had a special status and influence in local affairs. As acquisitive and litigious in their land-dealings as thegnly families, the tenth-century minster-priests at Horningsea (Cambs.) must have been prominent figures in the local society of shire and hundred.[116] So were their counterparts at Great Bedwyn (Wilts.), whom we find in the 930s witnessing manumissions and apparently writing documents for the local gentry.[117] In early eleventh-century Devon, slaves were ceremonially freed at crossroads after mass during summer, in the presence of 'all the minster-priests there' and possibly during mother-parish processions.[118] At Christchurch (Hants.) the narrative texts leave no doubt about the importance of its minster-priests in local religious life in the decades around 1100.[119] These are stray glimpses of an area of life which our mainstream monastic sources studiously ignore.

It is hard to measure how far people continued to see mother-churches as socially and devotionally important, even where the newer frameworks for religious practice were available to them. The five guilds whose tenth- and eleventh-century statutes survive were all focused on minsters: Great Bedwyn

---

[114] Below, p. 516; *Walt. Chron.* 66–8; Jolly 1996: 122, 148–9, 157, 161.

[115] Below, pp. 509–10. Early twelfth-century Waltham had 'two prebends which the canons had established from their own food-allowances for clerks who were to take turns at reading the Gospel at chapter masses, and who . . . were to be commissioned to organize or change the affairs of the church' (*Walt. Chron.* 70). In post-Conquest Beverley the vicars of the prebendaries had closely defined pastoral responsibilities (Palliser 1996: 212–14).

[116] *Lib. El.* 105–8, 420–1; above, p. 294.

[117] Meritt 1934; Dumville 1992*a*: 78–82, arguing that these memoranda date from the 920s–930s, and that Wulfgar's will (S 1533) was also written at Bedwyn; Pitt 1999: 144–5.

[118] Radford 1975: 6–7.   [119] Below, pp. 514–19; Hase 1988.

(Wilts.), Abbotsbury (Dorset), Cambridge, and (in two cases) Exeter.[120] These were lay associations, sworn to promote the welfare and drunken conviviality of their members, but religious functions were prominent: they returned members' bodies to the minster for burial, financed masses for their souls, and provided candle-wax or money at major feasts. Except for the federation of parish guilds in the later Exeter document, which linked rural communities to the cathedral by cutting across traditional parochial structures,[121] these bodies seem to have operated within the environment of the mother-parish. The continuities between such early religious brotherhoods and late medieval ones show how they could have kept devotion to minsters alive, not least through regular ritual and jollification at the ancient holy centres: much of our evidence for guilds before the thirteenth century comes from places that had been minsters. We have a vignette of the twelfth-century guild-brethren at Hartland (Devon): struggling to boil their pot in their house beside the graveyard of St Nectan's minster, then finding it occupied by the miraculous eel from St Nectan's holy well.[122]

The minds of guild-brethren, and Christians in general, must have focused on parochial loyalties at Rogationtide and the other great feasts of the year: did one celebrate and process with the greater community of the mother-parish, or with some nascent local one? On the Continent, Rogation processions could be used by the tenth century to affirm dependent communities' loyalties to their ancient mother-church,[123] and this principle underlies the 'recognition processions' to former minsters which are recorded after 1100, and which usually coincided with feasts on which processions were traditionally held.[124] At the old minster of East Dereham (Norfolk), a late eleventh-century visitor saw how

[120] Bedwyn: Meritt 1934. Exeter I: P. W. Connor, *Anglo-Saxon Exeter* (Woodbridge, 1993), 168–9. Abbotsbury, Cambridge, and Exeter II: B. Thorpe, *Diplomatarium Anglicum Aevi Saxonici* (London, 1865), 605–13; for Exeter II see also D. A. E. Pelteret, *Catalogue of English Post-Conquest Vernacular Documents* (Woodbridge, 1990), 110–14. For the character of the guilds see Rosser 1988a; Williams 2002: 22–4.

[121] The afterlife of these guilds can be traced in an episcopal mandate of c.1200 enforcing Pentecostal processions and oblations to Exeter cathedral, and ordering that every chaplain is to maintain a nominal roll of parishioners in each *mansio* in his parish, and be responsible on behalf of all who have a hearth and a means to pay for at least a halfpenny a head: F. Barlow (ed.), *EEA* xii: *Exeter 1186–1257* (Oxford, 1996), 170–1 (No. 188). This looks back to the statutes, which oblige the brethren to pay the canons yearly 1d. at Easter from each hearth. See Probert 2002: 146–8, 212, for the important conclusion that the Exeter guildships were specifically based at places *not* in Exeter's own mother-parish. [122] *Nectan*, 408–9. [123] Above, p. 225 n.

[124] In twelfth-century Hampshire, for instance, the inhabitants of chapelries attended the processions of their respective mother-churches at Winchester, Christchurch, Waltham, Southampton, and Carisbrooke: Biddle 1976b: 268–70; below, p. 519; *Winch. Acta*, 36 (No. 52); Hase 1988: 64 n. 34, 66 n. 71. The most common feasts were the dedication, Candlemas, the Ascension, Palm Sunday, and Pentecost. These cycles of processions to minsters should not be confused with Pentecostal processions to cathedrals, an apparently Norman innovation affirming episcopal authority (Brett 1975: 162–4; see however n. 121 above).

holy devotion had made a custom out of the rule that the people of Dereham and their neighbours should come together every year on the sixth day after the Lord's Ascension together with the priests and clergy, with banners and crosses, with candles and various offerings, and go in procession in sweet commemoration of their most kindly patroness Wihtburh, with inherited affection, and pray for her motherly aid for present and perpetual salvation, so that she might comfort her little family with more present affection.[125]

A glimpse of the division of the year into the 'ritual half' from Christmas to midsummer and the other, 'non-ritual', half[126] comes from Bampton (Oxon.), where the chaplain of a daughter-church founded *c.*1110–20 was obliged to attend the minster on a series of feasts starting with that of its own saint, St Beornwald, on 21 December and ending with that of its patron, St John the Baptist, on 24 June.[127] The sequence includes the Rogation days, implying that the chaplain was expected not only to visit Bampton but also to participate (leading his congregation?) in its processions. The exemption of the tenth-century ceorls of Hurstbourne Priors from work at midwinter, Easter, and Rogationtide looks like an earlier reflection of the same cycle,[128] and at Great Bedwyn in about 930 the mass-priest received a lamb or twopence from every two guild-brethren at Rogationtide, presumably for leading the procession.[129] The goods rendered by the king to Lambourn minster (which was dedicated to St Michael) at Michaelmas, Martinmas, and Easter[130] again suggest a sequence of festivals beginning with the patronal feast on 29 September.

These cycles of feasts and processions which embraced the whole mother-parish and emphasized its saints, and which communities from semi-devolved chapelries were encouraged or forced to attend, must have helped to retard the break-up of old devotional patterns. Compared with the examples just given, the restructuring of Rogationtide rituals at the level of the local parish is frustratingly elusive.[131] Some rural communities retained financial and practical duties to their old mother-churches centuries after they had acquired churches or chapels of their own.[132] What we cannot know

---

[125] Goscelin of Saint-Bertin, 'Vita S. Withburge', c. 5 (ed. Love 2004: 60–3).

[126] Bedingfield 2002 for the liturgical cycle from Christmas to Ascension Day; Phythian-Adams 1975: 21–5, and Hutton 1996, for folklorists' perspectives.

[127] F. Barlow (ed.), *EEA* xi: *Exeter 1046–1184* (Oxford, 1996), 24–6 (No. 25); cf. Blair 1994: 76–7.

[128] *RASC* 206. Cf. Wulfstan's comment that Easter, Rogationtide, and midsummer are the occasions when most people are gathered together: 'Canons of Eadgar', c. 54 (*C&S* 331–2).

[129] Meritt 1934: 345; see above, p. 440. The passage is ambiguous; common sense suggests that *gesamhiwen* should be translated as 'guild-brethren', not 'family members' or 'married partners', and that the text should be amended to *an geo[n]g sce[a]p*, 'a young sheep', not to Meritt's *an geo[n]g[or]scipe*, 'in discipleship'.   [130] Above, p. 449.   [131] Below, pp. 487–9.

[132] Below, p. 510.

is when, and how far, these ties lost their emotional force and became simply irksome.

Anecdotal evidence cannot really chart the varying gradient of allegiance between the centres and peripheries of mother-parishes. Even a very reduced minster would have been as important in 1100 to those who lived alongside it as it had been to their ancestors—it was their own local church—whereas inhabitants of peripheral zones in its former mother-parish might have lost interest in it completely. Other ex-minsters, by contrast, remained the ritual and devotional centres of multi-village territories down to modern times. In legal and institutional terms, the variation across the country between these two extremes reflects the broad geographical, demographic, and social patterns observed in the last chapter, though with anomalies conditioned by whether or not individual minsters had powerful protectors in the eleventh and twelfth centuries. Popular religious practice must have been moulded by this institutional framework, but is unlikely to have intermeshed with it straightforwardly. The emotional and spiritual hold of minsters could only be broken effectively once alternatives—more local, more convenient, and perceived to be at least as good—were on offer.

The local church as spiritual and social focus

The growth of such alternatives is most solidly, if indirectly, visible in the physical evidence of the church buildings and their churchyards, which in lowland England experienced a transformation during the eleventh century. The fabric of the small tenth-century timber churches was that of ordinary houses; the first Raunds church was rubble-walled but tiny, smaller than all but the smallest of the chapels of Atlantic Britain shown in Fig. 42. We do not know how any of these were finished or furnished, and their interiors could well have had a shrine-like atmosphere which set them apart; but their scale and technology was within peasants' everyday experience. The more permanent and aesthetically ambitious churches of the 'Great Rebuilding' must have had an impact hard to imagine today (Figs. 48, 49): they brought into the village a mode of architecture which for most people only existed at the local minster, or in the head town of the shire. They also introduced a clearer liturgical separation between clergy and people. In the primary one-cell church at Raunds, the priest at the altar was within touching distance of his congregation. The addition of an eastern cell around 1000 gave him a tiny presbytery to retreat into. But in a standard two-cell church of the mid eleventh century onwards (including the rebuilt Raunds) the eastern compartment was a fully-fledged chancel, removing both altar and celebrant out of the nave-space as in a great church.[133] It must indeed have seemed to local people that their community had acquired a 'little minster'. If imposing structures made religious sites more appealing (and in the early middle ages they generally did), the eleventh-century transformation of church buildings must have encouraged the re-focusing of loyalties.

It also seems likely that the rebuilt churches were conceived more clearly as community buildings, planned to accommodate the whole mass-hearing population as a primary rather than incidental function. In Worcestershire there is a broad correlation between the nave areas of Romanesque churches and the recorded Domesday populations.[134] This is perhaps a dubious calculation, since the more populous manors will have tended to be the more wealthy, capable of financing ambitious churches to raise their owners' prestige. Raunds, however, makes the practical impact clear. Twenty-nine people, more-or-less the adult population using the churchyard, could cram into the enlarged first church; the equivalent capacity of its eleventh-century replacement was 104, which must mean (unless there was some sudden influx of people) that everyone could now hear mass in comfort.[135] From the later tenth century the artistic repertoire of the great reformed churches gradually percolated to a more local level, and at least by c.1100 the naves of some ordinary two-cell churches were being enriched with elaborate painted schemes.[136] It is unknown how the interiors were organized, or whether they yet contained discrete altars for different parish groups,[137] but it is possible that provision of more space already encouraged the laity to think of the nave as 'theirs', as they would do by the end of the twelfth century.

In large churches by the tenth century, and even quite small ones from the 'Great Rebuilding', inscribed (and painted?) texts informed or inspired the literate.[138] The message on the south *porticus* arch at Breamore (Hants.), 'Her swutelað seo gecwydrædnes ðe' ('Here is made manifest the covenant to you'), evoked the rainbow of the covenant between God and Noah with its

---

[133] Boddington 1996: 22–5; Parsons 1986: 106–7 (which traces the further shift of the altar away from a position just east of the chancel arch towards the east wall). The 'Vision of Earl Leofric' describes the sanctuary fittings of a small church, St Clement's in Sandwich, around 1050 (Napier 1907–10: 184–6; Gatch 1993: 243–51). The altar stood away from the east wall, and in the space behind it, screened off by a heavy curtain, a cross stood on the floor on the north side, its base just visible below the curtain; Leofric and King Edward stood on either side of the sanctuary during mass.

[134] Bond 1988: 141–4. Some of the very small manors on the Surrey Downs had churches with conspicuously small naves: Blair 1991a: 134.   [135] Boddington 1996: 66.

[136] Gameson 1995: 245–8; Cather and others 1990, especially the contributions by Milner-Gulland, Taylor, and Park.   [137] But cf. Blair 1996c: 15, 17–18.

[138] Gameson and Gameson 1993: 1 and nn. 1–10; Gameson 1995: 70–6. The discoveries at Heysham (Potter and Andrews 1994: 117–21) show that high-status churches, even small ones, could have had painted inscriptions much earlier.

connotations of the Last Judgement.[139] By the later eleventh century, sundials and dedication inscriptions named patrons, priests, and masons, and fonts proclaimed the merits of baptismal washing.[140] It is unlikely, whatever view one takes of late Anglo-Saxon literacy, that such texts were accessible to most peasants. Yet they reinforce the sense of a thickening and a downwards percolation of literate Christian culture, founded on the buildings and endowments of the middle-ranking just as the birth of that culture had been founded three centuries before on the patronage of kings and nobles.

St Wulfstan's objection to the overshadowing nut-tree[141] implies some expectation, even at a local level, of the decorum befitting a sacred building. So, however unrealistically, does the programmatic literature. The altar is 'always to be clean and well draped and never soiled with mouse-droppings or with dung', all litugical fittings are to be kept clean, and a light should be kept burning in the church during mass.[142] Priests must not allow dogs, horses, or pigs within the churchyard (*binnan cyrictune*), and must refrain from wearing weapons in the church, or at least in the altar-enclosure.[143] Above all, they must restrain idle speech and behaviour in or near churches,[144] a point developed eloquently by Ælfric:

Christian men must often go to church, and one may not talk nor chatter inside God's church, because it is a house of prayer hallowed to God for the spiritual discourses. Nor may one drink nor eat foolishly inside God's house, which is consecrated so that one may partake of God's body with faith. But men very often behave foolishly, in that they will watch and drink madly inside God's house, and play disgracefully and defile God's house with scurrilous talking; but it would be better for them to lie in their beds than to anger God in that spiritual house. Whoever wishes to watch and to honour God's saints should watch in stillness and make no noise, but sing his prayers as well as he can; whoever wishes to drink and make a stupid noise should drink at home, not in the Lord's house.[145]

As well as implying that frivolous church attendance was seen as more of a problem than non-attendance, these comments suggest that churches had become public buildings to the extent of being used as taverns and club-houses, perhaps especially in the context of funeral wakes.[146] By barely

---

[139] Gameson and Gameson 1993, which suggests that major arches in other churches may have carried the same symbolism. See Okasha 1971: 56, for an alternative reading implying that the text continued, presumably on the facing arch. I am grateful to Matti Kilpiö for his comments.

[140] Okasha 1971: *passim*; Bond 1908: 107–13.   [141] Above, p. 382.

[142] Ælfric, 'First O.E. Letter for Wulfstan', c. 164; 'Canons of Eadgar', c. 42 (*C&S* 292–3, 328). Ælfric probably uses 'dung' figuratively, to mean general squalor.

[143] 'Canons of Eadgar', cc. 26, 46 (*C&S* 323, 329–30).

[144] 'Canons of Eadgar', c. 26 (*C&S* 323); cf. *Vercelli*, xx, ll. 5–7 (p. 332).

[145] *LS* xiii, ll. 68–86 (p. 288); 'Pastoral Letter for Wulfsige III', c. 105 (*C&S* 217–18).

[146] Below, pp. 503, 508; cf. Campbell 1986: 147.

visible stages, the emergent parish churches were becoming points for the orientation of rural life. Four sets of charter-bounds, one from 987 and the others after 1020, include 'church-ways' and 'church-paths' leading to ordinary local churches: a tiny glimpse of a new and smaller-scale ritual geography.[147]

A fundamental service which many local churches were discharging by c.1100 was baptism. Membership of the Christian people from infancy was assumed, and priests who failed to baptize newborn children were subject to penalties.[148] 'If an unbaptized child is brought suddenly to the mass-priest', urges Ælfric, 'he must baptize it immediately in haste, so that it does not die heathen.'[149] But where, around 1000, did this ceremony take place? Ælfric and the leechdoms mention the reservation of 'hallowed baptismal water', into which herb charms might be dipped.[150] Ælfric assumes that a church will have standing baptismal water, into which (*to þam fante*) oil is not to be put until a child is to be baptized,[151] though as usual he may have been thinking mainly of great churches. Like burial, baptism had a jurisdictional and topographical dimension: was it required simply that children should be baptized, or that they should be baptized in approved places?

The widespread use of monolithic stone fonts must indicate the stabilization of the baptismal rite in local churches. Anglo-Saxon fonts of any kind are, however, hard to find. The most convincing cases—though both open to dispute and both at major minsters—are Deerhurst (late ninth or early

[147] Manningford Abbots, Wilts., 987 (S 865: a footpath from Manningford church towards the east boundary); Newnham, Northants., 1021 × 3 (S 977, cf. Brown and others 1990–1: 97–8, 103: probably the way from Fawsley to Badby); Meavy, Devon, 1031 (S 963, cf. Hooke 1994: 199: a lane leading towards churches, Walkhampton and Sheepstor, in either direction); Evesham estates, Worcs. (S 80, S 1599, a forgery and a set of loose bounds, cf. Hooke 1990: 48–51, 410–12: a road from Pebworth to Church Honeybourne). One further set of bounds (S 1003, for Dawlish, Devon, in 1044, repeated *Regesta W. I*, 465 (No. 138); cf. Hooke 1994: 204–5) includes 'the street on the west side of St Michael's church'. Charford in South Brent (Devon) means 'church ford' (*P-N Devon*, i. 290).

[148] Ine, c. 2 (*Gesetze*, 90–1) imposes a heavy fine for failure to baptize within thirty days; Wulfstan seems initially to have followed this but then reduced the term to seven days, whereas his Northumbrian follower proposed nine: 'Canons of Eadgar', c. 15, *NPL* c. 10. 1 (*C&S* 319, 455; cf. Wormald 1999a: 397 n. 611). See Foot 1992a: 173–83 and Bedingfield 2002: 171–90, for the ritual and setting of baptism, and Page 1978 for vernacular rubrics for the rite. In the late Anglo-Saxon rite the child was dipped into the water three times (for the Trinity), and the priest put salt on the child's mouth: *Ælfric Supp.* xx, ll. 130–3 (p. 484); *Hom. Wulf.* viiib, ll. 22–4, 45–7 (pp. 172–3).

[149] Ælfric, 'Pastoral Letter for Wulfsige III', c. 71 (*C&S* 210). However, St Wulfstan had to baptize poor children whose own priests had demanded money: *Vita Wulf.* i. 7 (pp. 32–4).

[150] Jolly 1996: 95, 160, 164; see Jones 2001: 173–90, for these uses of *fantwæter*. Cf. Ælfric's story of a woman who dips her hair *on ðam fante* to work harm against her own children: 'Catholic Homilies', II. 2 (ed. M. Godden, EETS, ss 5 (1979), 15).

[151] Ælfric, 'Pastoral Letter for Wulfsige III', c. 129 (*C&S* 221); below, n. 162, for *fant* meaning 'baptismal water'.

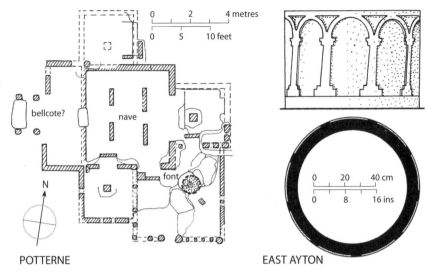

POTTERNE   EAST AYTON

52. Left: The excavated ground-plan of the timber church at *Potterne* (Wilts.), with an added *porticus* containing the impression of the stone font (after Davey 1964). Right: Drum-shaped font, probably eleventh-century, at *East Ayton* (Yorks.: author's survey).

tenth century?) and Wells cathedral (tenth century?).[152] A tub-shaped font of volcanic greenstone, whose fragments were re-used in the footings of a probably late eleventh- or twelfth-century chapel at Tintagel (Cornwall), might be claimed as pre-Conquest on these stratigraphical grounds.[153] At Barton-on-Humber the west *porticus* of the turriform church of *c.*1000 was equipped from the outset with a fixed font (of unknown construction) in one corner (Fig. 43).[154] Other excavated font-settings seem, however, to be entirely post-Conquest:[155] thus at Potterne (Wilts.) the surviving monolithic

[152] Bond 1908: 128, and Rahtz and Watts 1997: 146, for Deerhurst; Rodwell 2001: 149–60, for Wells. Views differ on whether the Deerhurst font was made as such (Carolyn Heighway and Richard Bryant pers. comm.), or whether it is recycled from a huge ninth-century cross-shaft (David Stocker pers. comm.; Drake 2002: 33). Several other fonts have been made, not necessarily at an early date, from Roman *spolia*, Anglo-Saxon cross-shaft sections, etc.: Bond 1908: 97–106, 129–31; Talbot Rice 1952: 147–8; Stocker 1997: 22–3.

[153] Thomas 1993: 108–9. This dating of the excavated structure is my own, not Thomas's: I believe it to be the chancel of a standard 'Rebuilding-period' chapel, and probably post-Conquest.

[154] Rodwell and Rodwell 1982: 298–9 and pl. XLIa. The excavation found the sub-base of the font with its construction pit and soakaway.

[155] At St Mary-de-Lode in Gloucester, the plaster setting for a font-base first appears in a late eleventh-century phase (Bryant and Heighway 2003: 117–22). In the small church of *c.*1100 at Bowthorpe (Norfolk), the font-drain was placed axially towards the west end of the nave, not in the integral round west tower (Beazley and Ayers 2001: 70–3), which weighs somewhat against the otherwise persuasive argument for west towers as baptisteries in Davidson 1998: 261–4.

font occupied a small annexe in the angle between the east and south *porticus* (Fig. 52), where its drain-pit has been excavated, but it seems unlikely that either the building or the bowl is much earlier than *c.*1100.[156]

English parish churches abound in relatively crude tub-shaped and drum-shaped fonts, which when they bear decoration, scenes, or (occasionally) inscriptions are evidently of the late eleventh or early twelfth centuries.[157] This raises a strong suspicion that the bowls which are perfectly plain, or have basic decoration such as cabling or arcading (e.g. Fig. 52), are not much older.[158] Monolithic fonts were probably an aspect of the 'Great Rebuilding' movement and became common when permanently built local churches did, during the later eleventh century. Portable containers of pottery, glass, or metal, which would have left no archaeological trace, could have been used earlier.[159] Some eleventh-century stone fonts seem from their shapes and decoration to imitate less permanent vessels: hoop-bound wooden tubs, and lead tanks with cable decoration.[160] The sixteen surviving twelfth-century lead fonts are distinctively English, and could be the tail-end of an older tradition.[161]

---

[156] Davey 1964. Note (ibid. 22) that the primary layer over the church site contained twelfth-century sherds; a building of this construction will have had a limited life.

[157] Bond 1908: 107–11, 131–43; Talbot Rice 1952: 158–51; Bond 1988: 149–50; Wrench 2003: 191, for the north. At Little Billing (Northants.), Potterne (Wilts.), and Partrishow (Brecon) are fonts bearing putatively pre-Conquest inscriptions referring to the makers or the baptismal liturgy, but only Little Billing has a serious chance of being earlier than *c.*1100: Okasha 1971: 97–8, 149. For a more optimistic view see Taylor and Taylor 1965–78: iii. 1064–5.

[158] Bond 1908: 125–6, and Stocker 1997: 21, suggest a pre-Conquest date for some others. But the view of Drake 2002: p. xv that 'almost no fonts survive which can safely be ascribed to the eleventh century' is supported by the occurrence of the compound *fantstan*, 'font-stone', only in post-Conquest texts: Jones 2001: 171–2.

[159] Early ninth-century Carolingian prescriptions, while preferring stone fonts, allow baptism to be performed with some other kind of vessel (*vas*) so long as it is reserved for this purpose: Haito of Basle, 'Capitula Ecclesiastica', c. 7 (*Capitularia*, i. 363); Leo IV, 'Homilia', c. 30 (ed. Migne, *PL* 115 (1881), col. 681). A word used twice by Ælfric, *fant-fæte* (literally 'font-vat': Jones 2001: 171), may be more appropriate to a metal container than to an immovable stone structure. An English scene of *c.*1000 shows Christ being baptized in a cauldron-like vessel (Wilson 1984: fig. 243).

[160] For stone fonts copying iron-bound casks, and Continental pictorial evidence for the use of barrels and cauldrons, see Bond 1908: 123–4, and Drake 2002: 1, 12, and pl. 3; some timber fonts survive in Norway (Drake 2002: 128–9). The striking popularity on Anglo-Norman stone fonts of the twisted rope moulding, which in architecture is only one in a repertoire of enriched mould-ings, may be a clue to lead prototypes: Roman and medieval lead coffins were often decorated by pressing actual ropes into the casting-sand (Weaver 1909: 208).

[161] Bond 1908: 77–87; Zarnecki 1957; Drake 2002: 170–4. The earliest surviving examples, prob-ably of the 1150s or 1160s, are very lavish and may mark the advent of rich decoration which caused them to be preserved later. There are late Romanesque lead fonts in Normandy, but one of them is cast from the same mould as an English font, and it seems likely that the fashion spread from England (Zarnecki 1957: 2–3). These fonts resemble in shape and size the circular lead baptismal tanks which are peculiar to late Roman Britain (Watts 1988), and which bear obvious Christian symbols: English ecclesiastics who found them could have identified them as fonts, and might have re-used or copied them. A number of ninth- to twelfth-century lead vessels with iron handles have

The possibility that small churches before *c.*1050 did have fixed containers for baptismal water therefore cannot be excluded. What seems certain, though, is that stone fonts rapidly became more widespread from that point onwards, and this in itself may tell us something about the growing importance of a fixed baptismal site at the heart of a churchgoing community.[162] Monolithic fonts may have appealed for their monumentality and fixedness, recalling fountainheads over holy springs. The infant St Rumwold, demanding baptism but spurning the 'urn or jar' offered by his father, pointed 'to a hollow stone lying not far off in a certain hut in the marshy valley nearby and ordered the servants who were standing around to bring it quickly and fill it with clean water'[163]—an episode which may reflect perceptions of the most appropriate kind of baptismal vessel when the story was written down in the mid eleventh century. It was perhaps then, at the same time as other conceptual shifts which this chapter tries to trace, that the parish font acquired its significance for the kindreds and successive generations who were baptized in it.[164]

Hierarchies between churches may be less at issue here than general ecclesiastical discipline over the laity. In England, unlike much of Europe, the right to baptize was never one of the central tests of independent parochial status, and there is no evidence that minsters claimed a monopoly.[165] It seems

been found, of which some are probably secular but others might have a liturgical function (Leslie Webster pers. comm. for unpublished finds; Weaver 1909: 20–2). A unique rectangular example found in the marshes of Willingdon (Sussex), now in Lewes Museum, bears on each long face an equal-armed cross enclosed by late interlace comparable to some early eleventh-century manuscript initials (Richard Gameson pers. comm.), and has sockets for iron hasps that could have held a lockable lid. The deposition of this and other late Anglo-Saxon lead vessels in marshes bears a curious resemblance to late Roman Christian votive practice (Petts 2003: 113).

[162] Here I am very grateful to Christopher Jones for discussing with me his work on the OE loan-word *font/fant* (now published as Jones 2001: esp. 164–70, 191–2), which, from a different starting-point, leads to a similar conclusion. No examples of the borrowing are recorded before the first half of the tenth century (the OE Bede, for instance, always uses a periphrasis or some native word such as *wielle*), and when it does appear in OE it seems generally to mean 'water(s)' or 'spring(s)' of baptism rather than a receptacle; nor is it clear that the term had popular currency before Ælfric adopted it around 1000.

[163] Love 1996: 100–2. (This passage is set at Kings Sutton: could it refer to the very strange font—gigantic, rough-hewn, and cut to a rudimentary cushion-capital form—which is still in the church there?) At about the same date, St Peter's minster at Northampton is envisaged as having a *baptiserium* with water standing in it: 'Inventio S. Ragenerii' (ed. C. Horstman, *Nova Legenda Anglie*, ii (Oxford, 1901), 729–30).

[164] Later in the middle ages, stone fonts, even if old and crude, seem to have been prized as enduring symbols of baptismal functions: they were often preserved through rebuildings, or ceremonially buried under their successors (Stocker 1997; Blair 1991*a*: 155).

[165] The dependent chapels of mother-churches often had Norman stone fonts: Bond 1988: 133 for Worcestershire; Blair 1991*a*: 52, 122, 155 for Surrey. Later medieval restrictions on fonts in chapels reflect the extension of universal Catholic discipline, and there is no evidence that they have any bearing on the English situation before 1100.

more important that the rite was now monumentalized, at a permanent stone structure within the walls of a church. While there is no means of proving that priests had previously baptized the laity at outdoor holy wells, it seems not unlikely; this practice, and that of filling fonts from holy wells, are recorded later in remote parts of Britain and may be archaic survivals.[166] Rather as a saint's shrine inside a church could be controlled as an open-air holy site could not, the rise of fixed internal fonts placed the rite of Christian initiation in the power of specific priests and specific lords. In giving the laity one more reason to regard a local church as 'theirs', the font within had a similar function to the family graves that were now accumulating outside the walls.

Changing burial practice in post-Viking England

The growth of churchyards, another step in the shift towards a more local parochial culture, happened against the background of structural changes to how burial was organized. In England it was pre-eminently the right to receive corpses which became the battleground and the test of status once different kinds of church began to compete for the allegiance of lay communities, and new manorial priests sought to bolster their meagre incomes with mortuaries. 'Some priests are glad when men die', complained Ælfric in about 1006, 'and they flock to the corpse like greedy ravens where they see a carcass, in wood or in field; but it is fitting for him to attend the men who belong to his parish at his minster; and he must never go into another's parish to any corpse, unless he is invited.'[167] Eadgar's concession of limited tithe-rights to the thegn's church with a graveyard is the first sign of this emerging politics of burial, which would have some bizarre manifestations in the twelfth to fourteenth centuries.[168] The tenth century may have been the first time when English people at large were told where they had to be buried.

The regulation of burial follows the broad tenor of change in the tenth- and eleventh-century English Church, but as so often it was Carolingian

[166] Quiller-Couch and Quiller-Couch 1894: 7, 8, 45, 67, 117, 124, 161, 182, 189, 203; Hope 1893: 83–4, 165, 169–70; Rattue 1995: 66–8. For instance, at Bisley (Surrey), parishoners were still baptized in St John the Baptist's well, not far from the parish church, into recent times (Blair 1991*a*: 111); at Halton (Lancs.) in the nineteenth century the baptismal water was brought to the church font from St Wilfrid's well (H. Taylor, 'The Ancient Crosses of Lancashire', *Trans. Lancashire and Cheshire Antiquarian Soc.*, 21 (1903), 89).

[167] Ælfric, 'First O.E. Letter for Wulfstan', cc. 182–4 (*C&S* 295–6); cf. his 'Pastoral Letter for Wulfsige III', c. 111 (*C&S* 218).

[168] Blair 1988*b*: 13; Blair 1985*b*. Below, pp. 518, 522 for examples of mother-church claims to receive corpses.

models that gave it definition and authority. From the mid ninth century, Frankish ecclesiastics were increasingly insistent that clergy should direct the practice and location of burial, and that the laity should be buried at their own proper churches.[169] The archaeological evidence suggests that by the tenth century these more prescriptive attitudes were being accepted in lowland England, whereas the old, unregulated practices of burial by family or neighbours continued in Wales and Cornwall.[170] Where the new principles applied, they brought with them a new definition of consecrated ground. 'Christian burial', near a place sanctified by relics or the mass, was of course centuries old by 900; but the bounded, exclusive plot of ground consecrated by a bishop, in which all faithful were to be buried and from which religious and social undesirables were to be shut out, had apparently not yet been invented. The conception reflects Continental notions of the inclusive Christian state, but the region of tenth-century northern Europe with the greatest political capacity to put ideals into practice (in this respect as with church dues) was England.

It is therefore less surprising than it might seem that the first European reference to consecrated ground for burial comes from Wessex, in a law of Æthelstan (*c.*930) which forbids an unreconciled perjurer to 'lie in a hallowed graveyard' (*ne binnon nanum gehalgodum lictune ne licge*).[171] Further, there are grounds for thinking that the liturgy which bishops used to consecrate graveyards, first known from pontificals of around the 970s, may have had an English origin; at all events the earliest extant European manuscripts are no older than the English ones.[172] The general lack of English liturgical books from the early to mid tenth century leaves the origins of the rite obscure, but if there were 'hallowed graveyards' in Æthelstan's Wessex there must have been some means of hallowing them. In this context, the consecrated cemetery can be seen as another instrument for defining and controlling the religious affiliations of the laity.

---

[169] Treffort 1996*a*: 165–7; cf. Hincmar's comment, above, p. 245. Paxton 1990: 127, 196–200, discusses the late Carolingian extension of death and burial liturgies to a wider lay community.

[170] Above, p. 63, for Wales. The most useful Cornish site is Mawgan Porth (Bruce-Mitford and others 1997: 63–70, 87–9), where a cemetery of perhaps some fifty long-cist graves lay 30 m. from a small tenth- and eleventh-century settlement. The excavators suggest a lost chapel, but there is no evidence for this, and the site is perhaps best interpreted as a lay cemetery which never *acquired* a chapel because it was abandoned in the eleventh century and masked by wind-blown sand. Cf. Fry 1999: 43–6, for non-church-associated burial in Ireland continuing into the late middle ages.

[171] II As. 26 (*Gesetze*, 164); Wormald 1999*a*: 307, for the date and possible context of this clause. See Gittos 2002*b*: 205–8, for the likely influence of Irish concepts of demarcated sacred space.

[172] Gittos 2002*a*: 55–61; Gittos 2002*b*: 195–201. Treffort 2001 comes independently to the same conclusion, which is endorsed by Zadora-Rio 2003: 12–13.

By the later tenth century it seems that churchyards normally had demarcated boundaries,[173] and the liturgies are notable for their stress on the exclu-
sivity of the zones thus enclosed. The bishop walks clockwise around the
perimeter, aspersing the cardinal points. His prayers emphasize that the
faithful who have been baptized, and have followed the Catholic faith
throughout their lives, can await the last trump there immune from all evil
influences.[174] This message of promise combined with exclusion drove a
wedge between Christian and unhallowed burial which is also visible in the
archaeological record. On the one hand, old secular burial locations which
were honourable but informal disappeared. Small, isolated groups of orientated and properly composed graves seem, on present radiocarbon evidence,
to occur only rarely after the earlier tenth century.[175] Evidently it was becoming unacceptable for Christians to be buried in their back yards, on hills, or
in ancient barrows and earthworks. This marks the final break with the
pre-Christian tradition of lay-controlled cemeteries, chosen more for their
ancestral or status associations than because the Church had blessed them.
Archaeology thus agrees with the legal and liturgical evidence in suggesting
an environment that was less informal, more tightly controlled, and more
conditioned by ecclesiastical as against traditional secular values.[176]

The other side of this coin was the proliferation of cemeteries that were
overtly shameful, servicing the penal system of an increasingly interventionist state, but located in just the kinds of places that had often been
chosen for elite seventh-century burials.[177] Groups of disordered corpses,

[173] Examples of excavated boundary fences and ditches are at North Elmham, Raunds, and
Trowbridge: Wade-Martins 1980: 185–6; Boddington 1996: 14; Graham and Davies 1993: 37–9.

[174] Gittos 2002a: 52–5; Gittos 2002b; Treffort 2001: 288–91, 297–9. In a similar spirit, according to William of Malmesbury, Dunstan enclosed the monks' cemetery at Glastonbury to make it
like 'a delightful meadow, free of the noise of any footstep. Truly can it be said of those who rest
here in their holiness: "Their bodies are buried in peace"': 'Vita Dunstani', i. 16 (ed. M.
Winterbottom and R. M. Thomson, *William of Malmesbury, Saints' Lives* (Oxford, 2002), 204–6).

[175] Above, p. 244. A cemetery at Lewknor (Oxon.) (Fig. 31) produced radiocarbon dates in the
ninth to tenth centuries (Chambers 1973, Chambers 1976), one at Kempston (Beds.) in the tenth
to eleventh (Dawson 1999). Cemeteries at Milton Keynes (Bucks.) and Fillingham (Lincs.) have
produced tenth- to early eleventh-century dates (Parkhouse and others 1996; Buckberry and Hadley
2001), but since both were axially aligned on nearby parish churches it seems likely that they were
under ecclesiastical control.

[176] For changing burial practices during the ninth to eleventh centuries (specifically in northern England) see Hadley 2000b and Hadley 2002a. A theoretical archaeological model, drawn from
a totally different cultural context (the Lower Illinois valley), 'links the development of specialized,
permanent and bounded areas for exclusive disposal of the dead to ritual affirmation of corporate
group control of crucial, restricted resources': J. E. Buikstra and D. K. Charles in Ashmore and
Knapp 1999: 203. This seems apposite to late Anglo-Saxon England, with its 'cellularization' and
growing pressure on resources.

[177] Reynolds 1998; Reynolds 2002; Semple 2002: 331–58; Semple 2004; cf. Geake 1997: 5, and
above, pp. 53–4. Reynolds's latest work modifies an earlier impression that special execution cemeteries were a tenth-century innovation. Nonetheless, the clear bipartite contrast between consecrated

some decapitated or with dislocated necks or bound hands, are now attested from the seventh century onwards but seem most prominent in the tenth and eleventh. They are often on hundred boundaries, and some overlie pre-historic barrows. Once, some such places had held the ambiguous associations of a pagan, but heroic and ancestral, past. By 1000 they seem to have been re-defined uncompromisingly as profane wastelands, fit only for the corpses of the condemned and lost: several execution cemeteries appear in charter-bounds as 'heathen burials', presumably in contrast to the 'Christian burials' of consecrated churchyards. Exclusion strengthens definition: by the mid tenth century, popular perceptions of the places in which baptized and law-abiding people could reasonably assume they would await the Last Judge-ment must have become sharper.

Nonetheless, in an age of complex transition from regional to local struc-tures the location of Christian burial might not be clear-cut. It was clearly not the case that everyone who died at peace with Church and law could expect, as of automatic right, to be carried to his or her parent minster. The early eleventh-century guild statutes of Abbotsbury and Cambridge oblige members to fetch home the body of a deceased brother, and in the former case this was explicitly to 'the minster' (though the steward's duty of finding out where the dead man had wished to be buried implies that other options remained possible).[178] While illustrating the continued importance of minster burial, this leaves one wondering what happened to the corpses of people who could not afford to belong to guilds. Mother-churches will have been more interested in receiving soulscots than corpses, and only interested in the corpses of those too poor to pay soulscots if allowing their burial else-where threatened vested rights. Nor is it obvious that minster communities will have relished giving house-room within their precincts to a steady flow of very plebeian corpses.

To solve this problem while safeguarding mother-church rights, licensed 'overflow' cemeteries had a place. In the 1090s all inhabitants of Milford (Hants.) were to be buried at Christchurch minster, except slaves and cottars who could be buried at Milford chapel on payment of 4d.; the only people who could be buried at Boldre, another of Christchurch's chapels, were

churchyards and 'heathen' burial-places after the 930s reflects greater regulation and a more uncom-promising ideology. It followed contemporary demands by the Frankish Church, beginning with the Council of Rheims in 900, that certain offences should be punished by publicly shameful burial (Treffort 1996*a*: 157–63), but in England it was also the instrument of a formidable criminal justice system. I am very grateful to Andrew Reynolds for discussions on this subject. Cf. Wormald forth-coming: ch. 9.

[178] Above, p. 454; Rosser 1988*a*: 31; Williams 2002: 23–4. I am grateful to Victoria Thompson for comments on this point.

'cottars and slaves of the land on which that church is founded, who were so poor that they did not have enough resources from which they could be carried to Christchurch'.[179] Something similar must be recalled in the thirteenth-century verdict that all landholding persons within a wide range of Pershore minster (Worcs.) were buried there, whereas the landless, for whom no mortuaries were payable, were buried at Little Comberton.[180] There was a satellite cemetery with hundreds of burials at Chimney (Oxon.), three miles from Bampton minster and on land granted to the Bampton clergy in the 950s, where radiocarbon dates from the skeletons fall between the mid tenth and mid eleventh centuries.[181]

On the other hand, the graveyards around some minsters continued to expand. Radiocarbon or stratigraphical dates falling between the late ninth and late eleventh centuries have been obtained from the outer zones of minster churchyards at Shipton-under-Wychwood (Oxon.), Crayke (Yorks.), North Elmham (Norfolk), and Pontefract (Yorks.).[182] It is notable that dates *after* the mid eleventh century seem uncommon from these outer zones, and that in all the cases just mentioned, as in several of the eighth-century minster cemeteries, the churchyard boundaries contracted again later.[183] Expansion and intensification of minster burial may be quite a specific phenomenon, happening at a time when general population growth coincided with a realization by the minsters that they must assert their rights or risk losing them. After 1000 the proportion of burials diverted to the new churchyards must have grown rapidly, and it was perhaps this which in turn caused the minster graveyards to shrink again.

The progressive shift from minsters to local churchyards is easy to observe, but hard to quantify or date: what proportion of thegns' churches in, say, 1000 had graveyards? Here the only measure, setting aside a very few excavations, is minor monumental sculpture, and this shows a fairly clear pattern. Up to 950 a variety of sculpture traditions, their spread stimulated by the Viking elites' rapid move to churchyard burial in late ninth-century

---

[179] Below, p. 518; Hase 1988: 56.

[180] *VCH Worcs.* iv. 162–3; Bond 1988: 133. Exactly this had been envisaged by Hincmar (cited Treffort 1996*a*: 166 n. 7) when he directed that each chapel 'atrii habeat, ubi pauperculi, qui suos mortos longius effere non possunt, eosdem ibi sepelire valeant'.

[181] Crawford 1989; Blair 1994: 73.

[182] Blair 1994: 66; Adams 1990; Wade-Martins 1980: 185–9; Roberts 2002: 73–4, 401–4. In the British west, the same phenomenon can be seen at Crantock (Cornwall) and Llandough (Glam.): Olson 1982; Selkirk 1996.

[183] Above, pp. 241–2. This phenomenon of churchyard contraction deserves further study. Zadora-Rio 2003: 13–16, suggests that in France—and perhaps by implication in England—it should be ascribed to changing conceptions of space, resulting in a smaller, more clearly bounded and more intensively used burial area, rather than to a declining burying population. On the other hand, the fact that the known English cases are nearly all minsters tends to favour the other explanation.

Northumbria,[184] were active in the north and midlands.[185] The later tenth century saw a new departure, with stereotyped grave-crosses and cover-slabs being produced on an altogether larger scale along the eastern edge of the limestone belt, notably in Kesteven, Lindsey, and the fens, culminating in the crude but prolific eleventh-century Barnack series.[186] In the south-east there was no significant slab or marker tradition before *c.*1000, but two localized eleventh-century groups, one in east Surrey and the other in west Sussex, use the local Greensands for rough, simple monuments in obscure little churchyards.[187] The established sculpture-producing zones of east Yorkshire, Durham, Northumberland, and the north-west did not, however, experience the post-950 boom in mass-produced stone grave-markers to anything like the same extent.[188]

Where it exists in quantity, this memorial sculpture is conclusive evidence for at least some local churchyards. Clearly a site with tombstones had burial rights, and it is probably right to assume that it had a church too (or just possibly that burial was an immediate and conscious prelude to church foundation): these monuments hardly ever occur outside later churches and churchyards.[189] In Lincolnshire, with its prolific tradition of post-950 mass-produced slabs and markers, some 15 per cent of medieval parish churches have sculpture from between the mid tenth and mid eleventh centuries; around Sleaford the proportion is as much as two-thirds, and north of Lincoln the sculpture reveals the distinctive 'ladder pattern' of parishes starting to form.[190] The Barnack and fenland groups, and to a lesser extent the crude south-eastern groups, likewise show the production-line dissemi-

---

[184] Above, p. 321. The Scandinavian contribution to this process needs to be seen against the background of the furnished Viking-age burials, some in churchyards and some not, which have been found scattered across England, with a concentration in the north-west (Wilson 1967; Biddle and Blair 1987; Biddle and Kjølbye-Biddle 1992; Hadley 1997: 89–92; Halsall 2000; Hadley 2002a: 214–28; Richards 2002: 157–65). What needs emphasis here is that these accurately reflect, on the present argument, the situation in late ninth-century England *in general*: a rapidly growing but still not exclusive preference for churchyards. By contrast the sculpture-marked graves were (so far as we know) in churchyards, the choice both of location and of monument suggesting correspond-ingly greater integration into Christian culture.   [185] Bailey 1980a; Lang 1984.

[186] Fox 1920–1; Butler 1964: 112–13; Tweddle and others 1995: 82–3; R. Cramp in Boddington 1996: 107–12; Everson and Stocker 1999: 46–7, 83–7; Stocker 2000: 180–3, 199–200; Stocker and Everson 2001.   [187] Tweddle and others 1995: 22–3, 82–8.

[188] Maps in Lang 1991: 6, Cramp 1984: 6, and Bailey and Cramp 1988: 4; Stocker 2000: 191–2; cf. *VCH Cheshire*, i. 276–8. It is notable that although these areas contain Anglo-Scandinavian hogbacks and small crosses, representing a considerable expansion from pre-Viking production, only York city has a tradition of mass-produced post-950 slabs and markers comparable to the east midlands traditions. The north-east did, however, have a tradition of small upright stones with crosses through the ninth to eleventh centuries: Cramp 1984: 7.

[189] R. Morris 1989: 153, which I find more persuasive than the contrary arguments of Everson and Stocker 1999: 72.

[190] Everson and Stocker 1999: 35–62, 76–80; Stocker and Everson 2001: 227–9.

53. Centralized burial and funerary commemoration: piled-up fragments of late Anglo-Saxon grave-markers at *Bakewell* minster (Derbs.).

nation of cheap monuments to a wide range of relatively unimportant sites in the late tenth and eleventh centuries. The zone in which there were enough small graveyards by *c.*1000–50 to create a mass-market for tombstones of minor gentry or clergy status can thus be defined as easterly England between the Humber and the Thames. By contrast, the phenomenon is apparent neither in the north, with its rich Viking-age sculpture tradition, nor in central Wessex, where manorial churches are again recorded relatively early.[191] The obvious conclusion is that minsters' burial-rights only collapsed on this scale in Lincolnshire, East Anglia, and the east midlands, where other evidence suggests that their rights in general had been eroded particularly heavily.[192]

But the destination of much of the sculptors' output was still the old minsters. Indeed, there is a clear tendency for many of the larger groups of post-900 slabs and crosses to occur at major pre-Viking sites: Bakewell (Derbs.),

---

[191] Above, pp. 385–6. Availability of stone can scarcely be invoked to explain these differences. The fens and Barnack products were disseminated widely into East Anglia, and similar workshops would surely have appeared in the Cotswolds if there had been a comparable demand in Wessex and the west midlands.   [192] Above, pp. 315–20.

Lastingham (Yorks.), Lowther (Westm.), and Lindisfarne (Northumb.) are among the more obvious cases (Fig. 53).[193] In Lincolnshire, maybe 40 per cent of surviving late pieces are at minsters.[194] Furthermore, the range and quality of material from minsters and from small churches is not—occasional prestige items apart—significantly different: the same workshops were supplying the whole market with the same basic products. While some of these memorials (especially at the minsters) were probably for clergy, many of them must have commemorated people of minor thegnly rank, of whom some were buried in their own graveyards but others still at the minsters. This is hardly surprising: local churchyards were not all founded at once, and there must always have been a tension between the prestige of minster burial—especially for old families with ancestral tombs—and the urge to found a mausoleum at the new family church. The law of 1008, or soon afterwards, which enforces payment of soulscot to the minster when the corpse was buried 'outside the proper parish'[195] may have been specifically with an eye to people of this kind, whose soulscots were worth fighting for even if their funeral instructions were hard to overturn.[196]

It looks as though stone monuments in local churchyards may largely commemorate the manorial family (or families, where lordship was divided): the quantity of material is rarely enough to suggest that a larger social group was involved.[197] At Wharram Percy (Yorks.) a cluster of eleventh-century slab-marked graves near the south-east corner of the chancel are surely those of the squire and his relatives.[198] A substantial thegn with several churches might choose to make one of them the site of his family tombs. Domesday Book lists six churches on the Hampshire and Berkshire manors held in 1066 by Cypping, and at one of the most valuable, Stratfield Mortimer, his son Æthelweard was buried under a big inscribed slab.[199]

[193] Cramp 1977: 218–25; J. Hawkes and P. Sidebottom, *Corpus of Anglo-Saxon Stone Sculpture VIII: Derbyshire and Staffordshire* (forthcoming); Lang 1991: 167–74; Bailey and Cramp 1988: 127–33; Cramp 1984: 194–208. Cf. above, pp. 311–16.

[194] Everson and Stocker 1999: 76 (50%); Stocker and Everson 2001: 226 (35%).

[195] Above, p. 444.

[196] Above, pp. 446–7, for the fluidity implied by the references to soulscot in wills. In the 1080s Steyning successfully asserted its burial rights (above, p. 450); Taunton claimed that the lords of its dependent territories were obliged to be buried there (DB Exon. 174); and the bishop of Worcester argued that tenants at Hampton owed churchscot and burial to his vill of Cropthorne (*Lawsuits*, i. 39 (No. 15)). But it is impossible to know how many minsters were able or concerned to enforce their rights so rigidly.

[197] Everson and Stocker 1999: 77: 'monuments like the mid-Kesteven covers . . . , or the Lindsey covers, or the South Kesteven shafts, may well have been the typical memorials to the late tenth-century resident aristocracy . . . [I]t is conceivable that the monuments belong to the parochial church founders themselves and are overt signs of those foundations.' Cf. Stocker and Everson 2001: 224–5.

[198] Bell and Beresford 1987: 56–8 and pl. VIA; Lang 1991: 222–3.

[199] Lennard 1959: 291; Tweddle and others 1995: 335–7. The slab can be dated stylistically to somewhere in the eleventh century; the inclusion of the patronymic in the epitaph suggests that

Even in small churchyards, space may have been structured to express hierarchy. At Raunds[200] the earliest burials (apparently from *c*.1000) were laid
out in orderly rows, arranged symmetrically around the church and leaving
a reserved strip against its walls. Two graves with decorated slabs lay not far
from the south-east corner of the chancel (Fig. 46), one in a reserved area
and probably with a standing cross at its head. Other evidently high-status
graves, including one in a stone coffin and several in wooden coffins, clustered in the same privileged zone immediately south-east of the church. Later,
infant burials encroached on the reserved strip,[201] and graves spread in less
regular rows to the boundaries of the churchyard, which was full and in the
first stages of re-use when burial stopped around 1100. Raunds is unique in
its completeness and fine detail, but elsewhere there are hints that monuments such as standing crosses were located to articulate space. At Brattleby
(Lincs.) a big cross stands in the centre of the churchyard, south of the church
and in line with its chancel arch, conceivably projecting across the churchyard the liturgical boundary between clergy and laity, or the social one
between lords and tenants.[202] Such arrangements, like the grouped churches
of split East Anglian townships, suggest that the formal planning of pre-
Viking minsters[203] was replicated in miniature by the 'still smaller minsters'
of the late tenth and eleventh centuries.

The landscape of ritual and cult: continuity and innovation

If the stabilization of baptism and burial at local churches was often achieved
through 'churchsoke' in the jurisdictional sense, it must in turn have encouraged 'church-seeking' in the spiritual and ritual sense. But we should not
envisage a religiosity focused exclusively on any church. People who had previously looked to their minster as the source of pastoral care, the regulator
of the ritual year, or the shrine of the local saint, may still have made more
regular day-to-day use of trees, springs, barrows, and other unofficial cult
sites surviving in the landscape. These habits are likely to have survived the
shift to local churches: lords wanting to exert discipline through their
churches, and bishops wanting to iron out unorthodox practices, had to

Æthelweard may have died before his father. The choice of Stratfield Mortimer, rather than Head-
bourne Worthy (with its impressive Crucifixion sculpture) which Cypping also held, must have
been a matter of personal preference.

[200] Boddington 1996: 36–7, 47–54; note the revised dating above, p. 391 n.
[201] This looks like a case of the widespread practice of burying infants under the eaves-drip; see
Wilson 2000: 216, for the idea that water running off the church roof conveyed some kind of
posthumous baptism.   [202] Everson and Stocker 1999: 70.
[203] Above, pp. 200–1, 398–9.

confront them. Even if they were merely an impediment to parochial formation—a rival system defying emergent church-centred loyalties—they
would be relevant to this chapter. But perhaps they had a more positive contribution. As an expression of long-standing solidarities in agricultural communities, popular social ritual and cult may often have been the foundations
on which new parish solidarities would be built; and there are indications
that both clergy and people assimilated them to the new order more easily
than we might expect.

To an extent, the new and more regulatory local structures must have
grown at the expense of other options: sacred springs could no longer be used
to baptize those entering the community, or ancient earthworks to bury those
leaving it. Intensified lordship may also have encouraged a privatization of
ritual space, noticed above in the building of churches over wells, barrows,
and Roman sites.[204] But perhaps these last cases are the most tangible examples of a wider pattern, one of assimilation rather than suppression. Fiscal
and jurisdictional control is achieved all the more easily when combined with
cultural tolerance. The best way to neutralize rival sources of spiritual power
was to re-label them as Christian, and then to encourage their incorporation
into rituals which the churchgoing body performed and their priests supervised; conversely, a new church was surely the more acceptable to its parishioners once they were convinced of its compatibility with older cultic sites
and activities.

In such a milieu the claims of elite and vernacular religion, and of lordship and collective action, could coexist and eventually grow together rather
than stand in rivalry to each other. The possibilities are illustrated by a region
of modern Mexico, a traditional society about as far from its own initial conversion as the eleventh-century English were from theirs, which has similarly
acquired parish churches against a background of older and more decentralized sites. Here standing wooden crosses identify a hierarchy of shrines at the
ceremonial nodes of social units, ranging from the individual household to
the entire *municipio*. Crosses also mark sacralized natural features, notably
mountains, caves, and water-holes, which are considered access-points to the
divine. Both the appearance of these shrines and the rites performed at them
are outwardly Christian, though the same can hardly be said of the underlying belief-system revealed by anthropological fieldwork.[205] This is a society

---

[204] Above, pp. 376–8.
[205] Vogt 1976: 6, 44–50; Vogt 1981. From Vogt's photographs of solemn-looking people kneel-
ing on the steps of tall crosses and offering prayers and incense, one would never guess that these
devotions are for the Earth Lord who lives underground riding a deer, or for ancestor-gods who
live in the mountains, eating their tortillas as the candles burn and smoking their cigarettes as the
incense rises.

where churches and Christianity have been imposed onto, but also assimilated into, a robust animistic cosmology.

To investigate whether late Anglo-Saxon England was anything like this we need to look both at the traditional sacred sites in the landscape and at those which had an explicitly Christian character, and to ask whether these were overlapping or mutually exclusive groups, whether they show similar or contrasting locational patterns, and whether the former were compatible or incompatible with parish-based religious discipline. The starting-point is the broad repertoire of originally pre-Christian sacred sites which repeats itself in animistic and polytheistic cultures the world over: deep places (caves, pools, springs), high places (hill- and mountain-tops), woods, trees. What is interesting is not that these sorts of places existed in England—it goes without saying—but how they related to their natural and cultural settings, how they changed over time, and how much room was made for them in 'official' Christian practice.[206]

The end-point is the much better-documented parish religion of the late middle ages. By then the kind of sacred geography that was earlier centred on minsters had been widely replicated at the smaller scale of the local parish, for instance in 'churchway paths', or in the crosses where Rogationtide processions paused to read the Gospel. Recent work, notably Gervase Rosser's, suggests not only that sub-parochial chapels were far more abundant than was previously thought, but also that they were more diverse in origin, many of them continuing to 'develop' long-standing cult places in the way described in the last chapter.[207] It has also emphasized the dynamic contribution to late medieval parochial life of 'voluntary' elements such as guild activity and communal chapel foundation, while at the same time noting official disapproval of do-it-yourself cult sites.[208]

This ambivalence, already visible in the late Anglo-Saxon sources, shows the tensions and overlapping loyalties of a society where 'unaltered' sacred places identified solely by lay devotions may always, down to the Reformation and sometimes even later, have been more common than we can ever know. Sites revered in folk-belief and those revered within a Christian framework were not discrete chronological layers: there was a very long continuum in which the first might or might not be converted to the second,

---

[206] A properly contextualized study of Anglo-Saxon sacred sites would need to take account of multiple regional variations in patterns of settlement, land-use, and territoriality: the present survey cannot be other than superficial. The sensitive account of sacred sites in the Mediterranean and its micro-regions in Horden and Purcell 2000: 403–60 illustrates what might be possible for England.   [207] Blair 1988*b*: 15–17; Blair 1991*a*: 154–7; Rosser 1991; Rosser 1996: 76–7.
[208] Rosser 1996: 77–9; Rosser 1991.

but either could be created or abandoned.[209] How flexible this process may in practice have been is illustrated by Heiki Valk's study of Estonia, on the late-converted periphery of Europe, where the official framework of parish churches, cemeteries, and chapels coexisted until recent times with a parallel sacred geography of stones, springs, and other natural sites. Communities, and individuals within them, believed simultaneously in the Christian system and in the minor supernatural beings of such places, so that 'the same congregation members who visited churches on Sundays made offerings to holy stones and house spirits'.[210] Late Anglo-Saxon England offers some hints at the same kind of protracted interpenetration—occasionally tense, perhaps more often tranquil—of official and vernacular modes of religious practice.

The conceptual geography of sacred centres and dangerous margins may have changed little in essentials through the Anglo-Saxon period: the wastes beyond the settled land, where there are bottomless meres and haunted barrows, are delineated in similar terms in 'Beowulf' and in post-medieval folklore.[211] But it is unlikely that centre/periphery and sacred/profane contrasts were incapable of readjustment, or that there was a consistent relationship between the forms and the ascribed functions of monuments. Anthropological studies have shown that people can invest landmarks with qualities—divine, magical, demonic, or social—which, though widely recognized, are both individual and flexible. Thus a community in rural Anatolia ascribes coexistent and shifting meanings, rather than fixed and exclusive ones, to the mounds and stones which surround its village: 'the archaeological landscape acts as a number of mnemonic points for individual and collective representations, and it is not always certain which particular mound or artefact will spark a response, nor that it will always be the same response.'[212]

Responses in the Anglo-Saxon countryside could well have been like this. Nonetheless, the gradual imposition of a Christian ideology must have caused wedges to be driven at certain points, splitting off sites that could be assimilated or accepted from those that were to be branded diabolical. This applies especially to the barrows and other ancient earthworks which, in the sixth and seventh centuries, had often been re-used for the graves of communities

---

[209] There were certainly some very late Christianizations of 'pagan' landmarks, such as menhirs, in which the perceptions of paganness were not necessarily very old either: Grinsell 1986.

[210] Valk 2003: 577.

[211] Semple 1998; Hope 1893: 71–2, 95–7, for late traditions of bottomless and diabolically haunted meres; Wilson 2000: 10–11, for the essential ambiguity of the 'wild margins'.

[212] Shankland 1999: 145. This is the kind of attitude that Effros 2001 recognizes in the re-use of Roman monuments in Gaul.

and elites. The transfer of regular burials to churchyards, leaving the old sites for the graves of criminals and outcasts, must have been an important stage in the marginalization of such landmarks from lay cult practice, and the accentuation of demonic as against ancestral or community associations. In such a desolate place the narrator of 'The Wife's Lament', perhaps a damned spirit, is forced to dwell: 'among a thicket of trees under an oak-tree in this earthen dugout (*eorðscræfe*). Ancient is this earthern abode (*eorðsele*), . . . the fortresses (*burhtunas*) grievously overgrown with briars, their habitations void of pleasures'.[213]

But old monuments in places set apart could have very different functions, as solemn sites for deliberation and judgement. At least for the laity, the contrast between these negative and positive attributes may have been less problematic than it seems to us: if communicating with the dead was one way of gaining wisdom, haunted mounds and moot-mounds were not necessarily exclusive categories.[214] Tyler Bell's locational analysis of Roman remains associated with churches or Anglo-Saxon burials shows not only that nineteen (out of a total of some 340 sites) adjoin parish boundaries, but also that nine of these are precisely where three or more parishes meet.[215] In some cases (including the *halig stow* at Fawler[216]), the boundary makes a kink from its natural line to touch the Roman site. This pattern cannot be coincidental, and implies that the Roman remains had some kind of focal significance, whether socially, economically, or topographically, for groups of estates or townships. Some of these may have been segments of earlier entities, in which case the Roman sites were originally central rather than marginal. On the other hand, Aliki Pantos's recent work on assembly-sites shows that hundredal and sub-hundredal meeting-places were often in just these kinds of places, perhaps considered common to all the interests involved but particular to none.[217] The importance of Bell's examples is to suggest that sites with ascribed ritual associations—either from burials in the past or from contemporary or future churches—could also be legal centres for groups of neighbouring communities. They illustrate a larger category of sites—shrine and meeting-place in one—which helps us to understand why one contemporary conceived the stopping-points of Rogationtide parish processions as 'spiritual moot-sites'.[218]

In the Christian context, a wide range of sites were considered 'holy' because of what saints did there, whether in life by performing miracles or

---

[213] R. F. Leslie (ed.), *Three Old English Elegies* (Manchester, 1961), 47–8; I follow here the interpretation of Semple 1998: 110–11. The idea of damnation implied by burial location is developed by Semple 2002: 331–58 and Semple 2004; cf. above, pp. 465–6.

[214] Semple 1998: 117–18; Pantos 2002: 96–104.   [215] Bell 2001: 211–23.

[216] Above, p. 377.   [217] Pantos 2002: 129–34.   [218] Below, p. 487.

receiving divine instructions (such as the many wells which burst forth when they prayed), or in dying by sanctifying the place with their blood (such as the lush grass on Oswald's death-site, or the hair that grew from the turf on Wigstan's).[219] Inherent in these stories, which are mainly versions of ubiquitous folklore motifs, is a deep ambiguity: does power reside in the saint or in the place?[220] A landscape feature which a saint creates, such as a well or tree, is by nature immovable, though it can provide relics in the form of water or shavings. Such legends had the potential both to Christianize existing sites of numinous power and to create new ones, and they suggest that a holy site required supernatural sanction, not simply the Church's approval and blessing, to be popularly regarded as such. Their ready incorporation into hagiography does not point to stress between elite and popular cultures, but on the contrary to a willingness on the part of local minster-priests to play the game by rules which their lay flocks would have understood.[221]

This interplay between educated Christianity and folk-belief is best illustrated by holy trees and holy wells, two ubiquitous kinds of site which span the whole range from overt paganism to full integration. Special trees could be assimilated to Christian culture through the hagiographical device of saints planting them: thus staffs driven into the ground by Aldhelm, Cynehelm, and Eadwold sprouted miraculously into huge ash-trees.[222] Disaster awaited anyone who felled the ashes in St Nectan's grove at Hartland (Devon).[223] As late as the 1680s a naturalist saw St 'Bertram's' (Beorhthelm's) ash-tree 'that growes over a spring which bears the name of the same Saint, in the parish of Ilam' (Staffs.), and found that 'the common people superstitiously beleive, that 'tis very dangerous to break a bough from it; so great a care has St Bertram of his Ash to this very day'.[224] In twelfth-century legend

---

[219] *HE* iii. 10 (p. 244); W. D. Macray (ed.), *Chronicon Abbatiae de Evesham* (Rolls Ser. 29, 1863), 332–4.

[220] At Belchamp Otton (Essex) a cross is made from a tree which grew where St Æthelberht pitched his tent, and set up on the same site; a nobleman tries to move it to his house, but it returns twice overnight and on the third attempt strikes him blind (Gerald of Wales, 'Vita Regis et Martiris Æthelberti', cc. 15–16: ed. James 1917: 233–5). This is a version of the much more common Spanish myth in which a statue of the Virgin Mary is found in an inaccessible cave and taken down to the local church, but insists on being venerated where found. As William A. Christian, Jr. puts it: 'The return of the image to its natural setting is the image saying: "No. I am not a relic; think again. Holy people you can move; I am showing you a holy place. You must face me there"' (Christian 1981*b*: 21). The rood dug up at Montacute (Somerset) might seem an exception; but it is *the rood itself* that decides to move to Waltham, and the smaller cross found with it is left behind (*Walt. Chron.* 2–16).

[221] Smith 1990: 326, 335, 342–3, makes a similar point with reference to Brittany.

[222] *GP* 384–5 (identified there as Bishopstrow by Warminster, i.e. 'ad episcopi arbores'); Love 1996: 58; C. Horstman (ed.), *Nova Legenda Anglie*, i (Oxford, 1901), 362–3.

[223] *Nectan*, 410.

[224] R. Plot, *The Natural History of Staffordshire* (Oxford, 1686), 207. For St Beorhthelm's cult see Blair 2002*a*: 515–16.

the site of King Oswald's martyrdom at Oswestry (Salop.) was marked by a spring and a health-giving sacred ash-tree, 'Oswald's tree'; a raven carried one of Oswald's arms to the tree and then dropped it, causing the spring to burst forth.[225]

The resonances of Woden/Oðinn, who (at least in his later Scandinavian guise) hung on a 'windy tree' and was associated with ravens, are unlikely to have escaped any late Anglo-Saxon mind. The ash was in fact the archetypal sacred tree of northern paganism,[226] and the recurrent choice of it in hagiographies shows beyond reasonable doubt that these associations were a veneer on a pre-Christian substratum. Sometimes the veneer was thin or non-existent. 'Holy trees' in place-names were not necessarily holy in the Christian sense, as becomes startlingly explicit when the charter-bounds of Taunton (Somerset) mention the 'ash-tree which the ignorant call sacred'.[227] It is worth pondering why the bishops of Winchester, who owned Taunton at the time, did not feel obliged to have it felled. That was exactly the response of a fourteenth-century bishop to a tree at Bisham (Berks.) containing the nest of a tame bird, where people left offerings in return for eye cures in the nearby well; yet even in the nineteenth century, great thorn- and oak-trees loomed over holy wells in Cornwall.[228]

Also in the case of the wells, but still more clearly, folkloric perceptions of their healing or miraculous powers coexisted with a long tradition of linking them to saints.[229] The Christianization of wells and springs had been a missionary device since Gregory of Tours,[230] and the prominence of wells associated with saints in eleventh- and twelfth-century English hagiography suggests that late Anglo-Saxon clergy encouraged the practice. But the 'holy' springs and streams of charter-bounds and place-names were not necessarily Christian, as is explicit in the case of those associated with goblins and auguries.[231] Incorporation continued: if 'St Helen's Wells' could originate as

---

[225] Rollason 1989*a*: 127; Stancliffe 1995*b*: 86–96.

[226] Davidson 1988: 170, 179. The world-tree Yggdrasil is repeatedly called an ash. Given the magical associations of elder (above, p. 380), it is interesting that St Cuthmann used it to make his prophetic cart-ropes (Blair 1997: 189).

[227] Smith 1956: i. 225; S 311: 'ad quendam fraxinum quem imperiti sacrum vocant.' This charter is a forgery, extant in a twelfth-century manuscript, but its bounds, like detailed charter-bounds in general, are presumably of pre-Conquest composition.

[228] Rattue 1995: 86; Quiller-Couch and Quiller-Couch 1894: 19, 169, 175–6.

[229] This paragraph owes much to Rattue 1995, where more evidence will be found.

[230] P. Brown 1996: 110.

[231] Six charter-bounds contain *(on) halgan wylle* and variants, sometimes in contexts indicating streams rather than springs (S 1819, S 310, S 352, S 615, S 961, S 1556); Smith 1956: i. 225, for the term in place-names. Names including *succa* and *puca*, 'goblin', and *freht*, 'augury', are: *scuccan hlaw, sceoca broces forda* (S 138, S 387); *pucan wylle* (S 108, S 508); and Fritwell, Oxon.; cf. Rattue 1995: 41–2, and Blair 1994: 18. For associations of severed heads with wells see Stancliffe and Cambridge 1995: 102–3, 170–1, 190–1.

Christian rationalizations of folklore during perhaps the tenth and eleventh centuries,[232] 'Lady Wells' may show the impact, from the twelfth century onwards, of the rising cult of the Virgin as a vehicle for assimilation, rather as do the miraculous Madonnas of Spain.[233] But it is unlikely that the non-Christian associations either died out or ceased forming. A high proportion of 'holy' wells and springs remained the property of supernatural forces other than Christ, his mother, or the saints: almost down to modern times, beliefs about healing and nature-spirits have been pinned on these most resilient of all sites of animistic power.[234]

The simple and obvious way to re-incorporate a sacred tree, stone, or other feature was to mark it with a cross, presumably to the accompaniment of suitable ritual.[235] Even a new free-standing cross may have seemed essentially similar, in scale and proportion, to traditional kinds of cult monument, which suggests one reason why crosses multiplied so readily.[236] The central question for present purposes is whether they were vehicles for new conceptions of articulating the landscape, or perpetuated old ones. Anglo-Saxon stone crosses away from church sites are very rare, but where they do survive in situ they seem normally to mark nodal points such as summits or junctions. The opulent eighth-century Lypiatt cross (Glos.) stands nearly a mile north-west of Bisley minster, at the point where the parish boundary crosses the Stroud–Bisley road.[237] The 'Elloe Stone' at Moulton (Lincs.), a large cross of *c*.1000, stood in an enclosure in the middle of a broad green lane on a parish boundary, and was the court site both for its wapentake and for crown pleas in southern Holland by the late middle ages.[238] There is a notable group of late Anglo-Saxon crosses in the upland parts of east Cheshire, Staffordshire, and Derbyshire, mostly on trackways, crossroads, and township bound-

---

[232] Above, pp. 379–80.

[233] Christian 1981*a*: 21. Cf. Walsham 1999: 227–31, for the incorporation of English wells continuing up to the end of the middle ages.

[234] Hope 1893 and Rattue 1995 for many examples. In the nineteenth century St Nun's Well in Cornwall was also known locally as the Piskies' Well, and an old man told a folklorist that pins were thrown there 'to get the good-will of the piskies' (Quiller-Couch and Quiller-Couch 1894: 179). See however the important reassessment of holy wells in post-Reformation England by Walsham 1999, who points out (pp. 238–46) that the purging of Catholic theology, combined with continued popular interest in hitherto Christianized wells, could have generated neo-magical and -folkloric practices which can be confused with pre-Christian survivals. The antiquity of specific 'unincorporated' sites should therefore not be assumed from late folklore evidence alone; it is nonetheless hard to doubt that there was, in general terms, a continuum in popular interest.

[235] Above, p. 227.   [236] Cf. Flint 1991: 257–63.

[237] Bryant 1990: 44–6. It was definitely in its present position by 1654.

[238] Everson and Stocker 1999: 70, 162–4; Pantos 2002: 338–9. Given that this cross looks like a standard south Kesteven grave-marker, there must be an element of doubt about its original location and function.

aries, and often very prominently sited on high ground in open moorland.[239] But were they instruments for defining emergent parishes?

In southern England and the south midlands, where crosses were presumably of timber and never survive, there are fourteen occurrences of *cristelmæl* (crucifix)[240] in charter-bounds from the 940s onwards, and a few others in place-names.[241] The strong impression given by this (admittedly small) corpus is that they generally stood on relatively important roads, especially where these crossed rivers or high ground.[242] The pattern suggests that they were not in the first instance boundary-markers (there should be many more such references if they were), but appear fortuitously through the incorporation of such nodal points in estate boundaries. This interpretation is reinforced by the uniquely informative physical evidence from Cornwall, which had a prolific tradition of virtually indestructible wheel-headed granite crosses from the late ninth century onwards. During the eleventh to thirteenth centuries, simple crosses were produced in their hundreds to mark routes, especially those leading to churches, and perhaps every church site, often standing prominently at the churchyard gate.[243] Where Cornish crosses

---

[239] *VCH Cheshire*, i. 275, 281 and works sited there. The Cleulow cross, on a hilltop mound at the head of a valley with wide views over Staffordshire and Cheshire, is a particularly striking case which may be compared with the 'Elloe Stone'. Several of the St Buryan crosses mark routes across unenclosed rough ground: Preston-Jones and Langdon 1997: 113, 121.

[240] The use of this term (literally 'Christ-image'), as against *rōd* or *rōd-tacn*, suggests an actual crucifix figure rather than merely a cross. The Old English Bede translates the description of Augustine's arrival, 'crucem pro vexillo ferentes argenteam et imaginem Domini Salvatoris in tabula depictam' (*HE* i. 25, p. 74), as 'bæron Cristes rode tacen sylfrene Cristes mæl mid him' (*OEB* 58).

[241] Charter-bounds: Christian Malford, Wilts., 940 (S 466); Buckland Newton, Dorset, 941 (S 474); Blewbury, Berks, 942 (S 496); Hawkridge, Berks., 956 (S 607); Perranzabuloe, Cornwall, 960 (S 684); Washington, Sussex, 963 (S 714); Newnham Murren, Oxon., 966 (S 738); Grimley, Worcs., 961 × 72 (S 1370, S 201, the latter a forgery); Nackington, Kent, 996 (S 877); Shipton-on-Cherwell, Oxon., 1005 (S 911); Shellingford, Berks. (S 1546, loose bounds); Bremhill, Wilts. (S 1575, loose bounds); Tardebigge, Worcs. (S 1598, loose bounds); Stoke Prior, Worcs. (S 60, an eleventh-century forgery). Place-names (references in E. Ekwall, *The Oxford Dictionary of English Place-Names* (4th edn., Oxford, 1960) and the relevant EPNS volumes): Christmas Hill, Warw.; Kersham Bridge, Devon; Kismeldon (Bridge), Devon. A field-name *Cristesmel* in Finstock, Oxon., occurs *c*.1160 × 90 and on the tithe-map (*Eynsham Cartulary*, i, No. 131, and information from Rosamond Faith).

[242] Of the fourteen *cristelmæls* in charter-bounds (above, n. 241), one was on a headland, two on fords, and five on routes (a *stræt*, a *herepæð*, a *hricg-weg*, a *stan-weg*, and a *mær-weg*); the phrase in S 738, 'andlang mær wege þæt up on wearddune þær þæt cristel mæl stod', indicates a notable landmark. Topographical analysis suggests that at least three of the remaining six (including S 911, on the main Woodstock–Bicester road and overlooking the Cherwell) stood on through-roads not mentioned in the charters. Cornish *crous*, 'cross', in the St Keverne bounds of 967 was on a stream and may have marked a crossroads or beacon (S 755; Hooke 1994: 38–9).

[243] Thomas 1967*a*: 86–100; Thomas 1978; Preston-Jones and Rose 1986: 159–60; Preston-Jones and Langdon 1997: 115–21, for the most recent attempt at a chronology. Thomas's map of Camborne shows the crosses mostly on routes radiating in to the central church, none on the parish boundary.

seem *not* to concentrate is on parish boundaries, as St Buryan illustrates very strikingly: nearly all its forty-two crosses were at intersections of tracks or streams with the main routes to the central church, but only one on the parish boundary, and none at all in the tenth-century charter-bounds which describe it.[244]

The hagiography, with its emphasis on saints' journeys in life and the landmarks created by them on the way, or on their journeys in death and the miraculous happenings at points where the corpses were set down,[245] strengthens this impression that routes were particularly important in ideas of the sacred landscape. Thus St Cuthmann's trail across west Sussex was marked by the stone near Bosham where he sat as a youth (known for its healing miracles), the meadow in the Arun valley where mowers laughed at him (cursed with rain in the mowing season), the spot where the ropes of his cart broke (Steyning minster), and the hole where his adversary Fippa was swallowed by the earth (Fippa's Pit).[246] The late Malmesbury tradition that a series of stone crosses along the Fosse Way marked the stages of Aldhelm's funeral procession in 709 illustrates (whether accurate or not) a conceptual link between the wayside crosses and the saint-legends.[247]

This siting of crosses and other ritual landmarks along routes, or at crossroads, fords, and the like, looks essentially traditional. The punctuation of long-distance tracks with holy trees, cairns, or other monuments is widespread in prehistoric cultures and modern indigenous ones,[248] and illicit rites at points along roads, such as crossroads, bends, and forks, are among those

---

[244] Preston-Jones and Langdon 1997: 111–13; Hooke 1994: 22–7. (See, however, Turner 2003: 187–9, which re-states the case for crosses as boundary markers in Cornwall.) St Buryan may be compared with the areas perambulated by the Ascension Day processions (*troménies*) of Brittany, for instance Gouesnou, which has crosses along the radial roads to the central church as well as around two phases of the *minihi* or zone of sacred space (Tanguy 1984). In the Welsh legal ritual of setting a cross on disputed land (Roberts 2001: 311–12), it was a token of the claim but not, apparently, a boundary marker.

[245] Cuthmann and Frithuswith are good examples of the first motif, Æthelberht, Cynehelm, Freomund, and Rumwold of the second: Blair 2002a: 484. The 'course of the hind' at Minster-in-Thanet (above, p. 144) is one exceptional case of an English saint-legend that does involve delineating a boundary.   [246] Blair 1997.

[247] *GP* 383–4. William of Malmesbury says that Bishop Ecgwine had set the crosses up along the funeral route (thirty-four miles from Doulting to Malmesbury, mainly on the Fosse Way and passing through Bath); that many miracles have happened at the crosses, all of which still stand; that they are called 'biscepstane, id est lapides episcopi'; and that one can be seen in the cloister at Malmesbury. A (rather unconvincing) attempt to identify them is [Browne] 1904–8; the most likely candidate still extant is the large cross of which fragments are now in Colerne church, though that dates from nearly a century after Aldhelm. Whether or not they were from Aldhelm's time, there seems no reason to doubt that William knew a series of Anglo-Saxon stone crosses standing along the Fosse Way at intervals of a few miles.

[248] The point comes out repeatedly in the essays in Carmichael and others 1994 and Ashmore and Knapp 1999.

most regularly condemned in early medieval Europe.[249] As in some more recently converted societies, it looks as though standing crosses and saint-associated landmarks were a new way of labelling old sorts of sites.[250] This is certainly not to say that they all replaced pagan equivalents: sacred marking of the landscape was probably as fluid as society itself, evolving as economic and social needs changed between the fifth century and the twelfth or later.[251] The point is not that individual sites remained static, but that—even when the grammar was becoming explicitly Christian—the same broad vocabulary continued to be used. If crosses in the landscape testified to a more thoroughly Christian society such as the late Anglo-Saxon homilists aspired to, they were apparently not instruments for delimiting its new territorial boundaries.

So familiar kinds of ritual marker were increasingly understood in a Christian context: saints' wells, ash-trees grown from their staffs, posts and pillars in the guise of crosses. These inclusive practices are not quite so remote from the hard-line principles of lawmakers and homilists as they initially seem. It is obvious that no official response to sites defined as 'pagan' could be other than hostile; what is striking is that in England the hostility seems so muted. The Christian tradition, from Caesarius of Arles onwards, of attacking veneration of wells, trees, and stones is notably absent until it appears at full blast around 1000 in the linked writings of Ælfric and Archbishop Wulfstan.[252] In 1005 × 8 Wulfstan wrote:

And it is right that every priest zealously teach the Christian faith and entirely extinguish every heathen practice; and forbid worship of wells, and necromancy, and auguries and incantations, and worship of trees and worship of stones, and that devil's craft which is performed when children are drawn through the earth, and the

---

[249] Flint 1991: 204–7; Wilson 2000: 40, 211, 215–16, 297, 354, 456.

[250] Above, n. 205, for Vogt's work on Mexico. O. V. Ovsyannikov and N. M. Terebikhin in Carmichael and others 1994: 72–81 discuss the nineteenth-century Christianization of the Samoyed clans in the Arctic tundra: crosses supplanted an earlier set of sacred markers, but were also set up on new sites of economic importance (e.g. fishing-shores or fields) or by houses. In both societies the pattern is fluid, and responsive to changing needs. Cf. the miraculous Marian images of rural Spain, 'discovered in the wild world at logical places for supplication and propitiation of the outside forces', and 'a kind of encoded recapitulation of the process by which rural pre-Christian notions of a sacred landscape reasserted themselves': Christian 1981*b*: 18–20, 149, 212–13.

[251] For the mutability of sacred landscapes in the Mediterranean, and the embeddedness of ritual space in patterns of production and distribution, cf. Horden and Purcell 2000: 403–11, 450–60. Note also Valk 2003: 578, on Estonia: 'It is possible to speak of the spatial expansion of non-Christian cult sites in the Christian Period: holy stones, trees or groves also exist in villages of medieval or post-medieval origin.'

[252] Cf. Flint 1991: 36–84, for the background tradition, and above, p. 226, for its invisibility in pre-Viking England. Re-working the 786 legatine statutes in the 940s, Archbishop Oda omitted, presumably as irrelevant, the clauses against heathen practices (*C&S* 68). For Ælfric's use of Caesarius and the Pseudo-Ecgberht Penitential see Meaney 1984: 129, and Meaney 1992: 110–11.

nonsense which is performed on New Year's day in various kinds of sorcery, and in sanctuaries (*on friðsplottum*) and at elder-trees, and in many various delusions in which men carry on much that they should not.[253]

In a similar vein, Ælfric complained that

some men are so blinded that they bring their offerings to an earth-fast stone, and also to trees and to well-springs, just as witches teach, and will not understand how foolishly they act, or how the dead stone or the dumb tree can help them, or give them health, when they themselves never stir from the place.[254]

A possible stimulus for these statements (one which may underlie the law against idol-worship—the first in England for three centuries—which Wulfstan drafted in 1020/1[255]) is the influx after *c.*990 of recently pagan Danes. But essentially we should see them in the general context of these authors' urgent demands for English society to clean itself up before Antichrist's imminent coming,[256] and not as evidence for rampant paganism. In any case, even Ælfric seems to have seen the merits of incorporation. He considered it diabolical to use magic, but legitimate to use the God-given powers inherent in nature and in holy things.[257] 'No Christian man is allowed to fetch his health from any stone, nor from any tree, unless it is the holy cross-sign, nor from any place (*stowe*), unless it is the holy house of God.'[258] In their cosmological basis the distinction between right and wrong rituals is profound, but Ælfric's formula opens the way for a substitution of symbols which could have left actual lay practice virtually unchanged. So easy a route to legitimization had precedent as well as convenience on its side: tenth-century reformers had read Bede, and knew Pope Gregory's advice to adopt existing cult places. A ritual landscape sown thickly with unacceptable sites of magical power could not be obliterated, but the sites could be made acceptable. If country people scraped moss from a stone or a tree, what better than to build a church or crucifix in the same place and let them scrape

[253] 'Canons of Eadgar', c. 16 (*C&S* 319–30; 319 n. 4 for sources and parallels). The slightly later 'Northumbrian Priests' Law' imposes a penalty 'if there is on anyone's land a sanctuary (*friðgeard*) round a stone or a tree or a well or any such nonsense': *NPL* c. 54 (*Gesetze*, 383; *C&S* 463).

[254] *LS* xvii, ll. 129–35 (pp. 372–4). This passage is based on the 'Pseudo-Ecgberht Penitential', II, 22, with echoes of Caesarius of Arles: A. L. Meaney, 'Ælfric's Use of his Sources in his Homily on Auguries', *English Studies*, 66 (1985), 486–7.

[255] II Cn. 5. 1 (*Gesetze*, 312; *C&S* 489): 'It is heathen practice if one worships idols, namely if one worships heathen gods and the sun or the moon, fire or flood, wells or stones or any kind of trees in woods.' The 'Northumbrian Priest's Law' (*NPL* c. 48: *Gesetze*, 383; *C&S* 461) also condemns 'worship of idols'. Cf. Eaton 2000: 94–110, for the suggestion that Roman altars deposited in church foundations may have been neutralized in this way because they had been appropriated for pagan worship or folk-magic.

[256] Below, n. 285.   [257] Jolly 1996: 72–95, for a survey of his views; cf. Flint 1991: 309–14.

[258] Ælfric, 'Catholic Homilies', I. 31 (ed. P. Clemoes, EETS ss 17 (1997), 450). Cf. Meaney 1984: 129–30.

moss from that? The story of St Wulfstan and the nut-tree suggests that some eleventh-century bishops took a severer view; but there is an ideological context here for the adoption of informal cult sites into the Church's official framework.

The rituals and folk-magic which centred on such places, and gave them their significance, were themselves an area of negotiation between normative Christianity and popular belief. In this period as earlier, official responses to ostensibly syncretic practices wavered between condemnation and assimilation. Ælfric deplored divinations and lot-casting (except in purely secular contexts), superstitions connected with propitious and unpropitious days, necromancy and clairvoyance, certain sorts of amulets, and in general the activities of 'wizards' and 'witches'.[259] To create an all-embracing Christian society it was essential to remove competitors, such as the wise-men and wise-women who may still have been popular in the countryside.[260] The attacks of Ælfric and Wulfstan on 'heathen songs' and drunken festivities at wakes and on feast-days[261] veer further across the boundary between sacred and secular, into jollifications (for instance by religious guild-brethren?[262]) which may have been raucous and unseemly, but were probably in no way pagan. A Christian reformation of manners, which would suppress alternative forms of social co-operation as well as alternative belief-systems, remained the ideal that it had been for Alcuin, but was a long way from reality.

In practice, injecting Christian doctrine into popular ritual involved compromising with vernacular tradition. This is especially clear from the surviving tenth- and eleventh-century remedies and charms, preserved principally in the 'Leechbooks' (*c.*900) and the 'Lacnunga' (*c.*1000).[263] Just as Ælfric allows a Christian to 'fetch his health' from a cross or a church, so these texts legitimize folk-magic by encapsulating it in a Christian framework. For example, a 'drink for a fiend-sick man' is made from herbs, church lichen, and lichen from a cross, has seven masses and three psalms sung over it, and is drunk from a church bell.[264] By such means some unpromising practices are brought within the Christian pale, such as the chanting of incantations

---

[259] Meaney 1984.   [260] Ibid. 135.

[261] 'Ælfric's Pastoral Letter for Wulfsige', cc. 112–13 (*C&S* 218); 'Canons of Eadgar', cc. 18, 68 (*C&S* 321, 335–6). These follow Carolingian attacks on *carmina diabolica* at wakes, e.g. Leo IV, 'Homilia', c. 40 (ed. Migne, *PL* 115 (1881), col. 681). Cf. Fry 1999: 81–8, for the ambivalent ecclesiastical responses to wakes and 'keening' in Ireland.   [262] Cf. Rosser 1988*a*: 32–3.

[263] Both edited in *Leechdoms*. The following owes much to the analysis of Jolly 1996, which I find helpful and, in its main lines, convincing. See also Meaney 1981: 38–65, for a discussion of the evidence for herb amulets in the medical texts, and Flint 1991: 115–16, 301–28. A similar incorporation of nature-magic, at a similarly late stage in the conversion process (in Mexico), is described by Gruzinski 1989: 120–1; see Wilson 2000: 20–4, 66 f., for some other cultures.

[264] 'Leechbook', I. 63 (*Leechdoms*, ii. 136–8); Jolly 1996: 147–8.

against ailments caused by elves, the writing on dishes of sacred words that are then washed off into the patient's drink, and the placing of concoctions on and under altars (which conjures up some bizarre images of church interiors).[265] It is unclear how far the surviving texts indicate practice in small rural churches: the manuscripts mainly come from Winchester, and the frequent references to multiple masses and daily hours imply large churches with books and well-formed liturgical routines.[266] No doubt less acceptable charms were used in the countryside but never written down, but the recasting of mainstream doctrine and observance in the idiom of traditional folklore, evident from the charms which we do have, must be more than just a literate fiction.

A text of around 1000 known as *æcerbot*, explaining 'how you may better your fields if they will not grow well or if some harmful thing has been done to them by sorcery or poison',[267] illustrates vividly how Christianity and folk-magic could fuse in envisaging supernatural protection of space. The petitioner cuts by night a sod from each of the four sides of the land, mixes oil, honey, yeast, and produce from the land with holy water, drips it three times on the bases of the sods, and repeats in Latin 'Grow and multiply and fill the earth, in the name of the Father and Son and Holy Spirit be blessed', and the Lord's Prayer. The sods are then carried 'into church, and let a mass-priest sing four masses over the sods, and let someone turn the green [sides] to the altar, and after that let someone bring the sods to where they were before, before the sun sets'. Laying a quickbeam cross marked with an Evangelist's name in each of the four holes, the petitioner says 'crux Matheus, crux Marcus, crux Lucas, crux Sanctus Iohannes', replaces the sods, repeats 'Crescite' and the Lord's Prayer nine times, turns to the east, bows nine times, and recites an English verse invoking God and St Mary to fructify the land. After repeating a sequence of standard liturgical prayers he commends the land 'to Christ and St Mary and the Holy Cross for praise and for worship and for the benefit of the one who owns that land and all those who are serving under him'. After boring a hole in his plough-beam he puts in incense, fennel, hallowed soap, and hallowed salt, and sets unknown seed

---

[265] 'Lacnunga', c. 76, 'Leechbook', I. 62-4 (*Leechdoms*, iii. 52-4, ii. 134-40); Jolly 1996: 138-9, 119, 147-9. It is interesting to compare these prescriptions with practices that still occurred at Cornish holy wells into the nineteenth century, such as divining the future by floating a rush cross on the surface of the well while reciting a verse, drawing sickly children through and around the water, or throwing a frantic person into the well and then taking him to church for masses to be said over him: Quiller-Couch and Quiller-Couch 1894: 13, 27-8, 55-6, 132, 137, 165, 171-2.

[266] Here I differ from Jolly 1996, who is more inclined to see the charms as the formulations of local priests rooted in peasant life.

[267] Ed. G. Storms, *Anglo-Saxon Magic* (The Hague, 1948), 172-87. See J. D. Niles (ed.), *Old English Literature in Context* (Cambridge, 1980), 44-56; Wilson 2000: 11-16, for several analogies for this charm in later popular culture.

provided by beggars on the plough. At this stage he recites another vernacular verse:

> Erce, Erce, Erce, earth's mother,
> May the all-ruler grant you, the eternal lord,
> fields growing   and flourishing,
> propagating   and strengthening,
> bright shafts,   millet crops,
> and broad   barley crops,
> and white   wheat crops,
> and all   earth's crops.
> May the eternal lord   grant him,
> and his holy ones,   who are in heaven,
> that his produce be guarded   against any enemies whatsoever,
> and that it be safe   against any harm at all,
> from poisons   sown around the land.
> Now I bid the Master,   who shaped this world,
> that there be no speaking-woman   nor artful man
> that can overturn   these words thus spoken.

As the ploughman cuts the first furrow he again invokes mother-earth's fruitfulness. A loaf baked from each kind of flour, and kneaded with milk and
holy water, is laid under the furrow as the field is blessed in God's name, and
the charm ends with threefold repetitions of 'Crescite', 'In nomine patris sitis
benedicti Amen', and 'Pater noster'.

Modern readers will notice first the magical and folkloric content of this
performance, but its liturgical borrowings and Christian cosmology are no
less remarkable. Power is indeed, as Ælfric had insisted, derived firmly from
God and his saints, who make mother-earth fruitful and protect it from
poison and witchcraft. It is meaningless here to try to distinguish 'pagan survivals' from 'Christian accretions', as Karen Louise Jolly has observed:

> Saints' relics, churches, and crosses sanctified the landscape, displacing or trans-
> forming pagan sites. Likewise in the charm remedies, holy water, prayers, the sign
> of the cross, and written liturgical formulas brought out the hidden virtues of herbs
> long known to have curative powers if properly prepared. The Christian charms were
> a logical product of the meeting of these two traditions . . . In the variety of ways
> that they combined folk practice and Christian ritual, the elf charms represent the
> literate edge of an ongoing acculturation process . . . [A]s liturgy got into the charms,
> and elves got into the liturgy, Christianity prospered and Anglo-Saxon traditions
> survived.[268]

---

[268] Jolly 1996: 171–4.

One form of Christian 'magic' has a direct bearing on parish origins. The clearest expression of communal religious activity in the landscape was the Rogationtide liturgy, the invocation of God's blessing on the spring crops which had strong undertones of weather-magic, and which in eighth-century England already involved exuberant lay participation.[269] It is no surprise that tenth-century reformers sought to make this occasion an overt demonstration of popular attachment to Christian symbols and solidarities. Homilists put a new emphasis on Rogation processions as a corporate devotional exercise for the laity, and Ælfric knew about their penitential origins in fifth-century Vienne.[270] But tenth-century England also had a tradition that St Peter had instituted them to replace pagan festivities on the same days: a reflection of awareness in contemporary Europe that the penitential observances overlay older perambulations around the ploughed land to invoke fruitfulness for the crops.[271] The most detailed description among several, in one of the late tenth-century Vercelli Homilies, enjoins the

observance of Rogation Days with our fitting procession and with song and with attendances at church (*mid ciricena socnum*) and with fasts and with almsgivings and with holy prayers, and we must carry our relics around our land, the . . . cross of Christ . . . Likewise we must carry the books which are called 'Gospel' . . . Also we must carry other holy relics that are the remains of holy men, of their hair or parts of their body or clothing, and with all these holy things we must go humbly around our land in these holy days. And our cattle (*ceap*) and our homeland (*eard*) and our woods and all our goods we must commend to God, and thank him for the prosperity which has come to pass.[272]

Following Caesarius of Arles, the late Anglo-Saxon homilists stressed that the Rogation Days were a time not only for severe penance, but also for soul-searching, listening to teachers, diligent church attendance, and visiting of relics (*mid cyricsocnum and . . . mid reliquiasocnum*) to expunge the year's sins.[273] As the English bishops had urged long ago at *Clofesho*, they were a time for walking with the relics, not for galloping, hunting, and feasting.[274] In a vision, Earl Leofric of Mercia (d. 1057) 'saw great crowds as on Rogation days, and they were all clothed in snow-white garments, in the same fashion that a deacon is when he reads the Gospel'.[275]

---

[269] Flint 1991: 187–9; above, p. 176. Bedingfield 2002: 191–209 is now the best account of the late Anglo-Saxon liturgical and homiletic material; cf. Hill 2000. For processional liturgies in general, see Gittos 2002a: 117–43.   [270] Bazire and Cross 1982: p. xxi.

[271] *Vercelli*, xi, ll. 1–8, xii, ll. 1–13 (pp. 221, 228); Bazire and Cross 1982: pp. xxi–xxii.

[272] *Vercelli*, xii, ll. 14–34 (pp. 228–9); Bazire and Cross 1982: pp. xxii–xxiv.

[273] Bazire and Cross 1982: pp. xxiv–xxv, 9–10, 27, 31, 91, 96; *Vercelli*, xix, ll. 160–3 (p. 325). As Bedingfield 2002: 196–7 observes, the liturgical elaboration of Rogationtide and the associated sermons are exceptional in being directed at the unlearned.

[274] Bazire and Cross 1982: pp. xxiv, 81, 83–4; cf. above, p. 176.   [275] Napier 1907–10: 182.

What Leofric probably had in mind was the practice, recorded later, of halting the procession for Gospel readings at a series of 'stations', analogous to the wayside crosses and calvaries used for this purpose in modern Catholic Europe. One homily mentions the various places (*on sunderlice stowe*) where the relics are set down, and in a remarkable simile compares them to sites of worldly pleading and judgement: just as disputants go to a moot-site to be reconciled, so people at odds with God use the Rogations as moot-days to make their peace with him at a 'spiritual moot-site' (*gastlice gemotstow*), which can be anywhere that the relics are placed.[276] Each processional stage is thus covered by a mantle of divine protection while the relics stand there, rather as a court enjoys a legally enforced peace while in session. For layfolk who saw the holy objects brought out to confer this power on a sequence of landmarks, the spectacle must have been as vivid as the homilist's language.

The identity of the stations in late Anglo-Saxon England is rarely stated, but it seems possible that they comprised exactly the sorts of places which this section has considered so far: popularly revered sites which priests were prepared to acknowledge, supplemented by crosses set up specially for the purpose. That this may be so is suggested by the widespread custom, recorded much later, of blessing wells and pools at Rogationtide and on Ascension Day; even Ælfric, believing as he did that Christ's baptism in the Jordan had left no water-source unhallowed, could not have objected.[277] The siting of some of the stations at nodal points such as crossroads, or the kinds of ancient monuments that were used as landmarks for assemblies, may have meant that some of the 'spiritual moot-sites' were also actual ones.[278] Every year, then, Rogationtide could have affirmed the equivalence of Christian and traditional sacred space.

But there is not the slightest hint that late Anglo-Saxon Rogation processions already involved 'beating the bounds', that is perambulating the hedges, ditches, rivers, and roads which marked parish boundaries. The original practice in early medieval Europe had been simply to walk around among the spring crops beseeching God's blessing, and this may still have been the form of English processions in the eleventh century, and indeed later.[279] The

[276] Bazire and Cross 1982: 72–3. I owe this point to Bedingfield 2002: 195, 201–2.

[277] Ælfric, 'Catholic Homilies', II. 3 (ed. M. Godden, EETS ss 5 (1979), 22). In early seventeenth-century Cheshire, 'when they went in perambulation, they did blesse the springs, that is, they did read a Ghospell at them; and did believe the water was the better'; the custom continued at Sunningwell (Berks.) until 1688 (Aubrey 1972: 189). For other folkloric memories of these practices see Hope 1893: 7, 42–3, 46–50, 63–4, 147, 159. Hilary Powell has pointed out an explicit reference to Rogation processions to a saint-cult site, a stone at Ebbsfleet miraculously marked with St Mildthryth's footprints: Goscelin, 'Vita . . . virginis Mildrethae', *c.*19 (ed. Rollason 1982: 132–3).

[278] Note, on the other hand, the rarity of place-names indicating the holding of assemblies at crosses: Pantos 2002: 67–8.

[279] For late medieval and early modern Rogationtide practice: Hutton 1996: 277–94; Rosser 1996: 82–3; Pounds 2000: 76–80; Wilson 2000: 38–9; Harte 2002. A complaint in 1235/6 that parish

detailed boundary descriptions in charters show that the perambulation of *estate* boundaries by village elders or manorial officials was ubiquitous from at least the ninth century. But tempting though it is to envisage Rogation processions and estate perambulations coalescing, thus fostering perceptions of the tenurial landscape as a parochial one, the rarity of explicitly Christian features in the huge corpus of charter-boundary terms is disconcerting: why are there no 'Gospel oaks' or the like? The overwhelmingly secular nature of the landmarks suggests that boundary perambulation was still, in the late tenth and early eleventh centuries, an essentially secular activity which had not yet been assimilated into liturgical ritual.[280] When crosses and other stations happened to coincide with parish boundaries it was probably because they marked liminal sites of ritual or assembly, not because they were boundary-points in themselves. The one hint of ritual boundary-marking comes, oddly enough, in the *æcerbot* charm, where the cutting of sods from the four sides of the land, and placing of quickbeam crosses in the holes, recalls the bounds-beating custom of cutting out turf crosses with a paddle.[281]

On the whole, it is more likely that Rogationtide used the existing repertoire of landmarks than that it was a tool for inculcating a new awareness of parish boundaries. This repertoire, as we have seen, was a vernacular one, reflecting the needs of people on the ground: routes, assembly-sites, power-

processions were inciting bloodshed by trying to outdo neighbouring parishes with their banners ('Mandate of Robert Grosseteste': F. M. Powicke and C. R. Cheney (eds.), *Councils and Synods II* (2 vols., Oxford, 1964), i. 205) indicates rivalry, but not necessarily boundary demarcation. The earliest reference to boundary ceremonies that I can find relates to that between Ashtead and Leatherhead parishes in Surrey (a relatively late one, since Ashtead church was founded soon after 1100 as a chapel of Leatherhead), which in a memorandum of 1450/1 runs to 'Frothynges Corner yn the este and so unto an hawthorne where stode a crosse of olde tyme att the whiche crosse bothe the processyons of Lederhed and Asshestede were wonte to sey theyr gospelles yn Rogacion Daies': Oxford, Merton College, muniment 5734. A map of Ashtead in 1638 marks the boundary stations with crosses (R. A. Leaver, 'John Lawrence's Survey Map of Ashtead', *Proceedings of the Leatherhead and District Local History Society*, 4. 10 (1986), 275–9). Harte 2002: 32–3, suggests an intermediate stage, in the late middle ages, when parish processions went out to boundary points and back again (as distinct from perambulating the boundary continuously), and the Ashtead/Leatherhead case would be compatible with this. I am grateful to Jeremy Harte for his advice.

[280] Contrast the supposed 515 foundation charter of Saint-Calais monastery (in fact a ninth-century forgery), where the donor is made to demarcate the estate with a series of new landmarks including crosses, in the form '. . . where we have ordered crosses to be made on the trees and stones to be placed under them' (J. Havet, 'Cartulaire de Saint-Calais', *Bibliothèque de l'École des Chartes*, 48 (1887), 209–47, at 210–13): none of the English charter-bounds is anything like this.

[281] Above, p. 484; J. A. Giles, *History of the Parish and Town of Bampton* (2nd edn., Bampton, 1848), 58. The *æcerbot* text seems to envisage that a substantial area of land (a whole estate?) will be protected in this way, since one of the prayers is for the landowner 'and all those who are serving under him'. Compare (earlier) the peripheral crosses of the Evangelists protecting the holy circuit in the Book of Mulling (Aitchison 1994: 234), and (later) folk-practices of signing crosses at the corners of land (Wilson 2000: 33, 99). Of course, these rituals have something in common with the liturgies for dedicating churches and churchyards.

ful or dangerous places on the community's margins. This is a peasants' rather than a landlords' vocabulary of demarcation, and it shows little trace either of Continental ideas of land-allotment or of Irish protected space. Sacred zones and routes to churches, not the boundaries of estates or townships, were indicated by crosses, as St Buryan strikingly illustrates.[282] To proto-parish communities, it may have been less important to mark their boundaries than to process along the routes and around the fields and landmarks that were the scenes of their everyday lives.

All of this tells us a good deal about the continuity of traditional sacred geographies, but disappointingly little about the emergence of local parishes. It is likely, on the whole, that the homilists still envisaged mother-parishes rather than local parishes as the essential processing communities: to that extent the new emphasis on Rogationtide merely affirmed the status quo. But at least we can recognize a new prescriptiveness, an insistence on the religious duty of all layfolk to belong to collectivities defined by worshipping in the same churches, venerating the same relics, and processing through the same landscapes: that is, to be 'parishioners'. Re-formulated and expounded in the tenth century for the benefit of minsters, these conceptions of exclusive belongingness to a specific church and its community eventually became tools for delineating a more local layer of parish organization.

Bishops, lords, and priests

The accent of this chapter so far has been on kings, landowners, and peasants, and there is indeed little sign of real changes brought about by bishops or priests through a power to compel rather than merely to influence. They were indispensable nonetheless: churches and parishes were different from other kinds of property or territory, and establishing new forms of parochial obedience would have been impossible without precedent, legitimization, and at least a show of regulatory authority. The laity may have been unwilling for their pastors to rule them, but they were influenced by the modes of seemliness and good conduct that they taught. The values propounded so eloquently by Ælfric may have been disseminated relatively widely, and no church-builder is likely to have been oblivious to the norms of proper behaviour set out in the prescriptive sources. If bishops and priests exhorted the laity to pay their tithes and other church dues, and to attend church regularly, church-owning laymen will not have thought this a bad thing.

---

[282] The point is again made by the the *troménies*, the Breton equivalents of English Rogation processions (Tanguy 1984): the cross-marked circuits that they perambulated were zones of sacred space, not in the first instance parishes or estates.

Ecclesiastical governance was not very strong in itself, but it could gain strength through alliance with local interests; before 1100 it could not be the driving factor, but it could be a defining one.

Yet it must be admitted that there is an extraordinary lack of coherent statements of principle—still more of practice—on such matters as diocesan governance, the lifestyles of priests, relations between neighbouring churches, and the duties of parishioners. The copious body of homilies, pastoral letters, tracts, and law-codes produced by Archbishop Wulfstan and Ælfric of Eynsham is the obvious exception,[283] but for several reasons this material can only be used with great caution as evidence for actual conditions. In the first place there is considerable repetition, both within Ælfric's own writings and because of Wulfstan's obsessive re-workings of his own, Ælfric's, and other material. Secondly, there is much recycling of earlier prescriptive statements on church organization and lay observances, extending from Caesarius of Arles through the Carolingian capitularies to Hincmar of Rheims and beyond: it is often hard to be certain that a statement is of specifically contemporary relevance, rather than repeated for its didactic or rhetorical value.[284] Thirdly, it can be unclear whether strictures and exhortations are being addressed to minster-priests or to the new parish clergy. Fourthly and most fundamentally, the principles are entirely programmatic: they urge a reformation of manners, but lack any serious mechanisms for putting them into practice.[285] Only with the 'Northumbrian Priests' Law', now re-dated to a generation after Wulfstan,[286] do we get some sense (in York diocese) of

[283] M. R. Godden and A. Orchard in *Encyc.* 8–9, 494–5 for a guide to the sources, and to the secondary literature on Ælfric, Wulfstan, and their pastoral theology. Hill 1992 is a judicious (and on the whole negative) assessment of the practical impact of the campaign; by contrast Jolly 1996: 58–70, a useful survey of the material in relation to local churches, may be slightly too inclined to take programmatic statements literally. See also Wormald 1999*b*: 225–51.

[284] For instance, the prohibitions on lay control and trading in churches, on the expulsion of priests without episcopal advice, and on the alienation of mother-church rights in V Atr. 10. 2 (*Gesetze*, 240–1; *C&S* 351), VI Atr. 13–15. 2 (*Gesetze*, 251; *C&S* 368), and *NPL* 20–2 (*Gesetze*, 381; *C&S* 457) come straight from Carolingian sources; Ælfric's statements that a priest may not leave 'his church to which he is consecrated' and go to another without his bishop's leave, that he may never hold two churches at once, and that no unknown priest from another diocese may celebrate mass or receive a church without the diocesan bishop's leave (Ælfric, 'First O.E. Letter for Wulfstan', cc. 207–10. *C&S* 301) are all based on earlier canons, including Hertford (672), c. 5 (*HE* iv. 5 (p. 350)). For Ælfric's recycling of Caesarius's attacks on idolatry see Meaney 1984. Cf. Wormald 1999*a*: 210–24, for the debt to Continental penitential literature.

[285] As with Wulfstan's lawmaking in general, his mind was fixed on the imminent coming of Antichrist: 'reassertion of divine precepts was now so urgent that worldly punishment was barely relevant' (Wormald 1999*a*: 451–5).

[286] In Patrick Wormald's view *NPL* is heavily influenced by Wulfstan but not his work; it could have been composed by Archbishop Ælfric Puttoc (1023–51) (Wormald 1999*a*: 208–10, 396–7). This re-dating makes sense of the hitherto puzzling discrepancies in tone, especially *NPL*'s more concrete references to diocesan administration and discipline.

episcopal intra-diocesan discipline backed up by sanctions. Yet these texts are not futile: they are mirrors of a fast-changing ecclesiastical world, in which the boundaries of the acceptable were shifting and good practice was being redefined, and they highlight several new concerns. In this indirect sense, they do have things to tell us about how bishops, lords, priests, and parishioners perceived their churches.

In 900 the great majority of English clergy either lived at, or were attached to, minsters. By 1000 it seems likely that significant numbers of priests were coming to be based at small manorial households and local churches. By 1100, though the minster-priests were probably still numerous, the priests of local churches may have outnumbered them substantially. The status of these people suggests that normally they were drawn from the rural population and chosen by their lords. Byrhtferth of Ramsey, Ælfric, and Wulfstan launched their initiatives for vernacular education in a world which presented a new opportunity and new problem: the 'backwoods priest' (*uplendisc preost*), ignorant, isolated, cut off from even the basic standards of learning and discipline which he would formerly have attained in a minster community.[287]

As individuals, the late tenth- and eleventh-century rural clergy are lost to us. We rarely know even their names, and those about whom Domesday Book is not impenetrably laconic are mostly associated with minsters.[288] To judge from the strictures against them, priests were often ignorant of Latin, unshaven, drunk, and quarrelsome, and in the habit of wearing weapons in church;[289] they could be alehouse-minstrels and entertainers, hunters, hawkers, and gamblers.[290] It is unlikely that even Ælfric and Wulfstan seriously thought that they could make priests give up their women, though they did their best to shame them into chastity.[291] Some priests may have

---

[287] Byrhtferth, *Enchiridion*, ed. P. S. Baker and M. Lapidge (EETS ss 15, 1995), 106, 110, 120, 138, 185; cf. Rosser 1992: 283. Byrhtferth aims to make hard things simple enough for these people to comprehend; he is unique in surviving texts in applying the word *uplendisc* to priests, which he does five times. The ninth-century Frankish attempts to cope with low-grade and sometimes servile priests who struggled to make ends meet, vividly surveyed by Nelson 1987, make a helpful background to the same problems and initiatives in England a century or two later.

[288] Lennard 1959: 288–338 is a meticulous analysis of the Domesday data; unfortunately he does not separate references to minster-priests and minsters from those to ordinary priests and churches.

[289] Ælfric, 'First O.E. Letter for Wulfstan', cc. 2, 185–200 (*C&S* 261, 296–9; cf. ibid. 245); *NPL* 34, 37 (*Gesetze*, 382; *C&S* 459).

[290] 'Canons of Eadgar', cc. 59, 65–6 (*C&S* 333–5); *NPL* 41 (*Gesetze*, 382; *C&S* 460).

[291] Ælfric, 'Pastoral Letter for Wulfsige III', cc. 13–23 (*C&S* 198–200); Ælfric, 'First O.E. Letter for Wulfstan', cc. 85, 147 (*C&S* 279, 289). I Cn. 6 omits V Atr. 9, which forbids priests to have sexual intercourse with women, but I Cn. 6. 2 states that 'they very well know' that they should not cohabit with women (*Gesetze*, 238, 288; cf. *C&S* 349 n.). The Northumbrian Priests' Law merely expects monogamy: 'if a priest leaves a woman and takes another, anathema sit!': *NPL* 35 (*Gesetze*, 382; *C&S* 459). Cf. above, pp. 361–2.

occupied themselves as traders, merchants, and reeves.[292] Maybe they needed such by-employment to make ends meet, especially in view of the injunction that every priest should 'in addition to learning, learn a handicraft': one wonders whether priesthood at the humbler level was normally a full-time job.[293] Perhaps the priests' guilds occasionally mentioned were in some sense substitutes for the minsters to which all priests had until recently belonged, giving local priests the social discipline of communities.[294]

We cannot assume that local priests were normally literate (especially in a period when we do not really know how literate the laity were), and standards are likely to have varied widely. It is possible that priests 'devolved' from minsters were more educated than those whom the laity selected from among their tenants or fellow-villagers, though if peasant priests acquired any education the minster-priests seem the obvious agents for providing it.[295] Many were certainly humble, even though the special powers which they professed, and revenues to which they alone had access, must always have set them at least slightly apart. Late tenth-century priests could be unfree, for Æthelgifu's will directs that 'Eadwine the priest is to be freed'.[296] Where eleventh-century glebes are visible they resembled standard local peasant holdings,[297] and in Domesday Book priests appear as ordinary people, sometimes lumped in with villans or bordars and sharing their plough-teams.[298] The priest 'might be a fairly substantial farmer without out-distancing the more prosperous of his rustic parishioners', like Wulfric, the early twelfth-century priest of Berwick St Leonard (Wilts.), with his half-hide of glebe, his tithes, his firewood, and his pasture for fifteen cows, sixty sheep, three horses, and fifteen pigs.[299]

Where lords were resident, priests of manorial churches would have remained very much members of their households. Even the thegn whose church lacks a graveyard is envisaged in Eadgar's law as having his own priest,

---

[292] Ælfric, 'Pastoral Letter for Wulfsige III', cc. 77-82, 102-3 (*C&S* 212, 216-17); Ælfric, 'First O.E. Letter for Wulfstan', c. 185 (*C&S* 296). However, these draw on Carolingian material and may not necessarily be contemporary comment.

[293] 'Canons of Eadgar', c. 11 (*C&S* 318), following Amalarius of Metz etc.; cf. Campbell 1986: 149.

[294] Priests guilty of certain offences were to be excluded from their colleagues' friendship and society (VIII Atr. 27; NPL 2. 1 (*Gesetze*, 266, 380; *C&S* 396, 452)), which may in practice have meant guilds; cf. below, p. 497.

[295] Cambridge, Corpus Christi College, MS 422, an eleventh-century liturgical compilation in eccentric Latin with rubrics in equally eccentric Old English, probably comes closer than any other surviving manuscript to the kind of book that might have been used by 'unlearned' priests: Page 1978.

[296] W. Æth, 8.   [297] Above, p. 409.   [298] Lennard 1959: 310-13.

[299] Lennard 1959: 329-30. But for evidently much poorer priests living on tiny inland holdings see ibid. 330-1, and Faith 1997: 165.

whom he must support from his own resources. Given that the priest of Ælfric the Small's church at Milford was provided by a minster, it is all the more striking that he was expected to behave socially as Ælfric's retainer: waiting on him respectfully, eating at his table, and attending him to the hundred.[300] Did thegns normally have their priests in tow when they visited the hundred court? If so, an advantage of summoning the priest, along with the reeve and six men from each vill, to the Domesday inquest would have been his familiarity with court procedures.[301] If not by status or substance, the local priest was marked out from other smallholders by his involvement in gentry circles and public business.

Small churches were 'owned' by the laity who built them. Yet they were rather more than *just* property, even though later medieval definitions of patronage and advowsons did not yet exist: lay lords' rights over churches were always tempered by social and moral expectations and obligations, if not by legislation.[302] The appropriate supervisor of a small church, as of a large one, was a priest, and assigning it to that priest with all assets seems to have become common practice in eleventh-century England. Sifflaed's will directs that her church of Marlingford (Norfolk) 'is to be free, and Wulfmaer my priest is to sing in it, he and his issue, so long as they are in holy orders'[303]—a case which illustrates how a church could pass openly and respectably to a line of hereditary priests. In such cases the glebe, tithe, and other assets presumably also came into the priest's hands. Domesday lists many churches, especially in Suffolk, where the glebes are said to be 'free', perhaps because the last generations of pre-Conquest landlords had made them rent-free as pious benefactions: the extant East Anglian wills seem to be doing exactly this.[304] Holywell church (Hunts.) was given to Ramsey in 1007 by its priest Gode, and the Londoners who gave their churches to Christ Church, Canterbury, during the eleventh century comprised both lay landowners and priests.[305] Symeon of Durham mentions a married priest called Feoccher who, around 1050, 'lived not far from the city [Durham] in a place where he had a church . . . One day many nobles and ordinary men met together in that place early in the morning to hear pleas, but before the court began they asked the priest to celebrate mass for them.'[306] This story

---

[300] Below, p. 518. When an early twelfth-century native of Compton Martin (Wilts.) returned to become priest there he joined the lord's household, eating at his table: John of Ford, 'Vita Beati Wulfricii Anachoretae Haselbergiae', c. 1 (ed. M. Bell, Somerset Record Soc. xlvii (1933), 14).

[301] Below, p. 502.

[302] See Reynolds 1994: 418, for a (perhaps slightly over-stated) attack on the whole notion of the 'proprietary church'. Wood forthcoming is a sustained exercise in rehabilitating the term.

[303] S 1525 (*Wills*, 92).   [304] Lennard 1959: 323–7; above, pp. 408–9.

[305] *Chron. Ram.* 85; Kissan 1940.   [306] *Symeon Lib.* iii. 10 (p. 172).

puts the accent on the priest's autonomous control of his church and on his public religious obligations (compromised in Symeon's eyes by his married state): this is Feoccher's church, and he is its lord even though he is also its priest.

Many priests may have acquired their churches through commercial transactions rather than pure piety. If a church was property of a special kind, there was a special way to profit from it: farming or selling it to the priest who was best placed to exploit its revenue-generating capacities. The practice of farming local churches to their priests for an annual revenue is conspicuous in Domesday Book,[307] which also leaves no doubt that churches could be bought and sold.[308] As well as leasing his assets a founding lord could shift his obligations, including the ongoing repair of the building. Eadwine, Æthelgifu's priest in the 990s, was 'to have the church for his lifetime on condition that he keep it in repair'.[309] Priests of this status can scarcely have built eleventh-century stone churches from their own resources, but they may have been expected to maintain them once their lords had put them up. An agreement of 1114 records that Hugh Gernun had built and endowed Chale church (IOW), but adds that 'the priest of Chale would do all service of the church, for the living and the dead, in books and vestments, in support and repair, even if it were to fall down to the foundations'.[310]

The gradual deflection of church dues from minsters to local churches, the growth of the tithe-paying economy, and the rise of endowment must have meant that the rural priests of small churches could eventually use them, as rich priests used minsters, for financial speculation. A clause in the 'Northumbrian Priests' Law', which forbids any priest under severe penalty to buy another priest's church, evidently envisages such dealing in the context of one-priest local churches.[311] Earlier, Ælfric had complained that 'some men sell even a church for hire, as though it were worthless mills, the glorious house of God . . . ; but it is unfitting that men make God's house like a mill for vile toll'.[312] The comparison is pointed: churches and mills appear side by side as estate assets in innumerable Domesday entries, but they also had it in common that they were detachable from the manorial nexus and

---

[307] Lennard 1959: 321-3. Cf. Bolnhurst (Beds.), where Tofig the priest held the church at the lord of the manor's will in the 1070s: *Regesta W. I*, 835-6 (No. 278).

[308] As at Huntingdon and Ipswich: DB i. 208, ii. 290-290ᵛ; cf. Barlow 1979: 192-3, and R. Morris 1989: 173.   [309] *W. Æth*, 8.   [310] Above, n. 112.

[311] *NPL* cc. 2-2.2 (*Gesetze*, 380; *C&S* 452-3). Susan Wood observes (pers. comm.) that 'buying another priest's church' sounds like annexing it by an offer to its lord, a practice condemned in Frankish texts known in England, e.g. *Theodulf*, c. 16 (pp. 320-1). Cf. above, n. 284, for the Continental sources of some similar prohibitions.   [312] *LS* xix, ll. 248-53 (p. 430).

could be subject to joint-profit agreements between lords and priests or millers.[313] To push the analogy further, both churches and mills could acquire geographical spheres of influence which, even if articulated by seigneurial authority, may have depended to a large extent upon the willingness of consumers to make use of the facility.[314] That the parallel came to Ælfric's mind as early as c.1000 offers a hint that small churches were starting to be perceived as assets before the stranglehold of minsters loosened, and even before the systematic rise of endowment.

For Ælfric and other reformers, the multiplication of rural churches and rural priests must have contributed massively to this worldliness and greed. The remedy, if any existed, can only have lain with bishops, who in theory had oversight and governance of the local religious affairs of their dioceses. Yet we learn virtually nothing of their involvement except from Archbishop Wulfstan, and what we learn from him is not really very impressive. The striking lack of any focused interest in the supervision of local clergy or parish life in early eleventh-century tracts on the episcopal office raises doubts about how often bishops were in a position to confront such problems.[315] Wulfstan set rigorous standards for candidates being examined for ordination (when the bishop was in a particularly strong position), but he was aiming to be 'more cautious about that than we have been hitherto' and we cannot know if the standards were often met.[316] Again, it is only in Wulfstan-associated texts that the obligation of priests to collect the episcopal chrism at the proper time,[317] to obey the bishop's or archdeacon's summonses, and to attend synods[318] are even enunciated. One wonders how far rural clergy

---

[313] Similar points are made by Lennard 1959: 319–20, Reynolds 1994: 164, and Aubrun 1986: 104. In Domesday Book mills are most common, and most frequently fractionalized, in some of the same areas as churches (Norfolk, Lincolnshire, Wiltshire), and sometimes mills and churches are fractionalized together.

[314] For this kind of argument in relation to mills, see Langdon 1994: 38–42; cf. Holt 1988: 36–69.

[315] 'Some Decisions at a Bishops' Synod'; 'Injunctions on the Behaviour of Bishops'; 'Admonition to Bishops'; 'Episcopus': *C&S* 402–22. (In 'Episcopus', c. 11 it is the parish priest, not the bishop, who regulates affairs 'ofer ealle þa scire þe he on scrife'.) Contrast this vagueness with, for instance, Hincmar of Rheims's provisions of more than a century earlier: McKitterick 1977: 63–4.

[316] 'The Examination of Candidates' (*C&S* 422–7).

[317] Wulfstan imposes a fine for the priest who 'does not fetch the chrism on the appointed day', and urges 'that each priest, when he fetches the chrism, knows to declare what he has done in prayers for the king and the bishop': Ed. & Guth. c. 3. 2 (*Gesetze*, 130; *C&S* 306); 'Canons of Eadgar', c. 70 (*C&S* 338); NPL c. 9 (*Gesetze*, 380; *C&S* 454). It is interesting that he also seems to have added the blessing of the chrism to a list of episcopal duties initially compiled by Ælfric: 'First O.E. Letter for Wulfstan', c. 115 (*C&S* 283). Forms for blessing the chrism occur in English pontificals from Dunstan onwards, but without any statement of which priests are expected to attend. Current work by Christopher Jones indicates the existence of a distinctive English *ordo*, associated with Worcester in Wulfstan's time.

[318] NPL cc. 3, 4, 6, 7, 44–5 (*Gesetze*, 380, 382; *C&S* 453–4, 460–1).

did bother to attend synods, except in the aspirations of the greatest English ideologue of the age.

In theory, bishops consecrated all churches and churchyards at impressive ceremonies in the presence of lay congregations.[319] Bishop Wulfwig of Dorchester (1053–67) is twice seen using the dedication ceremony as a theatre for public pronouncements, in one case conferring land on the new church and in the other affirming the monastic landlords' title to the estate.[320] There is evidence that the act of consecration could raise a church's legal status, but in practice some subordinate churches functioned without it.[321] The threat to withhold it, potentially the diocesan bishop's trump-card when confronted by a recalcitrant owner, may have been weakened by some owners' readiness to do without: an irate late eleventh-century Gloucestershire thegn was prepared to call St Wulfstan's bluff on this point.[322] The suspicion remains that while manorial lords doubtless recognized the spiritual and legal advantages of consecration, they could use unconsecrated churches without fear of reprisal. It is also unclear whether the principles that later prevented the calling-in of a compliant bishop from outside the diocese had any force before the 1070s.[323]

The means by which late Anglo-Saxon bishops might have enforced parochial discipline are in fact remarkably elusive.[324] There is no evidence for territorial archdeaconries and deaneries, nor for diocesan synods, until the 'Northumbrian Priests' Law', which in this respect points the way to the late eleventh-century reforms.[325] St Wulfstan's drive to replace uncanonical wooden altars with stone ones in the small churches of his diocese looks like

---

[319] Rollason 1988: 8–12, Lapidge 1991: 43, and Gittos 2002*a*: 192–230, for the church consecration liturgy; above, p. 465 for the churchyard consecration liturgy. According to the Life of St Wulfstan, 'the people were so seduced by the report of his preaching that you might have seen them flocking in droves wherever it was reported he was to dedicate a church': *Vita Wulf.* i. 14 (p. 50) (and cf. ii. 9, 15, 17, and 22 (pp. 78, 88–90, 94, 104)).

[320] Lower Heyford (Oxon.) and Studham (Beds.): above, pp. 388, 410. At Studham Wulfwig addressed an assembly including, as well as the thegnly donors, a royal staller and two sheriffs. Compare—earlier and on a much grander scale—Wilfrid's consecration of Ripon (*VW* c. 17, p. 36).

[321] Plymouth church was held in the 1040s as a subordinate chapel 'quia nondum dedicata erat' (below, p. 521). The Domesday jurors were asked whether the chapel at Stowmarket was dedicated, presumably because the fact had relevance to its status; and the subordinate chapel at Whistley (Berks.) was still undedicated in 1220 (above, pp. 398, 385 n.). Prohibitions of the celebration of mass in unconsecrated churches (*NPL* cc. 13–14, Winchester (1070), c. 8; *C&S* 456, 575) imply that it happened. Presumably consecration would have conferred legal advantages, including sanctuary and the penalty for breaking it.   [322] Above, p. 382.

[323] When St Wulfstan responded to lay proprietors' requests to consecrate their churches he was scrupulous in obtaining diocesan permission, but here as elsewhere his biographer presents him as a model: *Vita Wulf.* ii. 9, ii. 22 (pp. 78, 104). Cf. Brett 1995: 288 on the continuing, more limited right of bishops to consecrate churches on their own estates outside their dioceses.

[324] For this paragraph see especially Brett 1995: 282–5, 294–6.

[325] *NPL* cc. 4, 6, 44–5 (*Gesetze*, 380, 382; *C&S* 454, 460–1).

a serious attempt to impose proper standards, but is very late.[326] Here the English Church after 1070, with the emergence of a free-standing ecclesiastical law and a diocesan machinery to enforce it, stands in contrast to what had gone before.

Yet it still seems possible that a more focused and delimited conception of the priestly role to the laity was emerging around 1000. Ælfric, Archbishop Wulfstan, and the author of the 'Northumbrian Priests' Law' envisage individual priests as the moral leaders of local communities. Thus the teacher who refuses to learn 'misleads his parishioners (*hyrimen*) and himself along with them'; each priest is to announce in a synod if he knows anyone in his parish (*scriftscyre*) disobedient to God; and penalties are ordained for the priest who 'conceals what wrong is rife among men in his *scriftscire*' or who leaves the yearly dues undemanded.[327] Wulfstan thought that a corpse should be buried in its proper parish (*rihtscriftscire*), and that within their own parishes (*on heora scriftscirum*) priests should enforce just behaviour, even between lords and slaves, and should regulate weights and measures.[328] The ban on one priest taking from another anything belonging to him, 'neither in his church nor in his parish nor in his guild (*ne on his mynstre ne on his scriftscire ne on his gyldscipe*)', looks like a code of good-neighbourliness for the resident priests of adjacent parishes.[329]

We do not know at what level these regulations were meant to apply, or if realistically they applied at all, but they do at least point to a heightened sense of the individual priest as father of his own flock, the spiritual mentor of a well-defined group of people and their territory. Unless there was a large sphere of practice which written sources do not touch, bishops who wanted to encourage such attitudes had to persuade rather than compel. On the other hand, the people to whom priests ministered may have been more able to insist on reasonable standards of behaviour: especially if they were those priests' lords, but perhaps even if they were groups of peasant farmers. By slow stages, opinion may have been moving closer to something approaching later ideals of mutual obligation between parishioners and parish priest.

---

[326] *Vita Wulf.* iii. 14 (p. 128). The first English council to state the (by then ancient) rule that altars should be of stone is Winchester (1070), c. 5 (*C&S* 575), and Wulfstan's campaign could have been an immediate response to this. In Norway, wooden altars inlaid with stone slabs remained common until *c.*1200 (J. H. Jensenius pers. comm.).

[327] Ælfric, 'First O.E. Letter for Wulfstan', c. 174 (*C&S* 294); 'Canons of Eadgar', c. 6 (*C&S* 317); *NPL* cc. 42–3 (*Gesetze*, 382; *C&S* 460).

[328] I Cn. 13. 1 (*Gesetze*, 294; *C&S* 477); 'Episcopus', 10–12 (*Gesetze*, 478–9; *C&S* 421).

[329] 'Canons of Eadgar', c. 9 (*C&S* 318). Note that I have here translated *mynster* as 'church' rather than 'minster', which is subjective but seems required by the context: see above, p. 368.

Township, manor, and parish

From the strands of this chapter and the last, a chronology of change can be reconstructed. The thegn's bookland church makes its appearance in Eadgar's law of the 960s, soon after humble timber churches become visible archaeologically and mass-produced gravestones start to appear in ordinary churchyards. Around 1000, Ælfric was complaining about people feasting in churches and dealing in them like mills, Wulfstan was expecting priests to regulate affairs in their 'shrift-shires', Byrhtferth was trying to make life simple for 'backwoods priests', 'church-paths' were starting to appear in charter-bounds, and a slave-priest on a Hertfordshire manor was given a church and told to maintain it. Into the millennium, royal law acknowledged the existence of 'little minsters' and 'field-churches' while reserving church dues ever more insistently to minsters; Rogationtide processions probably still affirmed the integrity of the old rather than the new parishes, and use of minster graveyards was at its peak of intensity. The critical shift can be located during *c.*1030-80, when local churches were rebuilt to last, equipped with stone fonts and endowed with land, and when the minsters' monopoly over church dues went into drastic decline. With Lanfranc and the next generation of bishops, the growth of canon-law definitions and diocesan administration set the seal on the new order.

Except where it relies on physical evidence, this story has to be teased out of texts written by people to whom it was of virtually no interest. The local parish was built from below, with little official commitment to creating or defining it.[330] There is no sign that eleventh-century bishops saw it as their role to set parochial frontiers between neighbouring farms or manors which would withstand future ownership or land-management changes. Lacking overt definition, the parish community was founded on a range of seigneurial, economic, and social forces and was correspondingly fluid. It is also unrealistic to envisage it as the clear-cut entity of earlier Carolingian theory or later English practice. It may have been possible for an English villager in 1000 to belong to different (though doubtless overlapping) mass-hearing, guild-feasting, processing, and burying communities, and to resort for private devotions to sites which were not officially recognized at all. Local parishes grew within the shell of the old mother-parishes, the boundaries of which usually remained important even as the structures of authority and pastoral care within them fragmented. The fragmentation was driven partly by the varied structures of landholding and lordship between the mid tenth and early twelfth centuries, partly by the varied forms of settlement and economic

---

[330] Cf. Reynolds 1984: 79-80.

life. The first generations of parishioners must have had very diverse experiences of collective action and sense of community.

The most tangible sort of parish origin is tenurial, through manorial lords building churches and encouraging or pressing their tenants to attend and finance them. The jurors of 1086 saw the Stowmarket/Combs affair as an act of straightforward seigneurial encroachment: Nigel endowed Combs church by transferring eleven acres from the mother-church, and gave it a congregation by filching (*abstulit*) twelve sokemen there who 'used to be parishioners' of Stowmarket.[331] When Domesday Book observes that 'tithe and other church customs from Thori's land in Ropsley hundred [Lincs.] belong to St Peter's church',[332] it is defining parochial obligation tenurially. Early twelfth-century agreements between church-building lords and minsters are sometimes at pains to stress the dependence of the new devotional community on its secular lord: when Richard de la Mare built Alvescot chapel (Oxon.) within Bampton mother-parish he conceded 'that the men of Richard's land shall hear service there in such a way that no other parishioner of Bampton shall be received there', and at Hamnish Clifford (Herefs.) the villeins were only allowed to hear mass in the chapel in their lord's presence.[333]

But these relatively late and seemingly clear-cut cases may encourage too simple a view of tenure-based parish formation. The obligation to attend a particular church will in itself have created some sense of community, but it may have been a weak one if it cut across other solidarities.[334] And we can no longer, in the light of Rosamond Faith's work, think of even the 'classic manor' as a monolithic entity, uniformly under its lord's control.[335] A landowner able to demand 'church-suit' from his heavily dependent inland workforce may have had much less control over the free, geld-paying ceorls of the warland. His doubtless considerable influence over them will have interacted with autonomous choice, which is more likely to have pushed in the same direction if his church was admired for its beauty or holiness, or if his house and estate centre were central to the social and economic concerns of the township. The overlapping meanings of *circsocn* mirror the overlapping of township with manor: a villager used his community's fields, commons, alehouse, and church; a tenant might owe suit to his lord's court, mill, sheepfold, and church. But practice was not always dependent on duty: peasants under no obligation to grind their corn at the lord's mill, or to attend his church, may still have done both because they found them convenient and congenial.

---

[331] Above, p. 428; DB ii. 291ᵛ.   [332] DB i. 377ᵛ.
[333] F. Barlow (ed.), *EEA* xi: *Exeter 1046-1184* (Oxford, 1996), 25 (No. 25); Kemp 1988: 94 n. 38.
[334] Reynolds 1984: 92-3; cf. below, p. 510.   [335] Faith 1997: 56-152.

The voluntary element was probably strongest where manors and townships were not coterminous, but overlapped in complex and untidy ways.[336] The grouping of churches in the central zones of East Anglian townships, or even in single churchyards, is the odd but expressive result of individual proprietorship interacting with a sense of community. A lord/peasant dichotomy makes little sense in describing such groups of prosperous farmers, collaborating to establish their churches and presumably to appoint their priests. In dispersed settlement landscapes such as Devon, where some parishes look like amalgamations of farms and hamlets, it may have been a matter of attraction rather than compulsion, households making a free choice to attach themselves to one church rather than another and then establishing a family tradition. Often it must have been the economically most developed centre, or the dominant lord's residence, that emerged as the parish centre, though the pull of a revered holy site may sometimes have been decisive.[337]

If nucleated and dispersed settlements, unitary and fragmented townships, were variants on the parochial theme, towns were another. In their organization and culture as in their origins,[338] small urban parishes differed from rural ones in detail but not in kind. The contrast between eastern England, where tenth- and eleventh-century town churches could have their own graveyards from the outset, and the south-west and west midlands, where mother-churches often preserved a burial monopoly through the middle ages,[339] is just a facet of the broader regional variation in the decay of mother-church rights. When urban parish boundaries stabilized may have varied— in some towns perhaps as early as the twelfth century, in others much later—but their distinctiveness lies only in the fluidity and fragmentation of urban property.[340] Because so many town churches had been built simply to serve big houses and their dependent holdings, they tended to be left with minute 'parishes' and presumably minute congregations. If they made little

---

[336] Reynolds 1984, chs. 4 and 5; Pounds 2000: 276–84. For the diverse township structures of the northern Danelaw, and the complex overlapping of manor and township, see Hadley 2000a: 95–101, 108–15; where agricultural co-operation between neighbouring communities took place outside the manorial nexus (ibid. 212–13), this could be one basis for extra-seigneurial parish formation.

[337] In the area of West Alvington (Devon), both explanations may apply: Churchstow and Malborough look like old holy sites, but the other parish centres are mainly places with *tūn* names and high Domesday populations: see Faith forthcoming. In the cluster of manors called Tew in north Oxfordshire, it was the largest and most valuable which had acquired a church and was known as *Cirictiwan* ('Church Tew', now Great Tew) by the 1050s (S 1425; Blair 1994: 138–40).

[338] Above, pp. 402–7.   [339] Barrow 1992: 88–95; Barrow 2000a: 134–7.

[340] A case has been made that parish boundaries in Gloucester and perhaps Worcester had formed by the twelfth century (Baker and Holt 1998; for a modified re-statement see N. Baker and R. Holt, *Urban Growth and the Medieval Church* (2004)), but the evidence is open to more than one interpretation. Boundaries in Winchester remained fluid through the middle ages (Keene 1985: i. 123–6).

long-term pastoral or economic sense they could provide devotional foci for small groups, 'attractively cosy units within the wider civic community'.[341] In about 1100 the London churches of St Martin Vintry and All Hallows the Great were called 'the church of the porters (*bærmanne*)' and 'the church of the seamen', designations which are more likely to indicate their habitual users than their founders or owners.[342] Some of the Winchester churches may have been associated with guilds and guildhalls.[343] St Mark's in Lincoln has produced far more stone grave-markers than would a normal rural churchyard, and it has been argued for the east midlands generally that particularly large and diverse groups of tenth- and eleventh-century funerary sculpture commemorate members of merchant communities.[344] Urban churches may have been more cosmopolitan, perhaps richer, than rural ones, but they differed only in so far as their priests and congregations were different.[345]

One sign that people were thinking of small churches in the context of community, not just ownership, is the habit of describing them and their priests as belonging to vills or townships (*tūnas*). In late Old English usage *tūn* tends (though not unambiguously) to mean a place or township rather than a landholding, or at any rate to mean an entire economic or topographical entity which might either be one landholding or divided into several.[346] When Ketel (1052 × 66) bequeaths 'everything that is mine everywhere in that vill (*per on tune*) [Harling, Norfolk] except so much as I give to the church' he acknowledges the existence of a *tūn* of Harling—within which his own land is but a share—equipped with a church.[347] Eadwine's

---

[341] Reynolds 1984: 91.   [342] Schofield 1994: 35.

[343] Biddle 1976*b*: 333; the evidence is late, though.

[344] Gilmour and Stocker 1986: 55–62, 90–2; Stocker 2000: 187–9, 203–7; Stocker and Everson 2001.

[345] Cf. Andrén 1985: 250, on Danish towns: the 'principle of affiliation . . . is probably connected with churches being in the possession of individuals, the same phenomenon that occurred in the rural areas. . . . The sole specifically urban characteristic of the town was the "plurality" itself, which can be explained by the "rural" functioning of the town. In other words, the towns that held a large number of churches can be designated as "congested countryside".'

[346] J. Bosworth and T. N. Toller, *An Anglo-Saxon Dictionary* (Oxford, 1898), 1018–20, s.vv. *tūn* and compounds. The usages are too wide to allow a clear distinction; Ælfric translated *praedium* as *tūn*, and in some charters *land* in the sense of landholding seems to be synonymous with *tūn* (e.g. *RASC* 44, 52). Estate language tends, though, to reserve *tūn* for properties that were entire economic entities, as is explicit in such formulations as 'one-and-a-half hides in the *tūn* called Ditchford' (*RASC* 208). Maitland concluded that in Domesday book '*tūn*, it is clear enough, was translated by *villa*, not by *manerium*' (F. W. Maitland, *Domesday Book and Beyond* (Cambridge, 1897), 110).

[347] S 1519 (*Wills*, 88). Domesday Book duly shows the nine carucates of Harling divided into five shares, with Ketel's share (two carucates) including the church. Does this mean that the church was Ketel's sole and exclusive property and had no functions for the other shares of Harling (but in that case why does he not say '*my* church'?), or is this an illustration of Domesday terminology which reduces all relations to proprietorship and ignores community?

will (*c.*1050) leaves small bequests to churches in places where he held land but was evidently not the sole lord.[348] So when the East Anglian wills of Thurstan and Sifflaed mention four local churches as the *tunkirke*, a term which literally means 'church of the *tūn*' and equates with *ecclesia villae* used by Domesday Book in some Suffolk entries,[349] they represent them in rather different terms from, for instance, owner-based descriptions such as 'Blacemann's church'.[350] Predictably, these cases are East Anglian, but a series of royal procedural measures from 1009 onwards which present the priest, reeve, and selected villagers as officials or representatives of the *tūn/villa* suggest a general assumption that every *tūn* will have its priest, and that he will be one of its natural leaders.[351] A community to which this assumption applied must have been something like a parish.

People may thus have come to see themselves as parishioners for a variety of different reasons: because their communities were so self-contained that no alternatives were possible, because their lives were so influenced by the demands of an estate or the rhythms of its seigneurial household, because they liked their lord's or neighbour's fine new church, because they admired the priest or saw him as one of themselves, or because they had joined the church's processions and guild feasts. The more the solidarity of the parish coincided with other solidarities the stronger it was likely to be, and it is a reasonable assumption that it was strongest of all in a classic midland township with a single common-field system supporting a single nucleated village. That is certainly the perception of an anthropologist who has studied a comparable society (in rural Spain) at first hand:

[I]t is certain that the [nucleated] type of settlement plays a decisive role in the overwhelming importance of the village as a unit of activity. . . . The council is the legal body of the village, the parish is the religious body. . . . [E]very Sunday the villagers

---

[348] Above, pp. 408–9.

[349] Above, p. 408; S 1531, S 1525 (*Wills*, 80–2, 94); Darby 1977: 55. Cf. Carlton (Lincs.): 'decima et alie consuetudines de Carletune iacent in ecclesia eiusdem ville' (DB i. 377).

[350] Above, p. 385.

[351] VII Atr. 2. 5, VIIa Atr. 2. 3 (*Gesetze*, 261–2; *C&S* 377, 380): in the rescension known only in Latin translation, almsgiving and fasting are to be overseen by 'omnis presbiter et tungravius et decimales homines'; in the other, the alms are to be brought to church and divided 'be scriftes 7 be tunesgerefan gewitnesse'. The witnesses for the Domesday inquest were envisaged as including the priest, reeve, and six villagers from each vill ('per sacramentum . . . presbiteri, prepositi, vi villan[orum] uniuscuisque ville'): N. E. S. A. Hamilton (ed.), *Inquisitio Comitatus Cantabrigiensis . . . subjicitur Inquisitio Eliensis* (London, 1876), 97. In 'Leges Henrici Primi', c. 7. 7b (ed. L. J. Downer (Oxford, 1972), 100), the 'prepositus et sacerdos et quattuor de melioribus ville' can deputize for a lord or his steward in the shire court. In 'Leges Edwardi Confessoris', cc. 24, 24. 1 (*Gesetze*, 649), finders of lost property are to bring it before the church and summon the 'sacerdotem de ecclesia et prefectum de villa'; the reeve then sends to the four nearest vills 'propter sacerdotes et prefectos de villis, et ipsi prefecti adducant secum quisque tres vel quatuor de melioribus de villis'. See Campbell 2000: 208–10, on the possible public and official functions of 'village' reeves.

see their village as a social whole, and it has real meaning as a group of persons actively engaged together. The mass itself is set up as a common enterprise. Most of the village is there on the anniversary of the death of one of its members, rogations are said every year for the success of the crops, and various church festivals commemorate the different aspects of village life. The parish and the village are thus inextricably linked. . . . [T]he very boundedness of the village reinforces the sense of religious unity as nothing else could.[352]

On the other hand, it would be wrong to dismiss the autonomous role of a new church in building solidarities that would otherwise have been artificial and fragile.[353] As focus of loyalties and emotions, symbol of identity, or forum for debate, the church could have been all the more important where other central reference-points were lacking. In midland townships which were unified economically but divided tenurially, the church offfered a venue for meetings, as well as for worship, which was identified with the whole community.[354] But did English parish communities ever acquire their sense of identity *simply* through being parishioners, and if so, how far did their religious lives differ from those of more 'organic' townships? A strongly nucleated and bounded community was probably one in which the parish church most thoroughly eclipsed alternative religious sites, giving the religiosity of its individual members a more public and socially embedded character.[355] Did this mean that fewer 'undeveloped' cult places survived in the open-field townships of the midlands than elsewhere? And if so, did they survive better, even in the midlands, in mother-parishes that managed to resist fragmentation? These questions are part of a larger under-explored problem, the influence of the Anglo-Saxon past on patterns of local religious observance in the high middle ages and later.

Local parishes took their shape from secular forms of organization, but they did more than just reflect them. For a community to have its own church created a completely new kind of centre, and new opportunities for display and sociability. When Ælfric fulminated against eating and drinking, gossip, games, and raucous laughter in churches, he was describing some of the reasons why they were so important: a church could be shrine, alehouse, guildhall, and council-chamber all in one.[356] It was also permanent, and the mere passage of years enhanced its status. For instance, any church around

---

[352] Christian 1989: 18–20.   [353] Cf. Reynolds 1984: 90–3, 124–5, 143, 152.
[354] Cf. Rosser 1991: 181.
[355] Compare again Christian's study of modern rural Spain (1989: 67–8, 76–7), where the cult-images in the village churches not only have a clear ascendancy over others, but also have qualitatively different functions. Anyone can go freely and unobserved to remote shrines, but the church and its image are bound up with village solidarities and inter-village rivalries: devotions to them are statements of affiliation.   [356] Above, p. 458; cf. Campbell 1986: 147.

which people buried their dead, even as a duty, would in time be honoured as the site of ancestral graves. It only took a few generations for the various arrangements and compromises which were hammered out during the late tenth and eleventh centuries to be a parish's immemorial custom. By 1200 the parish church had become—as it often remains—the main repository of its community's history and identity. However fluid in origin, the parish as it consolidated became the determinant of other forms of collective action through many centuries.

Epilogue

The centrality of minsters to Anglo-Saxon Christianity is the main message of this book. Battered and reduced though they were through the ninth and tenth centuries, it was only in the eleventh and early twelfth that they decisively lost ground to the new order of local churches and the new forms of parochial life. These two successive modes of Church organization and culture were reflexes of successive social and economic regimes, but at the same time shaped them. Both were resilient because they had the flexibility to assume forms which were useful and congenial to patrons and parishioners, and rhythms which were in step with those of society at large. But this flexibility did not make them simply passive: in fundamentally important ways, they provided means of interacting ritually and socially, of defining groups or territories, of structuring habitation, of displaying piety or status in monumental form.

The adaptability of minster organization, and the depth of its cultural impact, can be seen in its capacity to absorb changing social and religious needs. In the seventh- and eighth-century era of heroic high culture and 'extensive lordship', minsters triumphed because their social ethos was so compatible with a people who were kindred-based but also hierarchical, and because their material needs and possibilities were so attractive to a primitive, food-render economy which was starting to respond to more sophisticated modes of production and consumption. Into the 'small shire' or *regio*, assessed in hides owing food-rents and looking for justice to a king's residence, the minster fitted naturally as a new kind of religious centre, drawing in its own renders and expounding God's law in return. Tenth-century 'cellularization', and the re-definition of communities at a more local level, prompted in turn a more localized form of Church provision. Although this involved a shift from multi-priest to one-priest churches, there is a sense in which the transformation was more in scale than in kind. With the 'Great Rebuilding', manorial churches in eastern and south-eastern England became the 'little minsters' which Æthelred II's law on compensation calls them: buildings with a physical presence, ritual importance, and sacral status setting them apart from any other kind of site or structure within their area of jurisdiction, even if that area was the territory of one township or manor rather than a whole *regio*.

But minsters were dynamic institutions rather than merely auxiliary ones: points of access to a new and exciting religious, cultural, and organizational world. During the seventh and early eighth centuries an extraordinary composite civilization was formed, which declined after its brief, spectacular flowering but left indelible marks on both England and Europe. As monuments and settlement nuclei, the minsters were revolutionary. There is persuasive evidence that parochial communities of some kind formed around them— even if the details of what it meant to be a parishioner before the tenth century remain largely obscure—and to this religious centrality was progressively added a social and economic centrality as commercial and, in the end, urban sites. The irony of the minsters' growing troubles after 750 is that they did their job of cultural and economic education only too well: they offered a lifestyle so attractive that the royal and magnate families who had founded and endowed them could not, in the end, abstain from repossessing both them and the wealth which they had generated.

Local churches, mainly added from the 950s onwards to existing settlements, were born into a more developed human landscape, and on a broad scale they were clearly less formative. Yet they were vehicles for bringing aspects of high culture to far more people, and their localized spheres meant that their role in the definition of micro-communities was correspondingly greater than that of the minsters. The emergent parish offered one context— alongside seigneurial, agricultural, and settlement change—for a re-grouping of society in the era of 'feudal transformation'. The extent of this re-grouping differed greatly between regions, and it was rarely if ever complete, but where it did occur a new kind of church was the permanent and increasingly prominent symbol of a new kind of community.

These processes were dynamic, and did not stop short in 1100: it remains to reflect briefly on the consequences of Anglo-Saxon developments for the religious and social fabric of later England. The crystallization of local parish communities, and the gradual extension of their collective activities into secular life, is of course the most obvious legacy. This book has, however, been concerned above all with minsters, and can appropriately end with them: the influence of that earlier organizational layer was far more tenacious and pervasive than is usually thought, and it contributed diversity, hierarchy, and eccentricity to a parochial system which would, if drawn on a clean sheet, have been more homogeneous.

To begin with the small churches, the tide of foundation flowed on into the middle years of the twelfth century: most parish churches which England contained before the Industrial Revolution existed by 1180, whereas only 50 to 60 per cent of them (at a very rough guess) may have existed in 1080. In this respect, the Norman settlement was more a stimulus to an existing trend than a new beginning. Where the Conquest did mark a turning-point was in opening a rather isolated England to the definitions and discipline of the new canon law.[1] Official language, and presumably perceptions, asserted for the first time the division of the English landscape into parishes with parish churches. Thereafter, a series of linked changes—the advent of archdeacons and rural deans, the flood of local churches into the hands of the new religious orders, the slow but steady percolation of Gregorian views on such matters as lay proprietorship and clerical celibacy—gave bishops an alto-gether tighter grip on the parochial affairs of their dioceses.[2] By 1180 a stable framework articulating the churchgoing and tithe-paying duties of the laity, founded on precise parish boundaries, a clear distinction between churches and chapels, and immunity from the ebb and flow of land-lordship, was being defined and enforced with growing bureaucratic precision in bishops' written judgements.[3]

Emancipated from the tenurial nexus within which it had developed, 'church-seeking' was now—in theory if not quite always in practice—a purely religious duty. But the identity forged through collective worship could in turn be re-deployed in more secular spheres. In 1138 the archbishop of York, rallying forces to fight the Scots, summoned the priest from every parish in the diocese, with cross, banners, and relics going ahead and his arms-bearing parishioners marching behind.[4] If the rhetoric of this occasion made it almost a crusade, the episode foreshadows the parish's later capacity to organize its members' public and secular obligations. During the thirteenth to sixteenth centuries it took on steadily increasing responsibilities and functions, many religious but others to do with politics, taxation, law-enforcement, and charity, which gave a broad range of people their strongest taste of communal action and self-government.[5]

---

[1] Brett 1995: 294–6; above, p. 451.

[2] Brett 1975: 112–31, 161–73; Scammell 1971; Kemp 1980; Kemp 1994.

[3] Blair 1988*b*: 13–15; Blair 1991*a*: 142–57 for a local study. The primary material has been pub-lished in various volumes of *acta*, currently being extended by the *English Episcopal Acta* series. Anglert 1995: 210–12, for the same developments, only slightly later, in southern Sweden.

[4] Richard of Hexham, 'De Gestis Regis Stephani', and Ailred of Rievaulx, 'Relatio . . . de Standardo' (both ed. R. Howlett, *Chronicles of the Reigns of Stephen, Henry II and Richard I*, ii (Rolls Ser. 82. iii 1886), 161, 182).

[5] For the functions of the parish from the late twelfth century onwards: Reynolds 1984: 90–100; Kümin 1996; Pounds 2000. An unusually early reference to a local parish as a collectivity is the gift to the canons of Southwark, no later than 1171, of land at Mitcham (Surrey) 'in qua domus eorum fundate sunt in eadem parochia, quam ex concessione et donatione totius parochie habent et possident' (British Library, Add. MS 6040, No. 16, ed. (inaccurately) *Winch. Acta*, 70 (No. 103). Note also a Devon charter of 1185, where the witness-list begins with local priests and ends '. . . et parochia de Finetuna' (Feniton): F. W. Weaver (ed.), *Cartulary of Buckland Priory* (Somerset Record Soc. xxv, 1909), 136–7 (No. 238); cf. Probert 2002: 201–2. For some other early cases see A. Brown, *Church and Society in England, 1000–1500* (Basingstoke, 2003), 90.

The steps from eleventh-century 'church-seeking' to these functions of the later medieval parish are not easy to trace. It is with a disconcerting suddenness that, in the early to mid thirteenth century, parishioners' financial duties become explicit in the principle of lay responsibility for the church fabric west of the chancel arch, and also—through what is likely to have been a lay initiative to keep collectively raised funds out of the incumbent's grasp—in the emergence of churchwardens.[6] The unrecorded beginnings of this process can, however, probably be glimpsed in the spatial re-structuring of parish church buildings: the sense of 'ownership' of a common ritual space, generated by an emergent collective identity and responsibility, could in turn strengthen it.[7] There is a parallel between the articulation of space in a small twelfth- or thirteenth-century manor-house and in a typical parish church after the 'Great Rebuilding': the nave, freely accessible and entered by lateral doors at the 'low' end, mirrors the hall, just as the chancel, reserved for the priest and his servers, mirrors the lord's chamber/solar.[8] If parishioners were sensitive to this analogy—as surely they were—it may have encouraged a view of the nave as 'their' hall equivalent to their lord's, a public but perhaps in some senses domestic space which could be beautified for recreational as well as devotional ends. It is hardly coincidence that in the later twelfth century, as the fashion for aisled manor-house halls rose,[9] large numbers of aisles with crude but highly stereotyped arcade capitals were added to parish naves: quarry-owners developed a new product for a new market, 'parochial' clients in both senses of the word. For many village communities the nave may have been the only communal indoor space, and the repeated thirteenth-century prohibitions of dispute-settlements, games, idle gossip, and general uproar there support the idea that parishioners had a tendency to use naves rather as their lords used their own halls.[10]

Meanwhile, as local parish communities won official recognition, the clergy of unreformed minsters gradually lost it: post-Gregorian conceptions of church organization and discipline left little room for them.[11] The followers of a mode of religious life which enjoyed widespread lay support up to the 1080s came, within a very short space of time, to be thought decadent and immoral: it could all too easily be said of them, as it was of the early

---

[6] Blair 1998a: 293 n. 52; Kümin 1996: 17–22.

[7] For church buildings as evidence for the emergent parish community, Davidson 1998 is fundamental; see especially pp. 108–26 for the shifting responsibility for maintaining the fabric.

[8] Grenville 1997: 90–1. The parallel would have been heightened by the commonly axial and orientated disposition of twelfth-century houses: Blair 1993: 2–7.   [9] Blair 1993: 13.

[10] Canterbury 1213 × 14, cc. 35, 60; Worcester 1229, c. 22; London 1245 × 59, c. 62; Exeter 1287, c. 21 (F. M. Powicke and C. R. Cheney (eds.), *Councils and Synods II*, i (Oxford, 1964), 31, 35, 174, 647, 1020); cf. above, p. 458, for Ælfric's similar complaints.

[11] Blair 1985a: 137–41, for this paragraph.

twelfth-century priests of Plympton (Devon), that they were more interested in ornamenting their women than in ornamenting their altars.[12] Against their new and exciting competitors for lay patronage and official favour, the Augustinian canons and the Cistercian monks, they had no chance, and indeed the Augustinians annexed several of the more prominent surviving unreformed communities.[13] As formally defined, most of the others sank obscurely during the twelfth century to the status of unusually large and wealthy parish churches. Only a few well-protected anomalies survived to shock the high-minded, as when the scholar Peter of Blois, taking up St Æthelwold's tune, described the old minster of Wolverhampton in about 1200:

The clergy there were completely undisciplined as though they were Welshmen or Scots, and so greatly had their life been overtaken by vice that their wickedness passed into contempt of God, peril to souls, infamy to the clergy . . . And while I was preaching the meaning of the Scriptures they would be singing their disgraceful songs . . . Indeed, fornicating publicly and openly they proclaimed like Sodom their own sin, and they took as wives each other's daughters and nieces.[14]

Yet alongside the great expansion of local parish life, the old 'minster-places' remained, as they remain today, the most widespread enduring legacies from early Christian England. Some were cities, others were villages or less, many were small market towns; but most of them, in one way or another, were distinctly different from ordinary settlements. Their religious life was different too, since although only a few of them were collegiate in a formal sense, they tended to retain complex groups of clergy: portionary vicars, multiple curates and chaplains, guild- and chantry-priests. Their churches, as rebuilt in the twelfth and thirteenth centuries, often copied monastic rather than parochial planning, with careful separation of clerical from parochial space, and perhaps an elaborate liturgy.[15] The resemblances which can be traced between late Anglo-Saxon minster-priests and the clergy of large late medieval parish churches, like those between the activities of the tenth-century parish guilds and those of their fourteenth-century counterparts,[16] indicate lines of continuity from early to late medieval religious modes.

Many ex-minsters of this kind, which tended to have the richest forms of participatory devotional life in the late middle ages, also had the largest rural

---

[12] Below, p. 522.   [13] See again the Plympton narrative, below, pp. 521–2.
[14] *The Later Letters of Peter of Blois*, ed. E. Revell (Oxford, 1993), 26; translation after Denton 1970: 148–9. Wolverhampton was one of the 'royal free chapels' which survived reform because of their exemption from diocesan interference. But for an altogether more sympathetic view of a secular college, by one of its own canons who lived to see it taken over by Augustinians, see *Walt. Chron.*
[15] Blair 1998a. Cf. Evans 1992 for a comparable development in Wales.
[16] Rosser 1988a; Rosser 1988b; above, pp. 453–4.

and small-town congregations, thanks to their former urbanizing role and the substantial survival of their mother-parishes. Some still provided pastoral care in ways that Bede would have recognized. At Chesterfield (Derbs.), a classic case of organic urbanization around a minster in a Roman fort, the parish guilds could claim in 1546 to exist partly

for the help and ministration of all manner of sacraments and sacramentals within the said parish, and other charitable deeds, for as much as the said parish is very large . . . and is divided into many hamlets and villages, being distant some two miles, some three miles or more from the said parish church, so that the vicar and his parish priest in the time of Lent and Easter and some other times cannot suffice to the ministration of behoveful matters.[17]

In mother-parishes like this—which during the Anglo-Norman era had survived both the melting of parochial authority and its reassertion (Fig. 54)—loyalties and resentments could resonate for centuries, as clergy and parishioners combined to uphold the honour of their district's old religious centre, or alternatively struggled to make sense of obligations which changes in settlement patterns, agriculture, or social orientation had rendered archaic.[18]

The map of parish boundaries as formed by 1200 was multi-layered and extremely complex, reflecting wide variations in economic and tenurial background, and in the survival or disappearance of mother-church rights. Usually, local parishes were relatively small and self-contained, but in less developed areas they could comprise substantial segments of former mother-parishes, and contain dispersed settlements with their own dependent chapels. The old dialogue between ecclesiastical centres and peripheries was thus transposed into the smaller-scale, more tightly supervised, and more rigid framework of later medieval parishes. Recent work has highlighted the co-operative aspects of the relationship between emergent parochial discipline and the devotional initiatives of the laity, and has seen in it less of a clash between vested interests and local independence, more of the vitality and widening choice of local religion.[19] These developments partially—but only partially—drew into the sphere of formal parish religion the substra-

[17] Riden and Blair 1980: 105.
[18] Blair 1985*b* describes such a contentious case (Bampton), and Kemp 1988 an exceptionally complex one (Leominster); for other post-Conquest disputes over the burial rights of mother-churches see Wormald forthcoming: ch. 8. To take one striking archaism, the parishioners of daughter-chapelries could remain responsible, well after the Conquest, for maintaining sections of the mother-churchyard wall. This continued to modern times at Prestbury (Cheshire), where the wall still contains stones marking the sections assigned to the various townships; at Chew Magna (Somerset), six daughter-parishes were still obliged to maintain specified sections of the wall in 1752 (Aston 1986: 58).   [19] Rosser 1991: 176, 182–3; Kümin 1996: 167–79; cf. above, p. 453.

54. A twelfth-century assertion of Lindisfarne's ancient parochial rights. By this agreement, complete with its 'votive knife', the lay lords of Lowick (Northumb.) concede 'that the monks of [Holy] Island should have the tithes of all things from the court of Lowick and from the vill, from whichever things yield tithes'. (Durham University Library Cathedral Muniments, 3.1.Spec.72; The Chapter of Durham Cathedral.)

tum of popular cult sites: their assimilation, for instance through Rogation-tide and guild activities, was a long-drawn-out process, doubtless acclerated by the gradual formation of a finer parochial mesh, but still nowhere near complete in 1100.

In these interchanges between 'official' and 'voluntary' structures, the ex-minsters had lost their exclusive role but may still have had a special one. Their parishes—the pared-down residues of older and larger territories— were still much more likely than others to be multi-focal, and to be well above average size; they consequently tended to contain abnormally large and varied constellations of subsidiary sites, and populations who were socially and economically diverse.[20] Much of this special character was lost with the widespread destruction of outlying shrines and chapels in the mid sixteenth century.[21] Yet the recurrent combination of two rather different inheritances from the past—centres of an urban or quasi-urban character, and heterogeneous and dispersed rural parishes over which those centres exerted a rather loose pastoral hold—gave some ex-minsters and their parishes a new and paradoxical distinctness as pockets of post-medieval religious dissent.[22] It may be slightly more than just an amusing irony that Oundle (Northants.), a minster founded by the great seventh-century champion of catholic orthodoxy, became a notable centre of Methodism.[23]

On the grass verge beside the parish church of Bredon (Worcs.), once King Offa's family minster, stands a stone obelisk dated 1808. The inscription reads: 'UPTON 6 Miles | PERSHORE 7 Miles | EVESHAM 12 Miles | TEWKESBURY 3 Miles | WINCHCOMB 10 Miles | CHELTENHAM 11 Miles'. In 1808, of course, these were the local market towns; but if there could have been such a signpost a thousand years earlier, it would have shown most of the same names and they would have designated minsters.[24] This example comes from a region which has very good Anglo-Saxon documentation and is relatively rural now, but it should in no way be thought atypical. Allowing for some differential growth and change, the map of local and regional centres in post-medieval England is a map of 'minster-places', drawn by the monastic founders of the seventh and eighth centuries.

[20] See for instance Blair 1988*b*: 15–17.
[21] Rosser 1991: 188–9. The last faint trace of devotion to 'unaltered places' involved healing wells, many of which were still used into the nineteenth or even twentieth century.
[22] Everitt 1972: 26, 31, 44–5; cf. Watts 1995: 100–10, 121–2. While I endorse the criticism by Rosser 1991: 176, an argument along the present lines does offer a context for what Everitt (1972: 45) defined—albeit in slightly misleading terms—as 'the association of Dissent with very early and very late settlements, or its relative absence from those of intermediate date'. Cf. Tiller 1987: p. xxv, for Dissent in 'boundary areas of large parishes' and 'decaying market towns'.
[23] Everitt 1972: 17, 29, 31; above, pp. 96, 251, for Oundle as Wilfrid's minster and as a territorial centre.
[24] The imaginary Anglo-Saxon signpost would probably have omitted Upton, and perhaps Tewkesbury; it would have added Beckford, Bishops Cleeve, and Ripple, which did not become market towns.

APPENDIX

Three Minor Minsters in the Eleventh Century: Reculver, Christchurch, and Plympton

The following exceptional texts, none of which is available in a modern edition, are printed and translated here for the light which they throw on small minsters in the last stages of their corporate existence, between the 1020s and 1120s. All are newly edited from the manuscripts or facsimiles. Punctuation, capitalization, and paragraph divisions are modernized. I am grateful to Richard Sharpe for advice on textual points.

(*a*) Archbishop Æthelnoth leases part of the demesne of Reculver minster (Kent), 1020 × 1038

Original: Canterbury Dean and Chapter, Chart. Ant. R. 17. S 1390; printed J. M. Kemble, *Codex Diplomaticus Aevi Saxonici*, 4 (London, 1846), 53–4; facsimile in W. B. Sanders, *Facsimiles of Anglo-Saxon Manuscripts*, i (Southampton, 1878), 22. Interlined words are indicated by \/. See above, p. 361.

[*chrismon*] In nomine domini nostri Jhesu Christi. Ego Ægelnothus peccator, servus servorum Dei et minister aeclesiae Christi, Anglorum quoque licet indignus archiepiscopus, notum volo esse omnibus nostre mortalitatis successoribus quod quandam terram dominicam Sancte Marie Raculfensis monasterii, .L. scilicet agros, in prestariam annuo duobus ministris meis, Alfwoldo et Ædredo, ex consensu fratris nostri Guichardi decani eiusdem aeclesie Sanctae Matris Dei, ut illam terram habeant non longius quam ipsi placuerit decano vel eius successori. Quamdiu vero eam tenuerint, singulis annis dent in ipso monasterio Deo famulantibus rectam decimam frugum et omnium pecorum que in ipsa terra nutriunt, et pro censu .L. denarios, et de subiectis pascuis .i. pensam caseorum, et siquid fracture contigerit. Ubi vero eidem fratri nostro decano vel eius successori visum fuerit ut illam terram possint fructificare dominicatui suo, recedant ab ea absque querela et contradictione, quia dominica est Sancte Marie, nec eam sibi vel posteris suis ullomodo possunt defendere. Quod si presumpserint, et ipsi et fautores sui iram Dei et excommunicationem omnium Dei fidelium incurrant, et legem patrie domino suo solvant.

Huius prestarie traditionis testes sunt fratres eiusdem monasterii, et quidam milites mei, qui subtus sunt ordinate descripti: Ego Guichardus subscripsi. Ego Fresnotus \monachus/ subannotavi. Ego Tancradus \monachus/ recognovi. Ego Milo \monachus/ assignavi. Ego Siward \miles/ contestificavi. Ego Godric \miles/ testis fui. Ego Wlwi \miles/. Ego Wlsige \miles/. Ego Radwine \miles/. Ego Ordnoth \miles/.

Ego Ælfric \miles/ \hog/. Ego Osward \miles/. Ego Ælfhelm \miles/. Ego Lefsona \miles/. Ego Ælfric \miles/ \quat'm'/. Ego Sibriht \miles/. Ego Ælwine \miles/.

Ego Haimericus presbiter iubente domno Ægelnotho archiepiscopo hanc cartulam conscripsi, die Nativitatis Sancti Johannis Baptiste.

In the name of our lord Jesus Christ. I Æthelnoth a sinner, servant of the servants of God and minister of Christ's Church, archbishop of the English though unworthy, wish it to be known by all inheritors of our mortality that [I have given] certain demesne land of St Mary's minster at Reculver, namely 50 acres, in yearly lease to two of my thegns, Ælfwold and Eadred, by consent of our brother Guichard, dean of the same church of the Holy Mother of God, on condition that they have that land no longer than it pleases the dean or his successor. While they hold it, they shall give yearly to God's servants in that minster a true tithe of produce and of all flocks which they breed on that land, and 50 pennies in rent, and a weight of cheese from the dependent pastures, and anything that may come if any [new land] is broken. Whenever it shall appear to our said brother the dean or to his successor that they can cultivate that land in their demesne, [the tenants] shall withdraw without any complaint or opposition—for it is St Mary's demesne—and may not in any way defend it on behalf of themselves or their heirs. If they presume to do so, both they and their accomplices shall incur God's anger and the excommunication of all God's faithful, and shall pay the legal penalty to their lord.

The witnesses to this assignment in lease are brethren of that minster, and certain of my knights, who are listed below in order: [*List of witnesses, comprising the dean, three monks with Flemish names, and thirteen knights with English names.*]

I Amery the priest have written this charter by order of the lord archbishop Æthelnoth, on the day of the Nativity of St John Baptist [24 June].

(*b*) The fortunes and parochial rights of Christchurch minster (Hants.) during *c.*1080–1120

The first passage, the Domesday Book entry for the canons' lands (DB i. 44) is a good illustration of how the commissioners of 1086 described clerical minsters. The other three passages are extracts from material in the fourteenth-century Christchurch Priory Cartulary: British Library, MS Cotton Tiberius D VI, part II, ff. 30ᵛ, 36, 36ᵛ. Passage (ii) is printed by R. Dodsworth and W. Dugdale, *Monasticon Anglicanum*, ii (London, 1661), 177–8; all are translated and discussed by Hase 1988.

(i) *The minster in Domesday Book (1086)*

See above, pp. 366–7.

Canonici Sancte Trinitatis de Thuinam tenent in ipsa villa v hidas et unam virgatam, et in Wit insula unam hidam. He hide semper fuerunt in ipsa ecclesia. Tunc \TRE/ se defendebant pro vi hidis et una virgata, et modo [*blank*]. . . . [*Lists rural resources.*] In burgo vi mansuræ de xiii solidis et iiii denariis. Ad hanc ecclesiam pertinet tota decima de Tuinam et tertia pars decimarum de Holehest. T. R. E. valebat vi libros, modo viii libros.

Alnod presbiter tenet de rege Bortel. In paragio tenuit de rege E. Tunc se defendebat pro una virgata et dimidia, modo similiter. . . . [*Lists rural resources*], et due mansure in Tuinam. Valuit v solidos, modo x solidos.

Alsi presbiter tenet de rege Bailocheslei. Ipse tenuit de rege E. Tunc se defendebat pro una hida et iii virgatis, modo pro iii virgatis tantum. . . . [*Lists rural resources.*] Valet et valuit xx^{ti} solidos.

In Bouere hundredo habuit ecclesia Sancte Trinitatis de Tuinam viii acras terre in Andret. Modo est in foresta hac terra.

The canons of the Holy Trinity of Twynham hold in that vill five hides and one yardland, and in the Isle of Wight one hide. These hides were always in [the possession of] that church. Then (in King Edward's time) it answered for six hides and one yardland, and now [*blank*]. . . . [*Lists rural resources.*] In the borough six houses at 13s. 4d. To this church pertains the whole tithe of Twynham and a third of the tithe of Holdenhurst. In King Edward's time [this property] was worth £6, now £8.

Ælfnoth the priest holds Burton from the king. He held it jointly from King Edward. Then it answered for one-and-a-half yardlands, now likewise. . . . [*Lists rural resources*], and two houses in Twynham. It was worth 5s., now 10s.

Ælfsige the priest holds Bashley from the king. He held from King Edward. Then it answered for one hide and three yardlands, now for three yardlands only. . . . [*Lists rural resources.*] It is and was worth 20s.

In Boldre hundred the church of the Holy Trinity of Twynham had eight acres of land in the Weald. This land is now in the [New] Forest.

(ii) *The internal history of the minster*

See above, pp. 362–6.

Relatu antiquorum orthodoxorum patrum, avorum, attavorum, tam clericorum quam laicorum, suis successoribus, de ecclesia Sancte Trinitatis que sita est in villa que vocatur Twynham et de conventu eiusdem ecclesie, huiusmodi verba traduntur verissima:

Tempore enim Willelmi Rufi in Anglia regnantis, prefuit quidam clericus nomine Godricus prefate ecclesie de Twynham, vita et honestate preclarus, cum xxiiij canonicis, more suo horas noctis et totius diei cotidie summo complentibus diluculo. Hunc etenim Godricum sui tunc temporis clerici non pro decano, quia nominis ignorantes, sed pro seniore et patrono venerabantur. Horum vero canonicorum talis ecclesiastica erat consuetudo, quatinus eiusdem Godrici senioris oblationes misse matutinalis et magne misse undecumque allate proprie absque alicuius forent participatione. Ceteras equidem oblationes, ante missas et infra et usque ad vesperas illatas, equanimiter inter se dividebant. Similiter et terris ecclesie adiacentibus, scilicet Herna, Buretona, Prestona, sub divisione participarentur. Preterea, canonicus missam quilibet celebrans omnimodas eiusdem misse oblationes, post cappe sue ablationem quousque eam indueret, sine alicuius haberet communione.

Huc accedente fortuna, Randulphus episcopus hanc ecclesiam cum villa a rege Willelmo impetravit. Cui, quoniam ibidem Deus in multis multa operabatur miracula, gazas multimodas et sanctorum reliquias contulit pretiosas. Tandem idem cupiens et disponens episcopus Randulphus prefatam Sancte Trinitatis ecclesiam de Twynham funditus eruere, et meliorem decentioremque cuilibet edificare religioni, Godricum eiusdem loci seniorem et totum in hiis convenit verbis conventum, ut ei, ad future perfectionem ecclesie, oblationes tantummodo ecclesiasticas peregrinorum et totius parochie tam vivorum quam mortuorum concederent, exceptis illis que cibi essent atque potus et suis terris forensibus, quousque eis ecclesiam plenam et perfectam et Deo dicatam cum oblationibus receptis redderet; interim vero eis victum inveniret insuper sufficientem. Cuius voluntati et dispensationi cuncti obsecundaverunt canonici, Godrico tamen seniori obvianti proterve et tamdiu contradicente, quousque ab ecclesia defugatum et per Angliam vexatum, nec regis nec episcopi sui gratiam et auxilium in hoc impetrantem; sed redeundo, pontificis Randulphi misericordiam exhorantem, in pristinum inter canonicos desub se idem ut fuit ante antistes constituit locum.

Fregit vero episcopus illius loci primitivam ecclesiam novemque alias que infra cimiterium steterant, cum quorumdam domibus canonicorum prope, locum ecclesie cimiterii et officinarum compe[te]ntiorem faciendum, et canonicis in villa congruum in mutationem ut dominus adaptavit locum. Fundavit equidem hanc ecclesiam episcopus Randulphus que nunc est apud Twynham, et domos et officinas cuilibet religioni. Obeunte canonicorum aliquo, eius beneficium in sua retinebat potestate, nulli tribuens alii, volens unamquamque dare prebendam religioni si eos omnes mortis fortuna in suo tulisset tempore. Obiit ergo vero Godricus senior non multo tempore post elapso, simul et decem ex conventu canonici, quorum prebendas ipsis xiiij^s remanentibus ad sui victus supplementum vita illorum superstite concessit episcopus. . . .

Very true words are passed down by the narrative of old [and] orthodox fathers, grandfathers, and great-grandfathers—both clergy and laity—to their successors, concerning the church of the Holy Trinity situated in the vill called Twynham and the convent of that church, as follows:

At the time when William Rufus reigned in England [1087–1100], a certain clerk named Godric, distinguished in his life and probity, presided over the said church of Twynham, together with twenty-four canons who, in accordance with their custom, daily observed the night hours and those of the whole day from dawn. At that time this Godric's clergy venerated him not as dean—for they were ignorant of the name—but as elder and patron. The ecclesiastical custom of these canons was this: all offerings at the morrow mass and the high mass went to Godric the elder as his own property, without anyone else taking a share, whereas they divided equally between themselves the other offerings, made before and after masses and up to vespers. They likewise shared by division the lands near the church, namely Hurn, Burton, and Preston. Furthermore, a canon celebrating a mass took all the offerings at that mass, between taking off his cope and putting it on again, without anyone else sharing them.

Fortune smiled on this place: Ranulf the bishop [of Durham, 1099–1128] obtained this church with the vill from King William. Since God was working many miracles there in many [people], he gave it manifold treasures and precious relics of saints. Then the same Bishop Ranulf desired and determined to destroy the said church of the Holy Trinity to its foundations, and to build one which would be better and more fitting for every [man of] religion. So he called together Godric, the elder of that place, and the whole convent, and asked them to give him, for the completion of the projected church, all the ecclesiastical offerings of pilgrims and of the whole parish both living and dead, excluding those which were of food and drink and their external lands, until he could return the church to them, whole and perfect and dedicated to God, with the offerings received; beyond that, he would meanwhile find them sufficient to live on. All the canons complied with his wishes and plans. However, Godric the elder impudently objected, and opposed him for a very long time, until, a fugitive from the church and harried through England, he obtained neither favour nor help from the king nor from his bishop [i.e. of Winchester]; but he came back and entreated Bishop Ranulf's mercy, and the bishop restored him to his former position, under himself, among the canons as he had been before.

Then the bishop demolished the original church of that place and nine others which stood within the cemetery, with houses of some of the canons nearby, in order to make a more fitting place of the church, cemetery, and offices; and as lord he appropriated for the canons a suitable place in the town as an exchange. Indeed, Bishop Ranulf founded this church which is now at Twynham, and houses and offices for every [man of] religion. When any canon died he retained the benefice in his control, not assigning it to any other, wanting to give each one of the prebends to [a man of] religion if death's doom should carry them all off in his time. So then Godric the elder died, and likewise ten of the convent not long afterwards, whose prebends the bishop granted to the remaining fourteen to augment their living during their lives. . . . [*The narrative goes on to recount the community's history from c.1100 until its regularization as an Augustinian priory in 1150.*]

(iii) *The mother-parish of Christchurch and the foundation of Milford church*

See above, pp. 383–4.

Alvietus decanus de Insula, et Elmerus, et plures alii, testificantur quod ab ortu cuiusdam fontis Otre nomine, qui oritur apud Lindehurst in virgulto Henrici filii H(ere)berti forestarii, usquequo defluit in mare, est totum parochia de Christi ecclesia; et omnes ecclesie que fuerunt et sunt citra fontem illum usque ad Dorsetam pertinent ad ecclesiam de Cristchurche, et decime [et] cherset.

Testificantur etiam quod apud Bolram non debent sepeliri nisi solummodo cotseti et servi de illa terra in qua ecclesia fundata est, et qui fuerunt tam pauperes quod non habebant tantum unde possint apportari apud Cristchurche; et tam liberi homines quam villani deberent vivi venire ad omnes festivitates ad Cristeschurche et decime illorum et cerset et oblationes, et mortui apportari et ibi sepeliri.

Testificantur etiam quod de Brokenherst pertinent decime ecclesie Cristeschurche.

Testificatur quoque Alvietus, qui interfuit, de dedicationi ecclesie de Melneforda, quod Alvricus parvus requisivit Godricum decanum, et per illum Walchelinum episcopum, ut posset inibi construere ecclesiam, eo tenore quod nichil perderet Cristchurche de antiqua consuetudine, scilicet decim(as) et cercet; et preter hoc dedit ad ecclesiam dimidiam virgatam terre quando dedicata fuit; et simul episcopus et Alvricus liberaverunt Godrico decano et canonicis Cristeschurche clavem cum ecclesia et terra. Sic definitum fuit in presentia episcopi ut servi et cotarii eiusdem Alvrici solummodo ibidem deberent sepeliri, et iiij denarios dare de sepultura. Et Godricus debet ibi mittere presbiterem; et presbiter debet habere corrodium suum ad mensam Alverici quotienscumque inibi esset residens; et presbiter debet convenienter exspectare Alvricum ad servicium sicut maiorem, et [ire?] cum illo ad hundred[um] quando illic moveret ad eundem ad hundred[um], et nichil amplius. Vidit etiam Alvietus quod Godricus ibi misit presbiterem quemdam de ecclesia Cristeschurche nomine Eilwi. Et Godricus ita tenuit ecclesiam in vita sua, et postea alii successores.

Ælfgeat dean of the Isle [of Wight], and Ælfmaer, and many others, witness that from the source of a certain stream called Otter, which rises at Lyndhurst in the thicket of Henry son of Herbert the forester, down to where it flows into the sea, everything is the parish of Christchurch; and all churches which were and are on this side of that stream as far as Dorset belong to the church of Christchurch, and tithes [and] churchscot.

They also witness that nobody should be buried at Boldre except only cottars and slaves of the land on which the church is founded, and who were so poor that they did not have enough resources from which they could be carried to Christchurch; and both free men and villeins ought alive to come to all feasts at Christchurch, and their tithes and churchscot and offerings [should go there too], and dead to be carried and buried there.

They also witness that the tithes from Brockenhurst belong to the church of Christchurch.

Ælfgeat, who was present, bears witness concerning the dedication of Milford church that Ælfric the Small asked Dean Godric, and through him Bishop Walchelin [of Winchester, 1070–98], if he might build a church there, on condition that Christchurch should lose nothing of its old custom, namely tithes and churchscot; and furthermore he gave half a yardland to the church when it was dedicated; and together the bishop and Ælfric delivered the key to Dean Godric and the canons of Christchurch together with the church and land. It was established in the presence of the bishop that only the same Ælfric's slaves and cottars should be buried there, giving 4*d.* for burial. And Godric should send [*or* put in] a priest there; and the priest should have his food allowance at Ælfric's table whenever he should be resident there; and the priest should wait suitably for service on Ælfric as his superior, and [go?] with him to the hundred when he sets out to go[?] to the hundred, and nothing further. Ælfgeat also saw that Godric sent [*or* put in] there a certain priest of the church of Christchurch called Æthelwig(?). And Godric held the church in this way during his life, as did others, his successors, afterwards.

(iv) *Recognition processions*

See above, p. 454.

Memorandum quod parochiani de Bolre, Brokenhurst et Lemynton', Mulleford, Middleton', Soppelei et Holnhurst tenentur singulis annis die Ascencionis, vel in Dominica sequenti, visitare hanc Ecclesiam Christi tanquam suam matricem ecclesiam cum cereis iuxta parochianorum numerositatem maioribus vel minoribus. Nam parochia[ni] de Bolre unum cereum precii iij s. viij d. portare debent; Brokenhurst unum cereum precii duorum solidorum; Lemynton' unum cereum precii iij s. vj d.; Mulleford unum cereum precii iij s. viij d.; Hordhull unum cereum precii duorum solidorum; Middelton' unum cereum precii iij s.; Soppelee unum cereum precii iij s.; Holnhurst unum cereum precii duorum solidorum. Tenentes autem de duabus Hurn', Bostell' et Ponte pro eodem die Ascensionis xvj d. nomine cerei deportant. Ryngwode unum cereum precii iij s. vj d., et Elingham unum cereum precii ij s. vj d., ex antiqua consuetudine et approbata portare tenentur.

Note that the parishioners of Boldre, Brockenhurst and Lymington, Milford, Milton, Sopley, and Holdenhurst are obliged yearly on Ascension Day, or on the following Sunday, to visit this Church of Christ as their mother-church with candles according to the number of parishioners great or small. For the parishioners of Boldre must bear a candle worth 3*s.* 8*d.*; Brockenhurst a candle worth 2*s.*; Lymington a candle worth 3*s.* 6*d.*; Milford a candle worth 3*s.* 8*d.*; Hordle a candle worth 2*s.*; Milton a candle worth 3*s.*; Sopley a candle worth 3*s.*; Holdenhurst a candle worth 2*s.* The tenants of the two Hurns, Bostall, and the Bridge bring 16*d.* for the same Ascension Day in lieu of a candle. By old and approved custom, Ringwood is obliged to bring a candle worth 3*s.* 6*d.*, and Ellingham a candle worth 2*s.* 6*d.*

(*c*) **The internal history of Plympton minster (Devon), and its parochial rights in Devon and Cornwall**

Seventeenth-century transcript from the lost Plympton Priory Cartulary: Bodleian Library, MS James 23, pp. 164–5. The present extract follows a series of notes and transcripts relating to twelfth-century grants by the de Redvers and de Vautortes families and the bishops of Exeter. The last section, on the parochial rights of Lanow (St Kew), is printed and discussed by Picken 1973–7; related texts are printed in R. Dodsworth and W. Dugdale, *Monasticon Anglicanum*, ii (London, 1661), 6–11; *EEA* xi: *Exeter 1046–1184* (1996), 19–24, 107–10; and *EEA* xii: *Exeter 1186–1257* (1996), 149–54. See above, pp. 361, 384, 496, 508–9.

Adiiciunt etiam canonici se ab antiquis audisse ecclesiam de Suthon' membrum fuisse Plimton' ecclesie antequam Normanni Angliam subiugasset. Dicunt etiam ipsum Reginald[um] de Valletorta primum supplicasse domino Galfrido priori Plimt' pro Thoma clerico, filio suo bastardo, ut eum admitteret in vicariam ecclesie de Suthon' sub annuo canonicis Plimton' ecclesie solvendo, et ut eum presentaret domino Willelmo [episcopo] Exon'; quod et factum est.

Item de hac ratione nituntur [*sic*] audita a Roberto clerico, filio sacerdotis de Suttuna nomine Dunprust, et ab aliis senioribus illius temporis: Tempore Aroldi regis Anglie, et Livingi episcopi Exon', et Godwini comitis Devonie, et Edrici vicecomitis, et Dodda hordre de Plimton', Alfegh fuit unus sacerdotum de Plimton. Habuit in prebenda sua et in communa sua capellam Sancti Andree de Sutton et parrochiam, et capella adhuc lignea erat. Filius vero Alfegh fuit Sladda sacerdos, et ipse tenuit predictam ecclesiam de Plimton', et post eum Alnodus sacerdos, et post Alnodum Dunprust filius eius; et ita Plimton ecclesia continue et pacifice tenuit ecclesiam de Suttuna tanquam capellam, quia nondum dedicata erat priusquam Normanni subiugassent sibi Angliam. Item post Dunprust Willelmus Bacini filius eius eam tenuit de Plimton', et post eum Thomas clericus, filius Reginaldi de Valletorta de filia Dunprust, qui post decessum Willelmi episcopi, et patris sui R[eginaldi] cui Rex Henricus primus dederat manerium de Sudtuna pro servitio suo, hoc recognovit in plenario capitulo Plimton', et in extremis agens clavem illius ecclesie resignavit Priori Johanni et canonicis Plimton' sub testibus.

Patet ergo Regem Henricum non dedisse Ricardo de Ridvers ius advocationis in Plimtona, licet eum multum iuverit in regno Anglorum et ducatu Normannie adversus fratrem suum Robertum Curthuse priorem natu, quem apud Tenechebrai bello devicit et in carcere quoad vixit tenuit. Sed cum prenominatus Willelmus de Warewast episcopalem cathedram Exonie adeptus est, impetravit a domino Rege Henrico primo ut ius advocationis in prefatis ecclesiis in perpetuum adtitularetur et carta illius confirmaretur episcopali sede Exon'; quod et factum est. Hec vero carta, et quedam alie Anglorum regum aureis litteris insignes de pertinentia memoratarum ecclesiarum ad capellariam regum, in Exon' ecclesia reservantur, quas nos vidimus et audivimus legi coram iustitiis Regis Henrici filii Matildis Imperatricis per Bartholomeum pie memorie Exon episcopum.

Willelmus igitur episcopus, cum subditorum et precipue clericorum vita et conversatione multas enormitates et scandala infirmorum abundare inspiceret (omnes vero incontinentia laborabant, et erat in hac causa ut populus sic sacerdos), Deo inspirante satagebat hoc vitium primo in maioribus ecclesiis corrigere. Erat [?scand]alum intollerabile cum sacerdotes publice uxores ducerent et, neglecto ornatu et cultu ecclesiarum, quasi de sola successione hereditanda cogitarent, et mulieribus non altaribus ornandis indulgerent. Coepit ergo tanquam bonus pastor, verbo sacre exhortationis et exemplo canonice religionis, ad castitatem et honestatem revocare. Primus vero ordinem canonicorum in Devonia et Cornubia per viros spectabilis vite instituit, et in ecclesia Plimton[ens]i et Bodmunensi et Lanstavaton' disposuit, et dominum Regem Henricum Primum ad confirmandum induxit.

Nos vendicamus septem villarum decimas quarum corpora habemus ad ecclesiam de Landeho, que sunt in eodem manerio regis de Landho, adversus Egglostetha que est in feodo Ricardi Bloiho. Harum prima dicitur Trebriðoc, secunda Trenkioh, tertia Serfontem, quarta similiter Serfontem, quinta Treursel, sexta Duunaunt, septima Bodwon. Illas ab antiquis audivimus ideo esse alienatas ab ecclesia de Landeho, tantum quia homines dictarum villarum timuerunt venire ad ecclesiam de Landho propter inimicitias homicidii cuiusdam, et ecclesia Sancte Tetha prope erat, tantum quia decimas illius temporis parvule erant, et clerici de Landho impot[ent]es et pigri ius suum prosequi. Ideo etiam omittebant de francoleinis suis annuatim donum et auxilium exigere, quod ut dicitur illi de iure debebant pendere: quoniam parvulum censum solvunt, scilicet de acra prima de ferlingo terre unum denarium, et modo nil amplius.

The canons add that they have heard from old [men] that 'Sutton' [i.e. Plymouth] church was a member of Plympton church before the Normans conquered England. They also say that the same Reginald de Vautortes I asked Dom. Geoffrey prior of Plympton, on behalf of his bastard son Thomas the clerk, to admit [Thomas] to the vicarage of Sutton on payment of a yearly [pension?] to the canons of Plympton church, and to present him to William [bishop] of Exeter [1107–37]; which was duly done.

In the same matter, the following things were heard from Robert the clerk, son of a priest of 'Sutton' called Dunprust, and from other elders of that time: In the time of Harold [I] king of England [1035–40], and of Lyfing bishop of Exeter [i.e. Crediton, 1027–46], and of Godwine earl of Devon [i.e. Wessex, 1023–53], and of Eadric the sheriff, and of Dodda steward (*hordere*) of Plympton, Ælfheah was one of the priests of Plympton. He had in his prebend and his commons the chapel of St Andrew of 'Sutton' and its parish, and the chapel was hitherto of timber. Ælfheah's son was Sladda the priest, and he held the said church of Plympton, and after him Ælfnoth the priest, and after Ælfnoth his son Dunprust; and thus Plympton church continuously and peacefully held 'Sutton' church as a chapel, for it was not yet dedicated before the Normans conquered England. Then, after Dunprust, his son William Bacini held it from Plympton, and after him Thomas the clerk, son of Reginald de Vautortes by Dunprust's daughter. After the death of Bishop William [in 1137], and of his own father Reginald (to whom King Henry I gave 'Sutton' manor for his service), Thomas acknowledged this in the full chapter of Plympton, and on his deathbed surrendered the key of that chapel to Prior John [1169–76] and the canons of Plympton in the presence of witnesses.

It is evident that King Henry [I] did not give Richard de Redvers the right of advowson in Plympton, even though he helped him greatly in the kingdom of England and duchy of Normandy against his elder brother Robert Curthose, whom he defeated in battle at Tinchebrai [1106] and imprisoned for life. But when the said William de Warelwast was raised to the episcopal throne of Exeter [1107], he besought of the lord King Henry I that the right of advowson in the said churches should forever be ascribed, and confirmed by his charter, to the episcopal seat of Exeter; which was duly done. This charter, and certain others of kings of England (notable for their gold letters) concerning the pertaining of the said churches to the royal chapelry, are preserved in the church of Exeter: we have seen them, and have heard them read before King Henry II's justices by Bartholomew bishop of Exeter [1161–84] of pious memory.

Then Bishop William saw that many outrages and scandals abounded in the life and behaviour of his feeble subjects, and especially clerics: for they all laboured in unchastity, and in this respect priest resembled people. Inspired by God, he strove to correct this vice first in the greater churches. It was an intolerable scandal[?] that the priests publicly took wives and, neglecting the embellishment and cult of churches, they meditated as it were on hereditary succession to estates, and they occupied themselves in decorating women, not altars. So he began, as a good shepherd, to recall them to chastity and truth by the word of holy exhortation and the example of canonical religion. He first established the order of [Augustinian] canons in Devon and Cornwall through men of distinguished life, and installed [it] in the church of Plympton [1121] and of Bodmin [c.1124] and of Launceston [1127], and involved the lord King Henry I in confirming [it].

We are claiming the tithes of seven vills from which we have the corpses at Lanow [St Kew] church, which are in the same royal manor of Lanow, towards *Egglostetha* which is in Richard Bloiho's fief. Of these the first is called Treburgett, the second Trekee, the third Suffenton, the fourth [Lower] Suffenton, the fifth Treroosel, the sixth *Duunaunt*, the seventh Bodwin. We have heard from old [men] that those [tithes] were alienated from Lanow church, partly because the men of the said vills were frightened to come to Lanow church on account of feuds arising from a killing, whereas St Teath's church was nearby; but also because the tithes were very small at that time, and the clergy of Lanow were weak and lazy in pursuing their rights. They likewise failed to exact from their franklins the yearly gift and aid which, it is said, they rightfully ought to have paid: for [the franklins] pay a small rent, namely a penny from the first acre of each farthingland, and now nothing more.

References

ABELS, R. P. (1988), *Lordship and Military Obligation in Anglo-Saxon England* (London).

ABRAMS, L. (1995*a*), 'The Anglo-Saxons and the Christianization of Scandinavia', *ASE* 24: 213–49.

——(1995*b*), 'Eleventh-Century Missions and the Early Stages of Ecclesiastical Organization in Scandinavia', *Anglo-Norman Studies*, 17: 21–40.

——(1996), *Anglo-Saxon Glastonbury: Church and Endowment* (Woodbridge).

——(1998), 'History and Archaeology: The Conversion of Scandinavia', in B. L. Crawford (ed.), *Conversion and Christianity in the North Sea World* (St Andrews), 109–28.

——(2000), 'Conversion and Assimilation', in Hadley and Richards 2000: 135–53.

——(2001), 'The Conversion of the Danelaw', in Graham-Campbell and others 2001: 31–44.

ADAMS, K. A. (1990), 'Monastery and Village at Crayke, North Yorkshire', *Yorkshire Archaeological Journal*, 62: 29–50.

ADAMS, R. McC. (1966), *The Evolution of Urban Society: Early Mesopotamia and Prehispanic Mexico* (London).

ADDLESHAW, G. W. O. (1953), *The Beginnings of the Parochial System* (St Anthony's Hall Publications 3, York).

ADDYMAN, P. V. (1973), 'Late Saxon Settlements in the St. Neots Area', *Proceedings of the Cambridge Antiquarian Society*, 64: 45–99.

AIRD, W. M. (1998), *St Cuthbert and the Normans* (Woodbridge).

AITCHISON, N. B. (1994), *Armagh and the Royal Centres in Early Medieval Ireland* (Woodbridge).

ALCOCK, L. (1988*a*), *Bede, Eddius and the Forts of the North Britons* (The Jarrow Lecture 1988, Jarrow).

——(1988*b*), 'The Activities of Potentates in Celtic Britain, AD 500–800', in Driscoll and Nieke 1988: 22–46.

ALI, J. R., and CUNICH, P. (2001), 'The Orientation of Churches: Some New Evidence', *AntJ* 81: 155–93.

ALLEN, D., and DALWOOD, C. H. (1983), 'Iron Age Occupation, a Middle Saxon Cemetery, and Twelfth to Nineteenth Century Urban Occupation: Excavations in George Street, Aylesbury, 1981', *Records of Buckinghamshire*, 25: 1–60.

ALZIEU, G. (1998), *Les Églises de l'ancien diocèse de Lodève au Moyen Âge* (Montpellier).

ANDERSON, E. R. (1991), 'The Uncarpentered World of Old English Poetry', *ASE* 20: 65–80.

ANDERSSON, H., and ANGLERT, M. (eds.) (1989), *By, Huvudgård och Kyrka* (Stockholm).

ANDERTON, M. (ed.) (1999), *Anglo-Saxon Trading Centres: Beyond the Emporia* (Glasgow).

ANDRÉN, A. (1985), *Den Urbana Scenen* (*Acta Archaeologica Lundensia*, 8° ser. No. 13, Malmö).

ANDREWS, P. (1992), 'Middle Saxon Norfolk: Evidence for Settlement 650–850', *Norfolk Archaeological and Historical Research Group Annual*, 1: 13–28.

ANGLERT, M. (1995), *Kyrkor och Herravälde* (Lund).

ARMSTRONG, P., TOMLINSON, D., and EVANS, D. H. (1991), *Excavations at Lurk Lane, Beverley, 1979–82* (Sheffield).

ARNOLD, C. J., and DAVIES, J. L. (2000), *Roman and Early Medieval Wales* (Stroud).

ASHMORE, W., and KNAPP, A. B. (1999), *Archaeologies of Landscape: Contemporary Perspectives* (Oxford).

ASTILL, G. G. (1978), *Historic Towns in Berkshire: An Archaeological Appraisal* (Reading).

——(1991), 'Towns and Town Hierarchies in Saxon England', *Oxford Journal of Archaeology*, 10: 95–117.

ASTON, M. (1986), 'Post Roman Central Places in Somerset', in Grant 1986: 49–77.

——and BOND, J. (1987), *The Landscape of Towns* (2nd edn., Gloucester).

ATSMA, H. (1976), 'Les Monastères urbains du nord de la Gaule', *RHEF* 62: 163–87.

AUBREY, J. (1972), *Three Prose Works* (ed. J. Buchanan-Brown, Carbondale, Ill.).

AUBRUN, M. (1986), *La Paroisse en France, des origines au XVe siècle* (Paris).

AUDOUY, M., DIX, B., and PARSONS, D. (1995), 'The Tower of All Saints' Church, Earls Barton, Northamptonshire: Its Construction and Context', *ArchJ* 152: 73–94.

AUSTIN, D. (1986), 'Central Place Theory and the Middle Ages', in Grant 1986: 95–103.

AYERS, B. S. (1985), *Excavations within the North-East Bailey of Norwich Castle, 1979* (*EAA* 28).

——(1994), *The English Heritage Book of Norwich* (London).

BAILEY, R. N. (1980*a*), *Viking Age Sculpture in Northern England* (London).

——(1980*b*), *The Early Christian Church in Leicester and its Region* (Vaughan Paper 25, Leicester).

——(1985), 'Aspects of Viking-Age Sculpture in Cumbria', in Baldwin and Whyte 1985: 53–64.

——(1991), 'St Wilfrid, Ripon and Hexham', in C. Karkov and R. Farrell (eds.), *Studies in Insular Art and Archaeology* (American Early Medieval Studies 1, Oxford, Oh.), 3–25.

——(1996*a*), *England's Earliest Sculptors* (Toronto).

——(1996*b*), '"What Mean these Stones?" Some Aspects of Pre-Norman Sculpture in Cheshire and Lancashire', *Bulletin of the John Rylands Library*, 78: 21–46.

——(2000), 'The Gandersheim Casket and Anglo-Saxon Stone Sculpture', in *Das Gandersheimer Runenkästchen* (Brunswick, 2000), 43–51.

——and CRAMP, R. (1988), *Corpus of Anglo-Saxon Stone Sculpture, II: Cumberland, Westmorland and Lancashire North-of-the-Sands* (Oxford).

BAKER, D. (1969), 'Excavations at Elstow Abbey . . . : Second Interim Report', *Bedfordshire Archaeological Journal*, 4: 27–41.

BAKER, N. (1980), 'The Urban Churches of Worcester: A Survey', *Trans. Worcestershire Arch. Soc.* 3rd ser. 7: 115–24.

——and HOLT, R. (1998), 'The Origins of Urban Parish Boundaries', in Slater and Rosser 1998: 209–35.

BALDWIN, J., and WHYTE, I. D. (eds.) (1985), *The Scandinavians in Cumbria* (Edinburgh).

BANNERMAN, J. (1966–8), 'Notes on the Scottish Entries in the Early Irish Annals', *Scottish Gaelic Studies*, 11: 149–70.

BARLOW, F. (1979), *The English Church 1000–1066* (2nd edn., London).

BARNWELL, P., BUTLER, L. A. S., and DUNN, C. J. (2003), 'The Confusion of Conversion: *Streanæshalch*, Strensall and Whitby and the Northumbrian Church', in Carver 2003: 311–26.

BARROW, G. W. S. (1973), *The Kingdom of the Scots* (London).

——(1975), 'The Pattern of Lordship and Feudal Settlement in Cumbria', *Journal of Medieval History*, 1: 117–38.

——(1983), 'The Childhood of Scottish Christianity: A Note on Some Place-Name Evidence', *Scottish Studies*, 27: 1–15.

BARROW, J. (1986), 'Cathedrals, Provosts and Prebends: A Comparison of Twelfth-Century German and English Practice', *JEH* 37: 536–64.

——(1992), 'Urban Cemetery Location in the High Middle Ages', in S. Bassett (ed.), *Death in Towns* (Leicester), 78–100.

——(1994), 'English Cathedral Communities and Reform in the Late Tenth and the Eleventh Centuries', in D. Rollason, M. Harvey, and M. Prestwich (eds.), *Anglo-Norman Durham* (Woodbridge), 25–39.

——(1996), 'The Community of Worcester, 961–c.1100', in Brooks and Cubitt 1996: 84–99.

——(2000*a*), 'Churches, Education and Literacy in Towns, 600–1300', in Palliser 2000: 127–52.

——(2000*b*), 'Survival and Mutation: Ecclesiastical Institutions in the Danelaw in the Ninth and Tenth Centuries', in Hadley and Richards 2000: 155–76.

BARTLETT, R. (1986), *Trial by Fire and Water: The Medieval Judicial Ordeal* (Oxford).

BASSETT, S. (1985), 'A Probable Mercian Royal Mausoleum at Winchcombe, Gloucestershire', *AntJ* 65: 82–100.

——(1989*a*), 'Churches in Worcester before and after the Conversion of the Anglo-Saxons', *AntJ* 69: 225–56.

——(ed.) (1989*b*), *The Origins of Anglo-Saxon Kingdoms* (Leicester).

——(1991), 'Anglo-Saxon Shrewsbury and its Churches', *Midland History*, 16: 1–23.

——(1992), 'Church and Diocese in the West Midlands: The Transition from British to Anglo-Saxon Control', in Blair and Sharpe 1992: 13–40.

——(1996), 'The Administrative Landscape of the Diocese of Worcester in the Tenth Century', in Brooks and Cubitt 1996: 147–73.

BASSETT, S. (1997), 'Continuity and Fission in the Anglo-Saxon Landscape: The Origins of the Rodings (Essex)', *Landscape History*, 19: 25–42.

——(1998), *The Origins of the Parishes of the Deerhurst Area* (The Deerhurst Lecture 1997, Deerhurst).

——(2000), 'How the West was Won: The Anglo-Saxon Takeover of the West Midlands', *ASSAH* 11: 107–18.

BATCOCK, N. (1988), 'The Parish Church in Norfolk in the Eleventh and Twelfth Centuries', in Blair 1988*a*: 179–90.

——(1991), *The Ruined and Disused Churches of Norfolk* (*EAA* 51, Gressenhall).

BATES, D. (1982), *Normandy before 1066* (London).

——(2000), 'England and the "Feudal Revolution"', *SSCI* 47: 611–46.

BATESON, E., and others (1893–1940), *A History of Northumberland* (15 vols., Newcastle-upon-Tyne).

BAXTER, S. (2003), 'The Leofwinesons: Power, Property and Patronage in the Early English Kingdom' (unpublished Oxford D.Phil. thesis, 2003).

BAZIRE, J., and CROSS, J. E. (eds.) (1982), *Eleven Old English Rogationtide Homilies* (Toronto).

BEAZLEY, O., and AYERS, B. (2001), *Two Medieval Churches in Norfolk* (*EAA* 96, Gressenhall).

BEDINGFIELD, M. B. (2002), *The Dramatic Liturgy of Anglo-Saxon England* (Woodbridge).

BEHR, C. (2000), 'The Origins of Kingship in Early Medieval Kent', *EME* 9: 25–52.

BELL, R. D., and BERESFORD, M. W. (eds.) (1987), *Wharram: A Study of Settlement on the Yorkshire Wolds, 3: Wharram Percy: The Church of St. Martin* (Soc. for Medieval Archaeology, London).

BELL, T. W. (1998*a*), 'A Roman Signal Station at Whitby', *ArchJ* 155: 303–22.

——(1998*b*), 'Churches on Roman Buildings: Christian Associations and Roman Masonry in Anglo-Saxon England', *MA* 42: 1–18.

——(2001), 'The Religious Reuse of Roman Structures in Anglo-Saxon England' (unpublished Oxford D.Phil. thesis).

BENSON, E. P. (ed.) (1981), *Mesoamerican Sites and World-Views* (Washington, DC).

BERESFORD, G. (1987), *Goltho: The Development of an Early Medieval Manor c.850–1150* (English Heritage, London).

BERNHARDT, J. W. (1993), *Itinerant Kingship and Royal Monasteries in Early Medieval Germany, c.936–1075* (Cambridge).

BETHELL, D. L. T. (1981), 'The Originality of the Early Irish Church', *Journal of the Royal Society of Antiquaries of Ireland*, 111: 36–49.

BHREATHNACH, E. (1998), 'The *Tech Midchúarta*, "the House of the Mead Circuit": Feasting, Royal Circuits and the King's Court in Early Ireland', *Archaeology Ireland*, 12. 4: 20–2.

BIDDICK, K. (1989), *The Other Economy: Pastoral Husbandry on a Medieval Estate* (Berkeley).

BIDDLE, M. (1973), 'Winchester: The Development of an Early Capital', in H. Jankuhn and others (eds.), *Vor-und Frühformen der europäischen Stadt im*

Mittelalter (Abhandlungen der Akademie der Wissenschaften: Philologisch-Historische Klasse, 3 Folge, Nr. 83, Göttingen), 229–61.

—— (1976*a*), 'Towns', in Wilson 1976: 99–150.

—— (ed.) (1976*b*), *Winchester in the Early Middle Ages: An Edition and Discussion of the Winton Domesday* (Winchester Studies 1, Oxford).

—— (1983), 'The Study of Winchester: Archaeology and History in a British Town, 1961–1983', *Proceedings of the British Academy*, 69: 93–135.

—— (1986), 'Archaeology, Architecture, and the Cult of Saints in Anglo-Saxon England', in Butler and Morris 1986: 1–31.

—— (1989), 'A City in Transition: 400–800', in M. D. Lobel (ed.), *The City of London from Prehistoric Times to c.1520* (Historic Towns Atlas 3, Oxford), 20–9.

—— and BLAIR, J. (1987), 'The Hook Norton Hoard of 1848: A Viking Burial from Oxfordshire?', *Oxoniensia*, 52: 186–95.

—— and KJØLBYE-BIDDLE, B. (1985), 'The Repton Stone', *ASE* 14: 233–92.

———— (1992), 'Repton and the Vikings', *Antiquity*, 66: 36–51.

———— (2001*a*), 'The Origins of St. Albans Abbey: Romano-British Cemetery and Anglo-Saxon Monastery', in M. Henig and P. Lindley (eds.), *Alban and St. Albans: Roman and Medieval Architecture, Art and Archaeology* (BAA Conference Trans. 24), 45–77.

———— (2001*b*), 'Repton and the "Great Heathen Army", 873–4', in Graham-Campbell and others 2001: 45–96.

———— (forthcoming), *The Anglo-Saxon Minsters at Winchester* (Winchester Studies 4. 1, Oxford).

BIERBRAUER, V. (2003), 'The Cross Goes North: From Late Antiquity to Merovingian Times South and North of the Alps', in Carver 2003: 429–42.

BISCHOFF, B., and LAPIDGE, M. (1994), *Biblical Commentaries from the Canterbury School of Theodore and Hadrian* (Cambridge).

BLACKBURN, M. (2003), '"Productive" Sites and the Pattern of Coin Loss in England, 600–1180', in Pestell and Ulmschneider 2003: 20–36.

BLAIR, J. (1985*a*), 'Secular Minster Churches in Domesday Book', in P. Sawyer (ed.), *Domesday Book: A Reassessment* (London), 104–42.

—— (1985*b*), 'Parish versus Village: The Bampton–Standlake Tithe Conflict of 1317–19', *Oxfordshire Local History*, 2. 2: 34–47.

—— (1987), 'Local Churches in Domesday Book and Before', in J. C. Holt (ed.), *Domesday Studies* (Woodbridge), 265–78.

—— (ed.) (1988*a*), *Minsters and Parish Churches: The Local Church in Transition 950–1200* (Oxford).

—— (1988*b*), 'Introduction: From Minster to Parish Church', in Blair 1988*a*: 1–19.

—— (1988*c*), 'Minster Churches in the Landscape', in D. Hooke (ed.), *Anglo-Saxon Settlements* (Oxford), 35–58.

—— (1988*d*), 'St. Frideswide's Monastery: Problems and Possibilities', *Oxoniensia*, 53: 221–58.

—— (1988*e*), 'Thornbury, Binsey: A Probable Defensive Enclosure Associated with St. Frideswide', *Oxoniensia*, 53: 3–20.

BLAIR, J. (1989), 'Frithuwold's Kingdom and the Origins of Surrey' and 'The Chertsey Resting-Place List and the Enshrinement of Frithuwold', in Bassett 1989 *b*: 97–107, 231–6.

——(1991*a*), *Early Medieval Surrey: Landholding, Church and Settlement before 1300* (Stroud).

——(1991*b*), 'The Early Churches at Lindisfarne', *Archaeologia Aeliana*, 5th ser. 19: 47–53.

——(1992), 'Anglo-Saxon Minsters: A Topographical Review', in Blair and Sharpe 1992: 226–66.

——(1993), 'Hall and Chamber: English Domestic Planning 1000–1200', in G. Meirion-Jones and M. Jones (eds.), *Manorial Domestic Buildings in England and Northern France* (London), 1–21.

——(1994), *Anglo-Saxon Oxfordshire* (Stroud).

——(1995*a*), 'Ecclesiastical Organization and Pastoral Care in Anglo-Saxon England', *EME* 4: 193–212.

——(1995*b*), 'Anglo-Saxon Pagan Shrines and their Prototypes', *ASSAH* 8: 1–28.

——(1996*a*), 'The Minsters of the Thames', in J. Blair and B. Golding (eds.), *The Cloister and the World: Essays in Medieval History in Honour of Barbara Harvey* (Oxford), 5–28.

——(1996*b*), 'Palaces or Minsters? Northampton and Cheddar Reconsidered', *ASE* 25: 97–121.

——(1996*c*), 'Churches in the Early English Landscape: Social and Cultural Contexts', in Blair and Pyrah 1996: 6–18.

——(1997), 'St. Cuthman, Steyning and Bosham', *Sussex Archaeological Collections*, 135: 173–92.

——(1998*a*), 'Clerical Communities and Parochial Space: The Planning of Urban Mother Churches in the Twelfth and Thirteenth Centuries', in Slater and Rosser 1998: 272–94.

——(1998*b*), 'Archaeological Discoveries at Woodeaton Church', *Oxoniensia*, 63: 221–37.

——(1998*c*), 'Bampton: An Anglo-Saxon Minster', *Current Archaeology*, 160: 124–30.

——(2000), 'Small Towns 600–1270', in Palliser 2000: 245–70.

——(2001*a*), 'The Anglo-Saxon Church in Herefordshire: Four Themes', in Malpas and others 2001: 3–13.

——(2001*b*), 'Beverley, *Inderauuda* and St John: A Neglected Reference', *Northern History*, 28. 2: 315–16.

——(2001*c*), 'Estate Memoranda of c.1070 from the See of Dorchester-on-Thames', *EHR* 116: 114–23.

——(2002*a*), 'A Saint for Every Minster? Local Cults in Anglo-Saxon England', and 'A Handlist of Anglo-Saxon Saints', in Thacker and Sharpe 2002: 455–565.

——(2002*b*), 'Anglo-Saxon Bicester: The Minster and the Town', *Oxoniensia*, 67: 133–40.

——(2004), 'Wells: Roman Mausoleum, or Just Anglo-Saxon Minster?', *Church Archaeology*, 5–6: 134–7.

——and Pyrah, C. (eds.) (1996), *Church Archaeology: Research Directions for the Future* (CBA Research Rep. 104, York).

——and Sharpe, R. (eds.) (1992), *Pastoral Care before the Parish* (Leicester).

Blinkhorn, P. (1999), 'Of Cabbages and Kings: Production, Trade, and Consumption in Middle-Saxon England', in Anderton 1999: 4–23.

Blockley, K., and others (1995), *Excavations in the Marlowe Car Park and Surrounding Areas* (*The Archaeology of Canterbury* 5, Canterbury).

——Sparks, M., and Tatton-Brown, T. (1997), *Canterbury Cathedral Nave: Archaeology, History and Architecture* (*The Archaeology of Canterbury* ns I, Canterbury).

Bodden, M.-C. (ed. and trans.) (1987), *The Old English Finding of the True Cross* (Woodbridge).

Boddington, A. (1990), 'Models of Burial, Settlement and Worship: The Final Phase Reviewed', in E. Southworth (ed.), *Anglo-Saxon Cemeteries: A Reappraisal* (Stroud), 177–99.

——(1996), *Raunds Furnells: The Anglo-Saxon Church and Churchyard* (English Heritage, London).

Boehmer, H. (1921), 'Das Eigenkirchentum in England', in H. Boehmer and others (eds.), *Texte und Forschungen zur englischen Kulturgeschichte: Festgabe für Felix Liebermann* (Halle), 301–53.

Bond, C. J. (1988), 'Church and Parish in Norman Worcestershire', in Blair 1988*a*: 119–58.

Bond, F. (1908), *Fonts and Font Covers* (London).

Bonnassie, P. (1994), 'Les *Sagreres* catalanes: la concentration de l'habitat dans le "cercle de paix" des églises (XIe s.)', in Fixot and Zadora-Rio 1994: 68–79.

Bonner, G. (1989), 'St. Cuthbert at Chester-le-Street', in Bonner and others 1989: 387–95.

——Rollason, D., and Stancliffe, C. (eds.) (1989), *St. Cuthbert, his Cult and his Community to AD 1200* (Woodbridge).

Bonnet, C. (1993), *Les Fouilles de l'ancien groupe épiscopal de Genève* (Geneva).

Bourne, J. (1987–8), 'Kingston Place-Names: An Interim Report', *Journal of the English Place-Name Society*, 20: 13–37.

Boyd, C. E. (1952), *Tithes and Parishes in Medieval Italy* (Ithaca, NY).

Boyle, A., Jennings, D., and others (1998), *The Anglo-Saxon Cemetery at Butler's Field, Lechlade, Gloucestershire:* i (Oxford).

Bradley, J. (1999), 'Urbanization in Early Medieval Ireland', in C. E. Karkov, K. M. Wickham-Crowley, and B. K. Young (eds.), *Spaces of the Living and the Dead: An Archaeological Dialogue* (American Early Medieval Studies 3, Oxford), 133–47.

Bradley, R. (1987), 'Time Regained: The Creation of Continuity', *JBAA* 140: 1–17.

——(1993), *Altering the Earth* (Edinburgh).

——(2000), *An Archaeology of Natural Places* (London).

Brett, M. (1975), *The English Church under Henry I* (Oxford).

Brett, M. (1995), 'The English Abbeys, their Tenants and the King (950–1150)', in *Chiesa e mondo feudale nei secoli X–XII: miscellanea del Centro di Studi Medioevali,* 14: 277–302.

Brink, S. (1996), 'Political and Social Structures in Early Scandinavia: A Settlement-Historical Pre-Study of the Central Place', *Tor,* 28: 235–81.

——(1998), 'The Formation of the Scandinavian Parish, with Some Remarks Regarding the English Impact on the Process', in J. Hill and M. Swan (eds.), *The Community, the Family and the Saint: Patterns of Power in Early Medieval Europe* (Turnhout), 19–44.

Britnell, R. H. (1981), 'The Proliferation of Markets in England, 1200–1349', *Economic History Review,* 2nd ser. 34: 209–21.

Britnell, W. J. (1990), 'Capel Maelog, Llandrindod Wells, Powys: Excavations 1984–87', *MA* 34: 27–96.

Brook, D. (1992), 'The Early Christian Church East and West of Offa's Dyke', in Edwards and Lane 1992*a*: 77–89.

Brooke, C. N. L. (1970), 'The Missionary at Home: The Church in the Towns, 1000–1250', *SCH* 6: 59–83.

——(1985), 'The Churches of Medieval Cambridge', in D. Beales and G. Best (eds.), *History, Society and the Churches: Essays in Honour of Owen Chadwick* (Cambridge), 49–76.

Brooks, D. A. (1988), 'The Case for Continuity in Fifth-Century Canterbury Re-examined', *Oxford Journal of Archaeology,* 7: 99–114.

Brooks, N. (1971), 'The Development of Military Obligations in Eighth- and Ninth-Century England', in P. Clemoes and K. Hughes (eds.), *England Before the Conquest* (Cambridge), 69–84.

——(1984), *The Early History of the Church of Canterbury* (Leicester).

——(1989), 'The Formation of the Mercian Kingdom', in Bassett 1989*b*: 159–70.

——(1992), 'The Career of St Dunstan', in Ramsay and others 1992: 1–23.

——(1995), 'The Anglo-Saxon Cathedral Community, 597–1070', in P. Collinson, N. Ramsay, and M. Sparks (eds.), *A History of Canterbury Cathedral* (Oxford), 1–37.

——(1996), 'The Administrative Background to the Burghal Hidage', in Hill and Rumble 1996: 128–50.

——(2000), 'Canterbury, Rome and the Construction of English Identity', in J. M. H. Smith (ed.), *Early Medieval Rome and the Christian West: Essays in Honour of Donald A. Bullough* (Leiden), 221–47.

——and Cubitt, C. (eds.) (1996), *St. Oswald of Worcester: Life and Influence* (London)

Brown, A. E., Gelling, M., and Orr, C. (1990–1), 'The Details of the Anglo-Saxon Landscape: Badby Revisited', *Northamptonshire Past and Present,* 8: 95–103.

Brown, M. P. (1996), *The Book of Cerne: Prayer, Patronage and Power in Ninth-Century England* (London).

——(2001), 'Mercian Manuscripts? The "Tiberius" Group and its Historical Context', in Brown and Farr 2001: 279–90.

——and FARR, C. A. (eds.) (2001), *Mercia: An Anglo-Saxon Kingdom in Europe* (London).

BROWN, P. (1981), *The Cult of Saints: Its Rise and Function in Latin Christianity* (Chicago).

——(1996), *The Rise of Western Christendom* (Malden, Mass.).

[BROWNE, G. F.], Bishop of Bristol (1904–8), 'The Aldhelm Crosses in Somerset and Wilts', *Proc. Clifton Antiquarian Club*, 6: 121–7.

BRUCE-MITFORD, R., and others (1997), *Mawgan Porth: A Settlement of the Late Saxon Period on the North Cornish Coast* (London).

BRÜHL, C. (1975–), *Palatium und Civitas*, i– (Vienna in progress).

——(1977), 'The Town as a Political Centre: General Survey', in M. W. Barley (ed.), *European Towns: Their Archaeology and Early History* (London), 419–30.

BRYANT, R. (1990), 'The Lypiatt Cross', *TBGAS* 108: 33–52.

BRYANT, R., and HEIGHWAY, C. (2003), 'Excavations at St. Mary de Lode Church, Gloucester', *TBGAS* 121: 97–178.

BUCKBERRY, J., and HADLEY, D. M. (2001), 'Fieldwork at Chapel Road, Fillingham', *Lincolnshire History and Archaeology*, 36: 11–18.

BULLOUGH, D. A. (1982), 'The Missions to the English and Picts and their Heritage (to c.800)', in H. Löwe (ed.), *Die Iren und Europa im früheren Mittelalter*, i (Stuttgart), 80–98.

——(1983), 'Burial, Community and Belief in the Early Medieval West', in Wormald and others 1983: 177–201.

—— (1985), '*Aula Renovata*: The Carolingian Court before the Aachen Palace', *Proceedings of the British Academy*, 71: 267–301.

——(1993), 'What has Ingeld to do with Lindisfarne?', *ASE* 22: 93–125.

——(1999), 'The Carolingian Liturgical Experience', *SCH* 35: 29–64.

BURNELL, S. (1988), 'Merovingian to Early Carolingian Churches and their Founder-Graves in Southern Germany and Switzerland' (unpublished Oxford D.Phil. thesis).

——and JAMES, E. (1999), 'The Archaeology of Conversion on the Continent in the Sixth and Seventh Centuries: Some Observations and Comparisons with Anglo-Saxon England', in Gameson 1999: 83–106.

BURTON, J. (1994), 'The Monastic Revival in Yorkshire: Whitby and St. Mary's, York', in D. Rollason, M. Harvey, and M. Prestwich (eds.), *Anglo-Norman Durham* (Woodbridge), 41–51.

BUTLER, L. A. S. (1964), 'Minor Medieval Monumental Sculpture in the East Midlands', *ArchJ* 121: 111–53.

——(1979), 'The "Monastic City" in Wales: Myth or Reality?', *Bulletin of the Board of Celtic Studies*, 28. 3: 458–67.

——and MORRIS, R. K. (eds.) (1986), *The Anglo-Saxon Church: Papers on History, Architecture, and Archaeology in Honour of Dr. H. M. Taylor* (CBA Research Rep. 60, London).

CADMAN, G. E. (1983), 'Raunds, 1977–1983: An Excavation Summary', *MA* 27: 107–22.

CAMBRIDGE, E. (1984), 'The Early Church in County Durham: A Reassessment', *JBAA* 137: 65–85.

——(1999), 'The Architecture of the Augustinian Mission', in Gameson 1999: 202–36.

——and ROLLASON, D. (1995), 'The Pastoral Organization of the Anglo-Saxon Church: A Review of the "Minster Hypothesis"', *EME* 4: 87–104.

CAMERON, K. (1968), 'Eccles in English Place-Names', in M. W. Barley and R. P. C. Hanson (eds.), *Christianity in Britain 300–700* (Leicester), 87–92.

——(1975), *Place-Name Evidence for the Anglo-Saxon Invasion and Scandinavian Settlements* (Nottingham).

CAMPBELL, E. (1996), 'The Archaeological Evidence for External Contacts: Imports, Trade and the Economy in Celtic Britain AD 400–800', in K. Dark (ed.), *External Contacts and the Economy of Late Roman and Post-Roman Britain* (Woodbridge), 83–96.

——and LANE, A. (1993), 'Celtic and Germanic Interaction in Dalriada: The 7th-Century Metalworking Site at Dunadd', in Spearman and Higgitt 1993: 52–63.

CAMPBELL, J. (1986), *Essays in Anglo-Saxon History* (London).

——(1987), 'The Debt of the Early English Church to Ireland', in P. Ní Chatháin and M. Richter (eds.), *Irland und die Christenheit: Bibelstudien und Mission* (Stuttgart), 332–46.

——(2000), *The Anglo-Saxon State* (London).

——(2003), 'Production and Distribution in Early and Middle Anglo-Saxon England', in Pestell and Ulmschneider 2003: 12–19.

CANHAM, R. (1979), 'Excavations at Shepperton Green, 1967 and 1973', *Trans. London and Middlesex Arch. Soc.*, 30: 97–124.

CARMICHAEL, D. L., HUBERT, J., REEVES, B., and SCHANCHE, A. (eds.) (1994), *Sacred Sites, Sacred Places* (London).

CARR, R. D., TESTER, A., and MURPHY, P. (1988), 'The Middle-Saxon Settlement at Staunch Meadow, Brandon', *Antiquity*, 62: 371–7.

[CARRIÉ, J.-M. (ed.)] (1996), *Les Églises doubles et les familles d'églises: Antiquité tardive*, 4.

CARVER, M. (1986), 'Sutton Hoo in Context', *SSCI* 32: 77–117.

——(ed.) (1992a), *The Age of Sutton Hoo* (Woodbridge).

——(1992b), 'Ideology and Allegiance in East Anglia', in R. Farrell and C. Neuman de Vegvar (eds.), *Sutton Hoo: Fifty Years After* (Oxford, Oh.), 173–82.

——(1998), 'Conversion and Politics on the Eastern Seaboard of Britain: Some Archaeological Indicators', in B. E. Crawford (ed.), *Conversion and Christianity in the North Sea World* (St Andrews), 11–40.

——(2001), 'Why That? Why There? Why Then? The Politics of Early Medieval Monumentality', in Hamerow and MacGregor 2001: 1–22.

——(ed.) (2003), *The Cross Goes North: Processes of Conversion in Northern Europe AD 300–1300* (York).

CASTAGNETTI, A. (1979), *L'organizzazione del territorio rurale nel medioevo* (Turin).

CATHER, S., PARK, D., and WILLIAMSON, P. (eds.) (1990), *Early Medieval Wall Painting and Painted Sculpture in England* (BAR Brit. Ser. 216, Oxford).

CERVANTES, F. (1994), *The Devil in the New World* (New Haven).

CHAMBERS, R. A. (1973), 'A Cemetery Site at Beacon Hill, near Lewknor', *Oxoniensia*, 38: 138–45.

——(1976), 'The Cemetery Site at Beacon Hill, near Lewknor', *Oxoniensia*, 41: 77–85.

CHAPLAIS, P. (1969), 'Who Introduced Charters into England? The Case for Augustine', *Journal of the Society of Archivists*, 3. 10: 526–42.

CHAPMAN, A. (1998), 'Brackmills, Northampton', *Current Archaeology*, 159: 92–5.

CHARLES-EDWARDS, T. M. (1974), 'The Foundation of Lastingham', *Ryedale Historian*, 7: 13–21.

——(1976), 'Boundaries in Irish Law', in P. H. Sawyer (ed.), *Medieval Settlement* (London), 83–7.

——(1989), 'Early Medieval Kingships in the British Isles', in Bassett 1989*b*: 28–39.

——(1991), 'From Conversion to Conquest' [review of works including Sims-Williams 1990], *Times Literary Supplement*, 8 Feb., 22.

——(1992), 'The Pastoral Role of the Church in the Early Irish Laws', in Blair and Sharpe 1992: 63–80.

——(1997), 'Anglo-Saxon Kinship Revisited', in Hines 1997*a*: 171–210.

——(2000), *Early Christian Ireland* (Cambridge).

——(2001), 'Wales and Mercia, 613–918', in Brown and Farr 2001: 89–105.

CHAUME, M. (1937, 1938), 'Le Mode de constitution et de délimitation des paroisses rurales aux temps mérovingiens et carolingiens', *Revue Mabillon*, 27 (1937), 61–73, and 28 (1938), 1–9.

CHIBNALL, M. (1958), 'Ecclesiastical Patronage and the Growth of Feudal Estates at the Time of the Norman Conquest', *Annales de Normandie*, 8: 103–18.

CHRISTALLER, W. (1933), *Die zentralen Orte in Süddeutschland* (Jena).

CHRISTIAN, W. A., Jr. (1981*a*), *Local Religion in Sixteenth-Century Spain* (Princeton).

——(1981*b*), *Apparitions in Late Medieval and Renaissance Spain* (Princeton).

——(1989), *Person and God in a Spanish Valley* (2nd edn., Princeton).

CHRISTIE, H., OLSEN, O., and TAYLOR, H. M. (1979), 'The Wooden Church of St. Andrew at Greensted, Essex', *AntJ* 59: 92–112.

CLARKE, H. B., and SIMMS, A. (eds.) (1985), *The Comparative History of Urban Origins in Non-Roman Europe* (2 vols., BAR Int. Ser. 255, Oxford).

————(1987), 'Analogy versus Theory: A Rejoinder', *Journal of Historical Geography*, 13: 57–63.

COATES, S. (1996), 'The Role of Bishops in the Early Anglo-Saxon Church: A Reassessment', *History*, 81: 177–96.

COLLIS, J. (1983), *Wigber Low, Derbyshire* (Sheffield).

CONSTABLE, G. (1964), *Monastic Tithes: From their Origins to the Twelfth Century* (Cambridge).

——(1982), 'Monasteries, Rural Churches and the *Cura Animarum* in the Early Middle Ages', *SSCI* 28: 349–89.

COPPACK, G. (1986), 'St. Lawrence Church, Burnham, South Humberside: The Excavation of a Parochial Chapel', *Lincolnshire History and Archaeology*, 21: 39–60.

COSTAMBEYS, M. (2001), 'Burial Topography and the Power of the Church in Fifth- and Sixth-Century Rome', *Papers of the British School at Rome*, 69: 169–89.

COULSTOCK, P. H. (1993), *The Collegiate Church of Wimborne Minster* (Woodbridge).

COWNIE, E. (1998), *Religious Patronage in Anglo-Norman England* (Woodbridge).

COX, B. (1975), 'The Place-Names of the Earliest English Records', *Journal of the English Place-Name Society*, 8: 12–66.

——(1994), 'The Pattern of Old English *Burh* in Early Lindsey', *ASE* 23: 35–56.

COX, J. C. (1911), *The Sanctuaries and Sanctuary Seekers of Mediæval England* (London).

CRAMP, R. J. (1976), 'Monastic Sites', in Wilson 1976: 201–52, 453–7.

——(1977), 'Schools of Mercian Sculpture', in Dornier 1977*a*: 191–233.

——(1984), *Corpus of Anglo-Saxon Stone Sculpture*, i (pts. 1 and 2): *Co. Durham and Northumberland* (Oxford).

——(1993), 'A Reconsideration of the Monastic Site at Whitby', in Spearman and Higgitt 1993: 64–73.

CRASTER, E. (1954), 'The Patrimony of St. Cuthbert', *EHR* 69: 177–99.

CRAWFORD, B. E. (1992), 'The Cult of St. Clement in England and Scotland', in *Medieval Europe 1992 Conference, Pre-Printed Papers*, 6 (York), 1–3.

——(ed.) (1996), *Scotland in Dark Age Britain* (St Andrews).

CRAWFORD, S. (1989), 'The Anglo-Saxon Cemetery at Chimney, Oxfordshire', *Oxoniensia*, 54: 45–56.

——(2004), 'Votive Deposition, Religion and the Anglo-Saxon Furnished Burial Ritual', *World Archaeology*, 36: 87–102.

CRICK, J. (1988), 'Church, Land and Local Nobility in Early Ninth-Century Kent: The Case of Ealdorman Oswulf', *Historical Research*, 61: 251–69.

CROOK, J. (2000), *The Architectural Setting of the Cult of Saints in the Early Christian West, c.300–c.1200* (Oxford).

CROOM, J. (1988), 'The Fragmentation of the Minster *Parochiae* of South-East Shropshire', in Blair 1988*a*: 67–81.

CROTHERS, N. (2000), 'Discovery of Tide-Mill at Nendrum Monastery', *Church Archaeology*, 4: 54–5.

CRUMMY, P. (1981), *Aspects of Anglo-Saxon and Norman Colchester* (CBA Research Rep. 39, London).

CUBITT, C. (1989), 'Wilfrid's "Usurping Bishops": Episcopal Elections in Anglo-Saxon England, c.600–c.800', *Northern History*, 25: 18–38.

——(1992), 'Pastoral Care and Conciliar Canons: The Provisions of the 747 Council of *Clofesho*', in Blair and Sharpe 1992: 193–211.

——(1995), *Anglo-Saxon Church Councils c.650–c.850* (London).

——(1997), 'The Tenth-Century Benedictine Reform in England', *EME* 6: 77–94.

——(1999), 'Finding the Forger: An Alleged Decree of the 679 Council of Hatfield', *EHR* 114: 1217–48.

——(2000), 'Sites and Sanctity: Revisiting the Cult of Murdered and Martyred Anglo-Saxon Royal Saints', *EME* 9: 53–83.

——(2002), 'Universal and Local Saints in Anglo-Saxon England', in Thacker and Sharpe 2002: 423–53.

CUNLIFFE, B. (1984), 'Saxon Bath', in Haslam 1984: 345–58.

DALLAS, C. (1993), *Excavations in Thetford by B. K. Davison between 1964 and 1970* (*EAA* 62, Gressenhall).

DAMMINGER, F. (1998), 'Dwellings, Settlements and Settlement Patterns in Merovingian Southwest Germany and Adjacent Areas', in Wood 1998: 33–106.

DANIELS, R. (1988), 'The Anglo-Saxon Monastery at Church Close, Hartlepool, Cleveland', *ArchJ* 145: 158–210.

DARBY, H. C. (1971), *The Domesday Geography of Eastern England* (3rd edn., Cambridge).

——(1977), *Domesday England* (Cambridge).

DARK, K. (1994*a*), *Discovery by Design: The Identification of Secular Elite Settlements in Western Britain, AD 400–700* (BAR British Ser. 237, Oxford).

——(1994*b*), *Civitas to Kingdom: British Political Continuity 300–800* (Leicester).

DARLING, M. J., and GURNEY, D. (1993), *Caister-on-Sea: Excavations by Charles Green, 1951–1955* (*EAA* 60, Gressenhall).

DARLINGTON, R. R. (1936), 'Ecclesiastical Reform in the Late Old English Period', *EHR* 51: 385–428.

DAVENPORT, P. (2002), *Medieval Bath Uncovered* (Stroud).

DAVEY, N. (1964), 'A Pre-Conquest Church and Baptistery at Potterne', *Wiltshire Archaeological and Natural History Magazine*, 59: 116–23.

DAVIDSON, C. F. (1998), 'Written in Stone: Architecture, Liturgy and the Laity in English Parish Churches, c.1125–c.1250' (unpublished London Ph.D. thesis).

DAVIDSON, H. R. E. (1988), *Myths and Symbols in Pagan Europe* (Manchester).

DAVIES, J. R. (2002), 'The Saints of South Wales and the Welsh Church', in Thacker and Sharpe 2002: 361–95.

DAVIES, W. (1978), *An Early Welsh Microcosm: Studies in the Llandaff Charters* (London).

——(1982), *Wales in the Early Middle Ages* (Leicester).

——(1983), 'Priests and Rural Communities in East Brittany in the Ninth Century', *Études celtiques*, 20: 177–97.

——(1988), *Small Worlds: The Village Community in Early Medieval Brittany* (London).

——(1992), 'The Myth of the Celtic Church', in Edwards and Lane 1992*a*: 12–21.

——(1994), 'Ecclesiastical Centres and Secular Society in the Brittonic World in the Tenth and Eleventh Centuries', in A. Ritchie (ed.), *Govan and its Early Medieval Sculpture* (Stroud), 92–101.

——(1995), 'Adding Insult to Injury: Property, Power and Immunities in Early Medieval Wales', in W. Davies and P. Fouracre (eds.), *Property and Power in the Early Middle Ages* (Cambridge), 137–64.

DAVIES, W. (1996), '"Protected Space" in Britain and Ireland in the Middle Ages', in Crawford 1996: 1–19.

DAVIS, R. H. C. (1972), 'The College of St. Martin-le-Grand and the Anarchy', *London Topographical Record*, 23: 9–26.

DAVISON, B. K. (1977), 'Excavations at Sulgrave, Northamptonshire', *ArchJ* 134: 105–14.

DAWSON, M. (1999), 'A Medieval Cemetery at Brook Drive, Kempston', *Bedfordshire Archaeology*, 23: 111–17.

DEANESLY, M. (1961), *The Pre-Conquest Church in England* (London).

——(1962), *Sidelights on the Anglo-Saxon Church* (London).

DEGREGORIO, S. (2002), '*Nostrorum Socordiam Temporum*: The Reforming Impulse of Bede's Later Exegesis', *EME* 11: 107–22.

——(2004), 'Bede's *In Ezram et Neemiam* and the Reform of the Northumbrian Church', *Speculum*, 79: 1–25.

DELAPLACE, C. (1999), 'La Mise en place de l'infrastructure ecclésiastique rurale en Gaule à la fin de l'antiquité (IVᵉ–VIᵉ siècles après J.-C.)', *Les Cahiers de Saint-Michel de Cuxa*, 30: 153–70.

——(2002), 'Les Origines des églises rurales (Vᵉ–VIᵉ siècles) à propos d'une formule de Grégoire de Tours', *Histoire et sociétés rurales*, 18: 11–40.

DEMOLON, P. (1986), 'Les Sépultures privilégiées mérovingiennes dans la France septentrionale', in Y. Duval and J.-Ch. Picard (eds.), *L'Inhumation privilégiée du IVᵉ au VIIIᵉ siècle en occident* (Paris), 57–68.

——(1990), 'Flandre', in Fixot and Zadora-Rio 1990: 59–62.

DENTON, J. H. (1970), *English Royal Free Chapels 1100–1300* (Manchester).

DETSICAS, A. P. (1976), 'Excavations at Eccles, 1975', *Archaeologia Cantiana*, 92: 157–63.

DÍAZ, P. C. (2001), 'Monasteries in a Peripheral Area: Seventh-Century *Gallaecia*', in Jong and Theuws 2001: 329–59.

DICKINSON, T. M. (1993), 'An Anglo-Saxon "Cunning Woman" from Bidford-on-Avon', in M. Carver (ed.), *In Search of Cult: Archaeological Investigations in Honour of Philip Rahtz* (Woodbridge), 45–54.

DIERKENS, A. (1981), 'Cimetières mérovingiens et histoire du haut Moyen Âge: chronologie—société—religion', *Acta Historica Bruxellensia*, iv: *histoire et méthode* (Brussels), 15–70.

——(1989), 'Prolégomènes à une histoire des relations culturelles entre les Îles Britanniques et le continent pendant le haut Moyen Âge', in H. Atsma (ed.), *La Neustrie* (Sigmaringen), ii. 372–94.

—— and PÉRIN, P. (2000), 'Les *Sedes Regiae* mérovingiennes entre Seine et Rhin', in Ripoll and Gurt 2000: 267–304.

DIMIER, M.-A. (1972), 'Le Mot *locus* employé dans le sens de monastère', *Revue Mabillon*, 58: 133–54.

DIXON, P., and STOCKER, D. (2001), 'The Southwell Lintel, its Style and Significance', in Graham-Campbell and others 2001: 245–68.

——Marshall, P., Palmer-Brown, C., and Samuels, J. (1994), *Newark Castle Studies: Excavations 1992–1993* (Newark).

Dodgshon, R. A. (1980), *The Origin of British Field Systems: An Interpretation* (London).

Dodwell, C. R. (1982), *Anglo-Saxon Art: A New Perspective* (Manchester).

Doehaerd, R. (1982), *Le Haut Moyen Âge occidental: économies et sociétés* (2nd edn., Paris).

Doherty, C. (1980), 'Exchange and Trade in Early Medieval Ireland', *Journal of the Royal Society of Antiquaries of Ireland*, 110: 67–89.

——(1982), 'Some Aspects of Hagiography as a Source for Irish Economic History', *Peritia*, 1: 300–28.

——(1985), 'The Monastic Town in Early Medieval Ireland', in Clarke and Simms 1985: 45–75.

Dornier, A. (ed.) (1977*a*), *Mercian Studies* (Leicester).

——(1977*b*), 'The Anglo-Saxon Monastery at Breedon-on-the-Hill, Leicestershire', in Dornier 1977*a*: 155–68.

Drake, C. S. (2002), *The Romanesque Fonts of Northern Europe and Scandinavia* (Woodbridge).

Driscoll, S. T. (1988), 'The Relationship between History and Archaeology: Artefacts, Documents and Power', in Driscoll and Nieke 1988: 162–87.

——and Nieke, M. R. (eds.) (1988), *Power and Politics in Early Medieval Britain and Ireland* (Edinburgh).

Drury, P. J. (1990), 'Anglo-Saxon Painted Plaster Excavated at Colchester Castle, Essex', in Cather and others 1990: 111–22.

——and Rodwell, W. J. (1978), 'Investigations at Asheldham, Essex', *AntJ* 58: 133–51.

Duby, G. (1953), *La Société aux XIe et XIIe siècles dans la région mâconnaise* (Paris).

Dumville, D. N. (1984), 'Some British Aspects of the Earliest Irish Christianity', in P. Ní Chatháin and M. Richter (eds.), *Irland und Europa: Die Kirche im Frühmittelalter* (Stuttgart), 16–24.

——(1992*a*), *Wessex and England from Alfred to Edgar* (Woodbridge).

——(1992*b*), *Liturgy and the Ecclesiastical History of Late Anglo-Saxon England* (Woodbridge).

——(1997), *The Churches of North Britain in the First Viking Age* (5th Whithorn Lecture, Whithorn).

Dunning, R. W. (1976), 'The Minster at Crewkerne', *Somerset Archaeology and Natural History*, 120: 63–7.

Dyer, C. (1985), 'Towns and Cottages in Eleventh-Century England', in H. Mayr-Harting and R. I. Moore (eds.), *Studies in Medieval History Presented to R. H. C. Davis* (London), 91–106.

——(1988), 'Recent Developments in Early Medieval Urban History and Archaeology in England', in D. Denecke and G. Shaw (eds.), *Urban Historical Geography: Recent Progress in Britain and Germany* (Cambridge), 69–80.

DYER, C. (1992), 'The Hidden Trade of the Middle Ages: Evidence from the West Midlands of England', *Journal of Historical Geography*, 18: 141–57.

EATON, T. (2000), *Plundering the Past: Roman Stonework in Medieval Britain* (Stroud).

EDWARDS, B. J. N. (1978), 'An Annotated Check-List of Pre-Conquest Sculpture in the Ancient County of Lancaster', *Lancashire Archaeological Journal*, 1: 53–82.

EDWARDS, H. (1986), 'Two Documents from Aldhelm's Malmesbury', *Bulletin of the Institute of Historical Research*, 59: 1–19.

——(1988), *The Charters of the Early West Saxon Kingdom* (BAR Brit. Ser. 198, Oxford).

EDWARDS, N. (1990), *The Archaeology of Early Medieval Ireland* (London).

——(1996), 'Identifying the Archaeology of the Early Church in Wales and Cornwall', in Blair and Pyrah 1996: 49–62.

——(2001), 'Early Medieval Inscribed Stones and Stone Sculpture in Wales: Context and Function', *MA* 45: 15–39.

——and LANE, A. (eds.) (1992*a*), *The Early Church in Wales and the West* (Oxford).

————(1992*b*), 'The Archaeology of the Early Church in Wales: An Introduction', in Edwards and Lane 1992*a*: 1–11.

EFFROS, B. (1996), 'Symbolic Expressions of Sanctity: Gertrude of Nivelles in the Context of Merovingian Mortuary Custom', *Viator*, 27: 1–10.

——(1997), 'Beyond Cemetery Walls: Early Medieval Funerary Topography and Christian Salvation', *EME* 6: 1–23.

——(2001), 'Monuments and Memory: Repossessing Ancient Remains in Early Medieval Gaul', in Jong and Theuws 2001: 93–118.

ELLIS, P. (1986), 'Excavations at Winchcombe, Gloucestershire, 1962–72', *TBGAS* 104: 95–138.

Essex County Council (1984), *Four Church Excavations in Essex* (Chelmsford).

ETCHINGHAM, C. (1991), 'The Early Irish Church: Some Observations on Pastoral Care and Dues', *Ériu*, 42: 99–118.

——(1996), *Viking Raids on Irish Church Settlements in the Ninth Century* (Maynooth).

——(1999), *Church Organization in Ireland AD 650 to 1000* (Maynooth).

EVANS, J. W. (1992), 'The Survival of the *Clas* as an Institution in Medieval Wales: Some Observations on Llanbadarn Fawr', in Edwards and Lane 1992*a*: 33–40.

EVERITT, A. (1972), *The Pattern of Rural Dissent: The Nineteenth Century* (Leicester).

——(1986), *Continuity and Colonization: The Evolution of Kentish Settlement* (Leicester).

EVERSON, P. (1977), 'Excavations in the Vicarage Garden at Brixworth, 1972', *JBAA* 130: 55–122.

——and KNOWLES, G. C. (1993), 'The Anglo-Saxon Bounds of *Æt Bearuwe*', *Journal of the English Place-Name Society*, 25: 19–37.

——and STOCKER, D. A. (1999), *Corpus of Anglo-Saxon Stone Sculpture*, v: *Lincolnshire* (Oxford).

——Taylor, C. C., and Dunn, C. J. (1991), *Change and Continuity: Rural Settlement in North-West Lincolnshire* (London).

Ewig, E. (1976), 'Les Missions dans les pays rhénans', *RHEF* 62: 37–44.

Faith, R. (1966), 'Peasant Families and Inheritance Customs in Medieval England', *Agricultural History Review*, 14: 77–95.

——(1994), 'Tidenham, Gloucestershire, and the History of the Manor in England', *Landscape History*, 16: 39–51.

——(1997), *The English Peasantry and the Growth of Lordship* (London).

——(forthcoming), 'Cola's *Tūn*: Rural Social Structure in Late Anglo-Saxon Devon', in R. Evans (ed.), *Lordship and Learning: Studies in Memory of Trevor Aston* (Woodbridge).

Fasham, P. J., Keevill, G., and Coe, D. (1995), *Brighton Hill South (Hatch Warren): An Iron Age Farmstead and Deserted Medieval Village in Hampshire* (Wessex Archaeology Report 7, Salisbury).

Faull, M. L. (1976), 'The Location and Relationship of the Sancton Anglo-Saxon Cemeteries', *AntJ* 56: 227–33.

Fell, C. E. (1995), 'Paganism in *Beowulf*: A Semantic Fairy Tale', in Hofstra and others 1995: 9–34.

Fellows-Jensen, G. (1985), *Scandinavian Settlement Names in the North-West* (Copenhagen).

——(1987), 'The Vikings' Relationship with Christianity in the British Isles: The Evidence of Place-Names Containing the Element *Kirkjá*', *Proceedings of the Tenth Viking Congress* (Oslo), 295–307.

Felten, F. J. (1980), *Äbte und Laienäbte im Frankenreich* (Monographien zur Geschichte des Mittelalters, 20, Stuttgart).

Fenwick, V. (1984), 'Insula de Burgh: Excavations at Burrow Hill, Butley, Suffolk, 1978–1981', *ASSAH* 3: 35–54.

Fernie, E. (1983), *The Architecture of the Anglo-Saxons* (London).

——(1988), 'The Church of St. Magnus, Egilsay', in B. E. Crawford (ed.), *St. Magnus Cathedral and Orkney's Twelfth-Century Renaissance* (Aberdeen), 140–61.

Février, P. A., and others (1980), *Histoire de la France urbaine*, i: *La Ville antique, des origines au IXe siècle* (Éditions du Seuil, [n. p.]).

Fisher, D. J. V. (1958), 'The Anti-Monastic Reaction in the Reign of Edward the Martyr', *Cambridge Historical Journal*, 10: 254–70.

Fisher, I. (1993), 'Orphir Church in its South Scandinavian Context', in C. E. Batey and others (eds.), *The Viking Age in Caithness, Orkney and the North Atlantic* (Edinburgh), 375–80.

——(1996), 'The West of Scotland', in Blair and Pyrah 1996: 37–42.

Fixot, M., and Zadora-Rio, E. (eds.) (1990), *L'Église, la campagne, le terroir* (Paris).

————(eds.) (1994), *L'Environnement des églises et la topographie religieuse des campagnes médiévales* (Paris).

Fleming, R. (1985), 'Monastic Lands and England's Defence in the Viking Age', *EHR* 100: 247–65.

FLEMING, R. (1993), 'Rural Elites and Urban Communities in Late-Saxon England', *P&P* 141: 3–37.

FLETCHER, LORD [E.], and MEATES, G. W. (1977), 'The Ruined Church of Stone-by-Faversham: Second Report', *AntJ* 57: 67–72.

FLETCHER, R. (1997), *The Conversion of Europe* (London).

FLEURY, M., and FRANCE-LANORD, A. (1998), *Les Trésors mérovingiens de la basilique de Saint-Denis* (Paris).

FLINT, V. I. J. (1991), *The Rise of Magic in Early Medieval Europe* (Oxford).

FOARD, G. (1985), 'The Administrative Organization of Northamptonshire in the Saxon Period', *ASSAH* 4: 185–222.

FOOT, S. R. I. (1989*a*), 'Anglo-Saxon Minsters AD 597–c.900: The Religious Life in England before the Benedictine Reform' (unpublished Cambridge Ph. D. thesis).

——(1989*b*), 'Parochial Ministry in Early Anglo-Saxon England: The Role of Monastic Communities', *SCH* 26: 43–54.

——(1992*a*), ' "By Water in the Spirit": The Administration of Baptism in Early Anglo-Saxon England', in Blair and Sharpe 1992: 171–92.

——(1992*b*), 'Anglo-Saxon Minsters: A Review of Terminology', in Blair and Sharpe 1992: 212–25.

——(1999), 'The Role of the Minster in Earlier Anglo-Saxon Society', in B. Thompson (ed.), *Monasteries and Society in Medieval Britain* (Stamford), 35–58.

——(2000), *Veiled Women* (2 vols., Aldershot).

FOREMAN, S., HILLER, J., and PETTS, D. (2002), *Gathering the People, Settling the Land* (Oxford).

FOSSIER, R. (1982), *Enfance de l'Europe* (Paris).

FOSTER, C. W., and LONGLEY, T. (1924), *The Lincolnshire Domesday and the Lindsey Survey* (Lincoln Record Soc. 19).

FOURACRE, P. (1979), 'The Work of Audoenus of Rouen and Eligius of Noyen in Extending Episcopal Influence from the Town to the Country in Seventh-Century Neustria', *SCH* 16: 77–91.

——(1995), 'Eternal Light and Earthly Needs: Practical Aspects of the Development of Frankish Immunities', in W. Davies and P. Fouracre (eds.), *Property and Power in the Early Middle Ages* (Cambridge), 53–81.

FOURNIER, G. (1962), *Le Peuplement rural en Basse Auvergne durant le haut Moyen Âge* (Clermont-Ferrand).

——(1982), 'La Mise en place du cadre paroissial et l'évolution du peuplement', *SSCI* 28: 495–563.

FOX, C. (1920–1), 'Anglo-Saxon Monumental Sculpture in the Cambridge District', *Proceedings of the Cambridge Antiquarian Society*, 71: 15–45

FRANKLIN, M. J. (1982), 'Minsters and Parishes: Northamptonshire Studies' (unpublished Cambridge Ph.D. thesis).

——(1985), 'The Identification of Minsters in the Midlands', *Anglo-Norman Studies*, 7: 69–88.

——(1988), 'The Secular College as a Focus for Anglo-Norman Piety: St. Augustine's Daventry', in Blair 1988*a*: 97–104.

FREKE, D. J., HOLGATE, R., and THACKER, A. T. (1987), 'Excavations at Winwick, Cheshire, in 1980', *Journal of the Chester Archaeological Society*, 70: 9–38.

FRY, S. L. (1999), *Burial in Medieval Ireland 900–1500* (Dublin).

GALINIÉ, H., and ZADORA-RIO, E. (eds.) (1996), *Archéologie du cimitière chrétien* (Tours).

GAMESON, R. (1995), *The Role of Art in the Late Anglo-Saxon Church* (Oxford).

——(ed.) (1999), *St. Augustine and the Conversion of England* (Stroud).

——and GAMESON, F. (1993), 'The Anglo-Saxon Inscription at St. Mary's Church, Breamore, Hampshire', *ASSAH* 6: 1–10.

GANNON, A. (2003), *The Iconography of Early Anglo-Saxon Coinage: Sixth to Eighth Centuries* (Oxford).

GARDINER, M. (1989), 'Some Lost Anglo-Saxon Charters and the Endowment of Hastings College', *Sussex Archaeological Collections*, 127: 39–48.

——and GREATOREX, C. (1997), 'Archaeological Excavations in Steyning, 1992–1995', *Sussex Archaeological Collections*, 135: 143–71.

GATCH, M. McC. (1993), 'Miracles in Architectural Settings: Christ Church, Canterbury, and St. Clement's, Sandwich, in the Old English *Vision of Leofric*', *ASE* 22: 227–52.

GEAKE, H. (1997), *The Use of Grave-Goods in Conversion-Period England, c.600–c.850* (BAR Brit. Ser. 261, Oxford).

——(1999), 'When were Hanging-Bowls Deposited in Anglo-Saxon Graves?', *MA* 43: 1–18.

——(2002), 'Persistent Problems in the Study of Conversion-Period Burials in England', in Lucy and Reynolds 2002: 144–55.

GELLING, M. (1978), *Signposts to the Past* (London).

——(1981), 'The Word "Church" in English Place-Names', *Bulletin of the CBA Churches Committee*, 15 (Dec.), 4–9.

——(1982), 'Some Meanings of *Stow*', in Pearce 1982*a*: 187–96.

——(1984), *Place-Names in the Landscape* (London).

——(1992), *The West Midlands in the Early Middle Ages* (Leicester).

GEM, R. (1975), 'A Recession in English Architecture during the Early Eleventh Century', *JBAA* 3rd ser. 38: 28–49.

——(1985), 'Holy Trinity Church, Bosham', *ArchJ* 142: 32–6.

——(1988), 'The English Parish Church in the Eleventh and Early Twelfth Centuries: A Great Rebuilding?', in Blair 1988*a*: 21–30.

——(1991), 'Tenth-Century Architecture in England', *SSCI* 38: 803–36.

——(1993), 'Architecture of the Anglo-Saxon Church, 735 to 870', *JBAA* 146: 29–66.

——and TUDOR-CRAIG, P. (1981), 'A "Winchester School" Wall-Painting at Nether Wallop, Hampshire', *ASE* 9: 115–36.

GILKES, O. J. (1997), 'Excavations at Rocky Clump, Stanmer Park, Brighton, 1951–1981', *Sussex Archaeological Collections*, 135: 113–25.

GILLINGHAM, J. (1995), 'Thegns and Knights in Eleventh-Century England: Who was Then the Gentleman?' *TRHS* 6th ser. 5: 129–53.

References

GILMOUR, B. J. J., and STOCKER, D. A. (1986), *St. Mark's Church and Cemetery* (The Archaeology of Lincoln XIII. 1, London).

GITTOS, H., (2002*a*), 'Sacred Space in Anglo-Saxon England: Liturgy, Architecture and Place' (unpublished Oxford D.Phil. thesis, 2002).

——(2002*b*), 'Creating the Sacred: Anglo-Saxon Rites for Consecrating Cemeteries', in Lucy and Reynolds 2002: 195–208.

GOUGH, H. (1992), 'Eadred's Charter of AD 949 and the Extent of the Monastic Estate of Reculver, Kent', in Ramsay and others 1992: 89–102.

GRAHAM, A. H., and DAVIES, S. M. (1993), *Excavations in Trowbridge, Wiltshire, 1977 and 1986–88* (Wessex Archaeology Report 2, Salisbury).

GRAHAM, B. J., (1987*a*), 'Urban Genesis in Early Medieval Ireland', *Journal of Historical Geography*, 13: 3–16.

——(1987*b*), 'Analogy and Theory: Some Further Thoughts', *Journal of Historical Geography*, 13: 61–3.

——(1998), 'The Town and the Monastery: Early Medieval Urbanization in Ireland, AD 800–1150', in Slater and Rosser 1998: 131–54.

GRAHAM-CAMPBELL, J., and others (eds.) (2001), *Vikings and the Danelaw: Select Papers from the Proceedings of the Thirteenth Viking Congress* (Oxford).

GRANSDEN, A. (1985), 'The Legends and Traditions Concerning the Origins of the Abbey of Bury St. Edmunds', *EHR* 100: 1–24.

——(1989), 'Traditionalism and Continuity during the Last Century of Anglo-Saxon Monasticism', *JEH* 40: 159–207.

GRANT, E. (ed.) (1986), *Central Places, Archaeology and History* (Sheffield).

GRÄSLUND, A.-S. (2003), 'The Role of Scandinavian Women in Christianisation: The Neglected Evidence', in Carver 2003: 483–96.

GREEN, D. H. (1998), 'The Influence of the Merovingian Franks on the Christian Vocabulary of German', in Wood 1998: 343–70.

GREGSON, N. (1985), 'The Multiple Estate Model: Some Critical Questions', *Journal of Historical Geography*, 11: 339–51.

GRENVILLE, J. (1997), *Medieval Housing* (Leicester).

GRIFFE, É. (1949), 'Les Premières "paroisses" de la Gaule', *Bulletin de littérature ecclésiastique*, 50: 229–39.

——(1975), 'A travers les paroisses rurales de la Gaule au VIe siècle', *Bulletin de littérature ecclésiastique*, 76: 3–26.

GRIFFITHS, D. (2001), 'The North-West Frontier', in Higham and Hill 2001: 167–87.

GRIMSHAW, A. (1983), 'Rizong: A Monastic Community in Ladakh' (unpublished Cambridge Ph.D. thesis).

GRINSELL, L. V. (1986), 'The Christianisation of Prehistoric and Other Pagan Sites', *Landscape History*, 8: 27–37.

GRUZINSKI, S. (1989), *Man-Gods in the Mexican Highlands* (English trans., Stanford, Calif.).

GUREVICH, A. (1988), *Medieval Popular Culture* (English trans., Cambridge).

HADLEY, D. M. (1995), 'The Historical Context of the Inhumation Cemetery at Bromfield, Shropshire', *Transactions of the Shropshire Archaeological and Historical Society*, 70: 143–55.

——(1996), 'Conquest, Colonization and the Church: Ecclesiastical Organization in the Danelaw', *Historical Research*, 69: 109–28.

——(1997), '"And they Proceeded to Plough and to Support Themselves": The Scandinavian Settlement of England', *Anglo-Norman Studies*, 19: 69–96.

——(2000*a*), *The Northern Danelaw: Its Social Structure, c.800–1100* (London).

——(2000*b*), 'Burial Practices in the Northern Danelaw, c.650–1100', *Northern History*, 36: 199–216.

——(2002*a*), 'Burial Practices in Northern England in the Later Anglo-Saxon Period', in Lucy and Reynolds 2002: 209–28.

——(2002*b*), 'Viking and Native: Re-thinking Identity in the Danelaw', *EME*, 11: 45–70.

——and RICHARDS, J. (eds.) (2000), *Cultures in Contact: Scandinavian Settlement in England in the Ninth and Tenth Centuries* (Turnhout).

HALL, D., and MARTIN, P. (1979), 'Brixworth, Northamptonshire—an Intensive Field Survey', *JBAA* 132: 1–6.

HALL, D. J. (1984), 'The Community of Saint Cuthbert—its Properties, Rights and Claims from the Ninth Century to the Twelfth' (unpublished Oxford D.Phil. thesis).

——(1989), 'The Sanctuary of St. Cuthbert', in Bonner and others 1989: 425–36.

HALL, R. (1994), *Viking Age York* (London).

——and WHYMAN, M. (1996), 'Settlement and Monasticism at Ripon, North Yorkshire, from the 7th to 11th Centuries AD', *MA* 40: 62–150.

HALL, T. A. (2000), *Minster Churches in the Dorset Landscape* (BAR Brit. Ser. 304, Oxford).

HALSALL, G. (1992), 'Social Change around AD 600: An Austrasian Perspective', in Carver 1992*a*, 265–78.

——(1995*a*), *Settlement and Social Organization: The Merovingian Region of Metz* (Cambridge).

——(1995*b*), *Early Medieval Cemeteries: An Introduction to Burial Archaeology in the Post-Roman West* (Skelmorlie).

——(2000), 'The Viking Presence in England? The Burial Evidence Reconsidered', in Hadley and Richards 2000: 259–76.

HAMEROW, H. (1991), 'Settlement Mobility and the "Middle Saxon Shift": Rural Settlements and Settlement Patterns in Anglo-Saxon England', *ASE* 20: 1–17.

——(1997), 'Migration Theory and the Anglo-Saxon "Identity Crisis"', in J. Chapman and H. Hamerow (eds.), *Migrations and Invasions in Archaeological Explanation* (BAR Int. Ser. 664, Oxford), 33–44.

——(2002), *Early Medieval Settlements: The Archaeology of Rural Communities in North-West Europe 400–900* (Oxford).

——and MACGREGOR, A. (eds.) (2001), *Image and Power in the Archaeology of Early Medieval Britain* (Oxford).

HANDLEY, M. (1998), 'The Early Medieval Inscriptions of Western Britain: Function and Sociology', in J. Hill and M. Swan (eds.), *The Community, the Family and the Saint: Patterns of Power in Early Medieval Europe* (Turnhout), 339–61.

HANDLEY, M. (2001), 'The Origins of Christian Commemoration in Late Antique Britain', *EME* 10: 177–99.

HANSEN, I. L., and WICKHAM, C. (eds.) (2000), *The Long Eighth Century* (Leiden).

HARDY, A., DODD, A., and KEEVILL, G. D. (2003), *Ælfric's Abbey: Excavations at Eynsham Abbey, Oxfordshire, 1989–92* (Oxford).

HARE, M. J. (1991), 'Investigations at the Anglo-Saxon Church of St. Peter, Titchfield, 1982–1989', *Proceedings of the Hampshire Field Club and Archaeological Society*, 47: 117–44.

——(1993), *The Two Anglo-Saxon Minsters of Gloucester* (The Deerhurst Lecture 1992, Deerhurst).

——(1997), 'Kings, Crowns and Festivals: The Origins of Gloucester as a Royal Ceremonial Centre', *TBGAS*, 115: 41–78.

HART, C. E. (1992), *The Danelaw* (London).

——(1995), 'The *Aldeworke* and Minster at Shelford, Cambridgeshire', *ASSAH* 8: 43–68.

HARTE, J. (2002), 'Rethinking Rogationtide', *Third Stone*, 42 (Spring), 29–35.

HASE, P. H. (1975), 'The Development of the Parish in Hampshire, particularly in the Eleventh and Twelfth Centuries' (unpublished Cambridge Ph.D. thesis).

——(1988), 'The Mother Churches of Hampshire', in Blair 1988*a*: 45–66.

——(1994), 'The Church in the Wessex Heartlands', in M. Aston and C. Lewis (eds.), *The Medieval Landscape of Wessex* (Oxford), 47–81.

HASLAM, J. (1980), 'A Middle Saxon Iron Smelting Site at Ramsbury, Wiltshire', *MA* 24: 1–68.

——(ed.) (1984), *Anglo-Saxon Towns in Southern England* (Chichester).

——(1987), 'Market and Fortress in the Reign of Offa', *World Archaeology*, 19. 1: 76–93.

HAVERCAMP, A. (1987), '"Heilige Städte" im Hohen Mittelalter', in F. Graus (ed.), *Mentalitäten im Mittelalter: Methodische und inhaltliche Probleme* (*Vorträge und Forschungen*, 35, Sigmaringen), 119–56.

HAWKES, J. (1995), 'The Wirksworth Slab: An Iconography of Humilitas', *Peritia*, 9: 246–89.

——(1999), 'Statements in Stone: Anglo-Saxon Sculpture, Whitby and the Christianization of the North', in C. E. Karkov (ed.), *The Archaeology of Anglo-Saxon England: Basic Readings* (New York), 403–21.

——(2001), 'Constructing Iconographies: Questions of Identity in Mercian Sculpture', in Brown and Farr 2001: 231–45.

——(2002), *The Sandbach Crosses: Sign and Significance in Anglo-Saxon Sculpture* (Dublin).

——(2003*a*), 'Sacraments in Stone: The Mysteries of Christ in Anglo-Saxon Sculpture', in Carver 2003: 351–70.

——(2003*b*), '*Iuxta Morem Romanorum*: Stone and Sculpture in Anglo-Saxon England', in C. E. Karkov and G. H. Brown (eds.), *Anglo-Saxon Styles* (New York), 69–99.

——and MILLS, S. (eds.) (1999), *Northumbria's Golden Age* (Stroud).

HAWKES, S. C. (1979), 'Eastry in Anglo-Saxon Kent', *ASSAH* 1: 81–113.

——(1981), 'Recent Finds of Inlaid Iron Buckles and Belt-Plates from Seventh-Century Kent', *ASSAH* 2: 49–90.

——and GROVE, L. R. A. (1963), 'Finds from a Seventh-Century Anglo-Saxon Cemetery at Milton Regis', *Archaeologia Cantiana*, 78: 22–38.

HEDEAGER, L. (2001), '*Asgard* Reconstructed? Gudme—a "Central Place" in the North', in Jong and Theuws 2001: 467–507.

HEIGHWAY, C. M., and BRYANT, R. (1999), *The Golden Minster: The Anglo-Saxon Minster and Later Medieval Priory of St. Oswald at Gloucester* (CBA Research Rep. 117, York).

HELMS, M. (1993), *Craft and the Kingly Ideal: Art, Trade and Power* (Austin, Tex.).

HENDERSON, C. G., and BIDWELL, P. T. (1982), 'The Saxon Minster at Exeter', in Pearce 1982a: 145–76.

HERITY, M. (1995), *Studies in the Layout, Buildings and Art in Stone of Early Irish Monasteries* (London).

HERREN, M. W. (1990), 'Gildas and Early British Monasticism', in A. Bammesberger and A. Wollmann (eds.), *Britain 400–600: Language and History* (Heidelberg), 65–78.

HEY, G. (forthcoming), *Yarnton: Saxon and Medieval Settlement and Landscape* (Oxford).

HEYWOOD, S. (1988), 'The Round Towers of East Anglia', in Blair 1988a: 169–77.

HIGGITT, J. (1979), 'The Dedication Inscription at Jarrow and its Context', *AntJ* 59: 343–74.

——(1995), 'Monasteries and Inscriptions in Early Northumbria: The Evidence of Whitby', in C. Bourke (ed.), *From the Isles of the North* (Belfast), 229–36.

HIGHAM, N. J. (1993), *The Origins of Cheshire* (Manchester).

——(1997), *The Convert Kings: Power and Religious Affiliation in Early Anglo-Saxon England* (Manchester).

——and HILL, D. H. (eds.) (2001), *Edward the Elder, 899–924* (London).

HILL, D. (1984), *An Atlas of Anglo-Saxon England* (2nd edn., Oxford).

——and COWIE, R. (eds.) (2001), *Wics: The Early Mediaeval Trading Centres of Northern Europe* (Sheffield).

——and RUMBLE, A. R. (eds.) (1996), *The Defence of Wessex: The Burghal Hidage and Anglo-Saxon Fortifications* (Manchester).

HILL, J. (1992), 'Monastic Reform and the Secular Church: Ælfric's Pastoral Letters in Context', in C. Hicks (ed.), *England in the Eleventh Century* (Stamford), 103–17.

——(2000), 'The *Litaniae Maiores* and *Minores* in Rome, Francia and Anglo-Saxon England: Terminology, Texts and Translations', *EME* 9: 211–46.

HILL, P. H. (1997), *Whithorn and St. Ninian: The Excavation of a Monastic Town 1984–91* (Stroud).

HILL, R. (1966), 'Christianity and Geography in Early Northumbria', *SCH* 3: 126–39.

HILLABY, J. (1987), 'Early Christian and Pre-Conquest Leominster', *Transactions of the Woolhope Naturalists' Field Club*, 45. 3: 557–685.

HILLABY, J. (2001), 'The Early Church in Herefordshire: Columban and Roman', in Malpas and others 2001: 41–76.

HILTON, R. H. (1982), 'The Small Town and Urbanisation: Evesham in the Middle Ages', *Midland History*, 7: 1–8.

HINCHCLIFFE, J. (1986), 'An Early Medieval Settlement at Cowage Farm, Foxley, near Malmesbury', *ArchJ* 143: 240–59.

——and THOMAS, R. (1980), 'Archaeological Investigations at Appleford', *Oxoniensia*, 45: 9–111.

HINES, J. (1990), 'Philology, Archaeology, and the *Adventus Saxonum vel Anglorum*', in A. Bammesberger and A. Wollmann (eds.), *Britain 400–600: Language and History* (Heidelberg), 17–36.

——(ed.) (1997*a*), *The Anglo-Saxons from the Migration Period to the Eighth Century: An Ethnographic Perspective* (Woodbridge).

——(1997*b*), 'Religion: The Limits of Knowledge', in Hines 1997*a*: 375–410.

Hinton, D. A. (1990), *Archaeology, Economy and Society: England from the Fifth to the Fifteenth Century* (London).

——(1998), *Discover Dorset: Saxons and Vikings* (Wimborne).

——and WEBSTER, C. J. (1987), 'Excavations at the Church of St. Martin, Wareham, 1985–86, and "Minsters" in South-East Dorset', *Dorset Natural History and Archaeological Society Proceedings*, 109: 47–54.

HODDER, I., and ORTON, C. (1976), *Spatial Analysis in Archaeology* (Cambridge).

HODGES, R., and HOBLEY, B. (eds.) (1988), *The Rebirth of Towns in the West, AD 700–1050* (CBA Research Rep. 68, London).

HOEKSTRA, T. J. (1988), 'The Early Topography of the City of Utrecht and its Cross of Churches', *JBAA* 141: 1–34.

HOFSTRA, T., HOUWEN, L. A. J. R., and MACDONALD, A. A. (eds.) (1995), *Pagans and Christians: The Interplay between Christian Latin and Traditional Germanic Cultures in Early Medieval Europe* (Germania Latina II, Groningen).

HOLLIS, S. (1998), 'The Minster-in-Thanet Foundation Story', *ASE* 27: 41–64.

HOLMES, C. (1999), 'From Pre-History to Domesday Book', in K. Tiller (ed.), *Benson: A Village through its History* (Wallingford), 15–44.

HOLT, R. (1988), *The Mills of Medieval England* (Oxford).

HOOD, A. B. E. (1999), 'Lighten our Darkness—Biblical Style in Early Medieval Britain and Ireland', *EME* 8: 283–96.

HOOKE, D. (1985), *The Anglo-Saxon Landscape: The Kingdom of the Hwicce* (Manchester).

——(1987), 'Two Documented Pre-Conquest Christian Sites Located upon Parish Boundaries', *MA* 31: 96–101.

——(1990), *Worcestershire Anglo-Saxon Charter-Bounds* (Woodbridge).

——(1994), *Pre-Conquest Charter-Bounds of Devon and Cornwall* (Woodbridge).

——and SLATER, T. R. (1986), *Anglo-Saxon Wolverhampton: The Town and its Monastery* (Wolverhampton).

HOPE, R. C. (1893), *The Legendary Lore of the Holy Wells of England* (London).

HOPE-TAYLOR, B. (1977), *Yeavering: An Anglo-British Centre of Early Northumbria* (London).

HORDEN, P., and PURCELL, N. (2000), *The Corrupting Sea* (Oxford).

HOWLETT, D. R. (1995), *The Celtic Latin Tradition of Biblical Style* (Dublin).

HUBERT, J. (1977), 'La Vie commune des clercs et l'archéologie', in id., *Arts et vie sociale de la fin du monde antique au Moyen Âge* (Geneva), 125–59.

HUGGINS, P. J., and BASCOMBE, K. (1992), 'Excavations at Waltham Abbey, Essex, 1985–1991: Three Pre-Conquest Churches and Norman Evidence', *ArchJ* 149: 282–343.

—— and others (1978), 'Excavation of Belgic and Romano-British Farm with Middle Saxon Cemetery and Churches at Nazeingbury, Essex, 1975–6', *Essex Archaeology and History*, 10: 29–117.

HUGHES, K. (1966), *The Church in Early Irish Society* (London).

HULL, P., and SHARPE, R. (1985), 'Peter of Cornwall and Launceston', *Cornish Studies*, 13: 5–53.

HUNTER, M. (1974), 'Germanic and Roman Antiquity and the Sense of the Past in Anglo-Saxon England', *ASE* 3: 29–50.

HURLEY, V. (1982), 'The Early Church in the South-West of Ireland: Settlement and Organization', in Pearce 1982*a*: 297–332.

HUTTON, R. (1996), *The Stations of the Sun* (Oxford).

IMBART DE LA TOUR, P. (1900), *Les Paroisses rurales du IVe au XIe siècle* (Paris).

JAMES, E. (1979), 'Cemeteries and the Problem of Frankish Settlement in Gaul', in P. H. Sawyer (ed.), *Names, Words and Graves* (Leeds), 55–89.

—— (1981), 'Archaeology and the Merovingian Monastery', in H. B. Clarke and M. Brennan (eds.), *Columbanus and Merovingian Monasticism* (BAR Int. Ser. 113, Oxford), 33–55.

—— (1992), 'Royal Burials among the Franks', in Carver 1992*a*: 243–54.

JAMES, H. (1992), 'Early Medieval Cemeteries in Wales', in Edwards and Lane 1992*a*: 90–103.

JAMES, M. R. (1917), 'Two Lives of St. Ethelbert, King and Martyr', *EHR* 32: 214–44.

JAMES, T. (1992), 'Air Photography of Ecclesiastical Sites in South Wales', in Edwards and Lane 1992*a*: 62–76.

JANKULAK, K. (2000), *The Medieval Cult of St. Petroc* (Woodbridge).

JENKINS, P. (1988), 'Regions and Cantrefs in Early Medieval Glamorgan', *Cambridge Medieval Celtic Studies*, 15: 31–50.

JEWELL, R. (2001), 'Classicism of Southumbrian Sculpture', in Brown and Farr 2001: 247–62.

JIGMEI, N. N. and others (1981), *Tibet* (London).

JOHANEK, P. (1987), 'Der fränkische Handel der Karolingerzeit im Spiegel der Schriftquellen', in K. Düwel and others (eds.), *Untersuchungen zu Handel und Verkehr der vor- und frühgeschichtlichen Zeit in Mittel- und Nordeuropa*, iv: *Der Handel der Karolinger- und Wikingerzeit* (Göttingen), 7–68.

JOHN, E. (1959–60), 'The King and the Monks in the Tenth-Century Reformation', *Bulletin of the John Rylands Library*, 42: 61–87.

JOHNSTON, A. G. (1993–4), 'Excavations in Oundle, Northants.', *Northamptonshire Archaeology*, 25: 99–117.

JOLLIFFE, J. E. A. (1933), *Pre-Feudal England: The Jutes* (Oxford).

JOLLY, K. L. (1996), *Popular Religion in Late Saxon England: Elf Charms in Context* (Chapel Hill, NC).

JONES, C. A. (2001), 'Old English *Fant* and its Compounds in the Anglo-Saxon Vocabulary of Baptism', *Medieval Studies*, 63: 143–92.

JONES, G. (1986), 'Holy Wells and the Cult of St. Helen', *Landscape History*, 8: 59–75.

JONES, G. R. J. (1976), 'Multiple Estates and Early Settlement', in P. H. Sawyer (ed.), *Medieval Settlement* (London), 15–40.

——(1992), 'The Multiple Estates of (Holy) Islandshire, Hovingham and Kirkby Moorside', in *York Conference on Medieval Archaeology: Pre-Printed Papers 8: Rural Settlement* (Medieval Europe 1992, York), 79–84.

JONES, M. J. (1994), 'St. Paul in the Bail, Lincoln: Britain in Europe?', in K. Painter (ed.), *'Churches Built in Ancient Times': Recent Studies in Early Christian Archaeology* (London), 325–47.

JONG, M. de, and THEUWS, F. (2001), *Topographies of Power in the Early Middle Ages* (Leiden).

JOY, C. A. (1972), 'Sokeright' (unpublished Leeds Ph.D. thesis).

KANER, J. (1993), 'Crayke and its Boundaries', in H. E. J. Le Patourel, M. H. Long, and M. F. Pickles (eds.), *Yorkshire Boundaries* (Leeds), 103–11.

KARKOV, C. (1997), 'The Bewcastle Cross: Some Iconographic Problems', in C. E. Karkov and others (eds.), *The Insular Tradition* (New York), 9–26.

KEENE, D. (1985), *Survey of Medieval Winchester* (Winchester Studies 2, 2 vols., Oxford).

KELLER, C. (2003), 'From a Late Roman Cemetery to the *Basilica Sanctorum Cassii et Florentii* in Bonn, Germany', in Carver 2003: 415–27.

KELLY, S. (1992), 'Trading Privileges from Eighth-Century England', *EME* 1: 3–28.

KEMBLE, J. M. (1849), *The Saxons in England* (2 vols., London).

KEMP, B. R. (1967–8), 'The Mother Church of Thatcham', *Berkshire Archaeological Journal*, 63: 15–22.

——(1968), 'The Churches of Berkeley Hernesse', *TBGAS* 87: 96–110.

——(1980), 'Monastic Possession of Parish Churches in England in the Twelfth Century', *JEH* 31: 133–60.

——(1988), 'Some Aspects of the *Parochia* of Leominster in the Twelfth Century', in Blair 1988*a*: 83–95.

——(1994), 'Archdeacons and Parish Churches in England in the Twelfth Century', in G. Garnett and J. Hudson (eds.), *Law and Government in Medieval England and Normandy: Essays in Honour of Sir James Holt* (Cambridge), 341–64.

KEYNES, S. (1985), '*Anglo-Saxon Architecture* and the Historian' [review of Taylor and Taylor 1965–78], *ASE* 14: 293–302.

——(1994), *The Councils of Clofesho* (Eleventh Brixworth Lecture: Vaughan paper 38, Leicester).

——and LAPIDGE, M. (1983), *Alfred the Great: Asser's 'Life of King Alfred' and Other Contemporary Sources* (Harmondsworth).

KIRBY, D. P. (1977), 'Welsh Bards and the Border', in Dornier 1977*a*: 31–42.

KIRBY, M. (1982), *Sanctuary: Beverley—a Town of Refuge* (Beverley).

KISSAN, B. W. (1940), 'An Early List of London Properties', *Trans. London and Middlesex Arch. Soc.* NS 8: 57–69.

KITZINGER, E. (1993), 'Interlace and Icons: Form and Function in Early Insular Art', in Spearman and Higgitt 1993: 3–15.

KJØLBYE-BIDDLE B. (1992), 'Dispersal or Concentration: The Disposal of the Winchester Dead over 2000 Years', in S. Bassett (ed.), *Death in Towns* (Leicester), 210–47.

——(1998), 'Anglo-Saxon Baptisteries of the 7th and 8th Centuries: Winchester and Repton', *Acta: XIII Congressus Internationalis Archaeologiae Christianae* (Vatican City), 757–78.

KLEINSCHMIDT, H. (1996), 'The Old English Annal for 757 and West Saxon Dynastic Strife', *Journal of Medieval History*, 22: 209–24.

KNIGHT, J. (1992), 'The Early Christian Latin Inscriptions of Britain and Gaul: Chronology and Context', in Edwards and Lane 1992: 45–50.

——(1996), 'Seasoned with Salt: Insular-Gallic Contacts in the Early Memorial Stones and Cross-Slabs', in K. R. Dark (ed.), *External Contacts and the Economy of Late Roman and Post-Roman Britain* (Woodbridge), 109–20.

——(1999), *The End of Antiquity* (Stroud).

KNOWLES, D. (1949), *The Monastic Order in England* (Cambridge).

KÜMIN, B. A. (1996), *The Shaping of a Community: The Rise and Reformation of the English Parish, c.1400–1560* (Aldershot).

LANG, J. T. (1978), 'Continuity and Innovation in Anglo-Scandinavian Sculpture', in J. Lang (ed.), *Anglo-Saxon and Viking-Age Sculpture and its Context* (BAR Brit. Ser. 49, Oxford), 145–72.

——(1984), 'The Hogback: A Viking Colonial Monument', *ASSAH* 3: 85–176.

——(1990), *The Anglian Sculpture of Deira: The Classical Tradition* (The Jarrow Lecture, Jarrow).

——(1991), *Corpus of Anglo-Saxon Stone Sculpture*, iii: *York and Eastern Yorkshire* (Oxford).

——(1993), 'Survival and Revival in Insular Art: Northumbrian Sculpture of the 8th to 10th Centuries', in Spearman and Higgitt 1993: 261–7.

——(1999), 'The Apostles in Anglo-Saxon Sculpture in the Age of Alcuin', *EME* 8: 271–82.

——(2000), 'Monuments from Yorkshire in the Age of Alcuin', in H. Geake and J. Kenny (eds.), *Early Deira* (Oxford), 109–19.

LANGDON, J. (1994), 'Lordship and Peasant Consumerism in the Milling Industry of Early Fourteenth-Century England', *P&P* 145: 3–46.

LANGEFELD, B. (1996), '*Regula Canonicorum* or *Regula Monasterialis Vitae*? The Rule of Chrodegang and Archbishop Wulfred's Reforms at Canterbury', *ASE* 25: 21–36.

LAPIDGE, M. (1984), 'Gildas's Education and the Latin Culture of Sub-Roman Britain', in Lapidge and Dumville 1984: 27–50.

——(1986), 'Latin Learning in Dark Age Wales: Some Prolegomena', in D. E. Evans, J. G. Griffith, and E. M. Jope (eds.), *Proceedings of the Seventh International Congress of Celtic Studies* (Oxford), 91–107.

——(ed.) (1991), *Anglo-Saxon Litanies of the Saints* (Henry Bradshaw Society, 106, London).

——and DUMVILLE, D. N. (eds.) (1984), *Gildas: New Approaches* (Woodbridge).

——and HERREN, M. W. (1979), *Aldhelm: The Prose Works* (Cambridge).

——and ROSIER, J. L. (1985), *Aldhelm: The Poetic Works* (Cambridge).

LEACH, P. (1984), *The Archaeology of Taunton* (Gloucester).

LEAHY, K. (1999), 'The Middle Saxon Site at Flixborough, North Lincolnshire', in Hawkes and Mills 1999: 87–94.

LEBECQ, S. (1989), 'La Neustrie et la mer', in H. Atsma (ed.), *La Neustrie* (Sigmaringen), i. 405–40.

——(2000), 'The Role of the Monasteries in the Systems of Production and Exchange of the Frankish World between the Seventh and the Beginning of the Ninth Centuries', in Hansen and Wickham 2000: 121–48.

LE GOFF, J. (1980), *Time, Work and Culture* (English trans., Chicago).

LE JAN, R. (2001), 'Convents, Violence, and Competition for Power in Seventh-Century Francia', in Jong and Theuws 2001: 243–69.

LE MAHO, J. (1994), 'La Réutilisation funéraire des édifices antiques en Normandie au cours du haut Moyen Âge', in Fixot and Zadora-Rio 1994: 10–21.

LEMARIGNIER, J.-F. (1966), 'Quelques Remarques sur l'organisation ecclésiastique de la Gaule du VIIᵉ à la fin du IXᵉ siècle, principalement au nord de la Loire', *SSCI* 13: 451–86.

——(1977), 'Le Monachisme et l'encadrement religieux des campagnes du royaume de France situées au nord de la Loire, de la fin du X à la fin du XI siècle', in *Le istituzioni ecclesiastiche della 'Societas Christiana' dei secoli XI–XII: diocesi, pievi e parrochie* (Miscellanea del Centro di Studi Medioevali VIII, Milan), 357–94.

——(1982), 'Encadrement religieux . . . de Charles le Chauve aux derniers carolingiens (840–987)', *SSCI* 28. 2: 765–800.

LENNARD, R. V. (1952), 'Two Peasant Contributions to Church Endowment', *EHR* 67: 230–3.

——(1959), *Rural England, 1086–1135* (Oxford).

LETHBRIDGE, T. C. (1936), *A Cemetery at Shudy Camps, Cambridgeshire* (Cambridge).

LEVISON, W. (1946), *England and the Continent in the Eighth Century* (Oxford).

LEYSER, H. (1984), *Hermits and the New Monasticism* (London).

LEYSER, K. J. (1979), *Rule and Conflict in an Early Medieval Society: Ottonian Saxony* (London).

LIEBERMANN, F. (1889), *Die Heiligen Englands* (Hannover).

LIEBESCHUETZ, J. H. W. G. (2000), 'Ravenna to Aachen', in Ripoll and Gurt 2000: 9–30.

LONGLEY, D. (1997), 'The Royal Courts of the Welsh Princes of Gwynedd, AD 400–1273', in N. Edwards (ed.), *Landscape and Settlement in Medieval Wales* (Oxford), 41–54.

LOSEBY, S. (1998), 'Gregory's Cities: Urban Functions in Sixth-Century Gaul', in Wood 1998: 239–84.

——(2000), 'Power and Towns in Late Roman Britain and Early Anglo-Saxon England', in Ripoll and Gurt 2000: 319–70.

LOVE, R. C. (1996), *Three Eleventh-Century Anglo-Latin Saints' Lives* (Oxford).

——(2004), *Goscelin of Saint-Bertin: The Hagiography of the Female Saints of Ely* (Oxford).

LOVELUCK, C. (1995), 'Acculturation, Migration and Exchange: The Formation of Anglo-Saxon Society in the English Peak District, 400–700 AD', in J. Bintliff and H. Hamerow (eds.), *Europe between Late Antiquity and the Middle Ages* (BAR Int. Ser. 617, Oxford), 84–98.

——(2001), 'Wealth, Waste and Conspicuous Consumption: Flixborough and its Importance for Middle and Late Saxon Rural Settlement Studies', in Hamerow and MacGregor 2001: 79–130.

LOWE, C. E. (1991), 'New Light on the Anglian "Minster" at Hoddom', *Transactions of the Dumfriesshire and Galloway Natural History and Antiquarian Society*, 3rd ser. 66: 11–35.

LUCY, S. (1999), 'Changing Burial Rites in Northumbria, AD 500–750', in Hawkes and Mills 1999: 12–43.

——and REYNOLDS, A. (eds.) (2002), *Burial in Early Medieval England and Wales* (London).

McCARTHY, M. R. (1996), 'The Origins and Development of the Twelfth-Century Cathedral Church at Carlisle', in T. Tatton-Brown and J. Munby (eds.), *The Archaeology of Cathedrals* (Oxford), 31–45.

MACGOWAN, K. (1996), 'Barking Abbey', *Current Archaeology*, 149: 172–8.

MACGREGOR, A. (2000), 'A Seventh-Century Pectoral Cross from Holderness, East Yorkshire', *MA* 44: 217–22.

McKITTERICK, R. (1977), *The Frankish Church and the Carolingian Reforms, 789–895* (London).

McNAMARA, J. (1994), 'Bede's Role in Circulating Legend in the *Historia Ecclesiastica*', *ASSAH* 7: 61–9.

MACQUARRIE, A. (1992), 'Early Christian Religious Houses in Scotland: Foundation and Function', in Blair and Sharpe 1992: 110–33.

MADDICOTT, J. R. (1997), 'Plague in Seventh-Century England', *P&P* 156: 7–54.

——(2000), 'Two Frontier States: Northumbria and Wessex c.650–750', in J. R. Maddicott and D. M. Palliser (eds.), *The Medieval State: Essays Presented to James Campbell* (London), 25–45.

——(2002), 'Prosperity and Power in the Age of Bede and Beowulf', *Proceedings of the British Academy*, 117: 49–51.

MAGILTON, J. R. (1980), *The Church of St. Helen-on-the-Walls, Aldwark* (The Archaeology of York 10. 1, London).

MALPAS, A., and others (eds.) (2001), *The Early Church in Herefordshire* (Leominster).

MARKUS, R. A. (1970), 'Gregory the Great and a Papal Missionary Strategy', *SCH* 6: 29–38.

——(1990), *The End of Ancient Christianity* (Cambridge).

MASON, J. F. A. (1963), 'Roger of Montgomery and his Sons (1067–1102)', *TRHS* 5th ser. 13: 1–28.

MASTERS, P. J. (2001), 'Church, Land and Lordship in West Sussex, 680–1200' (unpublished Leicester Ph.D. thesis).

MATTHEWS, J. F. (1982–3), 'Macsen, Maximus, and Constantine', *Welsh History Review*, 11: 431–48.

MAYR-HARTING, H. (1976), *The Venerable Bede, the Rule of St. Benedict and Social Class* (The Jarrow Lecture 1976, Jarrow).

——(1981), review of K. Schmid (ed.), *Die Klostergemeinschaft von Fulda im früheren Mittelalter*, *EHR* 96: 374–9.

——(1991), *The Coming of Christianity to Anglo-Saxon England* (3rd edn., Philadelphia).

——(1994), *Two Conversions to Christianity: The Bulgarians and the Anglo-Saxons* (The Stenton Lecture 1993, Reading).

MEANEY, A. L. (1964), *A Gazetteer of Early Anglo-Saxon Burial Sites* (London).

——(1981), *Anglo-Saxon Amulets and Curing Stones* (BAR Brit. Ser. 96, Oxford).

——(1984), 'Ælfric and Idolatry', *Journal of Religious History*, 13: 119–35.

——(1985), 'Bede and Anglo-Saxon Paganism', *Parergon*, NS 3: 1–29.

——(1989), 'Women, Witchcraft and Magic in Anglo-Saxon England', in D. G. Scragg (ed.), *Superstition and Popular Medicine in Anglo-Saxon England* (Manchester), 9–40.

——(1992), 'Anglo-Saxon Idolaters and Ecclesiasts from Theodore to Alcuin: A Source Study', *ASSAH* 5: 103–25.

——(2001), 'Felix's Life of Guthlac: Hagiography and/or Truth', *Proceedings of the Cambridgeshire Antiquarian Society*, 90: 29–48.

MEENS, R. (1994), 'A Background to Augustine's Mission to Anglo-Saxon England', *ASE* 23: 5–17.

MERDRIGNAC, B. (1993), *Les Vies des saints bretons durant le haut Moyen Âge* (Rennes).

MERITT, H. (1934), 'Old English Entries in a Manuscript at Bern', *Journal of English and Germanic Philology*, 33: 343–51.

METCALF, D. M. (1993–4), *Thrymsas and Sceattas in the Ashmolean Museum, Oxford* (3 vols., London).

——(2003), 'Variations in the Composition of the Currency in Different Places in England', in Pestell and Ulmschneider 2003: 37–47.

MILLS, S. (1999), '(Re)constructing Northumbrian Timber Buildings: The Bede's World Experience', in Hawkes and Mills 1999: 66–72.

MILNE, G. (1997), *St. Bride's Church, London: Archaeological Research 1952–60 and 1992–5* (English Heritage, London).

——and RICHARDS, J. D. (1992), *Wharram, VII: Two Anglo-Saxon Buildings and Associated Finds* (York Univ. Archaeol. Pubs. 9, York).

MOFFETT, L. (1994), 'Charred Cereals from some Ovens/Kilns in Late Saxon Stafford and the Botanical Evidence for the Pre-*burh* Economy', in J. Rackham (ed.), *Environment and Economy in Anglo-Saxon England* (CBA Research Rep. 89, York), 55–64.

MORELAND, J. (2000), 'The Significance of Production in Eighth-Century England', in Hansen and Wickham 2000: 69–104.

MORRIS, C. D. (1989), *Church and Monastery in the Far North: An Archaeological Evaluation* (The Jarrow Lecture 1989, Jarrow).

MORRIS, R. (1976), 'Kirk Hammerton Church: The Tower and the Fabric', *ArchJ* 133: 95–103.

——(1983), *The Church in British Archaeology* (CBA Research Rep. 47, London).

——(1986), 'Alcuin, York and the *Alma Sophia*', in Butler and Morris 1986: 80–9.

——(1988), 'Churches in York and its Hinterland: Building Patterns and Stone Sources in the Eleventh and Twelfth Centuries', in Blair 1988*a*: 191–9.

——(1989), *Churches in the Landscape* (London).

——(1991), 'Baptismal Places: 600–800', in I. Wood and N. Lund (eds.), *People and Places in Northern Europe 500–1600: Essays in Honour of P. H. Sawyer* (Woodbridge), 15–24.

——and CAMBRIDGE, E. (1989), 'Beverley Minster before the Early Thirteenth Century', in C. Wilson (ed.), *Medieval Art and Architecture in the East Riding of Yorkshire* (British Archaeological Association Conference Trans. for 1983), 9–32.

——and ROXAN, J. (1980), 'Churches on Roman Buildings', in W. Rodwell (ed.), *Temples, Churches and Religion* (BAR Brit. Ser. 77, Oxford) i. 175–209.

MORTON, A. D. (ed.) (1992), *Excavations at Hamwic, i: Excavations 1946–83* (CBA Research Rep. 84, London).

MÜLLER-WILLE, M. (1998), 'The Cross as a Symbol of Personal Christian Belief in a Changing Religious World', *Kungliga Vitterhets Hist. och Antikvitets Akad.* 40: 179–200.

——(2003), 'The Cross Goes North: Carolingian Times between Rhine and Elbe', in Carver 2003: 443–62.

MURRAY, A. (1992), 'Missionaries and Magic in Dark Age Europe', *P&P* 136: 186–205.

MUSSET, L. (1948), 'Les Villes épiscopales et la naissance des églises suburbaines en Normandie', *RHEF* 34: 5–14.

——(1961), 'Recherches sur les communautés des clercs séculiers en Normandie au XIe siècle', *Bulletin de la Société des Antiquaires de Normandie*, 55: 5–38.

NAPIER, A. S. (ed.) (1907–10), 'An Old English Vision of Leofric, Earl of Mercia', *Transactions of the Philological Society for 1907–10*, 180–8.

NASH-WILLIAMS, V. E. (1950), *The Early Christian Monuments of Wales* (Cardiff).

NEILSON, N. (1910), *Customary Rents* (*Oxford Studies in Social and Legal History*, 2, Oxford).

NELSON, J. (1979), 'Charles the Bald and the Church in Town and Countryside', *SCH* 16: 103–18.

NELSON, J. (1987), 'Making Ends Meet: Wealth and Poverty in the Carolingian Church', *SCH* 24: 25–36.

—— (1990), 'Women and the Word', *SCH* 27: 53–78.

—— (2001), 'Aachen as a Place of Power', in Jong and Theuws 2001: 217– 41.

NEWMAN, J. (1996), 'The True Provenance of the Woodbridge Sceatta "Hoard"', *British Numismatic Journal,* 65: 217–18.

—— (1999), 'Wics, Trade and the Hinterlands—the Ipswich Region', in Anderton 1999: 32–47.

—— (2003), 'Exceptional Finds, Exceptional Sites? Barham and Coddenham, Suffolk', in Pestell and Ulmschneider 2003: 97–109.

NIGHTINGALE, J. (1996), 'Oswald, Fleury and Continental Reform', in Brooks and Cubitt 1996: 23–45.

NOBLE, T. F. X. (2001), 'Topography, Celebration and Power: The Making of a Papal Rome in the Eighth and Ninth Centuries', in Jong and Theuws 2001: 45–91.

NORTON, C. (1998), 'The Anglo-Saxon Cathedral at York and the Topography of the Anglian City', *JBAA* 151: 1–42.

OAKES, C. M., and COSTEN, M. (2003), 'The Congresbury Carvings—an Eleventh-Century Saint's Shrine?', *AntJ* 83: 281–309.

O'BRIEN, E. (1992), 'Pagan and Christian Burial in Ireland during the First Millenium AD: Continuity and Change', in Edwards and Lane 1992a: 130–7.

—— (1999), *Post-Roman Britain to Anglo-Saxon England: Burial Practices Reviewed* (BAR Brit. Ser. 289, Oxford).

OEXLE, O. G. (1982), '*Conjuratio* et *ghilde* dans l'antiquité et dans le haut Moyen Âge', *Francia,* 10: 1–19.

OKASHA, E. (1971), *Hand-List of Anglo-Saxon Non-Runic Inscriptions* (Cambridge).

—— (1993), *Corpus of Early Christian Inscribed Stones of South-West Britain* (London).

OLSON, L. (1982), 'Crantock, Cornwall, as an Early Monastic Site', in Pearce 1982a: 177–85.

—— (1989), *Early Monasteries in Cornwall* (Woodbridge).

—— and PADEL, O. J. (1986), 'A Tenth-Century List of Cornish Parochial Saints', *Cambridge Medieval Celtic Studies,* 12: 33–71.

OOSTHUIZEN, S. (2001), 'Anglo-Saxon Minsters in South Cambridgeshire', *Proceedings of the Cambridgeshire Antiquarian Society,* 90: 49–67.

ORME, N. (1980), 'The Church of Crediton from St. Boniface to the Reformation', in T. Reuter (ed.), *The Greatest Englishman: Essays on St. Boniface and the Church of Crediton* (Exeter), 97–131.

—— (1991), 'From the Beginnings to 1050', in N. Orme (ed.), *Unity and Variety: A History of the Church in Devon and Cornwall* (Exeter), 1–22.

O'SULLIVAN, D. (1980), 'Curvilinear Churchyards in Cumbria', *Bulletin of the C.B.A. Churches Committee,* 13: 3–5.

—— (1985), 'Cumbria before the Vikings: A Review of Some "Dark Age" Problems in North-West England', in Baldwin and Whyte 1985: 17–35.

—— (2001), 'Space, Silence and Shortage on Lindisfarne: The Archaeology of Asceticism', in Hamerow and MacGregor 2001: 33–52.

——and YOUNG, R. (1995), *Lindisfarne: Holy Island* (London).

OZANNE, A. (1962–3), 'The Peak Dwellers', *MA* 6–7: 15–52.

PADEL, O. (1976–7), 'Cornish Language Notes: 5: Cornish Names of Parish Churches', *Cornish Studies*, 4/5: 15–27.

——(1978–9), 'Two New Pre-Conquest Charters for Cornwall', *Cornish Studies*, 6: 20–7, and 7: 43–4.

——(2002), 'Local Saints and Place-Names in Cornwall', in Thacker and Sharpe 2002: 303–60.

PAGE, R. I. (1978), 'Old English Liturgical Rubrics in Corpus Christi College, Cambridge, MS 422', *Anglia*, 96: 149–58.

——(1995), 'Anglo-Saxon Paganism: The Evidence of Bede', in Hofstra and others 1995: 99–129.

PAGE, W. (1914–15), 'Some Remarks on the Churches of the Domesday Survey', *Archaeologia*, 66: 61–102.

PALLISER, D. M. (1996), 'The "Minster Hypothesis": A Case Study', *EME* 5: 207–14.

——(ed.) (2000), *The Cambridge Urban History of Britain,* i: *600–1540* (Cambridge).

PALMER, J. B. O. (2002), 'The *Emporia* of Mid-Saxon England: Hinterlands, Trade and Rural Exchange' (unpublished Oxford D.Phil. thesis).

——(2003), 'The Hinterlands of Three Southern English *Emporia*: Some Common Themes', in Pestell and Ulmschneider 2003: 48–60.

PANTOS, A. (2002), 'Assembly-Places in the Anglo-Saxon Period: Aspects of Form and Location' (unpublished Oxford D.Phil. thesis).

PARKHOUSE, J., ROSEFF, R., and SHORT, J. (1996), 'A Late Saxon Cemetery at Milton Keynes Village', *Records of Bucks.* 38: 199–221.

PARSONS, D. (1986), '*Sacrarium*: Ablution Drains in Early Medieval Churches', in Butler and Morris 1986: 105–20.

——(1991), 'Stone', in J. Blair and N. Ramsay (eds.), *English Medieval Industries* (London), 1–27.

——(1992), 'The Cruciform Arrangement of Urban Churches: Some Possible English Examples', in *Religion and Belief* (pre-printed papers of Medieval Europe 1992 Conference, 6, York), 117–22.

——(1995), 'Early Churches in Herefordshire: Documentary and Structural Evidence', in D. Whitehead (ed.), *Medieval Art, Architecture and Archaeology at Hereford* (British Archaeological Assoc. Conference Trans. 15), 60–74.

——(1996), 'Before the Parish: The Church in Anglo-Saxon Leicestershire', in J. Bourne (ed.), *Anglo-Saxon Landscapes in the East Midlands* (Leicester), 11–35.

——(2000), 'Odda's Chapel, Deerhurst: Place of Worship or Royal Hall?', *MA* 44: 225–8.

PARSONS, D. M. (1916–17), 'A Hitherto Unprinted Charter of David I', *Scottish Historical Review*, 14: 370–2.

PAXTON, F. S. (1990), *Christianizing Death: The Creation of a Ritual Process in Early Medieval Europe* (Ithaca, NY).

PEARCE, S. M. (ed.) (1982*a*), *The Early Church in Western Britain and Ireland* (BAR Brit. Ser. 102, Oxford).

PEARCE, S. M. (1982*b*), 'Estates and Church Sites in Dorset and Gloucestershire: The Emergence of a Christian Society', in Pearce 1982*a*: 117–38.

——(1985), 'The Early Church in the Landscape: The Evidence from North Devon', *ArchJ* 142: 255–75.

——(2003), 'Processes of Conversion in North-West Roman Gaul', in Carver 2003: 61–78.

PEARN [BENNETT], A. M. (1988), 'The Origin and Development of Urban Churches and Parishes: A Comparative Study of Hereford, Shrewsbury and Chester' (unpublished Cambridge Ph.D. thesis).

PERCIVAL, J. (1997), 'Villas and Monasteries in Late Roman Gaul', *JEH* 48: 1–21.

PÉRIN, P. (1992), 'The Undiscovered Grave of King Clovis I', in Carver 1992*a*: 255–64.

PESTELL, T. (1999), 'An Analysis of Monastic Foundation in East Anglia, c.650–1200' (unpublished Ph.D. thesis, University of East Anglia).

——(2003), 'The Afterlife of "Productive" Sites in East Anglia', in Pestell and Ulmschneider 2003: 122–37.

——and ULMSCHNEIDER, K. (eds.) (2003), *Markets in Early Medieval Europe: Trade and 'Productive' Sites 650–850* (Macclesfield).

PETTS, D. (2002), 'Cemeteries and Boundaries in Western Britain', in Lucy and Reynolds 2002: 24–46.

——(2003), 'Votive Deposits and Christian Practice in Late Roman Britain', in Carver 2003: 109–18.

PHILLIPS, D., HEYWOOD, B., and CARVER, M. O. H. (1995), *Excavations at York Minster*, i: *From Roman Fortress to Norman Cathedral* (Royal Commission on Historical Monuments, London).

PHYTHIAN-ADAMS, C. (1975), *Local History and Folklore: A New Framework* (London).

PICKEN, W. M. M. (1973–7), 'The Manor of Tremaruustel and the Honour of St. Keus', *Journal of the Royal Institution of Cornwall*, NS 7: 220–30.

PIPER, A. J. (1986), *The Durham Monks at Jarrow* (The Jarrow Lecture 1986, Jarrow).

PIRENNE, H. (n.d.), *Medieval Cities* (trans. F. D. Halsey, New York).

PITT, J. M. A. (1999), 'Wiltshire Minster *Parochiae* and West Saxon Ecclesiastical Organization' (unpublished Ph.D. thesis, King Alfred's College, Winchester).

POHL, W. (2001), 'The *Regia* and the *Hring*—Barbarian Places of Power', in Jong and Theuws 2001: 439–66.

POTTER, T. W., and ANDREWS, R. D. (1994), 'Excavation and Survey at St. Patrick's Chapel and St. Peter's Church, Heysham, Lancashire, 1977–8', *AntJ* 74: 55–134.

POTTS, W. T. W. (1974), 'The Pre-Danish Estate of Peterborough Abbey', *Proceedings of the Cambridgeshire Antiquarian Society*, 65: 13–27.

——(1994), 'Brettaroum, Bolton-le-Sands, and the Late Survival of Welsh in Lancashire', *Contrebis*, 19: 61–76.

POUNDS, N. J. G. (2000), *A History of the English Parish* (Cambridge).

PRESTON-JONES, A. (1992), 'Decoding Cornish Churchyards', in Edwards and Lane 1992*a*: 104–24.

——and LANGDON, A. (1997), 'St. Buryan Crosses', *Cornish Archaeology*, 36 [issued 2001], 107–28.

——and ROSE, P. (1986), 'Medieval Cornwall', *Cornish Archaeology*, 25: 135–85.

PRINZ, F. (1965), *Frühes Mönchtum im Frankenreich* (Vienna).

PROBERT, D. W. (2002), 'Church and Landscape: A Study in Social Transition in South-Western Britain AD c.400 to c.1200' (unpublished Birmingham Ph.D. thesis).

PROUDFOOT, E., and ALIAGA-KELLY, C. (1997), 'Aspects of Settlement and Territorial Arrangement in South-East Scotland in the Late Prehistoric and Early Medieval Periods', *MA* 41: 33–50.

PRYCE, H. (1992a), 'Pastoral Care in Early Medieval Wales', in Blair and Sharpe 1992: 41–62.

——(1992b), 'Ecclesiastical Wealth in Early Medieval Wales', in Edwards and Lane 1992a: 22–32.

——(1993), *Native Law and the Church in Medieval Wales* (Oxford).

QUILLER-COUCH, M., and QUILLER-COUCH, L. (1894), *Ancient and Holy Wells of Cornwall* (London).

RADFORD, C. A. R. (1975), 'The Pre-Conquest Church and the Old Minsters of Devon', *Devon Historian*, 11: 2–11.

RAHTZ, P. A. (1976), 'The Building-Plan of the Anglo-Saxon Monastery of Whitby Abbey', in Wilson 1976: 459–62.

——(1979), *The Saxon and Medieval Palaces at Cheddar* (BAR Brit. Ser. 65, Oxford).

——(1991), 'Pagan and Christian by the Severn Sea', in L. Abrams and J. P. Carley (eds.), *The Archaeology and History of Glastonbury Abbey* (Woodbridge), 3–37.

——(1993), *Glastonbury* (London).

——and HIRST, S. (1974), *Beckery Chapel, Glastonbury, 1967–8* (Glastonbury).

——and MEESON, R. (1992), *An Anglo-Saxon Watermill at Tamworth* (CBA Research Rep. 83, London).

——and WATTS, L. (1997), *St. Mary's Church, Deerhurst, Gloucestershire* (Woodbridge).

————(2003), 'Three Ages of Conversion at Kirkdale, North Yorkshire', in Carver 2003: 289–309.

——HIRST, S., and WRIGHT, S. M. (2000), *Cannington Cemetery* (Britannia Monograph Ser. 17, London).

RAINE, J. (1863–4), *The Priory of Hexham* (2 vols., Surtees Soc. 44, 46).

RAMBRIDGE, K. (2003), 'Alcuin's Narratives of Evangelism: The Life of St. Willibrord and the Northumbrian Hagiographical Tradition', in Carver 2003: 371–81.

RAMSAY, N., SPARKS, M., and TATTON-BROWN, T. (eds.) (1992), *St. Dunstan: His Life, Times and Cult* (Woodbridge).

RATTUE, J. (1995), *The Living Stream: Holy Wells in Historical Context* (Woodbridge).

RAY, K. (2001), 'Archaeology and the Three Early Churches of Herefordshire', in Malpas and others 2001: 99–148.

RCHM(E) (Royal Commission on Historical Monuments (England)) (1982), *Beverley: An Archaeological and Architectural Study* (London).

References

REDFIELD, R., and SINGER, M. B. (1954), 'The Cultural Role of Cities', *Economic Development and Cultural Change*, 3: 53–77.

REICHEL, O. J. (1939), 'The Church and the Hundreds of Devon', *Transactions of the Devonshire Association*, 71: 331–42.

RENN, D. (1994), 'Burhgeat and Gonfanon: Two Sidelights from the Bayeux Tapestry', *Anglo-Norman Studies*, 16: 177–98.

RENNIE, E. B. (1984), 'Excavations at Ardnadam, Cowal, Argyll, 1964–1982', *Glasgow Archaeological Journal*, 11: 13–39.

REUTER, T., WICKHAM, C., and BISSON, T. N. (1997), 'Debate: The "Feudal Revolution"', *P&P* 155: 177–225.

REYNAUD, J.-F. (1996), 'Les Morts dans les cités épiscopales de Gaule de IV\u1d49 au XI\u1d49 siècle', in Galinié and Zadora-Rio 1996: 23–30.

REYNOLDS, A. (1998), 'Anglo-Saxon Law in the Landscape: An Archaeological Study of the Old English Judicial System' (unpublished London Ph.D. thesis).

—— (2002), 'Burials, Boundaries and Charters in Anglo-Saxon England: A Reassessment', in Lucy and Reynolds 2002: 171–94.

REYNOLDS, S. (1984), *Kingdoms and Communities in Western Europe, 900–1300* (Oxford).

—— (1994), *Fiefs and Vassals* (Oxford).

RICHARDS, J. (1999), 'What's so Special about "Productive Sites"? Middle Saxon Settlements in Northumbria', *ASSAH* 10: 71–80.

—— (2002), 'The Case of the Missing Vikings: Scandinavian Burial in the Danelaw', in Lucy and Reynolds 2002: 156–70.

RICHARDSON, H. (1984), 'The Concept of the High Cross', in P. Ní Chatháin and M. Richter (eds.), *Irland und Europa: Die Kirche im Frühmittelalter* (Stuttgart), 127–34.

RIDEN, P., and BLAIR, J. (eds.) (1980), *Records of the Borough of Chesterfield and Related Documents, 1204–1835* (*History of Chesterfield*, v, Chesterfield).

RIDYARD, S. J. (1988), *The Royal Saints of Anglo-Saxon England* (Cambridge).

RIGOLD, S. E. (1977), '*Litus Romanum*—the Shore Forts as Mission Stations', in D. E. Johnston (ed.), *The Saxon Shore* (CBA Research Rep. 18, London), 70–5.

RIPOLL, G., and GURT, J. M. (eds.) (2000), *Sedes Regiae (ann. 400–800)* (Barcelona).

RIPPON, S. (1997), 'Puxton (North Somerset) and Early Medieval "Infield" Enclosures', *Medieval Settlement Research Group Annual Report*, 12: 18–20.

ROBERTS, B. K., and WRATHMELL, S. (2000), *An Atlas of Rural Settlement in England* (London).

ROBERTS, I. (2002), *Pontefract Castle* (*Yorkshire Archaeology*, 8, Leeds).

ROBERTS, S. E. (2001), 'Legal Practice in Fifteenth-Century Brycheiniog', *Studia Celtica*, 35: 307–23.

ROBINSON, D. M. (1988), *Biglis, Caldicot and Llandough* (BAR Brit. Ser. 188, Oxford).

RODWELL, W. (1984), 'Churches in the Landscape: Aspects of Topography and Planning', in M. L. Faull (ed.), *Studies in Late Anglo-Saxon Settlement* (Oxford), 1–23.

—— (1993*a*), 'The Role of the Church in the Development of Roman and Early Anglo-Saxon London', in M. Carver (ed.), *In Search of Cult: Archaeological Investigations in Honour of Philip Rahtz* (Woodbridge), 91–9.

—— (1993*b*), 'The Battle of *Assandun* and its Memorial Church: A Reappraisal', in J. Cooper (ed.), *The Battle of Maldon: Fiction and Fact* (London), 127–58.

—— (2001), *Wells Cathedral: Excavations and Structural Studies, 1978–93* (2 vols., London).

——and RODWELL, K. (1982), 'St. Peter's Church, Barton-upon-Humber', *AntJ* 62: 283–315.

————(1985–93), *Rivenhall: Investigations of a Villa, Church and Village*, i–ii (CBA Research Reps. 55, 80, London).

ROGERSON, A. (2003), 'Six Middle Anglo-Saxon Sites in West Norfolk', in Pestell and Ulmschneider 2003: 110–21.

——ASHLEY, S. J., WILLIAMS, P., and HARRIS, A. (1987), *Three Norman Churches in Norfolk* (*EAA* 32).

ROLLASON, D. W. (1978), 'Lists of Saints' Resting-Places in Anglo-Saxon England', *ASE* 7: 61–93.

—— (1982), *The Mildrith Legend* (Leicester).

—— (1987), 'The Wanderings of St. Cuthbert', in D. W. Rollason (ed.), *Cuthbert, Saint and Patron* (Durham), 45–61.

—— (1988), *Two Anglo-Saxon Rituals: Church Dedication and the Judicial Ordeal* (Fifth Brixworth Lecture: Vaughan Paper 33, Leicester).

—— (1989*a*), *Saints and Relics in Anglo-Saxon England* (Oxford).

—— (1989*b*), 'St. Cuthbert and Wessex', in Bonner and others 1989: 413–24.

—— (1999), 'Monasteries and Society in Early Medieval Northumbria', in B. Thompson (ed.), *Monasteries and Society in Medieval Britain* (Stamford), 59–74.

——ROLLASON, D. W., GORE, D., and FELLOWS-JENSEN, G. (1998), *Sources for York History to AD 1100* (York).

ROPER, M. (1974), 'Wilfrid's Landholdings in Northumbria', in D. P. Kirby (ed.), *Saint Wilfrid at Hexham* (Newcastle upon Tyne), 61–79.

ROSENAU, H. (1983), *The Ideal City: Its Architectural Evolution in Europe* (3rd edn., London).

ROSENWEIN, B. H. (1999), *Negotiating Space: Power, Restraint and Privileges of Immunity in Early Medieval Europe* (Manchester).

ROSSER, G. (1988*a*), 'The Anglo-Saxon Gilds', in Blair 1988*a*: 31–4.

—— (1988*b*), 'Communities of Parish and Guild in the Late Middle Ages', in S. Wright (ed.), *Parish, Church and People* (London), 29–55.

—— (1991), 'Parochial Conformity and Voluntary Religion in Late Medieval England', *TRHS* 6th ser. 1: 173–89.

—— (1992), 'The Cure of Souls in English Towns before 1000', in Blair and Sharpe 1992: 267–84.

—— (1996), 'Religious Practice on the Margins', in Blair and Pyrah 1996: 75–84.

ROUND, J. H. (1890), ' "Churchscot" in Domesday', *EHR* 5: 101.

ROWLEY, T., and BROWN, L. (1981), 'Excavations at Beech House Hotel, Dorchester-on-Thames, 1972', *Oxoniensia*, 46: 1–55.

RUMBLE, A. R. (2001), 'Edward the Elder and the Churches of Winchester and Wessex', in Higham and Hill 2001: 230–47.

RUMBLE, A. R. (2002), *Property and Piety in Early Medieval Winchester* (Winchester Studies 4. iii, Oxford).

RUSHTON, N. S. (1999), 'Parochialization and Patterns of Patronage in 11th-Century Sussex', *Sussex Archaeological Collections*, 137: 133–52.

SANDRED, K. I. (1963), *English Place-Names in -Stead* (Uppsala).

SAWYER, B., and SAWYER, P. (1993), *Medieval Scandinavia* (Minneapolis).

SAWYER, P. H. (1978), 'Some Sources for the History of Viking Northumbria', in R. A. Hall (ed.), *Viking Age York and the North* (CBA Research Rep. 27, London), 3–7.

——(1981), 'Fairs and Markets in Early Medieval England', in N. Skyum-Nielsen and N. Lund (eds.), *Danish Medieval History: New Currents* (Copenhagen), 153–68.

——(1983), 'The Royal *Tūn* in Pre-Conquest England', in Wormald and others 1983: 273–99.

——(1988), 'Dioceses and Parishes in Twelfth-Century Scandinavia', in B. Crawford (ed.), *St. Magnus Cathedral and Orkney's Twelfth-Century Renaissance* (Aberdeen), 36–45.

——(1998), *Anglo-Saxon Lincolnshire* (Lincoln).

SCAMMELL, J. (1971), 'The Rural Chapter in England from the Eleventh to the Fourteenth Century', *EHR* 86: 1–21.

SCHARER, A. (1999), 'The Gregorian Tradition in Early England', in Gameson 1999: 187–201.

SCHLESINGER, A., and WALLS, C. (1996), 'An Early Church and Medieval Farmstead Site: Excavations at Llanelen, Gower', *ArchJ* 153: 104–47.

SCHMITT, J.-C. (1976), ' "Religion populaire" et culture folklorique', *Annales*, 31: 941–53.

SCHNEIDER, D. B. (1985), 'Anglo-Saxon Women in the Religious Life: A Study of the Status and Position of Women in an Early Medieval Society' (unpublished Cambridge Ph.D. thesis).

SCHOFIELD, J. (1994), 'Saxon and Medieval Parish Churches in the City of London: A Review', *Transactions of the London and Middlesex Archaeological Society*, 45: 23–145.

SCHULZE, H. K. (1967), 'Die Entwicklung der thüringischen Pfarrorganisation im Mittelalter', *Blätter für deutsche Landesgeschichte*, 103: 32–70.

SCOTT, I. R. (1996), *Romsey Abbey: Report on the Excavations 1973–1991* (Hampshire Field Club).

SCULL, C. (1991), 'Post-Roman Phase I at Yeavering: A Re-consideration', *MA* 35: 51–63.

——(1997), 'Urban Centres in Pre-Viking England?', in Hines 1997a: 269–310.

——(1999), 'Social Archaeology and Anglo-Saxon Kingdom Origins', *ASSAH* 10: 17–24.

——(2001), 'Burials at Emporia in England', in Hill and Cowie 2001: 67–74.

——and Bayliss, A. (1999), 'Radiocarbon Dating and Anglo-Saxon Graves', in U. von Freeden and others (eds.), *Völker an Nord- und Ostsee und die Franken: Akten des 48 Sachsensymposiums* (Bonn), 39–50.

[Selkirk, A.] (1996), 'Llandough', *Current Archaeology*, 146: 73–7.

Semmler, J. (1975), 'Pippin III und die fränkischen Klöster', *Francia*, 3: 88–146.

——(1982), 'Mission und Pfarrorganisation in den Rheinischen, Mosel- und Maasländischen Bistümern (5.–10. Jahrhundert)', *SSCI* 28.2: 813–88.

Semple, S. (1998), 'A Fear of the Past: The Place of the Prehistoric Burial Mound in the Ideology of Middle and Later Anglo-Saxon England', *World Archaeology*, 30: 109–26.

——(2002), 'Anglo-Saxon Attitudes to the Past: A Landscape Perspective' (unpublished Oxford D.Phil. thesis).

——(2004), 'Illustrations of Damnation in Late Anglo-Saxon Manuscripts', *ASE* 32: 231–45.

Settia, A. (1991), *Chiese, strade e fortezze nell'Italia medievale* (Rome).

Shankland, D. (1999), 'Integrating the Past: Folklore, Mounds and People at Çatalhöyük', in A. Gazin-Schwartz and C. J. Holtorf (eds.), *Archaeology and Folklore* (London), 139–57.

Sharpe, R. (1984a), 'Some Problems Concerning the Organization of the Church in Early Medieval Ireland', *Peritia*, 3: 230–70.

——(1984b), 'Gildas as a Father of the Church', in Lapidge and Dumville 1984: 193–205.

——(1992), 'Churches and Communities in Early Medieval Ireland: Towards a Pastoral Model', in Blair and Sharpe 1992: 81–109.

——(2002a), 'Martyrs and Local Saints in Late Antique Britain', in Thacker and Sharpe 2002: 75–154.

——(2002b), 'The Naming of Bishop Ithamar', *EHR* 117: 889–94.

Shaw, R. (1994), 'The Anglo-Saxon Cemetery at Eccles: A Preliminary Report', *Archaeologia Cantiana*, 114: 165–88.

Shephard, J. (1979), 'The Social Identity of the Individual in Isolated Barrows and Barrow Cemeteries in Anglo-Saxon England', in B. C. Burnham and J. Kingsbury (eds.), *Space, Hierarchy and Society* (BAR Int. Ser. 59, Oxford), 47–79.

Shoesmith, R. (1980), *Hereford City Excavations*, i (CBA Research Rep. 36, London).

——(1982), *Hereford City Excavations*, ii (CBA Research Rep. 46, London).

Simpson, L. (1989), 'The King Alfred/St. Cuthbert Episode in the *Historia de Sancto Cuthberto*', in Bonner and others 1989: 397–411.

Sims-Williams, P. (1975), 'Continental Influence at Bath Monastery in the Seventh Century', *ASE* 4: 1–10.

——(1982), [review of Davies 1978], *JEH* 33: 124–9.

——(1984), 'Gildas and Vernacular Poetry', in Lapidge and Dumville 1984: 169–92.

——(1988), 'St. Wilfrid and Two Charters dated AD 676 and 680', *JEH* 39: 163–83.

——(1990), *Religion and Literature in Western England, 600–800* (Cambridge).

SLATER, T. R. (1982), 'Urban Genesis and Medieval Town Plans in Warwickshire and Worcestershire', in T. R. Slater and P. J. Jarvis (eds.), *Field and Forest: An Historical Geography of Warwickshire and Worcestershire* (Norwich), 173–202.

——(1996), 'Medieval Town-Founding on the Estates of the Benedictine Order in England', in F.-E. Eliassen and G. A. Ersland (eds.), *Power, Profit and Urban Land* (Aldershot), 70–92.

——(1998), 'Benedictine Town Planning in Medieval England: Evidence from St. Albans', in Slater and Rosser 1998: 155–76.

——and ROSSER, G. (eds.) (1998), *The Church in the Medieval Town* (Aldershot).

SMITH, A. H. (1956), *English Place-Name Elements* (2 vols., English Place-Name Society 25–6, Cambridge).

SMITH, I. (1996), 'The Origins and Development of Christianity in North Britain and Southern Pictland', in Blair and Pyrah 1996: 19–37.

SMITH, J. M. H. (1990), 'Oral and Written: Saints, Miracles and Relics in Brittany, c.850–1250', *Speculum*, 65: 309–43.

——(1992), *Province and Empire* (Cambridge).

——(1995), 'Religion and Lay Society', in R. M. McKitterick (ed.), *The New Cambridge Medieval History*, ii: *c.700–c.900* (Cambridge), 654–78.

SMITH, N. (1989), 'England's Oldest House?', *Country Life*, 183. 35 (31 Aug.), 84–5.

SPEAKE, G. (1989), *A Saxon Bed Burial on Swallowcliffe Down* (London).

SPEARMAN, R. M., and HIGGITT, J. (eds.) (1993), *The Age of Migrating Ideas: Early Medieval Art in Northern Britain and Ireland* (Edinburgh).

SPUFFORD, P., and SPUFFORD, M. (1964), *Eccleshall: The Story of a Staffordshire Market Town and its Dependent Villages* (Keele).

STAECKER, J. (2003), 'The Cross Goes North: Christian Symbols and Scandinavian Women', in Carver 2003: 463–82.

STAFFORD, P. (1985), *The East Midlands in the Early Middle Ages* (Leicester).

——(1989), *Unification and Conquest* (London).

STANCLIFFE, C. E. (1979), 'From Town to Country: The Christianisation of the Touraine, 370–600', *SCH* 16: 43–59.

——(1983), 'Kings who Opted Out', in Wormald and others 1983: 154–76.

——(1995*a*), 'Oswald, "Most Holy and Most Victorious King of the Northumbrians"', in Stancliffe and Cambridge 1995: 33–83.

——(1995*b*), 'Where was Oswald Killed?', in Stancliffe and Cambridge 1995: 84–96.

——(1999), 'The British Church and the Mission of Augustine', in Gameson 1999: 107–51.

——and CAMBRIDGE, E. (eds.) (1995), *Oswald: Northumbrian King to European Saint* (Stamford).

STANFORD, S. C. (1995), 'A Cornovian Farm and Saxon Cemetery at Bromfield, Shropshire', *Transactions of the Shropshire Archaeological and Historical Society*, 70: 95–141.

STEIN, R. A. (1972), *Tibetan Civilization* (English trans., London).

STENTON, F. M. (ed.) (1920), *Documents Illustrative of the Social and Economic History of the Danelaw* (London).

——(1970), *Preparatory to Anglo-Saxon England* (ed. D. M. Stenton, Oxford).

STIEGEMANN, C., and WEMHOFF, M. (1999), *Kunst und Kultur der Karolingerzeit: Karl der Grosse und Papst Leo III in Paderborn* (3 vols., Mainz).

STOCKER, D. (1993), 'The Early Church in Lincolnshire', in A. Vince (ed.), *Pre-Viking Lindsey* (Lincoln), 101–22.

——(1995), 'The Evidence for a Pre-Viking Church Adjacent to the Anglo-Saxon Barrow at Taplow, Buckinghamshire', *ArchJ* 152: 441–54.

——(1997), '*Fons et Origo*: The Symbolic Death, Burial and Resurrection of English Font Stones', *Church Archaeology*, 1: 17–25.

——(2000), 'Monuments and Merchants: Irregularities in the Distribution of Stone Sculpture in Lincolnshire and Yorkshire in the Tenth Century', in Hadley and Richards 2000: 179–212.

——and EVERSON, P. (2001), 'Five Towns Funerals: Decoding Diversity in Danelaw Stone Sculpture', in Graham-Campbell and others 2001: 223–43.

STORY, J. (2003), *Carolingian Connections: Anglo-Saxon England and Carolingian Francia c.750–870* (Aldershot).

STYLES, D. (1936), 'The Early History of the King's Chapels in Staffordshire', *Birmingham Archaeological Society Transactions*, 60: 56–95.

——(1954), 'The Early History of Penkridge Church', *Collections for a History of Staffordshire 1950 and 1951* (Staffordshire Record Society), 3–52.

SWAN, L. (1983), 'Enclosed Ecclesiastical Sites and their Relevance to Settlement Patterns of the First Millennium AD', in T. Reeves-Smyth and F. Hammond (eds.), *Landscape Archaeology in Ireland* (BAR Brit. Ser. 116, Oxford), 269–94.

——(1985), 'Monastic Proto-Towns in Early Medieval Ireland: The Evidence of Aerial Photography, Plan Analysis and Survey', in Clarke and Simms 1985: 77–102.

TALBOT RICE, D. (1952), *English Art 871–1100* (Oxford).

TANGUY, B. (1984), 'La Troménie de Gouesnou', *Annales de Bretagne*, 91: 9–25.

——(1988), 'Les Paroisses bretonnes primitives', in *Histoire de la paroisse: actes de la onzième rencontre d'histoire religieuse* (Angers), 9–33.

TATTON-BROWN, T. (1980), 'St. Martin's Church in the Sixth and Seventh Centuries', in M. Sparks (ed.), *The Parish of St. Martin and St. Paul, Canterbury* (Canterbury), 12–18.

——(1986), 'The Topography of Anglo-Saxon London', *Antiquity*, 60: 21–8.

——(1988), 'The Churches of Canterbury Diocese in the Eleventh Century', in Blair 1988a: 105–18.

——(1998), 'Medieval Parishes and Parish Churches in Canterbury', in Slater and Rosser 1998: 236–71.

TAYLOR, A. (2001), *Burial Practice in Early England* (Stroud).

TAYLOR, H. M., and TAYLOR, J. (1965–78), *Anglo-Saxon Architecture*, i–iii (Cambridge).

THACKER, A. T. (1982), 'Chester and Gloucester: Early Ecclesiastical Organization in Two Mercian Burhs', *Northern History*, 18: 199–211.

——(1983), 'Bede's Ideal of Reform', in Wormald and others 1983: 130–53.

THACKER, A. T. (1985), 'Kings, Saints and Monasteries in Pre-Viking Mercia', *Midland History*, 10: 1–25.

——(1988), 'Æthelwold and Abingdon', in Yorke 1988*a*: 43–64.

——(1992*a*), 'Monks, Preaching and Pastoral Care in Early Anglo-Saxon England', in Blair and Sharpe 1992: 137–70.

——(1992*b*), 'Cults at Canterbury: Relics and Reform under Dunstan and his Successors', in Ramsay and others 1992: 221–45.

——(1995), '*Membra Disjecta*: The Division of the Body and the Diffusion of the Cult', in Stancliffe and Cambridge 1995: 97–127.

——(1996), 'Saint Making and Relic Collecting by Oswald and his Communities', in Brooks and Cubitt 1996: 244–68.

——(2001), 'Dynastic Monasteries and Family Cults: Edward the Elder's Sainted Kindred', in Higham and Hill 2001: 248–63.

——(2002), 'The Making of a Local Saint', in Thacker and Sharpe 2002: 45–73.

——and SHARPE, R. (eds.) (2002), *Local Saints and Local Churches in the Early Medieval West* (Oxford).

THOMAS, C. (1967*a*), *Christian Antiquities of Camborne* (St Austell).

——(1967*b*), 'An Early Christian Cemetery and Chapel on Ardwall Isle, Kirkcudbright', *MA* 11: 127–88.

——(1971), *The Early Christian Archaeology of North Britain* (Oxford).

——(1978), 'Ninth-Century Sculpture in Cornwall: A Note', in J. Lang (ed.), *Anglo-Saxon and Viking Age Sculpture and its Context* (BAR Brit. Ser. 49, Oxford), 75–83.

——(1981), *Christianity in Roman Britain to AD 500* (London).

——(1989), 'Christians, Chapels, Churches and Charters', *Landscape History*, 11: 19–26.

——(1993), *Tintagel: Arthur and Archaeology* (London).

——(1994*a*), *And Shall These Mute Stones Speak? Post-Roman Inscriptions in Western Britain* (Cardiff).

——(1994*b*), 'The Eastern Mediterranean and the Western Provinces: A British Perspective', in K. Painter (ed.), *'Churches Built in Ancient Times': Recent Studies of Early Christian Archaeology* (London), 269–78.

TILLER, K. (ed.) (1987), *Church and Chapel in Oxfordshire, 1851* (Oxfordshire Record Soc. 55).

TINTI, F. (2003), 'Dal *church-scot* alla decima: origine, natura e sviluppo dei tributi ecclesiastici nel'Inghilterra altomedievale', *Studi medievali*, 219–51.

TODD, M. (1987), *The South-West to AD 1000* (London).

TOLLEY, C. (1995), 'Oswald's Tree', in Hofstra and others 1995: 149–73.

TOY, J. (1983), 'The Commemorations of British Saints in the Medieval Liturgical Manuscripts of Scandinavia', *Kyrkohistorisk Årsskrift*, 91–103.

——(2003), 'St. Botulph: An English Saint in Scandinavia', in Carver 2003: 565–70.

TREFFORT, C. (1996*a*), *L'Église carolingienne et la mort* (Lyon).

——(1996*b*), 'Du *cimeterium christianorum* au cimetière paroissial', in Galinié and Zadora-Rio 1996: 55–63.

——(2001), 'Consécration de cimetière et contrôle épiscopal des lieux d'inhumation au Xe siècle', in M. Kaplan (ed.), *Le Sacré et son inscription dans l'espace à Byzance et en Occident* (Byzantia Sorbonensia 18, Paris), 285–99.

TRUDGIAN, P. (1987), 'Excavation of a Burial Ground at Saint Endellion, Cornwall', *Cornish Archaeology*, 26: 145–52.

TUCCI, G. (1980), *The Religions of Tibet* (English trans., London).

TURNER, D. (1997), 'Thunderfield, Surrey—Central Place or Shieling', *Medieval Settlement Research Group Annual Report*, 12: 8–10.

TURNER, S. (2003), 'Making a Christian Landscape: Early Medieval Cornwall', in Carver 2003: 171–94.

TWEDDLE, D., BIDDLE, M., and KJØLBYE-BIDDLE, B. (1995), *Corpus of Anglo-Saxon Stone Sculpture*, iv: *South-East England* (Oxford).

ULMSCHNEIDER, K. U. (2000), *Markets, Minsters and Metal-Detectors: The Archaeology of Middle Saxon Lincolnshire and Hampshire Compared* (BAR Brit. Ser. 307, Oxford).

——(2003), 'Markets Around the Solent: Unravelling a "Productive" Site on the Isle of Wight', in Pestell and Ulmschneider 2003: 73–83.

URBAŃCZYK, P. (2003), 'The Politics of Conversion in North Central Europe', in Carver 2003: 15–27.

VALANTE, M. A. (1998), 'Reassessing the Irish "Monastic Town"', *Irish Historical Studies*, 31: 1–18.

VALK, H. (1992), 'The Burial Grounds of Estonian Villages from the 13th to the 18th Centuries: Pagan or Christian?', *Tor*, 24: 203–28.

——(2003), 'Christianisation in Estonia: A Process of Dual-Faith and Syncretism', in Carver 2003: 571–9.

VAN DE NOORT, R. (1992), 'Early Medieval Barrows in Western Europe', in *Death and Burial* (pre-printed papers of Medieval Europe 1992 Conference, 4, York), 29–34.

——(1993), 'The Context of Early Medieval Barrows in Western Europe', *Antiquity*, 67: 66–73.

VERHULST, A. (2000), 'Roman Cities, *Emporia* and New Towns (Sixth–Ninth Centuries)', in Hansen and Wickham 2000: 105–20.

VINCE, A. (1990), *Saxon London: An Archaeological Investigation* (London).

VIOLANTE, C. (1986), *Ricerche sulle istituzioni ecclesiastiche dell'Italia centro-settentrionale nel Medioevo* (Palermo).

VOGT, E. Z. (1976), *Tortillas for the Gods: A Symbolic Analysis of Zinacanteco Rituals* (Cambridge, Mass.).

——(1981), 'Some Aspects of the Sacred Geography of Highland Chiapas', in Benson 1981: 111–42.

WADE-MARTINS, P. (1980), *Excavations in North Elmham Park, 1967–72* (*EAA* 9, Gressenhall).

WALSHAM, A. (1999), 'Reforming the Waters: Holy Wells and Healing Springs in Protestant England', in D. Wood (ed.), *Life and Thought in the Northern Church c.1100–c.1700* (*Studies in Church History Subsidia*, 12), 227–55.

WARD-PERKINS, B. (1984), *From Classical Antiquity to the Middle Ages* (Oxford).

——(2000), 'Why did the Anglo-Saxons not Become More British?', *EHR* 115: 513–33.

WAREHAM, A. (1996), 'Saint Oswald's Family and Kin', in Brooks and Cubitt 1996: 46–63.

WARNER, P. (1986), 'Shared Churchyards, Freemen Church Builders and the Development of Parishes in Eleventh-Century East Anglia', *Landscape History*, 8: 39–52.

——(1996), *The Origins of Suffolk* (Manchester).

WARNER, R. B. (1988), 'The Archaeology of Early Historic Irish Kingship', in Driscoll and Nieke 1988: 47–68.

WATTS, D. J. (1988), 'Circular Lead Tanks and their Significance for Romano-British Christianity', *AntJ* 68: 210–22.

——(1991), *Christians and Pagans in Roman Britain* (London).

WATTS, L., RAHTZ, P., OKASHA, A., BRADLEY, S. A. J., and HIGGITT, J. (1997), 'Kirkdale—the Inscriptions', *MA* 41: 51–99.

WATTS, M. R. (1995), *The Dissenters*, ii: *The Expansion of Evangelical Nonconformity* (Oxford).

WEAVER, L. (1909), *English Leadwork: Its Art and History* (London).

WEBSTER, L. (1992), 'Death's Diplomacy: Sutton Hoo in the Light of Other Male Princely Burials', in R. Farrell and C. Neuman de Vegvar (eds.), *Sutton Hoo: Fifty Years After* (Oxford, Oh.), 75–81.

——(2001), 'Metalwork of the Mercian Supremacy', in Brown and Farr 2001: 263–77.

——and BACKHOUSE, J. (eds.) (1991), *The Making of England: Anglo-Saxon Art and Culture AD 600–900* (British Museum exhibition catalogue, London).

WENHAM, L. P., HALL, R. A., BRIDEN, C. M., and STOCKER, D. A. (1987), *St. Mary Bishophill Junior and St. Mary Castlegate* (*The Archaeology of York*, 8.2, York).

WERNER, K. F. (1976), 'Le Rôle de l'aristocratie dans la Christianisation du nord-est de la Gaule', *RHEF* 62: 45–73.

WEST, S. E., SCARFE, N., and CRAMP, R. (1984), 'Iken, St. Botolph, and the Coming of East Anglian Christianity', *Proceedings of the Suffolk Institute of Archaeology and History*, 35: 279–301.

WHEATLEY, P. (1971), *The Pivot of the Four Quarters* (Chicago).

——(1972), 'The Concept of Urbanism', in P. J. Ucko, R. Tringham, and G. W. Dimbleby (eds.), *Man, Settlement and Urbanism* (London), 601–37.

WHITELOCK, D. (1941), 'The Conversion of the Eastern Danelaw', *Saga-Book of the Viking Society*, 12: 159–76.

WICKHAM, C. (1981), *Early Medieval Italy: Central Power and Local Society, 400–1100* (London).

——(1992), 'Problems of Comparing Rural Societies in Early Medieval Western Europe', *TRHS* 6th ser. 2: 221–46.

WILKINSON, D., and McWHIRR, A. (1998), *Cirencester Anglo-Saxon Church and Medieval Abbey* (Cirencester).

WILLIAMS, A. (1982), '*Princeps Merciorum Gentis*: The Family, Career and Connexions of Ælfhere, Ealdorman of Mercia, 956–83', *ASE* 10: 143–72.

——(1992), 'A Bell-House and a Burh-Geat: Lordly Residences in England before the Norman Conquest', in C. Harper-Bill and R. Harvey (eds.), *Medieval Knighthood IV* (Woodbridge), 221–40.

——(1997), *Land, Power and Politics: The Family and Career of Odda of Deerhurst* (The Deerhurst Lecture 1996, Deerhurst).

——(2002), 'Thegnly Piety and Ecclesiastical Patronage in the Late Old English Kingdom', *Anglo-Norman Studies*, 24: 1–24.

WILLIAMS, G. (2001), 'Military Institutions and Royal Power', in Brown and Farr 2001: 295–309.

WILLIAMS, H. (1997), 'Ancient Landscapes of the Dead: The Reuse of Prehistoric and Roman Monuments as Early Anglo-Saxon Burial Sites', *MA* 41: 1–32.

——(1998), 'Monuments and the Past in Early Anglo-Saxon England', *World Archaeology*, 30: 90–108.

WILLIAMS, J. H. (1979), *St. Peter's Street, Northampton: Excavations 1973–1976* (Northampton).

——(1984), 'From "Palace" to "Town": Northampton and Urban Origins', *ASE* 13: 113–36.

——SHAW, M., and DENHAM, V. (1985), *Middle Saxon Palaces at Northampton* (Northampton).

WILLIAMSON, T. (1993), *The Origins of Norfolk* (Manchester).

WILMOTT, T. (1986), 'Pontefract, West Yorkshire', *Bulletin of the C.B.A. Churches Committee*, 24: 25–6.

WILSON, D. M. (1967), 'The Vikings' Relationship with Christianity in Northern England', *JBAA* 3rd ser. 30: 37–46.

——(ed.) (1976), *The Archaeology of Anglo-Saxon England* (London).

——(1984), *Anglo-Saxon Art* (London).

WILSON, P. R., and others (1996), 'Early Anglian Catterick and *Catraeth*', *MA* 40: 1–61.

WILSON, S. (2000), *The Magical Universe* (London).

WILSON, S. E. (2003), 'King Æthelstan and St. John of Beverley', *Northern History*, 40: 5–23.

WINCHESTER, A. J. L. (1985), 'The Multiple Estate: A Framework for the Evolution of Settlement in Anglo-Saxon and Scandinavian Cumbria', in Baldwin and Whyte 1985: 89–101.

——(1987), *Landscape and Society in Medieval Cumbria* (Edinburgh).

WOOD, I. (1987), 'Anglo-Saxon Otley: An Archiepiscopal Estate and its Crosses in a Northumbrian Context', *Northern History*, 23: 20–38.

——(1990), 'Ripon, Francia and the Franks Casket in the Early Middle Ages', *Northern History*, 26: 1–19.

——(1994), 'The Mission of Augustine of Canterbury to the English', *Speculum*, 69: 1–17.

——(1995), *The Most Holy Abbot Ceolfrid* (The Jarrow Lecture 1995, Jarrow).

—— (ed.) (1998), *Franks and Alamanni in the Merovingian Period: An Ethnographic Perspective* (Woodbridge).

WOOD, I. (2002), 'Constructing Cults in Early Medieval France', in Thacker and Sharpe 2002: 155–87.

WOOD, S. (forthcoming), *The Proprietary Church in Western Europe* (Oxford).

WOODWARD, A., and LEACH, P. E. (1993), *The Uley Shrines: Excavation of a Ritual Complex on West Hill, Uley, Gloucestershire, 1977–9* (London).

WORMALD, P. (1976), 'Bede and Benedict Biscop', in G. Bonner (ed.), *Famulus Christi* (London), 141–69.

——(1978), 'Bede, *Beowulf* and the Conversion of the Anglo-Saxon Aristocracy', in R. T. Farrell (ed.), *Bede and Anglo-Saxon England* (BAR 46, Oxford), 32–90.

——(1982*a*), 'The Age of Bede and Æthelbald', in J. Campbell (ed.), *The Anglo-Saxons* (Oxford), 70–100.

——(1982*b*), 'Viking Studies: Whence and Whither?', in R. T. Farrell (ed.), *The Vikings* (Chichester), 128–53.

——(1984), *Bede and the Conversion of England: The Charter Evidence* (The Jarrow Lecture 1984, Jarrow).

——(1988), 'Æthelwold and his Continental Counterparts: Contact, Comparison, Contrast', in Yorke 1988*a*: 13–42.

——(1991), 'In Search of King Offa's "Law-Code"', in I. Wood and N. Lund (eds.), *People and Places in Northern Europe 500–1600: Essays in Honour of P. H. Sawyer* (Woodbridge), 25–45.

——(1993), *How do we Know so Much about Anglo-Saxon Deerhurst?* (The Deerhurst Lecture 1991, Deerhurst).

——(1999*a*), *The Making of English Law: King Alfred to the Twelfth Century*, i: *Legislation and its Limits* (Oxford).

——(1999*b*), *Legal Culture in the Early Medieval West* (London).

——(2001*a*), 'The Strange Affair of the Selsey Bishopric, 953–963', in R. Gameson and H. Leyser (eds.), *Belief and Culture in the Middle Ages: Studies Presented to Henry Mayr-Harting* (Oxford), 128–41.

——(2001*b*), '*On þa Wæpnedhealfe*: Kingship and Royal Property from Æthelwulf to Edward the Elder', in Higham and Hill 2001: 264–79.

——(forthcoming), *The Making of English Law: King Alfred to the Twelfth Century*, ii: *From God's Law to the Common Law* (Oxford).

——and others (eds.) (1983), *Ideal and Reality in Frankish and Anglo-Saxon Society* (Oxford).

WRENCH, R. (2003), 'Parochial Ministry and Lay Devotion in Northern England, 1000–1200' (unpublished Oxford D.Phil. thesis).

WYSS, M. (ed.) (1996), *Atlas historique de Saint-Denis* (Paris).

YORKE, B. A. E. (1982), 'The Foundation of the Old Minster and the Status of Winchester in the Seventh and Eighth Centuries', *Proceedings of the Hampshire Field Club*, 38: 75–83.

——(ed.) (1988*a*), *Bishop Æthelwold: His Career and Influence* (Woodbridge).

——(1988*b*), 'Æthelwold and the Politics of the Tenth Century', in Yorke 1988*a*: 65–88.

—— (1990), *Kings and Kingdoms of Early Anglo-Saxon England* (London).

—— (1993), 'Lindsey: The Lost Kingdom Found?', in A. Vince (ed.), *Pre-Viking Lindsey* (Lincoln), 141–50.

—— (1995), *Wessex in the Early Middle Ages* (Leicester).

—— (1998), 'The Bonifacian Mission and Female Religious in Wessex', *EME* 7: 145–72.

—— (1999*a*), 'The Reception of Christianity at the Anglo-Saxon Royal Courts', in Gameson 1999: 152–73.

—— (1999*b*), 'The Origins of Anglo-Saxon Kingdoms: The Contribution of Written Sources', *ASSAH* 10: 25–9.

—— (2003*a*), 'The Adaptation of the Anglo-Saxon Royal Courts to Christianity', in Carver 2003: 243–57.

—— (2003*b*), *Nunneries and the Anglo-Saxon Royal Houses* (London).

Young, B. K. (1977), 'Paganisme, Christianisation et rites funéraires mérovingiens', *Archéologie médiévale*, 7: 5–81.

—— (1986), 'Example aristocratique et mode funéraire dans la Gaule mérovingienne', *Annales*, 41: 379–407.

Zadora-Rio, E. (2003), 'The Making of Churchyards and Parish Territories in the Early Medieval Landscape of France and England in the 7th–12th Centuries: A Reconsideration', *MA* 47: 1–19.

Zarnecki, G. (1957), *English Romanesque Lead Sculpture* (London).

Index

English place-names are identified by reference to pre-1974 counties

Whitby (*Streanaeshalch*) (Yorks.) minster 72–3,
    99 n., 150, 311, 314–15
  site and buildings of 198 n., 199, 203, 204
  sculpture and small-finds from 140, 210,
    211, 216, 260 n., 320
  royal burials at 62, 72–3, 220, 229
  dependencies of 145–6, 212–13
  working brethren of 212–13, 255
  Prestebi in 314 n.
  Synod of 9, 79, 95
  see also Gregory
Whitchurch (Hants., Oxon.) 372
Whitchurch (Bucks., Devon, Heref., Salop.,
    Warw., Wales) 372 n.
Whitchurch Canonicorum (Dorset) 372
White Low (Derbs.) 173 n., 230, 232
Whiteparish (Hants.) 372 n.
Whithorn (Wigtown), British minster 28,
    372 n.
  Anglian churches and buildings at 30, 152,
    187, 200, 202, 203
  burials at 63, 229 n., 242
  crafts and commercial activities at 258 n.,
    260, 310
Widdington (Essex) 418 n.
'Wife's Lament' 475
Wigan (Lancs.) 309 n.
Wigheard, nobleman 89
Wight, Isle of 9, 87, 90, 167, 514–15
Wigstan, St 293–4, 315, 476
Wigwulf, Domesday tenant 401
Wihtburh, St 455
Wihtgar, son of Ælfric 414 n.
Wihtred, king of Kent 121 n., 167, 168 n.
Wihtric, East Anglian thegn or peasant 408
Wihtric, Domesday tenant in Suffolk 399, 401
Wilbraham (Cambs.) 386 n.
Wilcot (Wilts.) 416
Wilfrid, St, career of 92–9
  as bishop and nobleman 41, 57 n., 79–80,
    88, 110, 136, 173
  as monastic founder 85, 87, 89 n., 90, 110
  as head of monastic federation 48 n., 83,
    121, 145, 218, 219 n., 255 n .
  as architectural and cultural patron 92–3,
    138–40, 186, 190–1, 200, 201, 202, 216
  attitudes of to Britons 30–1, 187
  cult and sanctuary-zones of 142, 223, 314,
    463 n.
Wilgils, Northumbrian hermit-abbot 218
William I, king 359 n., 364, 450

William II, king 450, 515–17
William Bacini, Devon priest 520–1
William de Briouze 340 n., 450
William of Malmesbury 131, 143, 353, 465 n.,
    480 n.
William Warelwast, bishop of Exeter 519–22
William son of Wibert 410 n.
Willibald, St 162, 227
Willibrord, St 41
Willingdon (Sussex) 462 n.
Willington (Northumb.) 313 n.
Williton (Som.) 335
wills, Anglo-Saxon 299, 301–3, 318, 325–6,
    327 n., 354–5, 363, 372, 383, 386,
    407–10, 446
Wilton (Wilts.) 277 n., 325, 348, 441 n.
Wiltshire 151, 158, 267, 300–2, 303 n., 326 n.,
    350–1, 418
Wimborne (Dorset) 190 n., 195, 198, 302, 331,
    344
Winchcombe (Glos.) 122, 129, 159, 229 n.,
    287–9, 306 n., 344, 512
Winchester (Hants.), as post-Roman and early
    Anglo-Saxon centre 32, 271 n., 273 n.
  Old Minster (i.e. cathedral) 201, 229 n.,
    242, 300, 301, 351; estates of 394 n.,
    450 n.
  New Minster 301, 302 n., 342, 348, 351, 405
  Nunnaminster 348
  small churches in 387 n., 388, 402 n.,
    404–5, 407, 501
  parish boundaries in 500 n.
  processions to 454 n.
  MSS of charms from 484
  styli from 210 n.
  see of 79, 131, 328, 434–5, 445 n.
  Council of 451 n., 496 n., 497 n.
Windsor, Old (Berks.) 256 n., 278
Wine, bishop of London 79
Wineman, thegn or peasant 408
Wing (Bucks.) 128 n.
Wingham (Kent) 299
Winstone (Glos.) 420 n.
Winterborne Steepleton (Dorset) 419 n.
Winwick (Lancs.) 54 n., 309 n., 310, 342
Wirksworth (Derbs.) 165, 258 n.
wise-women and witches 170–1, 173–5, 483,
    485
Withington (Glos.) 105, 116 n., 130, 159
Wittering (Northants.) 413–14
Wittering (Sussex) 115